THE DIV

The Guide to Observing the Noahide Code,
Revealed from Mount Sinai in the Torah of Moses

Fourth Edition

by

Rabbi Moshe Weiner
Jerusalem, Israel

Authorized English version of the original Hebrew:

SHEVA MITZVOT HASHEM
(SEVEN DIVINE COMMANDMENTS)

Editing assistance and elucidations by
Michael Schulman, Ph.D.

With contributions by

Rabbi J. Immanuel Schochet, Ph.D.
Joe M. Regenstein, Ph.D.
Arthur A. Goldberg, J.D., B.C.P.C., C.R.S.
and Rabbi Shimon D. Cowen, Ph.D.

Translation assistance by Rabbi Yosef Schulman

a project of ASK NOAH INTERNATIONAL

Published and Copyright © 20′20-20′21 by Ask Noah International

Fourth Edition, ISBN 978-1-7333635-1-8

5 Elul, 5780 / August 25, 20′20

For information contact:

Michael Schulman, Executive Director
Ask Noah International
Email: SevenLaws@asknoah.org
Internet: https://asknoah.org

A note about our transliterations of Hebrew words:

The Hebrew letters ח *(ĥet)* and כ*(ĥaf)* (pronounced like the first sound in Hanukah/Chanukah) are typed herein as *ĥ*. A more common spelling is *ch*; therefore, use *ch* if looking up a reference name or text.

In this edition, we have placed the Editor's notes as added footnotes marked by an asterisk (*); these include commentary or additional information.

Other publications from Ask Noah International:

Sheva Mitzvot HaShem (Volumes I-III, in Hebrew)

Seven Gates of Righteous Knowledge: A Compendium of Spiritual Knowledge and Faith for the Noahide Movement and All Righteous Gentiles

Prayers, Blessings, Principles of Faith, and Divine Service for Noahides (English, Spanish, French, Portuguese, Dutch and Indonesian Editions)

Go(o)d for You: The Divine Code of 7 Noahide Commandments

To Perfect the World: The Lubavitcher Rebbe's Call to Teach the Noahide Code to All Mankind

With thanks to the One Above
the Directors of Ask Noah International express their gratitude to:

Rabbi Moshe Weiner,
who has stood on the shoulders of giants to thoroughly elucidate the Torah-based Noahide faith, and to produce the first codification of the Noahide Commandments, in his work Sefer Sheva Mitzvot HaShem;

Rabbi Jacob Immanuel Schochet, o.b.m.
who provided invaluable guidance, friendship, approbation and support to the Directors of Ask Noah International, along with expert contributions of explanations and daily prayers for Pious Gentiles, and to whom this book is dedicated;

the Schulman, Reisner *and* Weiner families,
who lovingly endured the unwavering commitment of the Directors of Ask Noah International to provide the Noahide movement with this book, as a foundation for faith and practical observance which is true to the Torah tradition extending back to Moses our teacher at Mount Sinai;

Rabbi Eliyahu Touger,
who believed in this project and helped establish its framework;

Rabbi Yosef Schulman,
who contributed the greatest amount of basic translation work;

Rabbi *and* Mrs. Berel Goldberg, *for their expert assistance;*

Laurel Tessmer *for the cover design and Part VII flowchart;*

Rabbis Shmuel Pollen *and* Eli Schulman *for their translation work.*

This Fourth Edition is dedicated to the blessed memory of

Howard (Chaim Menachem Mendel) Reisner ע"ה

yahrzeit 12 Nissan 5780 / April 6, 20'20

Founder and Co-Director of Ask Noah International;

and in loving memory of Jerry Brigham,
beloved and fondly remembered son, husband, father and grandfather;

and by Dr. Michael and Gilah Moritz – *May this work serve to hasten the time when "God shall be King over the entire earth; on that day God shall be One and His Name One." (Zechariah 14:9)*

[Abraham] planted an *eshel* in Beer-Sheba, and there he proclaimed the Name of God, God of the Universe. (Genesis 21:33)

"[Abraham] planted an *eshel* in Beer-Sheba" –
[What is this *eshel*? The Sage] Reish Lakish said: this teaches that he made an orchard and planted in it many types of fine fruit trees [to benefit the wayfarers]. [The Sage] Rabbi Nehemiah said: he built an inn [for the wayfarers, for lodging, food and drink].

"and there he proclaimed the Name of God, God of the Universe" –
Reish Lakish said: Do not read it as "he proclaimed;" rather, read it as "he caused to call." This teaches that our forefather Abraham caused the Name of the Holy One, blessed be He, to be called by the mouth of every passerby.

How? After [the wayfarers] ate and drank,
they stood up to bless Abraham.
He would say to them, "Was it then of *my*
food that you ate? You ate from the food
of the God of the universe.
[Rather, you should] thank, praise and bless
He Who spoke and caused the universe
to come into being."

They would ask, "What shall we say?"
He told them, "*Blessed is the God of the universe,*
from Whose bounty we have eaten."
So Abraham taught all people to recognize and call
in the Name of God, God of the universe.

(Tractate *Sotah* 10b and Rashi;
Midrash Rabbah Genesis ch. 54)

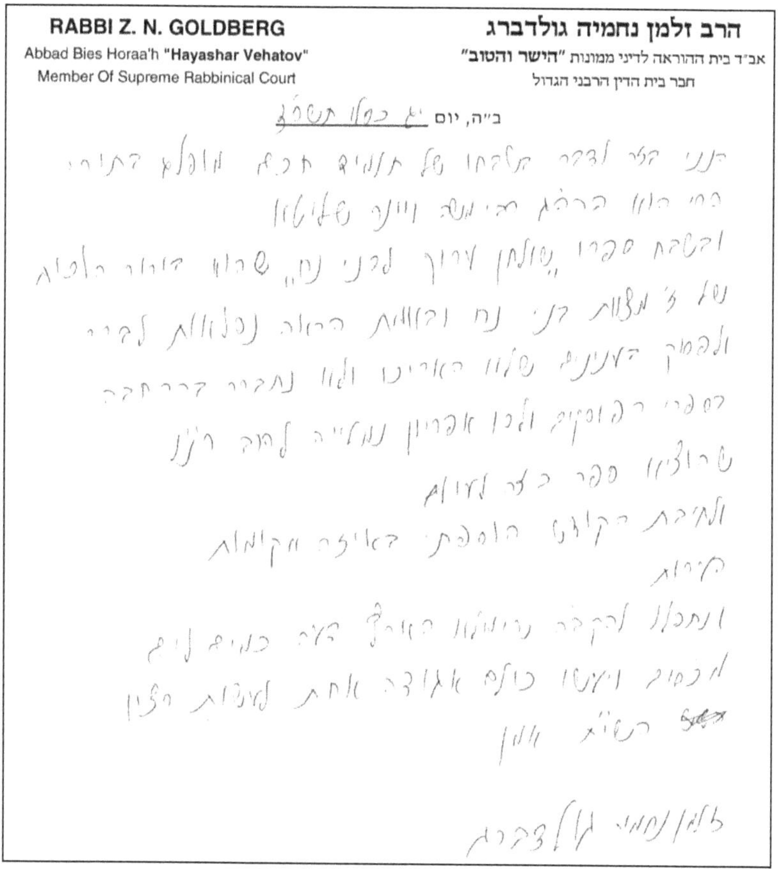
RABBI Z. N. GOLDBERG
Abbad Bies Horaa'h "Hayashar Vehatov"
Member Of Supreme Rabbinical Court
הרב זלמן נחמיה גולדברג
אב"ד בית ההוראה לדיני ממונות "הישר והטוב"
חבר בית הדין הרבני הגדול
ב"ה, יום

Approbation (*free translation*)

Kislev 13, 5767 / November 23, 2007

Behold, I am compelled to speak in praise of the great living scholar, the Rabbi *HaGa'on* Rabbi Moshe Weiner (may he live for many long and good days), and in praise of his book, a "*Shulĥan Aruĥ L'Bnei Noaĥ*," which is an elucidation of the Torah Laws of the Seven Commandments for the Children of Noaĥ. He truly showed greatness in his clear explanations and Torah-law rulings in matters that were not discussed at length or elucidated in breadth in the works of the Rabbinical authorities. Therefore I give my appreciation to the above Rabbi who put out such a book into the world. And for the love of the holy words, I have added comments in a few places. Let us pray to God that "the earth will be as filled with knowledge of God as water covering the sea bed [Isaiah 11:9]," and "all will form a single band to carry out the will of God, blessed be He."* Amen.

Rabbi Zalman Nehemiah Goldberg
Supreme Rabbinical Court of Israel

*From the Rosh Hashanah liturgy.

Shlomo Moshe Amar
Rishon Lezion Chief Rabbi Of Israel
President of the Great Rabbinical Court

שלמה משה עמאר
הראשון לציון הרב הראשי לישראל
נשיא בית הדין הרבני הגדול

בס"ד, ו' תמוז, תשס"ח
ס"ח/505-18-1

אגרת ברכה

ראיתי האי ספרא טבא דמריה טב ששמו הטוב **"שבע מצות השם"** שערך וחיבר הרה"ג **משה ויינר** שליט"א.

וראיתי שמלאכה גדולה ורבה להסביר את כל עניני ז' מצות בני נח, ועוד זאת עשה לטובה שכתב הכל בשפה קלה וברורה למען ירוץ הקורא בהם.

ואברכהו שחפץ ה' בידו יצלח להמשיך במלאכת הקודש להמשיך לחבר חיבורים בבריאות איתנה ונהורא מעליא.

ויהי רצון שיראה ברכה במעשה ידיו, שיכונו לשם ה' ברוך הוא.

המצפה לישועת ה' ברחמים.
שלמה משה עמאר
הראשון לציון הרב הראשי לישראל

שלמה משה עמאר · SHLOMO MOSHE AMAR · Rishon Lezion Chief Rabbi of Israel · הראשון לציון הרב הראשי לישראל

Approbation (free translation)

Shlomo Moshe Amar

Chief Rabbi of Israel and President of the Great Rabbinical Court

With the Help of Heaven
Tammuz 6, 5768 / July 9, 2008

Letter of Blessing

I saw the good book, well-written and aptly titled "*Sheva Mitzvot HaShem*," compiled and authored by the Rabbi and great scholar, Rabbi Moshe Weiner, may he live for many long and good days.

I have also seen the immense work that was required to explain all the matters of the Seven Commandments for the Children of Noaĥ, and this was done very well, written in simple, clear language, so that the reader can easily comprehend it.

I bless him that God should send him success in all his endeavors, to continue in his holy work, and to author and publish more works in excellent physical health.

And may it be God's will that he see blessing in the work of his hands, that it be for the sake of God, blessed be He.

Waiting for God's salvation and mercy,

Shlomo Moshe Amar
Chief Rabbi of Israel

BETH DIN ZEDEK

BETH DIN ZEDEK ECCLESIASTICAL JUDICATURE OF THE
CHICAGO RABBINICAL COUNCIL, INC.
2701 West Howard Street • Chicago, Illinois 60645
773/465-3900 • FAX: 773/465-6632

בית דין צדק דק"ק שיקגו והגליל
דמועצת הרבנים דשיקגו

הרב ישראל מאיר קרנו, ראב"ד מלפנים
RABBI ISRAEL M. KARNO
Av Beth Din Emeritus

הרב חיים דוד רעגענסבורג, זצ"ל, מייסד הבד"ץ
RABBI C. DAVID REGENSBERG, *of blessed memory*
Founding Av Beth Din

הרב גדלי' דוב שווארץ, ראב"ד
RABBI GEDALIA DOV SCHWARTZ
Av Beth Din

הרב אברהם מרדכי אברמסן
RABBI ALAN M. ABRAMSON
Menahel

בס"ד

ב' לסדר וארא תשס"ח

לכבוד הרב הג' ר' משה ויינר שיחי'
אחדשה"ט

נתכבדתי לראות ולעיין. בחיבורו הנקרא "ספר שבע מצוות השם." נרשמתי מאד על כל ציוני המקורות שהביא בספרו בבקיאות ממקורות הש"ס ומפרשיו. השתלשלות הבעיות היוצאות מכל החומר הנ"ל מראה על עמל המחבר בהשתדלותו לפתח ולפתור אותם. ד' ית' יחזק חילי' לאוריתא להמשיך עבודתו הק'.

ברגשי ברכה.

גדלי' דוב שווארץ

Approbation (free translation)

Monday, Tevet 22, 5768 / December 31, 2007

To the Respected Rav, the *Ga'on* Rabbi Moshe Weiner,

I was honored to peruse and learn his compilation titled "*Sheva Mitzvot HaShem*." I was deeply impressed by the copious citations in the book, which display a great erudition in the Talmud and its commentaries. The detailed development of issues in the material reflects on the author's tremendous effort to solve them. May God strengthen him in his Torah studies and in continuing his holy work.

With great respect,
Gedaliah Dov Schwartz
Head of the Rabbinical Courts,
Rabbinical Council of America
and Chicago Rabbinical Council

LETTER FROM RABBI J. IMMANUEL SCHOCHET

Rabbi of Congregation Beth Joseph
Toronto, Canada

Cheshvan, 5768 / October 2007

The world has undergone a fascinating revolution. For approximately three decades there has been an ever-growing interest in the *Sheva Mitzvot B'nei Noaĥ,* the "Seven Commandments for the Children of Noaĥ," revealed in the Torah of Moses.[1] A great number of Gentiles throughout the world have committed themselves to observe this universal "Noahide Code." Many of them are in touch with reliable Rabbis to learn about their religious obligations as "Righteous Gentiles." Unfortunately, there was very little authoritative material to guide even these Rabbis.

Throughout most of post-Biblical history, the Noahide commandments could not be widely promoted, for the obvious reasons of the restraints of the Jewish exile, especially under the duress of the threats from non-Jewish religions who dominated the governments throughout the Diaspora. These circumstances made it difficult even to apply the comment of Rabbi Yomtov Lipman Heller that if we are ordained to promote observance of the Noahide Code, how much more so then to use friendly persuasion to lead the hearts of all to the Will of their Creator.[2] With few exceptions, this has led to "neglect" of this important aspect of Torah.

Clearly, these restraints no longer apply, and this has been conducive to the development of the so-called Noahide movement. The search for clear information and guidance, however, is hampered by the lack of precise summaries of a Code for the Noahides. Thus, it is a tremendous merit for the organization *Ask Noah International*, directed by truly pious and responsible Jews, to be inspired to fill this vacuum.

---

[1] Maimonides, *Hilĥot Melaĥim (Laws of Kings)* 8:10. See also *Hilĥot Milah* 1:6, and the glosses of *Kesef Mishneh* and *Tzafnat Pane'aĥ*, ad loc.

[2] *Tosafot Yom-Tov* (Rabbi Yomtov Lipman Heller) on Tractate *Avot* 5:14, see there at length. Cf. *Tosafot*, Tractate *Ĥagigah* 13a, s.v. *ein mosrin*; *Sefer Ĥassidim*, par. 1124; R. Ovadiah Sforno, Commentary on Exodus 19:6; *Shu"t Tashbatz* III:133; and *Shu"t Ĥatam Sofer*, *Ĥoshen Mishpat*, no. 185. Note also *Midrash Vayikra Rabbah* 6:5, and its variant version in *Midrash HaGadol* on Leviticus 5:1.

In November, 2005, *Ask Noah International* brought together a team of highly qualified Torah-scholars to dedicate themselves to this goal. Rabbi Moshe Weiner of Jerusalem undertook to bring it to fruition. He devoted himself for two years to a thorough in-depth study of the Seven Noahide Commandments and succeeded in composing a historic text in Hebrew, *Sefer Sheva Mitzvot HaShem, Volume I*, in the style and format of the classic *Shulĥan Aruĥ* [Code of Jewish Law], to serve as a guide for the practical application and observance of their detailed laws by Noahide individuals, families and communities. The significance of this project cannot be over-emphasized, as ever more Gentiles seek to follow a lifestyle conforming to the Divine commands incumbent upon them.

Needless to say, this is an extremely sensitive undertaking charged with great responsibilities. Thus, Rabbi Weiner's work, *Sefer Sheva Mitzvot HaShem*, was submitted for review by the world-renowned Rabbinical authority *HaGa'on* Rabbi Zalman Nehemiah Goldberg (may he live for many long and good days), member of the Supreme Rabbinical Court of Israel, who graciously examined the text, adding numerous comments throughout, and granted his approbation.

All the scholars consulted have praised this work as a major achievement, which brings an important but neglected area of Torah to the forefront of Rabbinic attention. They emphasize, though, that it is yet more important to make all people aware of it, in concise and easily readable format, as an authoritative guide for their daily lives. The translators and editor of the English version of the *Sefer Sheva Mitzvot HaShem* are thus bringing the project to its first milestone, which is now serving as the basis for translation into other languages.

Immeasurably great is the merit of all those who are involved with, and supporting, this extra-ordinary endeavor, which no doubt will hasten the fulfillment of the prophetic vision of "the earth will be as filled with knowledge of God as water covering the sea bed" (Isaiah 11:9).

J. Immanuel Schochet
Toronto, Canada

TABLE OF CONTENTS

Additional chapters on Torah Laws relating to establishment of laws and courts by Gentiles, in *Sheva Mitzvot HaShem*, Part VIII:

  Appointment of Judges and Enforcement Officers, and the Qualifications Necessary to be a Judge

  The Law of a Judge Who Purposefully or Mistakenly Judges Incorrectly

  The Jurisdiction of a Noahide Court, and How to Appeal the Decision of a Noahide Court

  Summons to a Monetary Adjudication, and Representation by a Lawyer

  The Order of the Court Case

  Necessary Qualifications of Witnesses

  Giving Testimony, and Producing Documentation

  The Laws of a False Witness

  Laws of Inheritance

  Punishment of a Murderer

  Punishment for Infractions of the Other Noahide Laws

  Government Law

  Military Justice

EDITOR'S PREFACE

1. *The Noahide Code – a destination of convergent histories*

2. *Some background behind this effort*

3. *How the practical details of the Noahide Code are determined*

4. *How to use this book*

5. *How the past can be uplifted by disseminating this message*

1. The Noahide Code – a destination of convergent histories

1. *Praise the Lord, all you nations; extol Him, all you peoples.*
2. *For His kindness was mighty over us, and the truth of the Lord is everlasting; praise the Lord.* (Psalm 117)

This shortest Psalm consists of only two verses, which together encompass all humanity. Verse 1 encompasses all non-Jews, and verse 2 encompasses all Jews. These are the two intersecting vectors of the image of God within creation, and they are forever joined at a single point of unity, which is the simultaneously transcendent and indwelling Unity of God. This point of unity is not easily seen or felt, and that has been the case throughout most of the tumultuous history of the world. However, at one place, at one time, this point of unity was revealed, openly and miraculously, by our Creator Himself. He chose this in His wisdom, so that all of His children, the human race, could know and believe, remember and take it to heart, until the arrival of the Messianic Era. When that time arrives, it will happen because we will be ready – on God's terms – to receive Him as the King over the entire world. Such a fundamental revelation need only occur once, if it is unquestionably witnessed and recorded, and commanded by God to be preserved for posterity. That revelation took place at Mount Sinai, in the Hebrew year 2448 (1312 B.C.E.[1]).

At that time, the voice of God, the Name of God, and the Unity of God were openly revealed. But God, in His wisdom, saw it better to withhold from the individuals of the witnessing nation, the Jewish

---

[1] B.C.E. is Before the Common Era; C.E. is the Common Era.

people, an ability to continue living with the intensity of the revelation. Instead, He appointed Moses (*Moshe* in Hebrew) as His prophet, to receive and transmit all of His commandments for the future generations (Deut. 21-28). This included the recording of God's encapsulation of His Divine wisdom into written words, which can be absorbed and integrated within the limited human mind. This document, the Five Books of Moses, God called the *Torah*, which means "instruction," and He bequeathed it, along with its explanations, to the Jews as an eternal inheritance (Deut. 33:4). Along with this gift came the entrusting of a great responsibility, because the Torah does not "only" specify the 613 Jewish Commandments (of which the "Ten Commandments" are only a fraction). It also contains the Seven Noahide Commandments for all non-Jews, which God commanded to Noah sixteen generations earlier.

With the ascent of the Jews to nationhood in the Land of Israel, the surrounding nations, and especially the people from those nations who chose to take up residence in the Holy Land, returned to an awareness of the Seven Noahide Commandments. As the Jews encountered national successes and failures over the 440 years preceding the construction of the First Holy Temple by King Solomon, and the 410 years during which it stood, the appeal of the Noahide Code among the surrounding nations waxed and waned.

During the time of the Second Holy Temple (350 B.C.E.- 70 C.E.), a large movement of "Heaven Fearers" was active in the Roman Empire. These were Gentile adherents to the One God of Israel, who directed their religious loyalty to the Jewish Sages and the Holy Temple. It is nearly impossible to find any unbiased sources on this subject outside of the Talmud and Midrash, because after the Temple's destruction, these Torah-observant Gentiles became prime targets of the enforcers of the pagan Roman religion, and later of the missionizing activities of innovative new religions that began to challenge the Divinely appointed authority of the Torah tradition. The best non-Torah historical accounts of the "Heaven Fearers" are in the writings of Josephus.[2]

After the destruction of the Second Temple, and the Diaspora of the Jewish people among nations that were influenced by religions unfriendly to Judaism, it was necessary for the light and the eternal

---

[2] Josephus: *The Jewish War* 2:454,463 and 7:45; *Jewish Antiquities* 14:110 and 20:41; *Against Apion* 1:166,167 and 2:282.

promise of the Noahide Code to be preserved and guarded by the Jewish Sages within the writings of the Oral Torah tradition. Their Torah-law rulings and scholarly debates on the Divine obligations of the Gentile world would have been deemed purely academic over the centuries, were it not for the scriptural prophecies of universal peace and return to Torah observance that will occur in the Messianic Era.

Until Rabbi Elijah Benamozegh (1823-1900) in France, who used the title "Noahide" for observers of the seven commandments, there were no contemporary writings on the Noahide Code directed to the Gentile world. Although the seventh Rebbe of Lubavitch, Rabbi Menachem Mendel Schneerson (1902-1994), began delivering talks about detailed points of the Noahide Code from the beginning of his leadership in 1951, it was unexpected when, beginning in the 1980's, he put forth an urgent calling to the nations of the world to fulfill their seven commandments, and to the Jewish people at all levels to inform and influence Gentiles concerning the importance of this observance.[3]

2. Some background behind this effort

In response to the Rebbe's call, many Gentiles around the world began to seek information about how to correctly fulfill the precepts of these seven commandments. Also in response to this calling, Mr. Chaim Reisner of Pittsburgh, Pennsylvania, founded the *Ask Noah* organization in the mid-1990's. In 1999, I joined *Ask Noah* to provide Torah-true Noahide outreach, starting as the web master of the web site *asknoah.org*. Since then, these efforts have reached tens of thousands of Gentiles, and growing numbers of Noahide communities.

We soon saw that to fulfill the call for the nations of the world to return to the Noahide commandments, it would be necessary to have organized learning at the local level. We also learned of the Rebbe's efforts for a project to codify the Noahide commandments, in the spirit of the classic *Shulĥan Aruĥ* (Code of Jewish Law). To undertake this ambitious task, Mr. Reisner traveled to Israel in the summer of 2004, and met with several leading Rabbis and Torah experts, to present them with our plan, and to request their advice. He received positive reactions from each one, as exemplified by this letter from Prof. Nahum Rakover, former Deputy Attorney General of Israel:

---

[3] See *To Perfect the World: The Lubavitcher Rebbe's Call to Teach the Noahide Code to All Mankind*, pub. Sichos in English, 2016.

The Jewish Legal Heritage Society

B"H

י"ד-Elul-תשס"ד
8.31.2004

Mr. Chaim Reisner
Founder, Ask Noah
Pittsburgh, PA

Dear Mr. Reisner,

I was very impressed to hear about the projects that you are planning in regard to the Seven Noahide Commandments.

It is very important to produce a "Torah Code of Noahide Law", written by qualified Torah scholars, so Noahides will know their true obligations in detail.

Your other project, to open Torah academies for Noahides to learn about their Mitzvot, sounds very interesting and innovative. The students of these academies will be well acquainted with their obligations, and can become qualified teachers to disseminate the Noahide laws among the nations.

Sincerely,

N. Rakover

Prof. Nahum Rakover

With Rabbi Moshe Weiner's acceptance in 2005 to produce the foundation for this effort, an in-depth codification of the Noahide precepts, the goal became a reality. Volumes I and II of his *Sefer Sheva Mitzvot HaShem* (*The Book of Seven Divine Commandments*), were compiled in Hebrew during the next two years, with many points of scholarly advice from the renowned Torah authority, Rabbi Zalman Nehemiah Goldberg of Jerusalem. Volume I was published in 2008, Vol. II was published in 2009, and Vol. III in 2012. These are the source texts that Rabbi Weiner used to produce this English edition.

3. How the practical details of the Noahide Code are determined

Gentiles are obligated to fulfill the Seven Noahide Commandments because they are the eternal command of God, transmitted through Moses our teacher in the Torah. Since the explanation of every commandment in the Written Torah is established according to the Oral Torah,[4] as it was given over through Moses our teacher and transmitted from generation to generation through the Jewish Sages, it can thus be concluded that the rules which guide Torah-law decisions in regard to the 613 Jewish Commandments are the same rules which guide Torah-law decisions for Gentiles, aside from a few exceptions that are explained in this work. Rambam (Rabbi Moshe ben Maimon, or Maimonides, 1135-1204) was the first to codify these commandments, albeit in very concise form, and his rulings are known to be based on the same rules that guide the Oral Torah for the Jewish commandments, unless he stated a specific exception. This reasoning is born out by the numerous discussions in the Talmud that deal with the Noahide commandments.

In determining the Torah Law for Gentiles more comprehensively, Rabbi Weiner used the rulings in Rambam's *Mishneh Torah* as the main foundation, since Rambam is the principal Torah-law authority in this area. The importance of Rambam as a primary authority in the precepts of the Jewish people is well known. In the words of Rabbi Yosef Karo (1488-1575), author of the *Shulĥan Aruĥ* (the Code of Jewish Law): "For he [Rambam] is the most famous Torah-law authority in the world."[5] Thus, on any issue for which Rambam differed from only one other Torah-law authority, the opinion that Rabbi Yosef Karo decided upon for his *Shulĥan Aruĥ* was Rambam's.

---

[4] See the Introduction by Rabbi J. Immanuel Schochet to Part I of this work.

[5] Quoted from Rabbi Yosef Karo's Introduction to his book *Beit Yosef*.

This holds even more so for the precepts of the Noahide commandments, for Rambam is nearly the only *Rishon*[6] who took responsibility for authoritative teachings in this area. The other well-known classic Rabbinical works, such as *Tur* and *Shulĥan Aruĥ*, did not provide explicit rulings on Torah Law for Gentiles. Instead, we must gather insight from different points that they wrote regarding observance of Torah precepts for Jews, and these in turn imply their opinions about observance of Torah precepts for Gentiles. Therefore, Rambam is the main Torah-law authority whose opinion is to be considered in these matters, and therefore his opinion is given more weight than any other single authority. Still, exceptions can be found, and in *Sheva Mitzvot HaShem*, Rabbi Weiner extensively researched and cited the broad spectrum of Rabbinical sources. In the few cases where a majority of the other *Rishon* authorities and the *Shulĥan Aruĥ* all differ from Rambam, Rabbi Weiner decided the Torah Law according to their teachings, and not according to the opinion of Rambam.

In every case, Rabbi Weiner clearly explained the spectrum of sources, and the basis of his conclusions, in his footnotes for the text of *Sheva Mitzvot HaShem*. There are fewer footnotes in this English edition, and they are abridged, to limit the amount of technical Rabbinical discussion that is not relevant for most readers.

4. How to use this Fourth Edition

This edition has eight Parts; each contains chapters with numbered "topics." Thus, Part I, topic 6:1, refers to topic 1 of Chapter 6 within Part I. Numerous typing errors that were found in the Third Edition have been corrected, and an Appendix has been added on Torah laws that are particularly relevant for a Pious Gentile or a *Ger Toshav* who lives among Jews. Listings of the main precepts in each Part have been added from the book *Tishim Ĥukim (Ninety Laws)* by Rabbi Moshe Weiner. A number of points have been clarified, and some redundant sentences have been deleted, especially in Part II, Chapter 3. Editor's notes are added as footnotes marked by an asterisk (*); these include commentary or additional information. **The reader is advised that important information is included in many of the footnotes.**

---

[6] *Rishon* refers to leading Rabbis of 1000-1500 C.E. who succeeded the Talmudic Sages (200-500 C.E.) and Ga'onic Sages (589-1038 C.E.) in transmitting the Torah tradition. (See *Miraculous Journey*, by Rabbi Yosef Eisen.)

To make the footnoted citations of Rabbinic sources more meaningful, a bibliography for the book has been provided on our Web site, with short historical information on the source texts and their authors.[7] The sources are generally cited using our transliterations of their Hebrew titles. The exceptions are the citations of section titles in Rambam's *Mishneh Torah*, which are translated into English for the benefit of those who wish to look up the citations in a translation of *Mishneh Torah*. For this purpose, these translated titles match, or nearly match, the titles as they appear in the *Mishneh Torah* volumes that have been published in English by Moznaim (Brooklyn, New York; translated by Rabbi Eliyahu Touger). This series has been a valuable asset for our translation of the topics in *Sheva Mitzvot HaShem*, many of which follow the wording of *Mishneh Torah.*

In Part I, Chapters 1-4 present basic principles of Torah-based faith in the One God. These include acceptance of the truth of the Torah and acknowledgment that Divine rewards accrue from observance of God's will, and that the opposite (God forbid) accrues from deliberate, or sometimes careless, transgressions of His will. Chapters 5-6 and 8-9 present a practical and reliable guide to subjects that are of prime importance in the daily life of pious Gentiles: **Torah Study, Prayer, Moral Conduct, and Repentance.**

A few chapters in this edition have been shortened to one page: Chapter 7 in Part I, Chapter 4 in Part II, and Chapter 4 in Part V. This was done because detailed study of those subjects lacks practical relevance in our modern times. Those who are interested in further study are referred to the full chapters in the earlier editions or in the original *Sheva Mitzvot HaShem*. There, Gentiles who are interested will find more material from Torah sources, to learn more about how the general rules of the Noahide Code applied to those subjects, and about additional lessons and moral values that Torah teaches.[8]

Some topics in this book apply to both Jews and Gentiles, but it only comes to teach the Noahide Code. Thus, Jews should not use this text to determine their own obligations, which are more restrictive and numerous. Questions on Torah observance by any individual may be directed to observant Jewish Torah scholars, or sent to *AskNoah.org*.

---

[7] https://asknoah.org/wp-content/uploads/the-divine-code-bibliography.pdf

[8] For example, see the reference to the ancient idolatry of *Moleĥ* (Part II, ch. 4) in the Introduction to Part VI, on the Prohibition of Forbidden Relations.

5. How the past can be uplifted by disseminating this message

Finally, we need to address a point that arises in the minds of many Gentiles who accept and follow the truth of the Noahide Code. This is a question about Divine fairness: what can be said about Gentiles who never had access to awareness and information about the wellsprings of the Noahide Code, which is now finally being disseminated throughout the world? Surely many good people, who did many good deeds, passed on without having had the opportunity to know of, or much less observe, the Seven Noahide Commandments. Did they not deserve the opportunity to receive a portion in the future World to Come through faithful observance of the Noahide Code?

It is fundamentally important to recognize that God is fair and just, and therefore no deserving soul is denied the opportunity to earn a place in the World to Come.[9] God's ways, including how He accomplishes this, are ultimately inscrutable and beyond the understanding of mortals. However, on such a fundamental question, there must be answers that we can relate to on a practical basis. The growth of the world population has accelerated greatly over the past few hundred years, from 791 million in 1750, to 3 billion in 1959, to 7.8 billion in 2020. Thus, the world's population at this time, when the Noahide Code is finally being presented openly for all mankind, is surely more than able to contain the reincarnated souls[10] of all good and deserving Gentiles who have lived in the past. This may be God's way to give a soul an extra opportunity it deserves, to make amends and to become righteous.

Therefore, it will be a great service to every soul in the world today if we, together, will make this opportunity known and available. With God's help, through *your* help, we will accomplish this task, and very soon, with the coming of the Messiah, "the occupation of the whole world will be solely to know God,"[11] and "the earth will be as filled with knowledge of God as water covering the sea bed."[12]

---

[9] For a text that teaches numerous fundamental spiritual topics within Torah as they relate to Gentiles, see *Seven Gates of Righteous Knowledge*, by Rabbi Moshe Weiner, pub. Ask Noah International, 2017.

[10] See *Soul Searching*, by Yaakov Astor, pub. Targum Press, 2003.

[11] Rambam, *Laws of Kings* 12:5.

[12] Isaiah 11:9.

AUTHOR'S INTRODUCTION

by Rabbi Moshe Weiner

The Master of the universe commanded Adam, the first man,[1] on the day of his creation,[2] as it says (Gen. 2:16), "And the Lord God commanded 'the man' (*Adam*) ..." God commanded six precepts to Adam:

1) the prohibition against worshiping false gods;

2) the prohibition against cursing God's Name;

3) the prohibition against murder;

4) the prohibition against specific forbidden sexual relations;

5) the prohibition against theft;

6) the commandment to establish laws and courts of justice.[3]

The Creator added to these when He commanded Noaĥ not to eat flesh that was removed from a living animal,[4] as it says,[5] "And God blessed Noaĥ, ... But flesh, with its soul in its blood you should not eat." These seven precepts are called the Seven Commandments for the *B'nei Noaĥ* ("Children of Noaĥ," i.e. Gentiles, who are non-Jews).[6]

When Moses our teacher was called up on Mount Sinai, he received the Torah's commandments directly from the Holy One, blessed be He, together with their explanations. Moses received the entire Torah from God – both the Written Torah (the Five Books of Moses) and the Oral Torah. The Oral Torah is the explanation of all the commandments, which are very concisely recorded in those Five Books.[7]

---

[1] Tractate *Sanhedrin* 56b.

[2] It is explained in Tractate *Sanhedrin* 56b that all of the Noahide Commandments can be exegetically derived from Genesis 2:16, "And the Lord God commanded the man, saying, ...," which was stated to Adam in the Garden of Eden on the day of his creation; see Tractate *Sanhedrin* 38b.

[3] *This includes an obligation for leaders to inform their communities about the Noahide precepts.

[4] *Before the Flood, mankind was not permitted to kill animals for food or their other needs, nor to cut a limb from a living animal (Part IV, topic 1:1).

[5] Gen. 9:1,4. This applies to land mammals and birds; see Part IV, Chapter 1.

[6] Rambam, *Laws of Kings* 9:1.

[7] Rambam, *Introduction to the Mishneh Torah.*

Included in the Torah, God also repeated and gave to Moses the Seven Commandments for the Children of Noaĥ, along with their explanations and their details.

All the Gentiles of the world were henceforth eternally commanded to accept upon themselves and to fulfill these seven Divine precepts, because the Holy One, blessed be He, commanded them in the Torah, and He made known through Moses our teacher that the descendants of Noaĥ had previously been commanded to do them.[8]

These seven commandments have general rules and many details, and all of them are described in the Oral Torah, just as the 613 commandments (*mitzvot* in Hebrew; singular *mitzvah*) that the Jewish people were commanded to observe. The Jewish Sages and the faithful Rabbinical authorities in every generation are commanded to explain the Torah to the rest of the Jewish people. They are also commanded to explain the Noahide commandments to the Gentiles, and to teach them how these seven *mitzvot* should be fulfilled.[9]

We are not to rely on anyone else to provide explanations of any part of Torah, whether for Jews or Gentiles, aside from accepted Jewish Torah scholars, for they alone, as students of the earlier Torah Sages, are the authorities who explain the Oral Torah.[10] (Rambam describes the Torah Sages of the Talmud as "the mainstay of the Oral Torah.")[11]

In addition to observing the Seven Noahide Commandments with their many details, a Gentile is commanded to act in the proper ways that human intelligence would compel him, whether these are obligations to God or to other people, or to society as a whole. Even

---

[8] Rambam, *Laws of Kings* 8:11.

[9] *Tosafot*, Tractate *Ĥagigah* 13a, states that it is an obligation for the Jews to teach and inform the Gentiles of the Seven Noahide Commandments. (Due to the extreme difficulties of the extended Jewish exile, this was not possible in most societies until our recent generations.)

[10] *These are the Jewish Sages and faithful Orthodox Rabbis, whose responsa and teachings may be cited by laypersons.

[11] Rambam, *Laws of Rebellious Ones* 1:1. There were no drawn-out differences of opinion until the Supreme Sanhedrin ceased after the destruction of the Second Temple. Until then, a difference arose only about a matter (or a required degree of strictness) that was not received from Moses. When this arose, the Sages debated and established the Torah Law according to the majority in the Supreme Sanhedrin, and it was accepted by the Jewish people.

though Gentiles are not commanded in detail about these parameters of proper conduct, nevertheless, God carefully checks and judges all the ways of every person. There are actions for which the individual or the society is liable to be punished, since such behavior is not appropriate for the human race, even though it is beyond the scope of the Seven Commandments.[12] Societal morality is included in the commandment of "judgments" (*dinim*), by which the Children of Noaĥ were commanded to set up courts of law, and judges who will supervise and warn society about prohibited behaviors. But God will look upon the ways of an individual and judge him for his every action, even if he is not under the jurisdiction of a court of law, or if the court is not able to judge him, or if the court does not know about his behavior.[13]

The purpose of this book is to explain these seven commandments according to Torah principles and Torah Law, including both their general rules and their details, and also the moral obligations that are intellectually incumbent. All of this is in order to teach faithful Gentiles the way of God and the path in which it is proper for them to go, until they will merit through this the distinctions and the spiritual beauty of "the pious of the nations of the world."[14]

---

[12] *The true specialty of mankind is expressed in Tractate *Avot* 3:14: "He [Rabbi Akiva] used to say: Beloved is man, for he was created in the image [of God]; it is even a greater love that it was made known to him that he was created in the image [of God], as it is stated [Genesis 9:6]: For in the image of God He made man."

[13] Tractate *Sanhedrin* 104b relates the destruction of Sodom and Gomorrah. Even though idol worship and forbidden sexual relations were rampant there, in outright rebellion against God, His decree of their total destruction came because they punished any performer of charity and kindness with torturous execution. Hence it is obvious that God demands moral conduct from mankind, even though it is not explicitly commanded. Ramban on Gen. 6:2 explains why the Generation of the Flood was punished specifically because of theft, even though they violated all their commandments, because of theft is a logical prohibition that no one can negate by saying, "we did not know we were commanded." In Part I, see topics 3:8-9 and 4:6, and their footnotes.

[14] *These are Gentiles who earn eternal spiritual reward by accepting upon themselves to fulfill the Seven Noahide Commandments and being careful in their observance, specifically because the Holy One, blessed be He, commanded them in the Torah, and informed us through Moses our teacher that Noaĥ's descendants had been previously commanded to fulfill them.

The Basis for Fulfillment of the Noahide Code

Rambam explains in *Laws of Kings* 8:11: "...The Holy One, blessed be He, commanded them [the Seven Noahide Commandments] in the Torah, and informed us through Moses our teacher that Noaĥ's descendants had been previously commanded to fulfill them."

This means that even though Noaĥ's descendants were previously commanded to fulfill them – and this Divine command was not nullified in legal terms, and Gentiles are still obligated by the power of the original commands – nevertheless, there were more details added by God through Moses at the giving of the Torah at Mount Sinai. Clearly, the Noahide Commandments were commanded to Moses, because even though they were commanded previously to Adam and Noaĥ, they were never written down as Torah before Mount Sinai. Their recording in the Written Torah was through Moses, and their explanations and details as transmitted in the Oral Torah were given to Moses, as will be explained.

According to his above-cited ruling, Rambam explains that (a) the descendants of Noaĥ are obligated to observe their Seven Commandments because these were commanded to them by God through Moses, and (b) when the Torah was given by God through Moses, there was a spiritual dimension that He added for the Gentiles as well as for the Jews. The explanation of this spiritual dimension of the Noahide Code, which was added by God through Moses at Mount Sinai, is given by Rambam in *Laws of the Foundations of the Torah*, Chapter 8.

Rambam explains that we do not believe in Moses as a prophet because of the miracles he performed, since a prediction and a sign could be accomplished through sorcery, and thus it could be doubted. Rather, we believe in Moses and God's true Torah – against which there will never be a real challenge – based on the true testimony of what the entire Israelite nation saw and heard at God's giving of the Ten Commandments at Mount Sinai. They all witnessed with absolute surety that Moses heard his prophecies directly as the open speech of God, and that God gave Moses the Torah from Heaven. Therefore, if a subsequent "prophet" arises to challenge, change or nullify any prophecy of Moses, or any part of the Torah of Moses, we can know without any doubt that this person's words are false, as is well explained by Rambam. Therefore, the obligation to keep the Torah's commandments (the *mitzvot*)[15] is absolutely true, without doubt.

This is not known as a private tradition as were the earlier prophecies up to the time of Mount Sinai. Before the giving of the Torah, it was possible to think that perhaps another prophet could come and contest or deny the prophecy and words of an earlier prophet. Therefore, also in regard to the Seven Noahide Commandments, their existence is not absolute because they were commanded to Adam and Noaĥ personally from God. For it is possible that a later prophet could come and deny any of those commandments, and perform wonders and miracles to show his abilities, and thereby convince others that those earlier commandments had become nullified or changed. Rather, the absolutely true existence of the Noahide commandments, like the rest of the Torah, is only that they were commanded eternally by God Himself at Mount Sinai through Moses, as a true testimony.

Even though the testimony from Mount Sinai was directed to the entire Jewish people who heard and saw it directly, and the Gentile nations did not experience it directly, nevertheless, such a unique testimony to a group of millions of people is impossible to refute, and there never was again any occurrence of public Divine speech to an entire nation. All of the previous and later prophets received private prophecies (see Rambam's *Guide to the Perplexed*, Part II, ch. 35).

According to this, we can understand the words of Rambam in *Laws of Kings* 8:11, that "wise ones" of the Gentiles may be found who are keeping aspects of the Noahide *mitzvot* according to their intellect and their knowledge, or even because of the command to Adam and Noaĥ, but not because these commandments were reiterated and renewed by God at Mount Sinai. As Rambam writes in *Laws of Kings* 9:1, logic and wisdom dictate these precepts; i.e., it is possible to observe them on an intellectual basis without belief in the Divine command, or not because they were commanded to Moses, but rather because they were previously commanded. A Gentile who does so is called "wise," but he is not called "pious" (a "*ĥassid*" in Hebrew). Rambam teaches that if a Gentile observes these only from an intellectual standpoint, but not

---

[15] *There are 248 obligations and 365 prohibitions commanded for the Jews, and seven *categories* of prohibitions commanded for the rest of mankind. Beyond these seven categories of prohibitions, there are also fundamental and *universal* positive obligations, including: belief, faith and trust in God; turning to Him for one's needs; and creating a civilized world.

because of God's command to Moses, he will receive reward for his good deeds; but he has not earned a part in the ultimate spiritual reward of the future eternal World to Come, because that is obtained only by virtue of submitting one's actions to the will of God that He revealed in His eternal Torah of Moses, the "Tree of Life."[16]

However, the Divine command of the Noahide Code to Adam and Noaĥ stands and has not been nullified on a Torah-law basis, for, as Rambam states in *Laws of Kings* 8:11, Moses informed us in the Torah that the descendants of Noaĥ were previously commanded in them. Moses was commanded that mankind must be informed about this.[17]

Therefore, Rambam says clearly in *Laws of Kings* 9:1, "Six precepts were commanded to Adam ... it was added for Noaĥ ...," and these commands still stand. Therefore it is obvious that the primary commanding of the seven Noahide *mitzvot* was to Adam and Noaĥ. Beyond this, God added three new dimensions through Moses:

(a) The Torah's details of the Noahide commandments that were not revealed before Mount Sinai, as we will now explain.

(b) Their new strength as absolute and eternal commandments, which did not exist before Mount Sinai, as explained above.

(c) After Mount Sinai, it is impossible to add, subtract or change any of the Noahide Commandments forever, as will be explained below.

It is obvious that Moses explained the Torah's seven *mitzvot* that are for the Gentiles, and that the details they previously did not know were commanded to them by God with their explanations through Moses, at Mount Sinai. For example, after the Torah was given, a deliberate transgression of a specific Noahide commandment carries liability not only to punishment by God, but also to capital punishment by an

---

16 *For observing the Noahide Commandments based only on intellect, a Gentile's reward may be received during his life in this world, or in his after-life after the end of his physical life, or both. The eternal World to Come will begin with the general resurrection of the righteous who attached themselves to the Torah of Moses, which is called God's "Tree of Life" (Prov. 3:11-18).

17 *This was a direct command from God, in the same sense as (Leviticus 6:1-2): God spoke to Moses, saying, "Command Aaron and his sons, saying: This is the law ..." Thus, no group can validly claim that they may bypass acceptance of the Noahide Code from the Torah because their religion pre-dates Mount Sinai.

"authorized court" (see Part VIII, topic 1:11). But this is not commanded in Genesis as the definitive punishment for transgressions other than murder, in Genesis 9:6 – "Whoever sheds the blood of man …, his blood shall be shed …," which was commanded to Noaĥ.

Another example is the command regarding adulterous relations with a married Jewish woman. This was related in the Torah (Leviticus 18:6) as *"ish ish ..."* (any man), which Tractate *Sanhedrin* 57b explains as including Gentiles in the command prohibiting adultery with a married Jewess. This obligated Gentiles to take care in regard to the many Torah regulations and precepts that determine if a Jewess is considered married, and they have liability before an authorized court for these additional stringencies, even though Gentiles were originally commanded through Adam regarding adultery only as it applies to Gentile marriage. Hence, the cited command in Leviticus is to Gentiles (as a detail of their forbidden sexual relations), as well as to Jews.

These examples prove that the Torah that was given through Moses included the Noahide commandments, and also additional details that had not been commanded up to that point as part of a Noahide Code.

More so, it was also added through Moses for all mankind that the Noahide commandments will not change forever, and there will be no additions or subtractions. Until Moses, it was possible that God would let a prophet know that one of the commandments was nullified, or that a new commandment could be added (as God commanded the additional prohibition to Noaĥ of eating flesh that was severed from a living animal, and He commanded the additional precept of circumcision to Abraham).[18] But once Moses arose as the greatest prophet for

---

[18] Rambam teaches in *Laws of Kings* 9:1, "Thus, there are seven precepts [which were commanded to Noaĥ]. These remained the same throughout the world until Abraham, who arose and was commanded regarding circumcision, and he also ordained morning prayers. Isaac separated tithes and added a prayer service in the afternoon. Jacob added [a prohibition against eating] the sciatic nerve, and he also ordained evening prayers… Ultimately, Moses came and the Torah was *completed* by him." Thus, there were additions in the commands of God to His early prophets – first to Noaĥ and then to the three Patriarchs. The Patriarchs also added precepts from their own logic and for their own family, yet they violated no prohibition in doing so. This possibility did not continue after Moses completed the Torah, since also for the Children of Noaĥ, a prophet cannot add anything to the Torah, or create a new commandment or a new religion after Mount Sinai.

all time, and God commanded the precepts of the Torah through him, including the Noahide commandments, no true prophet will ever arise to change, or add to, or subtract from them, forever.

This concept is because of the special status of the "Torah of Moses," as Rambam describes and explains in *Laws of Foundations of the Torah*, Chapter 9. God sealed the Divine Commandments when He commanded mankind with the giving of the Torah to Moses, and He established that He will never send or command a prophet to alter any one of the Torah's commandments. This point, which God also commanded to Moses at Mount Sinai (Deuteronomy 13:1), established the Torah of the Jews as the source for His sealed commandments. This is true also in regard to the Seven Noahide Commandments, but only because of the unique transmittal of His commands to mankind through Moses at the public national revelation at Mount Sinai, as explained above. Without God's sealing of the Seven Noahide Commandments in the Torah, they would not truly be His eternal word, because of the possibility that they might be changed or added to.

This is the depth of Rambam's words (*Laws of Kings* 8:11): "Any Gentile who accepts the seven commandments and is careful to observe them is of the 'pious of the nations of the world' and will have a portion in the World to Come. **This is so provided that one accepts them and observes them because the Holy One, blessed be He, commanded them in the Torah and informed us through Moses our teacher** that the descendants of Noaĥ were originally commanded about them."

The true cleaving of a person to God can only be in a way that accords with the will of God, Who has given mankind a path of connection to Himself, and to a spiritually higher level of eternal existence that is inconceivable by natural means. This can only be achieved because God Himself, in His unlimited kindness, bestows this possibility to mankind. If one rationalizes the observance of these seven precepts and observes them based only on that reasoning, he may indeed be an intelligent person, and he may do many good deeds. But if one's observance is based only on human intellect, which is limited, it is definitely not connected with the eternally existing Divine Truth. Therefore, such an approach lacks the essential element of binding to God's will,[19] and, as the world has seen from tragic experiences, the person who follows that approach will be at increased risk of rationalizing an actual transgression.

Without proper explanation, a person may not automatically appreciate the special blessings that God has made available to mankind, nor how those blessings may be secured in the manner that Rambam shared: "provided that one accepts them and observes them because the Holy One, blessed be He, commanded them in the Torah and informed us through Moses our teacher ..." This is an eternal truth that God, in His infinite kindness, gifted to mankind at the event of *Matan Torah* (the "Gift of Torah").

---

[19] *In the Torah, there are statements by God to Moses, prohibiting Jews to do specific things that are prohibited in a general way for Gentiles. We cite such verses as sources or explanations for details of the Noahide commandments, but these are not intended to imply that Gentiles are commanded about any prohibition that God commanded to the Jews. Thus, particular prohibitions or directives, derived from an explanation on a Torah verse, can be understood as relating to Gentiles as God's will in general. This is the intention in this book – to cite verses from the Hebrew Bible as sources for Torah concepts and to provide their authentic explanations. This is a general point throughout the book, but there are exceptions when a verse actually relates directly to a commandment for Gentiles (see for example Part II, topic 1:1; Part III, topic 1:1; Part IV, topic 1:3). Usually in these cases, the author explains in the main text that this is an explicit scriptural commandment for Gentiles.

PART I

FUNDAMENTALS OF THE FAITH

This section explains details of the following nine obligations and six prohibitions that are based on fundamental principles which are implicit from the commandment to Gentiles that prohibits idolatry:

1. To know that there is a God, and that He created all that exists.

2. To accept the "yoke of Heaven" *(kabalat ol Malchut Shamayim)* and fulfill the Seven Commandments for Gentiles, according to their details and explanations within the Oral Torah.

3. To fear God.

4. To love God.

5. Not to prophesy falsely in the name of God.

6. Not to prophesy in the name of an idol, or to convince others to worship an idol or to transgress any of the Seven Commandments.

7. Not to listen to a false prophet, whether he prophecies falsely in the name of God or in the name of an idol.

8. To listen to a true prophet who speaks in the name of God, and to obey a true prophet's instructions.

9. Not to create a new religion or commandment. This includes the prohibition against a Gentile observing a sanctified day of ritual restraint, as it says (Gen. 8:22), *"lo yishbotu"* ("They shall not make a Sabbath").

10. Not to add to or subtract from the Seven Commandments, or any part of them, as they were given for Gentiles by God through Moses at Sinai.

11. Not to delve deeply into the study of parts of Torah that do not pertain to the Noahide Code. (This is also an offshoot of the commandment for laws and courts.)

12. To have faith and trust in God, which includes to pray only to Him and to ask Him to provide the things that one needs.

13. To praise and thank God, which includes that a person should thank God for his food and sustenance and for the things that happen to him.

14. To strive to imitate God's ways that were praised by the Prophets of the Hebrew Bible, and to improve one's temperament and character traits and establish them in the ways that are known to be correct in God's eyes.

15. To evaluate one's actions and repent for one's misdeeds, and to change one's ways for the better.

INTRODUCTION

The Foundation of the Noahide Code: The "Written Torah" and the "Oral Torah"

by Rabbi J. Immanuel Schochet

Any Gentile who accepts the seven commandments and is careful to observe them is of the "pious of the nations of the world" and will have a portion in the World to Come. This is so provided that one accepts them and observes them because the Holy One, blessed be He, commanded them in the Torah and informed us through Moses our teacher that the descendants of Noaĥ were originally commanded about them. But if one observes them only by virtue of common sense, he is not a Ger Toshav (Gentile "Resident," the Written Torah's term for one who takes on the Noahide Code)*, or one of the "pious of the nations of the world," but rather, one of their wise people.*[1]

The first five books of the Hebrew Bible (Genesis, Exodus, Leviticus, Numbers and Deuteronomy) are the very essence and substance of the "Written Torah."[2] They are also referred to as the "the Teaching of Moses,"[3] and in the vernacular as the "Five Books of

---

[1] Rambam (Maimonides), *Laws of Kings* 8:11. This ruling is based on the very early Rabbinic text *Mishnat Rabbi Eliezer*, section VI (ed. New York 1933, p. 121), as noted by Rambam himself in one of his responsa (*Teshuvot HaRambam*, ed. Blau, vol. I, no. 148): "The pious of the nations of the world are deemed pious if they observe the seven commandments enjoined upon the descendants of Noaĥ, in all their details."

[2] The term "the Written Torah" in a general sense refers to the whole body of the twenty-four Books of the Hebrew Bible. Its essence, however, is the *Ĥumash* (Pentateuch, or Five Books of Moses), for it alone contains all of the Divine precepts, and nothing may be added and nothing may be subtracted from it. Even genuine prophets cannot alter anything in the *Ĥumash*. Indeed, all later prophets or prophecies are verified by their complete conformity to the *Ĥumash*. It is the ultimate criterion: the falsehood of a prophet or prophecy is established by even the slightest divergence from the original words of the *Ĥumash*. Cf. Rambam, *Principles of the Faith*, no. 9; *idem, Laws of the Foundations of the Torah*, ch. 9.

[3] For example, Joshua 8:31-32 and 23:6; II Kings 14:6; Nehemiah 8:1.

Moses," as the Jewish people have an unbroken historical tradition to the very time of Moses that he is their author. Moses wrote these five books by Divine dictation: every word in them was dictated to Moses by God Himself.[4]

The belief in Moses as the ultimate and supreme prophet of God,[5] and therefore of the Divine origin of the Torah, is not based on claims by Moses or others, nor on the fact that Moses performed manifest miracles, supernatural signs and wonders. The authenticity of Moses is based on the public revelation at Sinai: God revealed Himself to the entire nation of Israel, at least three million people, and proclaimed before them the Ten Commandments.[6]

The entire Jewish people personally experienced that revelation, each individual in effect becoming a prophet, and each one verifying the experience of the other. With their own eyes they saw, and with their own ears they heard, as the Divine voice spoke to them, and also they heard God saying, "Moses, Moses, go tell them the following ..."[7] They did not receive the occurrence of that event and accept it as some claim or tradition of an individual, but they experienced it themselves. That public revelation, therefore, authenticated the *bona fide* status of Moses as a prophet of God, and the Divine origin of the instructions he recorded in the Torah. That, and that alone, is the criterion for the belief in, and acceptance of, Moses and his teachings, as God said to him, "I will come unto you in a thick cloud that the people may hear when I speak with you and will also believe in you *forever*" (Exodus 19:9).[8]

The "Written Torah" of the Five Books of Moses, however, which contains all the Divine precepts, presents a "problem," so to speak. Practically all of the precepts, the commandments and prohibitions,

---

[4] See Tractate *Sanhedrin* 99a. Rambam, *Principles of the Faith*, no. 8; *idem, Laws of Repentance* 3:8.

[5] See Rambam, *Principles of the Faith*, no.7; *idem, Laws of the Foundations of the Torah* 7:7.

[6] See Exodus 19:11, 20:1*ff.* and 19; Deuteronomy 4:12-13 and 35-36, and *ibid.* 5:2*ff.* and 19-21.

[7] See Rambam, *Laws of the Foundations of the Torah* 8:1.

[8] *Ibid.*, ch. 8. See also Rabbi Sa'adia Gaon, *Emunot VeDe'ot*, Introduction: ch. 6 (and see there also treatise III: ch. 6); Rabbi Judah Halevi, *Kuzary* I:87; *Sefer HaĤinuĥ*, Introduction.

appear non-understandable. Their practical applications are neither defined nor explained in the text. Consider, for example, these Jewish commandments:

There is a commandment of "circumcision," but one will not find an explanation in the Written Torah of what "circumcision" means – the where, what and how. Likewise there is a prohibition of "working" on the Sabbath, but there is no definition as to what constitutes forbidden tasks. There are commandments of fringes on four-cornered garments, and phylacteries placed on hand and head, but there is no explanation of how these are to be produced or how they are to be worn. There is also a mandate of ritual slaughter that renders *kosher* species of animals permissible for Jewish consumption, but there are no instructions for how this is to be performed. In fact, Deuteronomy 12:21 states, "slaughter ... as I have commanded you," yet nowhere in the Written Torah do we find the details of that command.

Moreover, the current division of the Pentateuch into chapters is a very late (medieval and non-Jewish) innovation. Indeed, this chapter-division is often blatantly inconsistent with the actual text. The fact that these divisions have become accepted universally is no more than a practical convenience for purposes of reference. The original text, to this day in all Torah-scrolls, is divided only into two kinds of sections or paragraphs, but without any written punctuation to separate the 5,845 verses from one another. Also, the Hebrew text consists of consonants only; there are no written vowels. Words without vowels are clearly ambiguous; they could be read in many different ways with altogether differing meanings.[9]

---

[9] In this context see *Kuzary* III:28-38 for Rabbi Judah Halevi's refutations of the Karaites, a sect which (like the Sadducees before them) claims to recognize the "Written Torah" only. He points out the inconsistencies and self-contradictions of their position, the unavoidable dependency on tradition. With regard to the traditional division of the Torah into sections, this is not related to facilitating easier readings. There are but 669 sections or paragraphs for the 5,845 verses, and they are of varying lengths. For example, the 148 verses from Gen. 28:10 to Gen. 32:3 form one single uninterrupted paragraph, and so do the 146 verses from Gen. 41:1 to Gen. 44:17! On the other hand, the 72 verses from Ex. 21:1 to 23:5 are divided into 18 paragraphs, and the 110 verses from Deut. 21:10 to 25:10 are divided into 44 paragraphs. Also, the 19 verses from Ex. 15:1-19, and the 43 verses from Deut. 32:1-43, have each verse broken up into separated components.

It follows that even with acceptance of the Mosaic origin of the Torah, the written Hebrew text before us is altogether incomprehensible. On the other hand, as the Torah has always been the primary text for knowing and practicing God's teachings and commandments, from the very days of its composition, it is clear that the Jewish people must have been informed from the outset as to how to read it, the meanings of its statements, and the definitions of its precepts. How so? By an oral tradition.[10] This tradition was revealed to Moses[11] and transmitted by him to the nation, and thereafter passed on from generation to generation.[12] It is called the "Oral Torah," and it was specifically *not* recorded in formal written texts until much later, in the Talmudic and Midrashic writings.[13]

(See Rambam, *Laws of the Torah Scroll* 8:4; Rabbi Simĥah, *Maĥzor Vitry, Hilĥot Sefer Torah.*)

[10] See *Kuzary* III:64-74 (as well as the reference in the preceding note). See also below, text relating to note 16.

[11] See Jerusalem Talmud, Tractate *Pe'ah* 2:4; *Midrash Vayikra Rabbah* 22:1.

[12] See Rambam, Introductions to his *Commentary on the Mishnah* and his *Mishneh Torah.*

[13] A number of texts discuss the reasons for the Divine injunction to keep this as an oral tradition; see, e.g., *Midrash Tanĥuma Ki Tissa* 34; *Midrash Shemot Rabbah* 47:1; Rambam, *Guide for the Perplexed* I: beginning of ch. 71; Rabbi Joseph Albo, *Sefer Ha'Ikarim* III:23; Rabbi Judah Lowe, *Tiferet Yisrael*, ch. 68-69. The historical change of eventually committing the Oral Torah to writing (the Talmud) was necessitated by the drastic deterioration of social conditions after the destruction of the Second Temple and the dispersion of Israel. (See Tractate *Temurah* 14b.) It became difficult for the Torah scholars to concentrate and rely on memory and transmission alone, and there was a serious threat that the tradition would be distorted and forgotten: "The number of disciples kept diminishing, ever new calamities came about, the Roman government expanded in the world, becoming ever stronger, and the Israelites wandered and became dispersed to the ends of the world. He [Rabbi Yehudah the Prince] therefore composed a [highly condensed] work [the *Mishnah*] to be available to all, so that they would be able to study it speedily and [the vast amount of details] would not be forgotten" (Rambam, Introduction to his *Mishneh Torah*). The continuing deterioration of social conditions necessitated the composition of the Talmud, and the later Rabbinical commentaries and codifications, in order to preserve the understanding of the Oral Torah for subsequent generations of Jews.

The "Oral Torah" includes the specific explanations of the "Written Torah." In reality, though, as the Torah is Divine Wisdom, it reflects the infinity of God:[14] "Its measure is longer than the earth and wider than the sea" (Job 11:9). Its teachings and meanings are innumerable, ranging from the traditional simple meaning of the actual text to the most profound mystical insights.[15] Moreover, the teachings of the Torah apply to all circumstances and conditions, at all times and in all places. Thus it would be impossible to contain this infinity in any finite depository. To this end the Almighty revealed to Moses a set of rules for valid hermeneutical interpretation, to draw legitimate conclusions from the established principles.[16] These rules underlie the Rabbinic analysis and discussions in the Talmud and later writings that explain how practical codifications and rulings are in accordance with God's will.

The Talmud recalls an incisive anecdote to illustrate the significance and centrality of the tradition known as the "Oral Torah:"

A Gentile came to the famous sage Hillel, and stipulated that he could believe only in the "Written Torah," rejecting *a priori* the "Oral Torah." Hillel patiently accepted the challenge and started teaching him the letters of the Hebrew alphabet: "This is an *aleph*, this is a *bet*, this is a *gimmel*, this is a *dalet,*" and so forth. The following day he

---

[14] The Sages expressed this in terms of: "the Holy One, blessed be He, and the Torah are one" (see *Zohar* I:24a; *ibid.* II:90b), in the sense that "Inasmuch as You are within them [the Divine Attributes which transcend creation], whoever separates one from another of these ten Attributes [which include Divine Wisdom], it is considered as if he had effected a separation in You [God forbid]" (*Tikkune Zohar*, Introduction II).

[15] Thus we speak of four dimensions of traditional meaning in the Torah: the simple meaning of the text, the allusions, the hermeneutical interpretations, and the mystical meanings. These four levels are summarized in the Hebrew acronym *PaRDe"S* (literally "orchard" or "garden") in context of the Talmudic passage in Tractate *Ĥagigah* 14b of the "four who entered the *Pardes*." See *Zohar Ĥadash*, *Tikunim* 107c; and *ibid.* 102b; *Zohar* I:26b, and *ibid.* III:110a and 202a. Ramban, Introduction to his *Commentary on the Torah*. See Rabbi J. I. Schochet, *The Mystical Tradition*, pp.36-38 and 119*ff.*

[16] See *Midrash Tanĥuma Ki Tissa* 16; *Midrash Shemot Rabbah* 14:6. These rules appear in *Torat Kohanim* (*Sifra*), introductory section; *Mishnat Rabbi Eliezer – Midrash Shloshim u'Shtayim Midot*, *parsha* I and II.

taught him the letters in reversed order. The Gentile protested: "This is not what you taught me yesterday!" Hillel responded:

"Obviously you must rely on me to know the truth. So, too, you must rely on me with respect to the 'Oral Torah'."[17]

In short, the "Written Torah" and the "Oral Torah" are inseparable. There is total interdependence between them. This affects not only Jewish Torah Law and practice, but also the Torah's Noahide Code.

In the "Written Torah" there are only three explicit verses containing precepts addressed to Noaĥ and his descendants: Genesis 9:4-6. Even these three require the traditional interpretation to extract their precise meanings. Without the "Oral Torah" tradition, it is equally impossible to have a codex of the universal precepts relating to Gentiles.[18]

To be sure, the prescriptions of the Noahide Code are, on the surface, self-evident principles required for appropriate (i.e. civilized) conduct. Common sense would seem to be sufficient to dictate their observance. Any rational person will readily concede that murder, stealing, illicit sexual relationships, and the absence of an authoritative legal system, and so forth, are harmful to human survival. It is impossible to have a society based on anarchy, with all people acting as they please. Thus from time immemorial, in places where the Noahide Code was forgotten, all groups of humans, from the most primitive to the most sophisticated, still devised some legal code of rules to define acceptable and unacceptable behavior for internal governance.

Those man-made systems, however, were – and are – no more than convenient social contracts to safeguard self-preservation. Individuals or societies that adopt them are indeed wise, for they serve practical or utilitarian purposes. They do not constitute, however, a sense of enduring morality, and they are most certainly devoid of any true religious significance.

This, then, is the substance of the ruling by Rambam (Maimonides) cited above to introduce our theme. Piety, repentance, righteousness, and reward of a hereafter are religious concepts. They have meaning in a religious context only.

The very idea of a Noahide Code *per se*, then, presupposes acknowledgment of both the "Written Torah" and its inseparable

---

[17] Tractate *Shabbat* 31a; for a similar incident see *Midrash Kohelet Rabbah* 7:8.

[18] See *Kuzary* III:73.

corollary of the tradition of the "Oral Torah." Without these there is no authentic Noahide Code. Without the foundation of a firm belief in the Revelation at Sinai of both the written text of the Torah and the authentic tradition[19] of its explication, there is no code prescribing a truly moral or religious system for mankind. Proper observance and understanding of the details of the Noahide commandments, therefore, presupposes implicit acceptance of both the "Written Torah" and the "Oral Torah."

---

[19] *There was a chain of transmission of the Oral Torah after the revelation at Mount Sinai, with a great spiritual leader and Sage in each generation who would lead a court of Sages to whom he taught the Oral Torah. In addition, they and their thousands of disciples taught the Oral Torah to the Jewish people in each generation. (See Rambam's Introduction to his *Mishneh Torah.*) These leaders who ensured the transmission of the Oral Torah were:

From the Lord God to:

(1) Moses our teacher, greatest of all Prophets
(2) Joshua, along with Elazar (son of Aaron)
(3) Phinehas (or Pinĥas, son of Elazar and High Priest)
(4) Eli the Judge and High Priest
(5) Samuel the Prophet
(6) King David
(7) Aĥiyah the Prophet
(8) Elijah the Prophet
(9) Elisha the Prophet
(10) Yehoyada the High Priest
(11) Zeĥariah the Prophet
(12) Hosea the Prophet
(13) Amos the Prophet
(14) Isaiah the Prophet
(15) Micah the Prophet
(16) Joel the Prophet
(17) Naĥum the Prophet
(18) Habakkuk the Prophet
(19) Zephaniah the Prophet
(20) Jeremiah the Prophet
(21) Baruĥ the Scribe

(22) Ezra the Scribe, whose court included the Prophets Haggai, Zeĥariah, Malaĥi and Daniel, as well as Ĥananiah, Mishael, Azariah, Nehemiah, Mordeĥai, Zerubavel and Shimon the Righteous.

(23) Shimon the Righteous, High Priest and Sage

(24-34) The main receivers of the Oral Torah in the following eleven generations are listed, for example, by Rambam in his Introduction to the *Mishneh Torah.*

(35) In generation 35, Rabbi Yehudah the Prince, a direct patrilineal descendant of King David, wrote down the Oral Torah in a brilliant abbreviated form, called the Books of the *Mishnah*, for widespread public use. Before this time, the Prophets and Sages who received the Oral Torah in each generation kept private notes on what they learned as oral lessons from their teachers. In the words of Rambam: "He (Rabbi Yehudah) gathered together all the traditions, all the enactments, and all the explanations and interpretations that had been heard from Moses or that had been deduced by the courts (of Prophets and Sages) of all the generations in all matters of the Torah; and he wrote the Book of the *Mishnah* from all of them. And he taught it in public, and it became known to all Israel; everyone wrote it down and taught it everywhere, so that the Oral Law would not be forgotten from Israel." See footnote 13 above for the societal challenges that prompted Rabbi Yehudah to undertake this challenge to preserve the Oral Torah.

(36-39) In the 36th generation, Rabbi Yoĥanan wrote down the Jerusalem Talmud in the Land of Israel about three hundred years after the destruction of the Second Temple. In the 39th generation (100 years later), the Sage Rav Ashe wrote down the Babylonian Talmud.

This historically well-known sequence proves that the Oral Torah, as recorded in the *Mishnah* and the Talmud, was transmitted orally from one leading Sage to another in an unbroken chain, as continually studied by hundreds of thousands of Jews in every generation, and that the conclusions in these and other books of the Oral Torah are the Word of God – this being the Oral Torah that was given to Moses at Mount Sinai. (See Rambam, *loc. cit.*)

CHAPTER 1

Awareness of God[1]

1. The basic foundation and the first principle of faith is to know that there is a Primary Being who brought all existence into being.[2] All of the entities in the spiritual and physical realms come into existence only from the truth of His Being.

2. This Being is the God of the universe and the Master of the entire earth. He controls the spheres and the entire universe with infinite and unbounded power that continues without interruption.[3]

3. This God is one, and only can be one, and not two or more. He is one with a complete unification that surpasses any of the types of unity that are part of the created realms; He is not one in the manner of a category that includes multiple individual entities, nor one in the manner of a body that is divided into portions or dimensions. Rather, He is completely unified, and there exists no unity similar to His within the created realms.[4]

If there were multiple gods, they would be limited to some type of spiritual body and form, because similar but distinct entities co-

---

[1] Based on Rambam, *Laws of Foundations of the Torah* 1:1-7.

[2] *In a note that Rambam wrote on his Commentary on the Mishnah, he explained, "Know that one of the great fundamental principles of the Torah of Moses is that our universe is a new entity, created and formed by God out of absolute nothingness … the non-existence of the universe before the beginning of time … proves God's existence absolutely, as explained in the *Guide for the Perplexed*."

[3] *God's complete knowledge and control of all creation extends to His continuous power of individual Divine Providence.

[4] *The created realms include the physical and the spiritual, to the peak of levels, and God's Unity transcends them all entirely. Thus it is impossible for a human or an angel to conceive of the true nature of His Unity. God has neither physical nor spiritual dimensions, as it is said (I Chr. 29:10-13), "Lord, Yours is [i.e., to You, in Your Essence, belong] the greatness, the power, the glory, the victory, and the majesty, even everything in Heaven and earth" – and none of these spiritual attributes are of His unknowable Essence.

existing on the same level are separated from each other through limitations that are associated with body and form.[5]

If God were to have body and form, He would be limited and defined, because it is impossible for there to be a body which has no limitation. Everything that has limitation and definition, by virtue of its body, also has a limited and bounded power. God's ability and power have no limitation or boundary,[6] so therefore His power cannot be the power of a body. And since He does not have a body or any form, He cannot be affected by any circumstances that can affect a body, as for example the effects of being separate from another entity. Thus it is impossible for Him to be anything other than one.

4. Just as His Existence is of an entirely different nature than that of the created beings, so too, His Truth is incomparable to the truth of the created beings. For all the created beings require Him, and He, blessed be He, does not require them. Therefore, the truth of His Being does not resemble the truth of any of their beings.[7]

This is implied by the words of the prophet (Jeremiah 10:10): "God your Lord is true" – i.e., He alone is true, and no other entity possesses truth that compares to His Truth. This is what is meant by the Torah's statement:[8] "There is nothing else aside from Him" – i.e., aside from

---

[5] *This limitation applies to the spiritual creations referred to as angels; see Rambam, *Laws of Foundations of the Torah* 3:3-8.

[6] *Why then are we not overwhelmed by the presence of unlimited Godliness? His infinite power includes His ability to limit the revelation of His Godliness to His creations. Note the explanation by Rashi on Gen. 1:1: "Originally it arose in God's thought to create the world with the attribute of stern judgment [i.e., with total concealment of Godliness]; He saw, however, that the world could not endure, so He combined with it the attribute of mercy." Rabbi Schneur Zalman explains in *The Gate to the Unity and the Faith* (ch. 5) that this refers to His revelation of Godliness to mankind through exceedingly righteous individuals (such as Moses) and the signs and miracles recorded in the Torah.

[7] *The truth of the existence of created beings is relative and subsidiary to, and a result of, the truth of His Being. For they exist only because, and as long as, it is His will that they exist. The creation and sustained existence of the spiritual and physical realms is only a result of God's creative speech (Genesis ch. 1).

[8] Deuteronomy 4:35; compare Deuteronomy 4:39.

Him, there is no true existence like His.

The Torah of Moses

5. Knowing this fundamental principle – the existence of God, blessed be He – was included in the commandment and the warning that prohibited idolatry to Adam the first man and all his descendants.[9]

The obligation of this knowledge is not only to hear and understand this precept once and to agree and set it in one's heart. Rather it is a continuous obligation for every person to think about and contemplate the existence of the Master of the universe and His greatness, in order to set the knowledge of God strongly in his heart and mind. One should constantly reflect upon this, as the righteous King David wrote, "I place God before me always; because He is at my right hand I shall not falter."[10]

This command of knowing and recognizing the existence of God includes acceptance of His Kingship and His constant authority (this is called "accepting the yoke of the Kingdom of Heaven"). This means that each Gentile is obligated to accept upon himself all things which he is commanded by God – i.e., this recognition, and the Seven Noahide Commandments and their details as transmitted in the Torah – because God, the Master of the universe, commanded them and

---

[9] Obviously the commandment to believe in one God and no other is included in the prohibition against serving idols, based on one of the Oral Torah's Thirteen Rules for exegesis: "from the negative, one can infer the positive."

In Tractate *Sanhedrin* 56b, it is shown that Adam was prohibited from serving idols by the words, "And the Lord God commanded the man ..." (Genesis 2:16), from which we infer that Adam was prohibited from rebelling against the One Who commanded. Rashi explains there that Adam was prohibited from serving idols from these words, with which the Almighty commanded Adam that His Godliness should not be associated with any other entity. This is also clearly cited by Rambam (*Laws of Kings* 8:10): "Moses was commanded by the Almighty to compel all the inhabitants of the world to accept the [seven universal] commandments given to Noaĥ's descendents." It is therefore obvious that all the nations of the world are commanded to believe in and recognize God.

[10] Psalms 16:8. See *Letter of Rambam (Iggeret HaRambam) to Rav Ĥasdai HaLevi* (pub. Lipsia, p. 24); *Likkutei Siĥot*, vol. 27, p. 246.

informed us of them in the Torah through the prophecy of Moses.[11]

6. Any Gentile who accepts these Seven Noahide Commandments, and is careful to observe them, is truly a pious individual of the nations of the world, and merits an eternal portion in the future World to Come. (And with this merit, the person will be included in the Resurrection of the Dead).[12] This applies only if he accepts them and does them because the Holy One, blessed be He, commanded them in the Torah, and made it known through Moses our teacher, that the Children of Noaĥ were previously commanded to fulfill them.[13]

However, if one fulfills the commandments of the Noahide Code only out of intellectual conviction (because his logic dictates them), he is forbidden by Torah Law to settle in the land of Israel,[14] and he is

---

[11] Rambam, *Laws of Kings* 8:11. See *Likkutei Siĥot*, vol. 26, p. 132 *ff.*, based on Rambam *ibid.* and *Laws of Forbidden Sexual Relations* 14:7 – "One needs a general acceptance of the yoke of Heaven as a preparation for keeping the 7 Noahide Commandments." (However, when Gentiles perform a precept, they do not need to specifically intend that they are doing it because God has commanded them; see *Likkutei Siĥot* vol. 7, p. 33, note 18.)

[12] See Rashi and *Tosafot* on Tractate *Rosh Hashanah* 16b-17a. They state that the Talmud's words beginning, "There are three groups for the Day of Judgment," refer to the Resurrection of the Dead. The Talmud is speaking in reference to both Gentiles and Jews, so it is apparent that Gentiles can have not only a part in the future World to Come, but also in the Resurrection of the Dead. Ra'avad, Ramban, and teachings of Ĥassidic leaders, are of the opinion that the main, eternal reward and revelation of Godliness in the future will be in the physical world, after the Resurrection of the Dead.

[13] Rambam, *Laws of Kings* 8:11.

[14] According to Rambam's *Laws of the Worship of Stars [and Idols]* 10:6, during the temporary diaspora of the Jewish people (during which the Jubilee cycle is suspended), no one can be accepted into the *legal* status of a Gentile "Resident" (*Ger Toshav* in Hebrew), even if he makes a declaration before three Torah-observant adult Jewish males that he accepts and abides by the Noahide Code. Nevertheless, for any Gentiles who do not accept and observe the Noahide Code, the Jews are commanded to expel them from the Land of Israel, and they are forbidden by Torah Law to dwell there (whether they are expelled or not). Ibn Ezra explains the simple meaning of Lev. 18:25-28, that the holiness of the Land of Israel cannot tolerate sinful inhabitants. From this it is clear that the spiritual standard of any inhabitants of the Land of Israel must be on a higher level compared to those who live elsewhere.

not counted among the pious individuals of the nations of the world.[15]

Deniers and Deviators from the Foundations of Faith

7. One who believes there is another god denies the basic foundation of faith, for knowledge of the existence, truth and oneness of the Master of the universe is the foundation upon which all else depends.[16] Such a person is a "deviant believer" (a *Min* in Hebrew) and in the category of those who believe in idols.[17] There are five categories of deviant believers (who deny a fundamental principle of faith in God):[18]

(a) one who says there is no deity (atheism), and the universe is not overseen;

(b) one who says there are two or more gods;

(c) one who says there is only one god, but having a body or a form;

(d) one who says that God was not the only First Existence and the Creator of everything, but rather there was a continuously existing primordial matter from which God formed the world;[19]

(e) one who serves an idol (or a star or constellation, etc.), that it should be an intermediary between him and God.

---

[15] See Rambam, *Laws of Kings* 8:11. However, if he fulfills the Noahide Code in practice, he is not liable to any punishment for this lack of belief.

[16] Rambam, in *Laws of Foundations of the Torah* 1:6, clearly gives his opinion that one is a deviant believer and an idol worshiper if he believes there is an independent power that is secondary to God. Other major Torah authorities held that this incorrect belief in an intermediary power is not forbidden to Gentiles (see Part II, topic 1:2). Yet one who believes this is not one of the "pious of the nations of the world," and he should be informed of his error if there is a possibility that he will correct his belief and keep the prohibition against idolatry to its fullest (in thought as well as in action).

[17] *Kesef Mishneh* on Rambam's *Laws of Repentance* 3:7.

[18] Rambam, *Laws of Repentance* 3:7. See Part II, topics 1:2 and 3:1,4.
As explained in Part II, topic 1:2, the difference of Rabbinical opinion regarding an intermediary for Gentiles is only in regard to whether such a **belief** is forbidden. But one who **serves** an intermediary transgresses according to all opinions. Hence, the wording of Rambam cited in (e) is accepted by all Rabbinical authorities.

[19] Ra'avad, on Rambam's *Laws of Repentance* 3:7.

8. There are three categories of "scorners:"

(a) one who says there is no prophesy at all and no communication of knowledge from God to the hearts of individuals;

(b) one who denies the prophesy of Moses our teacher;

(c) one who says that God does not know the actions of people.[20]

There are three categories of "deniers of the Torah":[21]

(a) one who says that the Torah's commandments are not from God (even if he observes some or all because they seem logical to him), even if he says that these commandments came from Moses himself (from his own intellect, and not as commandments from God);

(b) one who says that the Written Torah and its commandments were from God, but the Oral Torah and its explanations of the commandments were from Moses himself (and how much more so, anyone who says that the Oral Torah was introduced by persons other than Moses);

(c) one who says that God replaced any of the commandments He gave through Moses with another later commandment, or that His original Torah and its commandments were later nullified. (Included are those who say that the "first" Torah which was given to Moses was true and from God, but it was later nullified or changed.)

Each of these is a denier of the truth of the Torah.

9. The explanations of every precept that God commanded through Moses were also given directly from God to Moses,[22] and Moses gave these explanations orally to the Elders of Israel of that generation (in addition to teaching the entire Jewish people). This included not only the explanations of each commandment in a general way, but also details and measurements for the fulfillment of every precept, and the

---

[20] Rambam, *Laws of Repentance* 3:8.

*A "scorner" (*epicurus* in Hebrew) includes one who scorns the Torah or the Sages, or who shirks their teachings or authority. The Sages are those who transmitted the Torah's Oral Tradition since the time of Moses.

[21] Rambam, *ibid.* It seems clear from Rambam that a Gentile scorner, deviant believer or denier of the Torah does not believe in Moses' prophesy with all its details, so it is impossible for him to be truly observing the Noahide Code in accordance with Rambam's text in *Laws of Kings* 8:11.

[22] Rambam's Introduction to the *Mishneh Torah*.

specific rules for correct exegesis of the Written Torah. It was ordained by God that with this tradition, the recognized Sages of Israel[23] would clarify any future question about an explanation of a commandment, using these rules of exegesis. Therefore, the authentic Jewish Sages are the mainstay of the Oral Torah, and anyone who believes in Moses our teacher and his Torah must rely on them for explanations of the details of the Torah's precepts.

Anyone who denies their accepted rulings, meaning the Oral Torah, is also a denier of the Torah, as the term is explained above.[24]

10. If a deviant believer, scorner or denier (see above) has been taught about the truth of Torah, but he persists in these habits and false beliefs without repentance, his end will not be to receive a part in the World to Come,[25] but instead, as it says, "To the lowest world [the Purgatory] will the wicked return, all the peoples that forget God."[26] They are those who willfully dismiss the true God, like the deviant believers and the scorners, even though they did not serve idols, because they willfully dismiss the fundamental principles of faith [for Gentiles, about the One God and His commandments, prophecy, and the Torah]. Still, they are not liable to judgment by a court for this transgression, since a court may only punish for actions, but not for thoughts and beliefs.[27] God alone judges a person for heretical beliefs.

---

[23] *These were the members of the Supreme Sanhedrin which existed in the past, through an unbroken chain of ordination back to Moses. (This excludes false sages like the members of the heretical Sadducee Sanhedrin that temporarily existed in the days of King Jannai, c. 100 B.C.E.) Due to persecutions by the Romans, the Supreme Sanhedrin ceased many years before the Babylonian Talmud was completed. It will be renewed in the Messianic Era, when all people will be spiritually uplifted to serve God together (Zeph. 3:9).

[24] Rambam, *Laws of the Rebellious Ones* 1:1-2 and 3:3.

*Regardless of what argument is advanced, a person is a denier of the Torah (a *kofer* in Hebrew), if the ultimate result of his approach will be a negation of any of the Torah's precepts or fundamental principles.

[25] Rambam, *Laws of Repentance* 3:6.

[26] Psalms 9:18. *Sanhedrin* 105a refers this to the wicked ones of the nations.

[27] Rambam, *Laws of the Worship of Stars [and Idols]* 2:6, states that anyone who believes in idol worship insults God, yet he does not mention any physical punishment assigned for this false belief.

11. Any reference in this work to liability for "punishment by the Hand of Heaven" (i.e., from God) or "punishment by a court" is only intended to indicate a person's guiltiness and the liability of his soul. Permission for earthly judgment based on Torah Law applies only for a competent and empowered Torah-based court,[28] as provided by the Noahide commandment to establish Torah-based courts of law (see Part VIII, Chapter 1). Only an authorized Torah-based court has permission to apply any detail of the Noahide Code in placing a judgment of guilt upon a person.

12. All those who refuse to accept upon themselves to observe the Noahide Commandments are transgressors in God's eyes.[29] However, they should be warned to change their ways and fully accept these prohibitions.

Therefore, to help a person who is a denier of Torah or an idol-worshiper because of the habit of his upbringing, and has never known the truth because he has not learned it, it is incumbent on one who does know the truth[30] to teach him God's truth and the commandments that apply for him as a Gentile, and to correct and improve his ways.[31]

This effort and spiritual guidance is the proper path that Abraham

---

[28] We explain the meaning of an authorized Torah-based court in Part VIII, topic 1:11.

[29] Rambam, *Laws of Kings* 8:9, and *Laws of Circumcision* 1:6.

[30] See topic 3:1 below, that this applies for both Jews and pious Gentiles who know the truth and details of the Noahide Commandments, if they are able to explain these obligations persuasively.

[31] This is evident from Rambam, *Laws of the Rebellious Ones* 3:3, in regard to the Karaites of his time. Even though the Karaites deny the Oral Torah, *in Rambam's days* they were not judged to be deniers, since for many generations they were raised from their birth in that culture and compelled to follow that errant path.

It is also clear in Rambam, *Laws of Repentance* 3:14, that any person can return from his evil ways, do repentance and be forgiven by God, and therefore anyone who is liable – even to death by the Hand of Heaven – can repent and be saved from Divine punishment. But one who is convicted by an earthly court for a transgression that he committed cannot commute his legal sentence by repenting.

followed (as will be explained in Part II, topic 1:6).[32]

13. If there are deviant believers, scorners or deniers (as described above) who publicize their views that they do not believe in God or that they deny that the Torah is from God (yet they do not actually transgress any of the Noahide Commandments in practice because of fear of the government, or based on their concepts of morality or the like), a court does not judge them, since no physical transgression has been done (see topic 1:10 above).

---

[32] See Rambam, *Laws of Kings* 10:1, that a Gentile is liable for transgressing a Noahide commandment due to negligence, since he should have learned it. But it seems that Rambam is only referring to a situation in which the general community knows the law this person transgressed, yet he excluded himself and didn't learn it. If most of the members of the community don't know this law, one of these individuals is not liable unless he was previously warned, since it was impossible for him to learn it in his situation. Since the laws of God are true and just, such a person is not liable under these unavoidable circumstances.

It is clear that this only applies to the Noahide commandments that need to be taught (since they are not dictated by logic), such as details of the prohibitions against worshiping idols and eating flesh that was taken from a living animal. But for the logical prohibitions such as stealing and murder, it is obvious that a community is obligated to learn and know them, and individuals have no excuse for ignorance of the main points of these precepts.

But even for stealing, which is a logical prohibition, we find in the Book of Jonah that God sent Jonah to the Gentile city of Nineveh to warn them to return the stolen property they had in their possession, before they were to be destroyed by the Hand of Heaven for this sin (Jonah 3:8). From this we can conclude that for an entire community, a court should not rush to judge them, but rather they should first be warned and given the opportunity to correct their ways. Likewise, we see that God's judgment against the generation of the Flood was sealed because of robbery, because the prohibition of theft is a logical precept, and they could not be excused by claiming they had not learned about it (see topic 4:2 for details; also Rashi and Ramban on Genesis 6:13, and Ramban on Genesis 6:2). Nevertheless, before the Flood, Noaĥ was occupied in building the ark for 120 years, and during this time he repeatedly warned the people to abandon their sins (see Rashi on Genesis 6:14). Even though those events in the days of Noaĥ and Jonah involved Heavenly judgments, we can still learn from them about the appropriate conduct for a court to follow in regard to passing judgment.

CHAPTER 2

Proselytizers and False Prophets

1. If anyone comes to convince individuals or a community – by influencing, or with intellectual arguments, or by demonstrating supernatural powers or the like, or with false claims to be a prophet – to serve idols, or to nullify one of the Seven Noahide Commandments, or to add a commandment (in addition to the Seven Noahide Commandments transmitted by Moses), even if he says that God commanded that this should be done, it is forbidden to listen to him or to accept his words. All are obligated to remove and silence him by any necessary means.

A proselytizer is one who privately or publicly tries to persuade another person to serve an idol. Even if a proselytizer does not serve the idol(s) he promotes, he is among those that cause the public to sin.[33] Therefore, even if proselytizers cannot be judged for worshiping idols, the court needs to silence them from their proselytizing and return them to good, and if this is not successful, the court may judge them so that they should not continue to cause the community to err.

2. In Part II, it will be explained that one who serves idols is liable. Therefore, if one convinces others to serve him as an idol and tells them words such as "serve me," or "worship me," and they did worship him, then he is the idol himself, and both he and they are guilty, as are all those who serve idols. However, if someone did not serve this person as an idol, but only verbally accepted his words, then the person who said "worship me" is exempt from punishment by a Noahide court. (The verbal agreement is not considered as a real acceptance of his words but rather is assumed to be mocking him.)

If someone convinces a person that he should serve another person or thing as an idol, but the one who was misled has not yet served it, then even if he accepted verbally and said, "Yes, I will go and serve it," both of them are still exempt from punishment for their words.[34]

---

[33] Rambam, *Laws of the Worship of Stars [and Idols]* 5:1.

[34] See Rambam, *Laws of the Worship of Stars [and Idols]* 5:5. Although the proselytizer is liable to punishment by a Sanhedrin court, that precept for Jews does not apply to Gentiles (see *Minĥat Ĥinuĥ* Commandment 462).

3. A self-proclaimed prophet who convinces others to serve idols is liable. Whether he says, "This idol told me to serve it," or "God told me to serve idols," or words to this effect, he is a false prophet who has persuaded others to go astray.[35]

Even if he prophesies in God's Name to serve an idol only for a specific time, and even if he performs miracles and says that God commanded that people must serve the idol for only a short time, he has spoken unfaithfully toward God, as it says,[36] "and the sign or the wonder comes about, of which he spoke to you, saying, 'Let us follow the gods of others…' – do not hearken to the words of that prophet or that dreamer of a dream, for the Lord your God is testing you… The Lord, your God, shall you follow and Him shall you fear; His commandments you shall keep and to His voice shall you listen… And that prophet or that dreamer of a dream shall be put to death, for he has spoken fabrication against the Lord your God." Thus this person has come to contradict the eternal prophecy and Torah of Moses, and it is clear that he is a false prophet. All the apparent miracles he performs are just magic and sorcery.[37] The case of someone who says this in the name of God is not judged by a Noahide court, as explained below in topics 2:8-9. If he gives this false prophecy in the name of an idol, it is within the jurisdiction of a Noahide court to judge him.

4. Likewise, a self-proclaimed prophet who prophesies in the name of idols and says, "This idol or star told me that it is a commandment to do such and such," or "not to do such and such" – even if he cited a correct Torah law – is liable for committing the sin of false prophecy.[38]

---

[35] Rambam, *Laws of the Worship of Stars [and Idols]* 5:2.

[36] Deuteronomy 13:3-6.

[37] Rambam, *Laws of Foundations of the Torah* 9:1.

[38] It appears that one who prophesies in the name of an idol, i.e. by saying his prophecy in its name, is a main component of the idol worship itself. Since Gentiles are forbidden to practice idol worship or its offshoots, this false prophet is therefore liable. It appears from Rambam, who places this law in *Laws of the Worship of Stars [and Idols]* and not in *Laws of Foundations of the Torah*, that this is a part of the Torah law pertaining to idol worship. This is also clear because one who prophesies in the name of idols actually accepts them, and is liable like one who says to an idol, "you are my god." (See topic 3:23 in Part II, and Ramban on Deut. 13:2; 18:20.)

Even if he prophesies in the name of an idol but gives instruction to do a permitted mundane act or not to do so, or only predicts the future, he is nevertheless one who prophesies in the name of idols.[39]

5. It is forbidden to arrange a discussion or a debate with one who prophesies in the name of idols (or with one who prophesies in the name of God to serve idols; both have the same status as a false prophet), and he should not be asked to perform a sign or a miracle. If he makes a sign or a miracle on his own, one must not pay attention to it or think about it. Anyone who thinks about these so-called miracles, debating if they are true, is a sinner, since the false prophet obviously denies a foundational principle upon which everything in Torah depends, as it says,[40] "If a prophet or dreamer of a dream shall arise among you, and he will give you a sign or wonder, and the sign or the wonder comes about, of which he spoke to you, saying, 'Let us follow other gods, ... and we shall serve them!' – do not hearken to the words of that prophet or that dreamer of a dream ..."[41]

6. Likewise, a Jew or a Gentile[42] who claims that God sent him to add, remove or change a commandment from those that God gave through Moses (the 613 Jewish Commandments and the Seven Noahide

---

[39] This is included in the command (Deut. 18:20), "But the prophet ... who will speak in the name of the gods of others..." The general topic there (from Deut. 18:14-22) is speaking about two things: one who prophesies to do something as a temporary commandment, or to do some mundane act that is permitted to be done. Since, as explained above, this false prophet accepts the idol, it does not matter what he says in its name. Even if he relates a true command from God, which would appear to be a statement of truth, Rambam explains that it is still false prophecy if it is being said in the name of idols.

[40] Deuteronomy 13:2-4; see above in topic 2:3.

[41] Rambam, *Laws of the Worship of Stars [and Idols]* 5:7.

[42] See Rambam, *Laws of Foundations of the Torah* 9:1. It is clear from Rambam that all of these types of false prophets intend to contradict the Torah of Moses in some way, whether they prophesy in the Name of God or in an idol's name, or to change the Torah-based faith, and therefore they are liable. However, God will never send a prophet to command the nations to change their Torah laws even temporarily, whether the prophet is a Jew or a Gentile. However, it is possible for one to be sent to instruct a permitted action; see *Laws of Foundations of the Torah* 7:7, and *Iggeret Teiman*, p. 147.

Commandments), is a false prophet. This applies even if he says that God sent him to explain the observance of a commandment in a way that differs from the tradition that was received from Moses,[43] or that God sent him with a message that one of these commandments was only meant for earlier times, but nowadays God has changed or nullified it. He is liable for this false prophecy, since he is contradicting the prophecy and Torah that Moses received at Mount Sinai, which God promised that He will never change or nullify, or replace with a new doctrine.

7. A person who prophesies in the name of God, but lies in his prophecy, is in the category of a false prophet, as it says,[44] "But the prophet who says something in My name which I have not commanded him to speak, etc., ... that prophet shall die. If you will say in your heart, 'How can we know the word that God has not spoken?' What the prophet will speak in the Name of God and that thing will not occur and not come about – that is the word that God has not spoken; the prophet has spoken with willfulness; you should not fear him."

More specifically, a false prophet can be identified if he prophesies that a good event will come about and it does not come to pass, or if only part of the good that was promised comes to pass. This is because any good that God proclaims publicly (through a true prophet) will not be nullified, even if it is conditional, and this is a valid test for a false prophet.

---

[43] See Rambam, *Laws of Foundations of the Torah* 9:1. It appears to be clear that this ruling also applies if the person prophesies a correct explanation known in the Oral Torah, because after it was given to Moses, the Oral Torah does not reside in the Heavens (Deuteronomy 30:12), and God promised that He would not inform us of a matter of Torah Law in a prophecy (Deuteronomy 17:11), so it follows that the person is a false prophet.

*After Moses received the commandments from God, the definition of their observance was entrusted to the Sages of Israel in the Oral Tradition, and it left the context of any further prophetic revelation, as Moses taught: "For this commandment that I command you today, it is not hidden... it is not in the heavens... it is very near to you" (Deuteronomy 30:11-14; Tractate *Bava Metzia* 59). Subsequent prophets were sent to exhort people to keep the Torah, but not to add, change or nullify any of its commandments.

[44] Deuteronomy 18:20-22.

However, if a prophecy is given about punishments that will come, but they do not happen, the failure of this to occur does not nullify the possible validity of the prophet. For example, if a person declared as a prophecy that a certain person would die, or that in a certain year there would be a famine or a war, and the negative event did not occur, this is not proof that the prophet is false. Because the Holy One, blessed be He, is slow to anger, abundant in kindness, and forgiving of evil, it is possible that the person or the group of people repented and the sin was forgiven.[45] This occurred for the Gentile city of Nineveh, as written in the Book of Jonah. The prophet Jonah declared to the people that God would destroy their city, but the people repented from their evil ways (and made restitution to those whom they had wronged), and because of this God relented from destroying them.[46]

A person is a false prophet, and he is liable, if he prophesies in the name of God what he has not heard in a prophetic dream or vision, or if he hears a prophecy in the name of God from another person and then tells others that this prophecy was spoken to him by God.[47]

8. Even though a Gentile who prophesied falsely is liable in the judgment of Heaven, the Noahide Code does not include a commandment to judge false prophets,[48] and therefore a Noahide court does not

---

[45] *Or the retribution was delayed, as in the case of King Hezekiah, who was granted an extension of his life for fifteen years (Isaiah ch. 38).

[46] Rambam, *Laws of Foundations of the Torah* 10:4.

[47] Rambam, *Laws of the Worship of Stars [and Idols]* 5:8-9.

The laws regarding a false prophet also apply to Gentiles, as written in *Iggeret Teiman*, p. 149: "If a prophet stands up from among the Jews or the other nations and calls people to the religion of Moses [including calling Gentiles to observe the Noahide Code], and like Isaiah and Jeremiah and their kind, he does not add or subtract from them, we ask him for a miracle. If he gives one we believe him, and he is instated on the level of a prophet for us. However, if one thing is missing from his words, he is [a false prophet]."

*But if one merely says falsely that he had a predictive dream that was fulfilled, without claiming that it was shown to him by God, or by some idolatrous power, he is not acting in the manner of a false prophet. Rather, he is merely lying and deceiving, which is forbidden in general as immoral conduct (see topic 8:4).

[48] Responsa *Tzafnat Pane'aĥ*, Part II, ch. 138.

judge them. Rather, they are to be judged by a Jewish Supreme Sanhedrin when the required conditions are met.[49] When there is no valid Jewish Supreme Sanhedrin, or if for any other reason they cannot judge the case, if a Gentile prophesies in the name of God to serve idols, or to change one of the Seven Noahide Commandments or to make a new religion, a Noahide court may judge this false proselytizer if the situation requires. If he only prophesies in the name of God falsely, but does not say to add to or change any of the Torah's commandments, but instead he speaks about permitted things, it appears to the author that we may only warn him and trouble him, to convince him to stop this behavior. However, we also inform him that he is liable to death by the Hand of Heaven, and that he will be judged by God.

9. This only applies to someone who prophesies falsely in the name of God. But anyone who prophesies in the names of stars, constellations or other idols, is judged by a Noahide court like one who actually serves idols. For anyone who prophesies in the name of an idol says about it, in effect, "You are my god." (See below in Part II, topic 3:23.) Thus by his own words he accepts the service of the idol, and he is liable for this.[50]

---

[49] Rambam writes, in *Laws of the Worship of Stars [and Idols]* 5:9, that a Jewish false prophet was judged only by the Supreme Sanhedrin. It is unclear if this also applies to a Gentile false prophet. Even though a Noahide court cannot judge a false prophet, we can say – according to Rambam's statement in *Laws of Kings* 10:9 – that if he makes a new religion, the court can warn him that he is liable, and that he must stop this sinful behavior. And if he continues to be a stumbling block, they may remove him like any false proselytizer, for the benefit of society.

*The prescribed penalty can only be administered by a valid Jewish Supreme Sanhedrin of seventy-one Sages, if there is one that is meeting next to the Holy Temple in Jerusalem, as these are requirements for trying the case. The Supreme Sanhedrin abandoned the Temple Mount forty years before the Second Temple was destroyed, and as a result of the Roman persecutions, there ceased to be a valid Sanhedrin several generations before the Talmud was concluded. The institution of a valid Sanhedrin of seventy-one Sages will be renewed in the Messianic Era (may it come speedily, in our days).

[50] See above, footnotes to topic 4.

CHAPTER 3

The Prohibition Against Making a New Religion or Adding a Commandment

1. Moses our teacher gave the learning and explanation of Torah, and fulfillment of its 613 Jewish commandments, as an inheritance only to the Jews, as it says,[51] "The Torah which Moses commanded us is an inheritance for the congregation of Jacob," and to anyone who chooses to become Jewish through proper conversion. Likewise, Moses was also commanded by God to compel all nations of the world to accept the seven Noahide precepts that they had been commanded, and a Gentile who does not accept them is liable.[52]

This commandment to Moses to compel all the nations of the world to accept the seven Noahide precepts is not incumbent merely on the Jews, but also upon all the nations of the world; anyone who has the power to compel others to act in the correct way is obligated to do so.

---

[51] Deuteronomy 33:4.

[52] Rambam, *Laws of Kings* 8:10. It appears to the author that even though Rambam uses the words "to compel" only regarding these seven commandments, and does not include other obligations of the Noahide Code (e.g., the prohibitions against cross-mating animals and cross-grafting fruit trees, and observing worthy precepts in which the nations have a rational obligation, such as honoring parents and avoiding deception), nevertheless, it is logical that they must be compelled to keep the obligations that are placed upon them as part of their commandment to observe *dinim* (a legal code).

We have left out Rambam's statement, "one who accepts them is called a *Ger Toshav* (a *Gentile* '*Resident*' of the Holy Land)," and the laws of the *Ger Toshav*, because they do not apply while the observance of the 50-year cycle of Jubilee in the Land of Israel is suspended, as Rambam writes in *Laws of the Worship of Stars [and Idols]* 10:6. If a Gentile declares his acceptance of the Noahide Commandments before three observant Jewish men, it does not change anything in regard to his obligation to observe the Noahide Code, or his merit to be called one of the Pious of the Nations (*Ĥassidei Umot HaOlom,* in Hebrew). See *Likkutei Siĥot*, vol. 26, p. 134, which explains that this is the opinion of Rambam. This appears to also be the opinion of Rashba in *Torat HaBayit*, quoted in *Beit Yosef Yoreh De'ah* ch. 124, which says, "And we do not require him to accept them in front of a Jewish Court of three…" It seems clear that Rambam rules that nowadays, if a Gentile wants to act as a *Ger Toshav*, Jews should not prevent him from living in Israel.

If there is a court or government that has the authority, they must establish these seven commandments as an order and statute. If an individual has the ability to persuasively explain to Gentiles about their obligation, he is required to do so from this commandment to Moses.[53]

2. The general rule is that it is forbidden for a Gentile (an individual, and certainly a community which observes the Noahide Code) to add precepts from another religion or create a commandment based on his own decision. If he wants, he can seek proper conversion to become a Jew, or he can remain observant of the Noahide Code, without adding to or subtracting from the Noahide Commandments that he observes.

A Gentile may be deeply involved in study of Torah regarding the Noahide Code in which he was commanded (see Chapter 5), but one who delves deeply into other areas of Torah is liable. Also, if a Gentile abstains from weekday activities and makes a sabbath for himself, even on a weekday, he is liable. This includes one who establishes a "holy day" for himself, similar to the holy days and Sabbaths of the Jews (which are religious holidays, i.e. "holy convocation" days), during which he prohibits himself from work, since this is creating for himself a new religion.[54] Not only is taking on a sabbath day forbidden, but even the setting aside of any day for a specific religious observance or statute, such as one who establishes for himself a time to eat a special food as a precept (e.g., eating unleavened bread on Passover), or to fast on a specific day (e.g., the Jewish fast day of *Yom Kippur*), and the like. Even if he did not also set it aside as a sabbath or festival day (i.e., for refraining from work), this is considered as creating a festival and a religion from his own comprehension. However, if he sets up for himself a day of rest from work, not as a holy day but just as a break from work, it is permissible, for he is not establishing it as a religious precept from his own comprehension.[54]

If a Gentile does involve himself deeply in Torah study beyond the Noahide Code, or he curtails his activity in observance of a sabbath day, or he adds any other commandment upon himself, a court may chastise him and inform him that he is liable to death by the Hand of Heaven for this, but he may not be severely punished by the court.[54]

---

[53] This is obligatory based on the commandment for Laws and Courts; see the Preface to *Sheva Mitzvot HaShem*. See also *Kol Bo'ai HaOlam*, pp.155, 189.

[54] Rambam in *Laws of Kings* 10:9.

3. Any commandment connected to a Jewish holy day, such as eating unleavened bread on Passover, or waving a palm frond (*lulav*) or sitting in a *sukkah* booth on Sukkot, is forbidden for a Gentile to observe specifically on those days, because he is then making a holy day that he is not commanded in, and it is forbidden to make one's own holy day because of the prohibition against making a new religion.[55]

(However, if a Gentile is invited to the home of a Jew on the night of Passover, and he is served unleavened bread as the available food, or he is invited to eat a meal in a Jew's *sukkah* booth during Sukkot, there is no prohibition involved in this for the Gentile, since he is eating out of honor to the Jewish host, and not as a religious ritual for himself.)

4. The commandment of circumcision to Abraham was for the males of his own household, and for his male offspring that he would have after he received the commandment, as it says,[56] "You and your offspring after you for their generations." This does not include any direct descendants of Ishmael (and they can no longer be identified, as explained on the next page), as it says, "Whatever Sarah tells you, heed her voice, since through Isaac will offspring be considered yours."[57] It also does not include the descendants of Esau, since Isaac said to Jacob, "And God will give the blessings of Abraham to you and your descendants, that you may possess the land of your sojourns which God gave to Abraham."[58] This means that Jacob alone is the child from Abraham and Isaac who agreed to follow that religious path and unique Divine service. Thus Abraham's descendants through Jacob are commanded in circumcision. The descendants of Abraham's children from his wife Keturah, who were born after Ishmael and Isaac, are also obligated to circumcise their male children on the eighth day from birth.

---

[55] But if a Gentile wants to eat unleavened bread or sit in a *sukkah* booth for his physical pleasure (e.g., if he likes eating unleavened bread, or sitting in a *sukkah* for shade from the sun's heat), he is allowed to. This is so even during the Jewish festival days, since he does not intend at all to observe the Jewish commandment, but he does the action only for his physical satisfaction, and he is not establishing a festival for himself, as mentioned above in topic 3:2.

[56] Genesis 17:9.

[57] *Ibid.* 21:12, and Rashi there; Sarah was greater in prophecy than Abraham.

[58] *Ibid.* 28:4.

Since the descendants of Keturah became intermingled with those of Ishmael, all of them are obligated to circumcise their male children on the eighth day. However, the children of Keturah are not liable to punishment by a court for not observing this commandment, since it is not part of the Seven Noahide Laws.[59] (They are only commanded to circumcise the thick foreskin, but not the underlying covering of thin skin.[60] Once they have been circumcised, they are forbidden to extend back their skin to appear as if they are uncircumcised.)

5. A Gentile who is not from the descendants of Abraham who wishes to be circumcised, if he does so as a direct command of God, violates the prohibition of adding a religion or a commandment. However, if he has himself circumcised because he wishes to do so as a gift to God, he is permitted to do so, and he receives spiritual reward for doing so.[61]

6. If a Gentile wants to do one of the other commandments from the Torah in order to receive a **practical benefit** (but not as a direct commandment), we do not prevent him from doing so, even according to its correct laws for Jews (for example, if he desires to tithe for charity from his money or produce),[62,63] but with the following exceptions.

---

[59] Rambam, *Laws of Kings* 10:8. However, the male descendants of Keturah still receive spiritual excision if they remain uncircumcised (see Gen. 17:14).

[60] Rambam writes in a responsa (*Pe'er Hador*, ch. 60) that a Jew may circumcise the thick and thin foreskin of a Gentile if requested, and it appears that Gentiles may circumcise themselves and their sons in this way.

[61] We must conclude that Rambam considers circumcision to be different from the commandments that Gentiles are prohibited to keep because they would be adding a religious observance; see *Laws of Kings* 8:10 and 10:9. The reason may be that this command was given to Abraham before the Torah was given, and it was never nullified, as we see that the descendants of Keturah are still obligated in it. Thus, a Gentile who wishes to have himself or his son circumcised may do so, and he is included along with the nations that are in the covenant with Abraham, but he is not obligated to do so.

[62] Rambam *Laws of Kings* 10:10. See Radvaz *Hilĥot Melaĥim*, ch. 10.

[63] This applies even if he intends to do the commandment according to all the details of its Jewish laws. If he does the commandment not strictly in accordance with the prescribed details of Jewish observance, but rather only for a practical benefit he will derive, this is surely not a problem, as long as he does not intend to add this as a commandment or a religious practice.

However, if a Gentile observes any of the Jewish commandments from the Torah as a religious obligation (even if he does so from a desire to receive a spiritual reward), this is forbidden based on the prohibition of adding a commandment, and there is no spiritual reward to be derived from this.[64]

7. Gentiles are especially forbidden to perform commandments that require the holiness of a Jew, such as writing a scroll of the Torah or a *mezuzah* or phylacteries (*tefillin* in Hebrew).

The general rule is that any Jewish *mitzvah* between man and man, or between man and God, which has a reason and a logical benefit for a person or society, is permitted for Gentiles to perform. But this does not apply for any commandment that does not have a logical, natural benefit, but instead is a sign for the Jews (e.g., wearing ritual fringes *[tzitzit]* or phylacteries, or affixing a *mezuzah* on a doorpost),[65] or is a

---

His "reward" *(s'ĥar)* in this context refers to the practical benefit he receives from doing even just a part or an aspect of the commandment, if doing so brings a specific benefit for the person or his society.

A Gentile may validly choose partial observances of this type; for example:

- to circumcise only his thick foreskin, as opposed to the Jewish ritual circumcision which also includes removing the underlying thin foreskin;
- to marry a woman only to refine himself, without committing himself to have children or to engage in marital relations as a regular obligation;
- to return some lost objects, but not every type of lost object, or not to every person;
- to take upon himself an obligation to pray to God, but not on a daily or regular basis (which Jews on the other hand are obligated to do on a daily basis);
- to honor an old person or a Sage, but only if he recognizes the person's wisdom or achievements.

64 Rabbi Moshe Feinstein, *Igrot Moshe Yoreh De'ah* vol. 2, ch.7.

65 Radvaz on *Hilĥot Melaĥim*, ch. 10. See Rambam, *Laws of Tzitzit* 3:9 and *Shulĥan Aruĥ Oraĥ Ĥayim* ch. 20, that it is forbidden for a Jew to give or sell a Gentile *tzitzit*, so the ritual garment will not come to be used by a Gentile for the purpose of disguising himself as a Jew. Rema writes in *Yoreh De'ah* ch. 291, in the name of Maharil, that a Jew should not give a *mezuzah* scroll to a Gentile for the same reason. It appears that beyond this, there is a general reason that Gentiles should not be compared completely to Jews. Therefore, they should not perform uniquely commanded Jewish signs, such as those.

Godly statute for Jews without reason or benefit understood to a person. A Gentile should be prevented from performing such commandments and should be taught that it is improper for him to observe them.

It is not problematic that male Gentiles are allowed to have themselves circumcised as a spiritual observance (although it is meant to be a sign in the flesh of a Jew), since many Gentiles are circumcised for medical purposes, and not to add a commandment or a new religion. Thus, a male Gentile who wishes to be circumcised in order to refine his personality and his body and its desires may do so.[66] But if he is not descended from Keturah, he should not do so as a commandment.

8. The abovementioned rule applies only to Jewish commandments that are not duty-bound by logic (even if they have a logical reason) such as circumcision or tithes. However, those that are duty-bound by

---

See the *Ginat Veradim Oraĥ Ĥayim* Rule 2, ch. 28, which explains that Rebbi (Rabbi Yehudah the Prince) gave a *mezuzah* scroll to Artavon (a Roman Gentile) only to own, but not to be affixed to his door, for a Gentile has no purpose for this at all.

[66] See *Likkutei Siĥot* vol. 10, p. 139. Rabbeinu Baĥyai writes (on Genesis 17:13) that circumcision is comparable to offering a desirable sacrifice from one's body to God, and it can also accomplish a weakening of one's carnal desires (*Guide for the Perplexed,* Part III, ch. 49). These reasons are upright for every man for the purpose of controlling his nature, and likewise as a sacrificial offering, which righteous Gentiles are permitted to do. Therefore, if a Gentile wishes to have a circumcision for these reasons, and not as an obligation of observing a commandment, this is praiseworthy.

A Gentile may perform a Jewish commandment for a practical benefit, even if it is only indirectly – such as tithing for charity, which benefits society by supporting the poor and is a logical necessity; or returning a lost object, which helps to establish camaraderie; or sending away a mother bird before taking its young, which is having pity on animals. Since these actions have a benefit for him personally or for his society, they have practical justification, and he receives reward for performing them – both the practical benefit, and a reward from Heaven for doing a correct and good deed.

However, a Jewish commandment that has no physical effect on a person or society (such as *tzitzit*) accomplishes nothing for a Gentile. It follows that a Gentile would do this only because he desires to do a Godly commandment that he was not commanded, and thus he is adding a religion. He therefore receives no reward for this, and on the contrary, he would be committing a transgression that carries liability to punishment by the Hand of Heaven.

logic, such as honoring one's parents,[67] and kindness and charity,[68] are obligated to be kept by Gentiles, at least in a general way, because such is the correct way for a person to act, as befitting the image of God in which he was created. However, a Gentile may not keep them because it is a commandment to him from God, but rather because one is obligated to be a good, moral person.

Many prohibitions that are commanded upon Jews are obligations for Gentiles to observe based on logic, such as the prohibitions against hating others, taking revenge or bearing a grudge. A Gentile should observe these prohibitions out of human decency, and not as Divine commandments of their own. This duty is an absolute obligation upon Gentiles, and they are liable to be punished by God for transgressing these obligations and for acting against moral and logical practices, as the Generation of the Flood was punished in the days of Noaĥ.[69]

9. Gentiles are obligated to give charity, and whether as an individual or a community, they are obligated to be concerned about help for the poor and needy, to help them appropriately in any way possible. Sodom and Gomorrah were destroyed only on account of their refusal to uphold and help the destitute, and their outlawing of any charity or help for the poor; for this, God judged them to deserve annihilation.[70]

10. Gentiles are permitted to add any prohibitions in order to guard themselves against transgression, or to establish a correct and orderly society. This is desirous as a part of observing the obligations of the Noahide commandment to establish courts of law and develop proper societies in the world. Examples are societal restrictions against haras-

---

[67] See *Likkutei Siĥot* vol. 5, p. 154; it is possible that honoring parents is an intellectual obligation on a Gentile just like charity, which is necessary for the establishment of a proper society and proper laws (*dinim*). However, it is obvious that a Gentile is forbidden to embarrass his parents, since it is against logical human respect, as we can see from the story of Ĥam (Genesis 9:22), who disgraced his father Noaĥ. See *Pirkei Rebbe Eliezer* ch. 23.

[68] *Rokei'aĥ* 366, that also seems to say Gentiles are obligated to escort guests when they leave (referring to inviting guests also) as it is a logical obligation. *One's charitable donations should not go to fund activities that support idolatry, or drawing Jews or Gentiles away from faith in the Torah of Moses.

[69] According to Ramban on Genesis 6:2 and 6:13, and *Ĥiskuni* there, 7:21.

[70] Genesis ch. 19; Tractate *Sanhedrin* 104b; *Likkutei Siĥot* vol. 5, p. 155.

sing women and children, and punishments set for transgressing such laws.[71] The prohibition of adding a religion or a commandment does not apply to this, because it is part of keeping the Noahide obligations of establishing courts and laws, and proper societies in the world.

This only applies to restrictions Gentiles accept upon each other as communities, to avoid damages. But it is prohibited to add communal restrictions as if they were those commanded by God (for example, if a Gentile community would establish a law against eating meat from an unslaughtered animal carcass, as if it were a religious transgression like eating meat that was severed from a living mammal or bird), because that would be instituting a new religion.[72]

However, if an individual wishes to accept a restriction in order to gain a practical personal benefit or to refine his personality, then he is not establishing the restriction as if it were a prohibition for him that is commanded from God, and it is permitted. Otherwise, it is prohibited.

---

[71] Rashi on Genesis 34:7. See *Likkutei Sih̑ot* vol. 5, p. 190.

[72] That is to say, they wish to restrict the community in this additional manner as a religious precept. Similar to this would be a law against eating pork, which is permitted for Gentiles (and the same applies for an individual, if he adds it for himself as a religious precept). However, if a person wishes to restrict himself from eating meat from an unslaughtered carcass for the purpose of guarding his health, or from eating any pork or shellfish or any other food if he is disgusted by it (or for medical benefits), this is permitted.

An individual is allowed to additionally restrict himself for a religious purpose, if it is not in the manner of adding a new commandment. For example, a Gentile may restrict himself from eating any livestock or poultry meat, as a complete safeguard (stricter than is required) against the prohibition of eating meat that was severed from a living animal. Or, he may do this as a way to overcome a strong lust for fresh butchered meat, if he feels he will make himself more pleasing to God through this self-refinement.

The difference between the community and an individual is that an individual may set his mind and conviction to a specific personal purpose, but adding an unnecessary restriction upon the community is equivalent to instituting a decree with no logical purpose. From this we can conclude that a private person may choose to become a vegetarian, since this can be explained as a rationalization or an emotional desire, based on a personal aversion to the killing of living creatures for his food – which means that it is not based on a religious conviction. But to impose such a restriction on an entire community is definitely forbidden, because it amounts to adding a man-made decree that is unnecessary from a practical standpoint.

CHAPTER 4

Liability to Divine and Earthly Punishments

1. There are some essential aspects of the Noahide Commandments that carry liability as capital sins if they are transgressed, as a Divine decree. "There warning is considered their liability," meaning that from the time an adult becomes aware that one of these particular actions is prohibited, if he later willfully transgresses it, he will be liable to death in the judgment of God[73] (until he repents). The exact actions these are will be explained in each section. There are also many prohibitions in the Noahide Code that are not explicitly warned about, and one is not liable to death for transgressing them.[74] Both men and women are equally obligated to keep these commandments.[75]

2. A Gentile is only liable to death if he intentionally commits one of the actions that is a capital sin. If he errs without intention to transgress, he is not liable (for example, if a man enters a dark room and has relations with his neighbor's wife, thinking that she is his wife, or if one eats meat that was severed from a living animal, while mistakenly thinking that the animal had been killed).

Likewise, if he erred because he did not check well enough to know if his action would make him liable or not, this is not considered erring without intention. Rather it is close to a willful sin, since he should have checked and he did not. (For example, one who knows the prohibition against adultery, but he had relations for the sake of marriage without knowing that the woman was already married to another man. He should have checked carefully to find out if she was married or single, before having marital relations with her.)[76]

However, if he errs in judging his known action as permissible, this

---

[73] Rambam, *Laws of Kings* 9:14.

[74] This is clear from Rambam, *Laws of Kings* 10:6, in regard to cross-grafting different species of fruit trees or cross-mating different species of animals.

[75] Tractate *Sanhedrin* 57b.

[76] See Tractate *Makot* 9a and Rashi there (according to Rava). It appears that this is the case for adultery, since many women are married, and therefore a man is obligated to investigate whether the woman is single or married (this applies likewise for an action which might be idol worship or stealing).

is not considered as erring without intention, and it is close to being a willful sin[77] (for example, one who knows he is having relations with another man's wife but thinks that she is permitted to him, for he does not know the prohibition against adultery; or one who knowingly eats meat that was severed from a living animal, but does not know that it is forbidden). It appears that in such a case, he is only liable if he should have learned that it was forbidden and failed to do so, as when his community knows the Noahide Commandments. But in a community that does not know about the commandments that are not binding based on logic, and it is not possible for a resident to learn about them, he is not liable for transgressing them (but he also cannot be pious).

Rather, a Gentile should first be taught and warned also about those aspects of the Noahide Code that are based only on decrees from God, and only afterwards is he responsible for them. This applies in regard to the prohibitions against serving idols, forbidden relations, and eating meat that was severed from a living animal. However, for the main prohibitions against murder and stealing, and for the commandment to establish courts of justice, which are all logically binding, there is no exemption for not knowing that they must be observed.[78]

It also appears that there is no "erring" in regard to blasphemy. Once one knows that there is a God, and he knows His Name, it is logically clear that it is forbidden to curse God. (But if one does not know about God at all, or does not understand what he is saying – in Hebrew or other languages – his curse is not regarded as blasphemy; see Part III.)

3. A Gentile who is forced to transgress one of the Seven Noahide Commandments is exempt from liability to physical or spiritual

---

But in regard to the prohibition against eating meat from a living animal, a person may eat regular meat even if he does not inquire as to where it came from, since most food meat is not severed from a living animal. Since forbidden meat is uncommon, it appears that in this case one is considered faultless, since he is not obligated to be concerned with a small probability.

[77] Rambam, *Laws of Kings* 10:1.

[78] An example of a type of murder that might not be known as such is euthanasia, which logically could be viewed as a kindness if the person's physical suffering is ended. The rule here would be that in a community where the concepts of the Noahide Commandments are not known, one would be liable to death for acts known as homicide, but not for euthanasia.

punishment for committing the transgression. Even if one is being forced to serve idols, he is permitted to do so, and he is not obligated to give up his life to avoid this. This applies to the other Noahide commandments as well,[79] except for the prohibition against murder, for which a Gentile must submit even to being killed in order to avoid being forced to commit the transgression. (Regarding one who is being forced to injure another or to commit rape, see Part V, topic 2:5).

Just as it is permitted to transgress (other than committing murder, injury or rape) if coercers force one to do so on pain of death, so it is permitted to heal a person even if it involves a capital transgression, if it is a matter of life and death. A person is not obligated to give up his life in order not to transgress the commandments, other than for the exceptions cited above. (E.g., it is permitted to heal a person by feeding him meat that was severed from a living animal, if the person will die if he does not eat it and no other option is available. Neither the healer nor the patient is liable for this.[80]

If a Gentile is being forced to commit any act that is a capital sin within the Noahide Code, the question of whether or not he is permitted to give up his life in order to avoid the transgression is explained Part V, Chapter 2.

4. A Gentile is not obligated in precepts of the Noahide Code or their liability until he is knowledgeable and responsible for his actions. This age is 13 full years for a male, and 12 full years for a female (provided that they have produced two pubic hairs). Some opinions say that even a minor who is knowledgeable prior to this age is responsible.[81] One who is not knowledgeable, such as a deaf-mute, one who is mentally incompetent, or a minor, is exempt from any liability.[79]

5. One who is intoxicated is considered to be competent for all

---

[79] Rambam, *Laws of Kings* 10:2.

[80] See Part IV, topic 6:11.

[81] There is a debate between the later Rabbinic authorities regarding a set age for legal majority of Gentiles, or if there is no set age and it depends on the individual's mental maturity. From Rashi on Tractate *Nazir* 29b, the age of majority is a natural phenomena and not a decree of Torah Law, so there should be no difference between the age of majority for Jews and Gentiles. *S'dei Ĥemed (Pe'at Hasade Ma'areĥet Gimmel)* states that the simple interpretation of Rambam follows this opinion.

matters, and if he violates any of the Seven Noahide Commandments he is liable for punishment. However, if he reaches the intoxication of Lot (Genesis 19:33-35), at which point he is not cognizant of his actions, he is exempt from punishment.[82]

6. It is forbidden for a Gentile to mislead or convince another to sin. Therefore, it is forbidden to teach others to serve idols, or to seduce a man or woman to commit adultery, or to convince another person to murder or steal. Any action that necessarily causes or helps another person to violate one of the Noahide commandments is forbidden.[83]

Even if the one misled is unaware that he will be performing a prohibited action, it is still forbidden to cause him to violate the prohibition.[84] For example, if one had a piece of meat that was

---

[82] Rambam, *Laws of Marriage* 4:18; *Shulĥan Aruĥ Ĥoshen Mishpat* 235:22.

[83] It appears that this comes from the command to establish laws and courts, as Gentiles are commanded to influence others to keep the Noahide Commandments and not transgress them (e.g., by establishing a system of justice, with courts and police officers). A Gentile is permitted to do an act that causes but does not force someone to do wrong. It is forbidden for a Gentile to intentionally influence a person to violate a Noahide commandment, but it is not a capital sin. (One who hired an assassin is not liable for capital punishment by a Noahide court, but he is liable for punishment by God.)

[84] The Noahide Commandments not only prohibit a person from doing certain actions, but they also establish what deeds are undesirable and what situations God does not want to occur (see *Likkutei Siĥot* vol. 5, p. 159-160). The author holds that one who transgresses this by causing another to transgress is violating the commandment to establish laws (*dinim*).

The Divine commandments have two dimensions: (a) their *influence on the person* who accepts the "yoke of the Kingship of Heaven," which fixes and corrects his character and thoughts, etc., and (b) their *correction of the world*, so that the world will become more correct, just and refined, according to God's will. The second dimension considers the negative influence on both the person **and** the world when a wrong is done, even unknowingly. Based on this principle, *Or HaĤayim* on Genesis 20:6 explains the rebuke that God gave to Abimeleĥ in his dream, while he was being miraculously prevented from unknowingly committing adultery with Sarah, who was Abraham's wife: "I have saved you from sinning **to Me**" – i.e., "Even though you, Abimeleĥ, claimed to Me your innocence in this matter, since you did not know that Sarah was married, you should know that I saved you from doing the sinful act even unintentionally, because it would still be a sin against Me."

forbidden to be eaten because it was severed from a living animal (*eiver min ha'ĥai*), and he handed it to another person who thought he was receiving ordinary permitted meat to eat, this is prohibited. It is likewise forbidden to cause any other situation that resembles this.

Nevertheless, if one misleads another to transgress a commandment, the misleader is not liable for punishment by a Noahide court, unless the court sees a special need to enforce the commandment of *dinim* for the purpose of correcting the society (see topic 1:13 above). But he will be punished by God for misleading others and causing them to sin.

7. However, if one performs an action that may possibly cause or help another person to transgress, but he does not intend for this to happen (but instead his intention is for other reasons), there is no specific prohibition that prevents one from taking such actions. An example would be one who sells substances that idol-worshipers are known to use for their idolatrous rituals, but he does not know whether a particular customer has this intention in mind. The vendor may sell the substances to any customers, since his intention is for the sale, and he does not care what the customer might do with the product. But if it is known that a particular customer is buying this thing for the sake of idol worship, it is prohibited for the seller to assist him.

This only applies, however, when he is the only one providing the possibility for the other person to sin. But if this opportunity can be found without his assistance (e.g., if the product is legal and readily available in other stores as well), then even if he definitely knows that the intention of the customer is to commit idol worship with this product, then there is no prohibition against the sale (as it will be explained in Part II, topic 10:3). Still, it is pious to avoid doing things that could mislead another person to perform a prohibited act.

8. Just as a Gentile may not mislead another to sin, likewise if one sees someone violating one of the Seven Noahide Commandments or performing a related action which is forbidden by the Noahide Code, he is obligated to prevent the transgressor from continuing in the sin (if it is in his power to exert this influence without putting himself into danger, or even without considerable inconvenience). This is included in the commandment of *dinim* (establishing a judicial system) that is incumbent for Gentiles, as explained in topic 3:1. (See topics 8:7-8.)

[Note that topic 3:1 speaks about the obligation of authorities to uphold the Noahide commandments, by correcting and influencing the citizens in their observance, and by enforcing the laws.[85] But obviously that is only if the society as a whole is capable of accepting the commandment of *dinim*, and if the courts will judge correctly. **Here, instead, we explain the role of the individual**, and if there is no such court, there is definitely no major responsibility on an individual to stop another person from continuing to sin. (The responsibility of an onlooker to stop the murder or rape of a pursued victim by injuring or, if necessary, killing the pursuer, is addressed in Part V, Chapter 3.)]

If one is not able to stop a person from continuing to commit a sin, then the rules in topic 7 above apply as to whether one may assist the violator to continue.

9. Parents are obligated to provide education to their children, and specifically in the fulfillment of the Noahide Code.[86] This education for the children is an obligation within the commandment of *dinim*, to strengthen the observance of the Noahide precepts in the world.

---

[85] There are opinions that a Gentile may not be punished for not fulfilling a positive aspect of his commandments (e.g. *dinim*). But it is clear that one is obligated to separate another from committing a sin, if he can do so without being at risk, and he is not permitted to turn away and say that it is not his concern, as Rambam writes in *Laws of Kings* 9:14: "To judge… and warn the people." This is not specifically a warning for Gentiles not to transgress, but rather to teach them the details of the Noahide Code (see *Leĥem Mishneh*). It appears that it is also a logically clear obligation on all leaders of a society to teach the people the laws of the land, and surely the Divine precepts which they are commanded in – namely the Noahide Commandments. Therefore, it is logical that just as there is an obligation for the judges to enforce the laws and warn people about them, the same applies for all those who have the opportunity to prevent another from transgressing, and this is also included in the general precept "to compel all the nations of the world to accept the Seven Noahide Commandments," as is explained above in topic 3:1.

[86] *To the extent that his intellect can grasp, every child should be educated about the foundations of the Noahide faith, and about the infinite greatness of the King of kings, the Holy One, blessed be He, Who is the Source of life for every being. This education and training of the child, *before* he matures, will serve as a foundation of his service to God for his entire life, as it says (Proverbs 22:6): "Educate the child according to his way; even when he will be old he will not depart from it." See, for example, *The Principles of Education and Guidance*, by Rabbi Yosef Yitzĥak Schneersohn, pub. Kehot.

CHAPTER 5

Torah Study for Gentiles

1. The Torah as a whole is an inheritance from God for the Jews alone, and a Gentile who "delves" into areas of Torah that are unrelated to the Noahide Code is liable for punishment by the Hand of Heaven (as explained earlier in topic 3:2). In contrast, it was explained in topic 4:2 that a Gentile must learn and know what is prohibited and permissible for him. For if he would mistakenly commit a capital sin from one of the Seven Noahide Commandments because he didn't know of it, even if the action seemed to him to be permissible, still he has the status of one who sinned purposefully and is guilty, for he should have learned and he did not (except when it was not possible to learn; see topic 4:2).

From here we see that Gentiles are obligated to learn all the details of their seven commandments as they are found within Torah – that which God prohibits and that which He permits for them – and to be expert in all their details.[87] But it is forbidden for them to delve into the rest of the Torah that is not about the Noahide Code.[88]

Not only is it permissible for a Gentile to learn about the Noahide commandments, but regarding anything he is obligated to do (e.g., things that are intellectually obligatory, like giving charity or honoring parents), he is allowed to learn Torah sources that will help him know how to fulfill and understand his obligation in a practical and even outstanding way.[89] And even for Torah precepts that he is not

---

[87] Rashi and Meiri on Tractate *Sanhedrin* 59a. Rambam, *Laws of Kings* 10:1, says that a Gentile who mistakenly sinned because he did not learn is liable, so it is obvious that Gentiles must clearly understand **their** commandments. Rambam's statement (*ibid.* 10:9) about Torah study, "They may not delve into anything other than their... Noahide Commandments," means that within the broad Noahide Code, a pious Gentile may (and should) study deeply, including even in penetrating investigative learning, as will be explained.

[88] Tractate *Sanhedrin* 59a; Rambam, *Laws of Kings* 10:9.

[89] Meiri on *Sanhedrin* 59a, and Maharsha on *Avodah Zarah* 3a. This applies even if he only wishes to know about these Torah laws, but he does not intend to actually perform the permitted action. (But note topic 5:7 below.)

*It is obvious that *any* Torah learning should only be from correct translations by observant Jewish Torah scholars.

obligated in it at all but he is permitted to perform, it is permissible for him to learn the Torah laws that deal with those precepts.[90]

The difference between learning the Noahide Commandments and learning other topics in Torah is that in learning these commandments, a Gentile is obligated to understand them very well in all their details, and is even permitted to delve into this learning. But for the rest of the sources within Torah, even those that are permissible for Gentiles to read (see below), it is prohibited for even a pious Gentile to study them in a way of deep involvement and penetrating, investigative learning.

2. What is "delving into Torah"? It is learning only for the sake of acquiring the Torah knowledge itself (which is called "learning Torah for its own sake"). This means deep involvement in the study, and penetrating, investigative learning (*pilpul* in Hebrew; see below in this topic). This includes learning to deeply understand the detailed Torah laws, the deeper reasons for the commandments, or the depth of the intention of words of Scripture and Talmud, and not for any other goal.

One who learns for a goal other than these is not learning Torah "for its own sake." Rather, he is learning for the sake of a reward – that is, for the sake of some benefit that he will get from the information.[91]

---

[90] Rambam, in *Laws of Sacrificial Procedures* 19:16, states: "It is permitted to instruct and teach them how to sacrifice to the Almighty, blessed be He." Therefore, Jews may teach Gentiles the parts of Torah that relate to *optional* precepts in the Noahide Code, as well as the Noahide Laws and moral precepts (e.g., teachings of classical *mussar*). This can include instruction in proper understanding of these precepts, beyond their practical details.

[91] This difference is seen from what Rambam writes, that delving in Torah study is forbidden to a Gentile, as is the observance of a sabbath, because of the prohibition of adding a new commandment or religion. Even though the Talmud in Tractate *Sanhedrin* 59a says that this is like "having relations with a betrothed woman," or "stealing from the Jews," it appears that its intention is only regarding such a depth of Torah study that it is severely prohibited, more so than the general restriction that Gentiles should not take upon themselves an additional observance in a manner of a Divine commandment. Therefore, a Gentile who delves in Torah study to that extent is violating two prohibitions: (1) the general prohibition of adding a commandment, and (2) the specific prohibition of learning Torah in such depth that it is like having relations with "a betrothed woman" (a metaphor for the Torah), or stealing that which belongs to someone else (the Jewish people).

This is why the Talmud compares this level of Torah study to a capital sin. That comparison is relating only to the spiritual perspective (since this transgression is not punishable by a court of law).

It appears that the prohibition or permission to learn Torah in one way or another follows the general rule that was explained in Chapter 3 above: for any Torah commandment that has a reason and benefit for a Gentile to perform, it is permitted for him to do (and therefore he may also learn the details of its performance), and if it is a purely spiritual Jewish precept, it is prohibited for Gentiles to do. Likewise in regard to learning Torah, one who learns to obtain a benefit, like knowing the logical societal laws as the Torah gives them, is permitted to learn parts of Torah that are connected to this, on the level of the *Book of Damages* in the Mishnah, and the section *Ĥoshen Mishpat* in the Code of Jewish Law (the *Shulĥan Aruĥ*) which deals with laws of finance, financial responsibilities, personal and financial damages, and rules for a Jewish court *(Beit Din)*. Since he is learning this for his own benefit, and he is certainly not learning Torah "for its own sake" (*lishmah* in Hebrew), therefore this is not called "delving into Torah," and it is permitted.

Therefore, anyone who wants to learn specific parts of Torah in order to perform the logical commandments, such as honoring parents, returning lost objects, and giving charity, is not forbidden to do so, because he wants to perform these as righteous and upright actions, and not as spiritual statutes.

But if a Gentile only wants to learn Torah to know the special distinctions of the Jewish people and their Divine commandments, and he does not want to perform those Jewish precepts nor to study in consideration of conversion, this should be limited to study of the Written Torah, and not the Oral Torah (Mishnah, etc.) (This is why Moses wrote the Five Books of Moses in the 70 languages, to inform Gentiles about the Torah, so that they would know the special distinctions of the Jews and the Torah they received from God. See *Sotah* 35b as to how the Gentiles learned these translations by Moses.)

However, a Gentile who is involved in learning Torah "for its own sake" is adding on another commandment from which he has no practical benefit, and therefore is doing it only as a commandment of God, like one who puts on *tefillin*, or observes a sabbath, or fasts on Yom Kippur; all such observances are forbidden for Gentiles. This is what the Talmud refers to by saying that a Gentile who delves into Torah learning is reaching to a level of Torah that was "betrothed" only to the Jewish people and given as their exclusive possession, so he is liable for death by the Hand of Heaven. All of this is in accordance with the opinion of Rambam on this subject.

[These distinctions as to what types of Torah study are permitted or forbidden for a Gentile also apply if the Gentile is learning Torah from a Jew. See Tractate *Ĥagigah* 13, which is cited in the footnote to topic 5 below.]

The general rule is that it is obligatory for a Gentile to learn the seven commandments that he is commanded to do, and he should learn them very well, to know what is permitted and prohibited for him. He is permitted to learn them even in a way of "delving into them," meaning deeply learning in the Torah sources to understand their reasons and their details.

But for Jewish commandments of the Torah that he is allowed but not obligated to observe (see Chapter 3), he is allowed to learn about them for the sake of understanding them, whether from the text of the Written Torah or the Oral Torah, but not in a way of in-depth learning or penetrating investigative learning (i.e. *pilpul,* which is the Jewish style of learning Talmud). Rather, a Gentile is permitted to learn them from books in a language he understands, on topics that are written in a concise and clear way. An example would be a proper translation of the text of the *Mishneh Torah* by Rambam, which presents Torah-law decisions, but not the inner reasons or the details of how the derived rulings were decided by the Sages (including Rambam himself).[92]

However, here we are mainly speaking about a sincere and pious Gentile who wants to learn straightforward Torah teachings on his own in translated books. After the Torah was translated into Greek as the Septuagint, it is permitted to learn Torah in one's own language from a proper translation; see *S'fat Emet Ĥagigah* 13 and *Margaliyot Hayam Sanhedrin* 59a, note 4.

[92] Rambam wrote *Mishneh Torah* as a practical Torah-law guide, and his opinion is that from learning his *Mishneh Torah* one could know the final Torah Laws without the reasons. The Sages taught (Tractate *Kiddushin* 30a) that a Jewish person should divide his time for Torah study into thirds [i.e. three parts]: Written Torah [the Hebrew Bible], *"Mishnah,"* and *"Gemara."* *"Mishnah"* as a general term includes any part of the Oral Torah that is recorded for the sake of basic knowledge. This includes those texts that present the opinions of established Torah Sages on Torah Laws in brief, without their explanations, like *Mishneh Torah*, *Tur*, and *Shulĥan Aruĥ*.

However, sources that explain reasons for the Torah Laws, and texts that explain details of the *Shulĥan Aruĥ*, are included in the in-depth part of Torah that is called *"Gemara"* as a general term (which includes the Talmud, Midrash and Zohar), and Gentiles are restricted in regard to learning these.

According to this categorization, anything in the part of Torah that is *"Mishnah"* is permitted for a pious Gentile to learn for the sake of his obligatory or permitted observances. This is not delving into Torah. Rather, he is learning a text that teaches about Torah Law without its depth and reasons; examples include the following specific classic works:

If a Gentile does not understand what is permissible for him to learn, he should ask an observant Jewish Torah scholar to explain it to him.

Therefore, if one does not understand a point in any text that he may read or study that is mentioned in this chapter, he is permitted to ask a reliable and observant Jewish Torah scholar to explain it to him.[93]

3. **Gentiles are permitted to read the entire 24 books of the Hebrew Bible,[94] even with explanations of the simple meaning *(peshat)*[95] – e.g., by Rashi – in order to correctly understand the verses.** But it is forbidden for a Gentile to delve into study of the Written Torah (except for verses that discuss the Seven Noahide Commandments[96]).

Rambam's *Mishneh Torah*, Rabbi Yosef Karo's *Shulĥan Aruĥ*, and certainly the *Kitzur* ["Abridged"] *Shulĥan Aruĥ* by Rabbi Shlomo Ganzfried, and likewise the Tractates of *Mishnah* itself by Rabbi Yehudah the Prince, without its subsequent explanations.

However, explanations of *Mishnah* (e.g. by Rabbi Ovadiah Bartenurah) are part of *"Gemara,"* since they explain the reasons and depth of the *Mishnah*. The Talmud, and books by codifiers who write in depth about the reasoning of the Torah Laws (e.g., *Shulĥan Aruĥ HaRav*, the *Aruĥ HaShulĥan*, and the *Mishnah Berurah*), are definitely forbidden for Gentiles to learn in topics unrelated to their obligatory observance, for this is called "delving into Torah." This categorization is defined in *Maĥaneh Ĥayim* vol. 1, ch. 7.

93 It appears that it is permissible for a Jew to teach a Gentile single Torah laws that he asks about, or to answer a question in a specific area of Torah, without explaining the depth and reasons involved. See *Pe'ar Hador* ch. 60.

94 Rambam, *Laws of the Torah Scroll* 10:8: a Gentile may hold a Torah and read from it. See also *Ma'or Veshemesh*, beginning of *Ĥukat*.

95 It appears that main traditional *peshat* Jewish commentators of the Hebrew Bible (e.g., Rashi, Sforno, Ibn Ezra) are not included in the prohibition of Gentiles learning Torah in-depth as it is explained in *Shulĥan Aruĥ*, because there it talks about analyzing the text in-depth by comparing verses and explaining them, to draw out the points of Torah Law that are implied within them. But those commentators (such as Rashi) whose sole purpose is to explain the simple meaning of the text do not derive in-depth conclusions from the verses. If they occasionally cite words of the Sages (such as Midrash) to explain how a verse is to be simply understood, it appears that the Gentile must look at the main point that the commentator is presenting.

96 These are Gen. 1:26-30, 2:16-25 (and possibly ch. 3), ch. 4, 6:1-12, 8:15-22, 9:1-7. (Possibly the first two Torah portions, *Bereishit* and *Noaĥ*, are permitted for in-depth study, because they relate to humanity in general.)

It is obvious that it is permissible for a Gentile to recite verses from the Hebrew Bible as prayer, particularly the verses of Psalms.

4. If a question in Torah Law arises for a Gentile and the verdict is not explicit and clearly explained in the permitted sources, he does not have the ability or power to identify the correct ruling. Rather, he must ask a reliable and observant Jewish Torah scholar, for only they have permission to explain the Torah and decide what the correct Torah-law ruling is in any particular situation.[97]

5. The "secret" part of Torah that is called *Kabbala* is governed by the same principles as Talmud, regarding the parts a Gentile may learn.[98]

---

[97] This is concerning a questionable situation that requires a Torah-law decision, and deciding on an answer is equivalent to delving deeply into the Torah. More so, a Gentile may not be ordained to teach and expound the Torah, because that is solely the spiritual assignment of the Jews – to be deeply involved in Torah, and to delve into it for the purpose of deciding practical rulings on a Torah-law basis. This task is only given to observant Jewish Torah scholars who are trusted in their explanations of Oral Torah.

However, if a matter is easily understandable from learning about the Noahide Code and the conclusion is obvious, it appears clear that a Gentile is allowed to decide upon it for matters of personal practical observance. But it is essentially difficult to decide an exact conclusion for Torah law in general, and laypersons do not have the objectivity and breadth of Torah knowledge to be certain that they are making the correct ruling.

[98] For parts of *Kabbala* that do not relate to the Noahide Code, it is delving into Torah for its own sake, since Gentiles cannot learn anything practical from that, so there is no benefit for them. This is the simple meaning of Tractate *Ĥagigah* 13a, that Jews may not teach the "secrets" of the Torah to Gentiles, and therefore Gentiles may not learn it by themselves either. Also, one may not learn original *Kabbala* texts (e.g. *Zohar*) without a fitting teacher, and therefore automatically it is impossible for Gentiles to learn true *Kabbala* by themselves. They would need to be taught by Jews, which is forbidden for a Jew to do if it extends to parts unrelated to the Noahide Code.

*As in Talmud, the parts that relate to the Noahide Code, e.g. knowledge of the greatness of God, His Unity, etc., are permitted, and are recommended. These parts from the Talmud have already been quoted and explained in later works, e.g. in Rambam's *Mishneh Torah* and in this work. Likewise, these parts from *Kabbala* are explained in later books. Studying from original sources without guidance is impractical. See *Likkutei Siĥot* vol. 27, pp.246-7.

6. Even though a Gentile is obligated to learn the details of the Seven Noahide Commandments and the Noahide Code that he is commanded to follow, this learning itself is not in the category of a particular commandment (something that Gentiles are additionally commanded to observe). Gentiles do not have a Divine commandment of learning Torah, but this is rather an obligation that is included in the Noahide Commandments themselves. It is included in every Divine commandment that the one who is commanded should know and be involved in learning how to keep that commandment.

Therefore, when a Gentile learns a part of Torah for the purpose of observing a Noahide commandment, he receives a reward, in addition to the reward for observing the Seven Noahide Commandments themselves.[99] And even more so, since his learning Torah about the Noahide Commandments is connected to the particular commandment that it relates to, the learning is a fulfillment of a directive from God. Therefore, learning about the Seven Noahide Commandments is called a permissible "involvement" in Torah study,[100] and the reward for this learning and involvement in Torah is great.[101]

In brief we can conclude that there are three levels of Torah study:

a) Learning Torah "for its own sake," which is the aspect of Torah that is a betrothal and inheritance from God to the Jews alone, and is forbidden for Gentiles.

b) **Deep learning of the Seven Noahide Commandments and the full breadth of the Noahide Code *by pious Gentiles for the sake of observing their obligations*. Since a Gentile is commanded by God regarding the Noahide Code, and this includes the study of these precepts within Torah, the reward for this study is great; it is a spiritual reward that is like the reward as for observing the Noahide commandments.**

(The trendy matters called *"popular kabbala,"* and learning from false teachers, are fake, and this is not part of Torah at all. Furthermore, *Kabbala* must never be promoted or "observed" as a religion in and of itself.)

[99] Forward to *Naĥalat Ya'akov*, quoted in *S'dei Ĥemed*, vol. 1, ch. 112.

[100] The wording of Rambam in *Laws of Kings* ch. 10 is, "They may not be 'deeply involved' in anything other than their Seven Noahide Commandments," which follows the wording in Tractate *Sanhedrin* 59a.

[101] But this is not like the involvement of a Jew in learning Torah, as Meiri writes on Tractate *Avodah Zarah* 3, and Rashba on Tractate *Bava Kama* 38.

c) For other Torah study that is permitted for Gentiles but is not related to the observance of an obligatory precept, there is no great spiritual reward. Instead, there is the reward of the benefit it provides, like the advantages he can derive from the Jewish precepts and ethics that are permissible for him, which may be performed by Gentiles only for the sake of the practical benefit that will result.

If the Gentile is one of the "pious of the nations of the world" who keep the Seven Noahide Commandments as their part in the Torah of Moses[102] because he is commanded to do them, and he is careful in their proper observance according to the Noahide Code, and he is involved in learning the parts of Torah that relate to these seven commandments, he is indeed considered before God as being as honorable as a proper Jewish High Priest who served in the Holy Temple.[103] A hint to this is that Shem, the son of Noaĥ, was completely righteous,[104] and he was involved in Torah study.[105] Thus the verse praises him, saying, "he was a 'priest' [*kohen* in Hebrew] to God on High."[106]

7. But a Gentile who does not observe his seven commandments, even if he learns about them but not for the sake of fulfilling them, is indeed sinful, and he will be punished by the Hand of Heaven for this Torah learning.[107] If he serves idols (or follows other paths of heresy),[108] and nevertheless involves himself in Torah learning, he is liable for capital punishment by the Hand of Heaven.[109]

---

[102] *Sefer Mitzvot Katan ("S'MaK")* in the forward, and Meiri *ibid.*

[103] Tractate *Sanhedrin* 59a.

[104] See Tractate *Sukkah* 52b, and the explanation by Rashi there.

[105] Rashi on Genesis 25:22, according to the Midrash *Bereishit Rabbah* there.

[106] Genesis 14:18, based on Tractate *Nedarim* 32; Rashi on this verse says that "Malki-tzedek" was Noaĥ's son, Shem.

* *"Kohen"* in Scripture can also refer to a person of esteem; see II Samuel 8:18 about King David's sons.

[107] As implied from Meiri on Tractate *Sanhedrin* 59a.

[108] I.e. if he is viewed in Torah Law like one who serves idols; see Chapter 1.

[109] From the wording of Tractate *Sanhedrin* 59a, "An idol worshipper who is involved in Torah study is liable for death." Rambam explains, in *Laws of Kings* 10:9, that this refers to death by the Hand of Heaven.

CHAPTER 6

Serving God; Prayer and Grace After Meals

1. It has already been explained in topic 1:5 that it is incumbent on every person to try to achieve comprehension and understanding of the Creator according to his capability, and he should meditate always on the greatness of the Creator, and on His supervision over the whole creation, in order to awaken his heart to love and fear Him.[110]

What is this love and fear? When a person understands that God is the Creator of everything and keeps everything in existence at every moment, and that God created all people so they should honor and serve Him, and then he meditates on the infinite greatness of God according to his ability and understanding, he will come to love God. When one also contemplates the lowliness of any creation in comparison to the Creator of everything, he will realize God's infinite greatness, and awe and fear of God will fall upon him. A person will also be humbled by knowing that he is a small, lowly creation with extremely limited understanding, who is standing in God's Presence.[111]

This understanding and these meditations are the ways to recognize God and serve Him with love and fear. There is no true recognition without thought and contemplation, and true contemplation brings true emotions into the heart, and proper intentions for proper actions.

We find that part of the obligation to believe in and recognize God is the obligation one has to connect his intellect to his feelings, to bring himself to love and fear God, and accept an obligation to fulfill God's explicit will (the Noahide Code). Also included is the effort a person should make to follow correct paths and deeds that will be pleasing to God, even if there are no specific commandments that apply. God expects that if an adult person with developed intellect is blessed with the opportunity to learn of these ways, he will strive to follow them. (The Prophets of the Hebrew Bible revealed that these are ways of kindness, justice, mercy, righteousness, graciousness, and humility. These are basic examples, but one should strive to follow not only

---

[110] See *Likkutei Siĥot* vol. 27, p. 246. The command to fear God has a logical basis and is part of accepting and recognizing Him. It is included in the prohibition against blasphemy, as explained in Part III, Chapter 2.

[111] Based on Rambam, *Laws of Foundations of the Torah* 2:2.

these virtues, but any understood way that God wants a person to act.)

Therefore, a Gentile needs to serve God in his thought and emotions, to motivate himself often to love and fear God. How does one serve God? By arousing his will to focus his mind and heart, to direct his thoughts and opinions so that his actions will be in accordance with the will of his Creator. This will bring pleasure and satisfaction to God.

2. Included in the obligation to believe in and recognize the Creator of the universe is the trust that a person must place in God. With this trust, a person must have faith that God is surely concerned about him, and about all of His other creations, and that everything God does is for the ultimate good of the person, since God is the ultimate good. One aspect of this trust is that each of God's commandments will in truth be for the good of the person who is so commanded, and for the good of the entire world.

3. The main part of this service of the heart and mind is prayer.[112] Therefore one should always pray before God, to make requests to Him for all of his needs, and he should thank and praise Him always according to his ability. Another goal of this prayer and contemplation is to bring the person to know that there is nothing worthy of complete trust except the One God, Who is King of the universe.

Prayer, blessings and praise to God, even though they are not strictly required for Gentiles because they were not commanded explicitly in the Noahide Code to observe these things, are nevertheless an intellectual obligation, as explained in Chapter 3.

4. When a person prays, he should clearly express his words to God with his lips in speech if possible, and not only in his thoughts[113] (and this is a good deed). In a situation when a person is not able to speak for some reason, or the location is not a fitting place for prayer (see topic 7 below), he may pray in the concentration of his thought.

---

[112] Based on Rambam, *Laws of Prayer* 1:1. See *Kol Bo'ai HaOlam*, p. 45.

[113] Rabbi Moshe Feinstein, *Igrot Moshe Oraĥ Ĥayim* vol. 2, ch. 25. If he prays to God even in his thoughts alone, he has a reward for this as well, because he is fulfilling the obligation to believe in God. But from the outset, it is obviously better for a person to vocalize the words of his prayer (at least to the level at which the person himself can hear what he is saying).

A person can pray at any time of day, and in any fitting words that he chooses, but he should be careful not to use prayers that idol worshipers composed for their liturgies, because their intention for the prayer was surely to serve their idol. Even though one might recite the prayer for the sake of God alone, nevertheless, the liturgy of idol worshipers is an abomination to God.[114] For the same reason, a person should not pray to God if he is in a house of idol worship.

5. It is permissible for a Gentile to prostrate to God, whether he is doing so in prayer or not. If he prostrates to God when he is not praying, he should do it in a manner of honor and awe. And when he bows down to God, he should not include in this prostration any words other than prayer, thanks, or praise to God. (Also see Part II, topic 6:5.)

6. When a person prays before God, and when he wants to bless and thank God – e.g., to thank Him for his food,[115] for his life, for his recovered health, or for a miracle that was done for him – he should direct his mind and speech to say verses from the Hebrew Bible, or he should praise God in a way of honoring His blessed Name. With this manner of prayer, God's Name will be glorified. (Conversely, a person should not mention God while he is distracted or without thinking about what he is saying, as it would be degrading to the honor of God.)

Therefore it was Abraham's custom to teach all the people of the world that it is proper to thank and bless God's great Name, and not to assign this level of honor to any other presumed power or any created being, as it says (Genesis 21:33), "and there he [Abraham] proclaimed the Name of God, God of the universe." This means that Abraham caused the Name of the Holy One, blessed be He, to be called out to by all those who passed by, and he taught everyone to praise the Name of God.[116] Joseph also acted in this manner, as it says,[117] "God was with

---

[114] *Igrot Moshe ibid.* He compares it to the abomination of an animal brought as a sacrifice to God, after it was used for a sin (e.g., bestial relations, designation for idol worship, etc.; see *Sheva Mitzvot HaShem* Part I, topic 7:4).

[115] Even though there is no commandment for a Gentile to recite blessings for food or other things, it is nevertheless an intellectual obligation for one to thank God for the kindness that He has given him (see Tractate *Sotah* 10b.)

[116] Tractate *Sotah* 10b and Rashi there (as quoted earlier, on p. 4).

[117] Genesis 39:2-3 and Rashi there.

Joseph, and he became a successful man … his master perceived that God was with him, and in everything he did, God caused his hand to be successful." How did Joseph's master see that God was with him? Because the praise of God was always found in Joseph's mouth, and through this he would explain his success and publicize the Name of the blessed God to everyone. Likewise, Joseph told Pharaoh (Genesis 41:16), "It is God Who will respond to Pharaoh's welfare."

7. One's prayers should be said honorably, in order to honor God (even if God's Name is not mentioned). Therefore, it is meritorious to pray in honorable clothing.[118] One should not pray in filthy clothing, or with genitals uncovered, or in the presence of others who have their genitals uncovered. One should not pray where there is a bad smell or in a lavatory or bathing room, or within about 6 feet (1.8 meters) of excrement.

If one has no choice and has no other opportunity to pray, and he must make a request to God, and he is standing in a place where other people are unclothed, he should turn his body (or at least his head) in order not to see them, and then pray. If this is impossible as well (for example, one who is in a restroom and cannot exit), it is better to pray in his heart, and not utter God's Name in such a place.

8. One of the ways of serving God is to frequently mention His praise, and to bless and thank Him for all the good that He bestows on a person. Even though a Gentile is not commanded to bless God for the food that he eats, not before or after he eats, it is obvious by intellectual reasoning[119] that a person should thank and bless God for giving him his food, and also for giving him all his needs for existence.

How does one do this? Before he eats, it is proper to make a request to God that He please give him enough sustenance, and he should say words of praise and thanks for that which God gave him. It is permissible for him to say these blessings using the versions that the Sages instituted for the traditional Jewish liturgy,[120] as follows:

---

[118] *If people in the area would not appear before an eminent person without wearing shoes, he should not pray barefoot (unless it is an urgent situation).

[119] See Tractate *Berahot* 35a, that it is a logical obligation to bless God for benefit one receives from that which He bestows to the world. This was decreed by the Sages upon Jews, with liturgy and rules for reciting blessings.

[120] See *Shulĥan Aruĥ*, Rema and *Shulĥan Aruĥ HaRav Oraĥ Ĥayim* ch. 215.

Traditional Blessings Before Eating or Drinking[121]

Six blessings[122] correspond to the various categories of food. They belong to the type of blessing called "blessings for pleasures." We are reminded through these blessings to acknowledge God's kindness.

i. Before eating bread:
Blessed are You, Lord our God, King of the universe, Who brings forth bread from the earth.

Examples: leavened/unleavened bread, bagels, pita bread or rolls, if the flour is wheat, barley, rye, oats or spelt, and water is the main liquid.

ii. Before eating other cooked foods made from grain flour, or rice:
Blessed are You, Lord our God, King of the universe, Who creates various kinds of sustenance.

Examples: cakes, cereals, cookies, pastries, pasta, cream of wheat, and cooked rice or rice cakes (and unleavened bread if eaten as a snack).

iii. Before drinking grape wine or grape juice:
Blessed are You, Lord our God, King of the universe, Who creates the fruit of the vine.

iv. Before eating fruit of a tree:
Blessed are You, Lord our God, King of the universe, Who creates the fruit of the tree.

Examples: fruit (including dried fruit) of *perennial* trees, bushes, cacti and woody vines – such as apples, oranges, avocados, blueberries, cranberries, grapes, kiwi fruit, and nuts (except peanut, which is a root).

v. Before eating other edible plant produce:
Blessed are You, Lord our God, King of the universe, Who creates the fruit of the earth.

Examples: edible roots, leafy greens, vegetables - e.g. tomato, legumes; annual or perennial herbaceous fruit (e.g. melons, artichokes, bananas).

---

[121] One may answer "Amen" to blessings recited by a righteous Gentile, if said according to the versions instituted by the Sages, so it is permitted for a Gentile to say these blessings in these translated forms. See our booklet *Prayers, Blessings, Principles of Faith, and Divine Service for Noahides*, 7th ed. (also published in Dutch, French, Indonesian, Portuguese, and Spanish).

[122] Explanations and basic traditional rules are included in the next few pages.

vi. Before any other type of food or beverage:
Blessed are You, Lord our God, King of the universe, by Whose word all things came to be.

Examples: cheese, eggs, meats, mushrooms, fully processed foods (e.g. peanut butter, tofu, candy), drinks (except grape wine or juice); and any other food. **Use this blessing if in doubt as to which one applies.**

If the blessing for bread is said at the start of a meal:
The blessing for bread covers the entire meal, so other blessings are not said for the other foods or drinks (except the blessing for wine or grape juice, which is still said, because of the special distinction and quality of grape wine). This rule includes all types of food that may constitute the main meal. But desserts (for example, cake, fruit, or ice cream) are not considered part of the main meal, so one should also make the appropriate blessing on the dessert. Beverages served as dessert (whether they are served together with a food, like coffee with cake) or alone, are still included in the blessing over the main meal, and a separate blessing for them should not be made. (Wine or juice from grapes always receives its own blessing, since it has a special distinction, even during the main meal.)

If different foods will be eaten without bread:
The order of reciting blessings for each type of food is the same as the order of the list above (e.g., when beginning to eat mixed salad, first say the blessing over avocado, then tomato, then mushroom).

Basic Traditional Rules for Blessings Before Eating or Drinking

- A blessing may be said even if only a small amount of food or beverage will be consumed.
- Before beginning to recite one of these listed blessings for a food, one should determine which of the blessings is the correct one to say.
- After beginning to recite a blessing, do not interrupt with other words until the first bite or drink of that item is swallowed.
- Since Names of God are part of these blessings, and it is forbidden to say God's Names in vain, one should only say them under the necessary conditions. (When teaching them to a child, one may pronounce God's Names if needed, until the child has learned the words.)

• One should answer "Amen" immediately after hearing a blessing made by another person, if he is sure that the person is blessing only God. (But one does not conclude with "Amen" after his own blessing.)

• If several different foods in the same category will be eaten, say only one blessing that will cover all of them. For example, when eating apples and oranges say blessing (iv) only once. Make the blessing over the fruit that is more liked, and intend to include the others as well. Non-grape beverages are included when blessing (vi) is said for a food.

• After saying blessing (iii) over grape wine or grape juice, additional blessings before other beverages are not necessary, just as the blessing over bread exempts other foods and non-grape beverages. (Blessings said unnecessarily are said in vain, and are therefore forbidden.)

• If a dish contains different types of food mixed together, but one food is the main intention for the dish, only the blessing for the main food is said. (E.g., if tuna salad has pieces of vegetables, only the blessing for the tuna is said.) If the different foods are equally important, then a blessing is made only on the one that makes up the majority of the dish. **If the correct specific blessing is unknown, in doubt or forgotten, blessing (vi) can be said for any dish, to cover everything.**

9. After a person eats a satisfying amount,[123] it is fitting to thank and bless God for giving him his food. It is also proper to include thanks for his other necessities – e.g., his health, livelihood and existence. When a Gentile says prayers of grace after eating a filling meal, the final blessing to God should be the one that was taught by Abraham:

Blessed is the God of the universe, from Whose bounty we have eaten.[124]

Since a prayer of grace after a meal is optional for Gentiles and may be in any fitting words that the person chooses, the author has taken

---

[123] *One does not recite a "Grace after Meals" after eating a small snack.

[124] This was taught by Abraham to his Gentile guests, from *Midrash Rabbah Bereishit* ch. 54. It appears that it is not proper for Gentiles to recite the paragraph of Grace after Meals that was composed by Moses, for that Jewish commandment was not commanded to Gentiles. It is thus fitting for a Gentile to make a distinction, so it will be clear that he is not adding a commandment for himself. Also, most of the full Jewish prayer (with the several paragraphs that were instituted after the time of Moses) does not apply to Gentiles.

the initiative to write the following recommended liturgy that Gentiles may use, and many will find this to be helpful:

Recommended Grace after Meals for Gentiles

We offer thanks to You, Master of the universe, Who, in His goodness, provides sustenance for the entire world with grace, with kindness, and with mercy. He gives food to all flesh, for His kindness is everlasting.[a] *Through His great goodness to us continuously, we do not lack food,*[b] *and may we never lack food, for the sake of His great Name. For He, benevolent God, provides nourishment and sustenance for all, does good to all, and prepares food for all His creatures whom He has created, as it is said: You open Your hand and satisfy the desire of every living thing.*[c] *Blessed is the God of the universe, from Whose bounty we have eaten.*[d]

Please, Master of the universe, in Your mercy give us life and health, livelihood, and sustenance, so that we may thank and bless You always. Please do not make us dependent upon the gifts of mortal men nor upon their loans, but only upon Your full, open, and generous hand, that we may never be shamed or disgraced. Give thanks to the Lord for He is good, for His kindness is everlasting.[e] *Blessed is the man who trusts in the Lord, and the Lord will be his security.*[f]

One may continue to add requests and supplications to God at his own will.

Source texts: [a]Psalms 136:25. [b]Having concluded a meal. [c]Psalms 145:16. [d]*Midrash Rabbah Bereishit* ch. 54. [e]Psalms 136:1. [f]Jer. 17:7.

10. Similarly, there are other pleasures for which blessings of thanks to God were composed by the Sages, and these may also be recited:

When smelling sweet spices such as cinnamon or cloves:
Blessed are You, Lord our God, King of the universe, Who creates various kinds of spices.

On hearing news that is good for both oneself and others:
Blessed are You, Lord our God, King of the universe, Who is good and does good.

11. If a miracle occurs for a Gentile and he returns to that place after an interval of a month or more, he may recite:
Blessed are You, Lord our God, King of the universe, Who performed a miracle for me in this place.[125]

---

[125] See *Shulĥan Aruĥ Oraĥ Ĥayim* ch. 218.

If miracles were also done for him in other places, he may include those in his blessing as well, by saying:
Blessed are You, Lord our God, King of the universe, Who performed a miracle for me in this place, and in [such-and-such a place], and in [such-and-such a place]...

12. In the same way that a person should praise and bless God for all the good he receives, and recognize that these things are from Him,[126] likewise it is an obligation to recognize that also the hurtful and painful things one experiences are also directed by God. Even though a person can't fully understand why these difficulties are brought about, he should know and acknowledge that the ways of God are beyond the understanding of mankind. Everything that God does with a person is in truth an opportunity for the good of the person, as it says (Psalms 145:17) "God is righteous in *all* His ways."

Therefore, a person is obligated to acknowledge that all God's judgments are truly just.[127] One should not react to apparent tragedies by denying His existence or His constant watchful Providence, or by spurning Him in retaliation at the time when one experiences apparent evil, for that is the way of heretical and light-minded people who lack understanding.

13. The Sages did not fix a liturgy or times of prayers or supplications to God for Gentiles. Each person can pray to the One God in his own words in a language he understands. Psalms can be included, which are all prayers to God that were composed with holy inspiration. Many Gentiles seek guidance for prayer, so the following section is included.

---

[126] *A blessing to God by a Gentile is voluntary, since there is no penalty involved if the blessing is omitted. It may be expressed in any words the person chooses, when he has a desire and inspiration to do so with devotion. *However, prayers or blessings that would be made without intention and devotion to God are better left unsaid.*

[127] *Therefore, one should not take revenge or keep a grudge against a person who harmed him (see topic 8:10). It is proper for one to say, if his feelings have been aroused negatively regarding others: *"Master of the universe! I hereby forgive anyone who has angered or vexed me, or sinned against me, either physically or financially, against my honor or anything else that is mine, whether accidentally or intentionally, by speech or by deed"* (from *Tehillat HaShem* Jewish prayer book, *Prayer Before Retiring at Night*).

The following are some prayers that have been authorized by the author and Rabbi J. I. Schochet as recommended for pious Gentiles.

DAYTIME PRAYERS

On awakening, one should be mindful of the Holy One in Whose Presence he lies, as it says (Isaiah 6:3): "The whole world is filled with His glory."

After preparing oneself for prayer, recite (from the traditional liturgy):

I offer thanks to You, living and eternal King, for You have mercifully restored my soul within me; Your faithfulness is great.

Lord of the universe, Who reigned before anything was created – at the time when by His will all things were made, then was His name proclaimed King. And after all things shall be uplifted, the Awesome One will reign alone. He was, He is, and He shall be in glory. He is One, and there is no other to compare to Him, to call His equal. Without beginning, without end – power and dominion belong to Him. He is my God and my ever-living Redeemer, the strength of my lot in time of distress. He is my banner and my refuge, my portion on the day I call. Into His hand I entrust my spirit when I sleep and when I wake. And with my soul, my body too, the Lord is with me, I shall not fear.

Psalm 145 *(or any Psalms of praise; e.g. Psalms 67,100,145,146,150)*

A Psalm of praise by David: I will exalt You, my God the King, and bless Your Name forever. Every day I will bless You, and extol Your Name forever. The Lord is great and exceedingly exalted; there is no limit to His greatness. One generation to another will laud Your works, and tell of Your mighty acts. I will speak of the splendor of Your glorious majesty and of Your wondrous deeds. They will proclaim the might of Your awesome acts, and I will recount Your greatness. They will express the remembrance of Your abounding goodness, and sing of Your righteousness. The Lord is gracious and compassionate, slow to anger and of great kindness. The Lord is good to all, and His mercies extend over all His works. Lord, all Your works will give thanks to You, and Your pious ones will bless You. They will declare the glory of Your kingdom, and tell of Your strength, to make known to mankind His mighty acts, and the glorious majesty of His kingdom. Your kingship is a kingship over all worlds, and Your dominion is throughout all generations. The Lord supports all who fall, and straightens all who are bent. The eyes of all look expectantly to You, and You give them their food at the proper time. You open Your hand and satisfy the desire of every living thing. The Lord is righteous in all His ways, and benevolent in all His deeds. The Lord is close to all who call upon Him, to all who call upon Him in truth. He fulfills the desire of those who fear Him, hears their cry and delivers them. The Lord watches over all who love Him, and will destroy all the wicked. My mouth will utter the praise of the Lord, and let all flesh bless His holy Name forever.

Verbal acceptance of God's Unity and Kingship:

Almighty God, we accept upon ourselves that which is written in Your holy Torah: "You shall know this day and take to your heart that God [alone] is God, in the heavens above and on the earth below – there is none other!"[a] We affirm the precepts of "You shall love God, your God, with all your heart, and all your soul, and all your might;"[b] and "Fear God, your God, and serve Him, and in His Name [alone] shall you vow;"[c] and, as it is written, "Fear God and observe His commandments, for that is a person's entire duty."[d]

For devout prayer, asking God for one's needs in life:

Blessed are You, God, the Supreme Being who bestows abundant kindness. Please endow us graciously with wisdom, understanding and knowledge. Please accept our repentance, and forgive us for our errors and sins. Grant complete healing for all our wounds and ailments. Bestow upon us all the needs for our sustenance from Your bounty.

Hasten the day of which it is said: "God will be King over the entire earth; in that day God will be One and His Name One;"[e] "For then I will turn the peoples to pure language, so that all will call upon the Name of God to serve Him with one purpose;"[f] and "They will not harm or destroy on all My holy mountain, for the earth will be filled with knowledge of God as water covering the sea bed."[g]

Hear our voice, God, our merciful Father, have compassion upon us and accept our prayers in mercy and favor. *[Other requests to God may be inserted here.]* Blessed are You, God, Who hears prayer.

One may optionally say the **Prayer of the Repentant** *(see below).*

---

[a]Deut.4:39. [b]*Ibid.*6:5. [c]*Ibid.*6:13. [d]Ecc.12:13. [e]Zech.14:9. [f]Zeph. 3:9. [g]Is.11:9.

Psalm 20 *(This is also a Psalm for deliverance from illness or trouble. It may be said at any time, mentioning the name of the person in need.)*

For the choirmaster, a Psalm by David. May the Lord answer you on the day of distress; may the Name of the God of Jacob fortify you. May He send your help from the Sanctuary, and support you from Zion. May He remember all your offerings, and always accept favorably your sacrifices. May He grant you your heart's desire, and fulfill your every plan. We will rejoice in your deliverance, and raise our banners in the Name of our God; may the Lord fulfill all your wishes. Now I know that the Lord has delivered His anointed one, answering him from His holy heavens with the mighty saving power of His right hand. Some [rely] upon chariots and some upon horses, but we invoke the Name of the Lord our God. They bend and fall, but we rise and are invigorated. Lord, deliver us; may the King answer us on the day we call.

Psalms for the Seven Days of the Week

Levites would sing these in the Holy Temple. The first six were chosen for their relation to God's works on that day of the first six days of creation.

Sunday (*Psalm 24*): By David, a Psalm. The earth and all therein is the Lord's; the world and those who dwell there. For He has founded it upon the seas, and established it upon the rivers. Who may ascend the mountain of the Lord, and who may stand in His holy place? He who has clean hands and a pure heart, who has not used My Name in vain and has not sworn deceitfully. He shall receive a blessing from the Lord, and kindness from God, his Deliverer. This is the generation of those who seek Him, who seek Your Presence – Jacob, forever. Lift up your heads, O gates, and be lifted up, everlasting doors, so the glorious King may enter. Who is the glorious King? The Lord, strong and mighty; the Lord, mighty in battle. Lift up your heads, O gates; lift them up, everlasting doors, so the glorious King may enter. Who is the glorious King? The Lord of hosts, He is the glorious King forever.

Monday (*Psalm 48*): A song, a Psalm of the sons of Koraĥ. The Lord is great and exceedingly praised in the city of God, the mountain of His Sanctuary. Beautiful in landscape, the joy of the entire earth – Mount Zion, by the northern slopes, the city of the great King. In her citadels, God is known as a stronghold. For behold, the kings assembled; they advanced together. They saw and were astounded; they were terror-stricken, they hastened to flee. Trembling seized them there, pangs like a woman in difficult labor. With an east wind You shattered the ships of Tarshish. As we have heard, so have we seen in the city of the Lord of hosts, in the city of our God; God shall establish it forever and ever. We hoped, O Lord, for Your kindness, within Your Temple. Like Your Name, O God, so is Your praise to the ends of the earth; Your right hand is full of righteousness. Mount Zion shall rejoice; the daughters of Judah shall exult, because of Your judgments. Walk around Zion and encircle her, count her towers. Consider well her walls, behold her lofty citadels, in order that you may recount it to a later generation. For this is God, our God, forever and ever; He shall lead us eternally.

Tuesday (*Psalm 82*): A Psalm by Asaph. God stands in the council of judges; among the judges He renders judgment. How long will you judge wickedly, always favoring the evildoers? Render justice to the needy and the orphan; deal righteously with the poor and the destitute. Rescue the needy and the pauper; save them from the hands of the wicked. They do not know and they do not understand; they go about in darkness; all the foundations of the earth tremble. I said, "You are angelic, sons of the Most High are you all." But you will die as mortals, and you will fall like any prince. Arise, O God, judge the earth, for You possess all the nations.

Wednesday (*Psalm 94*): The Lord is a God of retribution; O God of retribution, reveal Yourself! Exalt Yourself, O Judge of the earth; render to the arrogant their recompense. How long will the wicked, O Lord, how long will the wicked rejoice? They continuously speak insolently; all the evildoers act arrogantly. They crush Your people, Lord, and oppress Your heritage. They slay the widow and the stranger, and they murder the orphans. They say, "God does not see, nor will the God of Jacob perceive." Understand, you senseless of the people; you fools, when will you become wise? Will He Who implants the ear not hear? Will He Who forms the eye not see? Will He Who chastises nations not punish? – He Who imparts knowledge to mankind. The Lord knows the thoughts of a person, that they are vanity. Fortunate is the man whom You chastise, O Lord, and from Your Torah You teach him – to grant him peace from days of trouble, while a pit is dug for the wicked. For the Lord will not abandon His people, nor will He forsake His heritage. For judgment will bring return to righteousness, and all those with upright heart will pursue it. Who will rise up for me against the wicked ones; who will stand up for me against the evildoers? If the Lord had not been my help, my soul would have soon dwelt in the silence [of the grave]. If I thought that my foot was slipping, Your kindness, Lord, supported me. When my worrisome thoughts multiply within me, Your comfort delights my soul. Can a throne of evil be associated with You? Those who make evil into law? They join together against the soul of the righteous, and condemn innocent blood. But the Lord was my fortress, my God, the strength of my refuge. He will turn their violence upon them, and destroy them through their own wickedness; the Lord our God will cut them off.

Thursday (*Psalm 81*): For the choirmaster, on the *gittit* instrument, by Asaph. Sing joyously to God Who is our strength; call out to the God of Jacob. Raise your voice in song, sound the drum, the pleasant harp with the lyre. Blow the ram's horn on the New Moon [of Rosh Hashana], the day appointed for [Israel's]

Holy Day. For it is a statute for Israel, the [day of] judging for the God of Jacob. He ordained it as a precept for Joseph when he went forth over the land of Egypt, when I heard a language that I did not know. [God says:] "I removed his shoulder from the burden; his hands were removed from the kettle. In distress you called, and I delivered you; you called in secret, and I answered you with thunderous wonders; I tested you at the waters of Merivah. *Selah.* Listen, My people, and I will attest to you; Israel, if you will listen to Me – no strange god shall be among you, neither shall you prostrate yourself to a foreign god. I am the Lord, your God, Who brought you up from the land of Egypt; open your mouth wide [with your requests], and I shall grant them." But My people did not heed My voice; Israel did not want [to listen to] Me. So I sent them away after their heart's fantasies, for following their own counsels. If only My people would hearken to Me, if Israel would go in My ways. In an instant I would subdue their enemies, and turn My hand against their tormentors. Those who hate the Lord would lie to Him, so their destiny will be forever. But He would feed him with the finest of wheat, and satisfy you with honey from a rock.

Friday (*Psalm 93*): The Lord reigns; He is clothed with grandeur; the Lord has clothed and girded Himself with might; He also established the world firmly that it shall not falter. Your throne is established from of old; You are eternal. The rivers have raised, O Lord, the rivers have raised their voice; the rivers have raised their raging waves. More than the sound of great waters, mightier than the waves of the sea, is the Lord mighty on high. Your testimonies are most trustworthy; Your House will be resplendent in holiness, O Lord, forever.

The following Psalm for Saturday speaks about the future Messianic Era:

Saturday (*Psalm 92*): A Psalm, a song for the seventh day. It is good to thank the Lord, and to sing praise to Your name, O Most High. To proclaim Your kindness in the morning, and Your faithfulness in the nights, with a ten-stringed instrument and with a lyre, with singing accompanied by a harp. For You, Lord, have made me happy with Your deeds; I sing for joy at the works of Your hand. How great are Your works, O Lord! Your thoughts are exceedingly profound. A boor cannot know; and a fool cannot understand this: when the wicked thrive like grass, and all evildoers flourish, it is in order that they may be destroyed forever. But You, Lord, are exalted forever. Indeed, Your enemies, O Lord, indeed Your enemies will perish; all evildoers will be scattered. But You will increase my might like that of a wild ox; I will be anointed with fresh oil. My eyes have seen my watchful enemies; when evildoers rise up against me, my ears have heard. The righteous will flourish like a date palm; he will grow tall like a cedar in Lebanon. Planted in the House of the Lord, they will flourish in the courtyards of our God. They will still be fruitful in old age; they will be vigorous and fresh – to declare that the Lord is just; He is my strength, in Whom there is no injustice.

A person on a trip away from his town may say the "Prayer for Travelers" *below.*

EVENING PRAYERS

Psalm 91 *(and any Psalms that ask God's protection, e.g. Psalm 121)*
Whoever dwells in the shelter of the Most High, who abides in the shadow of the Almighty: I say of the Lord who is my refuge and my stronghold, my God in whom I trust, that He will save you from the ensnaring trap, from the destructive pestilence. He will cover you with His pinion, and you will find refuge under His wings; His truth is a shield and an armor. You will not fear the terror of the night, nor the arrow that flies by day; nor the pestilence that prowls in the darkness, nor the destruction that ravages at noon. A thousand may fall at your side, and ten thousand at your right, but it shall not reach you. You need only look with your eyes, and you will see the retribution of the wicked. Because you [have said,] "The Lord is my shelter," and you have made the Most High your haven, no evil will befall you, no plague will come near your tent. For He will instruct His angels in your behalf, to guard you in all your ways. They will carry you in their hands, lest you injure your foot upon a rock. You will tread upon the lion and the viper; you will trample upon the young lion and the serpent. Because he desires Me, I will deliver him; I will fortify him, for he knows My Name. When he calls on Me, I will answer him; I am with him in distress. I will deliver him and honor him. I will satisfy him with long life, and show him My deliverance.

"Lord of the universe" – *see this prayer above.*[a]

Prayer of the Repentant

O God, I have erred, sinned and willfully transgressed before You, and I have done that which is evil in Your eyes, especially with the sin(s) of … (*state the specific sins or errors*). I am sincerely ashamed of my sins, and I repent and firmly undertake not to do so again.

Please God, in Your infinite grace and compassion, forgive my sins and transgressions and grant me atonement, as it is written: "Let the wicked abandon his way and the man of iniquity his thoughts; and let him return unto God, and He will show him compassion, and to our God, for He will pardon abundantly."[b] And it is written: "Do I desire at all that the wicked should die, says the Lord, God; it is rather that he return from his ways and live!"[c]

---

[a]From the traditional *Siddur* prayer book liturgy. [b]Is. 55:7. [c]Ezekiel 18:23.

Psalm 51: For the choirmaster, a Psalm by David, when Nathan the prophet came to him after he had gone to Bathsheba. Be gracious to me, O God, in keeping with Your kindness; in accordance with Your abounding compassion, erase my transgressions. Cleanse me thoroughly of my wrongdoing, and purify me of my sin. For I acknowledge my transgressions, and my sin is always before me. Against You alone have I sinned, and done that which is evil in Your eyes; [forgive me] so that You will be justified in Your verdict, vindicated in Your judgment. Indeed, I was begotten in iniquity, and in sin did my mother conceive me. Indeed, You desire truth in the innermost parts; teach me the wisdom of concealed things. Purge me with hyssop and I shall be pure; cleanse me and I shall be whiter than snow. Let me hear joy and gladness; then the bones that You have shattered will rejoice. Hide Your face from my sins, and erase all my trespasses. Create in me a pure heart, O God, and renew within me an upright spirit. Do not cast me out from before You, and do not take Your Spirit of Holiness away from me. Restore to me the joy of Your deliverance, and support me with a spirit of generosity. I will teach transgressors Your ways, and sinners will return to You. Save me from bloodguilt, O God, God of my deliverance; my tongue will sing joyously of Your righteousness. My Lord, open my lips, and my mouth will declare Your praise. For You do not desire that I bring sacrifices, nor do You wish burnt offerings. The offering [desirable] to God is a contrite spirit; a contrite and broken heart, God, You do not disdain. In Your goodwill, bestow goodness upon Zion; rebuild the walls of Jerusalem. Then You will desire offerings of righteousness, burnt-offering and whole-offering; then they will offer bulls upon Your altar.

One may conclude with verses of placing trust in God, before sleeping:

When you lie down, you will not be afraid; you will lie down and your sleep will be sweet.[a]

May I sleep well; may I awake in mercy.[b]

I entrust my spirit into Your hand; You will redeem me God, God of truth![c]

---

[a]Proverbs 3:24. [b]Traditional *Siddur* prayer liturgy. [c]Psalms 31:6.

Prayers for Specific Needs and Requests

A Prayer for Livelihood[a]

May it be Your Will, Lord, our God, that my provisions and my livelihood, and the provisions and livelihood of my household, be encompassing, appropriate and virtuous in Your hands. May we never be in need of the gifts of man nor of their loans, but only of Your hand which is full, open, holy and generous. And may my work and all my dealings be blessed and not destitute, for life and not for death. And may I merit that no desecration of the Name of Heaven occur through me, and that I may be among the charitable and those that influence for good to everyone at all times, and fill my hand with Your blessings and satiate me of your goodness. For You are blessed and bring blessings to the universe. The eyes of all look expectantly to You, and You give them all their food in its proper time. You open Your hand, and satisfy the desire of every living being.[b] Cast your burden upon the Lord, and He will sustain you; He will never allow the falling of the righteous.[c] Please lift my strength and raise my fortune so that I will be able to serve You wholeheartedly all the days of the world. Amen.

Prayer for Travelers[d]

This prayer is said outside the city from which one is leaving, on the first day of the journey. On subsequent days of the journey until reaching home again, the prayer may be recited every morning.

May it be Your will, Lord our God, to lead us in peace and direct our steps in peace, to guide us in peace, to support us in peace, and to bring us to our destination in life, joy, and peace
(*if one intends to return on the same day, add*: and return us in peace). Deliver us from the hands of every enemy and lurking foe, from robbers and wild beasts on the journey, and from all kinds of calamities that may come and afflict the world; and bestow blessing upon all our actions. Grant me grace, kindness, and mercy in Your eyes and in the eyes of all who behold us, and bestow bountiful kindness upon us. Hear the voice of our prayer, for You hear everyone's prayer. Blessed are You, God, Who hears prayer.

---

[a]From a prayer by Rabbi Moses Cordovero. [b]Psalms 145:16. [c]Psalms 5:23. [d]From *Siddur Tehillat HaShem with English Translation, Annotated Edition*, p. 85, pub. Kehot.

CHAPTER 7

Sacrificial Offerings

A Gentile is permitted to build an altar and offer upon it a *kosher*[128] animal or bird which he owns, as a (completely) burnt offering sacrifice to God.[129,130] Gentiles do not have any of the other types of scriptural offerings that apply for Jews in the Holy Temple, such as a "sin," "guilt" or "peace" offering.[131] The required details are explained in *Sheva Mitzvot HaShem*, Part I, ch. 7. Nevertheless, we *highly recommend* that Gentiles in our days *not* act on the permission within the basic Torah Law to offer sacrifices, for at least two reasons:

(1) In order to bring a sacrifice, one should be worthy to approach much closer to God (with a service that resembles the Jewish priests in the Holy Temple), which is something that is very difficult to achieve in our time. More so, a deed which one takes on voluntarily as an additional service to God must be done in an especially sincere and holy way. If the additional service to God is not performed by these higher standards, it will be considered as blemished before Him.

(2) It is obvious that this type of Torah-based Divine service should be instructed and supervised only by a reliable and expert Orthodox Rabbi, which is very difficult to arrange in our time.

However, a righteous Gentile may *study* these precepts (as explained above in topic 5:1) on a theoretical level, since he will learn more about each of the Seven Noahide Commandments and other aspects of serving of God, as they happen to apply within this subject.

---

[128] See Genesis 8:20; the sacrifices Noaĥ brought were only *kosher* species.

[129] From Rambam, *Laws of [God's] Chosen House* 6:15-16, a Gentile is forbidden to sacrifice on the Temple Mount even when the Temple is destroyed. The holiness of the Temple Mount is eternal, so no sacrifice may be offered there except according to Torah Law. At the Temple, when a sacrifice to God was brought there by a Gentile, it was offered for him by a Jewish priest.

[130] See Rambam, *Laws of the Sacrificial Procedures* 19:16 – "Gentiles are permitted to offer burnt sacrifices in any place" (except the Temple Mount), which implies that other types of sacrifices are forbidden for them to bring.

[131] See *Tosafot Rosh* Tractate *Yevamot* 71a, that a Gentile is forbidden to eat the meat of the Passover sacrifice by the commandment in Exodus 12:48.

CHAPTER 8

Obligatory Moral Conduct

1. Every person has natural traits, and there are other traits that one acquires by regularly habituating himself to act in these ways. A person must always evaluate his traits and strive to bring them toward the correct path.[132]

How so? One must especially strive not to become angered or to be an angry person, for these traits are despicable and they destroy one's life. Therefore, the Sages taught that anyone who gets angry suffers the departure of his intellect, and this type of a life is greatly lacking. If one is naturally an angry person, he should train himself not to get angry at all, and he should force himself to act with humility and patience toward others by habit, until he permanently acquires these good traits. Likewise with other character traits, one should evaluate himself truthfully to determine if he acts as a righteous person would, and he should correct himself to act in a way that finds favor in the eyes of God and in the eyes of other people.

2. A person should not be a buffoon or constantly despondent. Rather one should be happy, and should greet others with a happy countenance. Similarly, one should not be greedy, rushing for wealth and possessions, nor lazy and an idler from work. Rather, one should look upon others with a favorable eye, and be favorably looked upon by others. One should not have a quarrelsome or envious jealous temperament, or be possessed by desires, nor pursue honor. The Sage Rabbi Elazar HaKappar said (Tractate *Avot* 4:21): "Envy, lust and honor-seeking drive a person from [life in] this world."

3. If a person has one of these bad traits, how should he refine himself? One should habituate himself to the correct traits until they become habitual for him. He should force himself to perform actions that are morally and logically correct many times, until these actions are easy and the correct traits are set into his soul. For example, in regard to what we have written previously about the bad trait of anger, he should train himself that if he is hit or cursed, he should not arouse

---

[132] This chapter is collected from Rambam's *Laws of Attitudes (Hilĥot De'ot).*

his anger at all (that is, he should not answer back or fight about this, but he should accept it silently, against his nature), and he should habituate himself to do so until the anger is removed from his heart.

Likewise, one who is a buffoon and wastes his time with foolish jokes and lightheadedness which have no benefit, should distance himself from his friends who have these habits, and if he comes in contact with them he should close his mouth and stop from saying his usual foolish words. Instead, he should regularly act with seriousness, the opposite of his previous foolish ways.

4. It is forbidden for a person to tell lies, or act in a smooth-tongued and luring manner in order to deceive or persuade. One should not speak one thing outwardly and think otherwise in his heart. Rather, his inner self should be like his image that he shows to the world. He may not deceive people, and instead he should always pursue truthfulness.[133]

5. A person should direct his heart and the totality of his behavior to one goal, which is becoming aware of God, and searching to be close to Him and His just ways. How so? When involved in business dealings to make a profit, one should not think solely of gathering money to be rich, and certainly not just to hoard money for no purpose at all, as is the way of the stingy. Rather, he should earn his income with righteousness and honor, and his goal in this should be to have a healthy and strong body, to provide for the members of his household respectfully, and to do charitable deeds with his money as are logically expected, for his good and the good of others.

Likewise all his other actions should be intended for this goal, and he should not do things without any reason at all or for vain reasons, as Solomon the Wise said,[134] "In all your ways you should know Him, and He will straighten your ways," meaning that you should think through all your actions before they are taken, in order that they should definitely be for the goal of doing the will of God. With this effort, God will illuminate the correct path for the person, and will bestow success in it.

---

[133] *For more on this subject, see Part VII, topics 5:23-27.

[134] Proverbs 3:6, and *Metzudot David* there.

6. Every person by nature is very influenced by his friends and surroundings, and by nature he is drawn after those around him, to also act in their ways. Therefore everyone must befriend good people to learn from their worthy actions, and distance themselves from bad people in order not to learn from their bad actions, as Solomon said,[135] "He who walks with the wise will become wise, while one who associates with fools will suffer." Therefore one must also be especially careful about who his children and other household members are befriending, and what places they are frequenting.

7. Likewise, it is an obligation for every person to endeavor to influence those around him to observe those things that they are obligated in, in a way of friendliness and sociability. One who is able to distance those around him from doing wrong, has an obligation to do so, in order to support the foundation of a moral society that will be as God wishes, as the prophet says,[136] "The world was not created to be void, but properly settled."

8. If one who sees that his friend has sinned and is following an improper path, and he knows that he will be able to effectively rebuke him with words and return him to the correct path, he should do so. How should he rebuke him? He should rebuke him patiently with respectful and nice words, and he should not speak harshly or embarrass him (unless the one rebuking is a true scholar of human nature, who understands that in this particular situation, it is the correct way to influence him to be better, since each situation and person is different). His objective should be that his words should be accepted by the sinner's heart, and they should have the right effect. It is a very righteous deed to bring another to the merit of following the correct path, and one who accomplishes this does great good for humanity and brings God much pleasure.

If one begins to affectionately rebuke his friend but sees that his words are not being accepted, he should not admonish him further in order to embarrass him, which will cause a useless fight. Rather, he should distance himself somewhat from the person so that it does not seem that he is agreeing to and supporting his actions. Certainly, one

---

135 Proverbs 13:20.

136 Isaiah 45:18.

should never flatter sinners (unless he is in great danger that they might harm him otherwise).

9. One should always try to respect every person and show him honor, and speak about his honorable traits and deeds, but not about his disgraceful traits and deeds. Many fights in the world are brought about by people who spread tales, gossip and slander about others.

The Sage Ben Zoma said:[137] "Who is wise? One who learns from every person … Who is strong? One who subdues his [evil] inclination … Who is rich? One who is happy with his lot ... Who is honored? One who honors others …"

10. Likewise, a person should not take revenge or hold a grudge toward another. What is an example of taking revenge? If A asks for a favor from his friend B, and B does not agree to do it for A, and the next day, B asks A for a favor, and A answers to B, "I will not do this favor for you, just like you did not do one for me."

If A says, "I will do it for you, unlike you, who didn't want to do a favor for me before," he is holding a grudge.

A person must know that these traits, taking revenge or holding a grudge, are extremely bad, and they bring enmity and conflict between mankind. Almost every fight starts with something small which is not worthy of fighting over, and then it gets out of control, and hatefulness or arguing can end up in bloodshed or the like.

Instead, a person should overlook the bad traits of others, and do kindness to his friends until they all love him and his actions, and they will learn from him about the correct way to act. This is the truly good way in which it is correct to behave, and the true path by which it is possible to establish stable and productive societies which are based on good principles, and peaceful business dealings between people.

11. All the things explained in this chapter are only a small part and a few examples of a person's moral obligations. We have written this in brief, as an *introduction* for one who wishes to strive in gaining understanding and in following the correct ways with other people and with God.

---

[137] *Mishnah Avot (Ethics of the Fathers)* 4:1.

CHAPTER 9

Repentance

1. Every person is obligated to frequently search his own actions and make an accounting with his soul, to determine if he is acting in a correct way in God's eyes. If he finds that he acted wrongly, or if he transgressed God's will in one of his Seven Noahide Commandments, or he erred by not acting in a moral way, then he should change his ways and conduct, and he should accept upon himself that henceforth he will act in the correct way, and he will stop transgressing the commandments that God has given him.

2. **A person should have regret for doing wrong, and change his sinful ways, and ask for forgiveness from God for the sins that he transgressed.** This process, by which one asks and begs forgiveness from God, is called "repentance."[138] (God certainly accepts sincere repentance, and forgives the repentant sinner for his transgression.)

3. One should not think that his actions are already sealed before God, and since he sinned very much, it is impossible for him to return and become a righteous person. This is not true, for God is merciful and constantly anticipates that those who want to return to Him will repent and correct their ways. When they do, He accepts them fully and has mercy on them. When they repent correctly, and completely remove

---

[138] *Kol Bo'ai HaOlom*, p. 45, says that a Gentile is obligated in prayer and repentance as part of his commandment to believe in God and the negation of idols. It is possible that the obligation of repentance derives from the "essence of the commandment" – that it is a general obligation for a person to recognize God and His precepts, and therefore if one errs, he is required to correct his ways in order to keep God's commandments, from then on. (The "essence of the commandment" refers to a basic aspect of God's issuance of commandments to mankind: the very fact that mankind's Creator issues commands is the reason that mankind is obligated to follow those commands, above and beyond any specific details of what He has commanded. The obligation to repent is derived from the essence of the commandments themselves: the Divine commands are eternal, and they obligate the one who is commanded not only to adhere to them, but also to align and correct his deeds to be in compliance with his commandments.) See above, p. 93

themselves from their wrong actions, and they accept His Kingship and resolve to observe their commandments for the future, God forgives them for their sins and does not punish them for the past.

We find this exemplified by the city of Nineveh:[139]

> And the word of God came to Jonah son of Amittai, saying, "Arise, go to Nineveh, the great city, and proclaim against it, for their wickedness has come before Me." ... Jonah began to enter into the city ... and he proclaimed and said, "In another forty days Nineveh will be overturned!" And the people of Nineveh believed in God ... it was proclaimed and declared throughout Nineveh by the counsel of the king and his nobles, saying: ... "Both man and animal shall cover themselves with sackcloth, and they shall call out mightily to God. Everyone shall repent of his evil way and of the robbery that is in their hands." ... And God saw their deeds, that they repented of their evil way; and God relented concerning the evil He had spoken to do to them, and He did not do it.

Likewise, God said to Cain (Gen. 4:7), "If you better your ways, you will be forgiven," thus teaching about repentance, and that it was in his capability to return at any time he wished, and he would be forgiven.

4. Repentance helps to remove the sins between a person and God, such as one who serves idols, eats flesh that was severed from a living animal, or commits adultery. But for one who steals from his fellow, damages him or harms him, whether physically like hitting him, or emotionally like cursing him, in all these cases, his repentance is not effective until he appeases the person he wronged and asks forgiveness from him, and if the person agrees.

It is forbidden for a person who was wronged to be cruel and not let himself be appeased. Rather he should be forgiving and agree to pardon the one who sinned against him, if he asks for forgiveness with a complete and willing heart.[140] Afterwards, the sinner should regret his actions and ask forgiveness from God, and do correct repentance.

5. Just as a person needs to examine his actions to see if they are sinful, and repent from those which are, he likewise needs to search his personality for the bad traits he has, and to repent from those also and

---

[139] Jonah 1:1-2, 3:4-10. See Radak on Jonah 1:1.

[140] Rambam, *Laws of Repentance* 2:10.

correct his ways – such as traits of anger, hate, jealousy, sarcasm, pursuing money and honor, or pursuing physical desires and the like. These last traits are in some ways more evil than sins that merely involve action, for when one is drawn into these bad traits, it is very hard to remove oneself from them, and to distance one's self from the sins they inspire. Therefore the prophet said (Isaiah 55:7), "Let the wicked abandon *his* way, and the man of iniquity his thoughts; let him return to God, and He will have compassion upon him; and [let him return] to our God, for He will abundantly pardon."[141]

Even for an evil thought in which one planned to do a sin, but did not actually do it, one needs to repent, for God judges even a person's thoughts, and punishes for evil plans as well as for evil deeds.[142]

6. God judges all of one's actions. He punishes for unrepented wrong actions when and as He sees fit, and gives reward to those who do His will and keep His commandments and walk in the correct path, as befits a person whom God created in His image. One whose unrepented sins outweigh his merits is liable to die by the Hand of God [but He is forbearing and may choose to wait to see if the sinner will repent]. After one's passing, his soul ascends to its spiritual reward. If his unrepented sins outweigh his merits, his soul is first purged in *Gehinom*, and then goes to its reward (unless he was extremely wicked).

A country whose sins outweigh its merits is liable to be destroyed (and the righteous would be saved), as it says,[143] "And God said, '...because their sin [in Sodom and Gomorrah] has been very grave, I will descend and see: if they act in accordance with its outcry, etc.' "

In regard to the entire world as well, if the sins of humanity would become exceedingly greater than their merits, the wicked would be destroyed, as happened to the Generation of the Flood.[144] The wicked

---

[141] Rambam, *Laws of Repentance* 7:3.

[142] See Jerusalem Talmud Tractate *Pe'ah* ch. 1, and *Tosafot* Tractate *Kiddushin* 39b, that a Gentile is judged by God for dwelling on a bad thought.

[143] Gen. 18:20-21. [God had no need to "descend" in order to "see." He stated this to teach a lesson to judges that they must see the evidence in every case.]

[144] *God swore (Gen. 9:8-17) that He would never again bring a punishment of destruction on the whole world. This promise includes holding back from any worldwide destruction, not only by a Flood. Therefore, if the majority were wicked, God would punish the world as a whole in a lesser way.

would perish, and the righteous would be saved, as were Noaĥ and his family, as it is written, "God saw that the evil of mankind was great ... and God said: 'I will wash away man' ... But Noaĥ found favor ..."[145]

This reckoning is not calculated only on the basis of the number of sins and merits, but also takes into account their magnitude. There are some merits that outweigh many sins, as it says,[146] "Because something good for the Lord, the God of Israel, has been found in him ..." In contrast, a sin may outweigh many merits, as it states,[147] "One sin may obscure much good." The weighing of sins and merits is carried out according to the wisdom of the Knowing God. Only He knows how to measure merits against sins.

Therefore, a person should always look at himself as equally balanced between merit and sin, and the world as equally balanced between merit and sin. If a person performs one sin, he may tip his balance and that of the entire world to the side of guilt and bring destruction upon himself. If he performs one good deed, he may tip his balance and that of the entire world to the side of merit, and bring deliverance and salvation to himself and others.[148]

7. Every person[149] who desires and has motivation and understanding to stand before God, to serve Him and to gain knowledge about Him, and who goes in the correct path that God made for him, and who removes from upon himself the many calculations which people strive after, has become sanctified as "holy of holies." God will be this person's portion and inheritance forever, and he will merit to have his necessities met in this world, as did the Priests who served in the Holy Temple.[150] Thus said David, may he rest in peace:[151] "God is the portion of my inheritance and of my cup; You maintain my lot."[152]

---

[145] Genesis 6:5,7-8.

[146] I Kings 14:13.

[147] Ecclesiastes 9:18.

[148] Rambam, *Laws of Repentance* 3:4. See also Part VI, topic 7:22.

[149] *Likkutei Siĥot* vol. 13, p. 230: *"ish va'ish"* refers to Jews and Gentiles.

[150] This comparison is made above in topic 5:6, which explains that a Pious Gentile who involves himself in learning Torah in the area of the Noahide commandments is compared to a High Priest who serves in the Holy Temple.

[151] Psalms 16:5.

[152] Rambam, *Laws of the Sabbatical and Jubilee Years* 13:13.

PART II

THE PROHIBITION OF IDOLATRY

This section explains details of the following one obligation and nine prohibitions that are included in this commandment to Gentiles and its offshoots:

1. Not to worship any power other than God, which includes not to verbally accept upon oneself the dominion of an idol.

2. According to Rambam and Ramban: Not to believe in the false idea of a "partner" *(sheetuf)* with God, or to say words which imply that a *sheetuf* is true. According to *Tosafot* and Rema, a Gentile is not prohibited to believe in a *sheetuf* or to combine a *sheetuf* with God's name in an oath, but one who does is not a Pious Gentile.

3. Not to take interest in an idol or any ideas of idolatry, which includes not to contemplate an idol or the ways it is worshiped, not to read books about idolatrous doctrines or ways of service, and not to enter a house of idol worship except for a temporary practical need.

4. Not to take part in an idolatrous celebration, which includes not to eat food from such celebrations or from sacrifices to an idol.

5. Not to honor an idol by action or speech that shows honor or importance, including not to pray to an idol or take an oath in its name.

6. Not to make or own a three-dimensional statue of an idol of any size; as an offshoot of this, three-dimensional full or frontal figures of a person or angel are forbidden to have for decoration.

7. Not to set up or have an accessory to idolatry, such as a tree to worship or use for serving an idol; an offshoot is not to erect a pillar for people to gather at for any worship, or to have a stone to bow down on in worship.

8. Not to have any benefit from an idol or anything offered to an idol.

9. To destroy (or nullify) idols and their accessories that come into one's possession or domain.

10. Not to be involved in the rituals that idolaters perform as expressions of their beliefs, such as divination, soothsaying, witchcraft, necromancy, or consulting the *Ov* or *Yidoni*. This includes not to do things that are customary ways that idolaters show their beliefs, such as idolatrous tattoos and styles.

INTRODUCTION

by Rabbi J. Immanuel Schochet

Rabbi of Congregation Beth Joseph
Toronto, Canada

The concept of idolatry would appear to be an anachronism in our day and age, with no practical relevance in most countries. It recalls primitive societies of times long gone when paganism was rampant. For rational humans to worship artificial images fashioned by their own hands is so self-evidently absurd that one wonders how this could ever have happened. In reality, however, it is not so simple. For one thing, even nowadays one can still find remnants of such practices. Secondly, idolatry is not limited to man-made images, but may alternatively involve natural bodies such as celestial constellations, stars and planets, even animals and vegetation, or even fellow-humans, who are believed to be endowed with divinity. People, even in ancient times, developed sophisticated rationale to justify these practices.

Maimonides presents an anthropological analysis of how idolatry evolved:[1] initially there was no denial of the reality and supremacy of the One God and Supreme Being, Who created everything. Then people assumed that their submission to God obligates them to honor those natural forces (such as the sun, moon and stars) through which God benefits the world, and which "minister" before Him. Gradually this deteriorated to perceiving these forces as powers authorized to act independently of God, and the world's dependence on them would imply a rationale to worship them on their own – even while still recognizing the supremacy of God. The whole or partial worship of these forces eventually degenerated to a "substitute" worship of images that represent or symbolize them, and eventually led to these images themselves, on their own, becoming objects of worship.

Nowadays this appears to be a vestige of ignorance and naivety. Thus it seems strange that the eternal Torah should be so concerned about idolatry, to the point that it was found necessary to mandate so many cautions and prohibitions about its practices with all their corollaries, and about anything that savored of idolatry.

The answer is found in the generic Hebrew term for idolatry: *avodah*

---

[1] Maimonides (Rambam), *Laws of the Worship of Stars [and Idols]* ch. 1.

zarah. Literally it means "strange worship" (in the sense of being outside the boundaries of that which is permitted). In other words, the worship of anything other than God alone is an act of idolatry:

"The principal command with regard to idolatry is that one should not worship any of the created beings, neither angel nor sphere nor star, neither any of the four elements nor anything formed from them. Even if the worshiper knows that *HaShem*[2] is God and he only worships this creature in the manner that Enosh[3] and his contemporaries worshiped at first, he is still an idolater. It is against this that the Torah warns us when stating, 'Lest you lift up your eyes unto heaven and see the sun and the moon and the stars… which *HaShem* your God has allotted unto all the peoples' (Deuteronomy 4:19). This means: you might observe that these guide [sustain] the world, and God has allotted them to all peoples, as beings that 'live' and exist, and do not suffer decomposition as [all] other things in the world do, and [thus] conclude that it is proper to bow down to them and to worship them. Concerning this the Torah enjoins, 'Take heed to yourselves lest your heart be deceived' (Deuteronomy 11:16); that is to say, you should not be led astray through the reflections of your heart to worship these as intermediaries between you and the Creator."[4]

In his formulation of the "13 Principles of the Faith," Maimonides writes: "The Fifth Principle: [God] blessed be He, is the One that it is appropriate to worship and to exalt Him, and to make known His greatness and [the obligation of] obedience [to His commandments]. One is not to do so to any being lower than He – be it of the angels, the stars, the spheres, or the elements and what is compounded from them. For [all these] have been fashioned according to the functions they are to perform. They have no control or free will, but [function only] according to His Will, may He be exalted. One is not to relate to them as intermediaries through which to draw near to [God]. [Our] thoughts must be directed only to [God], may He be exalted, and anything other than [God] must be set aside. This is the fifth principle, the prohibition of idolatry, and the greater part of the Torah cautions us about this."

---

[2] *HaShem* (lit. "the Name") is the general non-sacred substitution in Hebrew for "the Lord" or "God."

[3] Enosh was a grandson of Adam. The practice of *avodah zarah* started in his time; see *Targum Yonatan* on Genesis 4:26, and *Sifre* on *Eikev*, section 43.

[4] Maimonides, *ibid.* 2:1.

Avodah zarah is not restricted to religious service of anything apart from the Godhead. It includes any assumptions of there being self-contained beings or forces that are not totally dependent on God and His Providence. This will be understood with an example: when driving in a nail with a hammer, the immediate agent of activity seems to be the hammer. In truth, however, it is not the hammer itself but the hand that holds it and the energy used by the hand. So, too, everything in the universe is forever altogether subject to God and His will.

To put one's faith into a belief that planetary constellations determine events and human fate (astrology), or that certain occurrences are indicative of predetermination, or to engage in any form of enchantment or sorcery (thinking that thereby one can manipulate future events), or consulting "spirits" (like séances), necromancy and other forms of divination – all these imply that there are other powers in existence which work on their own, independent of the continuous Divine Providence governing the totality of creation. Thus all of these are classified as *avodah zarah.*[5]

Human frailty is centered on self-interest, self-indulgence and gratification, the egocentric as opposed to the Theocentric. The powerful desire to control, direct and manipulate the unknown future, to circumvent the Divine "system," is extremely seductive. In effect, however, it betrays a lack of trust in God and undermines true belief in God, Who alone is the Creator and Sustainer of all beings, and Who alone is in exclusive charge of all that happens to them. *Avodah zarah* is thus denial of pure monotheism. It presupposes a polytheistic – or at least a dualistic – reality.[6] No wonder, then, that there are so many Torah laws, precepts and warnings dealing with *avodah zarah.* The Torah serves as the antidote to avoid idolatry's pitfalls, to guide us on the path of truth, and to help us live up to the fact that the human is created in the "image and likeness of God."

---

[5] See Maimonides, *ibid.*, Preamble (preceding ch. 1), and *ibid.*, ch. 6 and 11.

[6] This explains the many statements in the Torah tradition drawing a moral equivalence between certain attitudes and idolatry. E.g, pride and arrogance are regarded as tantamount to idolatry (*Sotah* 4b), as is losing one's temper (*Zohar* I:27b; Maimonides, *Hilĥot De'ot* 2:3), avoiding the giving of charity (*Ketuvot* 68a), dishonesty and deception (*Sanhedrin* 92a), etc. These imply some form of self-worship, and even when acknowledging God, also assuming a sense of self-sufficient importance (which thus constitutes dualism).

CHAPTER 1

The Prohibition of Idol Worship

1. The Master of the universe commanded Adam in the prohibition against serving idols,[1] as it says,[2] "And the Lord God commanded [upon] Adam ...," meaning that God commanded Adam to submit to His Divinity. The Sages explained that there are three meanings in this:

"I am God; do not exchange Me" – to rebel and replace Me with another god, which is the prohibition of idolatry.

"I am God; do not curse Me" – this being the prohibition of blaspheming God's Name, since for God's honor one must not disgrace and blaspheme Him.

"I am God; the fear of Me shall be upon you" – this being the obligation to fear God.

The prohibition of idolatry has two facets: the command to recognize and know God, and the prohibition against serving idols.

Anyone who does not recognize and believe in God is a "deviant believer" (see Part I, topic 1:7). Likewise, anyone who serves idols denies all of God's commandments (since he does not accept God's Sovereignty), as well as His honor and His True Existence.

2. The main prohibition against idol worship is not to serve one of the creations, be it an angel, a spiritual power, a constellation, a star or a planet, one of the fundamentals of the physical creation, a person, an animal, a tree, or any other created thing. Even if one *knows* that the Master of the universe is God, and he only serves a lofty creation and only in the mistaken manner that Enosh and his generation did (Gen. 4:26, as will be explained below in topic 4), this is still idol worship.

This concept is written in the Torah:[3] "Lest you raise your eyes to the heavens and see the sun and moon and the stars and the hosts of the heavens, and you are persuaded, and you bow down to them and serve them – those [celestial bodies] that God separated for all the nations under the heavens." This means that a person is able to err in his heart and believe that celestial bodies guide the world, and that God has

---

[1] Tractate *Sanhedrin* 56b; *Sifri* Numbers 15:23; Rambam, *Laws of Kings* 9:1.

[2] Genesis 2:16.

[3] Deuteronomy 4:19.

chosen them to be forever alive and existing without ever decaying, for the sake of the terrestrial world but unlike its way. From this false idea, one may come to think that it is fitting to bow down and serve them. Regarding this it says,[4] "Guard yourselves lest your hearts stray," meaning: be vigilant to avoid a mistaken thought, by imagining that these creations are acting as intermediaries between people and God.[5]

Therefore, a person is also an idol worshiper if he serves God along with another entity as an intermediary (see Part I, topic 1:7), even if he says that the Lord is the "main God," but he also serves another power. This is so regardless of whether one serves the intermediary alone, for example by bringing a sacrificial offering or bowing down to it, or if he brings a sacrifice and bows down and says that his service is for both God and the intermediary.[6] However, if a person serves only the Lord, but he also *believes* there is another power or god under the Lord's command that one should also have faith in and swear by, then he is called a "believer in an intermediary."

Great Rabbinical authorities throughout history debated whether the false belief in an intermediary is actually idolatry and therefore prohibited to Gentiles, or if it is not included in the basic Noahide prohibition of idol worship and therefore not forbidden for Gentiles.[7,8]

---

[4] Deuteronomy 11:16.

[5] Rambam, *Laws of the Worship of Stars [and Idols]* 2:1, explains the main concept of idol worship as the mistaken thought that it is God's will that we serve idols – unlike those who deny God's existence and imagine an idol as a deity. This is also the opinion of Ramban; see his explanations on Ex. 20:3, 22:19, and 23:25. Rashi (on Ex. 20:3) and some other Torah authorities maintain that the essence of idol worship is the physical action of worshiping an idol, rather than believing in the mistaken concept. This disagreement affects the question regarding belief in intermediaries, because according to Rambam this is the main thing that is prohibited as idol worship, and Gentiles are definitely forbidden to maintain this false belief. But Rashi holds this isn't the main prohibition, and from this follows the opinions of *Tosafot* (see below) that belief in an intermediary isn't forbidden for Gentiles.

[6] *Ĥiddushei HaRan Sanhedrin* 61b.

[7] *The majority opinion and practical ruling is that it is not forbidden; see topics 12:9-10 below. But it is unrighteous, i.e., the person is not one of the Pious of the nations of the world (see Part I, topic 1:7 and footnotes there).

[8] It is clear from Rambam's intentions (in *Laws of the Worship of Stars [and Idols]* 1:2, *Laws of Repentance* 3:7, and elsewhere) that this belief in an

intermediary power is also the essence of idol worship. In *Laws of Kings* 9:2, he concludes and writes that any act of idol worship that is a capital sin for a Jew is also a capital sin for a Gentile.

However, Rema on *Oraĥ Ĥayim* ch. 156 rules that the false *belief* in an intermediary is permitted for Gentiles, and in his *Darĥei Moshe (ibid.)* it is explained in detail in regard to traditional Christian doctrine, as quoted here:

> It is written in *Sefer Toldot Adam V'Ĥavah* by Rabbenu Yeruĥam: Rabbenu Yitzhak writes that it is permitted to accept an oath from a worshiper of Yeshua who swears in his religion ..., if he swears by "God" and does not mention the name of Yeshua, even if he mentions God's name in the oath with the intention of including Yeshua, because he still includes this with an intention for the Creator of Heaven and Earth. Even if he connects the name of God with his belief in the other power, nevertheless, it is not prohibited for one to cause a Gentile to mention his *belief* in an intermediary (even in an oath). Also the prohibition of "placing a stumbling block before the blind" does not apply, since it is not forbidden for Gentiles to believe in an intermediary. This is also written in *Tosafot* on Tractate *Beĥorot* 2b.

This is also written in *Tosafot* on Tractate *Sanhedrin* 63b and *Piske ha'Rosh Sanhedrin* ch. 7. The implication is that the *concept* of a divine trinity is actual idol worship, and swearing verbally in the names of God *and* another power would be forbidden for Gentiles. But if they mention *only* God, without saying clearly that they (also) mean Yeshua (or souls of others whom the person considers to be saints), it is considered in practical terms as combining God's power with an intermediary in an oath. *That* belief, and the mention of it, are not prohibited to Gentiles, and therefore if a Jew requires that a Christian should make an oath in God's name (only), it is permitted.

The explanation above (from *Tosafot* and Rema) is accepted by most later Rabbinical authorities (e.g., *Nodah Bi'Yehudah* vol 2, ch. 148). However, if one bows down before a physical statue or image, it is an act of idol worship.

This distinction between belief and actual worship is clear in the following section quoted from *Sefer Mitzvot Gadol* (*SMa"G*), Prohibition 1:

> One may not bring to mind the thought that there is any god besides the Lord, as it says [in the Ten Commandments, Exodus 20:3], "There shall not be for you other gods before Me," from which we see that the Torah forbids the taking of an oath in the name of an idol, and this includes belief in an intermediary, **even if one doesn't actually serve it**. In *Meĥilta* it says: "The inference that is clear from the verse [Exodus 20:4], 'You shall not make for yourself a carved image ...,' is not to create one. From where do I know that one should not keep in

> existence one that exists already? ... However, the verse's interpretation cannot be taken out of the simple meaning of the text."
>
> Furthermore, these words ..., "before Me" (i.e., "in My Presence"), are interpreted simply as the combining of God's name with the name of another. In Tractate *Sanhedrin* 63a it says that one who combines God's name with that of another will be "uprooted from the world," as it says (Exodus 22:19), "One who slaughters [sacrifices] to the gods will be destroyed – [this is allowed] only to the Lord alone."

The explanation of his words is that *Meĥilta* explains this verse, "There shall not be for you other gods before Me," to mean that one may not keep an idol in existence. However, the simple meaning of the verse is not referring to this. (Rather, the prohibition of keeping an idol in existence is learned from the verse, "You shall not bring an abomination into your house," as it is written by Rambam in *Laws of the Worship of Stars [and Idols]* 7:2). The simple meaning of the verse, "There shall not be for you other gods *before Me*," is that one may not have idols ("other gods") in any way, even in a way of an intermediary. He brings proof from Tractate *Sanhedrin* (*ibid.*), which explains that the verse cited above, "One who brings offerings to the gods will be destroyed – [sacrificing is allowed] only to the Lord alone," is referring to a punishment specifically for one who sacrifices or does some other *act* of idol worship. However, the prohibition itself applies even for one who does not actively serve idols, but accepts idol worship or swears by it. We see from this that the concept of an intermediary refers to believing that there is a partner along with God, as expressed either in one's thoughts or speech, and this does not necessarily need to be an active service.

This is the belief in an intermediary that (as *Tosafot* writes) is not prohibited to Gentiles, meaning to believe and swear in both God's name and another's name. However, it is not permitted for a Gentile to perform an active service of idol worship.

It is also clear from Rema in *Yoreh De'ah* ch. 141, that it is prohibited to benefit from even a plain crucifix icon unless it is nullified (see Chapter 8 below on nullification of idolatrous images, and the permissibility of a plain cross if it is only for decoration). Why would it be prohibited to benefit from this, if it is not an idol that is forbidden to Gentiles? Therefore it obviously involves actual idol worship, and the object needs to be nullified before it can be used for any benefit. Therefore there is no contradiction in the words of Rema, who writes (*Oraĥ Ĥayim* ch. 156) on belief in an intermediary; rather it is as explained above, that an intermediary is permitted for a Gentile only in belief and speech, but not in actual worship or service.

The conclusion of *Ĥatam Sofer* (on *Shulĥan Aruĥ Oraĥ Ĥayim* ch. 156) is, "The main opinion is that a Gentile is liable for worshiping an intermediary."

3. Idol worship does not only include the worship of an angel, a physical creation, or some natural or metaphysical power. If one accepts upon himself any created or imagined entity, spiritual or physical, as a deity, and he worships it and totally subdues himself to it, as a servant before his master, this is idol worship.

For example, those who worship spirits of the dead or any other spirits which they imagine to exist, are idol worshipers. Likewise, this applies if one worships any ideal that was imagined by some people to be a motivating reason for the universe, if he serves this spirit or ideal in the manner of those who bow down or bring incense to the ideals of "peace," "love," or "humanitarian rights."

The basic idea is that one who actually serves any part of the physical or spiritual creation (which includes everything except God Himself, Who is not created) is an idol worshiper. One should know that all these are natural created things, made for the sake of mankind, to help him in his service to God, and they were not created so that people should make them rulers over themselves. Those who exchange the secondary with the fundamental are transgressing the command (explained above in topic 1), "I am God; do not exchange Me."

4. What was the mistake of Enosh and his generation? In his days, mankind made a great mistake, and the wise men of that generation gave thoughtless and spiritually erroneous advice. They said that since God created the stars and the planets with which to control the world, and He put them in the heavens and treated them with honor, making them servants who minister before Him, it is therefore proper to praise them, glorify them, and treat them with honor. These people also said that it is the will of God that mankind should honor and make great those whom He magnified and honored, just as a king desires that the servants who stand before him will be honored, for doing so is an expression of honor to the king.

Once they thought this, they began to build places of worship for the stars and to offer sacrifices to them. They would praise and glorify them with words, and prostrate themselves before them, because by doing so, they would – according to their false conception – be fulfilling the will of God.

This was the essence of the worship of false gods, and this was the reasoning of those who worshiped them, and the explanation they gave. They did not say that there is no other god except for this star they were worshiping. This is what Jeremiah conveyed:[9] "Who would not fear You, O King of the nations? For [kingship] benefits You, for among all the wise men of the nations and in all their kingdoms, [it is known that] there is none like You. But in one concept they are foolish and stupid; the vain [idols] which they teach are but wood." This means that all people knew that God alone exists, but it was from their mistake and their foolishness that they said that this vanity of theirs (the concept of independent intermediaries and the worship of idols) was God's will.

5. After many years passed, there arose false prophets who said that God had commanded them to say to the people: Serve this star (or all the stars); sacrifice to it and offer libations to it, and build a temple for it and make an image of it, so that everyone – including the women, the children, and the general population – could bow to it.

A false prophet would inform them of a form that he had conceived, and tell them that this is the image of the particular star, claiming that this was revealed to him in a prophetic vision. In this manner, the people began to make images in temples, under trees, and on the tops of mountains and hills. People would gather together and bow down to the images, and the false prophets would say: "This image is the source of benefit or harm. It is appropriate to serve it and fear it." Their priests would tell them: "This service will enable you to multiply and be successful. Do this and this, or do not do this and this."

Subsequently, other deceivers arose and declared that a specific star, sphere or angel had spoken to them[10] and commanded them: "Serve me in this manner." The false prophet would then relate a mode of service, telling them: "Do this, and do not do this."

Thus, these practices spread throughout the world. People would serve images with strange practices – one more distorted than the other – offer sacrifices to them, and bow down to them. As the years passed, God's glorious and awesome Name was forgotten by the entire popula-

---

[9] Jeremiah 10:7-8.

[10] *In *Guide for the Perplexed*, Rambam explains that the stars and other celestial spheres influence our world, but they are also God's creations and have no free will of their own. Thus, they are no more than an "axe in the hands of a woodchopper," and should not be worshipped or served.

tion. It was no longer part of their speech or thought, and they no longer knew Him.

Therefore, all the common and uneducated people and their children eventually knew only the images of wood or stone which they were trained from their childhood to bow down to and serve, and in whose name they swore, and in whose temples they worshiped.

The wise men among them would think that there was no God other than the stars and spheres for whose sake, and in resemblance of which, they had made these images. The True God was not recognized or known by anyone in the world, with the exception of a few individuals: for example, Enoĥ, Methuselaĥ, Noaĥ, Shem and Eber.

The world continued in this fashion until the pillar of the world – Abraham the Hebrew[11] – was born.

6. After this mighty man was weaned, he began to explore and think. Though he was a child, he began to think incessantly throughout the day and night, wondering: "How is it possible for the celestial firmament to continue to revolve without having anyone controlling it? Who is causing it to revolve? Surely it does not cause itself to revolve!"

He had no teacher, nor was there anyone to inform him. Rather, he was mired in Ur Kasdim among the foolish idolaters. His father, mother, and all the people around him were idol worshipers, and he would worship with them. However, his heart was exploring and gaining understanding. Ultimately, he appreciated the way of truth and understood the path of righteousness through his accurate comprehension. He realized that there is One God who controls the celestial sphere and Who created everything, and that there is no other God among all the other entities. He knew that the entire world was making a mistake in worshiping creations. What caused them to err was their service of the stars and images, which made them lose awareness of the truth.

Abraham was forty years old when he became fully aware of his Creator. When he recognized and knew Him, he began to formulate the replies to the inhabitants of Ur Kasdim and debate with them, telling them that they were not following a proper path.

---

[11] *The word "Hebrew" (Genesis 14:13) identified him as a descendant of the prophet Eber (see Genesis 10:25); alternatively, it literally means "from over," since he came to the land of Canaan from over the Euphrates River.

He broke their idols and began to teach the people that it is fitting to serve only the God of the universe, and to Him alone is it fitting to bow down, sacrifice, and offer libations, so that the people of future generations would learn to recognize Him. Conversely, he realized that it is fitting to destroy and break all idolatrous images, lest people err and think that there is no One God, but rather only these images.

When he overcame them through the strength of his arguments, the king, Nimrod, desired to kill him, but he was saved through a miracle, and he left for Ĥaran. There, he began to call in a loud voice to all the people and inform that there is one God in the entire world, and it is proper to serve only Him. He would go out and call to the people, gathering them in city after city and country after country, until he finally arrived in the land of Canaan – proclaiming God's true existence the entire time – as it states (Genesis 21:33): "and there he proclaimed the Name of God, God of the universe."[12]

When the people would gather around him and ask him about his statements, he would explain them to each individual according to the person's understanding, until they turned to the path of truth. Ultimately, thousands and tens of thousands gathered around him. He planted in their hearts this great fundamental principle, and he composed texts about it.[13]

---

[12] *Abraham traveled from Ĥaran with his wife Sarah and "the souls they made in Ĥaran" (Genesis 12:5) – meaning the great number of people whose souls they had uplifted to righteousness, by teaching them to abandon idolatry and to accept the One God and His Seven Noahide Commandments.

The verse Genesis 21:33 can alternatively be understood to mean that not only did Abraham call in the name of the Lord, but he also motivated others to do so, as explained in Tractate *Sotah* 10a. See Part I, topic 6:6. Abraham proclaimed that God's name is *"E-l olom"* ("God universe"), to stress that there is no true separation between God and the universe. It is only an emanation of God's power, which is united with God Himself in total unity. With this realization, a faithful person will be motivated from love and awe of God to serve Him and do His will. See *Likkutei Siĥot* vol. 7 *(Vayak'hel)*.

[13] Topics 4-6 are quoted from Rambam, *Laws of the Worship of Stars* 1:1-3.

*From the time of Abraham's passing until the giving of the Torah at Mount Sinai, aside from the family of his grandson Jacob, we only find mention of righteous individuals, rather than entire communities. It seems that for most of the thousands of "people of the house of Abraham" whom he and his wife attracted, the couple's exceptional kindness only temporarily inspired them.

CHAPTER 2

The Prohibition of Turning to Idol Worship

1. The worshipers of false gods have composed many texts concerning their services, each sect describing what is the essence of its service, what practices are involved, and what are its statutes. It is forbidden for a person to read those books, or to think about them or any matters involved with them (except for specific purposes that are described below). On this matter it is said (Lev. 19:4), "Do not turn to the idols ...," and it is also said,[14] "[Be careful] ... lest you seek to find out about their gods, saying, 'How did these nations serve their gods...?' "

Therefore one should not inquire about the nature of their customary services, even if he himself does not serve them, because this might cause one to turn to the false god and worship it as its followers do, as the verse continues, "... so will I do likewise." For this reason, it is even forbidden to fix one's gaze upon the image of an idol.[15]

2. One is forbidden to listen to music of idol worship services, or to smell the aroma of idols or their incenses, or to gaze on the decorations and splendor of the idol or its ornaments, because a person benefits from all these things, and it is forbidden to benefit from idol worship, or to turn to it. If a person encounters things of this nature, he is not required to make a detour in order to avoid them, as long as he does not intend to benefit from these things or to gaze intently at them.[16] Clearly, it is forbidden to enter a house of idol worship (unless there are exceptional circumstances, or for one's own practical needs).[17]

The reason for these prohibitions is to guard against the danger of looking favorably toward any idols, so one will not be drawn toward their service, or to believe in them or the legends of their actions.

Nevertheless, one who wishes to look at an idol or a house of idol worship for purposes of business, or learning a craft, or to hear their

---

[14] Deuteronomy 12:30.

[15] Rambam, *ibid.* 2:2. From Rambam, *Laws of Kings* 9:2, all forms of idolatry are forbidden to Gentiles. See also *Sefer HaĤinuĥ* Commandment 26.

[16] *Shulĥan Aruĥ Yoreh De'ah* end of ch. 142, and Shaĥ there.

[17] See *Shulĥan Aruĥ Yoreh De'ah* 142:10 and 150:1; *Bircai Yosef* 142:15.

songs for such purposes, is not forbidden to do so.[18]

3. It is generally forbidden to participate in a wedding event that is held in a house of idol worship, or as a gathering in some other place, if the wedding ceremony is conducted through their priests, since they give praise and recognition to their idols. But if the ceremony is completely secular, and they only make the celebration with a gathering in a social hall (not in the sanctuary that is used for their worship services), and there is no service of idols involved, it is permitted to participate, even if a priest is attending the event.[19]

But if bad feelings, anger or hatred will arise if one does not participate in a wedding that is connected with idol worship – for example, if one's brother or sister is getting married in a house of idol worship, and most of the family will be participating – one is allowed to participate even if the others engage in idol worship in honor of the occasion. Obviously, an individual is forbidden to participate in any type of ceremony or prayer in which the idol is mentioned.[20]

However, if most of the wedding or gathering is focused on idol worship – for example, if the participants are very devout in their idolatry, and in each part of the celebration they will praise their idol and involve themselves with its worship – then even if bad feelings will be aroused, one may not participate.[21] One who eats from food that was used in a service for the idol is considered as if he accepts its

---

[18] However, this is forbidden for a Jew, because of the prohibition "Do not turn to the idols" (mentioned in topic 1). See topic 4, which explains that the basic reason for all the mentioned prohibitions in this chapter for Gentiles are precautions, lest one be drawn after an idol. But when there are practical reasons for a Gentile to enter a house of idol worship, it is permitted. This constitutes the basic difference between this command to Jews and to Gentiles. The Jewish prohibition, even though logically based, is obligatory in any case. But the Gentile is prohibited from a totally rational basis, so therefore in specific instances when there are other considerations in which the basic logic doesn't apply, the prohibition is lifted.

[19] Clearly one may enter a house of idol worship for his own practical needs.

[20] See *Shulĥan Aruĥ Yoreh De'ah* 148:9,12.

[21] See Tractate *Avodah Zarah* 8a, that eating from a sacrifice to an idol is considered to be an actual participation in its worship. Therefore, even the avoidance of anger or hatred can't be accepted as a valid reason to be lenient.

service.[22] Eating and drinking (especially alcoholic beverages) with the celebrants can bring one to actually serve the idol, as it is stated (Num. 25:2), "And they called to the people to come to the sacrifices of their gods, and the people ate and bowed to their gods."

It is likewise forbidden to participate in a celebration in which idolaters initiate a child or any person into the service of their beliefs. Even if they only do so as a custom from their ancestors, it is considered to be an actual service to the idol.[23]

4. All the books of deviant believers (see topic 1:7 in Part I) are forbidden to be read (except for specific purposes), for they are full of idolatry and denial of the True God. It is obligatory to destroy them, so that there will remain no remembrance of idol worship and heresy.[24]

The reason why one may not read the books of the deviant believers is because of the prohibition "Do not turn to the idols," meaning that it is prohibited to contemplate how to serve their idols. However, it is permitted to learn the actions and precepts of the idol worship from these books (or from those who serve it) if it is in order to keep away from those things, as the Sages explain the verse (Deut. 18:9), "Do not learn to follow the abominations of these nations," – it is forbidden to learn in order to do, but it is permitted to learn, understand and teach in order to be wary of a false prophet or magician who performs apparent miracles by magic in support of some idolatry.[25] It is also permitted to learn such things in order to be wary of them, and to save one's self from mistakenly transgressing the prohibition of idol worship.[26]

5. It is prohibited to study anything from a deviant believer who proselytizes others to serve the idol that he worships, for this brings one to heresy.[27] Similarly, the permission to learn about idolatrous

---

[22] Rashi on Exodus 34:15.

[23] See Meiri on Tractate *Sanhedrin* 64, about the idolatry of *Moleĥ*, in which a child is inducted into the service of those who believe in *Moleĥ*. From this can be derived a prohibition against any similar action within idolatry.

[24] *Shulĥan Aruĥ Oraĥ Ĥayim* 334:21. See Ch. 7 below; Gentiles are commanded to destroy (or nullify) idol worship and all items used for its service.

[25] Tractate *Shabbat* 75a, and Rashi there.

[26] *Torah Temimah* on Deuteronomy 18:9.

[27] *This refers to studying from the proselytizer himself.

practices in order to carefully avoid them, mentioned in the previous topic, only applies when it does not involve learning from someone who has a strong attachment to idol worship; rather, it only applies to learning factual information about topics of sorcery or idol worship that one might be likely to encounter, and usually this can be learned from books on these subjects.[28]

6. It is prohibited to engage in debates about matters of faith with deviant believers (those specifically mentioned in Part I, topic 1:7) and apostates (those who only go after the thoughts of their own heart and mind, and who don't take upon themselves the obligation to both recognize the Creator and accept the observance of His commandments for the Gentiles). It is also prohibited to listen to their heresies[29] or argue with them at all about the true faith, because in general their thoughts are still bound up with idol worship or atheism, respectively.[30] It is also prohibited to fraternize closely with them,[31] since they may lead one astray after their ways.[32]

7. It is forbidden for a person to ponder in his heart on concepts of idol worship, or to research idolatrous concepts in an attempt to discover if they are true or not (since they are certainly false). These are included in the Torah's prohibition, "Do not turn to the idols ..."

It is not only idol worship that one is forbidden to stray after. It is also forbidden for a person to dwell upon any thought in his heart that causes him to abandon one of the fundamentals of the Torah faith (for Gentiles, these are explained in Part I, Chapter 1). If one reflects on such thoughts and ideas without trying to remove his mind from them, he might start to be drawn after falsehood. For a person's knowledge is limited, and not all minds can completely understand the truth of God on an intellectual level. If every individual would go after the fancies

---

[28] Tractate *Shabbat* 75a and Rashi there; *Shulĥan Aruĥ Yoreh De'ah*, end of ch. 179 and Shaĥ there.

[29] *This includes, for example, recorded lectures (but see topic 4 above).

[30] Rambam, *Laws of the Worship of Stars [and Idols]* 2:5.

[31] *Tosefta*, cited in *Sefer Mitzvot Gadol (SMa"G)* and *Hagahot Maimoniot.*

[32] Tractate *Avodah Zarah* 27b.

of his own thoughts, the world would be destroyed by their short-mindedness.

How so? Sometimes a person strays after idol worship; sometimes he questions God's oneness, whether He is really one or two, or if He has a body. A person may sometimes think about a false prophesy, to question whether it is true or not. If he doesn't know the ways to arrive at the knowledge of the truth on his own, he will come to apostasy if he refuses to accept what is fundamental.[33] This is what the Torah says:[34] "Do not stray after your heart and after your eyes after which you stray," meaning that a person must not be drawn after his short-mindedness and come to think he can intellectually arrive at the truth.

8. One who accepts an idol as true, even though he does not serve it, is like one who curses and desecrates God's holy and mighty Name.[35]

9. Even though these thoughts involve serious prohibitions, since they can cause a person to turn away from God to the point that he will come to serve idols, or they can turn him into a deviant believer or an apostate, they are not punishable by an earthly court, since they are only a cause of idol worship, but they are not a forbidden action. A Gentile is only liable for the main prohibition of actually serving idols, as explained in the next chapter.[36]

10. One who thought about idol worship and decided to actively worship the idol, but he did not succeed in carrying out his planned act of worship, is punished by Heaven for his evil thoughts.[37]

---

[33] *This includes the historical facts of God's revelation at Mount Sinai, His speaking of the Ten Commandments to the Jewish nation, and His appointment of Moses to transmit the Written and Oral Torah.

[34] Numbers 15:39.

[35] Rambam, *Laws of the Worship of Stars [and Idols]* 2:6.

[36] It is clear that all the prohibitions mentioned in this chapter are not a part of the main prohibition against serving idols, and therefore they are not capital sins. In *Minĥat Ĥinuĥ* Commandment 213, it explains this likewise in regard to the prohibition, "Do not turn to the idols ..."

[37] Tractate *Kiddushin* 39b, and the explanation by *Tosafot* there.

CHAPTER 3

Which Actions Make One Liable for Idol Worship

1. A Gentile is forbidden to engage in *all* forms of idol worship.[38] However, if a person transgresses and worships an idol, this does not constitute a "capital sin" – one that could be punished by a Torah-based court – unless he serves the idol in the manner that is customary for its followers, or if he performs one of the four special rituals reserved for the service for God in the Holy Temple (topic 4 below).[39]

2. In this regard, there is no difference if the person serves a detached idol such as a statue, an attached thing such as a mountain, a sea, the sun or moon, another celestial entity, an animal or a person.[40]

3. For an idol that has many traditional ways of service, one is liable for performing any one of them. Idol worship that includes many steps in its manner of service – for example, (a) to take the blood of a sacrifice in a vessel, (b) to walk with it, and (c) to sprinkle it on an altar – causes one to become liable even if he did only one of these separate acts of service in his worship of the idol. It appears that this applies only to a main service itself, such as sprinkling blood; but other actions that are only preparations for the main service do not make one liable for a capital sin (although it is certainly forbidden).

---

[38] Rambam, *Laws of Kings* 9:2.

[39] The simple understanding of Rambam, *Laws of Kings* 9:2, is that the basic prohibition of idol worship, and the liability for this, are equal for Gentiles and Jews. This is also the opinion of *Nodah Bi'Yehudah* vol. 2, ch. 148.

[40] See Tractate *Sanhedrin* 60b regarding Exodus 22:19, "One who slaughters [sacrifices] to the gods will be destroyed – [this is allowed] only to the Lord alone." God reserved special services for Himself only, and if one uses any one of them for any type of idol worship, he has not reserved it for God alone. One who bows down to any idol is liable, based on Deut. 17:3, "and he will go and serve gods of others and prostrate himself to them, or to the sun or to the moon or to any host of Heaven [which includes angels], which I have not commanded." From this we see that bowing down is forbidden even if it is not the idol's traditional manner of service. This is the simple understanding of Rambam, *Laws of the Worship of Stars [and Idols]* 3:3: "But one who does one of the four [special] services for **any type** of idol worship ..."

4. What are the four special rituals referred to in topic 1? If one slaughters, burns an offering, pours a libation, or bows down in the worship of *any* idol, even if that is not its customary manner of worship, he is liable for a capital sin, because these are services that are specifically required for God in the Holy Temple.

The slaughtering referred to here is cutting the neck of a living being. About this it says,[41] "One who slaughters [a sacrifice] to the gods will be destroyed; [this is allowed] only to the Lord alone."

Bowing down is also only permitted to be done for God,[42] as it says, "For you shall not bow down to another god ...,"[43] and, "There shall not be for you other gods ... You shall not bow down to them or serve them."[44] This teaches that (a) **you shall not bow down to an idol**, even if this is not its customary manner of service, and (b) **you shall not serve them** in their usual manner of service.

5. One who bows down to an idol is liable for a capital sin if he prostrates totally and spreads his hands and feet to the ground (or floor), or only puts his face to the ground. But one who does not put his face to the ground, but only bends his head and body, is not liable for a capital sin unless it is the traditional manner of serving the idol. (However, it is prohibited regardless.)[45] One who bows down to an idol, even for only one moment, is liable once he puts his face to the ground.[46]

6. The capital sin of slaughtering to an idol includes cutting a living animal's throat, severing the back of the neck, or chopping the neck. [It appears that this applies for any tearing or cutting, even if done by hand (for example, with one's fingernail).] It applies for any animal or a bird, even if it is missing a limb or has any physical blemish.

The ruling that this also includes slaughtering a locust to an idol applies to any species of arthropod, reptile or amphibian that similarly

---

[41] Exodus 22:19.

[42] Rambam, *Laws of the Worship of Stars [and Idols]* 3:3.

[43] Exodus 34:14.

[44] Exodus 20:3-5.

[45] Rambam, *Laws of the Worship of Stars [and Idols]* 6:8. The liability for a capital sin is based on the similarity to the service in the Holy Temple. Thus, putting one's face to the ground is considered part of this prohibition.

[46] Rambam *ibid.*

has the appearance of a neck between the head and the body.[47]

7. Likewise, one who slaughters or chops the neck of a live person as an act of worship for any idol is liable for a capital sin for this service (in addition to his liability for murder).

One who performs such an action on a dead person or other dead creature, or cuts off part of a corpse, for idol worship is similarly liable if the idol's traditional service is any ritual with a corpse, in which case it is considered similar to slaughtering. If the traditional service is not with a corpse, this is not considered to be similar to slaughtering.[48]

8. If one cuts a living body in a manner other than slaughtering (whether death results or not) for idol worship, but this is not the traditional manner of service for the idol, the person is not liable for a capital sin. (Nevertheless, he will be liable to punishment for murder if he kills a person, or liable to other punishments that the courts may establish for injuring a person or an animal.)

After an animal is slaughtered to serve an idol, one who cuts up its limbs is exempt (even if slaughtering is the normal service for the idol) for in this case, this action is not considered similar to slaughtering.[49]

9. If one first slaughters an animal without the intention of serving an idol through the slaughtering, instead saying[50] that he will serve an idol only by sprinkling the animal's blood or burning parts of its body, he is liable for a capital sin even if he does not actually sprinkle any of the blood or burn any part of the animal (since he slaughtered the animal

---

[47] Tractate *Avodah Zarah* 51a. Any creature that appears to have a neck has the same ruling as mammals and birds in regard to slaughtering to an idol.

[48] This ruling for a corpse is like that for serving an idol by breaking a stick (topic 19 below), which is not a capital sin unless the idol's traditional manner of service is a ritual with a stick (e.g. by waving it or some other act).

[49] Cutting up limbs of an animal that was slaughtered in service to an idol is not comparable to a service by breaking a stick (topic 19). One who breaks a joint after the animal was slaughtered is not liable, as this is not comparable to a method of slaughtering in which the head is disjointed from the body.

[50] *Margaliot Hayam* on *Sanhedrin* 60b says that one is not liable in a court for this unless he verbalizes his intention. But it appears that if his intention is clear based on his actions, he is liable even if he didn't voice it (see topic 33).

as a step in serving the idol).[51]

10. In the act of slaughtering for idol worship, if one cut through a passage necessary for life (the trachea, esophagus, or a major artery or vein; see topic 6 above) by any amount, he is liable for a capital sin.[52]

The same applies for one who burns incense or other offerings or pours a libation as idol worship – in an act that carries liability for idol worship, there is no minimum amount below which one is not liable.

11. What is the ruling for two who participated in slaughtering one animal, whether one after another or together, with one or two knives?

If one slaughtered (and voiced his intention) for idol worship and the second had no such intention, the one who slaughtered for an idol is liable for a capital sin, and the other is not (regardless of the order in which they slaughtered). If both slaughtered for an idol (see next paragraph), whether for the same or a different idol, they are both liable.[53]

If an animal was already "fully slaughtered," whether or not the act of slaughtering was intended for idol worship, and another person then cut through a part that remained of the passages with an intention for idol worship, his act is not a capital sin (even if the animal was still convulsing), since the act of slaughter was already fully accomplished. (Here, "full slaughtering" means cutting through the majority of both the esophagus and the windpipe of an animal, or the majority of one of these for a bird, starting from the beginning of the cut.) The second person's action of cutting a remainder of the passages of the dying animal only served to hasten its death, and is not considered to be an act of slaughtering. (The same rule applies if one person cut the animal's neck up to the fully-slaughtered point without an intention for

---

[51] Any animal part that is fit to be consumed by the idol's altar fire is considered to be included as a sacrifice, and burning it as a service to an idol is therefore similar to the Temple service, as explained below in topic 20.

[52] Rambam, *Laws of the Worship of Stars [and Idols]* 8:1; one who slaughters for an idol by cutting through even a part of one of the vital neck passages of an animal has performed an action that makes the animal forbidden as designated for idol worship, and the person is thus liable for serving the idol.

[53] It is clear that two people who perform an act of slaughter both have a ruling of one who slaughters; see *Shulĥan Aruĥ Yoreh De'ah,* ch. 2 and ch. 5. Therefore it is considered slaughtering for idols, and it has been explained that there is no minimum in slaughtering to an idol for making one liable.

idol worship, and then he changed his mind and continued cutting through the rest of the passages with an intention for idol worship.)

This applies if it is done in the service of an idol that is not traditionally served by sacrificing animals or by cutting carcasses of animals, so the capital sin is in performing one of the Temple services in the worship of an idol. Then once the animal is fully slaughtered, any subsequent cutting is not considered to be an act of slaughtering.

However, if this was the idol's traditional manner of service, even if he slaughtered an animal that was convulsing in its death throes, or cut off its head[54] to serve the idol even after the animal's death, he is liable for a capital sin, since this resembles the act of slaughtering that is the traditional service for the idol (see topics 7 and 8 above).

12. If a person slaughters to a mountain or valley, the sun, moon or a constellation, a sea or river, an angel or the like, and intends to serve it, this is idol worship, and he is liable for a capital sin.

If he does not have an intention to serve the entity as an idol, but rather he only slaughters for the purpose of a healing remedy and the like, from the various foolish superstitions of idol worshipers, this is a transgression, but he does not incur liability for a capital sin.[55]

13. The same applies for one who slaughters to a demon, as it says, "And you shall not sacrifice any more sacrifices to the demons."[56] It

---

[54] For a Gentile, an animal that is convulsing in its death throes is to be considered as still alive, and it is forbidden for a Gentile to sever and eat meat from it, as is the rule for a living animal (Part IV, topics 3:2-3). Therefore, in this case, even the last bit of slaughtering as idol worship is considered as an action of sacrificing, and one is liable for this. But if the animal was already dead, and he only cut the neck a little but did *not* separate the head from the neck or break any joints in the neck, then he did not commit any meaningful action, and it is not comparable to breaking a stick to serve an idol that is normally served with a stick, so he would not be liable for a capital sin.

[55] See: Tractate *Ĥullin* 40a; Rambam, *Laws of Ritual Slaughter* 2:14; and *Shulĥan Aruĥ Yoreh De'ah* ch. 4 – whether one serves mountains, angels or anything else, if his intention is for obtaining success, luck or healing, or if he is serving it only from love or fear, then this is not an act of idol worship that one is liable for (although it is still forbidden). See topic 27 below.

[56] Leviticus 17:7; see Rashi there.

also says,[57] "They slaughtered to demons, not to God," which is idol worship, and the person is liable for a capital sin.[58] Also, anyone who serves a demon in the manner that its worshipers have established, or with one of the four previously mentioned Temple services, is committing a service of idol worship that makes him liable for a capital sin.

14. One who throws an animal from a high cliff for the service of an idol (in a manner similar to the Holy Temple ritual of the scapegoat on Yom Kippur, which God commanded to be pushed off a cliff) is liable for a capital sin if that is the idol's traditional manner of service.

If that is not the normal way of serving the idol, the person is liable for a capital sin if the normal manner of worship is by any service that is performed with an animal, and he throws it off a cliff in a way that kills it by breaking it into pieces, for this resembles slaughtering.[59]

15. One who brings a meal offering for an idol (e.g., of wheat or barley flour, gathering some of it by hand or with a vessel, even without the intention to burn it) is liable for a capital sin, since gathering meal is similar to slaughtering. This was also a service in the Holy Temple.

One who harvests grapes or cuts wheat (or any vegetation) for the sake of idol worship is liable for a capital sin if the idol's traditional manner of worship is by any service that is performed with vegetation. In this case, the harvesting is considered to be similar to slaughtering.[60]

---

[57] Deuteronomy 37:17.

[58] Ramban on Exodus 20:3, Leviticus 16:8 and 17:7.

[59] We see this from *Yoma* 64a and Rambam, *Laws of the Yom Kippur Service* 5:17, which explain regarding the scapegoat that was sent to be pushed off a high cliff as part of Yom Kippur service in the Holy Temple, that pushing it off to its death is considered to be its slaughter. Therefore, such an action for idol worship is also considered to resemble slaughtering: if the fall breaks its body into pieces, the person is liable for a capital sin if it is customary to use an animal for the idol's service. This ruling is like that of breaking a stick to serve an idol that is normally served with a stick (see topic 19 below).

[60] From Tractate *Avodah Zarah* 51a according to Rashi there, this is comparable to an idol that is normally served in some way with a stick, for which one is liable for a capital sin if he serves it by breaking a stick before it. In the case mentioned, serving the idol by harvesting or cutting any vegetation is comparable to breaking a stick.

16. Throwing something that breaks up and splatters for the sake of idol worship is included in the general prohibition of pouring a libation, because it is similar to the pouring of blood on the Altar in the Holy Temple. This applies to all liquids, such as blood, wine, oil, water, honey or fruit juice,[61] and to things like flour or meal that spread out when they are thrown.[62] If a person throws something for the sake of idol worship that is solid and does not shatter, like a stone or stick, this is not similar to pouring a libation, so he is not liable for a capital sin (unless this is the traditional manner of serving the idol).

17. Some lowly idols have traditional manners of service with manure or urine. If a person served such an idol by throwing moist manure that breaks up and splatters,[63] or he poured a container of urine before the idol, he is liable for a capital sin because these would be similar to pouring a libation for this type of idol. However, if this was done to serve another type of idol which is not served with these things, and they would instead be considered a degradation of the idol – even if it is normally served by pouring but not with these substances – this is not compared to pouring a libation at all, and the person is not liable.[64]

18. If one urinates or defecates before an idol, it is not considered as if he pours a libation, because anyone who does not pour with a vessel is not considered as if he is pouring at all, and he is therefore not liable

---

[61] Honey or juice, although they were not poured on the Altar in the Holy Temple, have the property of pouring, so this applies to them. The Sages debated as to whether just as one is liable for anything that is comparable to slaughtering, so too, one is liable for anything comparable to pouring, or if one is only liable if that is the traditional manner of serving the idol.

[62] Tractate *Avodah Zarah* 51a.

[63] Unlike the case of dry manure, which has the ruling of a stick, as stated below in topic 19.

[64] Rambam, *Laws of the Worship of Stars [and Idols]* 3:4. According to what he writes there in 3:5, "One who serves an idol in its way, even if he does so in a way of disgrace, is liable etc. … since this is its traditional service, he is liable [for a capital sin]," the repetition stresses his opinion that one is only liable if this is its traditional ritual. But if not, he is not liable (even if the degrading service was similar to one of the four special Temple services).

According to Rambam, one is not liable for serving an idol in one of the four manners of special Temple services unless it is done in a way of honor.

for a capital sin unless this was its traditional manner of service.[65]

Likewise, if one lets blood from a live creature before an idol, it is not considered as if he has poured a libation unless he first accepts it into a vessel and then throws it or pours it out to the idol.

However, if an idol's traditional manner of worship is to lacerate one's body or carve markings in one's body and let blood for its service, then one who does so is liable for a capital sin,[66] as its says,[67] "And they lacerated themselves, as was their way, with swords and lancets, until blood poured from them." (See topic 11:14.)

19. For an idol that is normally served with a stick, but not by throwing the stick (e.g., the customary service involves waving a stick before the idol), if one throws a stick before it, he is not liable for a capital sin. This is because it is not similar to the pouring of blood that was done as a service in the Holy Temple; a person who throws something as a service to any idol is liable for a capital sin if it is something that splatters like blood[68] (the exception to this is noted in topic 17 above).

However, one is liable for a capital sin if he breaks a stick before this idol (even if this is not the traditional manner of serving the idol with a stick), because for an idol that is served with a stick, breaking a stick before it is considered similar to slaughtering. If it is not customary to serve the idol with a stick, then breaking a stick before it is not considered like slaughtering, and one who does so is not liable.[69]

One who kills a fish in service to an idol by cutting it in a manner of slaughtering has the same ruling as one who serves an idol by breaking a stick.[70] If its traditional manner of service uses a fish for any ritual,

---

[65] Rambam, *Laws of the Worship of Stars [and Idols]* 7:18.

[66] Rashi on Tractate *Makot* 21a.

[67] I Kings 18:28 and Radak there.

[68] *Tur* and *Shulĥan Aruĥ Yoreh De'ah* 139:3.

[69] Rambam, *Laws of the Worship of Stars [and Idols]* 3:4, and *Shulĥan Aruĥ Yoreh De'ah* 139:3, based on the explanation of Rashi and *Tosafot* on Tractate *Avodah Zarah* 51a. (However, according to Ra'avad, a person is always liable for a capital sin for breaking a stick as a service to an idol, even if it is not customary to serve the idol in any manner with a stick, because in his view, breaking a stick is always considered to be similar to slaughtering.)

[70] Tractate *Avodah Zarah* 51a implies that a fish, which does not have a neck like that of a mammal or a bird, has the same ruling in this context as a stick.

the person is liable for a capital sin, and if not, he is not liable.[71]

20. One who burns something to any idol is liable for a capital sin,[72] because one of the four special services that are performed for God in the Holy Temple is the burning of sacrifices. A person is liable for any actions similar to these four in service to any idol, even if it is not the idol's customary manner of service (as explained above in topic 4). This applies even if one serves an idol by burning something that is unfit for burning on the Altar in the Holy Temple.[73] (However, if one burns something to serve an idol, but for that idol it is a degradation – for example, if he burns manure – he is not liable for a capital sin; this is similar to the ruling for one who pours out urine to an idol, as explained above in topic 17.)

Therefore, one who burns a person's living or dead body, or any part of a human body, as a service to an idol is liable for a capital sin, even if it is not the idol's traditional manner of worship.[74]

21. Something that is burnt completely and has turned into charcoal is not considered to be burned again by subsequently being returned to the fire.[75] But if it is not burnt completely, and can therefore be burned further after it was previously burned to serve an idol, then burning it a second time to serve an idol makes one liable as well.

Likewise, blood can be sprinkled and a liquid can be poured out repeatedly, even after they have already been sprinkled or poured out.

---

[71] This is the ruling of Rambam *ibid.*, and *Shulĥan Aruĥ ibid.* But in the opinion of Ra'avad, a person is always liable for this action.

[72] *Shulĥan Aruĥ Yoreh De'ah* 179:19.

[73] *Or Same'aĥ Hilĥot Avodat Koĥavim*, ch. 3. This is comparable to the ruling of *Tur Shulĥan Aruĥ*, that one is liable for any type of slaughtering, even for things that are not fitting to burn on the Altar (see topic 6 above).

[74] *Kesef Mishneh Hilĥot Avodat Koĥavim* 6:3 writes that one is liable for offering a person even if this is not the idol's normal service. Even though one is always liable for murder, the practical difference is that if it is combined with idolatry, the person is liable to punishment by God on two counts. There is also a practical difference as to whether one burned the body after someone else had killed the person, or if he burned just one limb of the body.

[75] See Tractate *Zevaĥim* 86a; Rambam, *Laws of Sacrificial Procedures* 6:3.

22. If one makes an offering to a demon, and through this he accepts it as a god – even if his final intent is to connect to it and [as he imagines] force it to do his will – he commits idol worship, and he is liable for a capital sin.[76] But if he did so for the purpose of doing magic, and he did not accept it as a god through his offering, it is still forbidden, but he is not held liable for idol worship.

23. One who verbally accepts upon himself any idol as his god is liable for a capital sin. This also extends to any created physical or spiritual entity, force or concept other than God Himself, even if it has not previously been associated with any idol worship.[77] This applies if he says to it, "you are my God," or other similar types of statements,[78] whether or not he is standing before a statue or image of the idol at the time. Even if he retracts his words shortly after his statement and says, "this is not my God," his retraction does not help, and he is liable.[79]

24. One who prays to an idol (verbally or in his thoughts), whether or not he is standing in front of its image, has served it, as it says,[80] "Then the rest of it [the refuse wood] he makes into a god as his graven image; he will bow to it, and prostrate himself *and pray to it, and say*, 'Rescue me, for you are my god!' " Therefore, verbal prayer to an idol makes one liable for a capital sin. (But one is never liable to punishment from a court for sinful thoughts alone. See Part I, topic

---

[76] One who burns an offering for a demon in order that it should do his will does not diminish the idol worship involved, since it is the way of idol worshipers to ask for good from their idols. This is not comparable to one who serves only out of love and fear, for then he does not accept it as a deity.

[77] *In the case of one who says, "I believe that such-and-such an idol is truly one of the gods," this in itself does not constitute an act of worship. However, it is a deification of the idol, as explained above in topic 2:8 – "One who accepts an idol as true, even though he does not serve it, is like one who curses and desecrates God's holy and mighty Name." Thus, if one accepts that there is some truth to an idol's deity, this is equivalent to one who "curses and desecrates" God, and this is forbidden (see footnote 81 below).

[78] Even though he has done no action (*Lehem Mishneh*), which is also clear from Rambam, *Laws of [Sacrifices for] Inadvertent Transgressions* 1:2.

[79] Rambam, *Laws of the Worship of Stars [and Idols]* 3:4.

[80] Isaiah 44:17.

1:10. See also topic 2:10 above. For praying to an idol in thought alone, one may be punished by God.)

Likewise, if one verbally praises the power or sovereignty of an idol in words which mean that he accepts it as a deity *over himself* (i.e., he accepts the idol as a divine power over himself, with words such as, "you are my god," or "it is my god," or any other words which show that he makes this acceptance), whether or not the idol is physically present before him, then he is liable for a capital sin.[81]

If one only praises and lauds the supposed deeds or beauty of an idol, or thanks it for his well-being, good fortune or happiness, or complains to it about his problems, but he does not verbally accept its divinity, then he is not liable for a capital sin, even though such speech is forbidden.

25. There are those who say that one who sings before an idol is liable for a capital sin, even if this is not its traditional manner of worship, because singing was a service in the Holy Temple as part of the sacrificial services and a preparation for them.

If the customary worship of an idol is to serve it by singing or playing musical instruments, then one who performs this service is obviously liable.

26. If a Gentile performs the service of an idol in its usual manner, even if it is in a degrading fashion (and his intent was only to degrade

---

[81] Praising an idol is forbidden from the prohibition against embracing, kissing or performing other honors for idols, as is clear from Rambam, *ibid.* 1:1: "They began to build temples for their idols and offer sacrifices to them. They would **praise and glorify them with words** and bow down before them." The only thing in this category that makes one liable for a capital sin is verbally praying to an idol, or making statements that constitute acceptance of an idol as a deity. But praises that one says before an idol which are not meant to be a service by worship, or an acceptance of it as a deity, do not make one liable. (See *Nekudot HaKesef Yoreh De'ah* ch. 148.) It appears from Rambam, *ibid.* 9:5, that one who praises an idol's power or sovereignty is obviously accepting it as divinity, and he is liable for this. But if one only praises an idol's supposed actions or image, and does things to honor those aspects of the idol, he is not liable for a capital sin, as this is not its main way of service.

it, and not to worship it), he is liable for a capital sin.[82] (How much more so is this the case for one who performs a traditional service for an idol that is in a way of honor, even if he did not accept it as a deity.)

However, if one performs a degrading ritual to an idol which does not have that particular ritual as its traditional manner of service, *and his intention is to degrade the idol* (even if this idol had a different type of degrading ritual service), this is permitted.[83]

If one sacrifices before an idol with the intention of causing anger, either from the idol itself or from its worshipers, because sacrificing is not its traditional manner of service, and he does not intend to accept the idol as a deity, he is exempt from punishment, but it is forbidden.

27. One who serves an idol out of love (for example, he desires this idol because its service is very pleasing to him), or who serves it from fear that it may wrong him (just as its worshipers believe that it has the power to do good or evil to a person), is liable for a capital sin if he accepts it as a deity.

If he serves it out of love or fear with its traditional manner of service, or with one of the four special services of the Holy Temple,

---

[82] Rambam, *Laws of the Worship of Stars [and Idols]* 3:5. He refers to a Jew who does not accept the idol as a god and intended to degrade it, but since he performed its traditional manner of service, his act is accounted as an accidental sin. Rabbi Meir Cohen, Rivash and *Kesef Mishneh* understand Rambam's words in this way, unlike *Leĥem Mishneh*. Therefore, it is clear that if he performs the traditional service of any idol, even if he does not accept it as divinity, he is liable for a capital sin – unless his intention is to derive personal benefit, such as one who serves out of love or fear, or as a superstition for healing. Therefore a Gentile would be liable for a capital sin whenever he voluntarily (purposefully) performs an idol's traditional manner of service. See topic 3:34 below.

[83] This is the implication from Tractate *Sanhedrin* 64a, as cited by *Kesef Mishneh*. It appears that this also applies to slaughtering, burning, and pouring out a liquid, which are like the special services in the Holy Temple, in that if one performs even these special services to anger or disgrace an idol (such as one who pours out urine or feces), he is exempt. Nevertheless, from the outset it is forbidden to use one of the special services for this purpose, so one is only permitted to degrade an idol with a different type of service. However, one who bows down before an idol is not disgracing it at all, and he is liable for a capital sin, as is explained in topic 28.

but he does not accept it as a deity, he is exempt from punishment.[84]

Likewise, if one serves an idol out of love or fear of a person, and does not accept the idol upon himself as a deity, he is also exempt.[85]

28. If one bows down to the statue or image of an idol, even if he does not verbally accept it as a deity, this activity itself is accepting it as a deity, and he is liable for a capital sin. Likewise, if one bows down to the sun, a star, a mountain or the like, and he states that he is bowing down to it, even though he does not mention that he is bowing down to it as a deity or accepting it as deity, he is liable for a capital sin.[86] (See topic 33 below, that one is liable to punishment in an earthly court for idol worship only if the intention is clear. One who prostrates himself before an idol is obviously worshiping it, but prostrating before a person might be for other reasons; see topics 29 and 30.)

29. It is forbidden to bow down to a person who makes himself into a god, just as for any other idol. If one bows down to the person out of fear or honor alone, and does not accept him as a deity, he is exempt from punishment.[87] Likewise, one who bows down to an idol

---

[84] Ramban writes on Tractate *Shabbat* 72 that the two situations of (a) a person serving an idol because of his love or fear (according to Rashi's opinion), or (b) a person serving an idol for some benefit it will bring to him (Rambam's opinion), are really one, and he agrees that one who serves an idol in such ways (for his own benefit) is exempt from punishment.

[85] Rashi, Ra'avad, Ran and Rivash in their explanations of *Sanhedrin* 61b.

[86] See Ritva on Tractate *Shabbat* 72b. One who bows down to an idol, even not accepting it as a deity, is liable for a capital sin. It appears that bowing itself is accepting the idol's divinity, as if the person said, "you are my god." The majority of opinions hold that no matter what the intention is while bowing down to an idol, this makes one liable for a capital sin.

[87] Rambam, *Laws of the Worship of Stars [and Idols]* 3:6, writes, "or one of the four services," which implies that one who bows down out of love or fear is also exempt. This refers to one who bows down to a person out of fear of him, or to give him honor, even if the person makes himself into an idol. The one bowing down is not accepting the other person as a deity so he is exempt.

*It is permitted to bow down to a person as an act of merely extending greetings, if that is the accepted custom (see Exodus 18:7). But in some cultures, the bowing in greeting is intended as a worship of the spirit within the other person, and it is forbidden to bow with this intention.

out of fear alone, and does not accept it as a deity, is exempt.

What type of fear are we discussing, by which one is not liable if he bows down to an idol because of it? By analogy, if a person is afraid of a king, since the king might kill him or be angry at him if he displeases the king, he will hasten to bow down in order to appease the king.

[Another example: if one finds himself in a crowd and they bow down to their idol, he will feel very uncomfortable to act differently from all the rest, or he may fear that they might cause harm to him if he does not copy their actions. It is still forbidden to bow down before the idol (unless it is obviously a situation of life or death),[88] but if one did so without accepting the idol, and he is only doing so out of fear from the crowd, his act is not a capital sin, and he is not liable for this.]

Likewise, a person is exempt from punishment if he does not accept an idol as a deity, but he bows down for this reason to an idol; or because he thinks that it is fitting to honor it for some reason; or because he is afraid in his foolish mind of the idol itself, and thinks that if he does not bow down to it, it can do evil to him.

30. If one encounters officers or priests who have images of idols on their clothes or hanging on a chain around their neck, or who carry an idol before themselves, it is forbidden to bow down to them or take one's cap off before them. A Gentile may, however, take off his cap before they arrive, thus allowing his head to remain uncovered as they approach. If it is known that everyone honors and bows down to an officer himself and not at all to the statue that he carries, it is permitted to bow down to the officer. However, it is always forbidden to bow

---

[88] *Elisha the Prophet ruled like this for the righteous Gentile Na'aman, who was the commander of the army of the idolatrous king of Aram (II Kings 5:15-19). After he recognized the truth of the God of Israel, he proclaimed before Elisha, "...your servant will never again offer a burnt-offering or any sacrifice to other gods, but only to God. May God forgive your servant for this [one] thing, however: When my master [the king] comes to the temple of [his idol] *Rimmon* to bow there, he leans on my arm, so I must bow in the temple ...; may God forgive your servant for this thing" (5:17-18). Tractate *Sanhedrin* 74a explains that Na'aman asked permission to bow in the idol's temple out of fear of the king, and asked if he must sacrifice his life and not bow. Elisha said "Go to peace" (5:19), which is explained in *Sanhedrin* (loc. cit.) as permission, because a Gentile need not sacrifice his life in order to avoid bowing down before an idol or in an idol's temple.

down to a priest of idol worship who carries or wears a picture or a statue of his idol, for this is surely honoring the idol.[88a]

31. There are many types of idol worship in which one presents objects before the idol, such as food or other honorable things. If this is an idol's traditional manner of service, one who does so is liable for the capital sin of serving idols. If these offerings are only brought as a decoration or honor for the idol, and the person is not actually serving the idol by this action, he is exempt from punishment. But it is nevertheless forbidden to do so, because it is forbidden to give any recognition or honor to idols.

32. It is forbidden to hug or kiss an idol, to sweep or clean before it, to wash, anoint, or dress it, to put shoes on it, or to honor it by other similar means,[89] since these things are included in serving the idol. But for this he is not liable for a capital sin, since these are not the way of serving it, but rather only ways of decorating and honoring it.

It is forbidden to light candles before an idol, since they provide a decoration for it, but this does not make one liable for a capital sin if this is not the traditional manner of its service.[90] However, if an idol's traditional manner of service involves any one of these things and the person does it, he is liable for a capital sin.

[88a] From Rema *Yoreh De'ah* ch. 150, and *Shulĥan Aruĥ Oraĥ Ĥayim* 113:8.

[89] Rambam, *Laws of the Worship of Stars [and Idols]* 3:6. It is explained in Rambam, *Laws of Kings* 9:2, that a Gentile is forbidden to embrace, kiss or honor an idol, or do any other activity of idol worship which is forbidden for Jews. For any idolatrous service that a Jew would be executed for, a Gentile is liable, and for any idolatrous service that a Jew would not be executed for, a Gentile is not liable – with the exception of embracing and kissing an idol, for which a Gentile is not liable. (If an action would make a Gentile liable for a capital sin, the Sages expressed this by saying that Gentiles are "warned against it.") Still, hugging or kissing an idol is forbidden for a Gentile, but it does not make him liable for a capital sin. See Meiri, Tractate *Sanhedrin* 58b.

[90] Candles placed before an idol are only a decoration, and not a type of service. See topic 9:12 below; even though this is not a service, it is still forbidden to derive benefit from candles placed before an idol, just like any type of offering to an idol. Lighting candles is not considered to be a service in the Holy Temple. Therefore, we do not classify this as one of the special services that are only allowed to be done for God (explained above in topic 4).

33. There is no liability for a capital sin for a Gentile who serves idols unless the way he served it is clearly a "service." This means that he either clearly performs a specific idol's ritual of service, for that specific idol, or he voices clearly that he is serving such-and-such an idol with its known service. However, if one performs the action and it is not recognizable as serving an idol, and if he does not vocalize that his intention is for the purpose of idol worship, then he is not liable to punishment from an earthly court for this transgression.[91]

34. A Gentile who serves idols in error is exempt from punishment. What is meant by erring? Either he did not know that this was an idol (for example, he bowed down to a statue while thinking that it is only an image for decoration or honor, and he did not know that it is an idol),[92] or he performed an action before a statue but he did not know that it is an idol that is traditionally worshiped in that manner. But if he knows that it is an idol, and that it is traditionally worshiped in a certain manner, but he errs and thinks that it is permissible to serve the idol in that way, he is liable. This is not considered erring, since he should have learned about this rule and didn't (see Part I, topic 4:2).[93]

If one is standing in a house of idol worship, and he mistakenly thinks that it is a place of prayer for God, and he errs and bows down there, he is not liable, since bowing down is only considered a service if he thereby accepts the idol as a deity. But the person who erred in

---

[91] See *Tosafot* on Tractate *Ĥullin* 40a, and *Tosafot* on Tractate *Avodah Zarah* 45a, which state that slaughtering to an idol clearly incurs liability even if it is not done before the physical idol; it is sufficient if one voices this intention or if there is other clear evidence of it. With bowing, one need not clearly state his intent to accept the idol as a deity, for as long as it can be seen from his actions that he is bowing down to it, the person is liable for a capital sin. Thus, one who bows down in a house of idol worship that has no idol in it is liable. This implies that one who bows down with intent to worship an idol is liable even if he does not bow down before the physical idol. If there is a physical idol in its house of worship, a person is liable for bowing there even if he intends to bow to God (unless he bows from fear for his life; see topic 29 above), as proven from Tractate *Keritot* 31a-b and Rashi there.

[92] See Tractate *Sanhedrin* 61b, and Tractate *Keritot* 3a and Rashi there, that if one does not accept the idol as a deity, his bowing is of no consequence.

[93] Rambam, *Laws of Kings* 10:1. A Gentile is not liable for this if his community doesn't know it is forbidden, and it was not possible for him to learn this.

this manner had an intention for God, and this is not serving the idol.[94] But if he knows he is standing before an idol and he bows down before it, he is liable even if his intention is to bow to God (see topic 28).

Likewise, if one serves a statue, knowing that it is an idol but thinking that its worshipers are exempt from liability because it is not made of gold or silver, and he thinks that idols made of other materials are permitted to be served, he is liable. This is not considered erring, since he should have learned that it is forbidden to serve an idol made of any material. For any situation in which a Gentile's mistaken transgression comes from his failure to gain knowledge of the Noahide Commandments if it is available to him, the error is also a sin.[95]

35. There are actions that are not idol worship at all, and yet it is fitting for one to distance himself from them, since it appears to others as if he is serving or honoring idols. For example:

If one gets a thorn stuck in his foot while in front of an idol, he should not bend down and take it out, since it appears as if he is bowing down to the idol. If his money fell out before an idol, he should not bend down and pick it up, since it appears as if he is bowing down to the idol; rather he should sit down or turn his back or side to the idol, and then pick it up.[96]

If there is a fountain with an idol placed there, he should not bend down before the idol and drink from the fountain, since it appears as if he is bowing down to the idol; if he can drink in a way that does not appear to be bowing down to the idol, it is permitted.[97] One should not drink water that is pouring out from an idol, since it appears as if he is kissing the idol.[98]

All these things are permitted in a situation of dire need,[99] since it is

---

[94] Tractate *Sanhedrin* 61b, and Tractate *Keritot* 3a.

[95] See Tractate *Keritot* 3b and Rambam, *Laws of [Sacrifices for] Inadvertent Transgressions* 7:1 – for a Jew this is erring in judgment, but for a Gentile, it is not considered erring, since he should have learned this laws and didn't.

[96] Rambam, *Laws of the Worship of Stars [and Idols]* 3:7; *Shulĥan Aruĥ Yoreh De'ah* ch. 150.

[97] Tractate *Avodah Zarah* 12a.

[98] Rambam *ibid.*

[99] *Minĥat Ĥinuĥ* Commandment 28: these are decrees of the Sages that do not apply to Gentiles.

clear and known that he is not serving the idol or honoring it, but rather he is involved with his own needs.

36. If a sect of idolatry became extinct, and it is no longer practiced in the world, one who serves the idol in its previous customary way but *does not* accept it as a deity is not liable (although there is a general rule that one who performs the customary ritual of an idol is liable even if he does not accept it as a deity; see topic 26 above). This case differs since the worship of this idol is now extinct, and it no longer has any specific service. Therefore, if a Gentile bows down before an idol whose worship became extinct in the world, with no thought to serve it, but instead he bows for the sake of God, he is not liable.[100]

Rabbi Zalman Nehemiah Goldberg holds that Gentiles have basically no obligation to follow rulings of the Sages in any matter. The author disagrees, and is of the opinion that Gentiles are definitely obligated by the commandment of *"dinim"* ("laws") to heed a court of law, and how much more so must they heed the basis of the Torah Law, which is the Oral Torah of the Jewish Sages. (But the author accepts the ruling of *Minĥat Ĥinuĥ* loc. cit., since in many matters, the Sages did not see a need, or declined for other reasons, to decree on a matter in regard to its application to Gentiles.) See the author's Preface to *Sefer Sheva Mitzvot HaShem* and his Introduction to this work.

[100] See Responsa of Rambam ch. 160, where he explains that the Muslims who bow down to God around the Ka'aba stone in Mecca (and in Rambam's time they would still specifically throw rocks at it, and not at any other statues) are not performing an act of idol worship, since their intention is only to bow down for God. In an earlier time (before Mecca was conquered for Islam), this stone was the base of a *Merculis* idol, and people used to throw rocks at it as its traditional worship ritual at that exact location. However, the Muslims who continued that custom had no intention for it to be a means of worshiping the stone as an idol.

If we explain that even if one intends to disgrace an idol and not accept it as a deity, he is still liable if his action is the customary manner of serving the idol, then why did the intent of the Muslims matter, and make them exempt from liability for throwing the stones in that location at Mecca? Rather, it must be because the worship of *Merculis* had already become extinct in the world by that time, as explained by Ran on Tractate *Avodah Zarah* ch. 3. But surely, if they had been throwing stones at it or bowing down to it while it was still being served by people in the manner of *Merculis*, they would have been liable. See topics 6:3,4 below.

CHAPTER 4

The Service of *Moleĥ*

1. *Moleĥ* is an ancient type of idol worship.[101] A person would kindle a great fire before the idol, and then the father would take one (or *some*, but not all) of his children and give the child to the idol's priests. They would then return the child to the father, and he would pass the child "through" the fire at his will, with their permission, walking in the midst of the flames.[102] He walked his child along from one side to the other. The father did not cremate his child to *Moleĥ* (in the manner that children were cremated in the worship of some other idols).[103]

2. There was another idol whose ritual was only to burn one's sons and daughters (which could be even all of them) in fire.[104] Even if one performs this for another idol that has a different traditional ritual, he is still liable for a capital sin as one who burns anything as an offering for an idol (in addition to liability for murder; see topic 3:20 above).

3. The practice of some midwives to take an infant in swaddling clothes, and put a spice which does not smell good on a fire, and wave the infant over it, is a type of passing through fire, and is forbidden.[105]

---

[101] This is clear from Rambam, *Laws of the Worship of Stars [and Idols]* 6:3 and *Kesef Mishneh* there; *Sefer HaĤinuĥ* Commandment 208; Rashi and Ramban on Leviticus 18:21; and Tractate *Sanhedrin* 57a.

*The worship of *Moleĥ* seems to be extinct today (see topic 3:36 above), so it is no longer an idol to be concerned about. We write about it for two reasons:

(1) The Torah is eternal, and from this study one may learn many values and practical points about other areas of Torah (see the notes to Part I, topic 7:1).

(2) It is important to know how low and degrading idol worship became, leading people to sacrifice even their own children. (Obviously this happened due to threats from the idol's priests that if they didn't do so, they would suffer some imaginary curse or damnation.) Even though the *Molecĥ* service did *not* have the ritual of sacrificing the child, still, the basis of all idolatries that are impressed upon a person (until they become accepted) are the same.

[102] *Rambam *ibid.*, and Rashi on Tractate *Sanhedrin* 64b.

[103] Rambam, *Laws of the Worship of Stars [and Idols]* 6:3.

[104] Deuteronomy 12:31, II Kings ch. 17, and Jeremiah 7:31 and Rashi there.

[105] Rambam, *Guide for the Perplexed*, vol. 3, ch. 37.

CHAPTER 5

Forbidden Statues, Images and Pillars

1. It is forbidden to make for oneself or for others a statue or an image of an actual idol[106] that people worship, whether one makes it himself, or tells others to make it for him, even if he does not intend to serve it, as it says,[107] "You shall not make for yourself a carved statue nor any image," and as it also says,[108] "Do not turn to the idols, and molten gods you shall not make for yourselves," meaning that others may not make them for you, and likewise you may not make them for others.[109]

2. It is forbidden to buy a statue or image of an actual idol, even if one does not intend to serve it, for it is forbidden to own, or keep on one's property, any type of idol, even if this particular person will not serve

---

[106] *This refers to a two- or three-dimensional material representation of something that is known and recognized to be served as an idol, by any of the types of idolatry that are currently practiced in the world. (If a non-permanent optical image – digital, video, hologram, etc. – is used to visualize an idol, and a person actually worships it or serves before it, the *equipment* used to produce the image is an *accessory* for idol worship, which also must be either destroyed or "nullified", as will be explained; see topic 7:3 below.)

[107] Exodus 20:4. It appears clear that this prohibition applies as well to Gentiles, since the Talmud in Tractate *Sanhedrin* 56b cites a debate as to whether the prohibition of idol worship for Gentiles applies only to serving idols, or also to making idols. Even though the final ruling follows the opinion that one is liable for a capital sin only from the time that he begins to serve an idol, but not from the time of making it, this does not necessarily argue that it is permitted to make a statue of an idol, and it is logical that both sides of the debate in the Talmud hold that it is prohibited to make an idolatrous statue.

The opinion of Rambam, in *Laws of Kings* 9:2, is clear: it is forbidden for Gentiles to make an idol, even for decoration. See Chapter 7 below, that the command to destroy idol worship and the prohibition against deriving benefit from it apply to Gentiles as well. This is derived from the main prohibition, as part of idol worship is making statues of idols, their service items, etc.

[108] Leviticus 19:4 and *Sifra* there, quoted by Rashi.

[109] Rambam, *Laws of the Worship of Stars [and Idols]* 3:9; *Sefer HaMitzvot* Negative Commandments 2 and 3.

at all.[110] This is included in the cited prohibition, "Do not turn to the idols," as explained above in Chapter 2.

3. It is also forbidden to make certain types of statues *for decoration*, even if there is no intent that they will be served, and even if they do not depict actual idols, as it says,[111] "You shall not make with Me, gods of silver and gold." This means there are certain statues that are forbidden to make for decoration, since erring people may mistake them for idols, and may come to serve them.

The only type of non-idolatrous statue that is prohibited to be made as a decoration is one with accurate three-dimensional features of a full frontal human form (i.e., a head together with a complete body, with all its limbs in nominally proper proportions even if only the front protrudes).[112] Therefore, one may not make a protruding human form

---

[110] Rashi on Exodus 20:3. A Gentile's idol that he made is forbidden to derive benefit from (so it must be destroyed or "nullified," as will be explained). Therefore, it is forbidden for any Gentile to possess an actual idol. (But see topic 7:4, that there is a possibility for a Gentile to be permitted to own an idol, if it was made by a Jew and it was never worshiped.)

[111] Exodus 20:20.

[112] Rambam, *Laws of the Worship of Stars [and Idols]* 3:10, which states, "when the image is protruding – for example, images and sculptures [that decorate the walls] of a hallway and the like;" these are obviously sculptured on one side only, and with their back side connected to the wall.

In regard to Gentiles, Rambam writes in *Laws of Kings* 9:2 that they are not allowed to set up a pillar, plant an *asherah* tree (a tree connected with idol worship), or make full-frontal human statues (with accurate features) for decoration. This means that all prohibitions of idol worship apply to Gentiles as well, including even these three things, and things similar to them, which are not themselves actual idol worship, but which may cause others to err and serve idols – namely, (1) pillars, which were used by the Hebrew Patriarchs for the service of God, but which are now forbidden since they may come to be used by other nations to mark gathering places for idol worship; (2) an *asherah* tree, which is not itself an idol at all, but only a decoration for the place of an idol's service, as Ramban writes (Deuteronomy 16:21-2) that it was planted by the doorstep of a house of idol worship to draw the masses of worshipers; and (3) full three-dimensional decorative human forms, which others may come to worship as idols, as explained by Rambam in *Laws of the Worship of Stars [and Idols] ibid.* See also Meiri on Tractate *Sanhedrin* 56.

in any material for decoration – for example, sculptures that are made to decorate a building or the like.[113]

4. It is permitted to make (non-idolatrous) decorative human images that are engraved or painted – for example, portraits that are painted (even on wood or stone), woven or embroidered (such as a tapestry).

---

[113] *Included in this are: (1) forms of human-like angels (for example, if wings are protruding from the back of a human body), and (2) mythical or other imaginary beings with *minor* non-human features added to a human body (e.g., a "medusa" that has snakes in place of the hair of the head, which is a slight change that retains the general human form).

However, if a significant change is made which clearly identifies the statue as non-human, it seems that it is not forbidden to make for decoration. For example, this applies if the statue is a human above the waist and an animal or fish (as a mermaid) below the waist, or if an animal's head or some other object is added alongside the human head. The Torah's prohibition specifies (Exodus 20:20): "do not make [the] forms that are with Me," meaning forms of humans or angels, who are the servants and messengers of God. But semi-human forms are not included in this prohibition, other than the multi-faced angel images that are described below, since those are ministering angels that are also "with Me." (Therefore, a statue of a full human body with an animal body and hind legs protruding from the back of the human form is forbidden to be made, because this includes a full human form, and the animal part is secondary.)

Even according to Rambam's logic that the Torah forbids making forms lest people come to worship them (and one can understand there is a logical argument for prohibiting forms of semi-human creatures that are famous from cultural mythologies), it is nevertheless obvious that there are limits to this prohibition, and not every form is forbidden to make. The precept itself only forbids the human or angelic forms.

The size of the form is irrelevant. If a *toy figure or doll* has an anatomically correct human form, we consider two types: (1) collector's pieces that are valued by adults, and which might be displayed for decoration – these can be made permissible by removing a feature, for example, by cutting off an ear (see topic 9 below regarding deformation of forms to make them permissible); (2) toys for children's play, which are permitted as they are, since they are not intended for decorative purposes (see topic 8 below). But if the toy's features are not accurate, the toy is permitted from the outset.

It is even permitted to make a three-dimensional *partial* human form – for example, just a complete head, or just a complete body without a head, or a human body in profile.

If one leaves something missing from the human image, for example, if he cuts off the tip of the nose or an earlobe, or he takes out one of its eyes, or if he omits the feature in the first place, it is permitted.

5. It is likewise forbidden to make forms of the angels of the "Divine Chariot" for decoration (which have the four faces of a human, ox, lion and eagle on one body); or forms which have the faces of a cherub (an angelic face like a human child), a human, a lion and an eagle on one body; or the form of any type of serving angel.[114]

Some opinions hold that images of angels have the same ruling as a human image, in that it is only forbidden to make a full frontal (three-dimensional) statue for decoration, but an engraving is not forbidden; other opinions hold that even an engraving of an angel's image is forbidden to make for decoration[115] (this would apply in topics 6-9 which follow). However, all hold that it is permitted to paint their images in color.

6. These human and angelic forms that are prohibited for decoration are forbidden whether they exist as a separate sculpture, or they are sculptured as protruding from the body of a vessel, or they are sculptured separately and fixed onto a vessel.

Not only a vessel is implied, but anything else, such as a cup, a finger ring, a nose ring, a necklace or the like. If they are protruding and complete forms (i.e., with at least the front half of a three-dimensional head and body, with nominally correct human proportions), they are forbidden.

7. This prohibition to make forms of humans or angels for decoration applies whether one makes them by his own handiwork or if others make them for him, and whether it is for his own benefit or if he makes

---

[114] *Shulĥan Aruĥ Yoreh De'ah* ch. 141.

[115] Ra'avad, on *Shulĥan Aruĥ ibid.*, holds that this engraving is not forbidden. Rambam, *ibid.* 3:11, and Ramban as cited in *Tur Yoreh De'ah* ch. 141, hold that it is forbidden.

them for others.[116] Regarding this, there is no difference between public or private objects – any human or angelic form that is prohibited for one individual Gentile to use for decoration is prohibited for all Gentiles of the general public.[117]

8. There is no prohibition of making these forms of humans or angels unless they are made exclusively for decoration. But if they are made for the purpose of business, it is permitted. Even if one made them for himself because he needed these images for purposes other than exclusively for decoration, this is permitted.[118]

Since we explained that it is forbidden to make these forms for others to use as decorations, how can it be permitted to do so for business? This can be so, for example, if the public buys them for their various uses, and the artisan makes them for the public, not knowing for certain whether they will use them for a forbidden or permitted use. However, if the artisan is certain that his customers want these images for decoration alone, it is forbidden to make them for the public, as explained above.

A currency coin that has a complete face protruding from it (even the face of a popular idol) is permitted to be made or used, since this is

---

[116] This is the opinion of Maharam Mi'Rutenburg (quoted in Ran and *Tosafot* on Tractate *Yoma* 54), who holds that it is forbidden from the Torah to make statues of humans or angels, whether for oneself or others, and he derives this (like the prohibition of making a statue for idol worship, as mentioned above in topic 5:1), from the verse "You shall not make statues of idols for yourself" – i.e., not for yourself or for others; this applies likewise in the prohibition "gods of silver and gold, you shall not make for yourself." This means "not for yourself, or for others." This is the opinion of *Tur Yoreh De'ah* ch. 141, and Shaĥ 141:22.

In practice, there is no permission to Gentiles for any of these things, and one must follow the ruling that whether one makes images for decoration for oneself or others, it is forbidden as a stumbling block that might cause others to err and serve them, as explained by Rambam (*ibid.* 3:10).

[117] *Meĥilta* Ex. 20:20; Tractate *Avodah Zarah* 43b; Rema *Yoreh Deah* ch.141.

[118] The author explains this by noting that it is prohibited to make these forms for decoration, lest they become a stumbling block, because someone might be attracted to make them into idols. But if a person needs to have them for some practical use, there is much less concern that this might happen.

strictly made for business.[119]

9. The forms specified above as forbidden to make for decoration are also forbidden to keep *for decoration*, if one found them or received them from others,[120] **unless he "deforms" them by detaching a feature from the form in order to make it incomplete, e.g. cutting off the tip of the nose or the like, in order that it can be recognized that it is not complete. Only after deforming the object in this way is one permitted to keep it in his possession for decoration.**[121] The concern is that they may become a stumbling block for others to err and think that they are for idol worship (see above in topic 5:3).

However, if one has a use for them that is *not* for decoration, it is permitted for him to make them, to benefit from them,[122] or to sell them to others to use them.

10. A form of any creature that is not worshiped, such as an animal, bird or fish, and in fact any form from nature, or even something similar to a dragon[123] – to the exclusion of a human or angel – is

---

[119] *Rema on *Yoreh De'ah* 141:3 explains that images on coins are similar to images on vessels; see topic 7:8. However, if the coin is minted only as a special medallion or a collector's item, and not for regular currency, it is prohibited if the form or image is an actual idol, or a full frontal human body.

[120] There is debate among the sages on this matter. It is forbidden for a Jew to possess any idols or human statues, whether because of a suspicion, or because of a Torah prohibition according to some opinions; therefore the same would to apply for a Gentile. As a practical matter, there might be no concept of something being prohibited for a Gentile because of a suspicion; nevertheless, since the making of idols is forbidden (from the ruling of Rambam that others might come to serve them), there is no difference between the ruling for making them and the ruling for possessing them.

[121] Tractate *Avodah Zarah* 43b mentions "put its eye out" – meaning that with this action, the statue becomes an incomplete form that is permitted to possess (since there is no suspicion that it will be served as an idol). See *Beit Leĥem Yehudah* on *Shulĥan Aruĥ Yoreh De'ah* 141:4 – **one needs to cut out a recognizable part of an idol in order to make it permitted to possess**.

[122] Rambam, *Laws of the Worship of Stars [and Idols]* 7:6.

[123] *Tur* and Rema *Yoreh De'ah* ch. 141. Although this form may be customarily served as an idol, the source verse only mentions forms of humans and angels as prohibited, so *making* a dragon form for decoration isn't forbidden.

permitted to be made, even if it is for decoration and even if it is a full, frontal, three-dimensional form.[124]

It is likewise permitted to engrave an image of the sun, moon, stars or constellations, even if one only intends for these to be decorations.[125] But if one makes a form for the purpose of idol worship, it has already been explained (topic 5:1 above) that it is forbidden because of the prohibition against making a statue or an image of an idol.

11. It is forbidden to plant an *asherah*, which is a tree with which idol worship is performed, or which is used for purposes of idol worship, even if the one who plants it only intends for it to be used for idol worship by others, but not for himself. (See topics 8:7-10 below, for descriptions of *asherah* trees.) It is also forbidden to plant a tree to be a decoration for idol worship, or to be a decoration for an altar that is used for idol worship.[126] (This is also an *asherah*.)

It is forbidden to build a house or altar for idol worship, or a platform to be used to stand an idol upon. The same applies for any vessels or ritual clothing which one knows will be used for idol worship.[127]

12. It is forbidden to set up a "pillar" (as it is called in the Torah), which is a structure, column or stone that is being designated for groups of people to gather around *for the purpose of their worship services*. Obviously, it is forbidden to set up a pillar whose sole

---

[124] Rambam, *ibid.* 3:11; *Shulĥan Aruĥ Yoreh De'ah ibid.*

[125] Rambam, *ibid.* 3:10-11, writes that from the Torah, the prohibition of making a form for decoration only applies to the form of a human or angel (as explained in topic 5:3 above). Like *Sefer HaĤinuĥ* Com. 39 and *SMa"G* Negative Com. 22, he holds that the prohibition, "You shall not make with Me..." applies only to the form of a human or angel, but not to forms and images of the sun and moon (which are not prohibited by the Torah). Especially according to Rambam's reason for prohibiting forms of humans or angels (because others might come to worship them), images of the sun and moon are not forbidden, since it is not customary for people to serve images of the actual sun and moon themselves, but rather statues of the gods which represent them. This is explained by Rambam in *Pirush HaMishnah Avodah Zarah* 3:3 (which is cited in Rema *Yoreh De'ah* 141:3) and in Shaĥ 141:8.

[126] Rambam, *ibid.* 6:9, and *Laws of Kings* 9:2.

[127] Rambam, *Laws of the Worship of Stars [and Idols]* 9:11.

purpose is for idol worship. But even if its purpose is only to serve God, it is forbidden. This applies whether one builds the pillar and sets it up, or if he designates a certain existing stone or structure, to be used as a pillar.[128]

A pillar is forbidden if it is being designated to locate any type of worship service. This applies even if it is also used in the service – either to sacrifice an animal upon it,[129] or to pour libations upon it (as

---

[128] Rambam, *ibid.* 6:6 and *Laws of Kings* 9:2. See *Sifra* Lev. 26:1, that both a statue and a pillar are included in the prohibitions "You shall not make ...," and "You shall not set up ..." Rambam explains (Negative Commandment 5) that "You shall not set up ..." refers to preserving and keeping the object, even if it was previously built. This is also the opinion given in *Sefer Mitzvot Gadol (SMa"G)*, Negative Commandment 42.

*But a house of prayer (such as a synagogue) is not included in the prohibition of a pillar, since it is a place that is designated specifically for people to pray without being disturbed. More specifically, it is forbidden to establish a pillar for the purpose of the congregating itself (which may be for any purpose), so that the pillar becomes transformed into a marker or a symbol of the gathering place, and it itself might then become transformed into a symbol of worship. This means that the peripheral presence of the pillar would become the basic factor in the worship. See the additional points in topic 6:4 below.

There is no prohibition against setting up a pillar for other purposes that are not for designating a place for worship gatherings. Therefore, pillars and monuments that mark historic locations, or honor special individuals or events in history, are permitted (Responsa *Minĥat Yitzĥak*, vol. 1, ch. 29).

[129] See Deut. 16:22. According to Rashi there, and *Sefer Mitzvot Gadol*, Negative Commandment 41, this refers to the prohibition of using a single stone as an altar for sacrificing, even for a one-time service. (Rambam does not explicitly list this as a negative commandment for Jews.) As Ramban explains there, this may be because it is already excluded according to the commanded requirements for building a sacrificial altar even outside the Holy Temple (such an altar may still be made and used by a Gentile for sacrifice to God, if it is built from multiple stones, and then after its use it is to be taken apart and the pieces should be buried; see *Sheva Mitzvot HaShem* Part I, topic 7:3). Rashbam explains there that this was a temporary command for Jews until the Holy Temple was built. According to Rambam's definition of a forbidden "pillar," it is definitely prohibited to establish a permanent pillar for the sake of anything associated with communal worship, including sacrificing upon it, even if it is assembled from pieces.

Jacob did before pillars were forbidden; see Genesis 28:18), or to burn incense upon it, or to bow down around it or beside it, or to call people to prayer or sermonize from it, or to use it for any other purpose connected to worship.[130] From this we conclude that it is prohibited to connect a pillar with any aspect of worship service.

It is also forbidden to designate a special fixed stone to bow down on. Therefore, although a Gentile may bow down and prostrate to God in any decent place (see Part I, topics 6:5-6), and on any type of floor (including a stone floor), it is forbidden to designate a *specific* stone, floor tile, or other fixed object to be bowed down upon.[131]

The essential concept of a forbidden pillar is that it is forbidden to establish an object for fixed and *enduring* use (as opposed to being a temporary marker), as a designated monument for communal worship (even for God).[132] This applies whether it is a natural object (e.g., a boulder, tree stump or log), or something that is chiseled out (as from wood or stone), molded (as from clay), cast (as from molten metal), shaped (as from beaten gold), formed (as from concrete or plastic), or

---

[130] See *Targum Yonatan ben Uziel Vayikra* 26:1, and Ramban on Deut. 16:22.

[131] *See Leviticus 26:1. Although Gentiles were not warned about this as a separate commandment, this is actually another form of the permanent pillars that are forbidden for them. As Rambam explains in *Laws of the Worship of Stars [and Idols]* 6:6 (and in *Guide for the Perplexed*, vol. 3, ch. 45, p. 379), there is one reason for prohibiting both things (a pillar and a prostration stone): because idol worshipers established them as innovated statues for their worship services. Also, there is another reason to forbid a prostration stone: eventually, people may come to bow down to the stone itself (see Ramban on Deuteronomy 16:22, and *Sefer HaĤinuĥ* Commandment 349). This is probably a basic logic for the prohibition of establishing a pillar, as reflected in the explanation by Rambam (*Sefer HaMitzvot* Negative Commandment 11): "the prohibition of making a pillar so that people will congregate there and honor it [the pillar]." This means that the pillar receives a status of holiness in the eyes of the common people, and some will then turn the pillar itself into an object of worship (i.e., an idol).

[132] *The simple meaning of the word for pillar in Hebrew, *matzeva* (from the root word *yatziv*), is something that is fixed, firm and enduring. An example is the mound of witness stones built by Jacob and Laban (Genesis 31:45-52), that Jacob described as a *matzeva*. (See Ramban and Sforno on Genesis *loc. cit.*, Ramban on Genesis 31:18, Rashbam on Genesis 31:13, and Sforno on Genesis 31:13 and Deuteronomy 16:22).

assembled from multiple pieces of any size (e.g., bricks, rocks or wood pieces), or even if it is an arrangement of multiple pillars at one site (e.g., as was done in ancient times at the site of Stonehenge). This is the type of pillar that was set up by Jacob to designate a place for communal worship of God (before pillars became forbidden), as it says (Genesis 28:18-22): [he] set it as a pillar, ... saying, ... "this stone that I have set as a pillar shall become a house of God ..."

A reason for this prohibition is that a group of people may eventually come to view and honor the object itself as "the stone," or "the pillar," or "the place" that they designate as a holy object or place by an *innovated religious statute* (see Part I, Chapter 3). Furthermore, some may begin to worship the pillar itself.

Despite the fact that Jacob set up a pillar for service to God (Genesis *loc. cit.*), when the Torah was given at Mount Sinai, the setting up of pillars for the purpose of any type of worship was forbidden by God, because it had become hated by Him, as it says (Deuteronomy 16:22), "And you shall not erect for yourselves a pillar, which the Lord, your God, hates."

The Sages explained that although this practice was beloved by God when it was done for His sake by Jacob, it later became hateful to Him when the Canaanite tribes made this into a customary practice for their worship of idols.[133]

13. A Gentile who makes statues or images of idols, for either worship or decoration, or who sets up a pillar to designate a place of worship, is not liable for punishment by a physical court. Nevertheless, a Noahide court should prevent people from engaging in these practices.[134]

---

[133] Rashi on Deuteronomy 16:22.

[134] Rambam, *Laws of Kings* 9:2.

CHAPTER 6

The Prohibition of Creating a New Religion

1. It was explained in Part I that the Seven Noahide Commandments, as commanded by God and revealed through Moses, have been incumbent upon mankind from the time of Noaĥ (before the giving of the Torah), and Moses was also commanded by the word of God to compel all the nations of the world to observe those basic precepts. After the commandments of the Torah and their explanations were given by God at Mount Sinai, people do not have permission from God to create any new religions.[135] If one creates or upholds a new religion, he is liable for this transgression, and he should be warned about this.[136] However, this transgression by itself does not make a person liable for capital punishment from a court[137] (unless he violates one of the Noahide Commandments through an act that is a capital sin).

Anyone who creates a new religion denies the command of God to all nations to keep the Seven Noahide Commandments, and transgresses the essential commandment of them all. Even if a new religion includes observing the Noahide Commandments, they are not being observed because they were commanded by God and revealed through Moses, but rather because of this newly created religion.[138] It is therefore forbidden to preserve any newly created religion.

---

[135] *This is explained clearly in the author's Introduction, as an outcome of God's promise that the Torah of Moses is eternal, and His commandment that it must not be changed by mankind.

[136] *It is obvious that one is only obliged to convey this information to the person if there is no danger in doing so, and follows the rules cited in Part I, topic 4:8.

[137] Rambam, *Laws of King* 10:9.

[138] This is clear from Rambam's opinion above, as is explained in *Igrot Moshe Yoreh De'ah* vol. 2, ch. 7.

*This prohibition includes religions that involve a nullification of part of the Torah or its commandments, or even one that accepts the details of the Seven Noahide Commandments, but adds additional commandments for Gentiles. See also Part I, topic 1:8.

2. The belief in a divine trinity is an idolatrous concept,[139] since it is a belief that God (or according to some, a second separate divinity)[140] has characteristic features, and the characteristics of a body.

3. The main doctrine of Islam is not idolatry, since it calls for belief in one God.[141] However, as stated above, it is forbidden to uphold an innovated religion that people introduced after Mount Sinai.

4. As explained in Chapter 5 above, if a religious statute is innovated to gather to the site of a specific pillar, this becomes the type of forbidden pillar that is mentioned in the Torah.

---

[139] Rambam: *Laws of the Worship of Stars [and Idols]* 9:4, *Laws of Forbidden Foods* 11:7, *Pirush HaMishnah* on the beginning of Tractate *Avodah Zarah* (in the complete text, not the censored version), and *Laws of Kings* 11:4. This is also clear from Rema in *Yoreh De'ah* 141:1 and ch. 150, which states that even plain crosses *which are bowed down to* have the ruling of an idolatrous image (see topic 7:10 below).

[140] Rambam, *Laws of Repentance* 3:7, rules that this is a type of idolatry, and thus did Ramban present in his famous disputation (*The Disputation at Barcelona*, pages 303, 310).

[141] Rambam *Laws of Forbidden Foods* 11:7; *Tur Yoreh De'ah* ch. 124 in the name of Rashba and the Gaonim; *Beit Yosef* and Rema *Yoreh De'ah* 146:5, all rule that Muslims are not idolaters.

However, see Ritva on Tractate *Rosh Hashanah* 17a, and on Tractate *Pesaĥim* 25, where he explains that believers in post-Sinai doctrines are "deniers of Torah" (defined in Part 1, topic 1:8) and "deviant believers" (defined in Part 1, topic 1:7), and are not among those who keep the Seven Noahide Commandments. (Traditional Christian doctrine rejects the continuing obligation to observe all of the Torah's eternal Divine commandments as such, both those which are for Jews and those which are for Gentiles, and also the need to repent to God Himself if a commandment is transgressed; traditional Islamic doctrine rejects the authenticity of the Five Books of Moses, and of the specific set of Seven Noahide Commandments – even though they may accept some or all of the Noahide Commandments in practice, but not as the basic command of God to mankind.)

An example is the Ka'aba stone[142] at Mecca;[143] since the congregating of people at this specific pillar, and the rituals, honor and

---

[142] See Ibn Ezra on Daniel 11:29 and *Yad Ramah Sanhedrin* 60, regarding the ritual service of the idol *Merculis* that was conducted there in earlier times. See the footnote to topic 3:36 above, quoting Rambam who says that although Muslims bow down around the Ka'aba stone, they are bowing to God and not to the stone itself, so therefore that does not constitute an act of idolatry. Nevertheless, it serves as the type of pillar which is explained above in topics 5:12-13.

[143] *This is opposite to the visiting and praying which takes place at the "Western Wall" in Jerusalem, for there is no Torah Law or Rabbinical obligation to congregate there or at the site of any other monument. The Torah obligation is for Jews to gather *in the Holy Temple* on the three Jewish pilgrimage festivals, if it is built and functioning on its established site, as they are commanded in (a) Deut. 16:16, "Three times a year all your males should appear before the Lord, your God, in the place that He will choose ..." (*cf.* Exodus 23:14-19), and (b) Deut. 31:10-13, "At the end of seven years ... during the *Sukkot* festival when all Israel comes to appear before the Lord, your God, in the place that He will choose, ... gather together [all] the people ... and their children ..."

Making a requirement for a specific place to worship, other than the Divinely sanctified Holy Temple when it is functioning, is an example of an innovated commandment. Also, one who relegates the Temple Mount to a status of secondary holiness in the world is accepting an innovated doctrine. This is one of the aspects of a forbidden pillar: designating a specific place as sanctified for obligatory congregating, other than the Holy Temple in Jerusalem. In contrast, the Holy Temple in Jerusalem is God's chosen place for the revelation of His Divine Presence, as stated (Psalms 132:13-14): "For the Lord has chosen Zion; He desired it for His dwelling place. This is My resting place forever, here I will dwell, for I have desired it." (See Rambam, *Laws of the Chosen House* 1:3.) Therefore, if one claims that there is some place with a more exalted presence of Divinity than at the site of the Holy Temple, that has the connotation of some other divinity which is not the One God of Israel, Who is the Source of the eternal Hebrew Scriptures.

The "Western Wall" is a remnant of the rampart around the Holy Temple, which was built in fulfillment of God's command in Ex. 25:8: "They shall make Me a Sanctuary ..." Therefore, both from the aspect of people visiting the site to pray there (including Gentiles; see Kings I, 8:41-2), and the structure itself, it is the opposite of the pillar that is forbidden by the Torah.

holiness that were connected with it, were made into statutes of a religion, it is the type of pillar that is mentioned in the Torah.

5. If during one's act of bowing down in prayer, he includes in this act an acceptance of someone as God's prophet, this is forbidden, since that would be including a created being in the intention for a prostration.[144] Permission is only given to mankind to bow down in worship if it is to God alone,[145] without combining any other being in the intention for bowing, so acceptance of a prophet through the act of bowing to God would be a form of service to an intermediary in practical terms. (Also, adding intention for another being in a service to God is a dishonor to Him, and regarding this it is written, "Anyone who combines God and an intermediary is torn from the world."[146])

6. Those who bow down or make offerings (for example, by burning incense) to an image of a person, or who pray to it, are idol worshipers. Even if the person did not declare himself or herself to be a god, those who make an icon or a god that represents the person and serve it are idol worshipers.[147]

---

[144] See *Ĥidushei HaRan Sanhedrin* 61b.

[145] *See topics 3:29-30, and commentary notes there, which explain this in more detail, and that it is permitted to bow before an idol out of fear for one's life, or to bow as a simple customary greeting to another person.

[146] Tractate *Sanhedrin* 63a. The Rabbinical expression "torn from the world" is based on Exodus 22:19, which states, "One who sacrifices [or worships] to idols [even if he combines it with intention for God] shall be destroyed."

*See Part I, topic 1:7. Conversely, "Satan" is the name of a prosecuting angel in the Heavenly Court (see Zeĥariah 3:1, Job ch. 1). Yet some say that he became an independent ruler over a realm of eternal damnation, and that he acts in opposition to God's will – i.e., that he is a separate god. This idolatrous concept is not even a belief in an intermediary (see topic 1:2 and the footnotes there), since it claims that Satan is not under God's control.

[147] *Likewise, those who serve pantheistic gods, by performing their various rituals, or by placing offerings of food, etc., before their statues, are idol worshipers. This applies even if one performs these rituals, but says that the Lord is the God of those gods that he is serving, or if he says that the idols represent God's own Divine attributes.

CHAPTER 7

The Obligation to Eliminate Idol Worship, and the Prohibition of Benefiting from It

1. It is an obligation to eliminate the worship of idols when it comes under one's domain, including its service, and all that is done for it and pertains to it, to the extent that the name of the idol should have no remnant left there,[148] as it says (Deut. 12:23), "You shall utterly destroy all the places where the nations that *you are dispossessing* worshiped their gods… you shall break apart their altars; you shall smash their pillars; and their *asherah* trees you shall burn in the fire; their carved images you shall cut down; and you shall obliterate their names [of those idols] from that place." (If an idol comes into one's possession, it should be either destroyed or "nullified," as explained in topic 3 below. Nullification of an idol is explained in topics 8:15-20.)

This obligation is placed both on the individual and the public as a whole. It is forbidden for one to preserve in his domain any worship of idols or things that pertain to it, and it is likewise the obligation of every government of every nation and its courts to remove all idol

---

[148] Rambam, *Laws of the Worship of Stars [and Idols]* 7:1. We see from *ibid.* 1:3 that this precept applies to Gentiles, since Abraham broke all of his father's idols, and taught others that it was fitting to break all the idols in order that no person would err and serve them. In Tractate *Sanhedrin* 90a, "break apart their altars" refers to the positive command regarding idolatry – that this obligation derives from the *prohibition*, and therefore it applies to Gentiles as well. It is likewise Rambam's opinion that Gentiles are not allowed to make idols or life-like statues of humans, and it was explained above in Chapter 5 that this prohibition refers to preserving their existence as possible objects of worship. This surely applies to an idol that was served.

The Torah relates (Genesis 35:2) that Jacob instructed his sons to hand over for burial all the idols they had taken from the city of Shechem. Ramban and Sforno explain that before these idols were taken from the city, they were made permissible by "nullification" – i.e. they were spoiled by damaging. (Ramban explains that by additionally burying the nullified idols in rocky terrain that would never be cultivated, so they would probably never be found, Jacob was observing additional scrupulous care in distancing his family and others from any connection with idols.) Thus they observed the commandment to nullify idols, and the prohibition against preserving idolatry, even in their time (as Gentiles, before the covenant at Mount Sinai).

worship from its borders, since it is forbidden to preserve idol worship in any place or time, as it says,[149] "You shall have no other gods *before Me*" – "before Me," meaning in any place or time that I, God, am there (i.e., everywhere and for all time), you shall have no other deities.[150]

2. It is not incumbent upon Gentiles to wage war with idolatrous nations, just for the purpose of eliminating their worship of idols.[151]

Some authorities[152] hold that it is permitted to steal another's idols in order to destroy them, and to prevent others from serving them. However, an individual should not do so since it causes strife; rather, the courts should be charged with that task. Nevertheless, if one did steal an idol for this purpose, he is exempt from punishment and any requirement to reimburse the idolater for the loss of the idol.

3. False deities, all items used in their service, offerings made to them, and all that pertains to them are forbidden to possess as such and derive benefit from, unless they are "nullified." All these aspects of idolatry are an abomination to God, as it says,[153] "You shall not bring an abomination into your house." One is obligated to either destroy or

---

The fact that Ramban mentions that the idols were nullified, before Jacob's sons took them from the city of Shechem and before they were buried, shows that he holds that it is an obligation for Gentiles to (at least) nullify idols.

How do we know this was not an extra stringency that Jacob took on because it would later be prohibited for a Jew to possess an idol that was not nullified? Ramban explains that Jacob buried the idols where they would not be found, but only *after* he made sure that they had been nullified. It is not possible for a Jew to nullify an idol (Rambam, *Laws of the Worship of Stars [and Idols]* 8:9); rather, Jacob fulfilled the *Noahide* obligation to nullify any idols that come into one's possession. Then, as a further stringency (similar to the future Jewish obligation), he removed the nullified idols from *possibly* being worshiped by others, in addition to their nullification, by burying them where they would not be found (which is equivalent to eliminating idolatry).

(Note that burial of an idol that is not nullified is not destruction of the idol, since there is at least some small possibility that it might be found intact.)

[149] Exodus 20:3.

[150] *Meĥilta* and Rashi on Exodus 20:3.

[151] Clearly, from Rambam, *Laws of the Worship of Stars [and Idols]* 7:1.

[152] Responsa *Shevut Ya'akov*, vol. 3, ch. 38.

[153] Deuteronomy 7:26.

nullify anything of this nature. It may be destroyed by grinding it and throwing it to the wind, burning it, throwing it into the deep sea, etc.[154]

If *any* Gentile (even a pious Gentile) nullifies *any* type of idol (by one of the methods that will be explained below), it is permitted for a Gentile to preserve and derive benefit from it after this nullification.[155]

[This is subject to the following limitations. (a) Nullification of an idol is accomplished only if it is done either by the Gentile who owns the idol, even if he is forced to do so, or by any Gentile if the owner agrees and gives his permission to do so. (b) A Jew cannot nullify an idol to make it permissible to benefit from it; if he does not find a Gentile to nullify it for him, he must destroy it (see topic 8:14 below).]

4. A statue (or any other form) that is made as an actual idol by a Gentile is forbidden as soon as it is created, as it says,[156] "The statues of their gods, you should burn in fire." As soon as a statue of an idol is made by a Gentile, it becomes forbidden and must be either destroyed or nullified.

In contrast, a statue that is made and possessed by a Jew is not forbidden until it is served. Even if a Gentile buys an idol from a Jew, it is not forbidden to derive benefit from it until someone serves it,[157] but one commits a transgression by preserving it as the idol, as explained above in topic 5:2. Its only manner of permitted use and benefit is to nullify it by damaging it to the extent that the features of the idol are destroyed. For example, a metal idol may be sold to someone who will definitely melt it down and utilize the metal for another use.

Objects that are prepared to be used in serving an idol or to beautify it, whether belonging to a Jew or Gentile, are not forbidden until they

---

[154] Rambam, *ibid.* 7:1-2 and 8:6, and *Shulĥan Aruĥ Yoreh De'ah* 146:14. It is clear that Gentiles are forbidden to benefit from things that are used for idol worship, based on their obligation to destroy idolatry, since preservation of something is the opposite of its destruction. This is found clearly in Rambam's explanation on Tractate *Avodah Zarah* 59b.

[155] Rambam, *ibid.* 8:9.

[156] Deuteronomy 7:25.

[157] Since an idol is only forbidden to a Gentile if it was made by a Gentile, and in this case it was a Jew who made the idol. But an idol made by a Jew *for a Gentile* is forbidden immediately, like the law of an idol made by a Gentile for himself (Rambam, *ibid.* 7:5).

are actually used for these purposes.[158]

5. One who makes idols for others, even though it is forbidden for him to do so (as explained in topic 5:1), is permitted to keep the profit he earns.[159] Even if he made an idol for himself (so it is forbidden to preserve and benefit from, and it must be destroyed or nullified), if he transgressed and sold it as an idol, he is permitted to use the money he received from the sale. Likewise, if one exchanged an idol (that was not yet nullified) for something that is not an idol, although he has transgressed, after the fact it is permitted to derive benefit from the item he received in exchange for the idol.[160]

6. It has been explained in Chapter 5 that it is forbidden for a person to make forms of humans or angels for decoration (with complete three-dimensional bodies and correct human features), or to preserve them. However, if these forms are used for decoration, it is still permitted to benefit from them. But any form or image made for idol worship is forbidden to gain any benefit from (as explained in topic 7:4 above). If forms or images of humans (or angels or any other creatures) are found, and it is unknown whether they were used for idol worship or just for decoration, one must decide according to the customs of the place and time. If it appears that these objects were probably used for idol worship, they are forbidden, and if not, they are permitted.[161]

How so? Any human figures found in villages of idolaters are forbidden for benefit, because it is assumed that they were made for idol worship, as figures in such villages usually are. Human figures

---

[158] Rambam, *ibid.* 7:4; *Shulĥan Aruĥ Yoreh De'ah* ch. 139.

[159] Rambam *ibid.*, 7:5.

[160] *Ibid.*, 9:18; *Shulĥan Aruĥ Yoreh De'ah* ch. 144; Shaĥ *Yoreh De'ah* 144:2.

[161] Shaĥ *Yoreh De'ah* 141:4. See topic 8:17 below, that if an idol worshiper forsook his idol in peace time, it proves that he has nullified it by deserting it. But if this was during a time of war, the idol is not considered nullified, because it could have been cast out reluctantly, or just left deserted, while the idolater was fleeing from danger (see for example II Kings 7:15). Therefore, any rulings in this and the following topics refer to cases when it is impossible to verify the status of the idol, such as a time of war or the like when its worshipers may have run away and left it. If, however, its worshipers can be found in its proximity, the idol's status is verified according to their account.

placed at the entrance to a city,[162] holding in their hand a stick, bird, ball or sword, or wearing wreaths or rings, are assumed to have been made for idolatry, as such figures usually are. Therefore, they are forbidden for benefit unless they are nullified. (All of the forms mentioned here are traditional idolatrous images. These symbols are intended to represent the power and dominion of the idol.) If other figures are found that are not normally idolatrous, it is assumed that they were made for decoration, and are permitted for benefit.[163]

7. This prohibition of benefit only applies if the questionable object is found in its original respectable fashion (so surely it was not nullified), and if there is still doubt whether it was made for either idol worship or decoration (e.g., as a monument). In contrast, forms and images found discarded in a marketplace, or among waste scraps or garbage, are permitted for benefit, since they are surely nullified;[164] how much more so for scattered parts or broken pieces of idols that are found in any condition or place.[165] (See topic 8:17 below.)

If one finds a hand, foot, or some other limb of an idol, or a statue of a star or constellation (meaning the idolatrous form associated with the star or constellation that was worshiped, such as a crowned king atop a chariot as a representation of the sun), and it was found *on its intended base*, then one may not benefit from it, since it definitely comes from an idol that had been worshiped, and it is not known whether it has been nullified (and therefore it is assumed that it was not nullified). Since it is not uncommon that idol worshipers will worship a separate limb from an idol, it is forbidden unless it is known that the idol's worshipers have annulled its status as their god. If it is found thrown on the ground away from its original place, it is permitted, since it is

---

[162] Shaĥ *Yoreh De'ah* 141:2.

[163] Rambam, *ibid.* 7:6; *Shulĥan Aruĥ Yoreh De'ah* ch. 141.

[164] See *milu'im* (notes) on *Shulĥan Aruĥ Yoreh De'ah* 141:7.

[165] See Tractate *Avodah Zarah* 41. For Jews, broken pieces of discarded idols are permitted (since there are multiple reasons to doubt if they are forbidden), but unbroken discarded idols are forbidden (since they only have one doubt, that they may not have been nullified). This only applies for Jews, upon whom the Rabbinical authorities added extra stringencies for cases when a *definite* prohibition likely applies to a particular item, but a doubt is present.

possible that it was nullified.[166]

It is obvious that this only applies when there is such a custom to worship pieces of an idol. But when the custom is never to worship pieces of an idol, then pieces are nullified automatically when they break off from an idol (even accidentally), and these pieces are permitted to benefit from. (See end of the next topic, and topic 8:17.)

8. If one finds gold or silver vessels, or silk cloths, on which there is a figure of a dragon, or the sun, the moon, a planet or a constellation (meaning the idolatrous images associated with the celestial spheres), or if one finds these images engraved on nose rings or ordinary rings (as all such items were considered important, and it was customary to make them for idol worship), then one may not benefit from them. If such images are found on other vessels, then those vessels may be used, because it is assumed that they were put there for decoration. Similarly, all other types of figures (such as an image of the actual sun or moon, or other animals) found on any type of vessel are assumed to have been put there for decoration and are permitted.[167]

However, this ruling exists only for vessels (which here include jewelry and clothing) whose purpose is unknown. If it is known that a vessel (even an unimportant one) was used for idol worship, or it was meant to beautify the idolatrous service, it is forbidden to benefit from it. If it is known that a vessel was not intended or used for idolatry, it is permitted for benefit even if it has the images described here.[168]

Nowadays, the ways of idolatry are different, and each sect follows its own statutes and rituals. Therefore, any vessels that appear to be used for idolatry, according to the current practices in a given place, are forbidden; if not, they are permitted.[169]

9. The above requirements apply only if one found such vessels in a respectable place. But if one finds them cast away, and it appears that they are ownerless or nullified – and surely if they are broken, since it is not a usual practice to use a broken vessel for idol worship – they are permitted.

---

[166] *Shulĥan Aruĥ Yoreh De'ah* ch. 141.

[167] Rambam, *ibid.* 7:8, and *Shulĥan Aruĥ ibid.*

[168] *Shulĥan Aruĥ ibid.*, and Shaĥ *Yoreh De'ah* 141:13.

[169] Remah *Yoreh De'ah* ch. 141.

10. Even plain crosses that are bowed down to are forbidden. But plain crosses worn as regular jewelry, that are only intended as a symbol and not for worship, are permitted for benefit[170] (unless they are used as aids in worship; also, a three-dimensional and accurate full-frontal human form of any size is not permitted for decoration, which includes jewelry; see topic 5:3 above).

Vessels and artworks that have images of crosses are forbidden to benefit from if they are generally used for idol worship, even if they are not respectable vessels. If they are generally used only for decoration in non-idolatrous contexts, they are permitted (even if they also include a two-dimensional human image).[171]

11. The general rule is that for any image or statue, or vessel or other accessory item, for which there is a doubt as to whether it was used either for actual idol worship, or as part of an idol-worship ritual, or for decoration of idol worship, one should assume that it was used according to the custom of the local area. If one is still in doubt, the ruling is lenient,[172] and it is permitted.

---

[170] Rema *Yoreh De'ah* 141:1.

[171] See Shaĥ *Yoreh De'ah* 141:6.

[172] This leniency for an item in doubt (as to whether it is permitted or forbidden) is because doubtful situations are decided leniently in basic Torah Law. (Rabbinical authorities ruled strictly on cases of doubt only for Jews.) Therefore, it is obvious that for Gentiles, doubtful situations are decided leniently.

Ĥatam Sofer (vol. 6, ch. 25) rules likewise. *Pri Megadim* states (in its introduction to *Shulĥan Aruĥ Oraĥ Ĥayim, seder hanhagot ha'shoel*, par. 42) that if there is doubt whether something is forbidden for a Gentile, it is permitted, even *up to* a one-to-one (50%) mixture of forbidden and permitted items, when the prohibited item is there but not distinguishable (in which case the entire mixture would be prohibited for a Jew, for whom the Torah rules strictly if it is definitely known that a prohibition is involved). In a case of one forbidden item mixed with one permitted item, one Gentile may even take one item and another Gentile may take the other item, so each one is benefiting from a item that might be prohibited with a doubt of up to 50%.

One cannot question this based on Rambam's *Laws of Kings* 10:8, which says that since Ishmaelites and the descendants of Keturah (Abraham's second wife, in Genesis ch. 25) became intermingled, they all are obligated in circumcision, which implies that a doubt is stringent for them. In that case, the descendants of Keturah are the majority (greater than 50%).

12. If idols or their associated accessories are mixed in with a majority of permitted items, the mixture is permitted. What does this mean? For example, this applies if an object that was worshiped as an idol got mixed up with some decorative figures, and it is not known which is the forbidden object; or if a goblet used for idol worship got mixed up with some other goblets and it cannot be recognized. If prohibited items of this nature became mixed together with a majority of permitted items, the whole mixture is permitted.[173]

How can this prohibited item be nullified in the majority, if it is still in the mixture, and someone will thereby derive benefit from it if the entire mixture is used? This is because the obligation to eliminate idols and their accessories does not fall on the material from which the item was made (as we see that if someone cut off an idol's head, a Gentile is permitted to benefit from its material, since the idol has been nullified for Gentiles). Rather, the only obligation is that there should not be any aspect of actual idol worship in the person's domain or possession, and this prohibition falls on the idol and the reminders of its existence as an idol, and not the material that composes it. If an idol becomes mixed in with permitted items, and it is not known which one is the idol, it has already been nullified, and its status has been annulled. The person who keeps or benefits from the mixture is not preserving or benefiting from the idol worship *per se*, but rather from the material that composes the object, and the material was never forbidden.

It is unclear if it is permitted to deliberately mix this type of forbidden item with a majority of permitted items in order to nullify it. How-

---

[173] This appears likely, since based directly from the Torah, every type of prohibited item or substance is nullified when it falls into a majority of indistinguishable items that are permitted. (In those cases for which Torah Law states that a prohibited item or substance does not become nullified as a simple minority in a mixture, it is referring to a prohibition that the Sages placed upon Jews, that they may not benefit from it.) See Tractate *Avodah Zarah* 73b. But it appears clear that in regard to the prohibition for a Gentile to benefit from items associated with idol worship, one considers only the status of the majority of the substance for another reason – namely, because the obligation for Gentiles is only to destroy the "name" (i.e., the remembrance) of the idol (which for Gentiles is not a separate obligation in and of itself, although it is for Jews). Since a Gentile who uses an item drawn out from an indistinguishable mixture does not have benefit from any recognizable idolatry, the mixture is permitted.

ever, if one did so, it appears that after the fact, it has already become nullified,[174] and it is permitted to benefit from the entire mixture.

The nullification of things that were sacrificed or offered to an idol, if they become mixed in a majority of indistinguishable permitted items, follows a different rule. See topics 9:17 and 9:18 below.

13. If forbidden forms, images, vessels, etc., were accidentally mixed with indistinguishable items that are permitted (so it is not known which of the items in the mixture were forbidden), and the permitted and forbidden items are present in the mixture *in equal amounts*, this mixture *as a whole* is forbidden, since there is no *majority* of permitted items to provide the nullification of the forbidden items. Nevertheless, it is allowed for one to destroy an amount of items from the mixture that is equal to the number of forbidden items that were originally there (one out of two, two out of four, etc.), and the remaining items will then become permitted for benefit (because of the doubt).

---

[174] It is unclear if a Gentile is allowed to make a mixture with an idolatrous item deliberately, since we find that a Jew cannot deliberately accomplish nullification of a prohibited thing in this way. Some Rabbinical authorities hold that this is a prohibition from the Torah and not a Rabbinical decree, as explained in *Shulĥan Aruĥ Yoreh De'ah* ch. 99 and Shaĥ there. According to this opinion, one is at least permitted to benefit from a mixture with a minority of forbidden items after the fact, but it is forbidden to make this mixture. This is because the Sages decreed a penalty upon *the person who made the mixture* with the prohibited substance – that *he* may not benefit from it, but it is permitted for others. Thus we can derive the concept that a mixture of forbidden and permitted items is permitted for Gentiles. Since we have not found a penalty for a Gentile in regard to this type of mixture of an idolatrous item, such a mixture is completely permitted after the fact.

It is possible that it may even be permitted for a Gentile to make this mixture deliberately, and this is not comparable to the ruling that one may not nullify a prohibition from the outset, since the penalty in that case is only upon the individual who desired to benefit from the prohibited item itself, and therefore he made the mixture. Here, however, where the actual substance is permitted to a Gentile, and the only prohibition is against preserving the "name" (remembrance) of the idolatry, we can say that there is no penalty, since this is a permitted act and one of the normal ways to nullify an idol. (An equivalent case of mixtures with meat that was severed from a live animal, which is prohibited to eat, is explained in Part IV, topic 6:10.)

The destruction of the necessary number of items may be done deliberately, and certainly it is sufficient if their destruction is accidental (for example, by falling into the sea, or being burnt, etc.). Even if the necessary number of items are:

(a) **lost from the mixture** (and even if the lost items are later found, if the same number of items from the mixture had already been consumed or sold, etc.; but if all the items from the mixture are once again intact in the possession of the original owner, the situation reverts to the original case), or

(b) **given away to another Gentile** (this should not be done from the outset, since this resembles deliberately making a mixture with idolatrous items as discussed in topic 12 above, and here also the person is causing a doubt to arise, in order to make a mixture permitted because of the doubt; but after the fact, each item is permitted because of the doubt),

then the rest are permitted because of the doubt. (See topic 11 above.)

If one adds indistinguishable permitted items (statues, vessels, etc.) into the mixture in order that the number of permitted objects will be greater than the forbidden ones, and thus the forbidden ones will be nullified, the mixture is permitted, as explained above in topic 12.[175]

14. It is forbidden to sit in the shade of an *asherah* tree or under it, whether it had been worshiped or whether there is an idol under it, since it appears as though the person is benefiting from idolatry and desires that it should be preserved. It is forbidden to walk under an *asherah* if there is another equidistant or shorter route that one could follow instead. But if there isn't another such route one could follow, he may pass under it (and it is better to do so running), since he has no intention of benefiting from the shade or the pleasant smell.

---

175 Deliberately mixing a forbidden item with permitted items in order to nullify it is questionable. But, in this case we may be more lenient, since the mixture originally happened accidentally, and we are only speaking about adding permissible pieces to make them the majority. The opinion of Rambam, in *Laws of Forbidden Foods* 15:27, and *Shulĥan Aruĥ Yoreh De'ah* 99:6, is that adding to a mixture after the fact is permitted in some cases.
*But if one sets aside some of the mixture items and designates them as prohibited for his own benefit, this accomplishes nothing, as the forbidden objects are still in his possession in the same ratio, and there is no change.

The same ruling applies for someone who is walking near a house or temple of idol worship, if he can hear the sound of the worshipers' music and singing. It is forbidden to pass by the building while the pleasant-sounding service is in progress, in order to avoid benefiting from it.[176] But if there isn't a different route that one can follow just as easily, and one does not intend to derive benefit (i.e. pleasure) from the music and singing, it is permitted to use a route that goes by that place.

15. Sticks taken from an *asherah* tree may not be benefited from. If they were nevertheless used to start the fire in a furnace or an oven, it is permitted to benefit from their heat or to cook over their coals.[177]

16. It is forbidden to derive benefit from a knife that was used for serving an idol. If one slaughtered an animal with a knife that was used for serving an idol, one may eat the animal. Similarly, if one transgressed and used other vessels of idol worship that are forbidden for benefit, for example, if one placed food in such a vessel or cooked food in it, the food is permitted.[178]

17. If there is a form or figure of an idol in the exterior surroundings or the interior of a bathhouse for decoration, and not for worship, it is permitted to bathe there.[179]

The prohibition of benefit from idol worship applies only to forms and figures that are regarded as gods that people worship, and not to figures they dishonor (for example, by urinating on a statue which stands next to a gutter). But if that is the customary way of worshiping the idol, then it is forbidden to enter that bathhouse,[180] because it is a house of idol worship.

---

[176] See above, topic 2:2.

[177] See *Taz Yoreh De'ah* 142:1.

[178] For Gentiles, Rambam rules in *Laws of the Worship of Stars [and Idols]* 9:18 that their profit and exchanges from idolatry are permitted for them, since it is not from the idolatry itself, as *Tosafot* writes on Tractate *Avodah Zarah* 64a, and as was noted in topic 5 above. In contrast, the prohibition for a Jew to benefit from anything that comes from idolatry is because for Jews, any such thing is considered to be (forbidden) like the idolatry itself.

[179] Rashi, *Tur Yoreh De'ah* ch. 142 and Shaĥ there.

[180] Rambam, *ibid.* 7:18, and *Shulĥan Aruĥ Yoreh De'ah* ch. 142.

CHAPTER 8

Aspects of Idolatry from which Benefit is Allowed, and Nullification of Idols

1. Any natural object that is not man-made and which was not physically altered in the service of an idol does not become forbidden for benefit, even if it is worshiped. Therefore, if idolaters worshiped mountains, hills, trees which grew naturally or were originally planted for a non-idolatrous purpose (e.g., for their fruit, shade, etc.), public or private springs (since they are attached to the ground[181]), a river, or an animal, then such things are still permitted for benefit (even though those who worship such things in nature are idol worshipers in the full sense, and are liable for a capital sin, as explained above in Chapter 3).

Therefore, it is permitted to eat fruits that grow on mountains, or on individual trees that were worshiped in their place of growth (see topic 8:7 below), and it is permitted to drink water from springs or rivers that were worshiped. Likewise, an animal which had been set aside for idolatry, whether to be worshiped or sacrificed, is permitted for benefit so long as its body has not been physically altered as a result of any act of idolatry being committed upon it.

However, if an act related to idolatry is committed upon an animal which involves a physical change in its body (as opposed to worshiping it from a distance, which does not involve any manipulation of the animal), then the animal becomes forbidden to benefit from.[182] For example, as soon as one begins to slaughter an animal for the sake of idol worship (which might involve cutting a vital passage in the animal's neck, or cutting a hole opposite its heart, in the manner of some idol worshipers), even if the act was not completed, the animal becomes forbidden for benefit, because it becomes an object that has been offered to an idol.[183]

---

[181] Shaĥ *Yoreh De'ah* 145:2, and Taz *Yoreh De'ah* 145:3

[182] *But if a person merely moves or waves it as a service of idol worship, this does not make the animal prohibited for benefit, since the body of the animal has not been changed. Likewise, if a person paints an animal or shears its hair as a service to an idol, the animal itself is not forbidden, because these are not permanent changes. **(For nullification of idol statues, see topic 16 below.)**

[183] Rambam, *ibid.* 8:1; *Shulĥan Aruĥ Yoreh De'ah* ch. 145.

2. If one sacrificed someone else's animal to an idol, or performed some other act of idolatry with it that physically altered it (for example, if one begins to make a slaughtering cut on his friend's animal for the sake of an idol), the animal becomes forbidden.

3. If someone bows down to the ground as an act of worshiping it, this does not make that area forbidden.

A hole, pit or cave that was dug as an act of idol worship may not be used, even if one did not yet bow down to it. If one wishes to nullify it, he must add back what was taken out. This is similar to the case of a house or stone, which is explained in topics 11 and 12 below.

4. A wave on a natural body of water that was bowed down to is not forbidden for benefit, but if one took the water out with his hand or with a vessel and had then bowed down to it, it is forbidden for benefit. Boulders that had been moved by natural causes, such as a landslide, and that were worshiped in the place where they came to rest, are permitted for benefit, because they are natural objects which have moved naturally, and not by the influence of a person.[184]

5. Something natural that is not altered by a person who worships it, such as a mountain, animal or tree, is permitted for benefit, but its "coverings" and "utensils" are forbidden for benefit[185] (see Chapter 9).

6. If a Jew set up one of his "bricks" (a generic term for any of his belongings) in order to bow down to it, but did not do so, and then a Gentile came along and bowed to it, it becomes forbidden for benefit, because its being set up to be worshiped was an act of dedication.[186]

However, if a Gentile set up a different brick that belongs to this Jew and bowed down to it, it does not become forbidden, because *one cannot make forbidden for benefit an object that is not his, even if he sets up or raises the object and worships it, as long as he doesn't make*

---

[184] Rambam *ibid.* 8:2; *Shulĥan Aruĥ ibid.* ch. 145; Shaĥ *ibid.* 145:1.

[185] *Examples of a "covering" are a cloth covering an item connected to a worshiped hill, or a silver tray placed on a mountain to ordain it as an idol. An example of a "utensil" is a fire pan for burning incense as a service of worshiping a beast.

[186] Rambam *ibid.* 8:3; Rema *Yoreh De'ah* ch. 139.

an alteration in the object itself.

How is this explained? In the first case, the Jew dedicated his own object *as an idol.* A Jew's *idol* only becomes forbidden when it is worshiped by him *or* someone else (even though it does not belong to the other person, since it was already designated as an idol, as explained above in topic 7:4). This is because an actual worship of the idol is needed to make it forbidden, if it belongs to a Jew. But in the second case, it is possible that the Jew only desired to dedicate the first brick as an idol, but not any of his other bricks.)[187]

It goes without saying that one who bows down to an object that is not his – like one who was walking on a public path and bowed down to a statue that was made for decoration – is liable for bowing down to it (see topic 3:28 above). But the object does not become forbidden for benefit, because one cannot make forbidden for benefit something that isn't one's own, if he doesn't alter it.

But if one alters an object as an act of idol worship – e.g. slaughtering an animal (mentioned in topic 8:1), or chiseling a stone or brick – it becomes forbidden, even if it does not belong to the worshiper.

7. A tree that was planted by a Gentile[188] for the purpose of being worshiped may not be used. The Torah calls this an *asherah.*[189]

If a tree was planted previously without this intention, and was later (a) trimmed or cut for the sake of idol worship, or (b) if one of its branches had then been bent down and forced into the ground in order to grow into another tree for idol worship, or (c) if a branch of another tree had been grafted to it for idol worship – and then if new growth came out from one of those parts that was prepared for idol worship, then the new growth is forbidden for benefit, and it must be cut off and destroyed (as are any parts that were trimmed or nurtured to grow for the sake of idol worship). However, the rest of the tree may be used.

Similarly, even though the trunk of a tree that had been worshiped does not become forbidden for benefit if it was not planted for this purpose (since it is considered to be a natural object that did not come about from an act of a person, as explained previously in topic 8:1) – nevertheless, all the shoots, leaves, branches or fruit that grew while

---

[187] Shaĥ *Yoreh De'ah* 139:1.

[188] Shaĥ *Yoreh De'ah* 145:4.

[189] Deuteronomy 12:3.

the tree was being served are forbidden, and must be destroyed.[190]

8. If idolaters harvest the fruit of a tree to make wine or beer that is used (or planned to be used) for the service of an idol (for example, for libations), or for drinking in the festive celebrations for an idol, then the entire tree is forbidden for benefit, and this is also called a type of *asherah*. The idolaters made the ritual wine or beer from its fruit, and this is a traditional procedure that is followed with an *asherah*.[191]

9. A tree that was planted in order to stand up an idol beneath it is forbidden for benefit all the time that the idol is under it, but if it is removed, the tree is permitted; this is because the tree itself is not being worshiped.[192]

10. Any tree (including a non-fruit tree) planted beside an idol, or beside an idol's altar or house of worship,[193] is a forbidden decoration for the idol, and is therefore an *asherah*. Likewise, trees that are brought into houses of worship to celebrate the birthday of Yeshua are forbidden as long as they remain there. In private houses or businesses, it appears that they are not forbidden for benefit if they bear no symbols of the religion, if they are only used as a custom and not as an aid in worshiping with prayers or songs. They would certainly be permitted for benefit after being discarded (a clear act of nullification).

11. A building is not something that is naturally attached to the ground, but rather its parts were originally disconnected from the ground, and afterwards became attached. Therefore, a building that was constructed by idolaters for the purpose of being served as an idol is forbidden for benefit and must be destroyed or nullified, and likewise for a building that was constructed for other purposes but was converted into an idol by being bowed down to.[194]

If a building was constructed for purposes other than idolatry, and it was later plastered for the purpose of becoming an idol; or if idols

---

[190] Rambam, *ibid.* 8:3; *Shulĥan Aruĥ Yoreh De'ah* ch. 145.

[191] Rambam *ibid.*, and *Shulĥan Aruĥ ibid.*

[192] Rambam *ibid.* 8:4; *Shulĥan Aruĥ ibid.*

[193] Ramban on Deuteronomy 15:21.

[194] Tractate *Avodah Zarah* 47b.

were later attached onto it so the entire building could be bowed down to; or if an addition was made that was bowed down to – then all that was added to convert it into an idol should be removed and destroyed, but the rest of the original (non-idolatrous) building is permitted. (If one removed only a significant part of the idolatrous addition, after the fact the rest is permitted, since by doing so, its connection to being worshiped was nullified.)[195]

A house into which an actual idol has been brought is forbidden until the idol is nullified, if the house was dedicated for the service of that idol. But if an actual idol was brought in only temporarily (or if it was brought in but the house was not dedicated for its service), the house is forbidden for use only as long as the idol is inside the house.[196] Once the idol has been removed, the house may once again be used.[197]

12. A stone that had been hewn for idolatrous purposes is forbidden for benefit. One nullifies it by damaging it. If, after having been hewn, it was sculpted or tiled for the sake of being worshiped, then even if the sculpted or tiled parts were in the very body of the stone, these parts are forbidden for benefit because they were made for idolatry. If someone removed the parts that had been added for idol worship, in order to damage and thereby nullify it, the stone becomes permitted.

A stone that an idolater set up to place an idol upon is forbidden to derive benefit from, since it was dedicated as a base for the idol. If it was set up only temporarily, it may not be used so long as the idol is standing upon it, but once the idol has been removed, the stone is again permitted for benefit.

---

[195] Shaĥ and Taz *ibid.* 145:3. This is sufficient even for those idolaters themselves, and therefore it applies for any other Gentiles as well; see topic 13.

[196] *This applies to private homes (see topic 2:2 above). However, minor children of idol worshipers are exempt from the prohibition to live in their parents' home when the idols are there. The prohibition does not apply if a building needs to be entered for the purpose of healing – for example, a hospital that contains idols.

[197] *Shulĥan Aruĥ ibid.* 145:3. This can also be noted from Gen. 24:31, "I have cleared the house." Rashi explains, based on Midrash *Bereishit Rabbah* there, that Laban cleared his father's house from idols before Eliezer, the righteous servant of Abraham, arrived there. This implies that Laban understood that Eliezer observed the prohibition to enter a house that had idols in it.

13. An object that was formerly an idol belonging to a Gentile is permitted for benefit if its status as an idol has been nullified. Any Gentile can fully nullify any idol for any other Gentile, whether it belongs to him or to any other person, even if he is compelled to do so against his own will. Even if one Gentile serves one idol, and a second Gentile serves a different idol, each is able to nullify the idol of the other. Even a nullification performed by a righteous Gentile who observes the Noahide Code is acceptable.[198]

The one who nullifies an idol's status must recognize the meaning of idol worship; therefore, a Gentile child or a significantly mentally deficient person cannot nullify an idol.[199]

14. A Jew cannot nullify the status of an idol, whether it is his or a Gentile's. A Jew's idol can never be nullified; it stays in its forbidden

---

[198] Rambam (*ibid.*, 8:9) explains that one who does not worship or submit himself to an idol cannot nullify it. It appears that this refers to a nullification that makes it permitted for a Jew. However, it becomes permitted for a Gentile even if the person who nullified the idol was not an idol worshiper.

See Tractate *Avodah Zarah* 44a: "Itti the Gittite came and nullified [the precious crown of Ammon, which was an idol]." Itti was a friend of David, and it is not logical that he would serve idols. Rather, he was a *Ger Toshav* (a Gentile "Resident" of the Holy Land who had declared before a Jewish Court that he would faithfully observe the Noahide Commandments). Nevertheless, he nullified the idols of the Philistines and Ammonites, as is explained there. Even if one would say that he was still an idol worshiper during the story of the wood of the Philistines, he surely was not serving idols in the second episode of Ammon (see Samuel II, ch. 5 and 12). Rather, we must say that from Torah Law itself, any Gentile can nullify any idol, even if he doesn't serve it, and especially if he is familiar with its ways; and although the Sages decreed that it cannot be nullified by a righteous Gentile who has resolved to worship only God, we can say that the Sages did not extend this decree to a case of significant need – for example, for the sake of a Jewish king (in this case, David). This is consistent with the fact that, for the sake of the needs of Jewish kings, the Sages set aside other Rabbinical decrees that they had placed upon Jews in general. Although Rashi on Tractate *Kedushin* 76b comments that Itti was an idol worshiper, it is possible that he means that Itti was *previously* an idol worshiper, and therefore had the ability to nullify an idol for any Jew, even though he (Itti) no longer served idols.

[199] Rambam, *ibid.* 8:9; *Shulĥan Aruĥ ibid.* ch. 146. See Part I, topic 4:4, regarding age of majority and conditions of mental incompetency.

state and must be destroyed. Therefore, if an idol belonging to a Jew came into the possession of a Gentile, who subsequently attempted to nullify its status, then the nullification is meaningless and the idol is forever forbidden for benefit.[200]

This only applies if the Jew actually served the idol. But if it was only in his possession and he did not serve it, and a Gentile bought it from him or received it as a gift, the Gentile can nullify its status.[201]

If the Jew owned the idol in partnership with a Gentile, the Gentile can nullify the status of his share in the idol, but he cannot nullify the Jew's share. (Therefore, the idol may be melted down or cut in two, so the part taken by the Gentile becomes permitted for him as being nullified, but the part taken by the Jew must be destroyed.)[202]

15. The nullification of an idol automatically includes any associated accessories (its decorations and all vessels used to serve it; even if these items belonged to a Jew, the Gentile's nullification of the idol nullifies the status of these as well).[203] But it does not nullify the idolatrous status of items that were offerings to the idol.[204]

---

[200] Rambam *ibid.* and *Shulĥan Aruĥ Yoreh De'ah* ch. 146.

[201] The ruling that an idol possessed by a Jew cannot be nullified is a decree of the Sages, as explained in Tractate *Avodah Zarah* 42a and *Yoreh De'ah* ch. 146, and this decree was only enacted upon the Jews, but not upon Gentiles, so any nullification is effective for any Gentile. A Gentile's nullification is effective for a Jew as well.

[202] *Shulĥan Aruĥ ibid.*

[203] Rema *Yoreh De'ah* 146:13. **An idol or its service vessels can be nullified by permanently damaging them in a way that demonstrates that they will no longer be used for idol worship, since their dignity and importance have been degraded** (or for vessels, if the idol they were used to serve has been nullified and thus degraded). See topic 16 which follows.

[204] This is based on Rambam, *ibid.*, and *Shulĥan Aruĥ ibid.* ch. 139, that (a) an offering to an idol can never be nullified by a *Jew*, and (b) an offering does not become nullified by nullifying the status of its idol (unlike the vessels used to serve an idol, which *are* nullified automatically through the idol's nullification, because they are secondary to the idol). It is explained in topics 9:17-19 below that an offering to an idol *can* become nullified for Gentiles, but not in the same way as an idol or vessels used to serve an idol. Items that are sacrificed or offered to an idol (and perhaps eaten as part of this service) are different – they are a distinct form of actual worship.

If the idolatrous status of only the associated accoutrements is nullified, the idol itself remains forbidden for benefit (until the idol itself has been nullified).[205]

16. **How is nullification of an idol performed? By cutting off the tip of the nose, ear or finger of the idol,[206] or smashing its face with a hammer even without removing anything.** A metal idol may be sold to a Jewish smelter (for he will surely melt it down). These are all methods of nullification.[207] Likewise, if a Gentile gave his idol as a deposit to a Jewish smelter, and the Gentile did not return to redeem it (unless the Gentile could not return due to some problem – for example, if he had to flee in a time of war), it is surely nullified.[208]

In contrast, if an idol was pledged or sold to a Gentile (even one who doesn't worship idols), or to a Jew who isn't a smelter; or if a building collapsed on it (even without any of its worshipers trying to retrieve it from the debris); or if it was stolen by bandits (even without any of its worshipers trying to recover it); or if it was smashed on an area other than the head – these are not methods of nullification.

Spitting at an idol, urinating in front of it, dragging it on the ground, or throwing feces on it are not acts of nullification.[209] Some Rabbinical authorities say that this applies only if one spat at the idol or urinated before it temporarily, whereas if one does so repeatedly, or even if he says that he is nullifying it and consents to do so, it is nullified.

But if a Gentile is being forced to nullify an idol, then merely voicing his annulment, or spitting or urinating on it, is not sufficient; only breaking or damaging the idol will nullify it.[210]

---

[205] Rambam *ibid.*; *Shulĥan Aruĥ Yoreh De'ah* ch. 146.

[206] **It appears that one needs to remove something consequential and noticeable from the idol – see topic 5:9 above and the last footnote there.**

[207] Rambam *ibid.* 8:10. In *Shulĥan Aruĥ ibid.* 146:8, there are differences of opinion in this regard, and for Gentiles the lenient opinion is followed.

[208] Shaĥ *Yoreh De'ah* 146:10.

[209] Rambam *ibid.* and *Shulĥan Aruĥ ibid.*

[210] Rema *Yoreh De'ah* 146:8.

17. An idol that has been deserted by its worshipers in a time of peace may be used for benefit, because a desertion of this nature is an act of nullification. However, if an idol is deserted in a time of war, it is not considered nullified and is still forbidden, because the worshipers probably deserted it only on account of the war.

Identifiable parts that have broken off an idol are forbidden for benefit until their status has been nullified.[211] It appears that this applies specifically in places where it is known that people serve broken parts of idols, like those who will serve a hand or other limb of an idol that represents a star or constellation (as explained earlier in topic 7:7). But other idols that do not include a practice of serving their broken limbs are surely nullified in this case.[212] (This is only the case if they were found in their original respectable fashion, when they surely were not nullified, and they were only broken accidentally. But if they were found discarded elsewhere, they are surely nullified through abandonment, as explained earlier in topic 7:7).

However, if a person (including a Jew) deliberately broke an idol into separated limbs, the idol has been nullified, and these parts are permitted for benefit.[213]

If the broken-off parts of the idol are such that any non-skilled person could easily reassemble them, then each and every part requires separate nullification. However, if even just one of these broken-off limbs of the idol had its status nullified, all of the parts are nullified after the fact.[214]

---

[211] Rambam *ibid.*, 8:11; *Shulĥan Aruĥ ibid.*

[212] This appears to be the ruling for Gentiles, and is not comparable to what is explained (by Rambam *ibid.* and *Shulĥan Aruĥ ibid.*) that for a Jew, it has yet to become nullified, and this is only from doubt. But for a Gentile it is surely nullified by itself.

[213] See Tractate *Avodah Zarah* 42a: for a Gentile, an idol that was smashed by a Jew is considered as if it was broken accidentally, which is accepted for a Gentile as a means of nullification.

[214] Based on Rambam, *Laws of Sources of Ritual Impurity* 6:4, we see that this is considered nullification in regards to the ritual impurity of an idol. Therefore, after the fact, it is considered a nullification for Gentiles as well. This is surely the case if a person did it knowingly and was not forced, and this is no less than the opinion of Rema (topic 8:16 above), that voicing the nullification alone suffices.

If the parts are such that a non-skilled person could not easily reassemble them, then if even just one limb of the idol had its status nullified, the status of the rest of the pieces is automatically nullified as well.[215]

18. If an altar that was used for idol worship became damaged, it remains forbidden for benefit unless the majority of the altar has been broken. An idol's pedestal that became damaged may be used. What is the difference between a pedestal and an altar? A pedestal consists of one stone or column, whereas an altar consists of many stones.[216]

19. Any stone that appears to have been thrown to a *Merculis* idol (or connected with its worship in some other way – for example, a stone that served as part of this idol) is forbidden, since it is part of the idol's worship ritual.[217]

How can the status of stones thrown to *Merculis* be nullified? If they have already been used for building purposes, or if they are found in the paving of a road, or for some similar secular purpose, they are permitted for benefit.[218]

20. How is the status of an *asherah* tree nullified?[219] Removal of a leaf, twig, stick or branch of the *asherah*, or any other unnecessary pruning, are all means of nullification. However, if it was pruned for a necessity, to improve or maintain the tree as an *asherah*, it remains forbidden for benefit, but the clippings may be used.[220]

---

[215] Rambam, *Laws of the Worship of Stars [and Idols]* 8:11; *Shulĥan Aruĥ Yoreh De'ah ibid.*

[216] Rambam *ibid.*, 8:12.

[217] Tractate *Avodah Zarah* 51a; Rambam *ibid.*, 7:16.

[218] Rambam *ibid.*, 8:12; *Shulĥan Aruĥ ibid.*

[219] *If an idolater who worshiped or served an *asherah* tree subsequently chopped up the tree or left it for disposal in a garbage dump, this constitutes a nullification of its status as an object of idol worship.

[220] Rambam *ibid.* and *Shulĥan Aruĥ ibid.*

CHAPTER 9

Objects Offered to Idols, and Decorations of Idols

1. It is forbidden to derive any benefit from an animal that has been offered (meaning slaughtered or killed[221]) for an idol. Everything from the animal's carcass is forbidden to benefit from – even its excrement, bones, horns, hooves and hide. Therefore, if there was a mark on an animal skin identifying it as coming from an animal that had been offered to an idol, then it is forbidden to derive any benefit from that skin. For example, such a mark could be a round hole that had been cut in the skin adjacent to the heart, in order to remove the heart (during an idolatrous sacrificial ritual). All hides like this are forbidden for benefit, as is anything else of similar nature.[222]

2. Likewise, wine poured out as a libation to an idol is an offering, and it is forbidden to drink or benefit from it.[223]

3. Any natural object (such as a star, mountain, tree or animal) that

---

[221] See *Or Same'aĥ* on Rambam, *ibid.* 7:3.

[222] Rambam, *ibid.*

[223] Tractate *Avodah Zarah* 29b; Rambam, *ibid.* 7:15 and *Laws of Forbidden Foods* ch. 11; Ramban on Tractate Avodah Zarah 59b in regard to Gentiles.

Rambam holds that the prohibition against benefiting from an item offered to an idol is understood from two prohibitions: (a) the general prohibition of benefiting from all types of idol worship, as the Torah says (Deut. 7:26), "Do not bring an abomination into your home," and (b) the separate prohibition, (Deut. 13:18) "Nothing of that which is condemned may remain in your hand," as he explains in *Laws of the Worship of Stars [and Idols]* 7:2. There is a separate prohibition for items offered to an idol, from the verse (Deut. 32:38), "[Where is their god,] the fat of whose sacrifices they would eat; they would drink the wine of their libations?" as explained in *Laws of Forbidden Foods* 11:1, and *Sefer HaMitzvot* Negative Commandments 25 and 194.

Ramban on Negative Commandment 194 says that the prohibition of benefiting from an item offered to an idol is not included in the prohibition of benefiting from the idol itself, but is rather a separate prohibition, from Exodus 34:15: "Guard yourself lest you make a covenant … and he will call to you and you will eat from his sacrifices." For implications of these specific sources, and the opinions of Rambam and Ramban, see footnotes 225, 229.

was worshiped as a deity, but which was not altered by the worshiper through an act of the idol worship, does not become forbidden for benefit (as explained above in topics 8:1-7). However, any "coverings" of a natural object that is served as an idol become decorations for idolatry, and are forbidden to benefit from (see note for topic 8:5).[224]

It is permitted to benefit from an offering brought to a star, the moon, a cloud, a mountain or a sea, or any other natural entity that is attached to the earth, and the offered item does not become forbidden (for example, an animal that was slaughtered as a means of serving a mountain as a deity).[225] (However, some of the Rabbinical authorities say that the offered item does become forbidden. But if one performed such a deed with the intention of bringing a healing, and he did not accept the entity as a god, they also agree that it is not forbidden.)

If one slaughtered with the intention of worshiping the angel of a star, mountain or sea, etc., the slaughtered animal is considered an offering for an idol, and it is forbidden for benefit.[226]

4. If an animal is worshiped as an idol, items offered to it as part of its idolatrous service are forbidden for benefit (e.g., fruit that is offered before it, or another animal that is slaughtered as part of its service).[227]

5. Meat or wine that had been set aside specifically to be offerings to an idol are not forbidden for benefit, even if they were brought into the temple of the idol. Once they have been offered, though, they have the status of a sacrifice. If the worshipers then moved them from the idol's temple to continue their service or to benefit from them (for example,

---

[224] Rambam, *Laws of the Worship of Stars [and Idols]* 8:7.

[225] *Shulĥan Aruĥ ibid.* 4:5. See Shaĥ *ibid.* 4:8 and 145:7, that there are dissenting opinions, as apparent from the opinion of Rambam (see topic 3:12 above). Possibly he holds that the only prohibition of a Gentile to benefit from an item offered to an idol is from the general prohibition of benefit from an idol, but something offered to a mountain is only forbidden from the verse (Deut. 32:38), "[Where is their god,] the fat of whose sacrifices they would eat; they would drink the wine of their libations?" which applies solely to Jews. Therefore, if a Gentile slaughtered for a mountain to serve it, it is possible that Rambam would agree that it does not enter the category of items offered to a man-made idol, and it is permitted for benefit.

[226] *Shulĥan Aruĥ ibid.* ch. 4.

[227] Rema on *Shulĥan Aruĥ ibid.* 145:8.

to eat them), they remain forbidden for benefit forever.[228]

6. Performing any type of "offering" that is customary for a sect of idolatry is considered part of its service, which makes one liable for idol worship (and the item offered becomes forbidden).

However, this does not mean that every type of item set before an idol is forbidden for any benefit. Only an item that is at least somewhat equivalent to the offerings that were brought for the service of God in His Holy Temple are forbidden to benefit from, if they are merely placed before an idol. These types of items become forbidden by being placed before an idol, even if it is not customary to serve that particular idol with that particular type of item.

An item cannot be considered offered if it was merely placed before an idol, unless it has a corresponding type of offering that is allowed for the Altar in the Holy Temple.[229] These items are: the meat of a cow, goat, or sheep, whether male or female; female or male doves;[230] oil, wine, flour, bread, water, salt, blood,[231] wheat sheaves or grapes (those which are fitting to make into a meal offering or wine), and

---

[228] Rambam *ibid.* 7:15; *Shulĥan Aruĥ ibid.*

[229] *Tur* and *Shulĥan Aruĥ ibid.* The opinion of Rambam is that *any* item placed before an idol is forbidden for benefit by Torah Law, and he clearly states this regarding fruits (*ibid.*). This does not necessarily apply only to something like those things that were offered on the Altar in the Holy Temple, or actions that are comparable to the service of the Altar. However, most opinions hold that an item placed before an idol is forbidden only if it is comparable to an item that was offered on the Altar, or if something was done to it that is comparable to a service in the Holy Temple. This argument is based on the reasoning and source for forbidding an offering to an idol, as is explained in the footnote to topic 2 above. According to Rambam, this prohibition is from the general prohibition to benefit from idol worship; therefore any type of offering to an idol is forbidden to benefit from, as is the idol itself. But according to Ramban and others, there is an explicit verse for this prohibition (Exodus 34:15): "Guard yourself lest you make a covenant … and he will call to you and you will eat from his sacrifices." This indicates that the offerings that are forbidden when only placed before an idol are those that are similar to one of the offerings that was brought in the Holy Temple.

[230] This does not apply to other types of meat – see *Taz Yoreh De'ah* 139:5.

[231] This is clear, since it was sprinkled on the Altar, and is really a type of food like oil, though it is forbidden for Jews to drink it.

olives that are fitting to make into oil.[232] All these are forbidden as offered items, even if they are only brought and set down before the idol, without any action performed with their actual substance (i.e., an action such as slaughtering an animal, or the like).

Bringing a live animal before an idol does not define it as an offered item, until a person serves the idol by performing an action with the animal that alters its substance (such as slaughtering); see topic 8:1.

7. Foods not cited specifically in the preceding topic (including other species of produce) do not become forbidden as offered items if they are *only* set down before an idol (even if this was the customary way to serve the idol). This is because they are not the types of items that were brought in the service of God on the Altar in the Holy Temple.

This applies so long as no action was performed with them resembling an activity that was part of the service in the Holy Temple.

But if one performed an action in the service of an idol with any item – if it resembles one of the Temple services of slaughtering, pouring a libation, or burning – the item becomes forbidden as an offering, and one may not derive benefit from it. For example, if one slaughtered (for an idol) any domestic or wild animal, bird or locust (whether or not the creature was a *kosher* species), it is forbidden as an offering, because the person performed an action with it that resembles the service of slaughtering that is to be done in the Holy Temple.

Therefore, if one cut vegetation as a service to an idol that is customarily served in some way with vegetation, this is comparable to the service of slaughtering in the Holy Temple, and the vegetation that is cut becomes forbidden. (See topic 3:15 above.)

If one served an idol by pouring (from a vessel; see topic 3:18 above) a libation of blood, wine, water or any respectable liquid (to exclude urine, putrid water and the like) this is considered offering, since it is an action that resembles the pouring or sprinkling of blood on the Altar in the Holy Temple. Likewise, burning any item before an idol defines it as an offered item, since this action resembles the burning of offerings that was part of the service in the Holy Temple.

---

[232] See Rosh on *Avodah Zarah* 50a, where Rabbi Yoĥanan holds that only *foods* become forbidden as "offerings" by setting them down before an idol. Incense and frankincense are non-food items, and are not considered offered items unless they are burned as a service to an idol. See topic 9:7 here.

All these types of actions, when they are considered to resemble the offerings made to God in the Holy Temple (i.e., they resemble slaughtering, pouring a libation, or burning), make one liable for a capital sin if they are performed in the service of an idol, even if it is not the customary way of serving the idol.[233]

8. If an idol is customarily served with a stick, and a person broke a stick before it, this action defines the broken stick as an offered item. This is because a stick is a significant item for this idol, so breaking it before the idol is considered comparable to slaughter. But if a stick is not customarily used in the rituals of the idol, it does not become forbidden; since the stick is not a significant item for the idol, breaking it is not considered to have any significance.[234] Likewise, for an idol whose ritual was customarily performed with urine, if one poured urine before it, it is forbidden for benefit as an offered item.[235]

9. Vessels or clothes and the like, that are items that were not brought upon the Altar of the Holy Temple, are not forbidden for benefit if they are merely brought or thrown before an idol. Therefore, if they were merely set down before an idol for its sake, they are permitted for benefit. But if it is unknown how they were used for the idol, it is assumed that they are decorations for it, which makes them forbidden for benefit.[236] If one tears clothing or breaks a vessel as a service to an idol, this is comparable to the breaking of a stick, so if this idol's customary ritual is any service with clothes or vessels, respectively, this is considered comparable to slaughtering.[237] Likewise, any burning of clothes as service for an idol is comparable to burning on the Altar.

---

[233] See *Tur* and *Shulĥan Aruĥ ibid.* ch. 139, in regard to slaughter of a locust.

[234] *Tur* and *Shulĥan Aruĥ ibid.*

[235] See topic 3:17 above in regard to pouring urine. There is no concept of forbidden pouring of this substance unless the idol was customarily served in this fashion (using urine in any way). If this is the customary ritual, then it would be a significant service for the idol, and therefore it would be classified as pouring a libation.

[236] *Shulĥan Aruĥ ibid.* ch. 139.

[237] See Meiri on Tractate *Avodah Zarah* 47 in regard to a sandal brought to an idol, which was originally set aside for this purpose.

10. Clothes, vessels or money found discarded in an irreverent manner on the top of an idol are permitted for benefit, but if they had been placed there in a reverent manner, they are forbidden for benefit, because they are decoration for idolatry. If, for example, one found a pouch suspended by a rope hanging from the idol, or a folded garment or a vessel upside down on its head, or similar situations, then one may use them, for they have been placed there in an irreverent manner. On the other hand, if one found on the head of the idol something of a type that was offered on the Altar in the Holy Temple, it is forbidden for benefit even if it was placed there in an irreverent manner.[238]

11. Any item that is forbidden when offered to an idol, if found inside a house of idol worship, or before an idol or in its enclosed area, whether arranged in an irreverent manner or not, is forbidden for use.

If one finds something of this nature outside of these areas in the nearby vicinity, and it is found in a reverent condition, and appears to be a decoration for the idol, it is forbidden; if not, it is permitted if it is an idol that is served in a reverent manner. But anything that might be an offering to an idol that is served in a degrading manner (for example, with excrement or by throwing stones at it), if found inside or just outside of their temples, is forbidden for benefit. This is because such idols are customarily served irreverently, and those who worship them are not careful to place their offerings in a reverent manner.[239]

12. Candles that were burning before an idol for its decoration[240] are forbidden for benefit. If the idol's priests put out the candles in order to

---

[238] Rambam *ibid.* ch. 7, and *Shulĥan Aruĥ ibid.*

(The latter ruling is unclear: the reason it is forbidden, although it was placed on the idol's head irreverently, is because it has already been offered. But in regard to Gentiles, its ruling should be as a decoration that becomes nullified through its use in an irreverent manner. If it is food, it is possible that even though it was nullified, others may not eat it, since one who eats of an offered food shows that he recognizes the idol, and its nullification only allows one to benefit from it in other ways, such as selling it.)

[239] Rambam *ibid.*; *Shulĥan Aruĥ ibid.*

[240] *Tosafot* on *Avodah Zarah* 50; *Shulĥan Aruĥ ibid.* See Rambam *ibid.* 7:15. They may be made of fat, which was an item burned on the Holy Temple's Altar, so it cannot be nullified if it is placed before an idol as an offering. If they are decorative only, even if they are made of fat, they can be nullified.

sell them, they have already nullified them,[241] but if the candles went out by themselves, they have not been nullified. If the priests sold the candles to one who doesn't worship that idol, they are nullified.[242]

Pieces of wax that are designated to make into candles for an idol's temple (even if they are placed before the idol with that intention) are permitted for benefit, since they are not decorations or offered items, and there is no *hekdesh* ("consecration") of an item that was merely dedicated to be used for idolatry.[243]

13. Priests' clothes that they wear upon entering their idol's temples are decorations for them and not for their idols, and they do not require nullification to make them permitted to benefit from.

Something that is worn upon the statue or image of an actual idol is called its decoration. Any vessels or rugs that are spread out before the idol for its decoration are likewise forbidden, and require nullification for them to be permitted for benefit.[236]

14. Flowers and spices that adorn an idol are decorations, and it is forbidden to benefit from them or to smell them.[244] Of course it is forbidden to smell the scent of incense that is burned for idol worship.[245]

15. A goblet that a priest used to pour wine to an idol (either as a drink for the idol, or as a means of worshiping it), or a pan that was used for burning an offering or incense, are vessels used for the idol's service, and it is forbidden to benefit from them unless they are nullified.[236]

---

[241] This is apparent from the words of the *Shulĥan Aruĥ ibid.* ch. 139: "since he put them out for his own sake" – meaning for the sake of the priest, from which we see that he has already nullified them. The same applies even if he sold them to others, and not specifically to a Jew. This is also implied from *Tosafot* on Tractate *Avodah Zarah* 50a and Ran there.

[242] See the last footnote to topic 15 below.

[243] *Shulĥan Aruĥ ibid.* This applies to those who dedicate wax to make candles, for there is no *hekdesh* (consecration) of items dedicated for an idol. However, if the pieces of wax were placed before the idol as a decoration or for their scent as part of its worship ritual, they are forbidden as a decoration, like a rose or myrtle that is used for that purpose (see topic 9:14).

[244] *Shulĥan Aruĥ ibid.* ch. 108; *Avodah Zarah* 12b: "a rose or myrtle by which they benefit from their scent," because of their function as decorations.

[245] *Tosafot* and Ritva on Tractate *Avodah Zarah* 12b.

Any vessel used for a service of idol worship or as a decoration for an idol, which one sold or gave away as a present to a non-idolater, has become nullified.[246]

16. Bread loaves that worshipers give to the priests of idols are permitted for benefit. They are not considered offered items, but rather as a gift for the priests.[236]

All types of breads, crackers, wine or other foods which are brought before an idol and then afterwards given by the priests to the worshipers are forbidden for benefit and eating, as offered items.

17. It has been previously explained in Chapter 7 that an actual idol, and items used for its service or offered to it, are forbidden to preserve, and there is an obligation to destroy them *(or nullify them)* so that there remains nothing left of idol worship or anything associated with it. If its decorations, or items offered to it, became mixed in with other indistinguishable items of the same type that are permitted, the forbidden items can become nullified in a majority of permitted items.

How does this rule work for a mixture of *offered* items? If pieces of offered meat became mixed with pieces of non-offered meat, or if libation wine that was poured for an idol became mixed with regular wine, the mixture is permitted if there is a majority of permitted substance.[247] However, one should dispose of an amount of the mixture equal to the amount of the forbidden pieces of meat, or the volume of

---

[246] *Tur* and *Beit Yosef* (*Yoreh De'ah* ch. 139). The sale of an idol's service vessel to a Jew nullifies it, and this is not comparable to the idol itself, which does not become nullified unless it is sold to a Jewish smelter (in the case of a metal idol). It appears that this also applies to someone that the idol worshiper knows does not serve idols, such a pious Gentile who observes the Noahide Code, since he surely will nullify it in such a case.

[247] Even though the ruling is that for Jews, an offered item cannot become nullified (so even if the forbidden item was mixed with a thousand times more of permitted items, it is all forbidden for a Jew), for Gentiles the general rule for an offered item is like that of all other idols and vessels used to serve them, which is that they *can* be nullified. How so? In a mixture they are nullified to the majority, since from the Torah Law itself, anything can be nullified in a majority. (From the basic Torah Law, even wine poured to an idol can be nullified in a majority; the stringency that the Sages added regarding the use of such a mixture by Jews does not apply to Gentiles).

forbidden wine, that became mixed with the permitted meat or wine. In this way, one forgoes the amount of benefit he would have had from the amount of the forbidden substance that became mixed in.

Why, in regard to the nullification of idol statues or their accessories in a mixture, is the ruling that the entire mixture is permitted (as explained in topic 7:12), but for a mixture of *offered food items* together with an indistinguishable permitted substance, one must dispose of an amount of the mixture that is equal to the original amount of forbidden substance?[248] This is because eating food is a pleasure for the body, and the person will also have pleasure from making use of some of the forbidden substance that is mixed in. Therefore, this mixing is not a true nullification, until one removes an amount of the mixture that is equal to the amount of forbidden substance that was originally present in the mixture. Consequently, the person will effectively not have any additional benefit from the forbidden substance.

If offered meat or wine became mixed with unlike items, such as meat that became mixed with vegetables, or wine that became mixed with water or a cooked dish, if the substance of the forbidden item is still recognizable, one may not eat from the whole mixture. If only its taste is recognizable, it is permitted to eat the whole mixture.[249]

---

[248] *Incense that became forbidden might come to be mixed with permitted incense, if the forbidden incense had been partially burnt and then it extinguished on its own. (See topic 9:7, that incense does not become an "offering" that is forbidden to benefit from until it is actually burned in service to an idol. But if it is only placed before an idol without burning, it is permitted to benefit from.) The mixture then becomes subject to the same rules of nullification as forbidden meat in a mixture, explained above, because of the physical benefit from the added forbidden incense. On the other hand, if the idol worshiper puts out the burning incense, that is an act of nullifying it (as in topic 12 above regarding candles, unless it is specifically the ritual of the idol's worship to only partially burn the incense).

[249] With unlike items, whenever the forbidden item can be distinguished, it cannot be nullified in a mixture. This is a Torah prohibition, as explained by Rambam, *Laws of Forbidden Foods* ch. 15. If one can only taste the forbidden item, Rambam's opinion is that the mixture is not forbidden from the Torah Law itself. Furthermore, it is explained below in Part IV, Chapter 6, that the Rabbinical ruling (that a noticeable taste of a forbidden substance renders the entire mixture forbidden to eat) was not extended to Gentiles.

18. It is forbidden to mix offered items, or libation wine poured for an idol, with a majority of permitted similar substance in order to nullify them and make it permissible to benefit from the prohibited substance through its nullification in the mixture.[250] Instead, they must be destroyed.

After the fact, if one did mix them in order to nullify them, he may dispose of the amount of forbidden items mixed, and benefit from the rest of the mixture.

19. For wine poured for an idol that later turned into vinegar, to the point that it is unfit for drink, and meat offered to an idol that became spoiled to the point that it is unfit for an animal to eat, it appears that this is considered nullification of the offering, since it is unfit for its designated purpose, and it is permitted for benefit.[251]

Furthermore, it appears to the author that although meat offered before an idol is forbidden to benefit from, if it is worthy for human consumption (by honorable people), still, one may feed it to animals, even if they are his own animals that he must feed. This is considered destroying and nullifying the idol's offering, since this type of benefit is not honorable or reverential for the idol. On the contrary, it is degrading the offerings and the worship of the idol.

---

[250] See *Yoreh De'ah* ch. 99, that one may not make a mixture from the outset in order to permit a forbidden food.

After the fact, it should be ruled according to topic 9:17, that one should throw away an amount from the mixture equal to the amount of forbidden pieces. This accomplishes that there is no additional benefit received from the forbidden substance. See the final footnote to topic 7:12 above, and Part IV, topic 6:10.

[251] This appears to be the ruling for Gentiles, since the taste of the wine or meat has already become lost, and does not have the name of "wine poured for idol worship," or "meat offered for idol worship," still associated with it. This is considered nullification for Gentiles, just as the nullification of the idol statue itself by cutting off its nose, etc. This was explained above in topic 8:16.

CHAPTER 10

The Prohibition Against Aiding Idol Worshipers

1. It has previously been explained in Part I, Chapter 4, that it is forbidden for a Gentile to cause another to transgress a prohibition of the Noahide Commandments. Therefore, it is forbidden for them to instruct others to serve idols, or to persuade or sway them to idol worship. Likewise, it is forbidden to support or be involved with anything connected to idolatry.

2. The restrictions listed below apply only to gatherings that are hosted by those who will serve their idol during its festival day, or to gatherings that are hosted as a personal celebration that will involve an idolatrous service or a ceremony with praise to an idol. But the restrictions do not apply to gatherings that are hosted on such occasions by those who are celebrating only out of a desire follow a longstanding custom, so long as they do not praise, thank or acknowledge any idols as deities.[252]

If one is afraid that others may be angry at him for not participating, or he is afraid of reprisals from the idol worshipers, it is permitted for him to attend and appear as if he is participating, for he is only flattering the idol worshiper, and does not attend out of any acceptance or recognition of the idol (see above, topic 2:3).

(a) On a day that idolaters celebrate as a festival for their religion or for praising one of their idols, it is forbidden to attend their celebration or support them. On a day that they celebrate by giving each other gifts that by their tradition are in honor of their idol, it is permitted to participate in this if it is considered by both parties (the giver and receiver) as only a custom, with no connection to the idol. But it would be better from the outset not to give gifts on that day, since it would be strengthening an idolatrous custom.

(b) If an idolater celebrates a personal occurrence, such as the marriage of a child, and in doing so makes a gathering in a house of idol worship, or elsewhere to hold a religious ritual service or to praise his idol, it is forbidden to attend the celebration.

---

[252] Rambam, *Laws of the Worship of Stars [and Idols]* ch. 9.

(c) On a day when someone in an idolatrous family has died and there is a commemorative funeral gathering, it is forbidden to attend if it is in a house of idol worship, or in a house dedicated to the idol, or if there are ritual items or incenses that are burned (because it is obviously being done for the purpose of their idolatry).

3. It is always forbidden to sell items that are directly connected to a type of idolatry, if they are sold to an idolater who practices that type of idolatry, or if it is in a place where that type of idolatry is practiced.

Items that are not directly connected to idolatry may be sold to idolaters, but if an idolater explains that he wants such an item for use in his idolatrous practices, it is forbidden to sell it to him, unless it is too unfit to be offered to the idol (since idolaters place a limit on how defective an item can be for their services to their idols). If a customer wishes to purchase a bulk of mundane merchandise in order to sell part of it to others, it is permitted to sell the merchandise to him, even though the others might want such items for use in idolatrous practices.

If items connected to idolatry got mixed up with items that are not, then one may sell the whole lot as one unit to idolaters (without investigating what use they will have for it), and one does not have to worry that they will separate the items which they accept for idolatry from the items they will reject for that use.[252] However, if the idol worshiper specifies that he agrees to purchase the whole lot because he will trouble himself to separate out that which is fit for idolatry, or if he cunningly mixes in items that will be used for idolatry with similar items that will not be used for that purpose, it is forbidden to sell the items to him if his intentions are clear.

Some say that if the idol worshiper would be able to buy the merchandise at the same quality and price from other merchants, there is no prohibition against selling it to him, since he can easily buy from the others as well.[253]

4. It is forbidden to join with idolaters in building a structure in which they will place their idols. One may, however, from the outset, construct a mundane building or courtyard that will contain such a

---

[253] There is no prohibition of placing a stumbling block before the blind in such a case, and the prohibition only applies if it is impossible for the worshiper to procure it in another way. See Shaĥ *Yoreh De'ah* 151:6.

structure.[252] It has been explained in Chapter 5 that it is forbidden to build a statue or temple of idol worship, or anything necessary for idolatry, but if one transgressed and did build it for the idolaters, one may nevertheless use the payment he receives for the work.

(A mundane structure is a place that is not designated solely for idol worship, and therefore it is permitted to be built, whereas a house of idol worship is solely dedicated for idolatry.)

5. If one's house is built next to a house of idol worship with a shared wall, and the shared wall falls down, he should not rebuild the wall on his own, for the house of idol worship will benefit freely from his effort and expense. Instead, he should collect his wages from them in payment for the part of his work that they will benefit from.[254]

6. If an idol has a pool or garden associated with it (and likewise any shop or any project whose profit is dedicated for the salary of the idol's priests or the idol's upkeep and maintenance), one may benefit from it only if he is not charged a fee, so he does not support the idol financially. But one may not benefit from it if one has to pay them (for example, if there is an "entrance fee" that will be a payment to the idol's priests). Even if it was owned partly by idolaters and partly by others, one may not benefit from it through paying for this opportunity.

If the profit from the payment will go to the public and not the idol itself, even if the public serves the idol, it is permitted to partake of this benefit even if one must pay a fee.

Some Rabbinical authorities say that this applies specifically when there is an idol in the pool or garden or courtyard, but if there is no idol in it, and the priests only collect profit from the entrance fee, it is permitted. However, if the profit goes directly to the upkeep and maintenance of an idol, or the expenses of its service (for example, to pay for the incense that is burned for it), all Rabbinical authorities say that it is forbidden to pay for partaking of this benefit.

7. If a town of idol worshipers is participating in a festival for their

---

[254] See *Shulĥan Aruĥ Yoreh De'ah* 143:1. It appears that as a Gentile, this person is permitted to do what he needs for himself (in fixing the wall), and he is not benefiting the idol worshipers for free. Afterward, it is not forbidden for him to benefit from the repaired wall, even though it is also benefiting the idol worshipers as a matter of course.

idol, and it has some shops that are decorated for the festival and others that are not, it is forbidden to buy anything in the decorated shops, since it is assumed that they are adorned for the sake of the idol worship (and if one buys merchandise there, he will be supporting its owners in their idol worship, or in their donations of funds for idolatrous purposes). But if one transgressed and did buy from them, he may nevertheless benefit from his purchase. He may, though, do business with those that are not decorated. (If there is no alternative available, or if it would be a hardship to travel to an undecorated shop, it is not forbidden to purchase a necessity from a decorated shop.)

8. It is forbidden to rent stores from idol worshipers, since one gives them profit (unless there is no alternative available). But if the profit falls to the ruling government, and it pays for the needs of an idol, it is permissible to rent the store.

9. It is forbidden to provide money to collectors of taxes or tithes for an idol. But one may pay a tax to a ruling power which stipulates that a certain amount from the tax will be used for the sake of idolatry.

10. One who buys a collection of items from an idol worshiper and finds among them idols or other forbidden images (that have clearly not been nullified), or books of idolatry, may return them to the seller and receive reimbursement, since they were accepted in error.

(Even though this is the basic rule, it is logical to say that it is a better option for the buyer to nullify the idolatrous items, if it is possible and it is not a difficulty, and then sell them, because returning them without nullification will possibly facilitate the seller and his other customers in acts of idol worship or things related to it.)

If children inherit from a parent who was an idol worshiper, and one child observes the Noahide Laws, and the other children serve the idol, the righteous child may not tell his siblings, "You take the idols (or the ritual items or books of idolatry), and I will take an equivalent amount of money." Rather, the righteous child must take his entire portion of the inheritance and then destroy or nullify the idolatrous items that are included, in order not to facilitate others in serving idols.[255]

---

[255] Inheritance to a Gentile is valid by Torah Law. Therefore, he immediately acquires any included idolatrous items and must not sell or exchange them.

CHAPTER 11

Practices that are Forbidden as Customs of Idol Worshipers

1. Just as Gentiles are forbidden to practice idol worship itself, so too they are forbidden to go in the customary ways of those who serve idols. These are ways and schemes in which the idol worshipers conduct themselves that are connected to and strengthen their beliefs.

The following are customary roles among those who worship idols: a magician, a diviner, a soothsayer, a witch, a charmer, a medium, a wizard or a necromancer. All these, even when they do not actually include idol worship in their practices, are branches of idolatrous services, and they cause and bring a person to serve idols.

About these it is said,[256] "There shall not be found among you one who passes his son or daughter through fire [referring to the service of *Moleĥ*, as explained above in Chapter 4], a diviner, a 'deceitful illusionist,' a soothsayer, a sorcerer [witch], an incantationist, one who inquires of *'Ov'* or *'Yidoni,'* or a necromancer, for these are abominations to God; anyone who does these..."[257]

All of these practices are forbidden. It is a great sin to engage in any

---

[256] Deuteronomy 18:9-12.

[257] Rambam, in *Laws of Kings* ch. 9, rules like the Sages in *Sanhedrin* 56b, that Gentiles are only commanded and "warned" about the Seven Noahide Laws and not other things. This is the ruling of Meiri (*Sanhedrin* 56b) and *Terumot HaDeshen* ch. 96. So although Gentiles are forbidden in all these practices that are offshoots of idolatry, they are not "warned" about them, since "warning" is a technical term (in this context) referring to explicit prohibitions (the Seven Laws) for which a Gentile is liable for a capital sin.

But if something is forbidden as an offshoot of the prohibition on items associated with idol worship, it does not make one liable for a capital sin. This can be seen from Rambam, *Laws of the Worship of Stars [and Idols]* 11:16, who writes about these practices, "All these things are only falsehood and lies with which the original **idolaters** deceived the Gentile nations, so the people would follow them [in their idol worship]." He also writes in his *Pirush HaMishnah Avodah Zarah* 4:7, that all of these things are sources of idol worship and its offshoots, meaning that they bring one to idol worship. This is the reason why Rambam included all these practices in his *Laws of the Worship of Stars [and Idols]*, since they bring one to serve idols. Therefore, it is clear that Gentiles should be prevented from practicing them.

of them, and the court is obligated to uproot these practices from among the people. Nevertheless, since Gentiles were not warned about them explicitly, none of them are in the category of capital sins.

2. The ancient rituals of *"Ov"* and *"Yidoni"* are practices of idol worshipers.[258] They include rituals of idol worship and sorcery, and are forbidden to Gentiles. Nevertheless, they do not make a Gentile liable for a capital sin, because he does not do them in order to serve the demon or the spirit of the dead which he calls upon (meaning that he does not do them with acceptance of these beings as deities). Instead, he performs these rituals as sorcery, and for his own benefit alone (see topic 3:22 above).

What is the ritual of the *"Ov"*? One stands and offers a certain incense, and holds the stem of a myrtle in his hand and waves it. He speaks words of magic that are known to those who practice this ritual, until he (the practitioner) hears a sound as if someone is speaking to him, and the voice replies to him about what he is asking. The voice seems to emanate from under the earth in a extremely low tone, that is not recognizable to the ear, but only perceived in thought.

Similar to this is the ritual of one who takes a skull of a dead person and offers incense to it, and then divines with it until he hears a very low voice coming from his armpit, and the voice replies to him.

Both of these constitute the ritual of the *"Ov."*

What is the ritual of the *"Yidoni"*? One places the bone of a certain bird named *yido'a* (in Hebrew) in his mouth, offers incense and performs other actions until he falls down into a type of faint and trance. The bone then seems to speak from his mouth about events that will happen in the future.[259]

---

[258] This is the wording of Rambam in *Laws of the Worship of Stars [and Idols]* ch. 6, and *Sefer HaMitzvot* Negative Commandment 9, that these are types of idol worship. Since the simple meaning of this is that they actually involve idol worship, why is a Gentile not liable for a capital sin if he practices one of these? This is because these types of service are done for private interest and not as an acceptance of an idol as a deity. In this respect, they are similar to a service performed only out of love or fear (mentioned in topic 3:27 above), and the prohibition comes only from the elements of witchcraft that are associated with the practice. The elements are forbidden to Gentiles as ways of idol worshipers, but not as acts of actual idol worship.

[259] Rambam, *Laws of the Worship of Stars [and Idols]* ch. 6.

Just as it is forbidden to practice the rituals of *"Ov"* or *"Yidoni,"* it is also forbidden to ask such individuals to provide advice through the practice of these rituals, and if one transgresses and does so, it is forbidden to act according to the advice that is received.[260]

3. Soothsaying involves those who follow signs, such as: "Since my bread has fallen from my mouth, or my stick has fallen from my hand, etc., I will not go to such-and-such a place today, for if I go, I will not be successful," or, "Since a fox passed me on the right-hand side I will not leave my house today, for if I do I will meet a swindler, etc."

This also applies to those who listen to the chirpings of the birds and follow these as signs, such as, "Because the birds chirped this way or that way, such-and-such will happen and such-and-such will not," or, "Because the birds chirped …, today it will be good to do this, but bad to do that, etc." Those who prognosticate by the actions of a rat or birds, or signs in the heavens (Jeremiah 10:2), are also practicing soothsaying. Similarly, one who designates signs for himself, by deciding that he will act this way or that way according to what transpires before his eyes, is also soothsaying.

Likewise, someone who tells a person that he will have bad luck unless he slaughters his rooster that called out in the evening, or his hen that made a sound like a rooster, is also soothsaying. All of these practices are forbidden.[261]

The practice of soothsaying also includes those who throw dice or coins, or draw cards, or do anything else that produces one result or another with a statistical probability, and follow these as signs, such as, "If it will fall a certain way, it is a sign for such and such, and if it will fall otherwise, it is a different sign."[262]

4. The prohibition of soothsaying applies when one sets a sign for himself and acts accordingly, and there is no natural or logical connection between the sign and the action he chooses because of it, or the course of non-action that he chooses, and it emerges that he

---

[260] Rambam *ibid.*, ch. 11.

[261] Rambam *ibid.*, and *Shulĥan Aruĥ Yoreh De'ah* ch. 179.

[262] *Sefer Mitzvos Gadol*, quoted in *Beit Yosef Yoreh De'ah* ch. 179. Though he explains that this is included in the prohibition of a diviner, it is clear that Rambam's opinion includes this as enchantment.

believes in folly.

In contrast, one who sets a sign for himself based on logical reasoning, as Eliezer the righteous servant of Abraham did (Genesis 24:12-14) by saying, "Let it be that the maiden ... who replies, 'Drink, and I will even give water for your camels,' [and acts with kindness,] her will You [God] have designated for Your servant, for Isaac." Likewise, if a person looks at a certain natural occurrence, from which he can logically deduce that the natural consequence will be such and such, and he decides to act accordingly or not to take action, this is not considered soothsaying.[263]

5. It is permitted to make statements such as, "This house that I built is a good sign for me," or "This spouse that I married is blessed, for once we married, I became rich," or "This animal that I bought is blessed, for once I purchased it I became rich," and the like. These statements are not forbidden, because by making them one has not decided upon a course of action, or refrained from doing something, based on a sign. Rather, one has accepted whatever it is as a good sign for what has already happened.[261] However, it is forbidden by the prohibition of soothsaying for one to designate a sign for himself, upon which he will decide upon a future action (to do this or not to do that, depending on how the sign turns out).[264]

6. If one built a house, or married a woman, or had a child, and then had success three times afterwards, he is permitted to consider this as a sign of his success, and it is permitted for him to set this as a good sign for the future to depend upon – i.e., that if he builds another house, or marries another woman (in a place and time that it is permitted to have more than one wife), or has another child, he will then have success, because this is not soothsaying; rather, the person sees it as an assurance of Divine assistance (a *mazal*).[265]

---

[263] Ran, as quoted in *Kesef Mishneh* (*Hilĥot Avodat Koĥavim* 11:4); *Nemukai Yosef* Tractate *Sanhedrin* end of ch. 7.

[264] This is implied from *Kesef Mishneh ibid.*, 11:5.

[265] Rashi on Tractate *Ĥullin* 95b; Rema *Yoreh De'ah* 179:4.

*A *mazal* is not a superstition, but a natural destiny which God has provided. Since this is a phenomena within the natural creation, there is a logical basis for allowing oneself to rely upon it, in the manner described.

Likewise, if one tests a medicinal charm three times and has success each time (such as through an amulet worn by a sick person), even though he doesn't know how it might work, but only that it is a repeatable good charm, it is permitted to use it based on this.[266]

7. It is permitted to ask a child who is learning the Hebrew Scriptures to recite a verse of his choice, and to act upon it, since this may be considered like a mild type of prophecy.[267]

8. It is forbidden to practice divination or to ask advice from one who practices it. Divination consists of performing particular actions in order to clear one's mind of all thoughts and matters, and concentrate transcendently until one starts predicting the future by saying, for example, "Such-and-such will, or will not, happen," or "It is fitting to do such-and-such, or beware of such-and-such." Some diviners touch or feel stones or sand and concentrate upon this; some crouch on the ground while moving or shouting; some stare into a mirror or lantern; and others hold a stick in their hands, leaning on it and knocking on the ground with it until their minds have cleared, and then they start speaking. Of this, Hosea said derisively in God's name:[268] "My people ask counsel from a piece of wood, and their staff declares to them."[269]

9. A "deceitful illusionist" is one who deceives the eyes of others and deludes them by appearing to do a supernatural thing which he does not really do.

One who performs acts of sorcery is called a sorcerer (or witch).

Both of these practices are forbidden.[270]

---

[266] *Tosafot* on Tractate *Bava Metziah* 27b; Responsa of Rashba chs. 413 and 825; *Darĥei Moshe Yoreh De'ah* ch. 179; Rambam, *Laws of the Sabbath* 19:13; *Pirush Ha'Mishnah Pesaĥim* ch. 4; and Tractate *Shabbat* ch. 6.

[267] Rema *Yoreh De'ah* ch. 179; *Taz* and Shaĥ *Yoreh De'ah* 179:5.

[268] Hosea 4:12.

[269] Rambam, *Laws of the Worship of Stars [and Idols]* ch. 11.

[270] Rambam *ibid.*; *Shulĥan Aruĥ Yoreh De'ah* 179:15. Rambam writes in *Guide for the Perplexed*, vol. 3 ch. 37: "A sorcerer is surely an idolater, even though his practice is done in strange and unusual ways that are different from the ways in which the masses worship their gods." Compare this to the rituals of *Ov* and *Yidoni*, which are explained in topic 11:2 above.

10. Astrology is not forbidden for Gentiles, i.e., to discern what is one's Divine *mazal* (a Divinely planned destiny), and to proceed with an action when it is apparent from the *mazal* that he will have success, or to refrain from an action when the *mazal* is opposing him.[271]

11. It is forbidden to practice incantations, which is the uttering of foolish, abnormal words that have no purpose, and he believes in his foolishness that these things will have some effect. Some even say that if one says these things over a snake or a scorpion, it will not be able to cause harm, and that if one says something over a person, the person will not be harmed. There is a similar practice of one who holds a designated object, such as a key or stone, etc., in his hand while speaking in order to project a power into his words. All such practices are forbidden. Likewise, it is forbidden for a person to sit opposite an incantationist and allow the utterances to be said over him, thinking that he has a benefit from these incantations, for by doing so he participates in the rituals of incantation.

---

[271] Based on *Shulĥan Aruĥ Yoreh De'ah* ch. 179, it would rule that it is permitted for Gentiles to practice astrology, as is the opinion of Ramban on Deuteronomy 18:9. Rashba chs. 413 and 825, and Ran on Tractate *Sanhedrin* 65b, rule that astrology is permitted even for Jews. Abram, before he became Abraham, was an expert astrologer (see Tractate *Nedarim* 32), from which we see that this practice is allowed for Gentiles.

Shulĥan Aruĥ Yoreh De'ah 179:1 rules against asking advice of stargazers or those who use lots or cards, as it says (Deuteronomy 18:13), "You shall be complete before God." This is a rule for Jews; Gentiles are not forbidden to follow astrology, but they are forbidden to take advice from lots or cards, etc.

On this distinction, it is clear from Tractate *Shabbat* 156 that there is a *"mazal"* (a Divinely planned destiny) for a Gentile which he may investigate, and the ruling of Rambam *ibid.* 11:8-9 that astrology is prohibited is only for Jews, who are commanded about the Oneness of God and not to put any faith in anything else at all. In contrast, there are opinions that Gentiles are not forbidden to believe in the false idea of a partnership with God (see topic 1:2 above), and surely by this opinion they are not forbidden to act based on their investigation of a *mazal*. Even Rambam, who forbids a belief in a divine partnership, says this only regarding a belief in the other entity as a deity; but he would agree that to investigate and act on one's *mazal* through natural means (for example, by astrological calculations) is permitted for a Gentile.

12. Likewise, one who uses whispering to gather snakes and scorpions or other animals, or flies or mosquitoes or the like, is an incantationist, and this is forbidden, even if his intentions are used to gather them into a desert or a place where they cannot cause harm. However, if they were chasing after him to harm him, it is permitted for him to cast a charm in order to save himself from them.[272]

13. It is permitted to whisper over the place where a snake or scorpion bit or stung a person, without using incantations, in order to give the injured person peace of mind and assurance. Even though this whispering itself doesn't have any healing power, it is permitted for its psychological benefits, because the injected poison is a danger to life (and the victim needs to be calmed).[273]

14. How are the dead consulted? One practice of necromancy is to consult them by fasting and then sleeping in a graveyard, so that a dead person will appear to him in a dream and answer his questions. There are others who consult with the dead by putting on specific clothes, burning incense and sleeping in a graveyard alone, so that a dead person will appear to them in a dream and speak to them.

The general rule is that it is forbidden for one to do anything to make a dead person appear to him and answer his questions.[274] Similarly, any "scientific investigations," séances or the like which include communicating with spirits of the dead are forbidden.[275]

15. It is the practice of some idol worshipers to make a mark on themselves or to tattoo their bodies as a sign of idol worship – for example, to show that they are servants who are sold to the idol and marked for its service. It is also their practice to cut themselves with vessels and wound their bodies, and to scratch themselves for their idols.[276] All these practices are rituals of idol worship, even though

---

[272] Rashi on Tractate *Sanhedrin* 65a; *Shulĥan Aruĥ Yoreh De'ah* ch. 179. and Shaĥ there.

[273] Rambam, *Laws of the Worship of Stars [and Idols]* 11:11.

[274] Rambam *ibid.* 11:13; *Shulĥan Aruĥ ibid.*

[275] See Responsa *Da'as Cohen* ch. 69. (This prohibition also includes communications with demons.)

[276] As it says in I Kings 18:28.

they are not its main rituals, and they are therefore forbidden as idolatrous practices if one intends it for idolatry.[277]

(One is generally forbidden to wound himself, with a few exceptions – for example, male circumcision and cosmetic surgery are permitted; see Part V, topics 6:5 and 6:6.)

It is also forbidden for one to wear a specific garment that is worn by idol worshipers in the name of their idol, if one intends it for that purpose.

16. There are those who cut their hair in ways prescribed by the practices of idol worship,[278] or shave their heads based on idolatrous practices.[279] If one cuts his hair this way and intends it for this idolatrous practice or for idol worship, this is forbidden. If he intends to do so only as a custom or for fashion, this is permitted.[280]

---

[277] Rambam, *ibid.* ch. 12, and *Kesef Mishneh* there.

[278] Rashi on Tractate *Avodah Zarah* 11b. See *Avodah Zarah* 29a, and Rashi and Rabbeinu Ĥananel there, and Rambam, *ibid.* 11:2 – since it is not permitted for a Gentile to have an idolatrous haircut, it is forbidden for a Jew to give him one, since it would cause the Gentile to err. However, it appears from *Kiryat Sefer* that this prohibition is because a Gentile who receives an idolatrous haircut may then go and perform some ritual (such as prayer, or praises and thanks) as a service for the idol.

[279] *Shulĥan Aruĥ Yoreh De'ah* 156:3.

[280] This is learned from Rambam, *ibid.* ch. 12, and *Sefer HaMitzvot* Negative Commandments 41-45, that this is the custom and ritual of some types of idol worship. It is therefore clear that it is forbidden to practice them, like other idolatrous rituals.

CHAPTER 12

The Prohibition of Swearing or Vowing in the Name of an Idol

1. It is forbidden to swear in the name of idolatry.[281] It is also forbidden to cause others to do so,[282] because this would give recognition to the idol

2. It is forbidden to swear in the name of an idol even if one intends it falsely, whether one swears regarding what one did in the past or about what one will do in the future, inasmuch as one thereby mentions the idol's name in a way of praise to others. It is also forbidden to swear in the name of a natural entity which others serve as an idol, even if he does not himself intend to serve it at all, and he only intends to swear by its constant existence. Nevertheless, since others consider it to be a

[281] Rambam, *Laws of Kings* 9:2, states that Gentiles are forbidden to practice idolatry in any way. Surely they are forbidden to swear in its name, as Rambam states in *Laws of the Worship of Stars [and Idols]* 5:10, in regard to Jews, that this is forbidden from the verse (Exodus 23:13), "… you shall not mention the name of other gods ..." These are forbidden for Gentiles, not from separate prohibitions, but rather from their general prohibition regarding all aspects of idolatry. For example, Rambam rules that Gentiles are forbidden to kiss or hug an idol (as explained in Tractate *Sanhedrin* 56b), even though this is not a capital sin, because anything associated with idolatry is prohibited. As this topic is explained in *Sanhedrin* 60b, this also includes one who verifies something or vows in the name of an idol.

This is likewise implied from Rambam, *Laws of the Worship of Stars [and Idols]* 1:2, "the image … in whose name they swore," for this is one of the ways of an idol's service, just as swearing in God's Name is an honor to Him, and is one of the ways of His service, as is explained by Rambam in *Laws of Oaths* ch. 11. It is also clear from Rambam, *Laws of the Worship of Stars [and Idols]* 2:6, that anyone who accepts a false god as true, even if he does not serve it, blasphemes and disgraces God, since one who vows in the name of an entity shows that he believes his vow is true, as demonstrated by his belief that the entity he vows upon is true and everlasting.

[282] Rambam *ibid.* 5:10. For Gentiles, there is no difference between one who swears, or one who makes others swear, for the prohibition of "you shall not mention, etc." (Exodus 23:13) means to give praise in mentioning idolatry. There is no difference if he praises an idol, or if he causes others to praise.

deity, it is forbidden to swear in its name, for it appears to others as if he swears by their belief. (Nowadays, when no one believes in the sun or stars as deities, one may clearly swear in their names; they are examples of lasting entities that were popular idols in the past.)

It is forbidden to lie, swear falsely, or take back one's word (except out of justified need).[283] One who does so is as if he serves idols.

3. It is forbidden to mention the names of idols in a way of praise, honor or importance,[284] as it says[285] "...you shall not mention the name of other gods, nor shall it be heard from your mouth."

A person should not tell his friend, "Guard this item for me next to such-and-such an idol," or "Meet me on the festival day of such-and-such an idol,"[286] in order not to mention the name of an idol in a respectable fashion.

4. Even though there is no prohibition in mentioning the name of an idol casually, it is unfitting that a person should make it his habit to mention such a name, since it brings one to be drawn after the idol or to respect it, which is forbidden, as mentioned above in topic 2:1, from the verse, "Do not turn to the idols ..." Therefore, it is permitted to mention their names if there is a personal need for it and it is not in a respectful way, and surely if the mention is to dishonor them.

Likewise, if one's intention is to mention an idol's name in order to

---

283 *Five situations are traditionally identified in which it may be permissible to deviate from telling the complete truth, if no promise or vow is involved: (a) to preserve peace between individuals, to avoid hurting someone's feelings, or to give comfort to a distressed person; (b) to avoid a situation that might lead to physical harm; (c) for the sake of modesty or to avoid appearing arrogant; (d) for the sake of decency; (e) to protect one's money or property from thieves or scoundrels.

Swearing falsely in God's name is extremely serious, and might only be considered if necessary to save a life. The same applies for reversing on one's promise, although procedures are available for nullifying a regretted vow or promise if it is justified (see Part III, topic 4:4).

284 The reason for the prohibition, "... you shall not mention the name of other gods ...," is to avoid praising them. But ordinary mention of an idol's name is not forbidden by Torah Law, as is the opinion of Rambam, *ibid.*

285 Exodus 23:13.

286 Tractate *Sanhedrin* 63b; Rambam, *ibid.*; Rashi on Exodus *ibid.*

learn or explain the customs of its worshipers (in order to avoid those things), or in order to avoid transgressing the prohibition of practicing any of their rituals, then it is permitted.[287]

5. It is permitted to mention the name of any idol that is written in the twenty-four Books of the Hebrew Scriptures,[288] such as *Pe'or*, *Bel*, *Nevo*, *Gad* and the like. This is because the person intends that the idol should be eternally nullified, and this is similarly the ruling for any idol that one intends to degrade or nullify.[289] This is an aspect of the permission to denigrate an idol.[290] However, it is forbidden to swear in the names of those idols, no matter what the intention is.[291]

6. It is permitted to mention people's names that are also names of idols, if one's intention is for the person's name alone.[292]

7. One should not say to an idol worshiper, "May your god be with you," or "May your god give you success," or "Do this for me in the name of your god," or the like, since it would give honor to the idol.[293]

8. A person who swears in the name of an entity shows his faith in the truth and everlastingness of the entity, such that it is a fitting thing to always rely upon. Therefore, if one Gentile wishes to swear in the name of an idol of his own accord, it is forbidden for another Gentile to accept such a vow, as this would appear to lend support to the entity in whose name the person swears.[294]

---

[287] Meiri on Tractate *Sanhedrin* 63.

[288] See *Sefer HaĤinuĥ* Commandment 86.

[289] *Likkutei Siĥot*, vol.23, p. 168.

[290] *Shulĥan Aruĥ Yoreh De'ah* ch. 147.

[291] *Tosafot* on Tractate *Sanhedrin* 63b.

[292] *If a Gentile was named after an idol by his parents, there is no special procedure required if he wishes to change his name. A person is the ultimate decider of his own name, and he merely needs to let his decision be known publicly, and follow the procedure required by the secular courts.

[293] Ramban on Exodus 23:13; *Taz* and Shaĥ *Yoreh De'ah* ch. 147.

[294] This can be seen from the ruling of the Rabbinical authorities on *Oraĥ Ĥayim* ch. 156, and *Ĥoshen Mishpat* ch. 182, in regard to the permission of accepting the vow of an idolater, from which it is clearly forbidden.

9. It was explained in Chapter 1 that some Rabbinical opinions maintain that a Gentile is not forbidden to believe in the mistaken concept of an intermediary to God, and this includes a belief that another entity exists that is fitting to respect because this is the will and honor of God. However, those opinions which say that this *belief* is not forbidden also admit that it *is* forbidden to perform any type of worship service for the supposed intermediary. Nevertheless, if such a belief itself is not forbidden, it is likewise not forbidden to swear in the Name of God combined together with the intermediary that one mistakenly believes in as another divinity, if it is done in the following way.

How would a person permissibly state such a combined vow? He would mention only that he vows in the name of "god" – where his *mental intention* is for both the true God and the intermediary which he has added. But it is forbidden to swear in the Name of God *and* the intermediary's name separately.[295] (Even if no one serves the intermediary as a separate idol, and it is served as a deity that is only secondary to God, it is forbidden for one to mention its name in a vow as a separate divinity, because it openly appears that he considers it to be his god.)

Clearly it is forbidden to vow by including a name of God with idolatry (meaning with the name of an idol that is not served as an intermediary to God, but rather it is served as a separate god).[295]

It appears that it is forbidden to swear in the name of an intermediary on its own.[296] (For example, it is forbidden to swear by Yeshua alone, even if the person considers this to be only an intermediary. The only permitted vow of the sort, as mentioned above, is to swear only in the name of "god", with the *intention* that is in reference to both God and Yeshua.)

10. Even though belief in an intermediary is not forbidden to Gentiles, this belief is not true. It is fitting for every person to see the mistake in this idea, which originated in the mistaken beliefs of Enosh and his

---

[295] This is clear from *Tosafot* and Rema, as explained in footnote 8 above.

[296] Even though the mistaken belief in an intermediary is not forbidden for Gentiles, in this type of vow one actually makes the intermediary into a separate divinity, which is forbidden. *Tosafot* and his contemporaries explained that a Christian's vow is not forbidden, because they usually intend to include *both* God and Yeshua in their ordinary vows to "god".

generation (mentioned before in topic 1:4), and to distance oneself from it,[297] especially since many of the great Sages determined that this belief is actual idol worship,[298] (and according to all opinions, it is considered to be idolatry for Jews). The permission is only for one who wishes to make others swear to something by their beliefs (for example, in a business deal); even if one knows that the one who swears will have intention for his intermediary as well, it is permitted to accept the vow, since there is no prohibition involved for a vow in which the name of actual idol worship is not mentioned.

11. However, in the future Messianic Era and the World to Come, the occupation of the whole world will be solely to know God,[299] as it says,[300] "For then I [God] will turn the people to a pure language, so that all will call upon the Name of God to serve Him with one purpose." And all will know that God alone exists, and that there is no other divinity aside from Him that is fitting to rely upon. Rather, all will depend on God alone, as the prophet says,[301] "God will be King over the entire earth; in that day God will be One and His Name One." This means that even His Name will be One and exclusive in the mouths of all, and there will be no belief in any other existence, even as an imagined intermediary to God, as it says,[302] "You shall know this day and take to your heart that the Lord [alone] is God, in the heavens above and on the earth below – there is no other!"

---

[297] See *Ma'agal Tov* (p. 162), which relates that Rabbi Ĥayim Yosef David Azulai explained and instructed a Gentile to distance himself from any belief in an intermediary and only to believe in God, from which we see that it is proper to instruct a righteous Gentile to believe in God alone.

It has been previously written (Part I, topic 1:7) that even for those Rabbinical opinions maintaining that *belief* in an intermediary is permitted for a Gentile, this only means that the person should not be considered as an idolater. But a person does not reach the spiritual level of a Pious Gentile as long as he is holding such a belief. (See Part I, topic 1:6 and footnotes there.)

[298] Rambam, quoted in footnote 8 above.

[299] Rambam, *Laws of Kings* 12:5.

[300] Zephaniah 3:9.

[301] Zeĥariah 14:9.

[302] Deuteronomy 4:39.

PART III

THE PROHIBITION OF BLASPHEMY

Including the Laws of Vows

This section explains details of the following one obligation and four prohibitions that are included in this commandment to Gentiles and its offshoots:

1. Not to curse God. An extension of this is not to curse any person.

2. Not to show contempt or disrespect toward God. This prohibition includes any mentioning of God's name in vain.

3. Not to destroy any writing that includes one of the holy Names of God, or something that is designated for a holy purpose, such as holy books or a synagogue.

4. Not to swear falsely. This prohibition includes saying a lie.

5. To fulfill an oath or vow that one verbalizes.

INTRODUCTION

by Rabbi J. Immanuel Schochet

Rabbi of Congregation Beth Joseph
Toronto, Canada

At the very center of this world is *homo sapiens*, the human being Divinely endowed with intellect. This intellect allows us analytical thought and examination of ourselves and the world around us. Without Divinely-endowed criteria for truth and moral values, however, our critical thinking is abstract and theoretical at best, and obviously susceptible to error.

Thus God revealed to mankind knowledge of His inscrutable Will by means of His prophets and the Torah, to know what is right and what is wrong, what is good and what is evil. The Divine revelation of the Torah at Mount Sinai, and the Divine designation of Moses as the foremost prophet for all time, set forth the ultimate test for the truth of future prophets, i.e., compatibility with the Torah and its eternal commandments. Even so, this legal and moral code is meaningful only when applying the other special gift endowed upon humans, namely freedom of choice to follow or reject proper conduct.

Open-minded and consistent reasoning readily leads to a realization that there must be a Supreme Cause for our most complex yet intricately precise world. Thus we arrive at the recognition and acknowledgment of God as Creator, Sovereign and Sustainer of the universe. This acknowledgment is not only an intellectual conclusion, but of itself has practical implications.

Noting that life, health and all human needs and blessings emanate unceasingly from the Creator, we must surely acknowledge this in thought, speech and action. We ought to express gratitude for the Divine benevolence on which we are continuously dependent, and make ourselves into worthy recipients thereof. This is the concept of worshipping God that applies equally to all, Jews and Gentiles alike.

The diametric opposite to this ideal of reverence for God is the crass and sinful conduct of deprecating God or His Sovereignty. This is referred to as blasphemy.

In common usage, the word "blasphemy" is generally defined as any form of uttered impiety, irreverence or sacrilege against God. These are acts of defiance seeking to impair the appropriate respect and reverence for God.

In the Torah the sin of "blasphemy" is circumscribed in terms of "cursing God." In this religious context, blasphemy is regarded as so unimaginable a rebellion and offensiveness that the traditional Hebrew terminology for it is the euphemism *birkat HaShem.* Literally this means *blessing The Name* (i.e., God), thus the very opposite of what it is used to signify. The Torah has two explicit references to this offense:

(a) Exodus 22:27 states, "You shall not curse God." The Hebrew word used here is *te'kalel*, from the root-word *kal*. It means "to degrade," to hold in light esteem and despise.[1]

(b) Leviticus 24:10-17 relates the incident of one who violated the cited injunction of Exodus 22:27, and the Divine edict declaring this to be a capital sin. Furthermore, it states there, "*ish ish* (any man) who curses his God shall bear his sin." Why the double expression of "*ish ish*" (literally: "a man, a man")? To include all mankind, both Jews and Gentiles. Blasphemy thus is prohibited to Gentiles as a capital sin even as it is for Israelites.[2]

This reiterates the earlier prohibition of the Noahide Code expressed in the all-inclusive verse of Genesis 2:16, "And *HaShem* [Y-H-V-H], God, commanded...": the citation of the Tetragrammaton Name[3] in this verse alludes to the prohibition of blasphemy to Gentiles.[4]

A Gentile would be guilty of this offense when uttering a blasphemous statement that invokes any of the explicit Divine Names in the Torah's Hebrew text (those which are forbidden to be erased

---

[1] Ibn Ezra and Ramban, *ad loc.*; Rashi on Deuteronomy 22:23.

[2] *Tractate* Sanhedrin 56a; Rambam, *Hilĥot Melaĥim* 9:1,3.

[3] The Tetragrammaton is the essential four-letter Name of God (Y-H-V-H), which was uttered only by the *kohanim* (Jewish priests) at certain points of their service in the Holy Temple of Jerusalem. Beyond this prescribed usage one is not allowed to pronounce this Name as it is written, thus also known as "the ineffable Name." In sacred service, as public Torah-readings, it is substituted by the Name *Ado-nai*, and in vernacular speech and writing by the Hebrew term *HaShem* (lit. "the Name"), which is also the general non-sacred substitution for the term "God." (In this and other Names of God in Hebrew, one or more dashes or apostrophes are inserted in the word to avoid writing an actual Divine Name that is forbidden to be erased or dishonored.)

[4] Tractate *Sanhedrin* 56b; Rambam, *Hilĥot Melaĥim* 9:1.

when spelled out in full, as explained in Chapter One below; for example, *Ado-nai, E-lohim, Y-ah,* etc., and of course the Tetragrammaton itself), or any appellation clearly referring to God (e.g., the Supreme Being, the Almighty, the Creator, the One Above, etc.), or "attributive" names – i.e., terms distinctly referring to the Divine attributes and identified with God (such as the Merciful, the Compassionate, etc.), *in whatever language it may be.*

(Normally one is punished only for offenses involving an action. The sin of blasphemy, however, is one of a very small group of offenses where speech on its own is deemed tantamount to criminal action. While actual articulation alone in this context will incur full penalty, blasphemous thoughts, too, are serious sins.)

Conceptually, blasphemy is closely linked to heresy and idolatry. Like the other Noahide Commandments, however, it is really a comprehensive category, which subdivides into a number of bylaws. By definition it involves not only a generic prohibition, but of itself implies a number of obligations. An early authority thus notes: "Do not err about the well-known enumeration of the seven precepts of the Children of Noaĥ as cited in the Talmud. In truth these seven are like seven comprehensive principles which contain numerous particulars."[5]

The very idea of there being a Divinely ordained "Noahide Code" presupposes an acknowledgement of (a) the existence of God; (b) the authority of God as Supreme Being; (c) the reality of Divine Revelation instructing mankind with regards to proper conduct (the bond or covenant between the Almighty and His creatures); and (d) the principle of Divine retribution, i.e., that man is accountable for obeying or disobeying these instructions, because a legal code devoid of consequences is ineffective.

More specifically, the Noahide prohibition of blasphemy derives from an acceptance of the supremacy and sovereignty of God which *ipso facto* demands respect or appropriate reverence for God. It follows then that –

(1) All Gentiles are subject to the precept of awe and reverence before God, more commonly referred to as the "fear of God." *Sefer HaĤinuĥ* states clearly: "This precept applies everywhere, at all times, and to the

---

[5] *Sefer HaĤinuĥ*, section 416 (ed. Chavel, section 424). Also note Tractate *Sanhedrin* 74b: "Them [the seven precepts] and all that pertains to them."

whole human species!"[6]

(2) A Gentile is not to use God's name in vain. To use God's name in vain (a Torah prohibition stated explicitly for Jews in the third of the "Ten Commandments") is closely allied with the principle of blasphemy. It is clearly a form of disrespect. This would then also include a prohibition to swear falsely. Thus we find in the Torah that from the earliest times the concept of an oath was regarded as a sacred obligation by Gentiles as well. (See for example Gen. 21:22*ff.*; ibid. 26:28*ff.*)

(3) A Gentile must likewise respect God's creatures, and thus one is not to curse or harm humans, for they are created by God "in His image and likeness" as it were. (The "image of God" within mankind is not the form of the human body, God forbid, which would be a false and idolatrous concept, but rather the unique capacity for intellect and speech that is possessed by the human enlivening soul, and its ability to distinguish between good and evil.)

"God created man in His image, in the image of God He created him, male and female He created them" (Genesis 1:27). This is reiterated in the Noahide Code in the context of the prohibition of murder: "Whosoever sheds the blood of man, by man shall his blood be shed, for in the image of God He made man" (Genesis 9:6). Thus it is also said of the Torah's "golden rule" to love your fellow as yourself (Lev. 19:18):

> Rabbi Akiva said, " 'Love your fellow as yourself' – this is the main principle of the Torah." Ben Azzai responded (quoting Genesis 5:1): " 'This is the book of the descendants of Adam – in the day He created man He made him in the likeness of God.' This is an even greater principle! [Thus, if you put another human being to shame, know and realize who you put to shame, for] He made him in the image of God!"[7]

---

[6] Section 432 (in ed. Chavel, section 430). Indeed one may add here that a Gentile ought not only attain the fear of God but also the love of God. Maimonides writes that the Israelite's commandment to love God (Deuteronomy 6:5) includes also an obligation "to call upon all mankind to His service and to have faith in Him. For if you love someone, you will praise and extol him and call upon people to love him as well..." There is, then, an implication that all mankind ought to love God.

[7] *Sifra* on Lev. 19:18 and *Bereishit Rabbah* 24:7. See *Likkutei Siĥot* vol. 17, p. 215.

CHAPTER 1

The Obligation to Respect God's Name, and What is Forbidden as Blasphemy

1. Gentiles are warned against "blessing God's Name" (the term is euphemistic, and means cursing God),[1] and they are liable for this. Adam, the first person, was warned about this, as it says,[2] "And the Lord God commanded [upon] Adam ..." This means that God commanded His Divinity and authority upon Adam. The three meanings of this statement are:

"I am God; do not exchange Me" – for another god, this being the prohibition of idolatry.

"I am God; do not curse Me" – this being the prohibition of blasphemy.

"I am God; the fear of Me shall be upon you" – this being the obligation to fear God. Fearing God is a part of the general commandment to guard one's self against committing blasphemy.[3]

This prohibition was again commanded explicitly in the Torah regarding Gentiles, as it says,[4] "*Any man* who will blaspheme his God shall bear his sin, and one who pronounces blasphemously God's Name[5] shall be put to death [by an empowered *Beit Din* court] ..."[6] Thus Moses received and transmitted additional details and clarifications about this Noahide prohibition.

2. What is the definition of "pronounces blasphemously God's Name"

---

[1] *I.e., stating that God should harm Himself (God forbid).

[2] Genesis 2:16.

[3] Tractate *Sanhedrin* 56b. Although the Talmud states there: "*My fear shall be upon you* – this is the commandment to establish *dinim* (courts of law)," this does not change the simple meaning. The main intent of "My fear" is that one should have "fear of Heaven" (i.e., fear of God). This obligation to fear Him is further understood to teach about the obligation to fear the courts.

[4] Leviticus 24:15-16.

[5] *This verse refers to the Explicit Name of God in Hebrew, which He revealed when He spoke the 10 Commandments at Mt. Sinai (Ex. 20:2).

[6] See Tractate *Sanhedrin* 56a: "***Any man** who will blaspheme* – this comes to include Gentiles ..."

in the above-cited verse, which refers to the Explicit Name of God?[7]

The Explicit Name of God is *either* the Tetragrammaton (which is represented by Y-H-V-H) or the Name *Ado-nai*[8] (meaning "Lord" in Hebrew, in the literal sense of Supreme Rulership). (Even though their articulations are different, these are two alternative expressions of the Explicit Name.)[9]

The capital sin of blasphemy is committed if a person clearly requests (with his mouth) a curse from God upon the Explicit Name. How? By invoking one of the holy Names of God, or one of His attributive names, against the Explicit Name (i.e., that God, as He is called by one of His Names, should do such-and-such a harm to Himself, as He is called by the Explicit Name).[10]

(See topic 3 below, about forbidden speech that is not a capital sin.)

One is liable if this is stated in a way of "May Yosai strike Yosai."[11] (The nickname "Yosai" is used as a euphemism, to avoid explaining this with the actual Explicit Name in such a negative context; using the euphemistic name Yosai does not carry any liability.) Equally forbidden are blaspheming in a way of "May Yosai curse Yosai,"[12] or "May the Merciful One (or Compassionate One, etc.) curse Yosai" (i.e., using an attributive name along with one of the expressions of the Explicit Name). This obviously applies if one cursed God's Explicit Name with the same Name, such as *Ado-nai* with *Ado-nai*.

What is considered a holy Name (other than the Explicit Name), and what is considered an attributive name? The holy Names of God

---

[7] The Hebrew word used in the verse, "one who pronounces blasphemously *(v'nokev)* God's Name," literally means both to clearly pronounce the Explicit Name, and to curse it, as is explained in Tractate *Sanhedrin* 56a, and Rashi on Leviticus 24:16.

[8] Rambam, *Laws of the Worship of Stars [and Idols]* 2:7.

[9] Rambam, *Laws of the Foundations of Torah* 6:2, states that, "The Name written Y-H-V-H is the Explicit Name, and is [also] written *Ado-nai*." On this, it is explained in *Kesef Mishneh* that it is only one Name, Y-H-V-H being its spelling and *Ado-nai* its pronunciation, and even though in other cases they are considered as two separate Names, that is only in regard to writing them, but not in regard to pronouncing them.

[10] Rambam, *Laws of Kings* 9:3.

[11] Based on Rambam, *Laws of the Worship of Stars [and Idols]* 2:8.

[12] Rashi on Tractate *Sanhedrin* 56a.

(specifically in Hebrew) are those that are forbidden to be erased after they are written down in a permanent fashion.[13] In addition to the Explicit Name (Y-H-V-H or *Ado-nai*), these Names are *Ai-l*, *E-lohim*, *E-loha*, *Sha-dai*, *Tziva-ot*, *Ehe-yeh* and *Y-ah*, as well as any variant of *E-lohim*, such as *E-lohehah* ("your God," if "your" is singular), or *E-lohaihem* ("your God," if "your" is plural), or *E-lohainu* ("our God")[14] – all these have the same holiness as the Name *E-lohim*.

The attributive names are "the Merciful One," "the Compassionate One," "the Creator," and the like,[15] and any other attributive name (**including a name in any language other than Hebrew**) by which a person clearly is referring to God, Who is the Creator of the universe.

3. If one cursed against any name of God, even the Explicit Name, without invoking against it another name of God, he is not liable for capital punishment by a court of law (although it is still forbidden).

Even if one says, "May Yosai strike Himself," since he did not clearly curse against the Explicit Name (nor did he invoke names of God twice, as the recipient and the source of the harm), he is not liable for punishment by a court.[16] If one cursed against a holy Name (that is forbidden to be erased) other than Y-H-V-H or *Ado-nai*, with another

---

[13] *Text characters encoded electronically, or projected optically or electronically, are not permanent forms of writing.

[14] Rambam, *Laws of the Foundations of Torah* 6:2.

*These are the Names of God in Hebrew (which is the "holy language"), with which God was called by the Israelite prophets through Divine inspiration, as recorded in the words of the Hebrew Bible.

[15] It is apparent from Rambam, *Laws of Kings* 9:3, that for cursing the Explicit Name with one of the other holy Names that may not be erased, a Jew is nonetheless liable. Thus, the only difference between the liability of Jews and Gentiles is regarding a "*kinuy*" (attributive) name, such as the "Compassionate One," the "Merciful One," and the like (as expressed by Rambam, *ibid.*, in that Gentiles are liable for blaspheming with a "*kinuy*" in any language, for which Jews are not liable).

[16] Rambam, *ibid.* His wording also supports this: "A Gentile who curses the Explicit Name **with** the Explicit Name or **with** an attributive name...," and not merely "A Gentile who curses the Explicit Name or an attributive name." This implies that a Gentile is liable for blasphemy only if he utters a two-part curse, with the Explicit Name as the object of the curse, and either with a holy Name or an attributive name being called upon to deliver the harm.

holy Name (for example, by saying "*Sha-dai* should hit *Tziva-ot*"), he is also not liable for punishment by a court. Even if one cursed against another of the holy Names by invoking the Explicit Name (for example, by saying, "*Ado-nai* strike *E-lohim*") he is not liable.

These curses against God are all forbidden to be said. But there is no capital sin for a Gentile to warrant a capital punishment unless one curses against the Explicit Name by invoking a name of God.[17]

4. One who blasphemes and then regrets his words and retracts them – even immediately – is still liable for capital punishment from a *Beit Din* court if he sinned by cursing God's Explicit Name, and it is proven by valid testimony.[18]

5. One who curses the Explicit Name by invoking against it a name of God in any language (whether with a translated name of God or His attributes, and likewise the wording of the curse may be in any language), is liable for a capital sin. If the words of the language he uses are clearly calling on God[10] to harm the Explicit Name, he is liable according to the definition of blasphemy. In particular, one is not liable unless he pronounces the object of the curse in correct Hebrew, as Y-H-V-H or *Ado-nai*. However, if a person translates this object of the curse into another language, he is exempt from punishment.[19]

6. If someone curses God in the name of idolatry (by saying, "May such and such an idol strike Yosai"), he is not to be judged or punished by a court, but he is still committing a grave sin, for which he will be punished by Heaven.[20]

A zealot is only given permission to strike down a blasphemer (one who verbally curses the Explicit Name of God) at the time he hears the

---

[17] This is as it says, "one who curses" (as explained in footnote 7), meaning that one mentions the Explicit Name and curses it with another name of God, but not that he uses the Explicit Name to curse a different name of God.

[18] Rambam, *Laws of the Worship of Stars [and Idols]* 2:9. Rabbi Y. Shteif, in *Mitzvot Hashem* p. 374, says this Torah Law also applies to Gentiles.

[19] This is because by definition, the "Explicit Name" implies the way that it is explicitly pronounced in Hebrew, the holy language. But a name for God in another language is only an attributive name, as explained by Rambam in *Laws of the Courts* 26:3, and *Shulĥan Aruĥ* in *Ĥoshen Mishpat* 27:1.

[20] Rambam, *Laws of the Worship of Stars [and Idols]* 2:9.

blasphemy being uttered, and only if he hears the blasphemy himself.[21] However, if he heard from others that a person blasphemed, or if he waits a short period of time after the transgression was committed, he has no permission to kill the blasphemer.

7. One who hears another person mention the Explicit Name and then he curses the Name that he hears, without mentioning the Explicit Name himself, is exempt from punishment, even if he cursed with the Explicit Name or with another holy Name.[22]

8. All the above explains when one would be liable in a *Beit Din* court. However, it is obvious that it is always forbidden to curse God in any other way, since that is included in the general sense of "blasphemous speech," and one who does so has committed a grave sin that is punishable by the Heavenly court, as it says, "Any man who will blaspheme his God shall bear his sin ..."[23]

Moreover, it is forbidden to speak of God in any degrading way, and this is also included in the general prohibition against blasphemy.[24] Even if one says unclear words that may or may not be understood by others, if he intends it as a disgrace to God, it is forbidden, and he is liable to be punished from Heaven for this.[25]

9. It is forbidden to write words of blasphemy or other insults towards God, which is included in the general prohibition of blasphemy.

---

[21] One need not blaspheme before an audience of at least ten for a zealot to be permitted to kill him. Rather, it applies when there is an audience of at least two witnesses other than the zealot himself. Thus, the total audience is required to be at least three, as Meiri says on Tractate *Sanhedrin* 81b.

*If the zealot asks for permission, he is not granted permission from the court to do so, and is instructed not to harm the blasphemer. For by the very act of requesting permission, he relinquishes his status as a zealot.

[22] See Rashi on Tractate *Sanhedrin* 55b.

[23] As explained in the footnotes to topic 1:1 above, based on Tractate *Sanhedrin* 56a, this prohibition applies to Gentiles as well.

[24] *Nevertheless, one should always be assured that through sincerely repenting to God and striving to correct his ways, he can be granted atonement for sinful thoughts, speech or actions.

[25] In *Mitzvot HaShem*, p. 375, Rabbi Yonatan Shteif explains that a Gentile is judged from Heaven for his thoughts as well as for his actions.

CHAPTER 2

Obligations to Revere and Fear God

1. Gentiles are commanded to fear and honor God.[26] This is included in the Torah's prohibition of blasphemy, as God commanded Adam (Genesis 2:16):
"I am God" – do not curse Me;
"I am God" – the fear of Me shall be upon you.[27]
It is obvious that the primary reason for the prohibition of blasphemy is the obligation to honor and fear God. Thus in the explanation of the verse,[28] "You shall not curse God," the Hebrew word for "curse" has the same root as the term for "disgrace."[29]

From this it can be understood that any action that causes a desecration of God's Name, and the opposite of bringing honor to God's Name, is forbidden. For this reason, the particular prohibitions discussed in this chapter are branches of the prohibition of blasphemy, although they were not spelled out explicitly for Gentiles in the Hebrew Scriptures.

2. One who swears falsely in God's Name[30] also desecrates His Name, as it says,[31] "You shall not swear in My Name falsely, and desecrate the Name of God; I am God," for by doing so one denies the truth of the One whose Name he swears by, since he effectively is saying that

---

[26] *Sefer HaĤinuĥ* Commandment 432: "For all people…"

[27] Tractate *Sanhedrin*, 56b.

[28] Exodus 22:27.

[29] Rashi, on Deuteronomy 21:23.

[30] See *Mishneh Li'Meleĥ Hilĥot Melaĥim* 10:7, which discusses whether false or vain oaths are included in the prohibition of blasphemy. However, the discussion is in regard to the prohibition and the punishment, since there is no clear warning to Gentiles in the Torah about such oaths. Nevertheless, this is forbidden based on logic, since swearing in God's Name in vain, and needless to say doing so falsely, is a disgrace to His Name, worse than uttering a Divine Name in vain (see topic 2:4 below). Therefore, oaths that are a disgrace to His Name are also forbidden.

[31] Leviticus 19:12.

just as his words are false, so is the existence of God false.[32] It is likewise forbidden to lie, or to falsely deny that he had promised or made an oath. Furthermore, one who changes his word is considered as if he serves idols[33] (except with justified need; see Part II, topic 12:2).

3. It is even forbidden to swear in God's Name in vain, i.e., to swear about something for which an oath is unnecessary (as will be explained in topic 3:12), since it is a disgrace to the honor of His Name to mention and swear by His Name in vain.[34]

Whether one swears by one of the Names of God, or by one of His attributive names, it is the same, as long as he clearly intends to mention God by this – for example, one who swears "by the One Whose name is the Compassionate," or "by the One Whose name is the Merciful" and the like, whether in Hebrew or in any way these attributive names are translated in other languages.[35] This is considered a vow in God's Name,[36] and if one does so falsely or in vain, he profanes God's Name.

4. Any mention of God's Name for naught is also forbidden, since this disgraces the honor of God, and one receives punishment from Heaven

---

[32] Rambam, *Laws of Oaths* 12:1; Ibn Ezra and Ramban on Exodus 20:7.

[33] Tractate *Sanhedrin* 92a. The prohibition against Gentiles lying or swearing falsely is not based on a specific warning, but rather on the logic that it is an obligation for them to act properly by honoring God's Name; see *Likkutei Siĥot*, vol. 38, p. 28, based on Ramban's commentary on Genesis 6:2,13.

*The explanation of the equivalence with serving idols (based on *Sefer HaĤinuĥ* Commandment 70 and *Ĥidushei Agadot* of Maharal on *Sanhedrin* 92) is that the world's existence is God's speech, which is continuously commanding that the world exist. Idol worship is like putting in God's mouth words He never said, i.e., that there would be some other being or force involved in the creation or sustaining of the world. (This is the concept of *sheetuf*, or partnership, as explained in Part II, Chapter 1). Humans were created in God's image, and to them God granted wisdom and the power of speech; therefore, they must uphold truth. False speech is equivalent to saying that God's speech also is not a definite Truth of Oneness, and that it can be corrupted (God forbid).

[34] Ramban on Exodus 20:7.

[35] See *Shaĥ Yoreh De'ah* 237:2; *Shulĥan Aruĥ HaRav Oraĥ Ĥayim* 85:3.

[36] Rambam, *Laws of Oaths* 2:2.

for this. Regarding this it is written,[37] "You shall not take the Name of God in vain; God will not hold guiltless one who takes His Name in vain" – meaning that a person remains guilty of this sin until he is punished by Heaven for profaning God's Name.[38] It is also said,[39] "To fear the honorable and awesome Name" – since from the obligation of fearing God, it is prohibited to mention His Name for naught.[40]

This applies specifically to the holy Names specified for Him (which may not be erased, listed above in topic 1:2), and even His names in other languages (e.g., the name "God").[41] But there is no prohibition of mentioning God's attributive names in vain, such as "Compassionate," "Merciful," and the like, or other "shared" names (such as the English name "Lord" which can also refer to a person, e.g., members of the British House of Lords), since they are not exclusively denoting God.[42]

5. What is meant by mentioning God's Name "in vain"? This means saying a Divine Name for no need at all. However, to mention it in a way of praise or prayer is permitted. It is likewise permitted to bless someone with God's Name, by saying "God bless you," and the like.[43]

Therefore, one who erred and mentioned God's Name for no reason should immediately praise and give honor to Him, in order that the mentioning of His Name should not be in vain. For example, if one said "God," he should immediately say, "Blessed is He forever," or "Who is great and very exalted."[44]

6. A person should always honor God's Name, in any language. When

---

[37] Exodus 20:7.

[38] Rambam, *Laws of Oaths* 12:1.

[39] Deuteronomy 28:58.

[40] Rambam, *ibid.* In *Mitzvot Hashem*, p. 382: Gentiles are forbidden to mention God's Name in vain, from the commandment to fear God.

[41] *Shulĥan Aruĥ HaRav Oraĥ Ĥayim* 85:3.

Rabbi Zalman Nehemiah Goldberg notes that in the Responsa of Rabbi Akiva Eiger, vol. 1:25, it is written that a Divine name in another language (other than Hebrew) is considered an attributive name, and therefore does not infringe the prohibition of mentioning God's Name in vain.

[42] Responsa of Rabbi Akiva Eiger, *ibid.*; *Minĥat Ĥinuĥ*, Commandment 69.

[43] *Shulĥan Aruĥ HaRav Oraĥ Ĥayim* 156:2, 215:3.

[44] Rambam, *Laws of Oaths* 12:11.

one does mention His Name, one should think about the reason and purpose for mentioning it, in order that it not be mentioned in vain. The Sages say,[45] "In any place one finds the mention of God's Name in vain, one finds poverty and death."

When one wishes to bless and thank God, one should direct his thoughts and words in order to say words of thanks and praise to honor God's Name. In this way the result will be that the Name of God is exalted, and not disgraced.

We see that Joseph acted in this way, where it says,[46] "And God was with Joseph and he was successful … And his master saw that God was with him, and all that he did, God made successful." Rashi explains how Joseph's master saw that God was with him:[47] "The Name of God was fluent in Joseph's mouth," – i.e., he would constantly credit his success to God and publicize His Name, as Joseph said to Pharaoh,[48] "God will give Pharaoh a favorable answer."

This was also the way of Abraham, to teach all the nations that it is fitting to praise and bless God's Name alone, as it says,[49] "and there he proclaimed the Name of God, God of the universe" – meaning that he caused all people he encountered to call (i.e., to pray and praise) in the Name of the Holy One, blessed be He, and he taught every person to pray to God and praise the Name of God.[50]

7. One who pronounces the Explicit Name according to its spelling, as written Y-H-V-H, will be "uprooted from the world."[51]

When a person reads scriptures containing God's Names, it is permitted to read them as spelled in any language,[52] except for the Name Y-H-V-H, which is forbidden to pronounce; rather, one should read it *"Ad-onai."* (Some are even more stringent, and do not to read God's holy Names as spelled even when reading scriptures, but rather

---

[45] Tractate *Nedarim* 7b.

[46] Genesis 39:2-3.

[47] Rashi on Genesis 39:3.

[48] Genesis 41:16.

[49] Genesis 21:33.

[50] Tractate *Sotah* 10b, and Rashi there.

[51] Tractate *Sanhedrin* 90a; Tractate *Avodah Zarah* 18a; Rosh on Tractate *Yoma* 8:19; *Tur Oraĥ Ĥayim* ch. 621.

[52] *Pri Megadim Oraĥ Ĥayim* ch. 215; *Mishnah Berurah* 215:14.

substitute *"HaShem,"* which literally means "The Name."[53] It appears that this applies only to God's Names written in the original Hebrew. But God's names in other languages are considered like attributive names and may be mentioned while learning. Thus there is no extra personal merit or honor to God in stopping oneself from pronouncing them as they are translated in other languages.)

8. One who curses any person with God's name in any language, whether he curses himself or others, or even a dead or evil person, has transgressed a prohibition, since he uses God's Name in vain.[54]

9. One who mentions God's name (in any language) and spits (in disgust), whether he does so before or after he mentions the name, has jeopardized his part in the World to Come.[55]

10. It is forbidden to mention any of the specified holy Names (which may not be erased; see topic 1:2 above), and even names for God in other languages, in a place where there is filth or in an undignified situation (for example, in a restroom or bathhouse, or where people are unclothed; see Part I, topic 6:7, for more details), since this is degrading to God's Name.

The word *shalom* in Hebrew is also a Name of God (based on Judges 6:24), and it is therefore forbidden to say *"shalom"* ("peace") as a greeting while one is in such a place. This applies specifically to saying it in Hebrew, but it is permitted to say the translation of the

---

[53] *Sha'arei Teshuva Oraĥ Ĥayim* ch. 215.

[54] *Minĥat Ĥinuĥ* Commandments 69, 231. In *Mitzvot HaShem* (p. 377), Rabbi Yonatan Shteif writes in the name of *Ĥemdat Yisrael* (on *Hilĥot Melaĥim* ch. 9) that it is forbidden for Gentiles to curse a judge, as this is included in the prohibition of blasphemy. This is also implied by Rashi on Tractate *Sanhedrin* 56b: "I am God – my fear should be upon you." This refers to fear of judges. It is also written in *Mitzvot Hashem* (p. 488) that it is forbidden for a Gentile to curse a Jew, which is included in the prohibition of blasphemy. And clearly, it is immoral to curse any good person.

[55] *Shulĥan Aruĥ Yoreh De'ah* 179:8. The *Shulĥan Aruĥ* (*loc. cit.*) says that one who utters a holy Name of God and then spits on a wound, thinking that this might be a cure, nevertheless has no part in the World to Come, because of the disgrace to God's Name. *Shaĥ* says there (179:11) that it is not forbidden for one to do this if he utters a translated name of God instead.

word *shalom* in other languages, since that is not considered God's Name.[56] One may, however, call a person by his given name *Shalom* in a bathhouse.[57]

Attributive names such as "The Compassionate," "The Merciful," "The Faithful" and the like, may even be mentioned in Hebrew in a bathhouse, even if one intends that it refers to God, since people are sometimes also described with these terms.[58]

11. It is forbidden to destroy holy Names and writings, as this is a disgrace to God's honor and profanes His Name.[59] The Hebrew Names which may not be destroyed are: Y-H-V-H, *Ado-nai*, *Ai-l*, *E-lohim*, *E-lohah*, *Sha-dai*, *Tziva-ot*, *Ehe-yeh*, and *Y-ah*, and any of the possessive versions of *E-lohim*, such as *Elo-heĥah*, or *E lohaiĥem*, or *E-lohainu* and the like; even to erase one letter from one of these Names is forbidden.[60]

However, if one only wrote part of a Name, such as "Shad" from *Sha-dai*, or "Eh" from *Eh-yeh*, or "Ado" from *Ado-nai*, since he does not complete the Names, he may erase them[61] if there is a need to do so. However, it is forbidden to disgrace them.

But *Shaĥ* definitely would agree that doing so for no reason is a disgrace, and forbidden, but not so severely. Mentioning one of God's holy Names and then spitting when there is no need is a less severe infraction, but it is also a disgrace, and is forbidden. This is similar to the case of erasing one of God's holy Names when there is no need, which is forbidden as explained in the last footnote to topic 12 below.

Some have a habit of uttering a holy Name of God and spitting upon a wound, but this is an infraction that is as severe as spitting in disgust. If an attributive name of God, including a translation, is used, it is also forbidden.

[56] This appears to be clear, as *Shalom* is not a Specified Name, since people also use it as a given name. Thus its translation, even if intended to refer to God, is only an attributive name, and may even be mentioned in these places.

[57] This leniency is granted because the intent is to say the person's name (*Shalom*), and not a name of God; *Shulĥan Aruĥ HaRav Oraĥ Ĥayim* ch. 84.

[58] *Shulĥan Aruĥ Oraĥ Ĥayim* ch. 85.

[59] *Minĥat Ĥinuĥ* Commandment 69 (in his *Kometz Minĥa*) writes that one who erases God's Name has done no less of a transgression than one who mentions His Name in vain, and both are thus clearly forbidden for Gentiles.

[60] *Shulĥan Aruĥ Yoreh De'ah* ch. 276.

[61] *Shulĥan Aruĥ* and Rema, *Yoreh De'ah* ch. 276.

12. It is likewise forbidden to write holy Names for no reason, as they may come to be disgraced, especially since their very writing for no reason is a disgrace to God.[62] It is even forbidden to erase (for no justified need) or disgrace one of the seven holy Names mentioned above when they are translated (or transliterated) in other languages.[63]

13. One may not disgrace a holy Name of God written in any language, for example, by putting it in the garbage or in an unclean place such a restroom (meaning a place that is designated and used for excrement or for baths or showers), and the same applies to all written verses from the holy Hebrew Bible.[64] If there is a need to dispose of them, one should bury them in a container, or conceal them in earthenware vessels, which is like burial.[65]

14. Likewise, it is forbidden to verbally mention God's Name, even in prayer, in an undignified place (see Part I, topic 6:7). This would disgrace the person's prayer and the Name he utters.

---

[62] See *Shulĥan Aruĥ HaRav* 32:14. (The author of our text compares this to mentioning God's Name for no reason, as explained above in topic 4, and according to this, in the opinion that holds that the prohibition against mentioning it applies even to its translation, this equality would apply to writing it as well. According to the opinion that permits it, cited in fn. 41, it appears that one may write it for no reason also, and it is only forbidden to disgrace it by throwing it out, as explained in *Aĥiezer* vol. 3, ch. 32.)

*An example of "justified need" is erasing a translated holy Name that is part of a written text, as part of the process of correcting or improving the text.

[63] From *Shaĥ Yoreh De'ah* 179:11 and *Shulĥan Aruĥ HaRav Oraĥ Ĥayim* 85:3, holy names in languages other than Hebrew may be erased – if a justified need arises to do so – but just to disgrace them is forbidden. Rambam, *Laws of the Foundations of the Torah* 6:5, writes that attributive names are like other holy writing and may be erased, and in *ibid.* 6:8, he writes that it is forbidden to burn or destroy Holy Writings. This means that if there is a justified need it is permitted, but not without reason.

[64] Rema *Yoreh De'ah* ch. 276.

*The same also applies to the texts of the Oral Torah, such as the Mishnah, Talmud, works of Torah Law, and any traditional Jewish prayer book (which is called a *Siddur* in Hebrew, meaning "order," because it gives a set order for the prayer services).

[65] See *Shulĥan Aruĥ Yoreh De'ah* 282:10.

CHAPTER 3

Laws of Vows and Promises

1. A Gentile does not have a specific commandment to fulfill any promises or vows he makes, and the Gentiles have not been warned against transgressing their words.[66] In any case, even though they were not commanded regarding this, as a thing which is obligatory according to human intelligence, every person is obligated to keep his word, and how much more so not to lie about the past.[67]

2. It is best for a person not to swear at all, even if he is not promising in the name of God or a term referring to God, and if he did swear, he is obligated to fulfill his words. Just as it is best for a person not to swear at all, it is also best for him not to make any vows, as he will find himself obligated to fulfill things that he may possibly be unable to fulfill, and then he will find himself lying about his words. If he does make such a vow, he is obligated to keep his words.[68]

3. However, someone who finds himself in a desperate situation can vow to God in his prayers, so that his promise and intended good deed should stand in his merit to save him from a desperate situation. In this situation, he should say: "I hereby vow that I will do such-and-such, if

---

[66] *Tosafot* in Tractate *Nazir* 61b. The commandment (Numbers 30:3) "… he shall not profane his word…" is directed to Jews. It appears that Rambam, in *Laws of Sacrificial Procedures* 3:2 (unlike the view of *Tosafot* in Tractate *Avodah Zarah* 5b), holds that the verse (Lev. 22:18) " *ish ish* [any man]…" only teaches us that a Gentile's sacrifice can be accepted in the Holy Temple, but not that a Gentile is obligated in any way to fulfill his word. Furthermore, Rambam himself does not mention anywhere that a Gentile must keep his promise to bring an acceptable sacrifice.

[67] *Mesheĥ Ĥoĥmah* Exodus 20:7; *Likkutei Siĥot* vol. 38, p. 28; Responsa of *Devar Yehoshua* vol. 1, p. 357. This is also clear from Jacob, who made an oath, and God required him to keep it (Genesis 28:20 and 31:13), and Joseph's vow to Jacob (Genesis 47:31 and 50:5-6). This is also clear from the Jerusalem Talmud, Tractate *Nazir* ch. 9, which discusses whether a Gentile can annul his vow, which implies that he must keep his vow, for otherwise there would be no need for annulment.

[68] Rambam, *Laws of Oaths* 12:12.

I will be saved from this problem." Perhaps in the merit of his promised vow, he will be saved.[69]

Similarly, it is proper and praiseworthy for one to make vows in order to correct his behavior and to properly redirect his opinions. How so? One who has a negative behavior trait or habit – for example, gorging on meat, or drinking a lot of wine or other intoxicating drink in an improper way – may make a vow that he will abstain from this thing for a certain amount of time. Or someone who fixates on seeking out wealth may vow that he will not accept any gifts for a certain amount of time. All such abstinences may properly be taken on with a vow in order to correct one's conduct. However, this is only on the condition that the person will first evaluate himself, to be confident that he is able to stand by his word, so he will not eventually transgress his vow and thus be guilty of lying.

Nevertheless, a person should not habituate himself to making vows, and he should not make many of them. Instead, he should try to separate from his improper behaviors, without making promises or vows.[70]

4. A Gentile who vows to bring a burnt offering to God must keep his word,[71] and so must one who verbally pledges money to charity.

5. Although Gentiles are commanded to honor God, it is permitted for them to swear in God's Name to prove that their words are true, for example, in the manner of an oath that a witness takes in court that he will give truthful testimony.

One is permitted to swear in the name of a noted person, such as a king or a respectable officer, or to swear by the life of such a person, or by one's own life. This we see from Joseph, who swore "by the life of Pharaoh."[72] It is also permitted to swear in the name of a well-known righteous Gentile, even if he is not truly righteous, but the

---

[69] This is learned from the conduct of Jacob, who made a vow in time of distress (Gen. 28:20). See *Shulĥan Aruĥ Yoreh De'ah* ch. 203.

[70] Rambam, *Laws of Vows* 13:24; *Shulĥan Aruĥ ibid.*

[71] *Tosafot* in Tractate *Avodah Zarah* 5b. This obligation is only based on moral human intelligence, and it is not a direct commandment.

[72] Genesis 42:15. One must conclude that in the days of Joseph, the pharaoh did *not* consider himself to be a god, unlike the pharaoh in the days of Moses; for otherwise, Joseph would not have sworn "by the life of Pharaoh."

masses believe he is a righteous and faithful person.[73]

6. Although it is permitted for a Gentile to vow by attaching a Name of God to another entity,[74] such as a king, a respectable officer, or his own life, it is not fitting to do so, since some opinions say that it is a degradation to combine God's Name with another. (The law regarding swearing in God's Name in combination with that of an idol or an intermediary is explained above in Part II, Chapter 12).

7. If a person is obligated to take an oath at the instruction of the court (or in another judicial framework), he is obligated to make a true oath. "True" implies two things:
(a) His words shall be true. Regarding the past he shall speak truth and not lie in his oath. Regarding a promise he makes about the future, he shall fulfill his promise.
(b) He is obligated to swear by something that is reliably true and not false. It has previously been described in this text in Part II, Chapter 12, that it is forbidden to swear by an idol, and in the case where he must swear by a deity, he should swear by the God of the universe, Who made the heavens and earth. Anyone who swears in one of His names, or attributive terms referring to God, is considered that he has sworn in the name of God.[75]

8. When someone swears by the Torah, or specifically the Hebrew Bible, by saying words equivalent to, "I swear by what is written in the

---

[73] See *Tosafot* on Tractate *Sanhedrin* 63b.

[74] *Tosafot* on Tractate *Sanhedrin* 63b; Rema *Oraĥ Ĥayim* ch. 156. However, it appears that Rambam, in *Laws of Oaths* 11:2, argues and forbids a Gentile to swear in the name of any intermediary being or power which he includes along with the Name of God, since by doing so one degrades and profanes the Name of God. Even though this prohibition is not spelled out by Rambam, it is clear that Gentiles are forbidden to do so for the above reason, for surely Gentiles are obligated to honor God and not degrade Him. The explanation of the Talmud's statement, "Anyone who combines the name of God with that of an intermediary is uprooted from the world," according to Rambam, applies to an intermediary which one does not consider to be a deity, as is explained in *Laws of Oaths* there. Thus, there is no difference with regard to which intermediary he swears by.

[75] See Rambam, *Laws of Oaths* 11:1.

Torah (or the Hebrew Bible)," or he takes hold of a scroll or book of the Torah in his hands, or only rests his hand on it at the moment when he makes his promise, it is considered that he swore by God's Name,[76] for the holy Names of God are written in the Hebrew Bible.[77]

If someone swears by God's holy Names that are written in the Books of the Prophets or Holy Writings (Hagiographa) that are part of the Hebrew Bible, or by God's holy Names that are written in any other holy books, this is considered swearing in the Name of God.[78]

9. If a court made a Gentile liable to swear under oath, but not with a Name of God, he should merely swear without mentioning a Name of God, or even one of His attributes (in any language).

Therefore when a court makes a witness liable to swear, he should only be made to do so without mentioning any of the Names, or attributive names, or attributes of God, and without placing his hand on a holy text or object.[79]

10. One who swears of his own accord, or one who hears an oath announced by others, and he affirms his acceptance by answering "amen," has made a vow and must keep his word, since anyone who affirms a vow by answering "amen" is as if he himself made the vow. Whether one answers "amen" or a word that bears the same meaning, such as "yes," or "I am obligated in this vow," or "I accept this vow," or any phrase that has the same meaning, one becomes bound by the vow which one affirms.[80]

---

[76] Placing one's hand on a holy book is considered as if he is holding it.

[77] Rambam *Laws of Oaths* 12:4; Rema *Yoreh De'ah* 237:6.

[78] Radvaz *Hilĥot Sh'vuot* 12:3; Rav Ĥai Gaon and Rashba cited by *Beit Leĥem Yehudah* on *Shulĥan Aruĥ Yoreh De'ah* ch. 212.

*On the other hand, swearing on a non-Torah book that is considered holy by a foreign religion is at least equivalent to swearing on an "intermediary" (a *sheetuf* in Hebrew); this was explained in detail in Chapter 12 of Part II.

[79] See Ra'avad on *Laws of Oaths* 11:13, in the name of the *Ge'onim* sages, that in later generations, Jewish courts nullified the practice of swearing in God's Name because of the severity of the punishment involved, as the *Shulĥan Aruĥ Ĥoshen Mishpat* 87:19 rules in regard to Jewish judges; it is therefore also fitting for Gentiles to conduct themselves likewise.

[80] Rambam, *Laws of Oaths* 2:1.

11. It is forbidden to swear in vain, for no purpose at all, whether one swears in God's Name or a term referring to Him, which is a desecration of His Name and is tantamount to swearing falsely in His Name. Even if a person swears in vain but not in God's Name, he at least profanes his words.

12. "Swearing in vain" denotes one of the following types of vows:

(a) One who swears about a known thing, in which there exists no doubt to its truth, like one who swears that a stone is a stone. Included in this category are those who hurry to swear when there is no true need for an oath;

(b) One who swears about a matter which all know is false, like swearing that a man is a woman, or a stone is gold, which is not only false, but needs no verification.

(c) One who swears to do something which he has no power to accomplish, like swearing not to sleep for three consecutive days and nights, or not to eat for seven days (or not to sleep or eat without giving a timeframe for his vow,[81] which implies that the vow exists forever), utters a vow in vain, since he will surely not be able to keep it.

One need not pain himself and deprive himself of sleep for one or two days until he goes against his vow, and likewise for deprivation of food; rather it is permitted for him to eat and sleep right away, for since his vow is in vain, his words are of no consequence.[82]

(d) One who swears about a prohibition he is commanded in (for example, swearing that he will eat flesh taken from a living animal, or steal, or commit adultery), has uttered a vain oath, since it is forbidden for him to keep his words, and he has no need to make such a vow.[83]

13. A person should not swear on the actions of others, that they will or will not do a future action, since he does not have the power to keep his words, and they are not bound by his vow,[84] unless they agreed to his words, in the manner described above in topic 10.

A man who swears to marry a woman, and vice versa, is not considered to have uttered a vain oath, since the intention is such that

---

[81] *Shulĥan Aruĥ Yoreh De'ah* 236:4.

[82] Rambam, *Laws of Oaths* 5:20.

[83] *Ibid.*, 1:4-7.

[84] *Ibid.*, 5:1-2; *Shulĥan Aruĥ Yoreh De'ah* ch. 236.

if the second person consents, then the first person will be obligated to keep the vow. When this happens, the first person does become bound by the oath. Likewise, in any case where one person swears on condition that a second person will do something, this oath is not in vain and is binding as soon as the condition is met.

14. It is permitted for a Gentile to swear to keep one of the Seven Noahide Commandments, even though he is already obligated in them, since he sees this as a necessary vow in order to encourage himself to keep the commandment.[85]

15. One who intends to swear and resolves a certain matter in his heart, but does not actually voice the commitment, is not bound by it as by a vow. Likewise, if one resolved in his heart to prohibit himself from doing a certain action, and erred and mentioned another vow which he did not intend, like one who intends to swear not to eat with person A, and erred and voiced a promise not to eat with person B, may still eat with both of them, as one is only bound by a vow which he both intends and voices in accordance; but resolve alone, or an errant spoken vow, are not binding.

If one resolved in his heart not to eat bread made from wheat, and then swore not to eat bread without specifying the type, he is only forbidden to eat wheat bread, as his heart and mouth were alike on this matter. In contrast, if one swears and says, "I swear such and such with your consent," he cannot say that he had other thoughts in mind, since his heart and spoken words were in accordance that the oath would depend on the consent of others. Therefore this is a complete vow, and

---

Rabbi Zalman Nehemiah Goldberg notes that such a vow is not necessarily in vain, for if it was, it would be considered in vain whether others kept the vow or not. The reason, it appears, is because one who swears to sin or do an impossible action intends that his vow should enable him to do so, and it is therefore said in vain.

In contrast, one who swears that others will do an action does not intend that they must do so, but rather that he knows the future and can predict that the others will do the action, and he does not necessarily swear for naught. Therefore, one who swears that rain will or will not fall the next day does not swear in vain, but rather swears on his ability of foresight, like a meteorologist who predicts the weather.

[85] Rambam, *Laws of Oaths* 11:3.

the consent of the others takes the place of his consent.[86]

16. If one swears or promises, and then rescinds his oath in a short period of time (equal to the time required to say, "Peace unto you, my teacher"), and says "I regret it," or "This is not a vow," or "I have reconsidered," and the like, then the vow is not binding. This is comparable to one who made a mistake, and did not really have intention in his heart for his vow.[87]

17. Likewise if others told him "Reconsider it," or "This is not binding for you," and he verbally accepts their words immediately (in the short time period defined above) by saying "Yes," or "I regret it," the vow is not binding. If he waits longer than this amount of time, he may not rescind his vow.[88]

18. If one swears verbally and reconsiders the vow in his heart before the specified time limit, but does not voice his regret, then he does not rescind it. If others told him, "Reconsider it," or "This is not binding for you," and he accepts their words in his heart during the specified time, he has accomplished nothing until he voices his intentions.[89]

19. There is a type of vow that is not made through speech, but is committed through action, in a community where this action is accepted as a vow, and this oath is binding with all the rules of a vow. For example, in places where a vow is communicated by an action at the time of the declaration – for example, by shaking hands, raising the right hand, or placing one's hand on a Hebrew Bible – then these actions are considered vows.

However, in places where businessmen commonly shake hands over a business deal, this is only considered an informal agreement and an endorsement of the deal, and it is not considered to be a vow.[90]

---

[86] *Ibid.*, 2:10-15.

[87] *Ibid.*, 2:17.

[88] *Ibid.*, 2:18.

[89] *Ibid.*, 2:19.

[90] *Shulĥan Aruĥ Yoreh De'ah* ch. 239; *Shulĥan Aruĥ Ĥoshen Mishpat* 81:28.

*Even a signed document that is recognized by a court is not a vow. It only serves to establish or validate a business agreement.

CHAPTER 4

Annulment of Vows and Promises, and Vows Made According to the Public's Understanding

1. If one makes a promise or vow to do a certain thing or not to do so, and he then regrets his vow and decides that he will be distressed if he holds himself to keeping it – or if something occurs later which he did not foresee, and he reconsiders his promise or vow because of this – then he may request annulment for the vow according to the instructions below. Once his vow becomes annulled, he is allowed to do a thing that he swore not to do, or he does not have to do the thing he promised to do.[91] Even if he swore to the promise by God's Name, he may request annulment for the vow.[92]

2. It has been explained in the previous chapter that a person should not rush to make promises or vows, and if one has already done so, he should keep his word and not annul his vow. He should endure distress to uphold what he swore verbally, rather than annul the oath (for anyone who swears and then annuls his vow is like a liar).[93] Only if one sees that the vow he uttered is causing him much distress, or if it becomes a stumbling block, or causes him or others to sin, should he then have the vow annulled.[94]

After the fact, if he requests annulment for his vow and receives it, even if it was not fitting for him to do so, he is then no longer bound by the vow.

3. One cannot annul his own vow;[95] rather others must annul it for him. Even one person can annul another person's vow, provided he is knowledgeable in the precepts regarding annulment of vows, and he

---

[91] Based on Rambam, *Laws of Oaths* 6:1.

[92] *Shulĥan Aruĥ Yoreh De'ah* ch. 228, 230.

[93] This can be shown from what happened to King Zedekiah, who was killed by Nebuchadnezzar for annulling the vow he swore to him, as explained in Tractate *Nedarim* 65a.

[94] Based on Rambam, *Laws of Oaths* 12:12 and *Laws of Vows* 13:25; *Shulĥan Aruĥ Yoreh De'ah* ch. 203.

[95] Rambam, *Laws of Oaths* 6:3.

knows what is considered valid regret from the outset, and how to find an opening for establishing that the necessary regret is there.[96]

Even a friend or relative, as long as they are knowledgeable in these laws, is allowed to annul a vow that a Gentile made.[97]

4. How is an oath annulled? The person who took the oath says before those who are annulling it: "I took an oath concerning such and such, and I have changed my mind. If I had known that I would feel so much discomfort concerning this matter, or that such and such a thing would happen to me as a result, I would not have taken the oath. If at the time of the oath, my understanding was as it is now, I would not have made the oath."

Those who are annulling the oath say to him: "Have you already changed your mind?" He answers: "Yes."

They then tell him: "The thing is permitted for you," or "The promise is released for you," or the like, with this intent and in any language.[98]

There is no annulment for a vow unless the one who made the oath regrets it and rescinds, declaring: "If I had known what I know now, or if I would have thought about this at the time of my vow, I would not have made it," and rescinds his vow in the presence of those who are annulling it.

Whether one comes forward to request an annulment on his own accord, or if another person initiates the annulment and asks him, "If you had known such and such at the time of your vow, would you have

---

[96] See Jerusalem Talmud, Tractate *Nazir*, beginning of ch. 9: Rabbi Yosay and Rabbi Avahu have the opinion that a Gentile does not need to request annulment from a scholar specifically, but may even do so from any ordinary person. The law follows their opinion, as seen from Tractate *Sotah* 36b, that Pharaoh said to Joseph, "Go and annul your vow." So we see that annulment of vows also applies to Gentiles. It appears that the annulment may equally well be made through an ordinary Jew or an ordinary Gentile.

[97] Rambam *ibid.*, 6:6; *Shulĥan Aruĥ Yoreh De'ah* 228:3. **Also, it should be done in person and not by telephone or video call.**

[98] This is the wording of Rambam (*ibid.* 6:5). It can be proven from the Jerusalem Talmud, Tractate *Nazir* (loc. cit.), that one needs to identify an opening for establishing that there is regret, without which the scholar cannot annul the vow.

made it?" and he answers "No," this is an "opening" for the other person(s) to annul his vow.[99]

However, if one says that he does not regret his vow, it is impossible to release him from it. Even if one regrets the vow at the current point in time but does not regret it from the time of its acceptance, and says that what he promised was good until now, and only in the future does he want to release himself from it, he cannot receive annulment.[100]

Therefore, if he himself does not express regret that he made his vow, the persons he approached to grant the annulment must discuss the matter thoroughly to see if there is any opening by which to say that he does indeed regret the vow to begin with or not, and they should delve deeply into the matter, and not hasten to annul the vow.[101]

5. The following rules apply when a person took an oath and does not regret it, and he came before a court to carry out his oath. If the judges see that releasing the oath will lead to a good result or the end of feuding (such as making peace between a husband and wife, or between two colleagues), and carrying it out will on the other hand lead to transgression and strife, they encourage the person to take the option of having his oath annulled.

They should discuss the matter with him, pointing out the negative consequences of his oath, until he regrets that he made it. If he changes his mind because of their words, they should release his oath. If he does not change his mind and upholds his oath, he must carry it out.

What is implied? If a person took an oath that he would divorce his wife, they should tell him: "If you divorce your wife, you will cause malicious gossip to circulate concerning her children, for people will say, 'Why was the mother of these children divorced?' Or it is possible

---

[99] *The court is ruling that the person made a mistake when he vowed by not realizing the truth of the situation, including the possible negative outcomes that could result.

[100] *Shulĥan Aruĥ Yoreh De'ah* 228:7.

[101] *Ibid.*, 228:4.

*Even though it was explained in topic 3 that even one person can release a Gentile's vow, nevertheless, when an opening is needed, it is fitting that it should be discussed among a "panel" of several knowledgeable persons to come to a decision as to whether it was truly a mistaken vow that warrants annulment.

that she may become remarried to another." If he says, "If I had realized this, I would not have taken the oath," they annul his oath. If he says, "All the same, I have no regret, and this is what I want," the court is unable to release him from his oath.[102]

6. We do not annul an oath because of something that had not occurred at the time the oath was made, and the person had no possible knowledge of it from the outset.[103] What is implied? For example, someone took an oath not to derive benefit from such-and-such a person, and that person later became the city's mayor. Since the person did not regret making the vow, even if he now says, "If I had known that this would occur, I would not have made the vow," his vow should not be annulled, for he still does not regret his original making of the vow.

However, if he regretted and said, "If I had known that this person was fitting for prominence and honor at the time of my vow, I would not have taken it," then this is a true and valid regret, and his vow can be annulled.[104] When does this apply? In regard to a normal occurrence, which a person could have foreseen as being possible at the time he made the vow.

A different rule applies if an unusual occurrence happens that one would not normally think of. Since this is a completely unforeseen condition, it should not be considered as an opening to allow the person to be granted annulment due to regret, since he does not regret that he originally made the vow. For example: if one swears not to derive benefit from such-and-such a person who was a healthy person, and that person dies unexpectedly and leaves an inheritance to the person who vowed, the court does not release him from the vow based on his statement, "If I had known that he would die, I would not have made this oath." Since the death of a healthy person is unusual, the person would not have thought about this possibility at the time of his vow.[105]

---

[102] Rambam, *Laws of Oaths* 6:10-11.

[103] *After the oath was made, something new arose, that the person could not have known or anticipated at the time of the oath.

[104] Rambam, *ibid.* 6:12.

[105] *Shulĥan Aruĥ Yoreh De'ah* 228:12.

Vows Made According to the Public's Understanding

7. One who swears or promises upon the knowledge of one or more other people, may not request annulment without their consent.[106] Therefore, a court should not release such a vow unless the person has previously received permission from the others for release of his vow.

If the court nevertheless released the person from the vow, or if the other people die (in which case it is impossible to request their permission to annul the vow), or if there was an overriding need that he must annul his vow, the court has permission to do so.[107]

8. A vow of a person who swears based upon the consent of the public at large can never be annulled, since it is impossible to receive consent from the public.[108] But if there was an overriding need for the person to rescind his vow, the court may do so even in such a case.[109]

One who takes an oath in public is not considered to have based his oath on their consent, until he says clearly that he made the oath based on the consent of the public.[110]

Vows Made in Partnership, or Under Duress, or by Mistake

9. If two people swore to each other to perform an action together, such as to make a partnership in business, or if a man and woman swore to marry each other, and one of the parties annuls the vow, the second is also not bound by the vow, since each person was only bound to begin with on condition that the other person keeps the vow.

If a man and woman became engaged with a vow and swore to get married at a specific time, or if two businessmen made a partnership

---

[106] *Since the vow was made on their knowledge and intention (see the end of topic 3:15), and releasing the vow is made possible by a regret from the beginning, the annulment must be granted with the agreement of all parties involved.

[107] Tractate *Nedarim* 65a *Tosafot* and Ran there; *Shulĥan Aruĥ ibid.* 228:20.

[108] *This is why Abimelech brought a *group* of his friends when he wished to convince Isaac to make an oath of mutual peace, even though Isaac respected the same oath that had been given by Abraham. (*Or HaĤayim* Gen. 26:26)

[109] Rambam, *Laws of Oaths* 6:8-9; *Shulĥan Aruĥ Yoreh De'ah* 228:21.

[110] *Shulĥan Aruĥ Yoreh De'ah* 228:23.

that is dependent on time, and this time passes, and one of the parties claims that he had no choice and did not purposefully put off the date, the second party may request annulment for his side of the vow (if he so desires), and the court may release him from it.[111]

10. This applies only if two people swore to each other to do something together. But if two or more parties swear to do a certain thing or not to do it, such as not to speak to or do business with a certain person, and one or more of them violated the oath, this does not release the other parties involved, since such a vow is not dependent on the consent of the others.

In contrast, if two people make an oath that is dependent on each one of them, such as an oath that they will go together to a certain place, and one violates the oath, the second is exempt from keeping his part in it, since this oath depends on the actions of both together, and is comparable to the cases in the previous paragraph.[112]

11. One who was forced to swear – for example, by being hit until he swore, or being pushed and forced against his will to make an oath – it is not a binding vow, and it does not need to be annulled.[113] This applies even if he was forced to swear by consent of the public.

12. Likewise, one who swore by accident or mistake – for example, one who swears that his wife and children should not benefit from him because they stole from his wallet, and then later finds out that they really had not stolen from him – is not bound by his vow. Similarly, if one thinks something positive or negative about such-and-such a person and therefore makes an oath regarding him, and later finds out that his assumptions were wrong (for example, one who thinks that a certain person was not attending a wedding, and pledged a thousand coins to charity "if this person was at the wedding," and later he finds out that this person was indeed there), then he has made a mistaken vow, and he is not obligated to keep his words. He is also not obligated to release his vow. All similar situations have the same ruling.[114]

---

[111] *Shulĥan Aruĥ Yoreh De'ah* ch. 236.

[112] *Ibid.*

[113] *Ibid.*, 232:15.

[114] *Ibid.*, 232:6.

PART IV

THE PROHIBITION OF EATING MEAT THAT WAS SEPARATED FROM A LIVING ANIMAL

Including Restrictions on Causing Suffering to Living Creatures, Mating Different Species of Animals, and Grafting Different Species of Fruit Trees

This section explains details of the following one obligation and five prohibitions that are included in this commandment to Gentiles and its offshoots:

1. If meat was severed from a living land mammal or bird, one may not eat from that meat while the creature is still alive. Included in this prohibition is not to inflict cruelty or unnecessary pain on any living creatures.

2. If meat was severed from a living land mammal or bird, one may not eat from that meat even after the creature has died.

3. To be guardians over nature and the life of all creatures, so that they will not be destroyed unnecessarily.

4. Not to cause mating together of two different species of animals.

5. Not to graft together two different species of fruit trees.

6. Not to unnecessarily castrate or neuter an animal.

INTRODUCTION

by Joe M. Regenstein, Ph.D.

Professor of Food Science
Head, Cornell Kosher and Halal Food Initiative
Department of Food Science, Cornell University

For most of us, the story of Noaĥ and the ark ends with the rainbow as God's sign of his covenant with Noaĥ. However, a covenant requires the input of two parties, so, yes, there are also the rules that humanity is required to obey as their contribution to the covenant. Although most of the precepts in the Hebrew Scriptures only apply to Jews, the Seven Noahide Commandments are considered a covenant with all of humanity – therefore it is important for everyone to understand these Divine laws, so that all may uphold their part in the covenant.

One of these Noahide Commandments is that which in Hebrew is referred to as *"Eiver Min Ha'ĥai"* ("Limb from a Living Animal"), which is the prohibition against eating flesh that was severed from a living animal. On the surface this seems like an easy concept to grasp, and it is. It is an important statement of the limitations imposed on each individual, in light of the broader scriptural permission for humanity to have "dominion" over the animals. It is also a statement of God's concern for the welfare of animals. Humanity's responsibility for animal welfare is further developed in the Hebrew Scriptures to encompass the broader concept of avoiding the infliction of unnecessary pain or suffering (*"tza'ar ba'alei ĥayim"* in Hebrew) upon living creatures, which is the concept of not doing any harm to animals unless there is a good reason to do otherwise. It is thus made clear that in God's judgment, to treat an animal cruelly is wrong. Therefore, Hebrew Scripture, by showing this caring for animals, also teaches by implication how much worse it is to treat people poorly. So, it is clear that by including *"Eiver Min Ha'ĥai"* as one of the Seven Noahide Commandments that are incumbent on all humanity, Hebrew Scripture is making a very powerful statement of God's vision for humanity.

In our generation, humanity has begun to re-examine many of its core values, and one outcome has been an increasing concern for establishing governmental and corporate standards for animal welfare (and for some, the relevance of animal rights in this process). So it is important that we now look closely and seriously at the guidance provided by the Torah's Noahide Code in this important area.

As has been the practice in Jewish law over the approximately 3300 years since the giving of the Torah through Moses, the implementation of any one of God's commandments has always been very carefully considered, including all of its details and ramifications. Throughout Jewish history, this process has been applied to the Noahide Code, just as it was to virtually all other subjects within the oral tradition of the Torah. Various expert Sages and Rabbis over the course of time taught and recorded their codifications, commentaries and responsa, and thereby provided clarifications and explanations of the fundamental texts of the Oral Torah, which include the *Mishnah* and Talmud, the *Mishneh Torah* of Maimonides (Rambam), etc. Furthermore, new situations arise over the generations that need to be ruled upon, based on the principles of the existing rulings that cover the full spectrum of Torah Law. Over time some opinions are accepted by the majority of leading Rabbis and become normative, while others are not widely accepted and assume the status of minority opinions.

This important volume reviews the many available traditional sources that deal with the issues of the Noahide Code for Gentiles. This section of the work then takes the broad principle of *"Eiver Min Ha'ĥai"* and presents the "meat" (pun intended) on this issue, covering its many details and extended topics in the traditional format of Rabbinical scholarship. The author has applied foundational principles from many sources to these issues, and in this process he has thus resolved standing differences of opinion on key points of practical observance, in regard to permission or restriction, and strictness or leniency. Thus, this work provides the reader with the most comprehensive and up-to-date guide for meeting, and understanding, the requirements of the Noahide Code.

For those seeking to live in accordance with the eternal commandments that God gave through Moses, the need to understand the implications of both the entire Noahide Code and this particular section is critical. As readers will see, many of the modern public issues being discussed in the realm of animal welfare with respect to slaughter, pre-slaughter handling, and post-slaughter waiting for the animal to expire, are covered by this detailed and well-written text. It now becomes a source for providing guidance to all consumers, along with the regulators and overseers of the modern meat industry, and it challenges us all to be concerned with improving the handling of animals – both on the farm and in our communities, and most importantly in the arena of the compassionate use of animals for human food. With the release of this work, this can now be approached in keeping with modern industry guidelines for animal welfare, while also meeting the ancient but continuously relevant rules of *"Eiver Min Ha'ĥai."*

Chapter 1

Permissions and Prohibitions for Gentiles Regarding Meat; Species for which Meat from a Living Animal is Forbidden

1. Adam, the first man, was granted dominion over all living creatures, as the Torah states (Genesis 1:28): "And you shall rule over the fish of the sea, the fowl of the sky, and every living thing that moves on the earth." This dominion granted to Adam was only for using animals to perform useful tasks, and he was not permitted to kill any creature for food.[1,2] However, he was permitted to eat from the carcass of an animal that had died naturally.[3] Just as Adam was not permitted to kill any creature to eat its flesh, he also was not permitted to cut off a part of it during its lifetime to eat from it.[4]

2. After the flood, Noaĥ was granted greater permission than Adam. The dominion granted to him entitled him to kill any creature to eat its

---

[1] Tractate *Sanhedrin* 59b.

[2] The author notes: from *Sanhedrin* 59b it appears that Adam's control over animals was only in regard to using them for his own needs. Nevertheless, he was forbidden to kill an animal even for his own needs (i.e. for his food). Surely, then, he was forbidden to cause needless suffering to an animal.

[3] Rashi on Tractate *Sanhedrin* 57a, and *Tosafot* on *Sanhedrin* 56b.

There is a discussion between the Sages as to whether Adam was commanded not to eat ***eiver min ha'ĥai*** (flesh from a living animal). Rashi and *Tosafot* explain there *(ibid.)* that Adam was not permitted to kill any animal for its flesh, but he was permitted to eat meat from an animal that had died naturally. Therefore, the prohibition of *eiver min ha'ĥai* for him (and his descendants before the Flood) only applied practically to eating flesh that became detached from a living animal due to injury or illness, since he was forbidden to cut a living animal **or to kill it in any way**. Rambam (*Laws of Kings* 9:1) maintains that the prohibition of *eiver min ha'ĥai* was not commanded to Adam at all, because he had no permission to eat meat; rather, it was first commanded to Noaĥ. However, it is clear according to all opinions that it was forbidden for Adam and his descendants to cut off a limb from a living animal, because of the suffering it would cause to the animal.

[4] Gen. 2:16 teaches that anything other than vegetation was forbidden for people to deliberately kill for food (until after the Flood, when mankind was permitted to eat meat; see Rashi on Gen. 1:29 and Tractate *Sanhedrin* 59b).

flesh, as the Torah states (Genesis 9:2-3): "The fear of you and the dread of you shall be upon every beast of the earth and every bird of the sky, upon everything that moves on earth and upon all fish of the sea; in your hand they are given. Every moving thing that lives shall be yours for food; like the green herbage I have given you everything."

Noaĥ and his descendants were granted permission to kill any type of animal in any way they desired, for the purpose of food. (Still, it is fitting for a person to have compassion toward animals and to kill them in the most painless manner possible. For mankind was not granted unrestricted permission to cause suffering to a living creature, as will be explained below in Chapter 7. Moreover, it is fitting for a person to distance himself from cruelty to the fullest extent possible.)[5]

Obviously there is no prohibition against a Gentile eating meat taken from the carcass of an animal that died naturally.[6]

3. Noaĥ was, however, forbidden to consume flesh that was removed from certain animals while they were still living (those specified in topic 1:6 below), as the Torah states (Genesis 9:4): "But flesh with its soul, its blood, you shall not eat." This refers to flesh separated from these live animals, while their soul is still in their blood.[7] This was an eternal, universal commandment for all the Children of Noaĥ.

4. There are various outstanding logical explanations which can be put forth for this prohibition. For example, the obtaining of such flesh is likely to be done in a way that would result in great pain to the animal.[8] Furthermore, it is a cruel behavior, which is a trait that people should strive to avoid. Nevertheless, it is from God's commandment, "But flesh with its soul, its blood, you shall not eat," that we learn that any flesh that is separated in any manner from the animals that are covered by this prohibition (see topic 6 below), during the time they are alive, is forbidden to be eaten.

---

[5] See Rambam, *Guide for the Perplexed,* vol. 3, ch. 17 and 48.

[6] Deuteronomy 14:21. See Rashi and Tosafot cited above in footnote 3.

*However one must guard his life (Part V, topic 7:1), and this includes not eating any tainted foods that would be hazardous to his health.

[7] Rashi, Tractate *Sanhedrin*, p. 59b.

[8] Ramban, on Genesis 1:29. However, the act remains forbidden even if the animal is rendered insensitive.

The Rabbinic term used to refer to this prohibition, ***eiver min ha'ĥai,*** literally means "limb from a living animal." However, the prohibition encompasses all flesh (meat, organs or limbs) separated from the designated types of animals while they are alive. This includes any flesh torn off during the animal's lifetime by a person (even if he bit the flesh off with his mouth),[9] or by another animal, or which fell off or was severed from the animal's body due to an accident or illness.[10]

5. After Noaĥ left the ark, humans were granted permission to kill any animals for food, or for the use of their body parts for beneficial purposes. However, neither Adam, Noaĥ, or their descendants were ever granted permission to injure, kill, or cause suffering to an animal for no useful purpose, and one who does so violates the prohibition of causing unnecessary pain to a living creature.[11]

For this reason, it is forbidden to skin an animal or cut out one of its organs during its lifetime,[12] even if one does not intend to eat from the part removed. Instead, if one requires the hide or the organ, one should

---

[9] See the discussion of Rebbi (Rabbi Yehuda the Prince) and Rabbi Elazar ben Shimon in Tractate *Ĥullin* 102b, about one who swallows a small living bird whole (whether he is guilty of eating *eiver min ha'ĥai*, which is meat taken *from* a living animal). All agree, however, that if a person bites off and eats flesh from one of the specified animals, he is liable (see topic 2:1).

[10] Rashi on Tractate *Sanhedrin* 57a, *Tosafot* (*ibid.* 56b), and Ran (*ibid.* 59b).

[11] Rabbi Zalman Nehemiah Goldberg notes that in Tractate *Ĥullin* 7b, Rabbi Pinĥas ben Yair said to Rebbi: "If one kills the mule, he will transgress the prohibition of wasting [something useful], and if he cuts off its hooves, he will transgress the prohibition of causing suffering to an animal." From this it appears that killing an animal is not included in the prohibition of causing unnecessary suffering to living creatures.

The author notes: it appears that the only proof from that source is that there is more suffering caused by cutting off the mule's hoofs, but there is still some pain inflicted by killing the animal. Rebbi would not kill the animal for no useful purpose, although it was mainly for the honor of Rabbi Pinĥas. He would sell its meat to a Gentile, or use it for some other purpose.

[12] *The restriction on causing needless pain dictates that one should kill the animal first. Questions arise about an organ transplant from a living animal to another animal or to a human, and if the transplanted organ would be *eiver min ha'ĥai*; see topic 4:10 and Chapter 7. Constraining an animal for continuous extraction of a bodily fluid is addressed in Chapter 7.

first kill it and then take the parts of its body that one needs.[13]

6. The prohibition against eating flesh taken from a living animal applies only to domesticated mammals, wild mammals, and birds.[14] In more general terms, these are all the animals for which there is a Torah-law distinction between their flesh and their blood. The *kosher* species status is of no consequence to this general prohibition.[15]

7. This prohibition does not apply to a *sheretz* animal (defined below), because there is no Torah-law distinction between consuming flesh or blood of a *sheretz*[16] (as is also the case for insect-like creatures, and all other creatures that are not included in the prohibition).[17]

Flesh separated from a living *sheretz* animal is allowed to be eaten by a Gentile.[18] It is, however, forbidden to separate a limb or organ from a living *sheretz* because of the suffering this causes to the creature, unless one's intent is that it is to be eaten for a therapeutic effect that will be lost if the creature is killed first.[19] The term *sheretz* refers to the eight creatures designated as such in Leviticus.[20] (The Hebrew terms for these creatures are: the *ĥoled,* the *aĥbar,* the *tzav,*

---

[13] Tractate *Ĥullin* 85b. (This is further discussed in Chapter 7 below.)

[14] *God also did not grant permission to eat human flesh, whether or not it would be removed while the person was alive (see topic 1:13 below). Note that these four categories of living beings are represented by the four faces of the *ĥayot* angels of the "divine chariot": the faces of the ox, lion, eagle and human (Ezekiel 1:10; see Rambam, *Laws of the Foundations of Torah* 2:3-8). Since these angels are elevated to the highest levels of the heavens, we can speculate that God gives an extra honor to their reflections in the physical world, through the Torah's universal restrictions on *eiver min ha'ĥai* and cannibalism.

[15] Rambam, *Laws of Kings* 9:13. (See Chapter 3 regarding *kosher*-slaughter.)

[16] The blood of non-*kosher* land mammals or birds is forbidden to Jews as "forbidden blood" under the prohibition (Lev. 12:26), "You shall not eat blood." As a substance, it is not defined as being within the category of non-*kosher* meat, as explained by Rambam, *Laws of Forbidden Foods* 6:1.

[17] Tractate *Sanhedrin* 59b.

[18] *Kesef Mishneh Hilĥot Melaĥim* 9:11.

[19] This is the same as for fish, as explained in topic 1:8 that follows.

[20] Leviticus 11:29-30.

the *anakah,* the *ko'aĥ,* the *leta'ah,* the *ĥomet* and the *tinshemes.*)[21]

8. The prohibition against consuming flesh from a living animal does not apply to fish, mollusks and insect-like creatures. It is not prohibited for a Gentile to consume them even while they are alive, whether to eat them whole or to cut off their limbs, organs, or flesh for food.[22] If, however, it is possible to kill these creatures first and then eat from them, one should do so, so that one does not cause unnecessary pain to the living creature, as explained below in topic 7:1. Nevertheless, if there are medical reasons that require one to consume meat or other parts from a live fish or crawling creature, it is permitted.[23]

The reason why the prohibition against eating flesh from a living animal does not apply to fish, insect-like creatures or a *sheretz* is because the prohibition is expressed in the verse, "But flesh with its soul, its blood, you shall not eat" (Gen. 9:4). This excludes creatures for which the blood is not considered separately from the flesh in the Torah's laws of foods that are allowed or forbidden for Jews.[24]

Even large sea mammals (for example, whales, dolphins and the like), which are included in the Torah's category of fish-like animals,

---

[21] *There is scholarly difference of opinion as to the identities of these animals. The one land mammal in this *sheretz* category that we can identify without question is the house mouse (Latin name *Mus musculus*). See the discussion of Leviticus 11:29-30 in *The Living Torah*, pub. Moznaim (3rd ed., June 1981, translation and commentary by Rabbi Aryeh Kaplan), which presents the Rabbinical opinions on these animals. (The application of the general precepts of *eiver min ha'ĥai* depends on a creature's classification as a mammal, and not on whether it is warm- or cold-blooded. The mole-rat, identified in *Aruĥ* as possibly being the *ĥoled*, is a cold-blooded mammal).

[22] *Tosefta*, Tractate *Terumos* ch. 9. The prohibition of Jews to eat *kosher* species of these creatures while they are still alive does not apply to Gentiles.

[23] *Hagahot Mordeĥai* on Tractate *Ĥullin*, ch. 3.

[24] This is like the permission to eat *eiver min ha'ĥai* from a *sheretz*, as discussed above (but there is no permission for inflicting unnecessary pain).

*This concept can only be appreciated in the context that the Seven Noahide Commandments are part of the Torah, which was revealed through Moses our teacher at Mount Sinai, as explained in the Introduction to this book. We see here that the concepts of Jewish Torah Law (*halaĥa*) apply to the details of the Noahide Commandments as well, even though the Torah's specific laws for Jews do not in general apply to Gentiles.

are therefore not included in the prohibition of *eiver min ha'ĥai.*[25] Likewise, all types of amphibians and reptiles are not included in the prohibition of *eiver min ha'ĥai* for the same reason.[26]

9. Mammals that dwell both in the sea and on the land are considered as wild land mammals and are included in this prohibition (e.g. seals, sea otters and sea lions).[27]

10. In the prohibition against eating meat from a living animal, rodents in general cannot be assumed to be included among the eight *sheretz* creatures that are listed in Leviticus (cited above in topic 1:7). Rodents in general must, therefore, be considered as wild mammals and not as *sheretz* animals, since we find that some rodents, such as squirrels, porcupines, etc., are considered wild mammals in Torah law.[28] Because of this doubt as to the identities of the named *sheretz* creatures in Lev. 11:29-30 as mentioned above in topic 1:7, no rodents other than the house mouse, which is definitely a *sheretz*, can be considered exempt from the prohibition of *eiver min ha'ĥai.*

Bats are considered to be in the same category as birds (Lev.11:19).

---

[25] See Rambam, *Laws of Forbidden Foods* 2:12.
*They are clearly defined *together* with fish in Gen. 1:20 ("Let the waters teem with swarming beings with living soul"), and in v. 21 ("the great sea giants and all the living soul that creeps, with which the waters teemed after their kinds"), which refers to beasts that live entirely in the water. Malbim extends this to all beasts that reproduce in water, even if they sometimes come out onto land, but there are other distinctions to consider.

[26] See Rambam, *Laws of Forbidden Foods*, ch. 6. All types of creatures, other than the specific ones for which a Jew has a separate prohibition against eating the blood (i.e. land mammals and birds), are not included in the prohibition of *eiver min ha'ĥai.*

[27] From Tractate *Ĥullin* 127a, if a mammal can travel on land by its own power, it is called a land mammal. It can be proven from Tractate *Kelim* 17:13 that a sea lion can receive the ritual impurity of an unslaughtered carcass *(neveila)*, which applies only to land mammals, because any beast which lives entirely in the sea does not receive Jewish ritual impurity. Since it is therefore a land mammal, it has the prohibition of *eiver min ha'ĥai*. In *Tzafnat Pane'aĥ* on Rambam, *Laws of Forbidden Foods* 2:12, it is explained that the sea lion is considered to be both a sea *sheretz* and a land mammal.

[28] Tractate *Kilayim*, ch. 8; *Sifra Torat Kohanim* 11:27.

11. When the prohibition applies, a Gentile is liable for punishment for eating even the slightest amount of an edible part (a limb, organ, flesh, fat, etc.) that was taken from the living animal.[29]

Blood from a living animal is not included in this prohibition.[30] A Gentile may drink blood that has already been extracted from a living animal, or cause an animal to bleed if he requires its blood for health purposes. He is, however, forbidden to cause an animal to bleed for the sake of drinking its blood as ordinary food, because of the suffering he will be causing to the animal. After the fact, however, a Gentile may consume blood that was collected in this manner.

It appears that the prohibition of drawing blood from an animal for the sake of drinking applies only if so much blood is drawn that the animal may die as a result. But drawing a small amount of blood from the animal, in a way that will definitely not result in its death, is permitted, if the person has an actual need for it, e.g. for drinking or medicinal purposes. This is because there is no Torah-based prohibition of causing pain to animals in a situation where the person has an actual need for it, as will be explained below in topic 7:2.

The prohibition of eating *eiver min ha'ĥai* applies to meat removed from living domesticated mammals, wild land mammals, and birds of any species. However, a Gentile is liable for a capital sin only for eating *eiver min ha'ĥai* meat from mammals (in the specific conditions explained in topics 1:12 and 3:1 which follow), but not from birds.[30]

12. Although cutting off flesh from a living animal is included in both the prohibitions of *eiver min ha'ĥai* and causing unnecessary pain to an animal,[31] a Gentile is not liable for capital punishment unless he eats from severed flesh while the animal is still alive.[32] The verse Gen.

---

[29] *This is because Gentiles are not subject to the principle for Jews that a Torah precept involving forbidden food does not make one liable for physical punishment unless a minimum amount of the food is eaten.

[30] Rambam, *Laws of Kings* 9:10, and the explanation of *Kesef Mishneh*.

[31] See Tractate *Bava Batra* 20a.

[32] It is also forbidden to cut flesh from a living animal and then eat it after the animal dies. See the last footnote for topic 3:2, and 3.4; if a Jew *kosher*-slaughters an animal and it is still convulsing, a Gentile is permitted to cut off a piece of it, but it is forbidden for him to eat it until after the animal has died (for there is no leniency to set aside the command to Gentiles in Gen. 9:4).

9:4, "But flesh with its soul, its blood, you shall not eat," indicates that a Gentile transgresses one of God's commands to Noaĥ only if he eats from the flesh of an animal that is still alive. But one who cuts off the flesh but does not eat from it is not liable to this penalty. If one person severs the flesh and another person eats it, the liability only applies to the one who eats the flesh. The person who transgresses by severing the flesh, but does not eat from it, is not liable for capital punishment.

Since the Torah places the liability exclusively on the eater (of the detached flesh of a live animal), the manner in which the flesh was removed is of no consequence. Accordingly, a Gentile who eats from *eiver min ha'ĥai* while the animal is still alive is liable regardless of whether the flesh was removed by him or by another, or even if it became detached because of injury or disease, or for another reason.[33]

13. Meat from a human (whether separated while the person was alive or after the person's death) was never permitted to be eaten.[34]

A Gentile is not allowed to cut off flesh of an animal killed by non-*kosher* means while its limbs are still convulsing, even if he will not eat the flesh until after the convulsing stops. Thus it is forbidden for a Gentile to (commit half of the transgression and) cut off a piece of an animal while it is still alive and healthy. The only reason permission is given for a Gentile to sever an animal's flesh immediately after *kosher* slaughter is that "what is permitted for Jews is surely permitted for Gentiles" (if a commandment is not violated). (The opinion of Rambam in *Laws of Kings* 9:13 differs; he says that even if a Jew *kosher*-slaughters an animal, any meat removed from it during the convulsions is from then on forbidden for Gentiles to eat.)

Though one can conjecture that the main prohibition is on cutting off flesh while the animal is still alive (see topic 3:1 below), the actual cutting of the flesh is forbidden as long as eating the flesh would be forbidden.

[33] *E.g., a part that was removed during a medical operation, or testicles of a castrated animal (such as "mountain oysters" from bulls), or a removed tail.

[34] *Yad Eliyahu* ch. 45; Malbim on Lev. 11:4. This is apparent from the commandments to Adam and Noaĥ, since Adam was given permission to rule over the animals, but not to eat them, and surely he was forbidden to rule over humans (by an act of kidnapping) and to injure them, for the purpose of eating a person. When God gave permission to Noaĥ to rule over animals, the prohibition against ruling over humans still stood; see *Ĥizkuni*, Gen. 9:5. This commandment to Adam was given in the positive form (Gen. 2:16): "You may eat from all the trees of the field" – to the exclusion of all non-vegetarian food. This distinction is explained in footnotes 3 and 4 above.

Therefore it is not permitted to eat from a limb, flesh or skin that was removed from a living human.

A Gentile is not forbidden to eat human blood that left the body, even while the person it came from is alive.[35] However, it is forbidden to injure a person (Part V, Chapter 6), so there is justification to forbid human blood, since permitting it may lead one to cause human injury.

It is allowed to benefit from part of a Gentile corpse if there is a definite need[36] – for example, for medical training or research, or organ transplants.[37]

It appears, however, that there is no direct prohibition against eating flesh from a human carcass. Nevertheless, this act might be considered a type of "ruling" over another human, and is not permitted; it may also lead to the sin of cannibalism, God forbid.

[35] Rambam, *Laws of Forbidden Foods* 6:2.

[36] *The permissibility or morality of "plastination" of skinned and dissected human corpses, for purposes of monetary profit and public display, is highly questionable. It is forbidden for Jewish bodies, which must be buried. In the author's opinion it is both immoral and a desecration of the "Divine image" within any person, and it should be considered in Torah Law as comparable to cannibalism, which is not permitted (see footnote 34).

[37] *Ĥatam Sofer Yoreh De'ah* ch. 336, and *Igrot Moshe Yoreh De'ah* 1:229, rule that it is not forbidden to derive benefit from a Gentile corpse. Some types of benefiting may be forbidden, however; see in footnote 34.

*Since Gentiles are not commanded that they must be buried in the earth, the option is open to plan for donation of organs after one's own passing, or the passing of a Gentile relative whom one has become legally responsible for. However, it must be noted that God's Torah defines life by the beating of the heart. Therefore, a Gentile who wishes to be an organ donor is encouraged to make a clear and legally binding stipulation (which may be in a so-called "Living Will") that no organs may be removed, and no life-support mechanisms may be discontinued (if they have already been applied), before the heart has permanently stopped beating. This is explained in more detail in Part V, topics 1:15-18 and 7:8.

From *Ethics of the Fathers* 3:14, "[Rabbi Akiva] used to say: Beloved is Man, for he was created in the Divine image. It is an even greater [act of] love that it was made known to him that he was created in the Divine image, as it states, 'In the image of God was man created' [Genesis 1:27]." This verse refers to all mankind. A practical lesson from this is that the human body should not be treated disrespectfully, even in death. We learn from Gen. 3:19 that the most respectful treatment for a human corpse is burial.

CHAPTER 2

Which Parts from Living Animals are Prohibited to be Eaten

1. For Gentiles, the prohibition against consuming flesh removed from a living animal encompasses not only entire limbs, but also any meat severed from the living animal.[38] The proof text, "But flesh with its soul, its blood, you shall not eat" (Genesis 9:4), does not mention a limb, even though the Hebrew term *eiver min ha'ĥai* literally means "a limb from a living animal."

The prohibition forbids eating any meat separated *from* a living land mammal or bird, so it does not apply when one swallows a whole small mammal or bird alive.[39]

2. Thus the prohibition of *eiver min ha'ĥai* includes a limb comprised of flesh, sinews (tendons) and bones (e.g. a paw or a foot), an organ that is entirely meat (e.g. the tongue, testicles, spleen or kidneys), and the animal's fat and similar parts. The prohibition applies regardless of whether one severs an entire limb or organ, or merely a portion of one,[40] and whether he ate the entire severed piece or only a part of it.

3. The prohibition of *eiver min ha'ĥai* applies only to one who eats severed meat. But if one chews severed bones or sinews and swallows them, he is not liable to punishment (although it is not permitted), for it

---

[38] Rambam, *Laws of Kings* 9:10 states, "A Gentile is liable for a limb or meat of any size." This teaches that (a) this prohibition for a Gentile is the same whether eating a whole limb or only a piece of meat, and (b) Gentiles have no minimum measurements for an amount of food that is prohibited.

[39] This is according to Rebbi (Rabbi Yehuda) in Tractate *Ĥullin* 102b, according to the explanation of *Tosafot*. This is unlike Rashi who says that the prohibition of *eiver min ha'ĥai* does apply to swallowing a whole living bird. Rambam, in *Laws of Forbidden Foods* 4:3, rules like *Tosafot*.

[40] Rambam, *Laws of Forbidden Foods* 5:2. Unlike the case for Jews, this prohibition applies for Gentiles whether the limb has sinews and bone within it or not, since Gentiles have no minimum quantities for forbidden food. [Jews are only guilty of a sin of eating *eiver min ha'ĥai* if they consume an entire severed limb; a Jew who eats only part of a severed limb commits a different sin, which is eating ***treifah*** ("torn") meat.]

is not considered an act of eating food.[41]

If one severs a limb in its entirety – flesh, sinews, and bones – or a portion of it, he is liable for eating from it as long as it has some meat on it, even if the majority is comprised of bones and sinews and is not fit to be eaten, provided that he ate at least some part of the meat. If one separates the meat from the bones, he is liable only for eating the meat, but not for eating any bones or sinews.[42] (One is, however, liable for consuming the marrow of the bones; see topic 2:7 below.)

A foreleg limb that naturally has only bone and sinews but no meat is forbidden as *eiver min ha'ĥai*, but it does not make one liable for punishment.[43]

4. This prohibition applies when one severs a limb from the body of a living animal, even though the act will cause the animal's death,[44] provided it does not kill the animal immediately. If, however, removing the limb or organ directly kills the animal, e.g. the act of cutting off its head or removing its heart, it is considered as if the animal was slaughtered by this act, and the prohibition against eating meat from a living animal does not apply.[45]

5. If one cut off the spleen, kidneys, or any other internal organs (or internal flesh[46]) of an animal while it was alive, and left the severed pieces in the cavity of the animal, they are considered as having been severed from the animal during its lifetime. If the animal is slaughtered thereafter, the organs severed previously remain forbidden.[47]

---

[41] *Pri Megadim, Siftei Da'at* 62:1. The prohibition only exists when one benefits in the normal manner of eating. Furthermore, the verse (Genesis 9:4), says, "You shall not **eat**, etc."

[42] Rambam, *Laws of Forbidden Foods* 5:3.

[43] See Tractate *Ĥullin* 128b according to Rebbi (Rabbi Yehuda the Prince); Rambam, *Laws of Sources of Ritual Impurity* 2:3.

[44] Rambam, *Laws of Forbidden Foods* 5:5.

[45] *Ĥaĥam Tzvi* (ch. 74), gives the reasoning for this: as soon as the heart (or head) is removed, it is impossible for the animal to continue living.

[46] Shaĥ *Yoreh De'ah* 62:5.

[47] *As will be explained in Chapter 3, once meat is placed in the category of *eiver min ha'ĥai*, it remains forbidden to be eaten forever.

If, however, one cuts off portions of a fetus, leaves them inside the mother's womb and then slaughters the mother, the portions of the fetus are permitted (see Chapter 5 below).[48]

6. An animal's fats, intestines and its stomach are considered as meat in all contexts.[49] The skin, intestines, gizzard and oviduct of a bird[50] are all included in the prohibition of *eiver min ha'ĥai*. As the crop is not edible,[51] one who eats it is exempt from punishment, although it is prohibited to do so.

7. Bones are not considered as fit for human consumption and are not considered as meat. Hence, if one eats from them after they were severed during the animal's lifetime, one is not liable for violating the prohibition against eating meat from a living animal. The above applies even if one ground the bones, chewed them, or cooked them.[52] This applies even to soft bones that are edible. Bone marrow, by contrast, is considered as meat.[53] Similarly, cartilage that is cooked until it is edible is considered as meat.[54]

8. Sinews are not considered fit for human consumption and are not considered as meat. Even soft sinews from a young animal are not considered as meat, since the sinews will harden as the animal gets older.[55] Therefore, one is not liable for punishment for eating them if they were removed from a living animal (although it is not permitted).

---

48 Rambam, *Laws of Forbidden Foods* 5:9; *Shulĥan Aruĥ Yoreh De'ah* 14.

49 This is explained by Rambam in *Laws of Forbidden Foods*, where fat is discussed in 5:5, and intestines are discussed in 4:19.

50 The skin of a bird is discussed below in topic 2:10. The other listed parts are discussed by Rambam in *Laws of Sources of Ritual Impurity* 3:10.

51 Tractate *Zevaĥim* 35a and Rambam, *Laws of Disqualified Offerings* 18:22, state that the crop is inedible; thus, the prohibition does not apply to it.

52 Rambam, *Laws of Forbidden Foods* 4:18. Regarding soft bones, see Rambam, *Laws of Sources of Ritual Impurity*, ch. 3, and *Laws of the Passover Sacrifice*, ch. 10.

53 *Tosefta*, Tractate *Pesaĥim* 6:8.

54 Rambam, *Laws of the Passover Sacrifice* 10:8, and the commentary of Ra'avad there.

55 Rambam, *ibid.*

9. An animal's hide is not considered as meat, and the prohibition against eating meat from a living animal does not apply to it.[56] This applies even if one cooked it thoroughly with spices.[57] However, soft skin, which is edible like meat, is included in the prohibition.

Included in the category of soft skin that is forbidden to be eaten if removed from a living creature is skin from: domesticated pigs, the hump of a young camel that has never carried a load, the area around the genitals of a female animal, the soft area on the underneath part of the tail,[58] and a fetus. These types of skin are considered as meat provided one eats them while they are soft. If the skin has already been processed and it has become hard, it is no longer considered as meat,[59] and one is not liable for punishment for eating it if it was removed from a living animal (although it is not permitted).

10. The skin of a bird is edible, and is like the bird's meat for all considerations.[60] The feathers, however, are not in the category of meat.[61] Eating the feathers with the skin is equal to eating the meat and the bones together, which is mentioned above in topic 2:3.

11. Horns, hooves and claws of animals or birds (even just the insides of these parts, which are soft), and a placenta are not considered as meat. The prohibition against eating meat from a living animal does not apply to them, and one is not liable for this.[62]

When is a placenta forbidden to be eaten? When it is removed from the body of a pregnant living mammal (or human) before it gives birth. After the mother gives birth, by contrast, the placenta in which the fetus was carried, and which is afterwards naturally expelled, is

---

[56] Rambam, *Laws of Forbidden Foods* 4:18.

[57] Tractate *Ĥullin* 77b, and Rashi there.

[58] Rashi on Tractate *Ĥullin* 122a.

[59] Rambam, *Laws of Forbidden Foods* 4:20-21.

[60] See *Mishnah Aĥarona* Tractate *Taharot* 1:4.

[61] Feathers are not in the category of flesh, as explained by Rambam in *Laws of Sources of Ritual Impurity* 3:9.

[62] Rambam, *Laws of Forbidden Foods* 4:18 and 9:7, and *Laws of Sources of Ritual Impurity*, ch. 1.

permitted to be eaten by Gentiles.[63] Similarly, if a pregnant animal dies or is slaughtered, the placenta is permitted.

If any part of an animal that is not considered to be edible meat (such as the horns, hoofs, thick skin, bones, sinews, placenta, toe nails, or even the nails of a bird[64]) is severed before the animal dies, one who eats them is exempt from punishment, but it is nevertheless forbidden to do so.[65]

12. An extra limb or organ (e.g. an extra finger or an extra lobe of the liver or lung) is considered as an ordinary limb or organ, and for these one is equally liable for the prohibition of meat from a living animal.[66] Even if the additional limb or organ would ultimately cause that animal's death, e.g. two livers or three hind legs, it is considered as part of the animal, and for these too one is equally liable for the prohibition.

---

[63] See Rambam and Ra'avad, *Laws of Forbidden Foods* 5:13, regarding Jewish dietary law for a placenta that partially emerged from a *kosher* animal, and then the animal was slaughtered. However, it seems that for Gentiles, anything (including a placenta) that is expelled naturally out of the body of an animal is considered to be a waste product and not meat, and is not restricted by the rules of *eiver min ha'ĥai.*

[64] Rambam, *Laws of Forbidden Foods* 4:18.

[65] *Ibid.*

[66] Rema *Yoreh De'ah* ch. 62.

CHAPTER 3

The Prohibition of Separating Meat from an Animal that is Living or in the Process of Dying, and Restrictions on Consuming such Meat after the Animal's Death

1. From the verse Genesis 9:4, "But flesh with its soul, its blood, you shall not eat," the meaning of "with its soul, its blood" is that its soul is invested in its blood. Thus God commanded Noaĥ that the prohibition of *eiver min ha'ĥai* applies to eating the flesh while the animal's soul is in its blood.[67] Therefore, eating severed flesh is counted as a capital transgression for a Gentile only while the land mammal (domestic or wild) from which the flesh was taken and eaten is still alive.

Nevertheless, the Sages decreed that the severed meat itself becomes forbidden forever and no one – even one who did not cut the meat from the animal – may eat from it, despite the fact that the animal from which the meat was taken has already died.[68] Once flesh, a limb, or an organ becomes considered "meat from a living animal" or "a limb from a living animal," it can never be removed from that category.[69]

2. From this verse we also know that as long as the animal's soul is in its blood, it is alive, and it is forbidden to remove any part of it to eat. This applies even if the animal is sick and has signs of terminal illness.[70] It also applies even if the sick animal has become so moribund that its death is imminent, for the animal is still deemed "alive" so long as there is even the slightest amount of life in it.[71]

---

[67] This is the explanation of Rashi and *Targum Yonatan* on the verse.

[68] The Sages made this decree so an individual would have no benefit or financial gain from cutting off flesh from a living animal. This provides a safeguard against nearly or accidentally transgressing the capital sin of eating *eiver min ha'ĥai* during the life of the animal, and also it safeguards against inflicting unnecessary suffering on living creatures *(tza'ar ba'alei ĥayim).*

[69] Tractate *Ĥullin* 121b.

[70] This can be learned from the case when an animal's limb is cut off, causing it to become a *treifah* (an animal with a fatal disease or injury), as cited by Rambam in *Laws of Forbidden Foods* 5:5, as explained in topic 2:4.

[71] A deathly sick creature is still considered to be alive (see *Shulĥan Aruĥ Yoreh De'ah* ch. 339, and Tractate *Ĥullin* 30a and 37a).

Thus, a Gentile who knowingly eats *eiver min ha'ĥai* that is severed from a living animal when it is moribund, or when it has a terminal illness or injury, is liable for a capital sin if the meat is eaten before the animal dies. However, this rule regarding dying animals applies only when the animal became stricken by a natural cause (for example: from old age or disease.)

The situation is different if the animal became mortally injured through an *action* which can kill it, and from which it will not survive. This applies whether the action was done by a human (for example: if a human slaughtered the animal); or whether it happened through Divine intervention (for example: a ferocious animal pounced on it and broke its collar bone); or if it fell and became fatally injured, as will be explained below in topic 11 (for example: if it fell and both its windpipe and its esophagus were cut). In one respect, a similar rule applies in that it is forbidden forever to eat any flesh that is severed from such an animal while it is still in its death throes. However, one who eats from a dying animal in such a condition, while it is still convulsing just before its death, is not liable for a capital sin if it resulted from an external action such as those cited.[72]

The difference between "deathly sick" and "moribund" (from a disease or old age), and "the throes of death" after being slaughtered for food, is that the sick animal became stricken without human intervention, and it is dying naturally; whereas if an animal is still convulsing after being slaughtered for food, its dying process has begun in a way that is permitted for a Gentile to have caused. This is also found in Tractate *Sanhedrin* 78a and Rambam, *Laws of Murderers* 2:7. But even if this death-causing act happened naturally (e.g. from an animal of prey), it is the beginning of its death process.

[72] Radvaz explains (on Rambam, *Laws of Kings* 9:13) that the prohibition of *eiver min ha'ĥai* is comprised of two types of actions: (1) the prohibition to sever and eat meat from a live animal, and (2) the prohibition to eat meat that was severed from a slaughtered animal that is still convulsing in the throes of death. Since a Jew is allowed to cut off meat from a *kosher*-slaughtered animal as soon as its esophagus and windpipe have been properly cut, a Gentile may surely do so. Likewise, according to Torah law from Mt. Sinai, a Gentile may cut off flesh from a fatally stabbed animal while it is still convulsing in its death throes, if this flesh will *not* be eaten until after the animal dies. However, the early Torah Sages forbade this, as it might lead to eating severed meat while the animal is still convulsing before its death, or even to eating *eiver min ha'ĥai* in other situations, which is forbidden.

Accordingly, if a Gentile slaughters an animal in any manner, it is forbidden to cut off meat or sever an organ while the animal is in its death throes, and any meat or organ severed at this time is forbidden to be eaten forever.[73]

3. A more lenient rule applies if an animal is authentically *kosher*-slaughtered for Jewish consumption. First we identify cases that *exclude* an animal from being accepted as *kosher*-slaughtered:
a) it is a non-*kosher* species;
b) it is a *kosher* species, but the slaughtering by the Jew is rendered ritually invalid due to an error that was made during the procedure;
c) it is a *kosher* species, but it is disqualified for *kosher*-slaughter while it is still living [for example: if the membranes of the gullet are perforated, or there is already a slit across more than half the diameter of the windpipe in the area that a *kosher*-slaughter cut could be made; or if either the gullet or windpipe is loosened and displaced.][74]

In these cases, the meat of the slaughtered animal is not *kosher*, and any flesh that is severed while it is still in its post-slaughter death throes is still forbidden to be eaten forever.[75] (See end of topic 3:11.)

4. The leniency applies if a Jew performs *kosher*-slaughter, as follows:

a) a *kosher* species of animal (those which have split hooves and chew their cud – for example, cows, sheep, goats and deer) or a *kosher* species of fowl (for example, a chicken, turkey or duck);
b) for the purpose of Jewish consumption;
c) in the Jewish ritual manner of slitting the majority of the gullet and windpipe with an extremely sharp knife.

As soon as the animal has been slaughtered according to these details, a Jew is permitted to remove flesh from this animal for food,

---

[73] *This applies even if the slaughter was performed by a Gentile in the ritual "Jewish" manner of neck slaughter, since the required spiritual dimension for actual *kosher* slaughter (the process called *sheĥita* in Hebrew) can only be accomplished by a sufficiently Torah-observant Jew.

[74] It is impossible to perform a valid *kosher* slaughter on an animal that is in one of these conditions. Therefore, as long as it is alive (i.e. the heart is still beating), its meat is subject to the prohibition of *eiver min ha'ĥai*.

[75] Tractate *Ĥullin* 121b; Rashba quoted in Shaĥ *Yoreh De'ah* ch. 27.

even while it is still convulsing **in its death throes**.[76] In this case, if a Gentile is acting as an agent or worker for a Jew, he is also permitted to remove flesh (even on his own initiative) from this animal immediately after the Jew's act of *kosher* slaughter (while the animal is still convulsing).[77] But it is forbidden for a Gentile to then eat the flesh until after the *kosher*-slaughtered animal actually dies and stops convulsing, since this flesh is still temporarily forbidden for Jewish consumption (due to the prohibition in Lev. 19:26).[78] In this situation,

---

[76] It appears, based on Maharshal (as cited in fn. to topic 6 below), that if a Gentile (if he is acting as a worker or as an agent for a Jew), severs anything from the animal that is slaughtered by a Jew under these conditions, then it is considered as if the Jew himself cut off the meat, and it is, therefore, immediately permitted for a Gentile to eat from it. But if a Jew slaughtered an animal for the purpose that it would be used by a Gentile, it is considered as if the Gentile killed the animal, and the same rulings regarding *eiver min ha'ĥai* apply to it as if it was the Gentile who performed the slaughter.

*The Torah defines the act of ritual *kosher* slaughter as the death of the animal, but any butchering during the short time that the animal is still sensitive to pain is highly discouraged. Also, it would not be consistent with standards of humane treatment in commercial slaughterhouses, which specify that the animal should be surgically insensitive before any further cuts are made. (It has been proven scientifically that the *kosher*-slaughter cut across the neck is painless to the animal if properly done; if the animal is calm when the slaughter is started, none of the bodily chemicals associated with a trauma reflex appear in the blood of the slaughtered animal.)

Note that the twitching of meat long after the cleaning of the carcass is a result of impulses from muscle cells that have yet to die. This can continue long after the death throes of the animal have ceased, and flesh removed from the carcass at that stage is not subject to the prohibition of *eiver min ha'ĥai*.

[77] Rashba, Rosh, *Tur* and Shaĥ *Yoreh De'ah* ch. 27, based on Tractate *Ĥullin* 121b. (In *Laws of Kings* 9:13, Rambam differs from this ruling.)

[78] See Tractate *Ĥullin* 33a and 121b: a Jew may only feed a Gentile from an animal which he (the Jew) is allowed to eat from at that time. This is a Rabbinical decree. Torah defines a *kosher*-slaughtered animal as immediately dead, so a Gentile would be able to eat from it while it was still convulsing (*mefarkeset*), if not for the fact that is forbidden to the Jew during that time, based on Lev. 19:26, "you shall not **eat** with the blood." This prohibits a Jew from eating the flesh while the slaughtered animal's life-blood is flowing, but it does not prohibit removing flesh. In other words, a Jew is forbidden to eat the meat of a *kosher*-slaughtered animal or bird before it is *physically* dead.

a Gentile may only eat the meat from the *kosher*-slaughtered animal starting from the time it becomes allowed for the Jew to eat the meat.

5. If a *kosher* species of animal had a terminal disease or injury which made it forbidden for Jews to eat, but it was nevertheless killed by a Jew through the *action* of ritual *kosher* slaughter, there are some Rabbinical opinions that a Gentile (just as a Jew) is permitted to cut off parts while it is still convulsing, just as is the case for regular *kosher* slaughtering, which is discussed in topic 3:4 above.[79] (Here, the slaughtering may be for any type of Jewish use, and not necessarily for consumption.) However, it appears to the author that a Gentile may not cut off parts from the terminally ill or injured animal (which had then received the act of ritual slaughter by a Jew), until after it dies and stops convulsing. But if a Jew cut off flesh while this animal is still convulsing, then, after the fact, he can give it to a Gentile for food after the animal has died and stopped convulsing. Still, as an initial preference, a Jew should not do so for a Gentile, but he should wait until after the animal stops convulsing.

If flesh is severed by a Gentile before this terminally ill or injured

---

[79] *Simla Ĥadasha* ch. 27, and *Pri Megadim Siftei Da'at* 27:2, both have the opinion that for *kosher* slaughter (i.e., *sheĥita*) by a Jew of a terminally ill or injured (i.e., *treifah*) animal, the rule that "anything permitted for a Jew is permissible for a Gentile as well" applies, and the Jew's act of *sheĥita* removes the status of *eiver min ha'ĥai* completely. This is because the Torah defines *sheĥita* by a Jew as "death" for a *kosher* species of animal.

The understanding of the Maharshal quoted in Shaĥ *ibid.*, and other Torah authorities, is that since the *treifah* animal is from the outset forbidden to be eaten by a Jew according to Torah law, this rule does not apply, and the Jew should not provide its meat for Gentile consumption until it stops convulsing.

Cutting flesh from this *treifah* animal is permitted for the Jew, immediately after the *sheĥita*. But the Jew may not feed it to a Gentile, or intend the *sheĥita* to be for this purpose, since it would be considered as if the Jew is slaughtering a Gentile's animal, and the Gentile would be forbidden to eat the flesh that was severed while the animal was still convulsing. (See topic 3:6.)

A Jew may cut flesh off of his convulsing *treifah* animal immediately after the *kosher* slaughter, if it is for a different purpose he would benefit from. After the convulsing stops, a Gentile may eat from flesh that was severed by a Jew during the convulsions. Still, a Gentile is forbidden to cut meat from the animal while it is convulsing and then eat that meat (at that time, or later).

animal stops convulsing, it remains forbidden to be eaten afterwards.

6. Moreover, even when a Jew slaughters a *kosher* species of animal (belonging either to a Jew or a Gentile) in the ritual *kosher* manner, if he slaughtered it for the sake of the use of a Gentile, the leniency mentioned in topic 4 above does not apply. Rather, it is regarded as the same as the slaughter of a non-*kosher* animal in regard to the precepts of *eiver min ha'ĥai*. As long as this animal is in its death throes, any flesh severed from it is forbidden to be eaten forever by a Gentile.[80]

7. Since the prohibition is dependent on the verse "But flesh with its soul, its blood, you shall not eat," and it is written, "The blood is the soul" (Lev. 17:11,14), this teaches that the soul of life is invested in the blood, which is circulated by the heart, meaning that the soul is based in the heart. Therefore, the moment of death for an animal is defined as the moment the heart ceases permanently to beat. **As long as the heart is still beating,** the animal is considered alive since its soul is still within it, and it is forbidden to cut off its meat or sever its limbs (except for the leniency explained in topic 3:4 above), even though its throat has been slit or another activity to kill it has been performed.

8. How can it be determined by observation that an animal has died? If it is lying lifeless and motionless, and is not breathing, we can assume that it has died[81] (but see topic 3:9 below). Similarly, if its jugular vein or another major blood vessel has been sliced through with an open cut

---

[80] Maharshal, Shaĥ *Yoreh De'ah* ch. 27. The reason given for this is that if a Jew properly slaughters an animal for himself or for other Jews, he actually makes this meat immediately permissible for Jews, according to the Jewish commandment of *sheĥita*, by which the animal is considered dead as soon as the act of *sheĥita* is performed. This removes the condition for *eiver min ha'ĥai*, and, therefore, it must be permissible also for a Gentile. But if he slaughters an animal for Gentile consumption, it is governed by the Noahide commandment that any meat removed within the duration of the convulsions may not be eaten by a Gentile until after the animal dies. (The Jewish sages added to this, and forbade Gentiles to cut off any flesh from this animal before the convulsions end, as one might come to eat from it.)

[81] Yoma 85a and *Shulĥan Aruĥ HaRav, Oraĥ Ĥayim* 329:3 state that the main life is in the heart, but signs of life are recognizable in the nose and breath, as it says "all that has life in its nostrils" (Genesis 7:22).

and the blood is no longer flowing out vigorously, but merely seeping out from the cut blood vessel, then the animal is dead.[82]

However, if the vein (even the jugular) is punctured with a stab instead of an open cut, it will bleed out more slowly. Since the animal is still alive as long as its heart is still beating, in this case one must check more carefully to determine if the heart is permanently stopped.

9. If an animal is killed as food for Gentiles, it may first be rendered unconscious by electric shock or the like. But if its reflexes and breath cease, this does not prove that it has died, since it may wake up.[83] Its death can be assured by making an open cut through a major vein or artery, and waiting until it has stopped bleeding vigorously.[84]

10. When the head of an animal is severed (its esophagus, windpipe, spine, and veins have been cut through), even if it is still attached by

---

[82] Rambam, *Laws of Forbidden Foods* 6:3.

[83] *Ĥatam Sofer Yoreh De'ah* ch. 339: a long period of stopped breathing is not proof of death for humans. See *Igrot Moshe Yoreh De'ah*, vol. 2, 146.

*For non-*kosher* slaughter, the main artery in the animal's neck should be cut so it will "bleed out." *Even if a strong electric shock is applied to kill the animal by cardiac arrest* (versus merely to facilitate the slaughter, or to render the animal insensitive), a further means such as decapitation or complete bleed-out is needed before skinning or butchering begins. This will insure that the heart has permanently stopped pumping, after which the animal is considered dead (even if the heart fibrillates for a little longer).

[84] *Dr. Temple Grandin, a humane-slaughter expert, shared the following in an on-line forum on April 23, 2002: "If an animal is completely bled out, the heart will be stopped. The [U.S.] Humane Slaughter Act states that the animal must be in a state of surgical anesthesia. In normal slaughtering procedures, the animal is bled out, … ideally [for] about five minutes. One of the most important factors to ensure a good bleed out is the skill of the person… In large plants with a power chain, there is an enforced bleed time. Small plants do not have this [and] ... must be very careful to allow the animal to completely bleed out prior to skinning or leg removal… [An animal can return to sensibility] if bleeding is poorly done... [So] plant management needs to supervise and do internal quality audits on animal handling and stunning… The [main] problem with sticking [for bleed out] is making an opening that is too small… [When the heart has stopped,] body movements can [still] occur… There are no humane slaughter regulations for poultry in the U.S., although there are voluntary industry guidelines."

the skin, the animal is certainly dead even though its heart continues beating for several moments. The prohibition against meat or organs removed from a living animal does not apply to it in this condition.[85]

11. As explained, if flesh is removed from an animal while it is still convulsing in its death throes, this flesh is forbidden for Gentiles to eat. Therefore, if flesh is removed from an animal while any of the following conditions apply, it remains forbidden to be eaten forever:

a) if the animal's backbone was broken at the base of the neck, with most of the flesh of the neck torn, but the head is not totally severed, and the windpipe, esophagus and most of the veins are still intact;
b) if its body was cut into two halves;
c) if a thigh and the adjoining socket was removed;
d) if it was torn "from the inside like a fish."[86]

In these cases, although the animal has no chance of living more than several minutes, as long as its heart is beating, its flesh is forbidden to be removed.[87] If a Gentile did sever a piece of meat from an animal while one of the above conditions existed, it is forbidden to eat that meat even after the animal dies. But one is not guilty of a capital sin in this situation, as explained in topic 3:2, based on the rules that apply while the animal is still convulsing in its death throes. If a Jew cut a piece of meat from an animal in this condition for his own need, it appears that a Gentile may eat from that meat after the animal dies.[88]

12. If a living animal is cut into two portions – although it has been previously explained that it is forbidden to cut off any limbs or pieces of meat until the animal dies – the two sides are not considered *eiver min ha'ĥai*, and, therefore, may be eaten after the animal dies.[89]

---

[85] Rambam, *Laws of Sources of Ritual Impurity*, ch. 4 and beginning of ch. 2. This case is full death, so the animal is not considered to be convulsing.

[86] *This means that its back is torn, and the spine is detached.

[87] See Rambam *ibid.*, which indicates that in such cases the animal is considered dead "while it is still alive," and is forbidden. The author notes: the animal is still alive in a practical sense, and any meat removed in these circumstances is forbidden to be eaten by a Gentile forever (see topic 3:2).

[88] See topic 3:5 above: if a Jew cuts off the piece of meat for his own consumption, he may offer it to a Gentile to eat after the animal dies.

[89] This is considered an act of slaughtering, which removes the prohibition.

Chapter 4

Maimed or Broken Limbs

1. The following precepts apply to a limb or flesh that has been maimed at the place where it is attached to the animal's body, but which has not been detached entirely. Instead, it is still attached somewhat to the animal's body and is hanging loosely from it.[90] If the hanging part can no longer heal as might an ordinary part of the body, there are some Torah authorities who consider it as flesh or a limb that is already severed from a living animal.[91] But the main opinion is that it is **not** considered to be severed from a living animal, as long as it never became totally detached during the animal's lifetime.[92] Hence, after the animal's death, a Gentile is permitted to eat from this flesh or limb that was hanging but still attached to the animal when it died.

2. As long as the animal is living, one may not cut off a hanging limb to eat it, even if the limb could not heal. Even if the limb fell off, it is

---

[90] Shaĥ and *Pri Megadim Siftei Da'at* 62:7.

[91] *Tosefta*, end of Tractate *Avodah Zarah*, *Eshkol Hilĥot Teraifot* ch. 20.

[92] Rambam writes in *Laws of Forbidden Foods* 5:6 that a hanging limb (hanging while the animal was still alive) is considered *eiver min ha'ĥai* even after the animal dies, and even if the animal received *kosher* slaughter, the hanging limb is still forbidden by Torah law, according to his opinion. Rashi and *Tosafot*, *Ĥullin* 74a, disagree with Rambam, saying that such a case is forbidden for Jews, but only by a decree of the Sages. For Gentiles, there is a difference of Rabbinical opinion as to whether such a prohibition exists.

The *Tzemaĥ Tzedek* (*Yoreh De'ah* ch. 63) and others hold that Rambam's opinion is that there is no prohibition for Gentiles to eat a hanging limb after the animal's death. But others disagree, including *Pri Megadim* (*Siftei Da'at* 62:9), and consider Rambam's opinion for Gentiles equal to the Torah law for Jews, that the animal's death causes the limb to be considered severed during its lifetime, and therefore prohibited to Gentiles as *eiver min ha'ĥai*.

Proof for the first opinion (the *Tzemaĥ Tzedek*) can be brought from the *Shita Mekubetzet Bava Batra* 20a, which quotes Rabbi Yosef Ibn Migash, who points out that there is no prohibition for a Gentile in this situation.

The lenient opinion should be followed, for several reasons:

(a) Most early authorities say clearly that the prohibition for a Jew to eat a hanging limb of a *kosher*-slaughtered animal is only a decree by the Sages upon Jews, and there is no clear prohibition stated for a Gentile.

still forbidden.[93]

Even if a Jew slaughtered it by the ritually *kosher* method but it is still convulsing, the hanging limb is forbidden for a Gentile until the animal dies. If the Gentile cut off flesh from the hanging limb while the animal was still convulsing, the flesh is forbidden forever.[94]

3. One may cut a hanging limb from an animal for veterinary reasons, or to feed to one's carnivorous animals (e.g., if it could not heal).

4. If, however, the hanging limb or flesh could still heal as an ordinary portion of the body, all Torah authorities agree that it is permitted to be

---

By original Torah Law, *kosher* slaughter makes it immediately permitted for a Jew to remove the flesh, but it doesn't apply for a Gentile (unless he acts as a Jew's agent). Although a Gentile may eat a hanging limb after the animal dies, this was forbidden for Jews by Rabbinical decree, as was cutting flesh from a hanging limb while the animal is still convulsing. Thus, a hanging limb is not considered severed during the animal's lifetime. If this flesh was prohibited for Jews by the Torah (instead of by Rabbinical decree), the Sages would have decreed that it is forbidden to be eaten forever by Gentiles. Rather, the Sages permitted a Gentile to eat flesh (after the animal's death) that was severed from a hanging limb of a convulsing *kosher*-slaughtered animal, since the risk that this could lead to a transgression of the actual prohibition of *eiver min ha'ĥai* (see footnote 72 above) is lessened.

(b) A hanging limb could not be forbidden to a Gentile and permitted for a Jew (in the original Torah Law), due to the general rule (*Ĥullin* 33a, *Sanhedrin* 59a) that Torah Law is always at least as strict for Jews as for Gentiles.

(c) For Jews, who have commandments regarding an animal after its death (regarding eating and spiritual impurity), there is a practical dimension to the rule that "death can confer a status of the limb having been severed while the animal is still alive." However, since Gentiles do not have these commandments, and their only prohibition from the Torah is the Noahide commandment against eating severed flesh while the animal is still alive, surely in the present situation where the animal is already dead, there is no reason to forbid a hanging limb.

[93] It is clear that it if it fell off while the animal is still alive, it is forbidden because of *eiver min ha'ĥai*, as explained above in Chapter 1.

[94] *Kraiti U'Plaiti Yoreh De'ah*, ch. 62, explains that in this situation there is no leniency, as opposed to when one severs a normal limb from a *kosher*-slaughtered animal that is still convulsing (topic 3:4), since the Sages forbid a Jew to eat from the hanging limb in such a case. See footnotes 78-80 above.

eaten after the animal is slaughtered or if it died in some other way.[95]

Similarly, all Torah authorities agree that the situations below are not in the category of a "hanging" or detached limb:

(a) a limb that has been dislocated, i.e., its bone has slipped from the socket joint where it is attached to the body, but it is still connected by its sinews;[96]
(b) a limb that has been crushed or pounded, but it can still heal;
(c) an animal's testicles that have been crushed or severed, but are left hanging in the scrotum and the scrotum is attached to the body (they are not considered to have been separated from the body, since they do not decay);[97]
(d) if a bone is broken and it does not cut through the flesh and does not protrude outward, but instead remains entirely covered by the animal's skin (for it is likely to heal).[98]

In all of these cases, after the animal dies or is killed, all authorities agree that it is permitted to eat from any part of the dislocated or injured limb.

5. The following laws apply when a bone has been broken and protrudes outside an animal's skin:

If the remaining skin and the flesh could cover the majority of the thickness of the broken bone and the majority of the circumference of the broken bone, were the bone to be returned to within the skin, the bone would most likely heal, and hence the limb is permitted.

If the remaining skin and the flesh would not cover the majority of the bone in this way, the portion of the broken limb below the break is considered as a maimed limb, and the difference of opinion mentioned in topic 4:1 above applies.[99]

In this instance also, one may follow the more lenient view. Thus under these conditions, as long as the broken limb was not separated from the animal's body in its lifetime, it is permitted after the animal's

---

[95] Rambam, *Laws of Forbidden Foods* 5:6; *Tur* and Shaĥ *Yoreh De'ah* 62:6.
*Regarding "mercy killing" of an injured animal, see topic 7:12 below.

[96] Shaĥ *Yoreh De'ah* 62:7.

[97] Rambam, *Laws of Forbidden Foods* 5:7.

[98] *Beit Yosef Yoreh De'ah* 55 in the name of Ra'avad.

[99] Rambam, *ibid.* 5:8; *Shulĥan Aruĥ Yoreh De'ah* ch. 55.

death. But if it was separated during the animal's lifetime or during the convulsions of its death throes, even the convulsions after Jewish *kosher* slaughter, it is forbidden, as explained in topic 4:2 above.

6. If a portion of the protruding bone splits off that is less than half of the bone's thickness and is separated from the body, and the remaining skin and flesh would be sufficient to cover the bone had that portion of the bone not fallen off, the remaining limb below the break is acceptable. If, however, the protruding bone splits and the portion that was separated off had the majority of the bone's thickness and/or circumference, the remaining bone is considered as if it has been cut off, because it will not heal. Hence, it is considered as a hanging limb,[100] and it is governed by the precepts cited in topics 4:1 and 4:2.

7. To determine whether the skin and flesh cover a majority of the broken bone, one should place the limb in its former position and then bring the flesh and skin together, and see if the majority is covered.[101]

The leniency above, allowing the flesh around a broken and protruding bone to be considered acceptable if the animal's flesh and skin covers the majority of its circumference and diameter, applies only when it is the flesh that could cover the greater part of that portion, and the skin is merely a secondary factor (to aid in the healing). If, however, the flesh and the skin play equal roles in covering the bone, it is unacceptable, because it will not naturally heal.

The above applies to a domesticated or wild mammal. With regard to a bird, by contrast, since its skin is soft, it is considered in combination with the flesh, and when the broken and protruding bone could be covered in this manner half with flesh and half with skin, the limb is acceptable.[102] If, however, it could be covered in this manner only – or primarily – by the remaining skin, it is not acceptable, even for a bird.[103] It appears, however, that one may be lenient and eat from a

---

[100] *Shulĥan Aruĥ Yoreh De'ah* ch. 55.

[101] *Rokeiaĥ, Taz Yoreh De'ah* 55:5.

[102] *Tur* and *Shulĥan Aruĥ Yoreh De'ah* ch. 55, based on Rashba.

[103] *Tur*, Rashba and Shaĥ, *Shulĥan Aruĥ Yoreh De'ah* 55:16. The leniency if the bone is covered only by skin is because there is a doubt regarding the law in Tractate *Ĥullin* 76b, and Rambam (*Laws of Forbidden Foods* 5:8) rules leniently to permit it. The rule that doubt is ruled stringently applies to Jews.

broken limb for which only the skin (without flesh) covered the majority of the broken bone, for either an animal or a bird.

8. The leniency in topic 4:7 above is accepted by all authorities, i.e. allowing the flesh of a broken and protruding bone to be acceptable when the majority of the bone's circumference and diameter is able to be covered by the remaining flesh, but this only applies when that is the ordinary pattern. When the bone is one that is never covered with flesh but rather merely with skin (for example, the knee), it is acceptable according to all authorities for it to be able to be covered just with the remaining skin.[104]

Even in other portions of the body where the majority of the circumference and diameter of the broken and protruding bone must be able to be covered by both skin and flesh for it to be acceptable according to all authorities, the leniency is granted in the following case: no flesh was available in that place to cover the bone in this way, rather only skin, but there were body fluids that would be between the skin and the replaced bone that the skin was able to retain.[104]

Soft sinews that will eventually become firm (and, needless to say, firm sinews) are not considered part of the flesh and are not included when reckoning the extent to which the bone is able to be covered.[105]

9. The flesh that is available to cover a broken and protruding bone must be healthy and largely contiguous. If, by contrast, there would be no large mass of flesh around the replaced bone, it is not acceptable if the flesh has one of the following conditions:
(a) it is in many small pieces around the bone;[106]
(b) it is very thin, or separated from the bone;
(c) it is perforated or slit in many places;
(d) it is crushed or decayed like flesh which a doctor would remove.

In these cases the flesh is not considered as a covering for the broken

---

[104] *Shulĥan Aruĥ Yoreh De'ah* 55:8.

[105] *Shulĥan Aruĥ Yoreh De'ah* 55:9.

[106] *I.e., when one would calculate the entire amount of flesh, it would be large enough to cover the greater portion of the bone. But it is not located in large sections, and is instead made up of many small pieces.

bone.[99] Similarly, in any instance where a doctor would say that the bone would not heal, it is forbidden according to the stricter opinion.[107] If, despite its initial condition, flesh regenerated and can now cover the majority of the thickness and circumference of the broken and protruding bone, the limb is acceptable.[108]

10. If an animal's limb was hanging or its bone was broken and protruding to the extent that it would have been forbidden, but it was repaired through surgery and healed, it is acceptable.[109] Even if the limb was severed from the body entirely, if it was restored through surgery, it is not forbidden as a limb separated from a living animal.

11. There is a Rabbinical opinion that maintains that when a land-mammal or a fowl is killed through a non-*kosher* neck slaughter in which the windpipe or gullet are slit, the lungs or the digestive tract organs are, respectively, forbidden to Gentiles as organs separated from the living animal. For since the windpipe or the gullet was slit, the lungs or the digestive tract organs are, respectively, no longer considered as attached to the body, but merely as contained within its body cavity (as in topic 2:5 above). According to this opinion, the windpipe and esophagus themselves are also forbidden, and *eiver min ha'ĥai* applies to those organs.

The prevailing Rabbinical opinion, however, is that these organs are not considered as having been separated from a living animal,[110] and from the outset the prohibition does not apply. Likewise, the prohibition does not apply for any glands in the neck (for example, the thymus gland) that may be severed from below or above by the

---

[107] This is implied from Rema *Yoreh De'ah ibid.*

[108] Rambam, *Laws of Forbidden Foods* 5:8.

[109] *Shulĥan Aruĥ Yoreh De'ah* 55:12, *Darĥei Moshe* and *Taz Yoreh De'ah* ch. 62, for since it healed, it was living flesh during the entire time. Since the only prohibition for Gentiles comes from taking flesh from the animal while it is still alive, it appears to be permitted to eat this type of injured limb after the animal dies. (However, an organ transplanted from a living animal to another animal, or to a human, will remain forbidden as *eiver min ha'ĥai.*)

[110] There is a discussion among the Sages in Tractate *Ĥullin* 33a, as to whether a Gentile may eat the intestines of a neck-slaughtered animal, since perhaps they are "severed" from the animal while it is still convulsing.

slaughter cut.[111]

12. This difference of opinion applies only when the neck slaughter was not *kosher*, e.g. if it was a non-*kosher* species, or if it was performed on a *kosher* species by a Gentile. If it was performed by a Jew as a *kosher* (ritual) slaughter for the sake of consumption by a Jew, all Rabbinical authorities agree that the lungs and digestive tract organs are allowed to be eaten by a Gentile according to Torah Law.[112]

Likewise, if a Gentile slaughtered an animal with a neck cut but did not cut the windpipe and esophagus completely, the lungs and digestive tract organs are still permitted, since they are not completely separated from the animal but are rather hanging in it, and they are permitted like a hanging limb, as explained in topic 4:1 above.[113]

It appears that practically, the ruling is that intestines are permitted for a Gentile regardless of the method of slaughter, and they are not considered to be hanging by themselves in the body cavity, for several reasons:
a) Most Rabbinical authorities do not hold that they are considered to be hanging by themselves, i.e. totally disconnected, within the body cavity. Even those who do hold this opinion do so only as a stringency because of a doubt, but this does not make something forbidden for Gentiles.
b) The entire consideration of that opinion is to say that the intestines are left like a hanging limb, which is permitted for Gentiles after the animal dies.
c) The entire problem of cutting off a limb while the animal is still convulsing is only a Rabbinical decree so that one should not come to eat the limb while the animal is still convulsing. See topic 3:2, footnote 72 above. In the case of internal organs, it is a very remote possibility that these parts would actually come to be eaten before the slaughtered animal has died.
d) Since neck-slaughtering of animals is permitted by the Torah for a Gentile, he is performing an action to permit the animal's limbs and intestines to be eaten, as opposed to the type of action that is forbidden, which is cutting off a limb of the animal while it is still alive.
e) Jewish slaughterers have always sold the carcasses that were incorrectly slaughtered, including the intestines, to Gentiles to reduce their financial loss. This proves that the prevailing custom has been the lenient view. Otherwise, the sale of these organs to Gentiles would be forbidden for Jews due to their prohibition of putting a stumbling block before "the blind" (Leviticus 19:14), i.e. before someone who is unaware ("blind") about a certain matter.

[111] *Pri Megadim Siftei Da'at* 27:2 only relates to laws of *kosher* slaughter.

[112] Tractate *Ĥullin* 33a and Rashba, as taught by Shaĥ *Yoreh De'ah* ch. 27.

[113] *Panim Yafot Parshat Tzav*, and *Ĥatam Sofer Yoreh De'ach* ch. 18.

CHAPTER 5

The Precepts Pertaining to a Fetus, and to Eggs

1. The prohibition of *eiver min ha'ĥai* from animals begins at the moment of birth, for the verse (Genesis 9:4) states "But flesh in its blood – its life – do not eat," which indicates that the life is in the blood. But for a fetus, prior to birth, its life is not (entirely) in its blood, but is instead dependent on both its and its mother's blood.[114]

Therefore, one who slices up a fetus while still in its mother's womb, and eats those pieces – regardless whether the pieces were removed before or after the mother's demise – will not be liable for a capital sin. However, there are circumstances in which the limbs and meat of a fetus are forbidden because it will appear to an onlooker as if the transgression of *eiver min ha'ĥai* is being committed.

2. A fetus which was born (alive) before its mother completed the period of gestation, although it cannot remain alive (without external support, and it is therefore considered a non-viable birth), is forbidden for a Gentile to eat from it while it is still alive; however, one is not liable for a capital sin if one ate flesh that was severed from it. Only after it dies naturally or is killed is it permitted to be eaten; if the fetus was dead upon birth, it is permitted as a carcass.[115]

3. The majority of mammals are born after the mother has completed the full period of gestation; thus, one who eats from a recently born animal is liable for a capital sin, since we do not rely on a doubt that this particular animal was born from an incomplete gestation. The reason for this is because we follow the majority of cases, and the majority of mammals are born alive after a full period of gestation.[116]

---

[114] This can be learned from the case of one who cuts off limbs from a fetus and leaves them inside the mother, as will be explained in topic 5:10 below.

[115] Rambam, in *Laws of Forbidden Foods* 4:4, explains that although this animal is born, since it cannot live, it is considered an unslaughtered carcass. Nevertheless, it appears that anything that has any life must be killed before it is eaten. (If doctors save this fetus and raise it in an incubator and it lives, it is clearly regarded as a completely live animal.)

[116] *S'dei Ĥemed* (*Pe'at Hasadeh Ma'areĥet Gimel* ch. 6): also for Gentiles, in Torah Law one should consider the situation for the majority of instances.

Nonetheless, if in a particular scenario there is reason to doubt that the animal was born after a completed pregnancy (for example, if it was apparent that the mother did not carry the fetus for the full term), one who eats from it during the first seven days of its life is not liable for a capital sin, because the status of the animal is in doubt.[117] If, however, the animal lived an entire week and is healthy, it is deemed a regular animal, and one who eats *eiver min ha'ĥai* from this animal before it dies is liable for a capital sin.

4. If an animal dies or is killed, it is permitted to eat a lifeless fetus that is found inside. If, however, the fetus is still alive, it is forbidden to eat from a detached limb or piece of the meat from the live fetus until it is killed. Otherwise, one would be violating *eiver min ha'ĥai.*

In this situation, if the fetus was carried for a full gestation, and therefore is viable, it is a living animal and one is liable for eating *eiver min ha'ĥai.* If the fetus was not carried for a full term, it is not considered viable, and though it is forbidden to cut and eat *eiver min ha'ĥai* from it, one is not liable (see topic 5:2 above).

If a Jew performs *kosher* slaughter on the mother animal, a Gentile who eats flesh from a live fetus found in its womb, that had gone through the full gestation period, is not liable, but one is forbidden to do so. (See also topic 3:4 with regard to one who eats from an animal that has been slaughtered by a Jew and is in its death throes.)[118]

---

*All marsupials give birth while the offspring is still in an early fetus stage, and the mother's pouch serves as an external womb. Since this is the normal manner in which these animals are born, one is liable for a capital sin if he eats flesh from a newborn marsupial after the normal gestation period, even though the animal is similar to an incompletely developed fetus.

[117] *Shulĥan Aruĥ Yoreh De'ah* ch. 15.

[118] *Pri Megadim Siftei Da'at* 13:3 expresses doubt as to whether a fetus taken alive out of its *kosher*-slaughtered mother's womb is governed by all the laws of *eiver min ha'ĥai* for Gentiles, or if the *kosher* slaughter of the mother permits the fetus to be eaten after it (the fetus) is killed in any manner, even by severing its limbs while it is still alive. This would apply only if it was done as an act of slaughtering, by removing a major limb that will cause immediate death of the fetus [see topic 3:12, the fn. there, and fn. 110(d)].

It appears to the author that such a live fetus is forbidden to be eaten by Gentiles as *eiver min ha'ĥai* until it dies or is killed. Regardless, for Gentiles, a live animal always has the prohibition of *eiver min ha'ĥai.*

5. An animal that was delivered by Cesarean section after a full period of gestation is considered a living animal,[119] and it must die naturally or be killed if meat is to be removed from it to be eaten. Any meat severed from an offspring after its delivery by Cesarean section, before it is killed or dies, is considered as severed from a living animal.

6. If the head of a living fetus emerges from the mother's body, the mother is considered as having given birth to a live baby. It is not necessary for the entire head to emerge. As long as its frontal head emerges (the part that is seen when looking straight on at the animal), it is considered as having been born alive;[120] at that point it becomes an independent entity from its mother (even if it retracted its head in to the mothers womb), and it is forbidden to cut from it a limb or meat while it is alive. Even if one cut off meat from a part of the live fetus that was still inside the mother's womb (after the majority of its forehead emerged) and left it in the mother's womb – regardless of whether the mother is alive or not – the meat remains forbidden, and is considered as if it was removed from a living animal.[121]

If the fetus dies in the womb after it has retracted its head, it appears that it is permitted to cut pieces from it and take them out while the mother is still alive (and surely one may remove the whole body) and eat them, as there is no prohibition of *eiver min ha'ĥai* in this case.[122]

Practically, the argument is not regarding the whole fetus (since in any case it isn't permitted to be eaten alive), but to pieces cut or torn off the fetus. According to the lenient side of the *Pri Megadim's* doubt, these are permitted for Gentiles, since its mother's *kosher* slaughter included the fetus inside as *kosher* meat. According to the other side of his doubt and this author's opinion, the mother's *kosher* slaughter has no effect on the fetus for Gentiles; therefore, as long as the fetus is alive it is like any other living mammal and is governed by the law of *eiver min ha'ĥai*. See footnotes 72 and 79.

[119] With regard to the prohibition of *eiver min ha'ĥai*, an animal born by Caesarian section is considered just like one that emerged by regular birth.

[120] *Shulĥan Aruĥ*, *Taz* and Shaĥ *Yoreh De'ah* ch. 14.

[121] *Shulĥan Aruĥ Yoreh De'ah* ch. 14.

[122] It is forbidden to cut a dead fetus from the mother's womb (as explained in topic 5:8) because it **looks like** the removal of *eiver min ha'ĥai*. However, when the animal was partially born and then retracted its head, it is considered independently an unslaughtered carcass and not the mother's flesh, and it does not have any prohibition of *eiver min ha'ĥai*.

7. If a fetus was born or removed from the womb alive and then the fetus died or was killed, or if it emerged stillborn, it is considered as an independent dead animal and may be then eaten by a Gentile.

8. If the fetus was dead in its mother's womb and it was removed from her body – whether through the birth canal or by a Cesarean section – while the mother animal was still alive, it is forbidden as meat taken from a living animal, although one who eats from it is not liable for a capital sin.[123] If the dead fetus was removed after the mother animal died, it is considered to be a carcass, and a Gentile may eat from it.

9. If a fetus is removed via Cesarean section before it has undergone a full gestational period, and thus it cannot live for more than a brief period (naturally, without external life support), it is not considered to be a "born" offspring. It is, therefore, forbidden to be eaten, as it is like a limb that was severed from a living animal. However, one who eats from it is exempt from liability for punishment.[124]

10. Detached pieces of the fetus that have not exited the mother's womb are not subject to the rules of *eiver min ha'ĥai*. Accordingly, if one severs limbs or flesh from a fetus while it is still in the mother's womb, but did not remove them from the womb, and then killed the mother or she died naturally, the pieces may be eaten.[125] (Furthermore, it appears that if the pieces were discharged from the mother's womb, they may be eaten.)[126]

But if one cut off a limb from the fetus and removed it from the mother, it is subject to the prohibition of *eiver min ha'ĥai*. Even if one severed the head of the fetus while it was still in the womb and then removed it, the same prohibition would apply (although eating this

---

[123] As will be explained in topic 5:10, a fetus in the womb is not considered an independently living animal, but rather it is forbidden since it resembles a living animal. This applies even if the mother is killed and is still convulsing.

[124] *Minĥat Ĥinuĥ* Commandment 452: a stillborn animal is like an unslaughtered carcass and has no prohibition of *eiver min ha'ĥai*, but it appears that it is forbidden, since it looks like one is eating the flesh of the mother.

[125] Rambam, *ibid.* 5:9; *Shulĥan Aruĥ Yoreh De'ah* ch. 14.

[126] As this is considered waste, and we do not say this is like the case of one who causes them to separate from the body by cutting them in the womb.

would not make a Gentile liable for a capital sin). It bears noting that there is no difference in this rule whether the fetus was alive or dead at the time the limb or head was severed, for while the fetus is still in the womb, it is reckoned as a piece of the mother's flesh, and it is, therefore, as if one cut off a piece of the mother's flesh.[127]

11. If the hand or foot of the fetus emerged from the mother while the mother was still alive, even if the limb remained outside the mother until the mother was slaughtered or died, it is not subject to the rules of *eiver min ha'ĥai* and is permitted, for it did not separate from the body of the fetus.[128] If, however, the limb that emerged was cut off while the mother was alive, regardless of whether the fetus is alive or already dead, or whether the mother was slaughtered or died while the fetus was alive, the severed limb is reckoned as *eiver min ha'ĥai* and is forbidden to be eaten (though one would not be liable for a capital sin).

If the limb that emerged from the womb was severed only after the mother and fetus died, it is considered as a carcass and may be eaten.

12. If the fetus exited the mother's womb feet-first, it is considered born when the majority of its body has emerged, and at that point it is no longer one unit with the mother.[129] (If it came out head-first it is considered born as soon as the majority of the forehead alone has emerged from the mother, as was previously explained.) Even the

---

[127] See *Leĥem Mishneh Hilĥot Ma'aĥalot Assurot* 5:11, which explains that this is forbidden for a Jew. According to what is explained in topic 5:1 above, it should be permitted for a Gentile, but nevertheless since it appears to an onlooker as if he cut off a piece of meat from the mother, it is forbidden.

The rationale is that the Torah Law for Jews reckons the fetus as a "thigh of the mother." Thus the fetus' meat becomes permitted for Jews through the mother's *kosher* slaughter, since the fetus is linked to its mother in receiving the slaughter to become *kosher* meat. Thus, as long as its mother is not *kosher*-slaughtered, the pieces of the fetus are *eiver min ha'ĥai* for a Jew, like pieces from the mother.

But for Gentiles, there is no link between the status of the mother and her fetus, and neither needs *kosher* slaughter, so the fetus is not considered a "thigh of the mother" in regard to *eiver min ha'ĥai*.

[128] *Tzemaĥ Tzedek Yoreh De'ah* 63:6; it is forbidden for a Jew because the emerged limb becomes *treifah*, but this is not forbidden to a Gentile.

[129] *Shulĥan Aruĥ Yoreh De'ah* 14:3.

minority part of the fetus which remained in the mother's body is also not considered as part of the mother. Therefore, if a limb was cut from the offspring at this stage of birth, it is *eiver min ha'ĥai* and thus forbidden to be eaten. If the offspring died during the birth process and then parts were severed from it, even the parts which remained in the mother (and which were later removed during the life of the mother) are not subject to the prohibition of *eiver min ha'ĥai*, for the dead offspring is a carcass and is, therefore, permitted (see topic 5:6 above).

13. If one limb exited and was severed, and then another limb exited and was also severed, the status of this meat depends on the following:

a) If the severed pieces constitute only a minority of the fetus, they are forbidden, for they are considered as *eiver min ha'ĥai* from the mother animal (as was explained previously in topics 5:10 and 5:11).

b) If the majority of the fetus exited and was cut off, it is considered as if it was born. Therefore, a piece of the fetus that remained in the womb, or was discharged, or was later removed from the womb, is considered to be a piece of carcass and is thus permitted.[130]

14. Though it was explained earlier in Chapter 1 that it is forbidden to cut off limbs from an animal even if one does not intend to eat them, it is however permitted to cut off limbs from a fetus to save its mother.[131]

15. If a beast of prey ripped off and swallowed a limb or meat from a living mammal or bird, and afterwards the injured animal escaped, but the beast of prey was killed and the limb or meat was removed from its digestive system, it is still considered as meat from a living animal and is forbidden, on the assumption that the animal whose limb or meat was swallowed is still alive. Needless to say, this applies if limb or meat was coughed out by the beast of prey.

This law applies only if the limb or meat is found in its totality (even if it has been cut up by the teeth of the attacker). If, however, it is found to be chewed up (but it still has the semblance of a limb or meat), it is only forbidden for the first 24 hours from the time it was swallowed. Once it has remained in the digestive system of the beast of prey for more than 24 hours, it is considered as waste and not

[130] Based on *Shulĥan Aruĥ Yoreh De'ah* 14:4.

[131] *Tiferet Yisrael* on Mishnah *Ĥullin* 4:6.

flesh.[132] (This ruling will only apply while the animal from which the limb or meat was ripped is still alive. If, however, it died prior to the removal of the swallowed meat from the abdomen of the beast of prey, it seems that the prohibition of *eiver min ha'ĥai* no longer applies.)[133]

16. The following rules apply if one struck a bird and caused an egg it was carrying to fall out.[134] If the egg is fully developed with both a white and a yolk (although the shell is not formed, and the egg is still in a soft membrane), it is permitted, for then it is already considered as independent from the mother.[135] If, however, the egg still requires the mother for development, it is considered as part of the bird organs,[136] and it is considered as flesh removed from a living animal.[137]

If a bird lays eggs naturally, even if they are not fully developed,[138] or one slaughters or kills a bird and discovers underdeveloped eggs inside that were still dependent on the mother, the eggs are permitted.

17. A chick that it is being formed in its egg, until it cracks the eggshell, is not considered a bird, but has the status of a *sheretz*-type

---

[132] See: *Taz*, *Pri Ĥadash*, and *Kraiti U'Plaiti*, *Yoreh De'ah* end of ch. 83; and *Shulĥan Aruĥ HaRav Orah Ĥayim* 467:63.

[133] This is because the separating of the limb was not done through a person, but rather by the beast of prey. The situation involved is after the death of the attacked (victim) animal, but during its life the limb was not available. As explained in topic 3:1, the basic prohibition is eating a limb during the life of the animal, but after its death it is only a Rabbinic prohibition. Therefore, it appears that for this situation, the Rabbis did not make a decree to forbid this. As well, after it was swallowed, there is a question as to whether something that was swallowed is still considered food, or if it is immediately considered waste. Therefore, it seems that this swallowed limb is permitted.

[134] *Birds, most reptiles (including most lizards, turtles and snakes), and monotreme mammals (the echidna and platypus) reproduce by laying eggs that have protective shells. The rules in this and the following topic apply equally to birds and to any other of these creatures and their eggs.

[135] The comparison to a Caesarian section can be found above, in topic 5:5.

[136] Rambam, *Laws of Forbidden Foods* 3:7.

[137] *Shulĥan Aruĥ Yoreh De'ah* 86, and *Minĥat Ĥinuĥ* Commandment 452.

[138] Though *Ĥatam Sofer* (*Yoreh De'ah* ch. 19) questions whether eggs might be forbidden to Gentiles as *eiver min ha'ĥai*, all other authorities permit it; the egg is naturally released when it is no longer part of the mother's body.

creature.[139] Thus, it appears that if one took it out of the egg and cut off a limb from it, the meat has no prohibition of *eiver min ha'ĥai.*

18. There is a difference of opinion with regard to worms that are found inside a mammal or bird, e.g. in its lungs, in its limbs, or beneath its skin during its lifetime. There are some opinions that maintain that they are considered as part of the animal's meat. Hence, if these worms remain alive after the animal's death, they can be considered as meat from a living animal. According to these views, it is forbidden to cook this meat together with these worms, for even after the worms die, they are forbidden. Other authorities, however, do not forbid these worms.[140] (Worms, or any larva, that grow in the meat of a carcass are permitted.[141])

19. This applies to worms that grow in an animal. On the other hand, worms that enter the animal's body from the outside, through its mouth, nose, skin and the like, are permitted and may be cooked with the animal's meat. If there is a doubt regarding whether they grew in the animal or entered from the outside, they are permitted.[142]

The reason is because it is only regarding Jews that there is a debate as to why bird eggs are permitted in general, since a Jew must eat only *kosher*-slaughtered meat, but eggs come from birds that have not been slaughtered. For Gentiles, who do not need *kosher*-slaughtered meat, the prohibition of *eiver min ha'ĥai* is not dependent on the laws of *kosher* slaughter. Since the egg is naturally released from the bird at the point when it is no longer a part of her body, it is not *"min ha'ĥai"* (severed from a living animal).

This explanation follows *Zeĥer Yitzĥak* ch. 33, which makes this distinction between the separate prohibitions of *eiver min ha'ĥai* for Jews and for Gentiles. See footnote 63 above.

[139] Rambam, *Laws of Forbidden Foods* 3:8 and *Shulĥan Aruĥ Yoreh De'ah* ch. 86; *"sheretz"* is defined in topic 1:7 above. Although it is forbidden to cut a limb from the chick because of the prohibition against causing pain to a living animal, it may still be permitted for the purpose of human healing.

[140] See *Pri Megadim Siftei Da'at* 84:42; *Mishbetzot Zahav* 84:21; Responsa of Rabbi Shneur Zalman ch. 15; *Tzemaĥ Tzedek* (*Yoreh De'ah* ch. 63); Responsa *Beit Shlomo* (*Yoreh De'ah* ch. 81); *Maharsham Daat Torah* (*Yoreh De'ah* 41:17).

[141] *Shulĥan Aruĥ Yoreh De'ah* ch. 84.

[142] Doubt in Torah law is ruled leniently for Gentiles; *Daat Torah ibid.* 41:14.

CHAPTER 6

Deriving Benefit from Meat Severed from Living Animals; Cases with a Doubt, and Mixtures with Forbidden Meat

1. Meat severed from a living mammal or bird is forbidden to be eaten. However, if meat does become severed, one is permitted to derive benefit from it.[143] For the Biblical proof text, "But flesh with its soul, its blood, you shall not eat," prohibits eating, but does not mention deriving benefit. Therefore, it is permitted to use such meat for work or any type of benefit other than eating.

2. Severed meat may thus be sold as non-food for profit. One may not, however, sell it to a person whom one knows will consume it, for that is considered as feeding him a prohibited substance, and Gentiles are forbidden to cause each other to transgress (see Part I, topic 4:7).

3. Torah prohibitions against eating involve eating a forbidden food in its ordinary manner and form. If meat has been processed and changed to the extent that it is no longer considered a "food," there is no prohibition, because it is no longer related to a normal way of "eating." Therefore, if a piece of *eiver min ha'ĥai* meat has been changed to the extent that it is no longer in the category of human food – for example, if it has been dried and made into a powder that itself would not be eaten in the manner of food – the prohibition is removed.[144]

4. When it is customary to eat the meat of a particular species of mammal or bird raw, the conditions on liability to punishment for eating meat removed from a living animal (topic 3:1) apply if the meat is eaten raw or cooked.

---

[143] Tractate *Pesaĥim* 22b; Maharil ch. 161.

*A Gentile commits a capital sin only by specific violations of the Noahide Laws. Still, governments may decide if, or how, violations of other aspects of the Noahide Code (e.g., cruelty to animals) will be punished.

[144] *Pri Megadim Yoreh De'ah* 62:1, 4. It appears that even if one used this powder to make normal food, it is permitted, as the original form is nullified.

*Thus the prohibition against eating *eiver min ha'ĥai* doesn't apply to most meat-derived vitamins, nutritional supplements, or gelatin products.

When, however, it is not customary to eat the meat of an animal raw, one is not liable to punishment for this unless the meat is cooked. Nevertheless, it is forbidden.[145]

It is not the ordinary practice to consume raw fat, so one who eats raw fat taken from a living land mammal is not liable to punishment.

If one cooks fat and makes it into an edible liquid, one is liable.[146]

One who drinks boiling fat is not liable, for this is not the common manner of consuming it, and it is not fit to be eaten in this state (i.e., this is not an edible form of the food). Nevertheless, it is forbidden.[147]

5. Even when there is no transgression of eating *eiver min ha'ĥai* meat, it is still forbidden to cut off meat or limbs from any living animal to derive benefit from them. Although God granted mankind dominion over the animals, He did not grant permission to cut off their limbs and flesh. Only when a limb or meat was found already severed is it permitted to use this for some non-food purpose.

6. One is only liable for punishment for eating meat that was taken from a living animal. If, however, one cooked the meat and consumed the sauce, or squeezed out the juices from the meat and drank that, he is not liable.[148]

Similarly, if one cooked this meat together with other foods and the forbidden meat imparted its flavor to those foods, one is not liable for consuming the other foods.

Likewise, if one sucks the juice from *eiver min ha'ĥai* meat but does not eat the meat, he is not liable.[149]

It is nevertheless forbidden to deliberately cook or mix meat that was severed from a living land mammal or bird with other foods, for the purpose of benefiting from the forbidden flesh. It is appropriate to forbid food with which such *eiver min ha'ĥai* meat was cooked. This

---

[145] See *Tosafot*, Tractate *Pesaĥim* 24b.

[146] Tractate *Pesaĥim* 24b; Rambam, *Laws of Forbidden Foods* ch. 14.

[147] *Ibid.* Even though a Gentile is liable for eating the smallest amount of *eiver min ha'ĥai*, this applies only when it is in an edible form.

[148] *Kraiti U'Plaiti* ch. 81; Responsa of Rabbi Shneur Zalman ch. 15; *Ĥatam Sofer Yoreh De'ah* ch. 106. The prohibition of a permitted food if it absorbed the gravy of a forbidden food is only a precept for Jews.

[149] This is not considered in Torah law to be a normal method of eating.

applies when one intentionally cooked meat taken from a living animal with other food. If, however, such meat accidentally fell into a pot and imparted its flavor into the other food, there is no reason to forbid the original food, but the forbidden piece of meat remains prohibited.[150]

7. If fat that was severed from a live animal was then cooked with other foods, and it became indistinguishable from the total dish, then the whole mixture may be eaten, for the forbidden fat is nullified in the general mixture. If, however, the fat's flavor is identifiable, even if the fat constitutes merely a minority of the total mixture and is completely blended with the rest of the dish, then the entire mixture is forbidden. For when the flavor of the forbidden fat is distinguishable, it is deemed as if the fat itself is apparent.[151]

It must be noted, however, that the abovementioned rule applies only when the fat was mixed with a different type of food. If, however, the forbidden fat was mixed with permissible fat that has the same taste, then the majority of the food becomes the decisive factor. If the majority of the mixture is permissible food, the mixture is permissible; if not, then it is forbidden.[152]

8. A Gentile does not have a prohibition in cases of doubt. Therefore, a Gentile transgresses only if he definitely recognizes that aspect of the action that is forbidden.[153] So, for example, if there is an unresolved

---

[150] Many later Rabbis agree that for Gentiles, the flavor is not considered as if it is the meat itself. See *S'dei Ĥemed* (*Pe'at Hasadeh Ma'areĥet Gimel* 6:18).

[151] See Rambam, *Laws of Forbidden Foods* ch. 15.

[152] *Ibid.* 15:4.

[153] *This is not the same as the case of topic 4:2 in Part I. There, topic 4:2 deals with an action that is definitely a transgression of the Noahide Code, but the person is unaware that he is committing that transgression.

An example would be a case in which a boy and his maternal sister were separated from each other as children. Years later, the grown boy met a woman and married her, not knowing that she was his sister. If he is unaware of this, he is not liable to punishment for having marital relations with her. Therefore, after the fact, he is not punished.

In the case discussed here of an accidental mixture of *eiver min ha'ĥai* meat with permitted meat, before the action of eating, the person is faced with a situation of doubt as to whether or not a piece of meat is forbidden. In this case, from the outset, the person is permitted to eat the doubtful meat.

doubt as to whether or not a piece of meat is *eiver min ha'ĥai*, it is permitted for a Gentile to eat it.[154]

9. If a piece of *eiver min ha'ĥai* meat accidentally became mixed with a piece of permitted meat and it is impossible to distinguish the forbidden piece, then there is a doubt regarding each piece as to whether it is permitted or forbidden. In such a case, a Gentile may eat any doubtful piece from the mixture.[155] Nevertheless, one Gentile may not consume the entire mixture, for then he is definitely consuming forbidden food.

The mixture may, however, be divided among two Gentiles, and each one is permitted to eat his share of the mixture.[156] Likewise, it is permitted to throw away one piece and eat the one remaining.

10. If a piece of *eiver min ha'ĥai* meat becomes accidentally mixed with two or more permitted pieces of meat and it is impossible to distinguish between them, we do not say that the forbidden substance is nullified and becomes permissible because of the larger amount of the permitted substance. It is still forbidden for one Gentile to consume the entire mixture,[157] even if he interrupts his eating (for example, if he eats part of it on one day and the rest on another day).

The leniencies mentioned above apply only when the forbidden meat and the permitted meat were mixed together accidentally. It is forbidden to purposely create such a mixture to enable the forbidden

---

[154] *S'dei Ĥemed Ma'areĥet Gimel Pe'at Hasadeh* 6:3.

[155] *If multiple pieces of forbidden meat became mixed with permitted meat, the entire mixture is forbidden if the majority is *eiver min ha'ĥai*. If less than half is *eiver min ha'ĥai*, one Gentile may eat from it until the number of pieces left is the same as the number of pieces of forbidden meat that were originally mixed in. Up to that point, there is a doubt regarding whether or not he has eaten forbidden food. But one Gentile may not have the intention to eat more than this amount, for then he will definitely be intending to eat *eiver min ha'ĥai*.

[156] See *S'dei Ĥemed*, *ibid*. See also *Pri Megadim* (introduction to *Oraĥ Ĥayim*): even if a prohibited piece of meat is within the mixture, so long as a doubt exists as to which piece is forbidden, the mixture is permitted for Gentiles (but one person may not eat all the pieces of meat).

[157] *Ĥatam Sofer Yoreh De'ah* ch. 19.

piece of meat to be permitted. If one does so, as a penalty he is personally forbidden to eat any meat from the mixture, and he is forbidden to benefit or derive pleasure from it in any way – for example, by selling it or giving it to his family, friends or pets.[158] It is, however, permitted for him to give it away for free to other Gentiles who might take from it, if it will be divided between two or more people.[159] Likewise, he may remove and discard at least one doubtful piece and give the remainder for free to one other Gentile.[160]

11. When there is a life-threatening situation and food is required, a Gentile may eat from meat severed from a living animal, for a Gentile is not required to sacrifice his life to uphold his commandments.[161]

---

158 This is logical. Just as a Jew is liable to a penalty for deliberately mixing forbidden items with a majority of permitted items (*Yoreh De'ah* ch. 99), the same prohibition should apply for Gentiles. If not, then the prohibition of *eiver min ha'ĥai* would come to be disregarded.

159 *In this case, he must notify the other Gentiles of the nature of this mixture of food, lest one person eat the whole mixture, which definitely will include forbidden meat.

160 *In this case, he does not have to notify the recipient that it might contain forbidden meat.

161 *Ĥatam Sofer Yoreh De'ah* ch. 70, and *Maharsha Nedarim* 31b. For a Gentile, the obligation to survive a life-or-death situation is an overriding duress; see Part I, topic 4:3.

Chapter 7

Restrictions on Causing Suffering to a Living Creature

1. As implied from the statement of the Torah,[162] "And you shall rule over the fish of the sea, the fowl of the heavens, and all beasts that swarm on the earth," Adam was granted dominion over all living things and given permission to use them to perform any labor or tasks.[163] Noaĥ was also granted permission to kill an animal to eat any part of its flesh, and to use portions of its body for other useful purposes (for example, its hide for clothing and its bones to fashion utensils).[164] Mankind was not, however, granted permission to kill or wound any animals purposelessly, or to cause them unnecessary pain.[165] This is not permitted with regard to any animal, even fish, *sheretz* creatures, reptiles, or other small crawling creatures.[166]

2. If animals are causing pain or discomfort to humans, it is permitted to harm or even kill them. For when there is an advantage to a person, it permits one to overlook the pain caused to an animal, as we see from the permission God granted to mankind to slaughter animals for food.

Therefore, if a person requires parts of an animal for medical reasons or for other human needs, there is no prohibition against causing the animal pain in the process, *if there is no other way available to fulfill*

---

[162] Genesis 1:28.

[163] Tractate *Sanhedrin* 59b.

[164] *Taz Yoreh De'ah* 117:4.

[165] See Ramban on Genesis 1:28, and *Guide for the Perplexed* vol. 3, ch. 48, which explain that a reason for *eiver min ha'ĥai* is because of the prohibition of causing pain to a living creature; therefore, where a human does not derive a necessary direct benefit from the pain, it is forbidden. In *Guide for the Perplexed* vol. 3, ch. 17, Rambam notes that this can be seen from the story of Bilaam and his donkey in Numbers 22:27-32, when the angel showed Bilaam that he was hitting the animal needlessly, and, therefore, asked him why he was causing the animal pain.

*The Rabbinical term for such an act is the causing of *"tza'ar ba'alei ĥayim,"* which is pain or suffering of living creatures.

[166] *Igrot Moshe Ĥoshen Mishpat*, vol. 2, ch. 47.

the need.[167] Therefore, it is allowed, for example, to remove the feathers of living geese if one requires feathers and does not have any others available. (It is, however, undesirable to do this, because it is an act of cruelty that causes much pain.)[168]

It is forbidden to skin a living animal, for this will surely cause the animal to die while suffering greatly in the process. Hence, it should first be slaughtered and then skinned.

If one needs only a small portion of the skin, which would not cause the animal to die, it is not necessary to kill it first;[169] however, this is only permitted in cases of dire need, as there is an element of cruelty in doing so. Similarly, if one needs a small fraction of an animal's blood, one may obtain the needed blood while the animal is alive.

3. If one wishes to kill any creature in order to eat it, he has no permission to be cruel and cause it *needless* suffering in the process. An example would be one who keeps birds, and when he wishes to prepare them for food he drops them alive into a pot of boiling water.

If there is a needed benefit for a person to do so, even such as the case of certain creatures whose taste is better when they are boiled alive, it is not forbidden to do so. If not, one is obligated to kill the animal first in a less painless way, even if this takes a little extra effort, since this is not enough of an excuse to permit causing such suffering to a living creature.[170]

4. It is permissible for a person to kill an animal or bird to feed his

---

[167] *Compassion also dictates that if possible, an animal should be made surgically insensitive before it is subjected to a major surgical procedure.

[168] Rema *Even HaEzer* ch. 5; *Shulĥan Aruĥ HaRav Hilĥot Ovrai Deraĥim* ch. 4; *Nemukai Yosef Bava Metzia*, end of ch. 2.

[169] This is like the rule of pulling feathers from birds, in which it is better when possible not to kill the bird, even if one causes it *temporary* pain. This can be seen from Tractate *Ĥullin* 7b; see footnote 11 above.

[170] See footnote 11 above: it is explained in *Sefer HaĤinuĥ* and Ran that the prohibition of causing pain to an animal also exists in regard to killing the animal in an unnecessarily cruel way. Only when there is a necessary benefit for humans is one not obligated to take the pain caused into account, and even then it is preferable to take the pain into account.

*A Gentile may cook (for food) an unbroken egg with the chick inside.

dogs or other carnivorous pets,[171] since he has responsibility for them. In contrast, it is forbidden to do so for ownerless dogs or wild beasts, since he derives no practical benefit from feeding them, and a human has no permission to kill one animal just for the sake of another.

5. It is not allowed to cause needless pain to an animal through any act that directly causes it suffering, even an act like removing its food to aggravate it. If, however, an animal is dying, feeling hunger, or suffering pain, a Gentile is under no specific obligation to relieve its suffering.[172] Nevertheless, it is proper to go beyond the letter of the law and show mercy to the created beings, by doing whatever is possible to alleviate their suffering (but see topic 12 below).

If an animal – even an ownerless animal – is starving, it is desirable to provide food for it, or to provide it with water if it is suffering from thirst. One may, however, strike the animal lightly to prevent it from returning to him continuously.[173] Needless to say, it is an act of cruelty for a person to refrain from feeding animals, fowl, or fish that rely on him for their sustenance.[174]

It is nevertheless forbidden to draw an animal into a fenced-in area where it cannot graze and will eventually die, for this is an intentional act of causing the animal pain.[175]

6. Similarly, it is permitted to strike an animal to prod it to perform work or other activities on behalf of a person. One is not, however, permitted to beat it severely (i.e., with cruelty).[176]

---

[171] *Shulĥan Aruĥ Yoreh De'ah* 1:5 and Shaĥ there; *Shulĥan Aruĥ HaRav Yoreh De'ah* 1:40.

[172] See *Shulĥan Aruĥ HaRav Hilĥot Ovrai Deraĥim* ch. 3, that shows that Jews are also not obligated to save an animal from death and hunger, and the Jewish obligation to unload a beast of burden that collapsed under its load is intended for human benefit; see Rambam, *Laws of Murderers* ch. 13.

[173] Tractate *Shabbat* 155b, and *Shulĥan Aruĥ HaRav ibid.*

[174] Rabbi Zalman Nehemiah Goldberg notes that the directive to Noaĥ (Genesis 6:21), "for you and them to eat," implies that there is no obligation for a Gentile to feed his animals before himself.

[175] *Nodah Bi'Yehudah* vol. 1 (*Yoreh De'ah* ch. 81), based on *Tosafot Sanhedrin* 80a.

[176] See *Shulĥan Aruĥ HaRav Hilĥot Ovrai Deraĥim* ch. 8.

7. One may poison a dog that causes harm, causing it to die,[177] and one may kill any beast or vermin that causes one aggravation.[178] Needless to say, it is permitted to banish pests from one's property.[179]

8. Similarly, it is permitted to kill any animal that causes hardship to people at large.[180] One is not, however, permitted to kill, or torture, an animal to increase one's honor or for sport or entertainment alone.[181]

9. It is permitted to perform sensible scientific experiments with animals to test drugs and other remedies, to determine whether they are possibly beneficial or safe for humans.[182]

10. If the wing of a fowl or the foot of an animal is broken but still attached, it is incorrect to remove it with the thought that it would be a stumbling block for others, as *eiver min ha'ĥai.* (See Chapter 4 above, which explains that a maimed or broken limb that is not detached from the body is permissible for a Noahide to eat after the animal is killed,

---

[177] *Baĥ* and *Taz*, *Yoreh De'ah* ch. 116.

[178] This is clear from *Shulĥan Aruĥ HaRav Oraĥ Ĥayim* 116:18, and *Igrot Moshe Ĥoshen Mishpat*, vol. 2, ch. 47.

[179] This is like the story in Tractate *Bava Metzia* 85a of the maid in the home of Rebbi (Rabbi Yehuda the Prince), who found young weasels in the house. Surely her intention to sweep out the pests was permitted by Jewish law. However, Rebbi protested that she should leave them be, because he wished to act piously (beyond the letter of the law).

*This includes, for example, the use of insecticides, insect traps, lethal or non-lethal rodent traps, and rodent poisons. However, methods that cause prolonged painful suffering to the trapped creature (such as glue traps for mice) should be avoided if there are other effective alternatives.

[180] *Pri Ĥadash Yoreh De'ah* 53:7, and *Pri Megadim Yoreh De'ah Mishbetzot Zahav* 53:9.

[181] It can be derived from the discussion in Tractate *Sanhedrin* 55 that one may not kill an animal for one's honor, since an animal is not even killed if it can be recognized as one which bestialized a Gentile. Though the donkey of Bilaam was killed for the sake of his honor (Rashi on Numbers 22:33), this may be different as he was honored as a prophet.

*This includes classic examples such as bullfighting, bull-baiting, bear-baiting, dog fighting and cock fighting.

[182] *Shevut Yakov*, vol.3, ch. 71. [Laws should be made to regulate such tests.]

and it does not fall under the prohibition of *eiver min ha'ĥai.*)

If one wishes to sell the animal to others for eating purposes, and there is a reasonable chance that they will cut off the broken limb while the animal is still alive and eat it, one should nevertheless leave the limb attached. The uncertainty of someone else transgressing the prohibition of *eiver min ha'ĥai* does not supersede the transgression of causing unnecessary pain to animals.[183]

It is obvious that one may remove a broken limb of an animal or bird for the sake of healing the injured creature.[184]

11. It is not allowed to tread on or drive a vehicle over a wounded or sick animal that is lying on the road. Instead, one should make a detour around it.[185] If one has no alternative way other than to step on or drive over the animal, it is permitted, as the needs of a human take priority.

Similarly, if one sees a healthy animal on the road, it is forbidden to drive into it or over it, if there is a safe alternative.

12. It appears to the author that a person has no permission to perform a "mercy killing" of an animal. If an animal is sick or injured, even it if will surely die, one should not kill it just because he desires to end its suffering,[186] but rather only if a needed human benefit can be obtained.

13. Hunting an animal is permitted only when it is necessary for human benefit, e.g., to eat the meat of the animal or use its hide or fur. Hunting merely for the sake of sport is not permitted because of the pain caused to the animal. This applies even to beasts of prey when they are in their natural habitat, where they do not pose a threat to humans. However, one is allowed to pursue and kill wild animals

---

[183] See *Pri Ĥadash ibid.* and *Pri Megadim ibid.* (This seems to be the ruling, as a Gentile is not commanded to remove something that could cause another to sin, and may not do so at the expense of causing pain to an animal.)

[184] From Tractate *Bava Batra* 20a and Chapter 1 above, it is forbidden to cut a limb from a living animal, but that is only when there is no purpose at all. But it is permitted for the purpose of healing the animal; see footnote 186.

[185] *Kesef Mishneh Laws of Murders* 13:11.

[186] Although one can say that this act causes no pain to the animal, this is still forbidden if it has no human benefit. One cannot say it is for the animal's benefit, as God did not assign humans to be judges over what is good for an animal in such a case; see Tractate *Bava Batra* 20a and *Tosafot* there.

when they approach an inhabited area, if there is a practical danger that they will cause physical harm to humans, or financial harm through destruction of livestock or physical property.[187]

Capturing animals and putting them in a zoo for human pleasure appears to be permitted, since this human benefit overrides the animal's discomfort. Likewise, it is permitted to raise docile animals in captivity, since a person has pleasure in seeing these animals, and it can alleviate a person's loneliness. This is not comparable to one who hunts animals needlessly, even though a person gets pleasure from hunting, since by hunting he derives pleasure from the actual suffering of the animal, which is forbidden. In contrast, for animals in a zoo or raised in captivity, the person derives pleasure from seeing or being with the animal, and a small discomfort caused to an animal by not living in its natural habitat is overridden by the benefit to the person (who has a pet) or to large numbers of people (who visit a zoo).[188]

14. A Gentile is not forbidden to castrate or neuter any male or female animal,[189] *if* it is done specifically to facilitate the use of the animal by humans, e.g., gelding a horse to make it easier to ride, or spaying a pet so it will not bear offspring in the owner's home.[190] (A reasonable effort should be made to reduce the amount of pain.) It is forbidden to perform such operations if there will be no direct benefit to a person.

15. It is permitted to de-claw an animal if this will benefit a person, for example, if it is needed to prevent the animal from causing damage.[191]

---

[187] *Nodah Bi'Yehudah* vol. 2 *Yoreh De'ah* ch. 10.

*However, the ruling government has the authority to limit the killing of particular species of wild animals (e.g., endangered species) in its domain.

[188] *Needless to say, a zoo or a pet owner should not subject an animal to cruelly inhumane conditions. Rather, there is a responsibility to provide a reasonable degree of comfort to the animal (and doing so will also increase the pleasure which people will be able to derive from the animal).

[189] Meiri on Tractate *Sanhedrin* 56, and this is the opinion of Rambam. In *Shulĥan Aruĥ Even HaEzer* 5:14, this is the majority opinion.

[190] It is clear that it is forbidden to castrate an animal in a painful way, such as tearing off the testicles. It is unclear if castration in a painless way is forbidden. Nevertheless, if there is no necessary benefit for humans, this is completely forbidden; see the footnote to topic 7:12 above.

[191] Tractate *Ĥullin* 7b; Tractate *Avodah Zarah* 11a, and *Tosafot* there.

CHAPTER 8

The Prohibition Against Mating Different Species of Animals

1. According to the Torah's Oral Tradition,[192] it is forbidden for Gentiles to cross-mate different species of animals[193] (and to cross-graft certain species of trees, as explained in the next chapter). Nevertheless, since these prohibitions are not explicitly stated in the Torah, the Torah does not make Gentiles liable to physical punishment for their violation.[194]

2. The universal prohibition against cross-mating of animals applies to causing the copulation of any male and female of two different species. This applies regardless of whether they are two different species of domestic animals, or two different species of wild animals, or if it is a domestic animal species and a wild animal species. This prohibition encompasses all species that humans can coerce or force to cross-copulate, including land and sea mammals,[195] birds,[196] and even reptiles and amphibians.[197]

---

[192] The words "Oral Tradition" here, quoted from the Rambam, refer to the Torah Laws given by God to Moses at Sinai that were not written clearly in the Torah, but instead were transmitted orally to the Jewish people by Moses. This is not a reference to later Rabbinical enactments of the Sages. See Rambam, *Introduction to the Mishneh Torah.*

[193] *Note that *hybridism* derives from the Latin *hybrida* (to insult or outrage).

[194] Rambam *Laws of Kings* ch. 10. A Gentile is liable for a capital sin only if he violates one of the specific seven Biblical Noahide commandments. Violations of other aspects of the Noahide Code (based on the Oral Tradition or later Rabbinical enactments by the Sages) are forbidden, but the Torah does not require these secondary transgressions to be punished in a court of law in the physical world.

[195] *Tur* and *Perisha Yoreh De'ah* ch. 297. But a prohibition of cross-copulation is not applicable to classes of creatures that in general do not mate by vaginal or cloacal copulation; see *Tosafot* on Tractate *Bava Kama* 55, regarding fish.

[196] Rambam, *Laws of Forbidden Mixtures* ch. 9; *Shulĥan Aruĥ Yoreh De'ah* ch. 297.

[197] See Tractate *Ĥullin* 127a. These are all creatures that the Torah mentions as part of creation with the term "according to its kind" (Genesis 1:21-25).

3. It is forbidden to cause animals of different species to mate,[198] even if the union cannot lead to procreation[199] (for example, if the two species cannot produce offspring from each other, and obviously if the mating of the two species can in general produce offspring, but the two individuals are physically unable for whatever reason, such as illness, injury, sterilization, or old or young age). This is implied by the verse[200] "Do not mate your animal with a different species," which instructs that the activity of directly causing copulation itself is forbidden, even if no procreation can occur.

This commandment does not encompass the act of copulating one male creature with another, although it appears that this violates the prohibition of causing unnecessary suffering to living creatures.[201]

4. It is forbidden to cross-mate not only one's own animals, but also those belonging to others[202] or which are ownerless. Similarly, one may not instruct others to cross-mate animals.[203]

---

198 *Even though this is a commandment specifically for Jews, according to the Oral Tradition it applies to Gentiles as well. Tractate *Sanhedrin* 60a teaches that in reference to the verse (Leviticus 19:19) "My statutes you shall observe: you shall not mate your animal with another species...," the Torah's statutes regarding general laws related to the creation are also incumbent upon Gentiles, so that making changes to the original order of creation is universally forbidden. (Furthermore, this calls into question the permissibility and scope of modern-day genetic engineering of animals. See topics 8:11 and 8:15 and the last footnote in Chapter 9 below.)

The Torah does not explicitly give a biological definition of a "species." In biology, *F1 hybrid* is the term for an offspring that results from the cross-mating of distinctly different parental types. The Sages gave many examples of nominally similar types of animals that are either the same or different species in regard to mating; see topics 8:6-10 below.

199 *Ĥatam Sofer Yoreh De'ah* ch. 297.

200 Leviticus 19:19.

201 Causing copulation of male creatures is not considered to be a form of mating, but nevertheless it seems to be forbidden, since it causes pain or distress to the violated animal.

202 Rambam *Laws of Forbidden Mixtures* 9:1.

203 This is because it is forbidden for one to cause another to sin, even if it is not his animal; see *Torat Kohanim* (Leviticus 19:19).

5. The prohibition against cross-mating animals involves any act that will directly cause their mating, be it inserting the male organ into the female organ, raising the male upon the female, or encouraging them to mate by other means.[204]

Nevertheless, it permitted to put males and females of two different species in the same enclosure. If they mate of their own accord, one is not obligated to separate them.[205]

If, however, one knows that a worker, partner, or the like will cross-mate them if they are in the same enclosure, it is forbidden to place them there.[206]

There are differing Rabbinical opinions as to whether it is forbidden to enclose a pair of different species together if it is known that they will certainly cross-mate – for instance, introducing a female donkey or mule into the corral of a male horse that desires to mate.[207] The resolution of this question remains in doubt, so from the outset it should not be done.

6. Even if two different species of animals or beasts appear similar and will be able to have offspring by mating, it is forbidden to cross-mate them.

Therefore, it is forbidden to mate a wolf and a dog, a fox and a *"kofri"* ("wild") dog (i.e. a "hunting" dog,[208] or in other opinions[209] a small dog that resembles a fox), a deer and a goat, a mountain-sheep and a domestic sheep, a horse and a donkey, a horse and a mule, a donkey and a mule, or a domestic donkey and a wild donkey.[210]

---

[204] *Perishah* and *Bi'ur HaGra Yoreh De'ah* ch. 297.

[205] Rambam, *Laws of Forbidden Mixtures* ch. 9; *Shulĥan Aruĥ Yoreh De'ah* ch. 297.

[206] Rema *Yoreh De'ah* ch. 297.

[207] There is an argument between *Baal Halaĥot Gedolot* who says it is forbidden, and other Rabbinic authorities who do not hold this opinion.

[208] Rambam *Pirush Hamishnah*, on Mishnah *Kilayim* 1:6.

[209] Rabbi Ovadiah Mi'Bartenura, on Mishnah *Kilayim* 1:6.

[210] Rambam, *Laws of Forbidden Mixtures* ch. 9; *Shulĥan Aruĥ Yoreh De'ah* ch. 297.

7. When the same species has a domesticated subspecies and a wild subspecies (for example, an ox and a wild ox, or a horse and a wild horse)[211] one may mate them together, because they are of the same species.[210]

Some wild dogs are permitted for mating with a domestic dog, as they are the same species.[212]

8. There is a difference of opinion as to whether domestic goats and wild goats are of the same species in this context of permission to cause them to mate.[213] The rule that is followed is that it is forbidden to mate them together.[214]

9. A buffalo (or bison) is a wild animal that is not the same species as a domestic ox. Hence the two may not be mated.[215] Similarly, a domestic pig is a different species than a wild boar.[216]

---

[211] *Mishnah Rishona* Tractate *Kilayim* ch. 8.

[212] Jerusalem Talmud, Tractate *Kilayim* ch. 1.

*The dingo seems to be one example of a wild dog that may be mated with a domestic dog. All breeds of domestic dogs (*Canis lupus familiaris*) are one species and may be mated. Even within the *Canis lupus* species of dogs, the Gray Wolf and Red Wolf types are considered distinct from the domestic and wild dog types, in terms of forbidden cross-mating.

In contrast, the thirty-six known species of wild cats are distinct from each other and from domestic cats (*Felis catus*), and the different species of cats should not be cross-mated. Recently, a fad has developed for expensive "designer" cats that are hybrids of domestic cats with wild cat species. If a hybrid cat of this type is produced, there are additional restrictions on what genealogies of cats it may be mated with; see topic 8:12.

[213] *Maggid Mishneh Hilĥot Ma'aĥalot Assurot* ch. 1, regarding the opinion of Rambam.

[214] See Rosh, Rashba, *Tur*, *Yoreh De'ah* ch. 80, and Meiri on Tractate *Ĥullin* 80.

[215] Although it appears from Tractate *Ĥullin* 80 that the buffalo and wild ox are of the same species, Radvaz on *Laws of Forbidden Mixtures* ch. 9, and *Tzemaĥ Tzedek* in his Novella on Talmud, Tractate *Kilayim*, rule clearly against this, based on the understanding of *Tosefta Kilayim* ch. 1, Rambam *Laws of Forbidden Foods* ch. 1, and *Shulĥan Aruĥ Yoreh De'ah* ch. 80.

[216] *Tosefta Kilayim* ch. 1.

10. Although a chicken, a peacock, and a pheasant[217] have similarities and graze together, they are considered as different species and may not be cross-mated.[218]

Similarly, a domestic duck and a wild duck are different species. This is evidenced by the fact that the testicles of a domestic duck are located within his body and those of a wild duck are outside. Hence these are two different types, and they may not be cross-mated.[219]

11. If one transgressed and cross-mated animals from two different species, it is permitted to consume the offspring and benefit from them in other ways, and to sustain them and raise them to maturity.[220]

If two crossbred offspring are born from the same types of parents (the parents being a similar pair of different species), it is permitted to mate these offspring together. For example, it is permitted to mate two mules together if each was born from a female donkey and male horse.

12. A hybrid offspring is considered as a separate species, and it is forbidden to be mated with an animal from the species of either of its parents. Moreover, a hybrid whose mother is from one species may not be mated with a hybrid whose mother is of the other species. Two hybrids whose mothers are of the same species may, however, be mated together.

For example, a mule is the offspring produced when crossbreeding a horse and a donkey. When the mother of one mule is a horse and the mother of another mule is a donkey, the two offspring may not be mated. Needless to say, the offspring may not be mated with the species of its mother or father. One may, however, mate together two mules whose mothers are horses, or two mules whose mothers are donkeys.

Torah-law sources explain that if one wishes to mate two mules but does not know the species of their mothers, the mules can be checked

---

[217] Rashi on Tractate *Bava Kama* 55a.

[218] Tractate *Bava Kama* 55a.

[219] Rambam, *Laws of Forbidden Mixtures* ch. 9; *Shulĥan Aruĥ Yoreh De'ah* ch. 297.

[220] Mishnah Tractate *Kilayim* ch. 8; Rambam and *Shulĥan Aruĥ ibid.*

for similarity by comparing their ears, tails, and voices.[221]

13. Similarly, the offspring of a cross-mated goat and deer (a "deer-goat")[222] is considered as a separate species, so it may not be mated with either of its parent species. Nor may a deer-goat whose mother is a deer be mated with a deer-goat whose mother is a goat, but two deer-goats whose mothers are of the same species may be mated. If there is a doubt whether the mothers of two deer-goats are of the same species or not, those deer-goats may be mated.[223] Similar concepts apply to a hybrid from a sheep and a goat, or from any other two species of cross-mated parents.[224]

14. The following principle applies when an animal gives birth to an offspring that resembles another species, e.g., an offspring of a horse that resembles a donkey, or an offspring of a donkey that resembles a horse. Even if it is possible that the mother could have conceived from a union with the species that the offspring resembles, unless one is certain that such a union took place, he does not need to be concerned with this. Rather, the questionable offspring may be considered to be of the same species as its mother, for the purpose of determining what animals are permitted to be mated with it.[225]

---

[221] Rambam and *Shulĥan Aruĥ ibid.* (It appears that the Sages knew the identifying signs for mules with the same species of mothers.)

[222] We use "deer-goat" for the hybrid offspring of a deer and goat, which some Sages identified with the name *ko'i* in Hebrew. The meaning of the term *ko'i* is the subject of dispute amongst the Sages (see Tractate *Ĥullin* 79), as to what species it is. In this volume we follow the terminology that *ko'i* means a hybrid of a goat and a deer. There are other opinions of Sages who said that *ko'i* is the name for some other separate natural species (and not a hybrid), and according to those opinions it is obviously ruled that one may not crossbreed a *ko'i* with a goat or deer.

[223] As noted above in topic 6:8, a doubtful case in Torah law is always ruled leniently with respect to its required observance by Gentiles. In the cases discussed here, it appears that the Sages did not know the identifying signs for deer-goat hybrids with the same species of mothers, although they did know these signs for mules (which are horse-donkey hybrids).

[224] *Tosefta Kilayim* ch. 5.

[225] *Ibid.*

When does the above apply? When we are certain that this mother bore the offspring. However, the fact that we find a young animal that is dependent on an adult female animal, and even if this adult female is nursing the young animal, this is not in itself sufficient proof that the adult female is the biological mother of the young animal. Rather, the young animal could have been adopted by this female, which is acting as its mother. Hence, in such an instance, we may assume the species of the offspring according to its appearance.[226]

15. A motivating rationale for the prohibition against cross-mating animals is not to change the natural order of animal species.[227] Hence, for two separate species which can crossbreed, it is also forbidden to inject sperm from one species into the womb of a female from the other species (i.e., artificial insemination),[228] or to produce a hybrid species in a laboratory vessel using sperm from one species and an egg from the other species.

If one transgresses and produces an animal from this cross-insemination, it is ruled to be a hybrid. One may only breed it with a like species of hybrid, and all the other precepts regarding hybrids apply to it as well (as in topic 8:12 above).[229]

16. It is permitted to have one bird sit on the eggs of another bird, since this does not involve any cross-mating. The mother bird of the different species is simply warming the eggs.[230]

---

[226] Rambam, *Laws of Forbidden Foods* ch. 1 and *Laws of [Entities] Prohibited to be Offered on the Altar* ch. 3; *Shulĥan Aruĥ Yoreh De'ah* ch. 79.

[227] Ramban on Leviticus 19:19.

[228] See *Minĥat Shlomo* vol. 3, ch. 98; also see the last footnote in Chapter 9.

[229] *Ibid.*

[230] Responsa of Rashbatz, vol. 2, ch. 58.

CHAPTER 9

The Prohibition of Grafting Different Species of Fruit Trees

1. The classic example of the type of cross-grafting that is forbidden is to graft a shoot from one type of fruit tree (e.g. an apple tree) onto another type of fruit tree (e.g. an orange tree). Similarly, it is forbidden to graft a fruit vine to a fruit tree, or a fruit tree to a fruit vine.[231]

2. It is permitted for a Gentile to graft a shoot of a fruit tree to a tree that does not bear fruit, or a shoot from a tree that does not bear fruit to a fruit tree. Similarly, one may graft a fruit vine to a non-fruit-bearing tree, or a shoot from a non-fruit-bearing tree to a fruit vine. Cross-grafting of two fruit-vine species is not forbidden.[232] Obviously, one may graft a shoot from one tree that does not bear fruit to another such tree; this is not the type of cross-grafting which the Torah forbids.[233]

3. Even if a graft never closes entirely and the grafted species merely derives nurture from the other, as the case when a fruit vine is grafted onto a fruit tree, the grafting is forbidden.[234]

4. The prohibition against cross-grafting includes grafting a shoot or a branch from one species of fruit tree to the trunk or branch of another, or cutting off a fruit tree at the stump and grafting the trunk of another fruit tree onto it. (It is irrelevant which end of the shoot or branch is

---

[231] Rambam *Laws of Forbidden Mixtures* ch. 1; *Shulĥan Aruĥ Yoreh De'ah* ch. 295. **See topics 9:11-12 below for definitions of these types of plants.** A "fruit" forms with internal seeds, unless it is a modern "seedless" variety.

[232] Rambam *ibid. Shulĥan Aruĥ Yoreh De'ah* ch. 295 writes that this is forbidden, but that is only regarding Jews. This is a Rabbinical enactment (for the Torah does not mention the phrase "to its kind" regarding non-fruit-bearing trees), and Gentiles were not included in this Rabbinical prohibition.

[233] Rosh, *Tur* and Rema *Yoreh De'ah* ch. 295 hold that all non-fruit-bearing trees are considered to be of one kind in this context. See topic 9:14 below.

[234] This is clear from the Jerusalem Talmud Tractate *Kilayim* ch. 1, which explains the opinion of Rabbi Yehudah that such a graft is permitted since it does not completely fuse. This implies that the Sages who differ say that although it does not completely fuse, it is still forbidden.

inserted into the other tree.)[235]

It is also forbidden to sow a fruit vine into the trunk of a fruit tree.[236]

5. There is no prohibition against bringing two fruit trees of different species together, as long as one tree is not actually grafted onto the other tree by human intervention. Even if ultimately they will combine and grow together as one, the person's actions are considered merely as a secondary cause, and a Gentile is not forbidden to do this.[237]

6. For Gentiles, the only applicable Torah prohibitions against growing mixtures of different species of plants[238] are those referring to the **grafts** listed above, which involve a species of fruit tree. It is, however, permitted to plant or sow any types of trees, vines, grains or vegetables side-by-side.[239] There is no prohibition against growing the different species together side-by-side in the same field or garden.[240]

Moreover, it is permitted to plant fruit trees of different species next to each other, even if they will graft onto each other by themselves.[241] As long as a person does not do the actual grafting, there is no prohibition if an otherwise forbidden graft develops on its own.[242]

7. The prohibition against cross-grafting does not apply to the roots of a fruit tree or any portion of the tree that is naturally underground.[243]

---

[235] *Tosefta Kilayim* ch. 1; one may not graft an olive branch onto a date tree.

[236] Mishnah *Kilayim* ch. 1; Rambam *Laws of Forbidden Mixtures* ch. 2.

[237] The prohibition of bringing two plants together in a way that causes them to graft together by themselves, discussed in *Tosefta Kilayim* ch. 1:7, is only a Rabbinic enactment for Jews, and is not forbidden for Gentiles.

[238] *Plants grown as mixtures, whether grafted together or planted together in a mixed garden or field, are called *"kilayim"* in Hebrew.

[239] Rambam *Laws of Forbidden Mixtures* ch. 1; *Shulĥan Aruĥ Yoreh De'ah* ch. 295.

[240] Tractate *Sanhedrin* 60a.

[241] Rashi *ibid.* This is similar to putting male and female animals of different species into the same enclosure. If one does nothing actively to encourage it, there is no prohibition against allowing them to mate. (See topic 8:5.)

[242] See Jerusalem Talmud *Kilayim* ch. 1, as explained by Rosh and *Tur Yoreh De'ah* ch. 295.

[243] Rosh, *Tur*, *Shulĥan Aruĥ Yoreh De'ah* ch. 295.

Any portion of the tree that grows above the ground is not considered a root, but as a part or extension of the trunk.[244] Therefore, if the trunk of a fruit tree is cut off, even cut off to the ground, it is forbidden to plant or graft a fruit tree of a different species or a fruit vine on its stump.[245]

8. One of the agricultural techniques practiced in the pre-Talmudic era was to bend down and bury branches of a tree or vine, bringing them out on the other side as a new tree or vine, in an attempt to increase the nurture received by the plant from the earth. If this is done with a fruit tree, it is forbidden to graft a shoot from another species of fruit tree or from a fruit vine onto the bent-down branch, even when the graft is under the ground. Since the bent-down branch usually grows above the ground, the prohibition against grafting applies.[246]

If a fruit-tree branch is buried in this manner (including a grape vine, which is soft yet categorized as a tree; see topic 11 below), one may sow a fruit vine in the earth which covers it, even though ultimately the extending roots will graft themselves onto the buried branch.[247]

9. As stated in topic 9:2, the prohibition against cross-grafting does not apply to a tree that does not bear fruit. Hence, it is important to know which trees are in the category of fruit trees and which are not.[248]

Spice trees are not considered as fruit trees, because they do not produce fruit that serves as food.[249]

Trees and vines whose fruits are not desirable and are not fit for human consumption are included in the prohibition if their fruit is fit

---

[244] Tractate *Bava Batra* 82a.

[245] See Rabbi Ovadiah Mi'Bartenura *Kilayim* ch. 1.

[246] The Rosh, *Tur*, and *Shulĥan Aruĥ Yoreh De'ah* ch. 295 hold that the prohibition of cross-grafting applies underground as well, as long as the graft can be considered as located on the trunk of the tree and not on the roots.

[247] As explained above in topic 9:5, there is no prohibition for Gentiles to indirectly cause the cross-grafting of these species. Even though Rabbinical opinions forbid this for Jews (Rosh, *Tur*, and *Shulĥan Aruĥ*), this does not apply for Gentiles.

[248] *Trees which bear edible nuts are considered fruit trees. For example, some societies have processed acorns for food, so oak trees are considered to be fruit trees in regard to the prohibition of cross-grafting.

[249] *Ĥatam Sofer Yoreh De'ah* ch. 287.

for use as animal fodder.[250]

A perennial rose bush is considered as a fruit tree, because jam can be made from its flowers.[251]

10. The prohibition against grafting different species of fruit trees onto each other applies even when the person's intent is not to produce fruit or to change the nature of the fruit.[252]

For that reason, it is forbidden to graft a branch from one fruit tree to another of a different species, even if either of the two trees is not producing fruit, either because it is old, its trunk has been cut off,[253] or it is a "male" of its fruit-tree species and, therefore, it does not produce the fruit.[254] If the two trees are still considered to be fruit-bearing species, the prohibition against cross-grafting still applies.

11. What is meant by a "fruit tree" and a "fruit vine" in the context of prohibited grafting?[255] Any perennial plant that has a trunk, with leaves and fruit growing from branches, is considered to be a fruit tree. This applies even if its trunk withers away in the winter and a new plant grows from its surviving roots every year.[256] Grapes, capers and

---

[250] Rash Mi'Shantz on Mishnah *Kilayim* 1:4, on the meaning of *"ĥizrad"* (a type of wild apple that is thrown to pigs). See in *Magen Avraham* ch. 204.

[251] See *Shulĥan Aruĥ Oraĥ Ĥayim* 204:11; *Magen Avraham* (*Shulĥan Aruĥ Oraĥ Ĥayim* 204:23); and *Shulĥan Aruĥ HaRav* 202:23 – one makes a blessing for "fruits of the ground" before eating it, which implies that it is a food. (See above, Part I, Chapter 6.)

[252] Mishnah *Kilayim* 1:7.

[253] This can be learned from the case of a sycamore graft, *ibid.*

[254] As it says "to its kind" regarding them (Genesis 1:11).

[255] *In this context a "fruit tree" refers to a fruit-bearing *ilan* in Hebrew, and a "fruit vine" refers to a type of fruit-bearing *yerek* in Hebrew. *Ilan* and *yerek* are the generic names for a tree and a vegetable, respectively.

[256] See *Tur* and *Shulĥan Aruĥ Oraĥ Ĥayim* ch. 203. In other contexts, a plant whose trunk withers is not considered a tree, as mentioned there. But from the Jerusalem Talmud Tractate *Kilayim* 5:7, it appears that the distinctions in topic 9:11 should be followed with regard to the fundamental definition of the categories of perennial *yerek* and *ilan*. It appears that any plant that does not have perennial roots, though it may send out shoots and fruits from its branches, is not considered a tree, according to all opinions.

cacti,[257] berry bushes,[258] blackberries and raspberries, and all other types of perennial bushes and "miniature trees"[259] are considered to be trees with regard to the prohibition of cross-grafting of fruit trees.

If the roots of the plant cannot survive in the ground from year to year in a favorable environment, it is not considered to be a tree, despite the fact that its leaves and fruit grow from its branches. However, a fruit plant with a sturdy stem that merely resembles a trunk is also included in the prohibition, so a banana plant is considered like a tree in terms of forbidden grafting.[260]

12. The type of fruit vines to which the prohibition applies are non-perennials that produce leaves and fruit on a thick vine that grows from the roots (e.g. tomatoes, melons, squash and cucumbers). It certainly does not apply to grain.[261]

13. There are several species of trees whose leaves or fruit resemble each other. Nevertheless, since they are distinct species, the prohibition against cross-grafting applies to them. For example, an apple and a hawthorn, a peach and an almond, and a plum and a jujube are separate species with regard to cross-grafting, even though they have some similarities.[262] Similarly, a citron is a different species than a lemon, and an orange is a different species than a grapefruit.[263] Indeed, all of the different citrus fruit are considered as distinct species and may not be cross-grafted.

---

[257] *Birkei Yosef Oraĥ Ĥayim* ch. 202 teaches that one should recite the blessing "fruit of the tree" before eating sabra fruit, so it is considered a tree.

[258] *Tosefta Kilayim* ch. 3 and Jerusalem Talmud Tractate *Kilayim* end of ch. 5; Rambam, *Laws of Forbidden Mixtures* 5:20; *Shulĥan Aruĥ Yoreh De'ah* 296:15.

[259] See *Tur* and *Shulĥan Aruĥ Oraĥ Ĥayim* ch. 203, regarding the blessing which is recited before eating fruit from miniature trees.

[260] *But it is not a real perennial tree, so its fruit is blessed as "fruit of the earth."

[261] See *Ĥatam Sofer Yoreh De'ah* ch. 287.

[262] *Shulĥan Aruĥ Yoreh De'ah* ch. 295.

[263] Responsa of Rema ch. 117; Levush *Oraĥ Ĥayim* ch. 649; Responsa of Maharam Alshaiĥ ch. 110; *Shulĥan Aruĥ HaRav Oraĥ Ĥayim* 648:31; *Ĥatam Sofer Oraĥ Ĥayim* ch. 207. See Ĥazon Ish (*Kilayim* ch. 2, 3).

14. Branches from different types of the same species of tree may be grafted onto each other. For example, it is permitted to graft a shoot from a white fig tree onto a dark fig tree, or from a golden apple tree onto a Macintosh apple tree. Likewise, pears have different families within the same species.[264] The same permission applies to grafting apple trees with wild apple (crabapple) trees.[265]

Thus it is permitted to graft one fruit tree with another from the same family, even if the two fruits are different colors or sizes, or if they have different names, like two types of figs or two types of apples.[266]

15. A hybrid fruit tree is considered as a new and distinct species, and its branches may only be grafted onto a hybrid of the same type.

A hybrid fruit tree may not be grafted onto either of the two species from which it was propagated,[267] nor may it be grafted onto a different hybrid fruit tree that was propagated from other species.[268]

16. It is forbidden to maintain a forbidden graft *before* it fuses. Therefore, if the grafted shoot has not fused to the root tree, the shoot of the different species must be removed.[269] However, once the fusion has occurred, there is no obligation to separate the graft.[270]

This applies for grafts of one species of fruit tree to another, in which instance the grafted shoot fuses with the root tree and they become a single self-maintaining entity. If, however, a fruit vine is grafted onto a

---

[264] *Shulĥan Aruĥ Yoreh De'ah ibid.*

[265] *Pisĥei Teshuva Yoreh De'ah* ch. 295 in the name of *Mishkenot Yaakov* ch. 66, and *Tzemaĥ Tzedek Yoreh De'ah* ch. 221, write that domestic apples are clearly the same species as wild apples with regard to grafting.

[266] *Shulĥan Aruĥ Yoreh De'ah ibid.*

[267] This appears clear from Jerusalem Talmud Tractate *Kilayim* ch. 1:4, which specifies that a certain hybrid comes from such and such a tree, and likewise from *Tur Yoreh De'ah* ch. 295. This implies that we need to know that it may not be cross-grafted with either of the two species used to create it. See *Ma'adanei Eretz Kilayim* p. 83.

[268] Though hybrids were not mentioned in the Torah, where it specifies each type "to its kind," they are fruit-tree species and may not be cross-grafted.

[269] *Shulĥan Aruĥ Yoreh De'ah* ch. 295.

[270] *When the graft has already fused, the transgression is considered as having been committed in the past, and it is not ongoing.

fruit tree, or a fruit tree is grafted onto a fruit vine, the grafted shoot will never fuse perfectly with the root plant. Hence, it is forbidden to maintain that graft, for to do so is an ongoing transgression.[271]

It is forbidden to replant a sapling onto which a forbidden cross-graft has been made, if the grafted shoot has not yet fused onto the root tree. If, however, the fusion has been completed, there is no prohibition in replanting the sapling.[272]

17. A hybrid fruit produced by grafting a branch from one species onto a tree of another species is permitted to be eaten, even by the person who made the forbidden graft. It is also permitted to take a branch from the forbidden graft and plant it elsewhere,[273] or to plant the seeds of the hybrid fruit to grow new trees.

18. When one grafts a shoot from one species of fruit tree to the trunk of another species of fruit tree after the trunk has been uprooted, it is forbidden to replant the trunk, for that would be the planting of a forbidden graft.

19. Even if a fruit tree is growing in a pot that is not perforated, the rules of forbidden cross-grafting still apply.[274]

20. The cross-grafting of a "grafting branch," in which the new-growth tip of a shoot from one fruit tree is inserted into a groove in the trunk of another species of fruit tree, in order to produce a branch that will bear hybrid fruit, is also forbidden.[275]

Cross-pollination of the flowers of different species of fruit trees, or injecting the hormones or sap from one fruit tree into a fruit tree of a

---

[271] See Responsa *Yehuda Ya'aleh* ch. 350; *Ĥatam Sofer Likutim* ch. 25; *Ma'adanei Eretz Kilayim* p. 70.

[272] See *Ma'adanei Eretz* p. 214, quoting the Responsa of Rabbi Avraham Yitzchak Kook and Rabbi Ĥayim Yehuda Auerbach.

[273] *Shulĥan Aruĥ Yoreh De'ah* ch. 295.

[274] Har Tzvi, *Zera'im* vol. 2, ch. 24.

[275] *Tzitz Eliezer* vol. 1, ch. 16. (*Ma'adanei Eretz*, p. 74, argues that this type of grafting is permitted because it is only comparable to drawing out the sap of the trunk into the grafted shoot; thus the grafted shoot could not be sustained independently by itself from the ground, as would the shoot of a true species.)

different species, is permitted.[276] This is not considered as cross-grafting one tree with another.[277] (But seeds from the hybrid fruit will grow into hybrid fruit trees that are considered to be a distinct species.)

---

[276] *There is no explicit source that indicates that genetic modification of food plants is prohibited. After the fact, once modified varieties of produce have been created, there is certainly no prohibition in using them in accordance with the guidelines of this chapter.

[277] This can be seen from Rashi on Tractate *Pesaĥim* 56a. Although Ĥazon Ish (*Kilayim* 2:16) writes that this is comparable to cross-mating animals, one can make a possible distinction between the two cases:

The only prohibition for Gentiles regarding plants is to do an action of cross-grafting, which must include the fruit trees themselves. But cross-mating animals carries a prohibition in any case where the natural order is changed, and it includes anything that will cause a change in the species, including by artificial insemination. See also *Minĥat Shlomo* vol. 3, ch. 98.

Even though the prohibitions of cross-grafting trees and cross-mating species resemble each other in some respects, and both share the same rationale – not to change the design of nature – cross-mating of animals is more severe. The forbidden cross-grafting of trees only applies when the graft is visually observable. Therefore, the planting of two species in close proximity, so their roots will combine underground, is permitted (see topics 9:6-8). This is because the usual method of cross-grafting trees is done in a visually observable way.

However, the prohibition of cross-mating animals is more severe in the following regard. Causing the birth of a hybrid species of animal is a change in nature that may or may not result from the cross-mating. However, the action of cross-mating of two different species, even if they cannot produce an offspring, is also prohibited, because this unnatural mating is itself a change of the natural order, regardless of the outcome. So creating a new animal species, and changing the natural order of mating that God made in the world, are both prohibited, regardless of how the change is made. But for all different types of vegetation, there isn't any prohibition at all for Gentiles to sow or plant them together side-by-side, so the general attitude toward cross-grafting of vegetation is more lenient.

Furthermore, mankind was not given permission from God for unlimited control over animals (see Chapters 1 and 7 above), and cross-mating is a type of unnecessary control. In contrast, Gentiles are not forbidden to waste or cut down trees unnecessarily on a limited scale.

*Yet we see that as a practical matter, many modern governments have instituted laws to preserve the growth of trees – for example: for managed harvesting as a natural resource, for preservation in local or national parks, for beautification of towns and cities, to protect the landscape against erosion and the atmosphere against pollution, and to maintain a habitat for wildlife.

In general, concern for the environment should be rational and consistent with one of the main accomplishments that God desires of mankind: *"yishuv olam"* – efforts by each individual and group to contribute to the making of a "settled world" for the people of all nations, with societies that function properly and morally in God's eyes, harmoniously with each other, and responsibly with the natural world and its bountiful resources.

May it be God's will that this text will help to bring this to fruition.

PART V

THE PROHIBITION OF MURDER AND INJURY

This section explains details of the following three obligations and seven prohibitions that are included in this commandment to Gentiles and its offshoots:

1. Not to murder a human being.

2. To save oneself or another person from a pursuer.

3. Not to commit elective abortion.

4. Not to commit suicide.

5. Not to hire, send or incite someone (or even an animal) to murder.

6. To exile oneself if he killed another person accidentally, in order to atone for this.

7. Not to wound or physically damage another person or oneself. This includes not to castrate oneself or another person, and not to leave one's property in a condition that may harm other people.

8. To guard one's potentially harmful entities (such as his animals, or a fire that he lights on his property) from causing harm to others.

9. Not to communicate (in speech or in writing) words that will cause harm to a person.

10. A man is not to spill his semen "in vain", nor allow this to be done to him. (More details of this prohibition are provided in Part VI, Chapter 5.)

INTRODUCTION

by Michael Schulman, Ph.D.

Director, Ask Noah International
and United Noahide Academies

Modern democratic societies struggle to reconcile the concept that everyone is *endowed* by their Creator with "certain unalienable rights," which are associated with individual freedoms, with the evidence that the Creator *commanded* certain boundaries that neither an individual nor a society is free to disregard. The perfectly balanced answer to this dichotomy between mankind's essential rights and essential obligations is found in the Noahide Code of Seven Universal Commandments. Among these commandments, the prohibition of murder and mayhem (serious personal injury) is probably the most obvious and, on the surface, the most straightforward. The specific commandment prohibiting Gentiles from committing murder can be found in God's communication to Noaĥ (Gen. 9:5-6), "… of man for his brother, I will demand the soul of man ... Whoever sheds the blood of man, by man his blood shall be shed; for in the image of God, He made man." God reinforced this commandment when He transmitted the Torah from the heavens to Moses on Mount Sinai.

As the preceding sections of this book have shown, each commandment is linked to recurring fundamental concepts in the Hebrew Bible. For example, Gen. 1:27 states, "And God created man in His image; in the image of God He created him; male and female He created them." This teaches that each person in some sense contains a reflection of God, and therefore possesses a dimension of holiness. Taking a human life diminishes a measure of the Divine image that is present in the world, and without God's permission it is strictly forbidden. At the same time, murder is an act of extreme rebellion against God Himself, Who blessed mankind "to be fruitful and multiply and fill the earth" (Gen. 1:28), and "He did not create it for emptiness; He fashioned it to be inhabited" (Isaiah 45:18).

In addition to sinning against the Divine and destroying the victim's physical existence, a person who murders harms many others as well. The tragic loss of a person's life afflicts his loved ones, his friends and his associates. But even physically, the effects of murder extend across time and space. We learn this from the world's first act of murder. When Cain murdered his brother Abel, God responded by asking Cain (Gen. 4:10), "What have you done? The voice of your brother's 'bloods' [the literal translation] cry out to Me…" The use of the plural "bloods" is meaningful. It teaches that one who murders another also "kills" that person's would-be descendents for all generations to come. Who but God can know where those descendants would have lived or what good they would have brought to the world? All that potential for good throughout the future has been lost because of the violent act. Even if the victim would not have subsequently had any children, the Jewish Sages teach that all of a person's great or small good deeds are the spiritual fruits that he adds to the world. Therefore, the Sages taught that someone who causes the destruction of one person's life from the world is considered as if he destroyed an entire world, and conversely, someone who saves or sustains one person's life in the world is considered as if he saved an entire world.[1]

Here we have two paradigms. In one, murder represents an attack on the Divine image present in the world. In the second, murder represents on attack on a fellow physical person. Which aspect of the sin is worse? The Torah provides the answer in Gen. 11:1-9, which describes the episode of the Tower of Babel, when the people of the world united to challenge God. For this purpose, they built a giant tower with its top reaching up toward the heavens. Yet rather than destroy the people for their openly rebellious act, God simply confused their language, which forced the people to abandon their audacious plan. However, earlier in the Torah (Gen. 6:13), we find that God told Noah, "The end of all flesh has come before Me because the earth is filled with violence." At that time, God destroyed mankind through the flood because of their pandemic violence that included bloodshed,

---

[1] Mishnah *Sanhedrin* 4:5 (Rambam's version, in his commentary there; see R. Kapach's edition). See also Rambam, *Mishneh Torah, Laws of the Sanhedrin* 12:3. This is also the version of this Mishnah in the Jerusalem Talmud, Tractate *Sanhedrin* 4:9 – "Therefore [the first human being] Adam was created alone in the world, to teach that someone who causes the destruction of one person's life is considered as if he destroyed an entire world, and someone who saves/sustains one person's life is considered as if he saved/sustained an entire world." (The original Hebrew uses the word *keyaim*, which includes the alternate meanings "save" and "sustain.")

theft, and sexual crimes. It is clear that murder and mayhem assault the spiritual foundation upon which mankind as a whole exists, more so than direct rebellion against God!

Yet what constitutes the sin of murder? What acts are included in that category, and what acts are not? Are there times when killing is permitted, or even mandated, by the Torah? Does a person ever have the "right" to end his or her own life? What about engaging in activities that are inherently life threatening, or accepting donor organs from living persons who will not regain consciousness? In the pages ahead, we see that God provided ample instructions for how the commandment should be fulfilled in any circumstances.

Furthermore, this discussion has thus far addressed only the physical act of taking a human life. Are there acts that don't involve physical harm, but which are spiritually equivalent to murder? For example, can one be guilty in the eyes of God for destroying another's reputation, or subjecting him to humiliation? What if the publicized damaging information is true? These questions, as well as many more, are addressed in the upcoming pages of this section on the Prohibition of Murder and Injury.[2]

Specifically, "Murder and Injury" covers obvious issues such as homicide (whether premeditated murder or accidental manslaughter), suicide, euthanasia, and causing serious physical injury. It covers issues such as the Torah laws regarding permissible acts of self-defense, endangering one's life to save another, and death caused through criminal or unavoidable negligence.[3] The prohibition of injury also extends to nonphysical attacks such as slander, embarrassment, and causing emotional harm. Even though many of the precepts relating to murder and injury are complex, an underlying theme can be summarized in one sentence. It is known as Hillel's "Golden Rule" of the Torah, and it simply states, "That which is hateful to you, do not do to your fellow. The rest is the explanation; go and learn."[4]

---

[2] *In this section, the order of Chapters 4 and 5 is reversed from the order in which they appear in the Hebrew text of *Sheva Mitzvot HaShem*, Vol. II.

[3] We also find specific transgressions within all of the Seven Noahide Commandments for which *courts of law* have an essential right to apply capital punishment, if they are rightfully empowered to do so.

[4] Hillel the Elder, in Tractate *Shabbat* 31a.

But how could Hillel's sweeping statement encompass even the Torah precepts that forbid certain actions that seem to be purely matters of personal concern? These include medical issues at the forefront of modern societal debates, such as advance directives ("Living Wills")[5] for health care decisions, transgender operations, choosing between different means of reproductive sterilization, and other personal matters that are addressed in this section. Therefore, we must conclude that a person should reject certain free-will choices because they are hateful to one's *inner* self, and even in inflicting them upon one's own self, the person is harming a "fellow" whom he should be concerned for. King David gave us the answer to this puzzle in Psalms 146:2, which reads literally:

I will sing to God with "my life;" I will
chant praises to my God with "my other."

This teaches that a person is a composite of two entities – a "life," which is the spiritual soul, and an "other," which is the physical body. To sin against God's commands is hateful to the soul itself, because it bears the painful spiritual consequences of the sin. Therefore, a person should not even inflict injury upon his own body, the "fellow" that God has appointed to be bound up with his soul.

By thus committing to observe both the obvious and the inner dimensions of Hillel's Golden Rule, each person can hasten the time when God will reveal the fulfillment of His promise (Isaiah 11:9), "They will not harm or destroy on all My holy mountain, for the earth will be filled with the knowledge of God as water covering the sea bed."

---

[5] See Editor's note to topic 7:8 in this section.

CHAPTER 1

Details of the Prohibition of Murder

1. A Gentile is forbidden to commit murder or bloodshed, and would be liable to the death penalty for this in a court of law,[1] as God commanded Noaĥ,[2] "But your blood of your souls I will demand; of every beast I will demand it; but of man *(adam)*,[3] of man for his brother, I will demand the soul of man *(adam)*. Whoever sheds the blood of man *(adam)*, by man *(adam)* his blood shall be shed; for in the image of God He made man *(adam)*."

The Sages explained:

(a) "… your blood of your souls I will demand" refers to one who commits suicide.

(b) "… of every beast will I demand it" refers to one who places another person before an injurious animal so it will kill him.

(c) "… of man for his brother" refers to one who sends another to kill. For all these three cases, the verse states, "I [God] will demand," which refers to punishment by God.[4]

(d) "Whoever sheds the blood of man" refers to one who kills actively and deliberately.[5]

(e) "Whoever sheds the blood of *adam* within *adam*" refers to one who kills a human fetus, which is "a person within a person."[6]

(f) "… his blood shall be shed" refers to the judgment of capital punishment that is meted out by a court of law.[7]

The reason for the prohibition of murder is clear and simple: it is necessary since God desires the world that He created to be inhabited

---

[1] Rambam, *Laws of Kings* 9:4.

[2] Genesis 9:5-6.

[3] *In most contexts of the simple meaning of the Hebrew Scriptures, this term refers to any human being, as we see from Genesis 1:27, "And God created man *(adam)*...; male and female He created them."

[4] Rambam, *Laws of Murderers* 2:3, the source being Rabbi Yoĥanan in Midrash *Bereishit Rabbah* ch. 34.

[5] Rambam *ibid.*

[6] Tractate *Sanhedrin* 57b; Rambam, *Laws of Kings* 9:4.

[7] Tractate *Sanhedrin* 57a; Rambam *ibid.*

and settled, and not destroyed and desolate,[8] as is stated,[9] "He did not create it for emptiness; He fashioned it to be inhabited." Also, no person should presume that he has mastery over others to be able to take their lives or injure them according to his own will or desires. Rather, a person should recognize that there is a Master and Creator of everything, Who directs the world and judges its inhabitants. A person should respect the life, property and honor of his fellow human beings and not harm them, and know that the authority over human life is in the hands of God alone, and human beings do not have this authority or discretion in their own right.[10]

2. "Whoever sheds the blood of man" refers to one who murders directly, and to one who murders indirectly. In both cases the murderer is liable for a capital sin.

What is direct murder? This refers to someone who brings the death through his own power – for example, if the murderer grasps a sword or a lethal stone[11] and strikes the victim with it; or if the murderer, with his own hands, strangles the victim, or applies fire to the victim and burns him, or holds the victim under water until he drowns, or gives the victim a lethal injection. Even if the victim fell into water, and an adversary only *prevented* him from coming out of the water until he had no more strength left and then he drowned, this would be an act of direct murder. Since the adversary killed directly with his own power, he is a murderer.[12]

What is indirect murder? This refers to someone who commits an act that actually causes a victim to die, but he does not kill the victim directly through his own power – e.g., if a person tied up a victim and left him to be killed by a lion or other injurious animals; or he tied up the victim and left him to starve to death;[13] or he tied up the victim and left him in a place that would ultimately become so hot or cold that the

---

[8] Rambam, *Laws of Murderers* 4:9; *Sefer HaĤinuĥ* Commandment 34.

[9] Isaiah 45:18.

[10] Rather, we must follow God's directives in matters of life and death, as taught by the precepts of God's Torah.

[11] I.e., a stone that is sufficiently large and massive to inflict a fatal injury.

[12] Rambam, *Laws of Murderers* 2:1 and 3:1-9.

[13] Rambam, *Laws of Kings* 9:4.

victim would die; or he put the victim in a container that would cause suffocation, and all similar things.[14] Though his action did not directly cause the victim to die, nevertheless, since it caused a condition to occur in which the victim *would surely* die, he is considered to have shed blood and murdered through the power of his actions, and he is liable to be punished for this capital sin in a court of law.

3. What is the difference between one who murders directly and one who murders indirectly?

A direct murderer is liable for the ***action*** of murder, and therefore a concept of "murder after murder" exists. What is this? This occurs when a first attacker delivers a lethal blow to a person, and the injured victim is in the process of dying. A second attacker then delivers another lethal blow to the victim, before he dies from the first blow. Both attackers are considered murderers, and both are liable to be punished for this in a court of law, as explained below in topic 15.

But if a first person sets up the indirect death of a victim, and then a second person comes and delivers a mortal blow to the victim, or even if the second person subjects the victim to another situation of indirect murder that will cause the person to die sooner – either by augmenting the original process or by setting up a new process of indirect death – then the second person becomes the indirect murderer and is fully

---

[14] See Rambam, *Laws of Murderers* 3:10, that a Jew who kills indirectly is exempt from capital punishment by a Jewish court, but he is still considered a murderer and liable to punishment by the Hand of Heaven. The prohibition of murder for Jews is based on Leviticus 24:17, "If he [one individual] strikes any person mortally, he should be put to death." In this verse, "strikes" excludes one who causes death indirectly, and the Hebrew for "any person" (*kol nefesh adam*) can also mean "all the soul of the person," which excludes one who did not accomplish the mortal blow on his own. The Noahide prohibition, however, stems from Genesis 9:6, "Whoever sheds the blood of man," which includes bloodshed that only partially contributes to a murder.

It appears that in Ramban's commentary on the Torah, he disagrees somewhat with Rambam based on the verses Gen. 37:22-26, in which Reuben tells his brothers not to "shed the blood" of Joseph, but rather to throw him into a pit, which is a lesser and more indirect form of murder. But Judah tells them that this is also murder. Ramban interprets that although causing indirect death is considered murder for Gentiles, it carries a lesser form of punishment than execution by a court of law, similar to the Torah Law for a Jew.

liable for this, and the first person is exempt from capital punishment by a court of law.[15] This is because an indirect murderer is not liable to capital punishment on account of his particular action, but rather for the nature of an outcome that happened on account of his action, and in this situation, the action of the first person is not the deliberate cause of the actual death of the victim at the time when it happened.[16]

One example is when a first person tied up a victim in a pit, and then opened a source of water into the pit, so the water would eventually rise to a level that would cause the victim to drown. Afterwards, a second person opened up another source of water into the pit with intent to cause the victim to drown. The second person came with intention to murder and caused the drowning of the victim to happen sooner. In such a case, only the second person is liable to capital punishment by a court of law, since he is the one who has the deliberate responsibility for the actual death of the victim. The first person is not liable to capital punishment by the court, for although his actions had the ability to eventually cause death, in actuality they were not the deliberate cause of the death at the time when it happened.

It appears that even if the second person changed the process by which the victim would die, but instead of advancing the victim's death he (with intent to kill) caused it to happen later, he is still the only one who is liable for capital punishment for the indirect murder. In the above example, if the first person opened up the source of water into the pit, and the water had a strong enough flow to surely drown the victim in one hour, and the second person came with intention to kill, but instead reduced the flow of water to a level that brought the

---

15 *But since the first person intended to murder, he is liable to be punished by God. This applies for all cases in this chapter. One who acted with intention to murder, but is exempt from punishment in a court of law, it still liable to punishment by God if he does not repent. See topic 1:8 below.

16 This is based on the explanation in the previous topic. The liability of a Gentile to execution by a court of law for indirect murder is limited to his being the one who is deliberately responsible for causing the victim's death. Therefore, the court is to determine which person's action was the deliberate cause of the actual death of the victim, and only the one who committed that action is liable by Torah Law. (As explained in topic 1:8, the court can decide to punish both the one whose deliberate action actually caused the victim's death, and the one who provided assistance for this action.)

victim's death in two hours, it appears that the second person is the only one who should be subject to capital punishment in a court of law.

However, if a first person ties up a victim in a enclosure and lights a flame there that will reduce the oxygen inside to a level at which the person will die of asphyxiation, or if he opens a flow of non-reactive gas into the enclosure such that the victim will asphyxiate,[17] and then a second person makes a small opening in the enclosure that is not enough to save the person, but it will delay the process of death, then the first person is still fully liable but the second person is not liable, since the second person's action did not at all cause the death.

4. If a second person transforms a first person's act into an act of murder, the second person is liable. For example, if a first person pushed someone into a pit and there was initially a ladder there that could have been used to climb out, and a second person removed the ladder with intent to kill; or likewise, if a first person threw a spear at someone who was holding a shield, and a second person pulled away the shield, then if the victim died from starvation in the pit or by the spear, then the second person is considered to be the murderer and is liable to capital punishment in a court of law,[18] while the first person is exempt from capital punishment.

This applies even if the victim put himself into the situation (e.g., he descended into a pit of his own accord when the ladder was there, or if someone put himself at risk in some other hazardous situation while taking appropriate measures for safety), and the murderer took away his victim's means of saving himself (e.g., by removing the ladder from the pit), thus putting the victim in a situation of certain death.

However, if a first person lethally shoots and thereby mortally wounds a victim, and there is a doctor available who could heal the victim, but a second person prevents the doctor from doing so, only the shooter is liable to be punished by a court for murder, and not the

---

[17] Compare Rambam, *Laws of Murderers* 3:9, stating "he placed a person in a house or cave and filled it with smoke until [the victim] died," which describes a case of direct murder. The cases cited here are indirect murder, since it is only the lack of oxygen that kills (and not the flame that was lit, or the non-reactive gas that was flowed in).

[18] From Rambam *Laws of Murderers* 3:11; these are cases of indirect murder.

second person.[19] The act of murder was only done by the shooter who directly caused the death, and the second person only prevented the victim from being saved.

This case is dissimilar to the previous cases of indirect murder by a person who removed a ladder that could save a victim in a pit, or a person who pulled away a shield that could save a victim from a spear. In the case of a "pit," we are discussing a situation in which the pit is not so deep that a person would have a fatal injury from the fall, but it is too deep and steep for the person to climb out of on his own. Pushing a person into such a pit does not directly kill the victim. Rather, the death is caused through an external circumstance, for example starvation, etc.[20] Therefore, a person who removes a ladder that could save the victim is the one who causes the victim's death, and not the one who pushed the victim.

Likewise, a person who throws a spear at someone who has a protective shield is not committing a fatal action.[21] It is the person who removes the shield who performs the act that causes the inevitability of the victim's death. However, if the victim has no shield, the spear thrower becomes a direct murderer when the victim dies from the spear wound, and not at the time when the spear was thrown. In that case, the spear thrower caused the death to become inevitable. But in the previous case in which a shield was pulled away, the cause of the death that resulted from the spear thrower's action could have been avoided if not for the deliberate intervention of the person who pulled away the shield with intent to kill.[22]

If an attacker mortally wounds a person, but the victim is saved by a doctor, the attacker is not judged as if he had actually murdered.

---

[19] The ruling in Tractate *Sanhedrin* 77b, that if there is an available doctor who has medicine to heal, the injurer is not liable, applies only to Jews.

[20] *But if the pit is so deep that a person who is pushed in dies from the force of the impact, this is direct murder, and the murderer is liable in a court of law.

[21] *If the victim with the shield tried but failed to block the spear, the thrower is liable for direct murder. If the victim removed the shield on his own, or if he had no shield and willfully moved himself in front of a thrown spear that would otherwise have missed him, he is guilty for suicide, and the thrower is not liable for direct or indirect murder.

[22] This difference is explained in Tractate *Sanhedrin* 77b.

5. One who sent others to kill, or one who has hired an assassin to kill, is considered to be a murderer when the victim is killed, and he is liable to the punishment of death from God, as it says (Genesis 9:5), "of man for his brother, I [God] will demand the soul of man." Here, "of man for his brother" refers to one who sends others to kill, and "I will demand" refers to punishment by God, but there is no liability to capital punishment by a court of law.[23] [One who sends another to kill is considered a pursuer (see topic 1:8 below), and governments are empowered to deter this through civil laws and harsh punishments.]

It appears that even if someone gives bad advice to another person, knowing that this advice will cause the person to come to death, he is considered as if he sent him to his death, and he is liable to punishment by God,[24] just as one who hires a mercenary to kill.

6. If one intended to kill or to send a mercenary to kill, but the murder was not accomplished, regardless of how it was prevented, then the would-be murderer is not liable for capital punishment in court, since he did not actually murder. Still, he is liable to punishment from God for his evil intentions.[25]

7. What is the meaning of the statement (Genesis 9:5), "of every beast will I demand it"? This refers to one who *places* a victim [unbound] in front of a lion or other wild animal in order that the animal will kill him. The verse implies that a person who does so is liable to punishment from God, but not to capital punishment by a court of law.[26]

---

[23] Rambam, *Laws of Murderers* 2:2, states this law regarding a Jew, and does not make any amendments in *Laws of Kings* regarding Gentiles, so it seems there is no additional stringency for Gentiles in this area. See *Minĥat Ĥinuĥ*, Commandment 34, and the responsa of *Sho'el U'Maishiv*, in accordance with Rabbi Yoĥanan's opinion in Midrash *Bereishit Rabbah* ch. 34.

[24] See *Or HaĤayim* Genesis 4:8.

[25] See Part I, topic 9:5, and *Or HaĤayim* Genesis 20:6.

*This punishment is lesser than death by Divine agency, since in actuality there was no murder.

[26] Rambam, *Laws of Murderers* 2:3. However, Rambam writes in *Laws of Kings* 9:4 that if a Gentile *bound* a victim and placed him in front of a lion that then killed him, this is murder that is liable to capital punishment, as it is explained above that a Gentile is liable for indirect murder.

What is the difference between this case and the one in topic 2, in which one who causes another to die through indirect means is liable for capital punishment? Under the Noahide Code, a Gentile would not be liable to capital punishment for causing a person's death in this way unless he placed his victim in front of the wild animal in such a way that the victim had no means of escape, such as if he bound a victim and left him in front of a lion, whereby these actions are directly, and inevitably, leading to the victim's death. However, if the victim was able to attempt escape, and the animal nevertheless caught and killed him, the perpetrator is only liable to be punished by God.

Likewise, one who places the mouth of a venomous snake on a victim, so that the snake bites and kills him, is considered to have directly caused the death.[27] But if the victim was only placed in the vicinity of the snake, and he had a means of escape, the perpetrator is only liable to punishment from God if the victim is killed. In any case where the victim is able to escape death, such as if someone pushed a victim into the sea[28] in an area where he would be able to swim to land and survive, but instead he drowned, the perpetrator is only liable for punishment from God, but not capital punishment from a court of law.

The same law applies if a killer placed poison before a person, so the unaware victim would drink it and die. Even if the killer lied to the victim, saying that it was a normal beverage, he is exempt from execution by a court (but liable for punishment from God), because his action of setting down the poison did not cause the victim's death. Rather, the victim died through his own mistaken action. (But if the killer poured the poison down the victim's throat, it would be a case of direct murder, with liability to punishment from a court.)

It appears that Rambam chose the words (*Laws of Murderers* 2:3), "of every beast will I demand it – this refers to one who *places* a person before a wild animal so it will tear him," in reference to Gentiles. This wording indicates that the wild animal forcefully overpowers and kills the person – meaning that the victim is not bound, and he has a possibility to escape. The perpetrator of this death is liable to punishment by God; but not to *capital* punishment in a court of law. In contrast, if the victim is bound and cannot escape from the wild animal, it is considered as if the perpetrator directly caused the death, and he is liable to capital punishment in a court of law.

[27] See Rambam, *Laws of Murderers* 3:10, and *Kesef Mishneh* there.

[28] See Rambam, *Laws of Murderers* 3:9.

8. In the cases in topics 5 and 7,[29] the court is not *obligated* to put the perpetrator to death, but the ruling power is permitted to make a *general law* that allows for punishment by execution in these types of cases for the benefit and/or safety of the society. Similarly, if the court deemed it necessary to execute this more indirect killer as a special case due to overriding needs of the time, it may do so.

If neither the ruling power nor the court puts such a perpetrator to death (since no laws have been made for doing so under these conditions, or as a matter of policy), it is still incumbent upon the court to punish him severely, or to imprison him for many years, or to sentence him to different forms of anguish, in order to discourage others from thinking that they too could bring about the death of their enemies by more indirect means and be exempt from punishment.[30,31]

Likewise, one who hires mercenaries to kill, but they are prevented from doing so, deserves to receive significant punishments from a court of law, even though he is not liable to capital punishment. This is said concerning one who has sent or hired murderers just one time (or even twice, in special circumstances). However, one who follows this path and does so regularly is considered a "pursuer" of people's lives, and the court or any individual is obligated to kill him at any opportunity, in order to save lives (as will be explained in Chapter 3).[32]

9. It is forbidden to murder *any* human life: a man or a woman; an adult or a minor; a free person or a slave;[33] a deaf, handicapped, deformed, aged or physically or mentally ill person;[34] or even a fetus in its mother's womb.[35] A Gentile who kills any of the above is a murderer and is liable to capital punishment by a court of law.

---

[29] However, regarding topic 6 above , that one who intends to kill but is not able to carry out that intention is liable to punishment from God, it appears that a court or the ruling power has no permission to punish him for his evil plans; see Part I, topic 1:10.

[30] Rambam, *Laws of Murderers* 2:5.

[31] See *Or Same'aĥ Rambam*, *Laws of Kings* 3:10.

[32] This is clear from *Shulĥan Aruĥ Ĥoshen Mishpat* 388:15, and *Shaĥ* there.

[33] Rambam, *Laws of Murderers* 2:10.

[34] *Minĥat Ĥinuĥ*, Commandment 34.

[35] Rambam, *Laws of Kings* 9:4.

Abortion

10. One who hits a pregnant woman and kills her fetus,[36] or a doctor who performs an abortion by which the fetus cannot possibly live,[37] or a doctor who gives the mother medicine for the purpose of aborting the fetus or killing it in place, or a pregnant woman who did this herself,[38] are all liable to be punished for murder in a court of law.

However, one who hits a woman in another area of her body, which causes her to weaken and subsequently miscarry, is not liable in court unless he has intention with his action to cause the miscarriage, and the miscarriage was inevitably a result of the blow (see topic 5:7 below).

One who hires a doctor to perform an abortion is considered as one who hires a mercenary to kill, and this is punishable by God.[39]

11. An implanted embryo is not judged to be a human life until 40 days after conception. Until then, its substance is considered like mere water,[40] but during that time, it is still forbidden within the prohibition of murder to cause an abortion, and God will seek justice for the destruction of the implanted embryo.[41] Nevertheless, within 40 days after the egg is fertilized (the moment of conception), a killer of an im-

---

[36] Rashi on Tractate *Sanhedrin* 57b.

[37] If the aborted fetus might survive in an incubator, but the doctor does not intend this, and it isn't done, this is considered murder; see topic 4 above.

[38] Since the abortion-inducing medicine will surely take effect in her body, it is tantamount to the case where one pushes a victim into a pit where he will surely die from hunger or lack of air, and this is direct murder for a Gentile.

Although Rambam, *Laws of Murderers* ch. 6, differentiates between a murder caused directly from one's own power or that comes as a result of one's actions, this difference applies only for inadvertent killing by a Jew.

[39] See *Kli Ĥemda Parshat Shemot*, paragraph 4, which holds that even though a Gentile who hires others to kill is liable to be punished by God, this only applies if the victim is a born person and not a fetus; in the author's opinion, this reasoning does not appear to be valid.

[40] Tractate *Bechorot* 47b; *Shulĥan Aruĥ Yoreh De'ah* 305:23.

[41] In this case, as for any murder, the blood of the victim and of the would-be descendants are all avenged, as God said to Cain (Gen. 4:10): "The voice of your brother's *bloods*, they cry out to Me…" Based on *Sanhedrin* 37a, Rashi explains this as "his blood and the blood of his [would-be] descendants."

planted embryo is not liable to capital punishment by a court of law.[42]

12. Even if the mother has emotional justification for not wanting the pregnancy (for example, in cases of rape or incest), aborting the fetus is forbidden according to the severity of the prohibition of murder.[43]

If it is known that the child she is carrying will be born with a fatal illness or defect, it is nevertheless forbidden to abort the fetus, and one who does so is a murderer.[44]

It would appear that if it is medically proven that the fetus will be miscarried or not born alive, or that it will be born but will die within 30 days, then one who transgresses and aborts such a fetus is not liable to capital punishment from a court of law.[45]

13. A pregnant woman whose own life is at risk because of her pregnancy is permitted to have an abortion (see topic 3:7 below).

The use of methods that prevent conception from happening is permissible for Gentiles, as explained below in Chapter 9.

14. One who kills a born child that *could not* have lived for 30 days after birth, due to a serious illness or defect, is exempt from liability to

---

[42] Responsa of *Beit Shlomo Ĥoshen Mishpat* ch. 132; *Aĥiezer* 3:65; *Ĥemdat Yisrael Hilĥot Melaĥim* 9:7. (In medical terminology, the transition from an implanted embryo to a fetus is complete at the ninth week after conception.)

[43] See Responsa of *Ĥavot Yair* ch. 31, who gives no permission for abortion even in the first 40 days, even for an embryo conceived out of wedlock; *Tzitz Eliezer* vol. 9, ch. 51, permits this for a Jew. *Igrot Moshe Ĥoshen Mishpat* vol. 2, 69:3, states that for a Gentile this is permitted in a dire case.

[44] *Igrot Moshe Ĥoshen Mishpat* vol.2, ch. 69 and 71. *Sridei Aish* vol. 1, ch. 162, permits abortion for a Jew in the first 40 days if the child will have a permanent illness or defect that will impede normal living; it appears that the same applies for Gentiles and there is allowance for them to do so, but requests for this permission should be judged very carefully because of the severity of the prohibition of murder if it is done without correct justification.

[45] This is based on the case described in topic 14, when it is medically determined in accordance with Torah-law standards that a born child would have been a short-lived and nonviable. Liability to capital punishment for the transgression of abortion of a fetus applies if it has no defect that would preclude the child from being capable of living for at least 30 days after a full-term birth. See Responsa of Radvaz vol. 2, ch. 695, in regard to Jews.

capital punishment.[46] If, however, the child could live at least 30 days after birth, even if only through medical intervention, it is considered viable, and one who kills it is liable to capital punishment.

Euthanasia

15. Killing a mortally sick or injured person or a *"goses"* (the Hebrew term for a dying person who has become moribund and whose death is imminent) is considered murder, and this carries liability to capital punishment.[47] If a victim was close to dying as a result of one person's act of murder, and *another* person dealt the victim a final blow (e.g. decapitation), both are liable by the court if they intended to kill[48] – the

---

[46] This is the ruling of Rambam, *Laws of Murderers* 2:6 regarding a Jew, and *Minĥat Ĥinuĥ* Commandment 34 and *Maharam Shik Oraĥ Ĥayim* ch. 142 write that the same applies to a Gentile. (Nevertheless, it is still forbidden to do so, within the prohibition of murder.) The difference between a nonviable child and a mortally wounded living person (for whose murder one would be liable to capital punishment) is that the mortally wounded person has already gained the distinction of viable living, as opposed to a newborn child that emerged so unhealthy that it cannot gain the distinction of viable living.

(The ruling is unclear for a fetus that will be born prematurely and then placed in an incubator – especially when there is a good chance that it will fully develop – as to whether a Gentile who aborts this fetus is liable to capital punishment. On one hand, this fetus should be considered as living, since it has a better chance for survival after its premature birth than a mortally wounded person. Conversely, an underdeveloped fetus that will be born prematurely does not yet have the potential to be born as a "viable living person." The ruling is likewise unclear regarding a woman who died with a 9-month old fetus in her womb: is one who destroys this fetus liable to capital punishment, since it is possible for the fetus to be pulled out alive from the mother? Or is he exempt from capital punishment, since it would die if it is left alone? It appears that in both cases, one who aborts the fetus is exempt from capital punishment because it will not be born as a viable living person, as can be seen from the Responsa of Radvaz vol. 2, ch. 695.)

[47] Rambam, *Laws of Kings* 9:4 and *Laws of Murderers* 2:7.

[48] Meaning that each knew that his actions would cause the victim to die. A person is not exempt from punishment if he hastens someone's death to lessen the suffering (even for a victim who was mortally injured by another person); see topic 17 below. See Part I, footnote 78, regarding one who inadvertently neglected to learn the precepts of a Noahide commandment.

last perpetrator,[49] since he made the final murderous blow, and the first,[50] since his actions would surely have brought death without the actions of the second. (This is "murder after murder" in topic 3 above.)

However, one who hastens the death of a "living carcass"[51] is exempt from capital punishment by a court.[52] (Examples of a "living carcass" are one whose body was split in two, or whose back was ripped from behind "like a fish," or whose thigh with its cavity was removed, or whose neck and most of the surrounding flesh was broken

---

49 *Minĥat Ĥinuĥ* Commandment 34; *Or Same'aĥ Hilĥot Rotze'aĥ* 2:4; *Igrot Moshe Ĥoshen Mishpat* vol. 2, ch. 73.

50 Rabbi Zalman Nehemiah Goldberg agrees that the second person who struck and subsequently killed a mortally wounded victim is liable; and therefore it is also correct that one who kills a *goses* is liable, even according to the Sages (Tractate *Sanhedrin* 78) who hold that a *goses* who came to his situation as a victim of a person's action is judged to be the same as a mortally wounded person.

However, he questions if the first of two people who struck a mortally ill victim is liable, for a Jew who struck a victim first is exempt if a second person then struck and thereby killed the victim (and is therefore liable for the murder). Also, *Tosafot* on Tractate *Sanhedrin* 78a asks why the first of two people who struck a *goses* should be exempt, if most people in a *goses* condition will not recover. *Tosafot* answers there that Torah Law requires a striker to be held in jail until it is determined if the victim died from his action. Thus it stands to reason that we don't automatically make the first striker liable just on the basis that in the majority of cases a *goses* will die, and therefore it is considered that only the second (final) striker has killed the *goses*. It is unclear from the opinion of *Tosafot* if a Gentile who is the first of two who strike a *goses* is exempt on the same grounds, or if the majority rule is followed, making the first striker also liable, since he gives what is considered a lethal blow – which is the opinion of *Yad Ramah* on *Sanhedrin* 78.

The author responds that there is no source in Torah for requiring a Gentile to be jailed while it is being determined if his action will result in a victim's death. (Although there is obviously a logical allowance for a Noahide court to do this, it has no bearing on whether or not the person will be liable according to Torah Law.) Rather, the Torah Law for Gentiles follows the majority of situations, as *Tosafot* writes. See topic 20 below.

51 See Rambam, *Laws of the Principal Impurities* ch. 2.

52 A person in this condition is considered to already be dead, and not in the category of a *goses*. A *goses* is still considered fully alive, as explained in *Shulĥan Aruĥ, Even HaEzer* ch. 121 and *Yoreh De'ah* ch. 370.

– before the person dies, i.e., while the heart is still beating.)

16. It is forbidden to even *touch* a dying person, even to close his eyes, since doing so might hasten the person's death, which is forbidden within the prohibition of murder.[53] (It is clear that one would not be liable as a murderer for touching a dying person, especially since it is not certain if these actions cause death; rather, the Sages warned about this as a possible harm to a *goses*.)

However, one who is trying to revive a *goses*, or to lessen his suffering, is clearly allowed to touch the stricken person in the course of trying to save or help him,[54] and indeed it is commendable to do so.[55] However, from the moment that a doctor knows that it is impossible to help the *goses* at all, it is forbidden to touch him.

17. Mercy killing is forbidden, even if the patient is suffering and wants his life to be terminated. Even if it is clear that the person will not emerge alive from his current sickness, it is forbidden to kill him, and one who does is a murderer (see topic 2:1 below). Nonetheless, one does not have to *prevent* a terminally-ill or mortally-injured person from dying, and it is permitted to *allow* him to die (from that illness or injury that will be fatal if left untreated) if this is his true wish,[56] provided that he is an adult and this is his clear-headed decision, and

---

[53] *Shulĥan Aruĥ Yoreh De'ah* ch. 339. This law applies as well for Gentiles.

[54] *Shvut Yaakov* vol. 1, ch. 13; *Biur Halaĥa* ch. 329; *Igrot Moshe ibid.*

[55] See Responsa of *Tzitz Eliezer* vol. 13, ch. 87, and vol. 14, ch. 103.

[56] Gentiles are not obligated in the Jewish commandment (Lev. 19:16), "Do not stand [passively] by your brother's blood," so they aren't required to save a Gentile or Jew who does not want to be saved. There is no commandment to lengthen one's life if he can only live a short time and with suffering, since his life cannot be saved. If he does not want to be saved, a Gentile is not obligated to save him, even if it is possible. This is clear from *Tosafot* on *Sanhedrin* 59a in regard to saving the life of a mother at the expense of the life of her fetus. Although it will be explained in Chapter 6 that a person has no jurisdiction over his own body for harming himself, we are discussing here the issue of preventing the application of a life-support system. One who is terminally ill and suffering, and does not want to continue living, is not obligated to prolong his suffering in order to prolong his life; therefore, he is permitted to put himself in a **passive** situation where his terminal illness will take its natural course, if he will not be actively violating any commandment.

he knows his true condition. The prohibition is only against actively killing a person, e.g., by removing or turning off a life-support system.

However, if one in this situation says that he wishes to die, but his mind is not sound, or he is being coerced or is not making clear-headed decisions, the above case does not apply. It appears that it is forbidden to let the person die of his own choosing, and it is obligatory to take the medically necessary steps to save his life.[57]

Even if there is no hope for a patient, and the relatives do not wish to prolong his suffering, they do not have any permission to withhold medical treatment. (This does not apply to a patient who was put on a ventilator machine, but he has entered clinical death and does not have any heartbeat; in such a case, one may turn off the ventilator, since the person is not considered to be alive.[58])

18. If a person is nearing death (or still in good health) and he expresses a wish that if he falls into a near-death condition, some parts of his body should be removed for transplant donations before he dies (before his heart has permanently stopped beating), it is forbidden to do so, even though in that condition he would surely die in a short time regardless of what is done. This is obvious, since the operation will or might hasten his death (and it is not done for the purpose of healing).[59] See topic 7:8 below for more regarding organ donation.

Causing Mortal Injury, and Partners in Murder

19. If one mortally injures a person, even though the victim only dies later as a result of the injury, then the injurer is considered a murderer.[60] (It is unclear whether he is liable to capital punishment by a court of law before the victim dies, or if he is only deserving to be

---

[57] See *Igrot Moshe Ĥoshen Mishpat* vol. 2, ch. 73-5.

[58] Responsa of *Tzitz Eliezer* vol. 13, ch. 89.

[59] *Igrot Moshe Yoreh De'ah* vol. 2, ch. 174.

[60] It is unclear if one who willfully mortally injures another is liable for capital punishment, on the basis that at some later time the victim will die as a result of this injury.

See Responsa *Sho'el U'Maishiv* vol. 5, ch. 10, that a Gentile is liable for an act of murder, even if the immanent death is not yet fully accomplished.

punished by God. After the victim dies, he is definitely liable for punishment by the court.)

20. Ten people who hit one individual, one after another, and killed him are all murderers and are all put to death,[61] if each of the ten hit with a lethal blow. Those in the group who did not hit with a blow that had the capacity to kill are exempt from capital punishment.[62]

What is the ruling if two people strike a victim to his death, one after the other, and neither had the power to kill him on their own? If the first person's striking would not have killed the victim, but it weakened him enough so that the second person's strike killed him, then only the second person is liable as a murderer.[63]

If one person throws a victim off a roof, from which the victim would certainly die, and another person held a sword beneath the falling victim, onto which the victim fell and was killed before hitting the ground, both of the attackers are considered murderers.[64] (This is like the case of attackers who strike a victim, one after the other, each with a lethal blow.)

21. Two people who committed one act of murder simultaneously (for example, if together they pushed a victim off a high cliff, or together held a victim under water until he drowned, or together lethally struck

---

[61] Rabbi Zalman Nehemiah Goldberg notes that if 10 Jews hit one victim simultaneously and killed him, all are exempt from execution. In Tractate *Bava Kama* 10b, Rashi explains that since it is not known who killed the victim, and the same should apply for Gentiles, for whom the law is lenient in a case of doubt as to a capital sin.

The author cites Tractate *Sanhedrin* 78a, Rashi's explanation there, and Rambam *Laws of Murderers* 4:6, that a Jew in such a situation is exempt due to the verse (Lev. 24:17) "A man who hits one of all men," which teaches that a Jew is only liable for killing a victim solely from his own actions. A Gentile is liable by the commandment (Genesis 9:6), "One who spills the blood of man," which implies any amount of murder – individually or shared. This is also found in *Torat Ben Noaĥ* p. 34. Therefore, any one of the Gentile attackers who puts enough power in his strike to kill is liable for murder.

[62] See topic 23 below.

[63] Meiri on Tractate *Sanhedrin* 78.

[64] Tractate *Bava Kama* 26b, comparable to the discussion in Tractate *Sanhedrin* 78 of ten people who lethally hit one person.

a victim with one club or sword) are both considered murderers and are both liable to capital punishment,[65] if *both* of the attackers could have accomplished the murder with his own power, or if *neither* of them could have accomplished the murder individually.[66]

However, if *only one* of the attackers had the power on his own to

---

[65] See Rambam *Laws of Murderers* 4:6, and *Kesef Mishneh* there, that this is equivalent to the law for ten people who consecutively struck one victim with lethal blows and killed him. A Jew is exempt from capital punishment for this unless he is the last attacker, according to the traditional meaning of the verse (Lev. 24:17), "A man who hits one of all men." This is unlike the Noahide Code for a Gentile, who is liable for being any one of those who lethally struck the victim, as explained above in footnote 61.

[66] The concept of two people who sinned simultaneously and were only able to do so with both their efforts has different applications in Torah, depending on the nature of the sin involved.

See Rashba on Tractate *Bava Kama* 53b, who differentiates between two cases. If ten people struck a victim simultaneously, and the victim died as a direct result, then each one is only responsible for a part of the end result. But if two people push a victim off a cliff, the resulting death is one full action caused by both of the attackers together, and they are both fully responsible. Even Rambam, who disagrees with Rashba and regards the judgment of both instances to be the same (see the previous footnote), does so only in regard to a Jew who murders, for whom there is a special exception based on the verse "A man who hits one of all men." But for Gentile attackers, Rambam would agree that each individual who lethally struck is fully liable to punishment. Furthermore, since a Gentile is also held responsible for indirect murder, even in the first case cited by Rashba (ten attackers striking simultaneously), a Gentile would be liable to punishment for this, since the actual death resulted from the striking done by each individual.

In conclusion, it appears that if two Gentiles struck a victim simultaneously and caused him to die, if ***neither or both*** of the attackers were capable on their own of killing the victim, then both are liable to capital punishment.

If one of the two was exempt from punishment due to some other factor (even if the death could only have been caused by both of them acting together), such as a minor acting together with a mature person, then only the one who can be held liable should receive capital punishment.

If *more than two* Gentiles are involved together in killing a victim, and *none* of these attackers could accomplish the murder individually, but only when they all participated together, they are all considered as "assistants to murder," and they are not liable to capital punishment.

commit the murder, while the other was not capable of doing it on his own, only the one with the capable power is liable to capital punishment from a court.[67]

22. The same rules apply to two people who together perform one action that causes a victim to die, even if only indirectly (as explained in topic 1:2 above). Both are liable to capital punishment for this in a court of law, with the limitations explained in topic 21.

23. All that has been mentioned above in topics 20-22 only applies when the power and effect of each person in the shared act of murder are clearly known. However, if ten people struck one person and it is unclear which of them caused the actual death, or if attackers pushed a victim into a pit or a furnace, and it is unclear which ones actually exerted the force sufficient to kill, and which ones only assisted without contributing to the lethal effect, then all the attackers involved are exempt from receiving the death penalty from a court of law.[68]

(This is based on the principle that when three people can accomplish one activity *only with their equal participation*, each if them is considered in Torah Law to be the third person who only assists, who is considered unneeded and therefore exempt from punishment.) Likewise, if only one of them was capable of killing the victim on his own, the two (or more) incapable ones are only considered assistants, and are not liable to capital punishment. (See the following footnote.)

[67] It is held throughout the Torah that one who assists in a sin but has no ability to accomplish the deed on his own, is judged in a court of law as if he has not committed an offense, as explained in Tractate *Shabbat* 93; Rambam, *Laws of an Impure Person who Enters the Temple* 5:18; and Responsa of *Ĥaĥam Tzvi* ch. 82. Regarding Divine punishment, it is unclear whether an assistant to murder is regarded with the same severity as one who commits murder of his own accord; he may not even be as liable as one who sends a mercenary to kill. See *Or HaĤayim Bereishit* 37:31, who implies that in the case of the ten Gentiles who together killed a victim, all of them are not liable to capital punishment in court, but they are all liable to punishment by God. This implies that they are all liable to the same punishment (death), but only by Divine retribution. It appears that if the king or the court deemed it fit to execute assistants to murder, based on the particular situation, they are entitled to do so; see Responsa of Rivash, ch. 251.

[68] *Sanhedrin* 80a; the rule of exemption due to doubt also applies to Gentiles.

24. One who intends to kill one particular person, and kills another person instead, or one who throws a stone into a group of people and kills one of them without targeting a particular victim, is considered a murderer.[69] Likewise, if two Gentiles threw stones or shot at a group of people and killed some of them, but it is unclear which person killed which victim, both are liable as murderers since they have each killed a person.[70]

25. Although a person has committed an action for which he is liable for capital punishment, it is forbidden for any other person to kill him; only a court has jurisdiction to judge and punish that transgressor for his actions. One who does kill a transgressor (other than a murderer) before he stands trial is himself judged as a murderer.[71]

---

[69] See Rambam, *Laws of Murderers* 4:1, that in this case a Jew would be exempt from capital punishment, since his judgment is based on the details of Deut. 19:11, which specifies "lying in wait for him" (*Kesef Mishneh*, based on Tractate *Sanhedrin* 79), but this is not said regarding Gentiles, as explained in *Minĥat Ĥinuĥ* Commandment 34:8. It is also implied by Rambam, *Laws of Murderers* 6:10, that a Jewish murderer who intended to kill one person, but instead killed another, is considered close to having murdered willfully, and cannot receive protection in a City of Refuge. In such cases of an unintentional murder that is close to being willful, a Gentile is liable for capital punishment by the court, as explained below in Chapter 5.

[70] It is clear that regarding the Noahide Code, it is not necessary to know which victim the murderer killed, as long as it is known that he murdered.

[71] See *Sefer HaĤinuĥ* Commandment 409, regarding a Jew. The *Minĥat Ĥinuĥ* explains there that it is clear that this does not apply within Torah Law to a Gentile who witnesses another Gentile committing a capital sin, since a Gentile can receive the death penalty based on one witness and one judge, and since a Gentile witness can become a judge of that case, a Gentile who sees a capital sin committed by another Gentile can also be the judge and mete out capital punishment based on the ruling he makes. *Minĥat Ĥinuĥ* also writes in Commandment 410 that a Gentile who kills another Gentile who served an idol or willfully transgressed one of the other Seven Noahide Commandments, is exempt, for he has killed one deserving of death; the above reasoning is also mentioned there. However, to the author, it seems unlikely that a person is actually allowed to proceed right away to execute the transgressor, without first having the testimony accepted in a proper court proceeding.

In general, if a court has *already* sentenced to death a Gentile for a capital sin within the Noahide Laws, and another person kills this transgressor before the execution, he is exempt from punishment.[72]

In the case of a Gentile who kills without being forced to commit the lethal action, whether he murdered intentionally or with liable negligence (according to the guidelines of Chapter 5 below), one who kills him before he has been tried in court is not liable to punishment (although it is forbidden to do so).[73]

Rabbi Zalman Nehemiah Goldberg notes that this appears to also be the reasoning of *Tosafot Avodah Zarah* 64b. Also, not everyone is qualified to be a judge (or a witness) in a court proceeding. So it is clear that the permission for a Gentile witness to become a judge in such a case is *only* for one who thoroughly knows the detailed laws of the Noahide Code, and the Torah-law process of administering this justice.

Although the injunction "The murderer shall not die until he stands in court to be judged" (Num. 35:12) is said regarding Jews, it is still logically incumbent upon Gentiles, for otherwise everyone would take the law into their own hands, and there would be no standards of objective laws in the world.

[72] *Sifri Bamidbar* 35:31. This is also clear from Rambam, *Laws of Sanhedrin*, 14:8.

It appears that this *only* applies specifically to a judgment of death prescribed in Torah, i.e., a case in which the convicted Gentile violated one of the specific Seven Noahide Commandments. If, however, an attacker kills one who is sentenced to death only for transgressing a law of the land, he would be considered no less a murderer than one who killed a mortally injured person, for which he would be liable to capital punishment.

[73] Even one who kills unintentionally "has no blood," as the verse (Numbers 35:27) is explained, as written by Rambam, *Laws of Murderers* 5:10. This is learned *a fortiori* from the case of a Jew who leaves his City of Refuge after he committed unintentional murder. It is considered that he "has no blood" (i.e., there is no liability for one who kills him), and surely this applies before he arrives at the City of Refuge; how much more so for one who kills a Gentile murderer, for whom there is no City of Refuge. (The exception is a *Ger Toshav* Gentile who kills unintentionally in a time when the Jubilee cycle is observed and Cities of Refuge exist in the Land of Israel; see Num. 35:9-28. But still, the Torah Law for a *Ger Toshav* is equal to that for a Jew who murdered unintentionally, before he escaped to a City of Refuge; see *Sheva Mitzvot HaShem*, Part V, Chapter 5.)

CHAPTER 2

Suicide, and Sacrificing One's Life for One of the Seven Noahide Commandments

1. One who takes his own life intentionally is a murderer and is liable to punishment by God for the capital sin of murder, as it is stated,[74] "But your blood of your [own] souls I will demand." This refers to one who took his own life, who is judged by God, and his soul is punished in *Gehinom*[75] for his act of suicide[76] (with the exceptions explained in the following topics).

Even one who is enduring great physical suffering from illness or an injury, and will surely die because there is no available cure for him, or one who is suffering great degradation, embarrassment or depression, is forbidden to commit suicide.[77] Likewise, others are not permitted to kill him as an act of mercy, even upon his request, as explained above in topic 1:17.

2. One who is about to be caught by enemies and is certain that they will torture and kill him (and he has no natural means of being saved) is permitted to take his own life before he is attacked, as it says, "But your blood of your souls I will demand" – the word "but" implies the exclusion of a case when suicide is permissible.[78]

---

[74] Genesis 9:5.

[75] *Ĥizkuni* Genesis *ibid.*

[76] Rambam, *Laws of Murderers* 2:2,3; Rashi on Genesis *ibid.* See *Kli Ĥemda Noaĥ* topic 3, who debates whether a court gives the death penalty to one who mortally wounds himself.

[77] See *Tosafot* on Tractate *Bava Kama* 91b; *Yam Shel Shlomo Bava Kama ibid.* ch. 59; *Ĥatam Sofer Yoreh De'ah* 326:3; *Ĥatam Sofer Even HaEzer* 69. **This only applies to one whose suffering is not being inflicted directly and physically by another person.** For the case of a Gentile who is being mortally wounded by another person, see topic 2 and the following footnote.

[78] *Bereishit Rabbah* 34; *Orĥos Ĥayim*, cited by *Bedek Habayit Yoreh De'ah* 157; *Baĥ* and *Shaĥ Yoreh De'ah* 157.

The permission these sources give applies to a Jewish victim who might be faced with torture that he could not withstand, that might cause him to succumb to "desecration of God's Name" (see end of footnote 83). A Jew is obligated to "sanctify God's Name" for the sake of three specific Jewish commandments, and one who fails to do so desecrates God's Name. On the other hand, a Gentile has no such obligation; see Part I, topic 4:3. Therefore, avoiding desecration of God's Name might not be a valid reason to permit suicide for Gentiles. It can be said that the opinions above citing *Bereishit Rabbah* were only giving one example of a situation when there is permission for a person to take his own life – when the person would be tortured *to death* – but there are also other specific cases in which anyone (including a Gentile) is permitted to do so, as discussed in this chapter.

This can be seen from the fact that in the verse regarding King Saul's death (I Sam. 31:4), there is no reference in his reason for committing suicide that it was because he feared that he might desecrate God's Name. Rather, it was because he was terrified that from defeat on the battlefield, his capture would lead to his torture, or to humiliation of the kingship of Israel (see Radak's commentary on I Sam. *ibid.*, and Rashi on II Sam. 1:9). Likewise, Midrash *Bereishit Rabbah* says that the word "but" in the cited verse comes to exclude King Saul, and then says separately that it also excludes the voluntary martyrdom (in Daniel ch. 3) of Ĥananya (Shadraĥ), Mishael (Meshaĥ) and Azaryah (Abed Nego). This implies that King Saul was permitted to commit suicide for reasons that did not apply to Ĥananya, Mishael and Azaryah, who accepted to be killed in sanctification of God's Name (Daniel 3:16-21), i.e., in compliance with God's commandment that a Jew must not bow down to an idol in the presence of 10 other Jewish men, even if he is faced with death.

Further proof can be brought from Rambam, *Laws of Mourning* 1:11, that one should not eulogize or mourn for one who commits suicide. Nevertheless, one who committed suicide under duress similar to King Saul may be mourned, as in II Sam. ch. 1, when King David mourned for King Saul.

(The last proof is debated by many later Rabbinical authorities. Some argue that it is possible that King Saul was not permitted to commit suicide, but since it was done out of fear and duress, he did not receive any punishment from God, and this is why King David was allowed to mourn him. Or perhaps King David mourned out of honor for the kingship and the nation, and because of his love for King Saul's son Jonathan. But the main opinion seems to be that King Saul was permitted to commit suicide in that situation.)

See Tractate *Avodah Zarah* 18a regarding the martyrdom of Rabbi Ĥanina ben Tradyon, who was burned alive by the Romans. His disciples asked him to open his mouth so that the fire would enter and end his suffering sooner, but he would not agree to do so. However, he did allow the Roman executioner (who was a Gentile – see Maharsha *ibid.*) to stoke the flames and remove the wet wool from upon his heart, in order to hasten his death. *Igrot Moshe Ĥoshen Mishpat* v. 2, 73:3, asks how this Sage was permitted to allow

The victim is even permitted to ask someone else to take his life (even before the unavoidable attack occurs),[79] and the person who is asked is permitted to comply.

---

a Gentile to hasten his death. It appears that he did not want to open his mouth out of his own righteousness, but since he was permitted by Torah Law to do so, he allowed the Gentile executioner to hasten his death. [Even though a Gentile would be liable if this was committed as an act of malicious murder, when the executioner did this and then committed suicide by jumping into the flames with Rabbi Ĥanina (apparently as an act of sanctifying God's Name), his soul was granted a Divine reward.]

Since a Gentile may hasten a Jew's death when the Jew is or will imminently be enduring *physical suffering from attack or torture* that is surely leading to death without any hope of escape – *if the suffering Jew requests this himself with a rational mind*, then the same is surely true for hastening another Gentile's death *under the same circumstances*. The same applies if a Gentile takes his own life in these circumstances.

This permission is given **only** if the one who wishes to commit suicide is being physically tortured by other people, and his death is unavoidable at their hands. But if his suffering is resulting from other situations of Divine Providence (for example, illness, or accidental injury, or emotional distress), he may not commit suicide to end his suffering sooner, nor may another person assist him in this or do it for him, even at the request of the suffering person. (Rationale for this distinction may be brought from the law of a *rodef* – the Hebrew term for one who pursues with intent to kill. Even though murder is prohibited, anyone may kill a *rodef* if that is the only way to stop him from murdering. In a situation where the victim cannot save himself by overpowering the *rodef*, just as he would be permitted to kill the *rodef* in self-defense, he is likewise permitted to commit suicide.)

[79] It appears clear that just as it is permitted to commit suicide *in that type of situation*, it is also permitted for the person to ask someone else to kill him, and the person asked is permitted to comply. This is like the case of King Saul, who was mortally wounded and requested his servant to kill him (I Samuel 31:4). See Ritva on Tractate *Avodah Zarah* 18a in name of *Tosafot*.

However, King David executed King Saul's servant (II Samuel 1:14-16) because he killed the mortally wounded King Saul. It seems unlikely to the author that the servant was forbidden to do so because of a detail of the prohibition of murder, for King Saul himself, who acted according to the Torah Law, asked for this (in order to shorten his suffering and avoid being captured and humiliated by the enemy before he died). Rather, there were other reasons that David executed the servant, that were specific to that case.

3. It seems that one is permitted to commit suicide to save oneself from being taken into captivity or slavery.[80] How much more so is one permitted (but not required) in order to save oneself from sexual abuse, rape or forced prostitution.[81]

4. With one exception, a Gentile is not required to sacrifice his life to avoid transgressing one of the Seven Noahide Commandments; i.e., a Gentile is *permitted* to transgress in order to avoid being killed. See Part VI, topic 1:10, and Part VII, topic 4:1; see also Part II, topic 3:29, and Part IV, topic 6:11. [Alternatively, topic 9 below explains the circumstances under which a Gentile is permitted to give up his life to avoid transgressing any of the Seven Noahide Commandments.] The one exception is in regard to committing murder. Even if one is

---

[80] See Tractate *Bava Batra* 8b, that "captivity is worse than death by the sword or starvation;" see also topic 3:10 below. This also appears to be the reasoning of the *Beit Leĥem Yehudah Yoreh De'ah* ch. 355.

However, Ĥida in his responsa *Ĥayim Sha'al* vol. 1, ch. 46 (quoting *Knesset HaGedolah Yoreh De'ah* ch. 157), rules that a Jew may only commit suicide to avoid being murdered, but not to avoid being tortured. This is also the opinion of the *Beit Efraim Yoreh De'ah* ch. 76. And despite the Talmud's words that captivity is as bad as "all forms of death" (Tractate *Bava Batra ibid.*), there is no guarantee that one will die in captivity. Therefore, although the Torah Law is that one may consider one who pursues to take a person captive as having intentions for murder, so the pursuer may be killed in self-defense, we don't find a source implying that one would be permitted to avoid captivity by committing suicide.

Nevertheless, (a) the above opinions are only expressed regarding Jews, and (b) aside from captivity equaling "all forms of death," it can also be considered worse than other types of suffering if it is a captor who would force his captive to do whatever he wishes.

It therefore appears to the author that for a Gentile, just as it is permitted to save oneself from captivity by taking the life of the pursuing captor, it is also permitted to take one's own life to be saved from captivity (except if the captivity is a legal sentence of punishment decreed by a court); see topic 2:9.

[81] See *Tosafot* on Tractate *Avodah Zarah* 18a, regarding the group of Jewish children who committed suicide after being captured by the Romans for the purpose of sexual slavery, after the destruction of the Second Temple. It is considered that the children acted righteously and sanctified God's Name, and it appears that permission to do so also applies for Gentiles.

threatened with losing one's own life or with excruciating torture beyond endurance,[82] nonetheless, he must submit to being tortured and/or murdered rather than murder another human being. The reason for this is to comply with the common-sense dictum, "Who says that your blood is redder (than that of your fellow)?"[83] (It is not due to any obligation to more strongly uphold the *Divine commandment* against murder, compared to the other six Noahide commandments from God that are associated with this leniency. The practical difference between these two ways of reasoning will be explained below in topic 8.)

5. Even if a person is being forced to kill someone who is already dying, or an embryo in its mother's womb, he should rather let himself

---

[82] See Tractate *Ketubot* 33b: "suffering severe torture is worse than death."

[83] Tractate *Sanhedrin* 74a. See *Parshat Deraĥim* p. 28, based on Rambam, *Foundations of the Faith* ch. 5, that it is logical that one must give up his life rather than murder, so this must apply to Gentiles. This is also clear from the Jerusalem Talmud, Tractates *Shabbat* ch. 14 (end) and *Avodah Zarah* 2:5.

However, some authorities (see Meiri on Tractate *Sanhedrin*, end of ch. 8) note that Rambam, *Laws of Kings* 10:2, writes that a Gentile may transgress rather than be killed, and he does not distinguish between any of the Noahide Laws; these authorities therefore infer that murder is also included.

Still, the ruling of Rambam (*ibid.*) is apparently only a reason why murder is like the other Noahide Laws, in that Gentiles are not *commanded* to sanctify God's Name, even for the purpose of avoiding murder. Hence, the reason that the prohibition of murder outweighs a Gentile's own life is not because of the severity of the sin to God, but because of the logical moral reasoning, "Who says that your blood redder than that of your fellow?"

The difference (discussed in the Jerusalem Talmud, Tractate *Terumot* ch. 8, and *Yoreh De'ah* ch. 157) is that if attackers tell a group of Jews to hand over an individual Jew to be killed, or else they will all be killed, Torah Law forbids them to hand him over, even on pain of death of many people. But a group of Gentiles may do so in this case (because the blood of many people is "redder" than that of just one person). The difference is that by Torah Law, a Jew may violate his commandments if necessary to save his life, with the exception of three prohibitions – murder, idolatry, and sexual relations that are forbidden as capital sins – even though for the latter two, there is no common-sense dictum of "Who says that your blood is redder than that of your fellow?" Gentiles are not obligated to observe this point of Jewish law, but they are obligated by the dictum, "Who says that your blood is redder ...?"

be killed than kill the sick or dying person or the embryo.[84]

It would appear that the same applies to injuring another person. One should let himself be killed[85] if he is being forced to injure another person or commit rape[86] of a male or a female person, rather than commit the act in order to save his own life.

---

[84] See *Minĥat Ĥinuĥ* Commandment 296, which is uncertain as to the Torah Law in this situation; *Nodah Bi'Yehudah Ĥoshen Mishpat* ch. 59 forbids this. *Igrot Moshe Ĥoshen Mishpat* vol. 2, 69:1, is uncertain in regard to a fetus (although he originally leans to forbid it). Regarding a person who is mortally wounded or a *goses* (in the throes of death), he completely forbids the murder, which is also the opinion of *Tzitz Eliezer* vol. 9, 17:6, vol. 10, 25:5.

[85] Rabbi Zalman Nehemiah Goldberg views the law as unclear in regard to whether one must let himself be killed if he is being forced to injure or rape.

The author finds reason why it should at least be *permitted* for the person to let himself be killed to avoid this, and not considered as a prohibited suicide, because of the dictum, "Who says that your is blood redder than that of your fellow?" This can be seen *a fortiori* from Tamar (Gen. 38:25), who submitted herself to be executed rather than embarrass Judah (since publicly embarrassing a person is likened to murder). However, it is unclear whether a person is *obligated* to give up his life to avoid injuring or raping another.

See *Pisĥei Teshuva Yoreh De'ah* 157:16, that cites Radvaz vol. 3, ch. 627; *Yad Avraham Yoreh De'ah* 157, based on Rambam, *Laws of Marriage* 21:11; *Or Same'aĥ* on Rambam, *Laws of Murderers* 7:8; and *Igrot Moshe Yoreh De'ah* vol. 2, 174:4, who all write that one is *not required* to lose a limb (for example, a hand or a foot) in order to save another person's life. *It therefore appears to the author that a Jew or a Gentile may not cut off or break another person's limb or commit rape to save his own life, and the common-sense dictum, "Who says that your blood is redder than that of your fellow?" would apply even to the other person's limb.* Nevertheless, some sources say that this is permitted [Maharam Ĥaviv in *Tosefet Yom HaKippurim* (Tractate *Yoma* 82b); *Kli Ĥemda Parshat Teitze* p. 236.] (In any event, one who is forced to transgress on pain of death is **not** to be judged or punished by a court of law for committing the forced act – including homicide, as explained in topic 7 below, even though one who **kills** under duress is held accountable in the judgment of Heaven.)

[86] Pursuit for the purpose of raping is tantamount to pursuit for the purpose of murdering. See Rambam, *Laws of Murderers* 1:10-15, who says this is learned from the verses Deut. 22:26 (a consecrated maiden who is raped in a field), and Lev. 19:16 ("you shall not stand [idly] by the blood of your fellow").

6. The above only applies if the person is being forced to physically commit direct or indirect murder. However, if one is being forced to stand in a certain spot[87] where his body will be used by others as an instrument for murder, there is no obligation to give one's life up to save the intended victim, since the murder is being done through the actions of others.

It need not be mentioned that one is not obligated to give up his or her life to save another person's life. Nevertheless, it appears permissible to do so.[88]

7. If a person committed homicide because another person was threatening his life (or limb or severe torture), this killer has committed an offense and is a murderer and will be punished by Heaven. However, a court of law does not have permission to punish him, because he was severely pressured.[89]

8. If a group of Gentiles is told, "Give over one of your group to be killed, or else all of you will be killed," they have no permission to hand over one person from the group, for the reason given in topic 4. However, if the murderers singled out their victim, and will either kill that one particular victim or the whole group, it is permissible to hand over the one victim, since it cannot be said that the victim's blood is "more red" than that of the whole group.[90]

9. Although a Gentile is not obligated to sacrifice his life for the sanctification of God's Name[91] (i.e. to avoid committing idolatry or

---

[87] Tosafot on Tractate *Sanhedrin* 74b; Rema *Yoreh De'ah* ch. 157.

[88] This is discussed at length in the footnotes for this topic in *Sheva Mitzvot HaShem*, Vol. II, p. 370. See topic 9, and the footnote to topic 3:20 below.

[89] Rambam, *Laws of Kings* 10:2.

[90] See the last footnote to topic 4 above.

[91] See Tractate *Sanhedrin* 74b, from which it can be learned that although a Gentile is not commanded to sacrifice his life so as not to transgress one of the Noahide commandments, it is, nevertheless, still considered a sanctification of God's Name if he does so, and even if there are no witnesses. Therefore, this should be permissible (but not required) for a Gentile in either a public or a private situation.

one of the other capital sins prohibited by the Noahide commandments, at the cost of his life), it is permissible for him to do so, and this is not considered suicide.[92] It appears that this applies even if he is being forced to transgress the commandment in private.

Likewise, if one is being forced through torture to transgress one of the Seven Noahide Commandments, and is unsure whether he will be capable to withstand the suffering, it is permissible for him to take his life so as not to transgress, and this is not considered suicide.[93] This permission only applies to avoiding a transgression for which a Gentile would be liable to capital punishment in a Noahide court, if it were committed willfully.

---

[92] See *Shulĥan Aruĥ Yorah De'ah* ch. 157, which rules this way regarding a Jew. *Parshat Deraĥim* writes that the same applies to a Gentile, and cites *Bereishit Rabbah*, ch. 34, as a source.

We can also take a proof from Abraham, who allowed himself to be thrown into a furnace by Nimrod, instead of being forced to commit idolatry. (Since Abraham was not Jewish within the Divine Law, this proves that what he did is permitted for Gentiles, and it is not considered to be like suicide.)

See Rambam in *Laws of Kings*, 10:2 – "A Gentile who is forced... is **permitted** to transgress" – to prove that it is not an obligation to transgress in this case, and the Gentile may give up his life instead. See *Maharatz Ĥayot* on Tractate *Sotah* 11b, and *Mesheĥ Ĥaĥma Parshat Vezot HaBraĥa.*

It appears that just as it is permitted for a Gentile to give up his life at the hands of others [who will kill him] in order to avoid transgressing a capital sin, it is also permitted for one to take one's own life in this case, and this is not considered suicide.

[93] See *Bereishit Rabbah*, ch. 34: "but" excludes the case of Ĥananya, Mishael and Azarya (Daniel ch. 2). *Orĥot Ĥayim* [quoted in *Bedek HaBayit* of *Beit Yosef Yoreh De'ah* ch. 157] brings two explanations. One is that they went on their own into the furnace, since they were afraid they would succumb to idolatry through torture, and the second explanation is that they were thrown in by the Gentiles, but they were forbidden to throw themselves in. *Tosafot* on Tractate *Avodah Zarah* 18a quote only the first explanation.

CHAPTER 3

Laws of a Pursuer and Self Defense; Saving the Life of a Woman in Danger from Childbirth

1. One who murders intentionally is to be brought to the court and judged for his sin. Before he is brought to court and judged, he may not be killed by those who witnessed the murder, or by those who see him and identify him as the one whom they were told is a murderer.[94]

This only applies if he has already murdered. However, if someone (an adult or a child) is chasing another person, male or female, adult or child, with intent to kill the person, it is an obligation[95] to save the one who is being chased. This is so even if the one being pursued can only be saved by taking the life of the pursuer. This applies whether the one who is saving is someone who sees the chase, or the one who is being chased. The Sages learned from the verse,[96] "Whoever sheds the blood of man, by man his blood shall be shed," that it is permissible to save the one being chased by taking the life of the pursuer who is chasing a person with intent to murder.[97] The main reason for this is that it is logical for the one being chased to try to save himself at all costs from the pursuer, and likewise for the intended victim's friends and relatives who witness the pursuit. For this should be a civilized world, and it is expected that each group (family, community, etc.) will to try to save itself from its attackers.[98] This rule is a branch of the Noahide

---

[94] Rambam, *Laws of Murderers* 1:5.

[95] The law of a pursuer applies for Gentiles, from Rambam, *Laws of Kings* 9:4 – if maiming a limb will not stop the pursuer, it is permissible to kill the attacker. This is seen also from Tractate *Sanhedrin* 57a. In the *Minĥat Ĥinuĥ* Commandment 296 (and *Ĥemdat Yisrael* on Rambam, *Laws of Kings* 9:4; and *S'dei Ĥemed Pe'at Sadeh* vol. 3, 6:13) there is a discussion regarding a Gentile saving another person who is being chased. These opinions decide that since this is logical, there is no need for support from a verse.

[96] Genesis 9:6.

[97] See Tractate *Sanhedrin* 72b. Rashi's explanation bases this on Gen. 9:6, "by *adam*" (in Hebrew), meaning mankind in general. The Talmud explains there that saving a pursued person is also an obligation for Gentiles, and not just permissible. However, Rambam does not mention this as an *obligation*.

[98] See *Sefer HaĤinuĥ*, Commandments 237 and 600.

prohibition against murder. Namely, one should not let an attacker kill whomever he wishes, but he should protect the one who is being chased in any possible way, and if there is no alternative, he should kill the attacker in order that the one being chased will not be killed.[99]

2. The law of a pursuer does not only apply to one who chases to kill a victim directly (e.g., with either his hands or a weapon). It even applies to one who is proceeding to kill a victim by indirect means, such as one who is trying to lock his victim in a place where he will die of hunger (as explained in topic 1:2). Other examples would be someone who is traveling to hire an assassin to commit a murder, or someone who sets a killer dog or wild animal on the pursued victim. All of these are cases of pursuing with intent to kill, and a person may take action to prevent the homicide by using any means (without killing or maiming any bystanders). It is an obligation upon everyone who is able to save the pursued victim, and one may kill the pursuer if that is the only possible way.[100]

---

[99] Gentiles have no clear commandment to save one who is pursued (for Jews there is a separate verse, Lev. 19:16, "Do not stand by your brother's blood"), but from Rambam, *Laws of Kings* 9:4, it is at least *permissible* to save the victim by killing the pursuer. *Minĥat Ĥinuĥ, S'dei Ĥemed* (cited above) and *Aruĥ LeNair* (on Tractate *Sanhedrin* 72) say that this law must be one that logically applies to Gentiles, and is only permissible, but not obligatory.

However, it appears that it is also obligatory for a Gentile to save one who is pursued, even though there is no explicit commandment for this. It seems to be included in the Noahide precepts regarding murder (see Chapter 7), based on what is written in Part I, Chapter 3, that Gentiles are *obligated* in matters that are logically binding, such as charity and acts of kindness, and there is no greater kindness than saving one who is being pursued for murder.

See Rabbi Ĥayim HaLevi (on Rambam, *Laws of Murderers* ch. 1) (and *Ĥemdat Yisrael* on Rambam, *Laws of Kings* ch. 9), who says that this is an obligation that stems from the Noahide precepts regarding Courts of Law.

A difference for Gentiles is that if the onlooker knows he can save the victim from some of several pursuers, yet the others will still kill their victim, he is only morally, but not legally obligated to stop some of the pursuers.

[100] This can be learned from the law of an informer, as explained in Tractate *Beraĥot* 58a and *Shulĥan Aruĥ Ĥoshen Mishpat* ch. 388. This is also written by *Minĥat Ĥinuĥ* Commandments 296 (part 25) and 600, *Aĥiezer* vol. 1 ch. 19, and *Or Same'aĥ* on Rambam, *Laws of Murderers* 1:8.

3. It is not permissible to save someone by killing his pursuer unless this is the only way to save the victim. If it is possible for one to save the victim without killing the pursuer – for example, by appeasing him or confusing him with words, or by wounding him, as by cutting off his hand or foot – and instead he killed the pursuer, this is considered murder with liability to capital punishment.[101]

Even if the one being chased saves himself by killing his pursuer, when he could have saved himself by injuring the pursuer's limbs, he is considered a murderer and is liable to capital punishment.[102]

4. One who blackmails another to either do a certain action or else be killed is considered a pursuer. The victim does not need to listen to what the blackmailer wishes him to do, but is rather permitted to kill him, since he is the same as a pursuer (for example, a robber who threatens to kill if he is not given money).

This applies if the victim was being forced to do something that is forbidden or only permissible. If he is being forced to keep one of the Noahide Commandments, since he is obligated to keep them, killing the person who is forcing him to do so would constitute murder.[103]

5. One who pursues a mortally wounded person to kill him is considered to have intent to murder, and it is permissible to kill the pursuer in order to save the mortally wounded person.[104]

6. One who pursues a pregnant woman, intending to strike the mother in order to kill (abort) the fetus, is considered in Torah Law as a real pursuer, and it is permitted to save the fetus like any other pursued person.[105]

---

[101] Rambam, *Laws of Kings* 9:4.

[102] As a practical matter, the pursued person may be too harried to calculate whether he can save himself by merely injuring the pursuer. However, if it is clear that this option is available, he is obligated to do so, and if he does not utilize this opportunity but rather kills his pursuer, he is judged as a murderer.

[103] See *Tzitz Eliezer* vol. 9, ch. 17, topic 2:7.

[104] It appears clear to the author that since a Gentile is liable for capital punishment if he kills a mortally wounded person, it is permitted to prevent him from doing this, by deadly force if needed, just as any other case of a pursuer.

[105] Based on topic 1:10, that murder of an embryo is fully murder.

7. If a woman is at risk of dying in childbirth (due to her fetus), it is permitted to kill the *unborn* fetus[106] and remove it from her to save her life, because it is as if the fetus is pursuing her to kill her. But if its head has already emerged,[107] since it is already born, it is forbidden to harm it, for one does not have permission to choose one life over the other, and this risk in childbirth is the nature of the world.[108]

If taking no action against the fetus would result in *both* the mother and the fetus dying, or if it is clear that the child will be nonviable no matter what,[109] or it will be stillborn, it is permissible – if necessary to save the mother's life – to kill the fetus, or the nonviable child even if the head or most of the body has come out.[110,111]

---

[106] *Intact dilatation and extraction ("D & X," commonly referred to as "partial-birth abortion") of a fetus would not be permitted unless it is the only way medically available to save the mother. In 1996, a select panel convened by the American College of Obstetrics and Gynecologists found no circumstances when this is the only available option for saving the mother. (This document is available on http://mrc.org.) If it is possible to save the mother without killing the fetus, and yet the fetus was killed from the outset, it is considered a case of murder.

[107] *In Torah Law, a child has been born when its forehead, or the majority of its body, has emerged from the birth canal (*Shulĥan Aruĥ Ĥoshen Mishpat* 287, *Shulĥan Aruĥ Yoreh De'ah* 14).

[108] Rambam, *Laws of Murderers* 1:9.

[109] *Tiferet Yisrael Bo'az*, Tractate *Ohalot*, end of ch. 7. This law is comparable to the case in which murderers singled out their victim from a group, and will either kill that one victim or the whole group. It is permissible to hand over the one victim, since it cannot be said that the victim's blood "is more red" than that of the whole group (see topic 2:8, and footnote 83).

[110] *Panim Meirot* vol. 3 ch. 8, and *Tiferet Yisrael ibid.*, and the *Mishnah Aĥarona* Tractate *Ohalot* there. Although they write about a Jew, it appears that the same law would apply to Gentiles. See *Igrot Moshe Ĥoshen Mishpat* vol. 2, 69:2, who explains that unless the head of the child has emerged, it cannot be considered to be as alive as the mother. This logic would apply here, if it is known that after the head emerges, the child will be nonviable.

Rabbi Zalman Nehemiah Goldberg notes that it appears that if a child will be stillborn, this is correct. If it is not stillborn, but it will die in any case (as a result of the birth process), it is still a completely live person (even if it is medically equivalent to a mortally wounded person). He thus brings the following question. If the danger from the labor is a "natural process by the

8. Where two people are each trying to kill each other, it is permissible for others to help one of them by killing the opponent as a pursuer.[111]

9. There is no "law of a pursuer" for a Gentile who wishes to commit a sin in general (other than murder). If a Gentile is determined to commit idolatry, eat a limb from a living animal, or steal money or the like, one may not prevent the person from sinning by injuring him.[112] One should rather warn the would-be violator about the severity of his forbidden action, and if he still sins, he can be judged in a court of law.

Likewise, if it is clear that a pursuer wishes only to strike a victim non-lethally[113] or to sever a limb, or if it is a man pursuing for the

---

Hand of Heaven," in which either the child or the mother would die, but not both, then the child would not be classed as a pursuer. Then it is not clear that it should be treated differently than the law of a mortally wounded person, in which case a Gentile would be liable for murder if he kills it. So in this case, would it be forbidden to kill the emerging child to save the mother's life, even though taking no action will otherwise cause the death of both?

The author responds that the Talmud, in Tractate *Sanhedrin* 72b, only instructs no intervention in a case of a natural process in which one of them will live and the other will die (as for example, in Gen. 35:16-20, when Rachel died giving birth to Benjamin, after most of the child's body had already emerged). But if the child will be nonviable no matter what, at least the mother should be saved, even by killing the child if that is the only way.

[111] See topic 7, in which a woman's life is being threatened by her childbirth. See Tractate *Sanhedrin* 72b, that if the head of the child or most of the body has come out, one may not harm it, since it is a natural process that is threatening the mother's life. However, this rule does not apply if both the mother and the child are "pursuing" each other. In the Jerusalem Talmud, Tractate *Sanhedrin*, end of ch. 8, the reason given for the prohibition of killing the child after its head has emerged is only due to the fact that we do not know who the pursuer is. However, if it is clear that each is endangering the other's life, it is permissible to kill the emerging child to save the mother.

[112] Rambam, *Laws of Murderers* 1:11.

[113] This is the apparent intention of the verse in Deut. 25:11-12, "You shall cut off her hand," since the woman is a pursuer who is in the act of injuring a man in his private parts, as explained in Rambam, *Laws of Murderers* 1:7-8, even though she is acting to save her husband from his attacker. From this it is clear that one may only kill a pursuer whose intention is to kill. This is also clear in *Or HaĤayim* on Deuteronomy *ibid.*

purpose of rape (i.e., a man who is pursuing a Gentile woman to rape her, whether or not she would be a forbidden partner for him within the Noahide Code, as for example the wife of another man, or if a man is pursuing another man to commit sodomy), a Gentile may not save the victim by killing the pursuer.[114]

Therefore, if it is clear that the pursuer doesn't intend to kill, it is forbidden to kill him. However, it is permissible for an onlooker, or the victim in self-defense, to injure the pursuer to prevent him from committing injury[115] or rape.

However, if there is a possibility that the pursuer actually intends to kill (or even if he doesn't intend to kill, but his action may turn into a life-threatening situation for any reason), then the usual ruling of a pursuer applies, that one do anything to the pursuer to save the victim, and if there is no other choice, he may kill the pursuer, as stated by the Sages[116], "One who comes to kill you, precede him and kill him", meaning that if there is a possibility that the pursuer comes to kill,[117] one should quickly kill the pursuer first, and not wait to verify that he indeed intends to kill.

10. Likewise, one who is being pursued for the purpose of enslavement is surely permitted to save himself, even by taking the life of his pursuer.[118]

11. A pursuer who is legally a minor has the same ruling, and may be killed if that is the only way to save the victim.[119] Likewise, a pursuer

---

[114] See *Minĥat Ĥinuĥ* Commandment 296, who says that it is clear that for Gentiles there is no Torah-law obligation to save a Gentile victim from a pursuer who has non-lethal intent, and therefore it is forbidden for a Gentile to kill someone who is pursuing a Gentile for rape, even if it is for forbidden relations.

[115] *Shulĥan Aruĥ HaRav, Laws of Bodily Damage*, topic 2.

[116] Tractate *Sanhedrin* 72a.

[117] This is clear from the Talmud *ibid.*, " 'If the sun shines on him' – if it is clear to you that he comes to kill…," and Rambam, *Laws of Theft* 9:5.

[118] Rabbi Zalman Nehemiah Goldberg notes that it appears that this applies only if there is a possibility that the enslavement will lead to death.

[119] Rambam, *Laws of Murderers* 1:6.

who is a deaf-mute or mentally challenged may be killed[120] if that is the only way to save the victim.

12. If someone attempts to break into a house secretively for the purpose of robbery, whether by day or night, it is permitted to kill him[121] (except in certain situations that are explained below). This is learned from Ex. 22:1 that states, "there is no blood for him" [i.e., it is permitted to shed his blood; since he is ready to kill in the process of his robbery, therefore, he is also permitting himself to be killed as a pursuer if he is discovered]. Therefore, if a defender of the home or business (the owner or any other person) kills the robber, he is not liable. If a person reasons that the robber is ready to commit murder, it is permitted for anyone to kill the robber in any possible way. This applies whether the robber comes through a tunnel,[122] or a door,[123] or is found on the roof or in the yard, or in any place where occupants of the building can usually be found.

How can we permit a person to take the life of a robber if he only comes for money? This is because it is assumed that if the house owner stands up and tries to prevent the robbery (which is the natural way of the world), the robber will kill him. Therefore, if someone enters another person's house to rob him, it is as if the robber is pursuing the owner to kill him. For this reason, it is permitted within the Noahide Code to kill the robber (and indeed, it is a moral obligation) if there is a risk to the life of the house owner, regardless of whether the robbery is being committed by a minor or an adult, or a man or woman. (This applies only in a case where there is a concern that the minor or woman may be coming with the intent to kill if discovered, and that he or she has the capability to do so.)

However, if it is clear to the person inside who encounters the robber that the robber will not kill him, it is forbidden to kill the robber, and if one does so, he is considered a murderer. (Therefore, if it is clear that

---

[120] *Minĥat Ĥinuĥ* Commandment 600.

[121] Rambam, *Laws of Theft* 9:7.

[122] *In the language of Torah Law, this is the classical expression (based on the language of Exodus 22:1) for referring to a thief who is trying to steal by entering a building secretively, by any means.

[123] *Maggid Mishneh, Laws of Theft ibid.*

the robber is only coming to steal money or belongings, without readiness to kill in the process, and he is fearful and will submit if he is discovered in the act – like the behavior of a minor child who steals secretly but who isn't prepared to kill – it is forbidden to kill him.)

Therefore, if a father comes secretly to rob his son, and it is clear that if this son tries to stop him, he will not kill his son, then he is not considered a pursuer. If the son kills him anyway, the son is considered a murderer, and is liable to capital punishment for this (because in general, a father will have mercy on his son; however, if it is known that the father is cruel and will not have mercy, then he is assumed to be a pursuer, and it is permissible to kill him if he is discovered robbing). Likewise, if a robber is breaking into the house of his known close friend, and it is clear that he does not come with readiness to kill, he is not considered a pursuer, and it is forbidden to kill him.[124]

On the other hand, a son who robs his father's home is assumed to be a pursuer (since in general, a son has less mercy for his father than his father has for him). Therefore, the father or another person is permitted to kill the son when he is caught breaking in.

13. However, if a thief enters secretly into a garden, field or animal pen, it is forbidden to kill him (i.e., he still "has blood"). Since it is unlikely that the owner will be found in these places, it is assumed that the thief comes only to steal, without being ready to kill.[125]

14. If a robber is leaving from the building (or apartment or office) where he stole, and the owner or someone else finds him leaving, whether or not he is holding any stolen money or objects, then it is forbidden to kill him. He has the status of "having blood" (i.e., others are not permitted to kill him) because he has turned his back to leave, and there is no risk that he will be a pursuer. Likewise, if a robber is discovered and surrounded by people who will capture him, so it is clear that he presents no danger to the owner,[126] then even though he is

---

[124] *Ibid.*

[125] Rambam, *Laws of Theft* 9:12.

[126] *Shulĥan Aruĥ HaRav, Laws of Bodily Damages*, topic 13.

still on the property of the one he is stealing from, he is not considered as a pursuer, and it is forbidden to kill him.[127]

If a robber stole and the house owner is chasing him to retrieve his money or belongings, the owner is permitted to strike the robber to retrieve his stolen property (as will be explained in topic 6:10), but it is forbidden to kill the robber in order to get back what was stolen.[128]

Also, if witnesses catch a robber in the act of entering a house to steal, it can be assumed that the person will not go ahead and steal, if doing so would make him liable to capital punishment from the court system.[129] Nevertheless, if it is clear that he is not paying heed to the witnesses, and he continues with his intentions, he is considered a pursuer and it is permitted to kill him.

15. Within Torah Law, even one who pursues *unintentionally* has the status of a pursuer. The person in danger of being killed by the pursuer may act to save himself, and he may kill the pursuer if this is the only way.[130] It is clear that this also applies to one who is forced to pursue another; he still has the legal status of a pursuer, and the pursued person may save himself, or another person may save him. If there is no other way, the pursuer may be killed.[131]

(Even though we have written in topics 2:4-5 that it is forbidden to kill another person in order to save one's own life, because of the principle, "Who says that your blood is redder than that of your fellow?" – that is only if the other person is not pursuing him; rather, it applies when others are telling him that if he does not commit that murder, they will kill him. However, if one is in a situation such that if he does not kill a person who is unknowingly putting his life in danger, he himself will be killed, then he is considered to be pursued (and the

---

127 Rambam, *Laws of Theft* 9:11.

128 *Shulĥan Aruĥ HaRav, ibid.*

129 *Maggid Mishneh* and *Shulĥan Aruĥ HaRav, ibid.*

130 This can be learned from the case of a woman whose life is threatened in childbirth, because the fetus surely has no intention to murder; see *Tiferet Yisrael Boaz*, Tractate *Ohalot*, end of ch. 7.

131 This can be learned from the law regarding a woman in mortal danger from childbirth. The fetus may be taken from her womb to save her, even if it will certainly kill the fetus. See *Minĥat Ĥinuĥ* Commandment 296, part 26.

other person has unwittingly become a pursuer). If necessary, he may save himself by killing the pursuer, even though the pursuer is not intentionally endangering him.)

16. Therefore, this will apply if one is driving in a highway full of fast-moving cars, where it is not possible to stop suddenly or move to the right or left without causing a serious accident, and a person on foot suddenly moves into the middle of the highway lane. If a fatal accident will probably occur if the approaching driver suddenly stops or swerves, it is permissible for the driver to continue forward and fatally strike the person who is suddenly in his lane, because that person is considered to be a pursuer.[132]

If one is driving on a road and a pedestrian is suddenly encountered in the car's lane, the pedestrian is not considered to be a pursuer if the driver *can* stop or swerve without causing a fatal accident. In this case, the driver is forbidden to strike the pedestrian, and must do everything possible to avoid this, even if he will have to crash his car by swerving off the road and thereby suffer a nonfatal injury.

---

[132] Rabbi Zalman Nehemiah Goldberg comments that the concept introduced here is that a person can be considered a pursuer due to his life-threatening inaction, if he is not taking the needed action to prevent the death of the one whose life is endangered because of his presence in a certain location (e.g., a pedestrian who moves into a lane of fast-moving heavy traffic and stops there).

It is possible that the person only came to be a pursuer by default, because of his own action of placing himself in this situation.

This can be compared to one who illegally enters a full boat that cannot take his additional weight and starts to sink. If the rightful occupants on the boat are in danger of drowning, they may throw him off since he is considered a pursuer; see Rema *Ĥoshen Mishpat* 380:4. Although in the case of the pedestrian, the person's very existence in that spot is making him into a pursuer, it appears that there is no difference.

The author adds that it can also be explained that in this situation, one may act "in the way that the world is regularly run." For example, just as one cannot save a fetus at the expense of the mother's life, so too, one cannot make the driver on the busy highway liable for preserving his own life in an expected way, despite the fact that his decision not to act (i.e., not to abruptly stop or swerve on the fast-moving crowded highway) will cause the pedestrian's death. (See *Tzitz Eliezer* vol. 15, ch. 70.)

In some situations, a person may be legally driving a vehicle in an area where others have equal rights to be present on foot, and the driver is required to be alert for others who might come into his path. (This could apply, for example, to someone driving an off-road motorcycle or a snowmobile in a wilderness area.) In this case, the driver has no right to drive over and possibly fatally injure a pedestrian whom he encounters suddenly in his path, even though he may have to sacrifice his own life to avoid the collision, because the pedestrian in this case is not a pursuer, any more than the driver is. So this reverts to the principle of "who says your blood is redder than his."

17. In any case where there is a chance, a person should try to warn the intentional or unintentional pursuer and stop him without physical intervention. If this is not possible, he may intervene physically to save the one who is being pursued.[133]

See topic 3 above, that if a person can save the pursued by hurting the limbs of the pursuer, and yet he kills the pursuer, he is a murderer.

18. Anyone who kills a pursuer in a permissible way should not be sentenced or fined at all by a court, since he has no liability.

19. In any case in which an onlooker (a rescuer) tries to permissibly save the victim by killing the pursuer, but the pursuer overpowers and kills the rescuer, he is liable for this as a murderer. The pursuer is not considered as one who is being pursued, since he should have desisted from his forbidden action of pursuing his victim.[134]

---

[133] *Tur*, *Shulĥan Aruĥ Ĥoshen Mishpat* ch. 425, and Rambam, *Laws of Murderers* 1:7.

[134] *Mishneh LiMeleĥ* on Rambam, *Laws of Murderers*, ch. 1; *Minĥat Ĥinuĥ* Commandment 600. It is clear that we are referring to a case in which the pursuer knows that the rescuer is attacking him in order to rescue the pursued person. But if the pursuer is unsure about why this person (the rescuer) is coming to kill him, he is not liable to capital punishment for defending himself by killing the rescuer (as might be the case, for example, if a person is judged as a pursuer at all times because he repeatedly hires others to kill, as explained in topic 1:8.)

20. If a sick person is *actively requesting* to be killed in order to alleviate his physical suffering, even though it is forbidden to listen to him (see topic 1:17), anyone who comes to fulfill this requested euthanasia is not considered a pursuer and it is forbidden to kill him, since the suffering sick person is expressing his desire not to be saved.[135] Therefore, anyone who kills the "mercy killer" to prevent this from happening is a murderer, and is liable for capital punishment (as is the "mercy killer" if he commits the euthanasia, which is forbidden).

21. One who is about to commit suicide is not considered to be a pursuer; although he is liable in God's judgment for committing a capital sin, he is like any sinner who may not be prevented through murder from sinning, as explained in topic 9. It appears that it is also forbidden to harm his limbs in order to save his life.[136]

(It is clear that if the person has become mentally ill and is endangering his own life, he is not considered as one who is liable for committing suicide, and it is an obligation to save his life, like that of any other sick person.)

22. The Torah laws regarding murder in time of war are discussed in *Sheva Mitzvot HaShem*, Volume 3 *(Dinim)*, Chapter 16.

---

[135] See *Minĥat Ĥinuĥ* Commandment 34, section 13, which debates whether (within the Torah Law for Jews) one may kill a pursuer if the pursued person wishes to die. It appears that for Gentiles, saving a pursued person is a morally based concept that has a non-incumbent nature, so there is no permission to kill the pursuer in this case.

*However, if the sick person is not conscious or mentally competent at the time, or is not able to communicate this wish for any other reason, and only expressed this desire for euthanasia verbally or in writing at some earlier time, then one who comes as a "mercy killer" may be a pursuer. In all cases, a mercy killer should be stopped.

[136] For Gentiles, for whom there is no commanded obligation of "do not stand idly by your brother's blood," it appears that they are not required to save someone who does not wish to be saved.

CHAPTER 4

An Accidental Killer's Obligation for Exile

A Gentile who *accidentally* kills a person has a moral obligation to pray for forgiveness from God, and to seek *kapara* (atonement and cleansing) for his soul from the stain of this accidental but grave sin that occurred through him, since he bears some responsibility. For if he had been more careful, this death could have been avoided.

As part of his request for forgiveness and *kapara*, he should go into a voluntary self-imposed exile from his place of residence.[137] This is the correct way, which applies in all places and at all times, even if there is no blood-redeemer[138] chasing him, due to the severity of the wrong that he has perpetrated. If he does not exile himself and he does not feel remorse and ask for forgiveness from God, God will punish him for the blood he spilled, even though it was done by accident.[139]

---

[137] *It seems that Gentile courts should teach this concept, and encourage one who killed unintentionally to exile himself from his city and his local friends, to a new place. See Rashi on Genesis 9:5, where he clearly emphasizes this point, and Tractate *Sanhedrin* 37b. It is significant that God imposed exile upon Cain after he killed his brother Abel (Genesis 4:12). Genesis 4:17 states that after Cain went into exile, he "became a city-builder, and he named the city like the name of his son *Ĥanoĥ*." Thus we see that the exiled manslayer may settle in a new town, continue to raise his family, and pursue a career. If a teacher goes into exile, his students are permitted to accompany him, to continue receiving their education from him.

A further insight is given in *Vedibarta Bam: And You Shall Speak of Them*, vol.1, in the name of Rabbi Shmuel Pesach Bogomilsky: the name *Ĥanoĥ* is from the Hebrew word *ĥinuĥ*, meaning education. Through being exiled, Cain came to realize the debased state he had fallen to, and he understood that without proper education from childhood, a person may go astray and even commit the most horrific crimes. Therefore he gave this name to his son, and to the city he built, to publicize the obligation of educating one's children from infancy about right and wrong, and that one should be active in support of a morally proper education for all the children in one's city.

[138] *Torah laws of Cities of Refuge and Gentile blood-redeemers are included in *Sheva Mitzvot HaShem*, Part V, ch. 5. These are not relevant in societies today where the government laws forbid anyone to act as a blood-redeemer.

[139] See Rashi on Genesis 9:5; Rabbeinu Beĥaye on Genesis 4:12.

CHAPTER 5

Laws of Intentional and Unintentional Killing, and Killing Through Negligence or Under Duress

In this chapter, we discuss what is considered intentional murder or a nearly-intentional accident – for both of which the perpetrator would be judged as liable for capital punishment in a Noahide court – and what is considered a complete accident, for which a Noahide court would not give capital punishment. We also differentiate the situations of one who killed unintentionally but could have prevented the death (and therefore he should go into exile to atone for this act – see Chapter 4 above), and the case of one who commits unforeseeable manslaughter and is therefore exempt from all punishment or exile (and therefore a blood-redeemer[140] may not kill him, and surely no one else may avenge the death).

(*Sheva Mitzvot HaShem*, Part V, Chapter 5, explains the permission in Torah Law for a relative who a blood-redeemer to avenge the death of one who was killed by intentional murder, or by a nearly-intentional or clearly-preventable accident. It also explains the Torah Law that in the Biblical era before the northern Ten Tribes of Israel were exiled, a Jew or a *Ger Toshav* who killed accidentally, and was therefore not liable to capital punishment, received asylum in the Land of Israel through exile in a City of Refuge[141]).

1. There are four levels of intention for causing a person's death:

(a) One who kills intentionally from the outset. It is explained in Part I, Chapter 4, that in the Torah Law for a Gentile, if one would claim, "I had no knowledge that this action was forbidden, since I did not learn about that," he is liable for his deliberate action and is considered as one who sinned intentionally, and he is liable to be judged in a court of law and punished for his transgression. The leniency for one who

---

[140] *As it applies to the cultural norm in any society, application of this principle is subject to the laws of the ruling government. This is emphasized and explained in *Sheva Mitzvot HaShem*, Part V, Chapter 5.

[141] *See Numbers 35:9-28. The exile of an accidental manslayer in a City of Refuge in the Land of Israel was a means for his atonement.

never had an opportunity to learn does not apply for murder or theft, which are logically dictated (see Part I, topic 4:2). Therefore, a murderer who says, "I did not know that it is forbidden to murder," is still liable for capital punishment before a court of law, just as a murderer who acted intentionally.[142]

(b) A fatal accident due to such gross negligence that the liability is close to that of an intentional murder – i.e., if there was clearly a need for some precaution to be taken to avoid a fatal situation, yet it was not taken. In such a case, the negligent Gentile is judged in a Noahide court as an intentional murderer.

(c) A fatal accident in which a Gentile killed inadvertently, and without negligence, yet if he had been more careful and taken precaution to avert the cause of another person's accidental death, it could have been prevented.[143] In this case, he is exempt from capital punishment in a court of law.[144] Although a court should not apply capital punishment for one who kills unintentionally and without negligence, nevertheless, since causing a person's death is a very severe act, and this person did not take the necessary precautions to ensure the safety of the one who was killed,[145] he needs to atone for his action. Therefore, there are cases in which a person who murders unintentionally is obligated go into exile to receive atonement (see Chapter 4 above).[146]

(d) A completely unpreventable manslaughter, for which the outcome was completely unforeseeable in time for a person to take any precautions, and yet the death occurred through him; in such a case, he is exempt from any punishment.

---

[142] Rambam, *Laws of Kings* 10:1, and *Laws of Murderers* 5:4.

[143] *This level (c) includes one who operates a vehicle while under the influence of drugs or alcohol, and as a result of his impaired ability, he causes a fatal accident.

[144] Rambam *ibid.*, and Ramban on Tractate *Makot*, p. 9.

[145] Rambam, *Laws of Murderers* 5:4 ("a person must always take responsibility for his conduct"); Rashi on Tractate *Sanhedrin* 57a ("Whoever sheds human blood, even unintentionally, the Torah considers it fully murder. But Torah is nevertheless lenient [if the act is unintentional] and does not decree liability to capital punishment"); *Sefer HaĤinuĥ* Commandment 410.

[146] See also Rambam *Laws of Kings* 10:1.

2. Anyone who neglected to take necessary precautions, and thereby his actions caused a person to be killed, is considered as if the action was intentional, and the murderer is liable to be sentenced to death in a court of law.[147]

For example, if one intended to kill an animal, but instead he killed a person who happened to be in the place of the animal, he is considered to be an unintentional murderer.

However, if there was someone close by the animal originally, or it was in a place where there were many people, and he intended to kill the animal but instead he killed a person, this is close to an intentional murder, because he should have been more careful, in order to avoid killing any person. In this case, he is therefore liable to the death penalty from a court of law.[148]

If, however, there are not usually any people passing through an area, and therefore a person was not careful to look before throwing a stone, and on this rare occasion there was a person passing through and the stone killed him, then the person is considered an unintentional murderer and is not liable in court. However, it cannot be said that this was unpreventable, since the person throwing the stone could have looked or loudly announced what he was about to do.

If the person looked before throwing the stone, and did not see any passersby, and after throwing the stone, a person suddenly came into the area and was hit and killed by it, this occurrence was unpreventable.

---

[147] Any Gentile who kills with a near-intentional act is liable to capital punishment. Rambam explains this in *Laws of Kings* 10:1 and *Laws of Murderers* 5:4, regarding a Gentile who intended to murder but claimed ignorance of the prohibition. Tractate *Makot* p. 9 compares this to someone who should have been careful and did not take necessary precautions. This is also clear from Rambam, *Laws of Murderers* 6:5, who says that one who causes a death by not taking necessary precautions is considered as murdering intentionally. This is also written by *Aruĥ Lanair*, Tractate *Makot* 9a.

[148] See Rambam, *Laws of Murderers* 6:10; Tractate *Makot* 7b; *Tosafot* on Tractate *Makot* 9a; *Tosafot* on Tractate *Sanhedrin* 77b; and Meiri on Tractate *Makot* p.9. These all discuss a person who should have looked (to see if there was a risk of harming anyone) and acted to avoid accidental manslaughter, and therefore he is considered to be liable, just as if he killed intentionally.

Likewise, if one intended to kill an animal with a knife, and knowing that there are people in the vicinity, he took the necessary safety precautions, but in an unpreventable occurrence the knife in his hand slipped and killed someone, there is no liability for the action.[149]

3. It has been previously explained in topic 1:24 above that if one intends to kill a particular person, and then a different person happens to stand in the first person's place and is killed instead, or if one throws a stone into a crowd of people and kills any one of them – both of these are murderers and are liable to capital punishment by a court if convicted.

Therefore, it is logical that even if the second person came unexpectedly and took the place of the intended victim, the one who threw the stone is equally responsible, since the first action that was taken was one of intent for murder, and therefore he is liable to the death penalty from a court.[150]

4. Above in Chapter 1, it was explained that one who kills intentionally, either directly or indirectly, is a murderer. These two cases are likewise equal for unintentional murder. If one kills directly or indirectly by an act that is considered close to being intentional, he is liable to capital punishment by a court. If the act is completely unintentional, whether killing directly or indirectly, the manslayer is exempt from a court penalty.

Therefore, if one's actions directly cause a person's death (such as one who ties up another person and then places him in the sun to die of heatstroke or leaves him to die of hunger, and even if he only intended to make the person suffer), this is considered bordering on intentional murder. Even if the perpetrator forgot the tied-up victim, who subsequently died, there is still full liability, since a person must always take responsibility for his conduct. Therefore, the perpetrator is liable like one who committed intentional murder. Likewise, if the perpetrator tied up a victim with the intention to kill him by starvation,

---

[149] The details of this situation will be discussed in topics 11 and 12.

[150] Meiri on Tractate *Makot*, p. 9, regarding the Torah Law for Gentiles: any case in which an action starts off with negligence is judged as negligence, even if it finishes with unavoidable results.

and then was prevented from saving the victim who subsequently died, he is considered in court as a murderer, since that was his original intention (although circumstances occurred that kept it from being prevented).[151]

However, if there was no intention for murder, but rather only to cause suffering, and he was subsequently prevented from untying the victim who then died, this is comparable to unintentional murder, and the court does not give a sentence of the death penalty.

If one tied up a person in an area where the tide will usually rise and cover the person, or where lions are plentiful in the area and there is a significant chance that they will find and kill the victim, and the person dies from these predictable circumstances – even if the perpetrator merely did not take the necessary precautions to avoid the lethal situation, and even if he did not know these dangers were there – this is considered close to intentional murder, for which he is liable for capital punishment.

However, consider the case of a person who was tied up in an area where lethal circumstances *might* happen, but the perpetrator was depending on conditions being as usual in which a danger would not occur. If the lethal circumstances *did* happen, and they caused the victim's death, then the one who bound the victim and left him there is considered as having committed a lethal action unintentionally, and the court should not sentence him to capital punishment.[152]

---

[151] Meiri on Tractate *Makot* p. 9, *ibid.*

[152] *Minĥat Ĥinuĥ* Commandment 410 (part 9) states: if a *Ger Toshav* ties up a person before a lion (which is indirect murder), or in any case in which he killed accidentally, he should go into exile. A Gentile who murders intentionally (even through an indirect act) is liable for the death penalty (see above in Chapter 1), and therefore the same law should apply – he needs to go into exile.

See Rambam, *Laws of Murderers* 5:2, who writes that an accidental murderer did not need to go into exile if the victim did not die right away, because it is possible that some other cause brought about death (based on Tractate *Gittin* 70b; see *Tosafot* there.) It appears that the reference is to a Jew, who in this case would not have had to be exiled, and the point being made is that the blood-redeemer has no permission to kill him.

5. If a blind person throws a stone into an area where a seeing person would be required to look and take precaution (since the area is usually populated) and the stone killed someone, the blind perpetrator is considered to have acted in an intentional fashion.[153]

6. If one intended to hit and injure a person but not to kill him, but the blow did kill him, he is not liable to punishment from a court if his blow did not have the amount of power that would be expected to kill the person. (For example, he hit him with a small stone which a healthy person would not die from, or he hit him with his fist on a place on his body which would normally not bring about death). It is ruled that this was an accident, and that the victim did not die from the blow, but from another cause. Even though he intentionally hit him, he is not considered to have intentionally or negligently caused his death.

However, if the victim could have died from that type of blow, then even if the attacker only planned to hurt, but not to kill, he is a murderer and is liable to capital punishment, for the victim died by his hand[154] (for example, an attacker intended to hit the victim on his calves with an implement or stone which was not capable of inflicting lethal injury when used in that manner, but it was capable of killing if it would hit in some different place, e.g. the head, and it went unexpectedly onto the victim's head and killed him).

But in this case, if the attacker hit the victim on his calves (which would normally not cause a lethal injury) and the victim died, the perpetrator is exempt because his actions alone could not have caused death (and as explained in topic 1:7, one whose actions merely assist another person's death is not considered a murderer).

---

[153] See Rambam, *Laws of Murderers* 6:14, that a blind person (a Jew or a *Ger Toshav*) who killed by accident was exempt from exile, since this is considered close to unpreventable. Therefore, if a seeing person killed due to his negligent actions, so that in the Noahide Code he would be liable to capital punishment and would not go into exile, then a blind person as well would be liable to capital punishment for his negligence in not taking the necessary caution.

[154] See Rambam, *Laws of Murderers* 4:2, who calls this an intentional murder in the Torah Law for Jews (and therefore it is clear that the same would apply for Gentiles).

7. If a person hit a pregnant woman and killed (aborted) her fetus, knowing that the woman was pregnant, whether the intended victim was the woman or the fetus, the perpetrator is liable as a murderer. It appears that even if the person intends to strike with a force incapable of killing the woman, but clearly capable of killing the fetus, he is considered to have acted in a way that is close to intentional murder, and is liable. But if the person did not know that she was pregnant, and only intended to injure the woman, and yet unintentionally killed the fetus, there is no death penalty for this action.[155]

8. If an attacker hit a victim who then became sick from the blow, and expert doctors examined him and determined he would die from the injury, then even if the victim started to recover, but in the end he died from the blow, the attacker is considered a murderer and is liable to capital punishment.[156,157]

9. Even if one has permission to hit another person (see Chapter 6 below), such as a parent who may discipline a child, or a teacher who may discipline a student, this can only be a small blow in the way of rebuke and teaching. But if a Gentile parent hit and injured his or her child who then died as a result, or likewise for a Gentile teacher and his or her student, it is considered intentional murder and carries liability to capital punishment, because the person should have been careful.[158]

This is also clear from Meiri on Tractate *Makot* p. 9, who gives the ruling that for any unpreventable murder which is started by negligence, a Gentile would be liable.

[155] See *Minĥat Ĥinuĥ* Commandment 410, part 9: a *Ger Toshav* in Biblical Israel who accidentally killed the fetus of a *Ger Toshav* woman would go to a City of Refuge.

[156] Rambam, *Laws of Murderers* 4:5.

[157] See the last footnote to topic 5:4 above.

[158] See *Tosefta Bava Kama* 9:3: if the youth was hit more than he could bear, the father or teacher is liable, as it says in Rambam, *Laws of Murderers* 2:14. This is explained in *Tashbatz* vol. 3, ch. 82, that a teacher or doctor who *intentionally* injured more than is required to accomplish his permitted goal is liable to capital punishment.

For example, if a father is teaching a trade to his son, or a teacher is teaching a pupil, and from time to time the child is struck in order to make him behave and learn, then if the son or pupil is killed completely unintentionally, the father and the teacher are exempt from going into exile, since they were involved in carrying out the good deed of educating the child.[159]

(This could happen, for example, if the father or teacher mistakenly uses a larger stick than is appropriate. But in any other type of situation, one who strikes another without taking the necessary precautions against lethal injury is liable).

10. If a doctor who has official[160] permission to practice medicine was trying to cure an unhealthy person, and he gave a *generally-accepted* treatment for that particular medical condition but it unintentionally killed the patient, he did not commit unintentional murder. Rather, it is an unpreventable death, since he was correctly trying to cure the patient. Even if it is known that the correct medical treatment carries a risk of death (for example, surgery), the doctor still has a responsibility to try and cure the patient, and therefore he is not called a murderer if he correctly used the generally-accepted treatment.

However, if a doctor was directly using his hands on a patient to treat him, and as a result of the doctor acting incorrectly he killed the patient

---

[159] See Rambam, *Laws of Murderers* 5:6, who states, " 'to chop wood' – that is a permitted act; this comes to exclude a [Jewish] father who strikes his [Jewish] son, or a [Jewish] teacher who strikes his [Jewish] student… for they unintentionally killed while performing a commandment." It appears that this applies to Gentiles as well, since in such cases as these, they are doing a positive action that they are morally obligated in (although it is not commanded to them within Torah), and therefore when an accident is involved, it is considered unpreventable.

This also appears to be the opinion of *Tashbatz* cited in the previous footnote: a doctor who applied an accepted treatment, but it accidentally killed the patient, is equated to a father or teacher whose reasonable discipline killed the child, and therefore, a doctor – even though he is not obligated (by a strict Torah commandment) to help but is only doing so as a good action – is exempt if his patient is killed by the medical treatment. (See topic 10 which follows.)

[160] *Aruĥ HaShulĥan Yoreh De'ah* ch. 336.

(for example, if a surgeon incorrectly performed an operation), he has committed unintentional murder,[161] since he should have been more careful.[162] It appears that this only applies if he killed by using his hands.

In contrast, if a doctor administered a wrong medication and it killed the patient, it is an indirect murder (as explained above in topic 1:7).[163]

However, if a doctor who was not licensed (or there was a more competent licensed doctor available) caused death through a treatment he administered, then even if he only wanted to help the patient, this is an instance that began with his neglecting to leave the treatment to a certified doctor. Therefore, even if it is unpreventable in the end, he is liable to be sentenced for murder.[164]

It need not be said that if a doctor killed on purpose through a hands-on treatment, that he can be considered a murderer.[165]

11. What type of killing is considered completely unintentional, yet the one who killed should go into exile? This occurs if one should have been more careful and taken precautions to avoid the person's death.

There are three levels of accidents:

(a) An accident that is nearly intentional, since there was clearly a need for precaution yet none was exercised; in such a case, it has been explained that the one who killed is judged in court as an intentional murderer.

---

[161] See *Tashbatz* vol. 3, ch. 82.

[162] *Shulĥan Aruĥ Yoreh De'ah* ch. 336. The statement there regarding a Jewish doctor, "If it is known to him that he erred and killed, he must go into exile," means that he knows that he gave the wrong treatment. But if the professional assessment is that he gave a reasonable treatment, he need not go into exile. This is also clear in *Birkei Yosef Yoreh De'ah* 336:6 and *Aruch HaShulĥan ibid.*

[163] See *Tashbatz ibid.*, and *Birkei Yosef Yoreh De'ah* 336:7, who leave this undecided. Their discussion applies only to someone who did this intentionally; if it was done unintentionally, he does not go into exile.

[164] This is the implication of *Shulĥan Aruĥ Yoreh De'ah* ch. 336, which states "he is considered a murderer," and this is also mentioned in *Aruĥ HaShulĥan Yoreh De'ah* ch. 336.

[165] *Tashbatz ibid.*, and *Shaĥ Yoreh De'ah* 336:2.

(b) An accident that nears unpreventable circumstances, since the perpetrator was unaware that his actions could lead to death. Such a murderer is exempt from the death penalty.

(c) An accident in which one should have been more careful and taken precautions to avoid the murder, which then could have been prevented. (In this case, a *Ger Toshav* would be exiled,[166] as explained in *Sheva Mitzvot HaShem*, Part V, Chapter 5.)

12. The following example is given in the Torah (Deut. 19:5). If someone was cutting wood in a forest and didn't look to see if anyone was nearby, and when he brought the axe down to strike the wood,[167] the metal blade slipped from the handle (or the axe slipped from his hand, or it knocked out a wood chip that fell *below* the level where the woodchopper was standing[168]), and a person who was passing by was hit and killed, then the woodchopper is considered an accidental murderer. This is because people are not usually found in the forest, and therefore his lack of caution is not out of negligence (for which a person would be liable).

Nevertheless, since others are permitted to be there, and caution would have prevented the lethal accident, this is not considered unpreventable.[169] The woodchopper is completely exempt only if he looked around and shouted warnings to caution anyone who might be in the area, and then in an unpredictable accident, a person was killed.[170]

---

[166] Rambam, *Laws of Murderers* ch. 6.

[167] Specifically with a downward motion, and it need not hit the wood. If the accident occurs in this way, the woodchopper should go into exile.

[168] *Sifri Devarim* 19:5.

[169] This is based on the explanation of Deuteronomy 19:5 according to the Sages, in the Mishnah of Tractate *Makot* 7b. This is also the opinion of Rambam, *Laws of Murderers* 6:15.

[170] This is comparable to the law of one who sticks his head into the path of a dropped stone, as explained in the Mishnah of *Makot* 8a, and in this case, the woodchopper is exempt from exile. In any situation for which a Jew was exempt from going into exile because the lethal accident was unpreventable, a *Ger Toshav* would also be exempt, as implied in *Makot* 9a and by Meiri's explanation there (regarding one who killed accidentally by an upward motion of the axe, or by the chip flying upward).

However, if the woodchopper saw a person below the level of the area where he was chopping wood and did not warn the person at all, and one of the accidents described above happened and killed the person, this is considered an accident due to gross negligence. For this, the woodchopper is liable to receive the death penalty, since it was his negligence alone that caused the lethal accident.[171]

If the axe blade got stuck in the wood and then the axe fell down (not during the action of the woodchopper bringing down the axe to cut into the wood) and it killed a person who was below,[172] or if a chip of wood flew out from the chopping[173] and a nearby person who wasn't below the chopping area was struck and killed, these are considered unpreventable whether or not the woodchopper took precautions, and the woodchopper is completely exempt. The reason is because this occurrence is unusual and could not have been foreseen.

13. In a similar fashion, if a person breaks down a wall or throws a stone in a place where people are not expected to be found at all, and by an unusual occurrence there was another person there who was killed by this, it is considered to be an unpreventable occurrence, and the first person is exempt from punishment.

If there are people who occasionally walk in that area, though, and on this occasion there was someone walking by who was killed, this is considered to be fully accidental manslaughter.[174] And if it is a place where people are always found, such as a public thoroughfare, and the perpetrator did not take caution and killed someone, it is considered close to intentional negligence, and he is liable to capital punishment.

---

[171] For any case in which a Gentile is obligated to watch out for others, he is liable for capital punishment if there is a fatal accident because he does not do so, as explained in Tractate *Makot* 9a.

[172] This is Rambam's (*ibid.*) interpretation of the Mishnah of *Makot* 7b that states: "The metal blade slips off from the wood being cut" – meaning that the axe got stuck in the wood, and when the cutter loosened his grip, it fell and killed someone (as interpreted by Malbim on Deut. 19:5). This is considered as being unpreventable, because it did not happen during a descending chop with the axe.

[173] Rashi's explanation of Tractate *Makot* 7b, according to the opinion of the Sages. It is clear that Rambam as well holds that this is unpreventable.

[174] This is comparable to the case of a woodchopper in the forest.

If the person looked and saw that there was no one there when he threw the stone, and once he threw it another person's head emerged and was hit, the person who threw the rock is considered to have brought about an unpreventable lethal accident, and he is exempt.[175]

14. If one enters into the courtyard or store of another without permission, and the owner, who was working there at the time, accidentally dropped (or threw down, without looking) an object on the one who entered, and this killed him, the owner is not liable since he need not take caution about this, because there is no permission to enter.

On the other hand, if it is permissible for another person to enter there, but other people are only found there intermittently (as in a forest), the lethal accident in such a place would be considered fully accidental.[176] However, if people are found there constantly, the owner who killed is liable for not taking caution.

15. If someone is *raising* a barrel up towards a roof and the rope snaps, and the barrel drops on someone and kills him – or if a person is *ascending* a ladder and a rung breaks, and he falls on someone and kills him – it is considered to be an unpreventable murder (if he reasonably assumed that the rope or the ladder was in good condition and strong enough), and the person is exempt from punishment.

However, if someone is *lowering* a barrel or *descending* a ladder, he should be taking extra caution, since a heavy object is involved, and he is just guiding the downward pull of gravity, instead of concentrating his cffort to work against gravity (as when he is raising a heavy object). Therefore, if he or an object he is lowering drops and falls onto another person and kills him, it is deemed a fully accidental but preventable manslaughter.[177]

---

[175] Rambam, *Laws of Murderers* 6:6-9.

[176] Rambam, *Laws of Murderers* 6:11. (Rambam's phrase "if he has permission" refers to a case in which the owner had no idea that the other person entered, but since he is permitted to do so, the owner should have taken precautions. But if he noticed someone entering, this is close to intentional murder. This is also clear from Tractate *Bava Kama* 32b).

[177] See Rambam, *Laws of Murderers* 6:12.

16. Consider the case of a butcher who, while cutting meat, raised the cleaver backwards to gain more force to cut through a bone, and killed a nearby person who had permission to be in the butcher shop. If the person was killed by the force of the butcher swinging backwards, the butcher need not go into exile. But if the person was killed in the swing forward (including the upward swing from the back before the cleaver descends), the butcher committed a preventable accident (and should go into exile).

It is a general rule of the Torah that if the intended objective of the lethal action was a descending motion, even if it started with an ascending motion, the person who accidentally killed while doing this action should be exiled, to atone for not taking caution. If the intended objective of the lethal action was an ascending motion, even if it started with a descending motion, the person who did this action would be fully exempt, as this is considered an unpreventable accident.[178, 179]

17. A blind person who mistakenly threw a stone into a place where people are not commonly found, in a situation where a seeing person would have needed to go into exile to atone for this action, the blind person is exempt, since his blindness puts his act in the category of unpreventable error.[180]

18. Within Torah Law, one who killed his enemy by mistake did not have permission for protection in a City of Refuge, since it can be

---

[178] Rambam *ibid.* The simple interpretation of the Talmud in Tractate *Makot* 9a is that this also applies for a *Ger Toshav*, as Meiri says there as well.

[179] The rule is that if the objective of the lethal action was to achieve a descending motion, even if it started with an ascending motion, then the person who accidentally kills by this action should go into exile. The reason for this is because he should have taken caution at the beginning of the motion, due to the extra force he was about to put into the downward motion.

[180] Rambam, *Laws of Murderers* 6:14.

assumed that the killing was done intentionally.[181] This law refers only to exile in a City of Refuge, and not to judgment in a court of law.[182]

19. Wherever the word "exempt" is mentioned in this chapter, the reference is to an exemption from punishment in court, just as any other person who sins through unpreventable circumstances. In such cases, a blood-redeemer has no permission to kill the accidental offender, and if he does so, he himself is considered a murderer and is liable to capital punishment.[183]

---

[181] *Ibid.*, 6:10.

[182] In a court, this would be deemed unintentional manslaughter, for a Jew or a Gentile, since in this situation no more precaution could have been taken. However, the assumption is that there would be some degree of intention involved, for which going exile in a City of Refuge would not atone.

[183] *Ibid.*, 6:3.

CHAPTER 6

The Prohibition of Causing Personal Injury or Damage

1. Just as it is forbidden to murder, it is likewise forbidden to harm any person,[184] whether male or female, old or young. This applies not only to physical harm, such as wounding or bruising, but also to emotional harm, such as scaring, terrifying,[185] or embarrassing a person (for example, stripping a person in public). It includes causing suffering[186] in any way, and damaging a person through speech[187] (as will be explained in Chapter 8). All these types of harm are forbidden.

---

184 *Panim Yafot Parshat Leĥ Leĥa*; *Ĥidushei Hafla'ah* end of Tractate *Kidushin*; *Likkutei Siĥot* vol. 5, p. 146.

Panim Yafot learns this from Tractate *Bava Kama* 91b, which explains the verse (Genesis 9:5) "But, your blood of your souls I will demand ...," to mean that it is forbidden to injure another person. Although the Talmud *ibid.* rejects this claim, saying that murder is forbidden as a distinct form of injury, since its final statement is that injuring is forbidden, it is possible to say that this is the source for its exegesis.

Surely, the words "But, your blood (etc.)" imply that it is forbidden for a Gentile to injure another person or even himself, since this verse also refers to suicide. The explanation of this verse (from Rashi, Ibn Ezra, and Sforno – and see Part IV, footnote 34) is that although it is permitted for a Gentile to kill an animal for human needs, it is forbidden to kill a human for the same purpose. From this it can be learned that since even an animal, which is permitted to be slaughtered, may not be treated inhumanely by cutting off a limb before its death, then surely a human, whose murder carries liability to capital punishment, must not be injured. In other words, the prohibition against causing needless human suffering can be learned from the prohibition against causing needless suffering to animals (see Part IV, Chapter 7).

185 Tractate *Bava Kama* 56a; Rambam, *Laws of Injury and Damages* 2:7.

186 *Likkutei Siĥot* vol. 5, p. 147.

187 Rabbi Zalman Nehemiah Goldberg notes the following point.

In Chapter 8 below, it is explained that this is part of the Noahide prohibition against murder. It is logical that all types of physical injury can be likened to stealing, as we see from the *Tur*, beginning of *Laws of Injury* (*Ĥoshen Mishpat* ch. 378), and Rabbeinu Yonah on Tractate *Avot* (*Ethics of the Fathers*) 1:1.

One who raises a hand against another with intention to hit the person, even if he does not actually do so, is called a sinful person.[188]

2. These matters are a branch of the prohibition of murder, stated in the warning of the verse,[189] "One who spills the blood of man," since any type of harming is an offshoot of spilling blood, even if it does not result in the murder of the person.

Although a Gentile is not liable to capital punishment for harming another person without murdering, still, it is an obligation to penalize anyone who harms or causes suffering to another person. This transgression, and the details of this obligatory penalty, are explained in *Sheva Mitzvot HaShem*, Volume 3, on the Noahide commandment for Courts of Law *(Dinim)*,[190] and below in Part VII, Chapter 10, on the prohibition of rape.

3. A Gentile who maliciously strikes a Jew, causing even the most minimal damage, is liable to death by Divine punishment, although he

---

It is questionable if embarrassment can be considered like stealing, although the Torah obligates a Jew who embarrasses another to make restitution – even though there is no monetary damage (*Minĥat Ĥinuĥ* Commandment 49, part 38, leans toward the ruling that a Gentile cannot be liable to make restitution for causing another person embarrassment.) See Part VII, topics 11:1-2 and the footnotes there.

188 Tractate *Sanhedrin* 58b; Rambam, *Laws of Injury and Damages* 5:2.

189 Genesis 9:6.

190 See Ramban on Gen. 34:13, who holds that Gentiles are prohibited from injuring others because of their commandments regarding societal laws (*dinim* in Hebrew) and stealing, and therefore this is a capital prohibition. This opinion is initially cited by Ran on Tractate *Sanhedrin* 58b, but he finally agrees with Rambam that it is not included in the prohibition of theft.

The question posed by Ran (against Rambam's opinion) is that a Gentile who strikes a Jew is liable to death by the hand of God (Tractate *Sanhedrin* 58b; see topic 3 that follows), but according to Ramban, a Gentile who strikes anyone, including another Gentile, is liable because injuring is tantamount to theft; if so, why does Tractate *Sanhedrin loc. cit.* specify "a Jew"?

It can be answered that he differentiates between an injury that causes a loss of money – and therefore can be compared to the capital offense of stealing – and an injury that causes pain but no monetary loss.

is not liable to receive capital punishment in a Noahide court.[191]

It is also possible that Ramban sees extensions of two prohibitions in injury: murder and stealing. The difference is (a) where there is no loss of money involved, and (b) in regard to injuring oneself. The prohibition of murder applies even if it is self-inflicted, based on the verse "But, your blood of your souls I will demand," whereas one is not liable for causing monetary loss to oneself.

See *Ĥelkat Yoav, Kava Kashyata* ch. 18, who questions Rambam's logic, saying that there would be no need to instate a death penalty for killing a fetus if the penalty already exists for causing injury to the mother, which Ramban would compare to the capital sin of stealing. There is, however, a practical difference: where there is no loss of money, such as one who aborts the fetus of one's own slave, or a woman who aborts her own fetus, the only capital sin is the offense of murder.

See *Ĥemdat Yisrael Hilĥot Melaĥim* ch. 10, topic 47, who clearly holds that if there is monetary damage incurred with the injury, the perpetrator is liable for the capital offense of stealing, and that in this regard, both Rambam and Ramban agree. (The *Tur* and *Rabbeinu Yonah* brought by Rabbi Zalman Nehemiah Goldberg above in footnote 187 concur.) However, he is skeptical in regard to Rambam's opinion, since Rambam doesn't mention openly any prohibition of stealing in regard to injury.

See *Levush Ĥoshen Mishpat* ch. 378, which says that injury is considered stealing, but is different in its liability, as can be seen from the Torah Law that a Jew is not liable to receive lashes for causing injury, but he is liable to this if he steals. The understanding is that a robber actually enters into the other's property and gains from the other's loss, as opposed to injury, where the perpetrator has no gain from his sin. This reasoning is also mentioned in *Leĥem Mishneh* on Rambam, *Laws of Injury and Damages* 5:9. It can therefore be assumed that although injury falls within the category of stealing, it is not a capital offense for Gentiles.

[191] Rabbi Ĥanina in Tractate *Sanhedrin* 58b; Rambam, *Laws of Kings* 10:6. (Rambam mentions "idol worshipers," but it is prohibited for any Gentile.)

It is unclear, since there is liability to punishment from God for this, if one who kills the striker is exempt. *Or Same'aĥ*, on Rambam *ibid.*, implies that this is true. This is also the simple understanding of Rabbi Ĥanina's statement (in Tractate *Sanhedrin* 58b.), which is the source that teaches that a Gentile who strikes a Jew is "liable to death," as can be seen from the fact that Moses killed the Egyptian who was striking an Israelite (Ex. 2:11-12). However, Rabbi Ĥanina does not specify (*loc. cit.*) whether the liability is in a court of law, or from God.

4. Just as it is forbidden to harm another person, it is also forbidden to harm oneself,[192] as it says,[193] "Your blood of your souls I will demand." Just as it is learned from this verse that it is forbidden to commit suicide (as explained above in Chapters 1 and 2), it is likewise forbidden to harm oneself.[194]

The body of a person is not self-possessed,[195] and a person therefore has no right to harm himself without due reason, in the manner that one may do to his own property. Even if a person has given permission to another to harm him, it is forbidden for the other to do so.[196]

This also includes a prohibition for one to cause himself suffering for no reason, since the body is not one's own possession. But if there is a purpose in it, such as toil for making a living, it is surely permitted.[197]

[It is not considered there that the Israelite slave was in danger of being killed from the beating, in which case the Egyptian taskmaster could have been killed according to the law of a pursuer (see topic 3:1 above)].

See Rambam, *Laws of Injury and Damages* 5:3: "A Gentile who strikes a Jew is liable to capital punishment, as it states [Ex. 2:12]: And he [Moses] turned this way and that [and saw that there was no man], and he struck [killed] the Egyptian." However, Rambam, *Laws of Kings* 10:6, states "A Gentile who strikes a Jew is liable to death [from God] for causing even the most minimal damage. Nevertheless, he is not executed [by a court]." It is questionable why Rambam mentions this in *Laws of Injury and Damages*, and why he changes his wording. It seems clear that in *Laws of Injury and Damages*, he refers to the law that an empowered Jewish court could give the death sentence. In *Laws of Kings* 10:6, Rambam cites the rule that a *Noahide court* cannot execute a Gentile who strikes a Jew, despite his liability to death by the hand of God.

192 *Panim Yafot* and *Likkutei Siĥot ibid.* in footnote 206; see Rambam, *Laws of Injury and Damages* 5:1.

193 Genesis 9:5.

194 Tractate *Bava Kama* 91b, and as mentioned in footnote 206.

195 Tractate *Bava Kama* 90b; *Shulĥan Aruĥ HaRav, Laws of Bodily Damage* topic 4.

196 *Shulĥan Aruĥ HaRav ibid.*; *Ĥavot Yair* ch. 163; *Le'Or HaHalaĥa* (by Rabbi Shlomo Zevin), p. 318 *ff.*

197 *Shulĥan Aruĥ HaRav ibid.*

This is also the opinion of Rabbeinu Yonah in *Sha'arei Teshuva* section 3, topic 82, based on Gen. 9:5, "But, your blood of your souls I will demand ..."

5. It is only forbidden to cause harm in any way of disregard to the body. But it is permitted if done in order to heal or enhance the body – such as surgery done to heal a sick person, or even plastic surgery for purposes of beautification.[198]

6. A male Gentile may have himself circumcised, and a Gentile parent may have his or her male child circumcised.[199]

7. A father may use *reasonable* physical punishment (for example, a short spanking that inflicts no damage) to reprimand his children who

---

Presumably this is according to Tractate *Bava Kama* 91b, and therefore accordingly, this law would apply to Gentiles as well. Even if it is to be assumed that this is only a righteous behavior, and the verse does not give a command but is rather a support for this way of action, it is clearly morally logical and therefore binding for Gentiles, as explained in this work (Part I, Chapter 3) and by Rambam, *Laws of Personality Development* ch. 3, that one who afflicts himself for no reason is going on an evil path.

*For this reason, it is permitted to participate in sports that have a nominal degree of risk for injury, similar to different types of widely accepted work that have some risk, that many people will accept in order to earn an income. But if the aim of the sport is to injure another person, it is forbidden.

198 *Igrot Moshe Ĥoshen Mishpat* vol. 2, ch. 66 and 73.

199 See Tractate *Avodah Zarah* 10b for the story of the Gentile Ketiah bar Shalom, who circumcised himself. The Talmud raises no objections to this, implying that it is permissible. Also, Rambam, *Laws of Kings* 8:10, says that a Gentile man may take this upon himself. This can also be seen from the statement in Rambam, *Laws of Kings* 10:8, that the descendants of Keturah (who are obligated in circumcision) are intermingled with the descendants of Ishmael, and therefore all of their males should be circumcised. From this we see that the prohibition of physically damaging oneself (if there is no obligation or benefit to do so) does not apply in this case.

This seems to contradict the *Hafla'ah* (mentioned above in footnote 206) who says that Abraham did not circumcise himself until he had an express Divine command to do so, because of the Noahide prohibition of harming oneself – for if so, how could any male Gentile (other than the intermingled descendants of Keturah and Ishmael) be allowed to circumcise himself nowadays? It is possible that the answer is that any male Gentile may have a circumcision as a universal way of serving God, whereas before this commandment was given to Abraham, it did not constitute a service to God.

are minors (see the next topic for what age range this applies) in order to educate them, including to teach them to have good conduct, since this responsibility is placed upon the father. (In the absence or unwillingness of the father, the mother may assume this responsibility.) As well, if one's children do not listen to him, he may punish them physically to a reasonable degree – even if this is only for his [the father's, or her] own good at the moment – in order that they should learn to listen to him, since this is for the children's own good in the end. If the father's children are obeying him and respecting him, he may not strike them, just as he may not strike any other person.

Likewise, an orphan who is a minor, and is placed under the responsibility of a guardian, is considered like a son in regard to education. The guardian may physically punish him to educate and discipline him, in the same manner as a parent.[200] (However, since the guardian of an orphan does not naturally have the same love for the child as a parent would, he must take extra precaution against punishing the child beyond the limited amount that is needed for the child's own good).

8. A father should not hit an adult child, even one who is disobedient, since this may causes the child to rebel against him, and this is considered like "putting a stumbling block before the blind."[201]

At what age does this aspect of adulthood start? Some opinions say at 22 years,[202] while others say that it depends entirely upon the child's

---

This is comparable to what Rambam writes in *Pirush HaMishnah* on Tractate *Terumot*, end of ch. 3, that a Gentile can receive reward for his righteous actions. Therefore, at least for this reason, there is no prohibition against male circumcision because of self-inflicted injury. See also Part I, topics 3:4-5 and footnotes there.

[200] *Shulĥan Aruĥ HaRav, Laws of Bodily Damage* topic 4.

[201] *Shulĥan Aruĥ Yoreh De'ah* 240:20.

The question of whether or not the prohibition of "putting a stumbling block before the blind." applies to Gentiles is dealt with in Part I, footnote 83. However, regarding the actual ruling on the matter, it is clear that hitting an adult child is not considered education, and therefore doing so would be just like striking any other person. For both Jews and Gentiles, this is forbidden.

[202] Rema *Yoreh De'ah ibid.*

maturity.[203] If the child is already married, one should not strike him even prior to the specified age.[204] It is clear that it is forbidden to strike an adult daughter just like a son.

9. Likewise, a teacher who is educating a minor student, in a field of study or trade, may strike the student in order to teach him. Both a father who strikes his child, and a teacher who strikes his student, must do so only in a light manner without cruelty. To strike a child strongly or with cruelty is not the way of education, but rather anger and revenge, and it is forbidden.[205]

10. It is permitted for a person to strike someone who comes to harm him, if he cannot fend off the attacker in any other way. This also applies if someone comes to steal from him or damage his property, or if a trespasser enters his house or field without permission. It is permitted to strike the attacker, the thief or the intruder in order to protect himself or his possessions, if there is no other recourse.

However, if one can fend off an intruder in another way, it is forbidden to strike him. Likewise, if someone cursed or even struck a person in the past, it is forbidden to take revenge against him physically, since this is only permitted as an act of defense at the moment, and not for revenge.[206]

11. It is forbidden for a husband to cause suffering to his wife,[207] and it need not be stated that it is forbidden to hit her, since she was joined with him as a wife, not as a slave. If a man's wife is causing him intolerable suffering or cursing him, he should divorce her if he cannot refrain from hitting her or tormenting her to cause her anguish.

---

[203] Ritva as cited by *Birkei Yosef* on *Yoreh De'ah ibid.*

[204] *Pitĥe Teshuva Yoreh De'ah* 240:17.

[205] *Shulĥan Aruĥ, Yoreh De'ah* 245:11: *Shulĥan Aruĥ HaRav, Laws of Torah Study* 1:13.

[206] *Shulĥan Aruĥ HaRav, Laws of Bodily Damage*, topics 2, 3.

[207] *Likkutei Siĥot* vol. 5, p. 147, and p. 236 in the notes. If a Gentile *feels* seriously or chronically compelled to strike his or her spouse, the couple should seek effective marriage counseling or else divorce, since it is preferable to do so rather than causing ongoing suffering to one's spouse.

12. A master may not strike a servant who is slacking in his duties, in order to subdue him into doing a desired task.[208]

13. One who injured or embarrassed another, even with words, does not receive full atonement for the distress he caused just through the restitution determined by a court. His sin is only forgiven when he asks forgiveness from the injured person and appeases him. It is not proper for the person who was harmed to be cruel and unforgiving. Rather, when he sees that the person who harmed him truly wishes to seek his forgiveness, he should pardon him.[209]

---

[208] *Shulĥan Aruĥ HaRav, Laws of Bodily Damage* topic 4.

Rabbi Zalman Nehemiah Goldberg notes that it appears that if one sold himself as a slave, the master may chastise him physically, but only with a rod or a strap that will not cause bodily damage, as explained by Rambam, *Laws of Murderers* 2:14.

[209] Rambam, *Laws of Injury and Damages* 5:9-10; *Shulĥan Aruĥ HaRav Laws of Bodily Damage* topic 6, based on Tractate *Bava Kama* 92a, which records the story of King Abimeleĥ (Genesis ch. 20). He was obligated (and so instructed by God) to ask forgiveness from Abraham for abducting his wife. Clearly, this law applies to Gentiles as well as Jews.

CHAPTER 7

The Prohibition of Endangering Oneself or Another, and the Obligation to Save a Person's Life

1. It is forbidden to place oneself in danger, such as fasting longer than the body can stand,[210] or other types of endangerment to life or health.

It is likewise forbidden to place others in danger, or cause a hazard for the community, such as to dig pits and the like in public property, or to keep dangerous animals in an area where others frequent, since another person may be harmed through these actions. Likewise, a person is obligated to erect a fence around the accessible roof and porches of his house in order that no one will fall from them.[211]

A person must guard his own potentially harmful entities, such as a fire lit in his own property, or his animals such as cattle, from entering into another person's property and causing damage.

If one's bull habitually gores people (it has been witnessed goring people three times), and then it once again gores a person, though the owner does not receive the death penalty, as he did not take any direct action through not guarding his bull (see topic 1:7 above), nevertheless the court is obligated to give him a severe penalty for causing death through his irresponsibility.[212]

---

[210] See *Shulĥan Aruĥ, HaRav Oraĥ Ĥayim* 618:111, that one who fasts to the point of mortal danger violates the verse, "But your blood of your souls I will demand." Therefore, it seems that this law is a part of the prohibition against suicide, which is also binding on Gentiles.

[211] *Rokei'aĥ* ch. 366.

[212] See Rambam, *Laws of Monetary Damage* ch. 10, who holds that in the Noahide Code, the ox is not killed and its owner has no liability. However, Ramban, on Genesis 9:2, holds that by Torah Law, an ox of a Gentile that kills another Gentile must be killed, as it says there, "of every beast will I demand it."

It is unclear if a king or a blood-redeemer has permission to kill the animal's owner, since it is written (Ex. 21:29-30), "... the owner [of the ox] shall die, in that a fine will be imposed upon him ..." which means that the Jewish owner is liable to death by the Hand of Heaven, but he receives atonement through paying a fine.

2. Likewise, it is forbidden to give bad advice to a person, that will cause him harm, as it says[213] "Before a blind person, do not put a stumbling block" – meaning that if a person is "blind" in a certain matter, do not give him wrong advice in that area which would cause him to be unwittingly damaged.

3. It is an obligation on every person to save another person from bodily or life-threatening damage. If one sees another person walking in a dangerous area, he must alert the other person, and if one sees

---

Now, since in Torah Law, Gentiles do not have the rules of fines for violations of their Noahide Commandments, the owner should be regarded as any other murderer who is liable to death by the Hand of Heaven, who can be executed by decree of the king or killed by the blood-redeemer. And though it is possible to say that since a Gentile's ox has a more lenient judgment than the ox of Jewish person, so the owner also should not be liable, nevertheless, inasmuch as the owner did cause death through his negligence, it is logical that he is liable for death by the Hand of Heaven (and he can therefore be killed by a king or the blood-redeemer).

It appears that if there is no other recourse to protect oneself from this habitually dangerous animal, its owner is considered a pursuer and he may be killed so that he does not let his animal run free. It is clear that it is permitted to kill this dangerous animal (even though it belongs to someone else), since it is a danger to the public, as discussed in Part IV, topic 7:8.

[213] Leviticus 19:14, and this is logically prohibited.

Rabbi Zalman Nehemiah Goldberg notes that it is clear that the verse "Before a blind person, do not put a stumbling block," does not constitute a Torah-law prohibition upon Gentiles, as explained by *Tosafot* and *Rema Yoreh De'ah* 151, and Tractate *Avodah Zarah* ch. 1, that one may sell an item used for idol worship to a Gentile if there is no suspicion that he will use it in this function, and this is even permissible if it is known that he will sell it to a third party who will surely use it in idol-worship. In the comparative case for a Jew, there would be a prohibition on the original seller because of, "Before a blind person, do not put a stumbling block."

On the other hand, it is possible that it is even forbidden for a Gentile to give another person bad advice, because it can be considered stealing, since it can cause the person to suffer a loss. Misleading one to sin, however, does not constitute this prohibition, since the one who is sinning is responsible for his own actions. This is explained by *Aĥiezer* and by the Ponovizer Rav (Rabbi Shlomo Kahanaman).

another person drowning, he must attempt to save him in any way that he is able.[214]

The obligation is only to expend effort, but a Gentile is not obligated to spend money to save another person[215] if he will not be reimbursed. However, one is obligated to spend money to save another person with the assumption that it will be paid back, and it is obvious that one can use the victim's own money to save him.

One is not obligated to put himself in mortal danger to save another person.[216]

4. A doctor is obligated to heal his patients to the best of his capability, whether they are gravely ill or having a minor health problem, and he is permitted to charge for the money and time spent on treatments, and for his expertise. A doctor who holds back treatment (*for reasons other than a lack of reimbursement*) is an evil person. If the sick person dies because of this withholding of treatment, this is morally equivalent to murder by the standards of God and mankind. However, the doctor's lack of action should not be judged by a court as a capital crime;[217] see topic 1:17 above.

---

[214] This can be logically deduced from the law that permits one to kill a pursuer, which shows that it is a moral responsibility – and therefore, one which applies to Gentiles as well. This is also implied from Tractate *Sanhedrin* 72b, where it is explained, based on the verse Gen. 9:6 ("Whoever sheds the blood of man, by man his blood shall be shed"), that one is *obligated* to save the victim by taking the life of the pursuer. This obligation is included in the Noahide prohibition of murder. This logic can be found in *Ĥasdei David Tosefta* of *Korbanot* ch. 13, that it is a positive obligation deduced from the negative commandment that prohibits murder.

[215] *Shulĥan Aruĥ HaRav, Laws of Bodily Damage* topic 8.

Rabbi Zalman Nehemiah Goldberg notes that it appears that the obligation to expend effort to help another person falls under the category of returning a lost object (in which Gentiles are not obligated), as explained in Tractate *Sanhedrin* 73a and *Shulĥan Aruĥ HaRav ibid.*

The author responds that although it is true that this obligation and that of saving another's life are the two sources in this area regarding Jews, and they are both not binding for Gentiles, they are still obligations within the prohibition of murder, or from pure moral logic.

[216] *Shulĥan Aruĥ HaRav, Laws of Bodily Damage* topic 7.

[217] *Shulĥan Aruĥ, Yoreh De'ah* ch. 336.

5. If one overhears people planning to do evil to another person, it is obligatory to warn the intended victim, or to appease the plotters from carrying out their evil plans if possible (with words, or money on the condition to be reimbursed).[218]

6. If one is in mortal danger, it is permissible to save oneself by expending another person's money, but only on condition that the money or property used will be returned. If one is not in mortal danger, it is forbidden to save oneself from any disease or suffering by using another person's money or property without permission, even if reimbursement is intended. It need not be said that it is forbidden to save one's own money or property by expending that of another person.[219]

7. Just as it is permissible to save oneself by expending another person's money or property, it is likewise permissible to save a third party by using a different person's possessions.[220]

It appears that such an action with another person's possessions is permissible even if it is in order to save someone's limb that is not necessary for maintaining his life. This applies whether it is one's own limb, or that of a third person. For more details on these points, see Part VII, Chapter 4.

It appears clear based on moral logic (and possibly due to the positive aspect of the prohibition of murder, which is the obligation to save another person's life) that if there is no significant loss to the doctor and the patient has no money to pay, the doctor must save the patient's life, and otherwise this constitutes a sin of murder.

[218] *Shulĥan Aruĥ HaRav, Laws of Bodily Damage* topic 8.

[219] *Shulĥan Aruĥ Ĥoshen Mishpat* 359:4; *Shulĥan Aruĥ HaRav, Laws of Stealing* topic 2.

[220] See Tractate *Sanhedrin* 74a, which says that one who is chasing a pursuing attacker to save the victim and damages property in his chase is exempt, and that although by law he should be liable, such a judgment would cause that no one would want to save another person. This is written by Rambam, *Laws of Injury* 8:14. It is logical that it is no less permissible to save another person's life by a third person's money, than it is to save one's own life in this manner.

8. A person is not obligated to donate a kidney or another organ (even if removing the organ is not life-threatening) in order to save another person. This is a matter completely dependent on personal choice.[221]

However, to remove a heart or liver from a terminally ill person as a transplant for another person is fully murder, even if the donor will die in a short time. This applies even if the second person will also not live without the donated organ, since certainly there is no permission for one to save one person's life by taking another person's life.[222]

---

[221] See Responsa of Radvaz vol. 3, part 627, who writes clearly that one is not obligated to give up a limb to save another person. This is also written by *Yad Avraham Shulĥan Aruĥ Yoreh De'ah* ch. 157, who proves it from Rambam, *Laws of Marriage* ch. 10. See also *Or Same'aĥ Laws of Murderers*, ch. 7, and *Igrot Moshe Yoreh De'ah* vol. 2, ch. 174. Nevertheless, it seems that just as one may remove an organ to save one's own life, it is also permissible to donate an organ to save another person's life. This reasoning is cited by *Tzitz Eliezer* vol. 9, ch. 45, and vol. 10, ch. 25, topic 7.

This can be seen from Tamar's willingness to give up her own life rather than embarrass Judah – for if she could be permitted to give her life for his honor, it is surely permissible for one to donate a limb to save another's life.

Rabbi Zalman Nehemiah Goldberg notes that the proof from *Yad Avraham* is that one is not obligated to donate an organ that is necessary for life; but it may be obligatory to donate a kidney. It is also unclear if one must donate blood to save another; it may be obligatory, since it causes no loss to a donor.

*It is important for a Gentile to have a "Living Will," to be protected from euthanasia. The following is from a Rabbinically-approved Living Will text for Gentiles:

"Jewish Law to Govern Health Care Decisions: I am a Gentile. It is my desire, and I hereby direct, that all health care decisions made for me be made pursuant to Jewish law as it pertains to Gentiles as determined in accordance with strict Orthodox interpretation and tradition. By way of example, and without limiting in any way the generality of the foregoing, it is my wish that Jewish law as it pertains to Gentiles should dictate the course of my health care with respect to such matters as performance or non-performance of cardio-pulmonary resuscitation if I suffer cardiac or respiratory arrest; initiation or discontinuance of any particular course of medical treatment or other form of life-support maintenance, including tube-delivered nutrition and hydration; and method and timing of determination of death. If any question arises as to these requirements, I direct my agent to consult with __(name)__."

[222] *Igrot Moshe Yoreh De'ah* vol. 2, ch. 174.

CHAPTER 8

The Prohibitions of Embarrassing Another Person, Evil Gossip, and Talebearing

1. Just as it is forbidden to harm someone (as part of the prohibition against murder, as explained in Chapter 6), it is also forbidden to cause another person suffering through one's speech. This is morally and logically binding, as Hillel said as a summary of the *entire* Torah,[223] "What is hateful to you, do not do to your friend."

It is forbidden to humiliate or embarrass another person, even if only with words, or to call another person by a name that is embarrassing to him, or to tell him something that is embarrassing to him.[224]

The Sages said,[225] "One who causes his fellow to pale in public does not have a portion in the World to Come," meaning that (a) one is

---

[223] Tractate *Shabbat* 31a.

[224] See Rambam, *Laws of Personality Development* 6:8. It appears that all these precepts are a branch of the general prohibition of murder and harming another person, and therefore they apply to Gentiles as well as Jews. This is also explained by Rabbi Yonaton Steif, *Mitzvot HaShem*, p. 175, 490.

Rabbi Zalman Nehemiah Goldberg comments that there is no source which clearly shows that Gentiles are obligated by these Jewish precepts. It may be inferred from the story of Tamar, who risked her life so as not to embarrass Judah (Gen. 38:25), but perhaps she did so because Abraham, Isaac and Jacob and their families kept the Torah's Jewish commandments before they were given through Moses. A similar instance can be seen from Ezekiel 16:49-50: "Behold, this was the sin of Sodom … She and her daughters [the surrounding villages] had pride, overindulgence in bread, and peaceful serenity, but she did not strengthen the hand of the poor and the needy. And they were haughty, and they committed an abomination before Me, so I removed them in accordance with what I saw." According to the Midrash, one example of their abominations was the severe court-ordered punishment of a girl who violated their law against giving charity. Thus, because the people in the metropolis of Sodom forbade and punished acts of charity, they were destroyed by God (even though there was no Divine commandment to give charity). This question needs further examination.

[225] Tractate *Bava Metzia* 59a. See the responsa *Divrei Yatziv Yoreh De'ah* ch. 51, that it is possible to learn from the story of Tamar (Gen. 38:25) that Gentiles are forbidden to embarrass one another.

forbidden to insult another person with words to an extent that his facial appearance changes, and (b) this is punishable by God.

2. It is forbidden to go around gossiping about people, and this is described as talebearing – collecting information and then going from one person to another, saying, "This is what so and so said," or "I heard such and such about so and so," or "So and so said such and such about you," or "Such and such was done to you by so and so," etc. Even though these words may be true, this type of behavior destroys the world, for doing so has the ability to cause death and murder.[226] We can learn this from the story of Doeg the Edomite, who informed King Saul that the Jewish priests in the town of Nov had helped David. Saul was angered and killed all these priests (for which Doeg was cursed by David and died by the hand of God halfway through his natural life).[227]

3. A person who transgresses in this way is called a talebearer (a *raĥil* in Hebrew, from Lev. 19.16). The one who listens to his gossip is punished[228] – and more so than the talebearer – unless he sees that these words are recognizably true, *and* that it is necessary for him to hear the gossip in order to be able to guard himself or others from harm. (For example, one may listen to a reliable warning that someone is planning to damage him physically or financially.)[229]

---

226 Rambam, *Laws of Personality Development* 7:1-2; *Shulĥan Aruĥ HaRav Oraĥ Ĥayim* 156:10.

A proof can be brought for this from the verse (Genesis 37:2), "... and Joseph would bring negative reports of them to their father," which resulted in his brothers' plot to kill him. The simple meaning of the verse is that telling evil gossip is a sin (even though Joseph had a good intention for doing this), as can also be seen from the explanations by Rashi and Sforno there, as well as in the Jerusalem Talmud, Tractate *Peah*, ch. 1, p. 4a.

227 I Samuel, ch. 22; see also Tractate *Sanhedrin* 106b (explaining Psalms 55:24, that Doeg died at age 35, which was only half of his destined lifetime of 70 years.)

228 *For this reason, God provided a person with earlobes below each of his ears, to be able to quickly close off his ears from hearing gossip.

229 *Shulĥan Aruĥ HaRav*, *ibid.*

4. It is a terrible sin, and even more so than merely talebearing, to tell evil gossip (*lashon harah* in Hebrew), which is telling a derogatory thing about another person, even though it may be true. What is considered evil gossip? Any informative or derogatory statement that would cause harm to another person's body or possessions, or that would cause him anguish or distress if he heard those words, or if he knew they were heard by others. This applies whether or not it is told in the presence of the person whom it is about.

If someone made such statements in the presence of at least three other people, the matter is assumed to become public knowledge. If one of those three people later tells this to another person, it is not considered evil gossip if he does not intend to spread the matter and publicize it further.[230] But if someone made such statements before just a few or even many people, and he warned them not to speak to others about the matter, then any one of those people who he spoke to and warned still commits evil gossip if he spreads it further.[231]

5. The sin of one who listens to evil gossip is more severe, and it is punished more, than the sin of the one who tells it.[232]

6. Evil gossip (topic 4) and talebearing (topic 2) apply whether they are committed in speech or in writing.[233] Communication of derogatory matters about a person by any method is in the category of talebearing and evil gossip.[234] Similarly, if someone publicizes matters of evil gossip (verbally or by other means), without giving any details

---

230 Rambam, *Laws of Personality Development* 7:5.

231 *Sefer Mitzvot Gadol* and *Hagahot Maimoni*; *Shulĥan Aruĥ HaRav Oraĥ Ĥayim* 156:11.

232 Rambam, *Laws of Personality Development* 7:3.

233 *See topic 14 below regarding stories in the public media.

234 *Ĥofetz Ĥayim, Laws of Lashon Harah*, ch. 1.

*In our days, telephones, text messaging, email and the Internet make it possible to gossip instantaneously, from one end of the world to the other, and with great numbers of people. For this reason, a person must be especially vigilant to guard himself from giving over or accepting any type of gossip while he is using these electronic communication technologies. This includes not only communication by words, but also sharing pictures and videos that convey derogatory information about a person.

of whom this information is about, and afterwards he gives hints or signs about whom his gossip was referring to, he is committing talebearing or entirely evil gossip.[235] If he tells the gossip without saying whom it is about, but he knows with certainty that the identity of the person he referred to will become known as a matter of course, this is also evil gossip.

7. The prohibition of evil gossip and talebearing applies when it is the intention of the gossiper to harm another person's body or possessions, or to embarrass him with his words, or even when he simply wants to publicize a matter and he has pleasure from its denigration of others.

However, it is permissible to relate a prohibited or negative action committed by a person, to someone whom it is proper to tell, in order that he should be able to influence that wayward person to act in a proper way. This is only on the condition that it is told in a way that reflects his intentions for the good of that other person.[236]

8. Similarly, it is permissible to publicize the character of an evil person and his evil deeds, so that other people will be warned about him and will take care not be harmed by him, since the intention is to save others from harm.[237]

9. It is also permissible for a person to tell about a truthful matter in order to clear himself, regarding an evil action that others wrongly suspect that he did, even though he will be revealing something about another person. This only applies if he has no other way to clear himself except to reveal the truth about who actually committed the deed.[238]

---

[235] *Ĥofetz Ĥayim*, *Laws of Reĥilut*, ch. 1.

[236] *Ĥofetz Ĥayim*, *Laws of Lashon Harah*, ch. 4.

[237] *Ibid.*

[238] *Ĥofetz Ĥayim*, *Laws of Lashon Harah*, ch. 10, based on Tractate *Erĥin* 16b, and *Laws of Reĥilut*, ch. 5. [Tamar acted in an exceedingly righteous manner (more than was required) so as not to embarrass Judah (as explained in Tractate *Sotah* 10b), since it was fully permissible by Torah Law for her to say that she became pregnant from Judah in order to save her own life.]

For this reason, it is also permissible to examine and search out information about a specific person, to find out if he is honest or not, in order to be protected from trickery or when doing business with him in trade and business transactions or the like. Similarly, it is permissible for the one being questioned to give advice and tell things regarding the one whom he is asked about, in order to advise the questioner for his own good and to keep him from harm, because in any case their intention is only for the good of the one asking, and not to put down the one about whom they are asking.[239]

10. It is also permissible for a person to tell, in the presence of another person, about evil things that were done to him – for example, that someone stole from him – if it will help him to be able to bring a court case to save his money.[240]

11. We have explained that it is forbidden for a person to accept evil gossip, meaning that it is forbidden to hear these things. If one sees that someone is coming toward him to tell him such things, he should prevent the gossiper from saying them. If the gossiper will not heed him, he should walk away. But if he knows that the person who wants to tell him such things is faithful to him, he should first listen briefly to examine whether or not these things the person wants to tell are for his benefit – i.e., if this is coming as a warning to him so he can guard himself from harm, or to alert him to a problem he can fix, or so he can provide help for the person who is being spoken about. If this is not the case, he should refuse to listen to these words. Even if he already heard this tale, if these are words of evil gossip and talebearing, it is still forbidden for him to accept them, meaning to decide that these things are true, and to act according to them – for example, to now distance himself from the person about whom this gossiper spoke such and such. But if he recognizes that these words are true, it is permitted for him to be more careful in the future because of them.[241]

12. It is permitted to hear something even though it is evil gossip, if the

---

[239] *Ĥofetz Ĥayim*, *Laws of Lashon Harah*, ch. 4, and *Laws of Reĥilut*, ch. 5.

[240] *Ĥofetz Ĥayim*, *Laws of Lashon Harah*, ch. 10.

[241] *Ibid.*, ch. 6.

intention of the teller and the listener is to gather advice on how to make peace between people in an argument.[242]

13. It is forbidden to sit or stand together with evil gossipers, for most of their words are talebearing and evil gossip, and it is known that certainly this will very likely be included in their words. If a person was already compelled to be in a group of such people, and they are speaking such words and he cannot get away from them, he should not participate in their conversation at all. He should not show agreement or happiness about what they are saying, and he should decide not to accept any of their evil gossip or talebearing.[243]

14. Many forms of public media (newspapers, magazines, television, radio, Internet, etc.) publicize evil gossip and talebearing. It is permissible to read or watch them, even though one is hearing evil gossip and talebearing, because these things are already publicized and have became common knowledge (see topic 4). Nevertheless, it is not fitting for this to be a person's main interest and attention. It is only if the person saw or heard this by chance, and he did not go delving into the matter, that there is no transgression involved.

It is not even forbidden to tell others about gossip that was publicized through the media, but it is a bad trait to feel good about, or to feel benefited by, the failures and shortcomings of other people. Such a trait is unfitting for an upright person. However, it is forbidden to receive a subscription to a media publication if its main business is evil gossip and talebearing. Furthermore, these types of publications should not be supported.

If the publication's main business is not evil gossip or talebearing, but it includes these types of reports as interspersed minor additions, it is permitted for one to support and subscribe to such media. Nevertheless, one should protest the wrongdoing they commit by publicizing evil gossip. It is explained in Part I, Chapter 4, that whoever can safely protest a sinful policy and urge that it be eliminated is obligated to do so, in order to improve the opinions of others, and to improve the world.

---

[242] *Ibid.*
[243] *Ibid.*

CHAPTER 9

Reproductive Sterilization, Contraception, Emitting Semen "in Vain," and the Severity of the Sin of Murder

1. Reproductive "sterilization" refers to a surgical severing within the reproductive organs, which makes it impossible for the person to accomplish conception (the fertilization that produces an embryo). It is forbidden to sterilize one's self or someone else, because this is an act of destruction of the human body. This prohibition applies to sterilization of men and women, children and adults.[244] However it is permitted for a Gentile to use a medicine whose purpose is to promote contraception (i.e., infertility from the outset, so that conception does not take place), since this does not cause a physical destruction of any organs[245] (or of a fertilized egg). Likewise, it seems that elective female tubal ligation is also not forbidden for Gentiles, because this action does not irreparably destroy the woman's reproductive anatomy (and it can be reversed by a subsequent minor surgery).[246]

2. Sterilization may be performed if there are overriding considerations for safety or health. If a man cannot or will not be restrained from criminally forcing himself sexually upon other people, it is permissible for the court to order him to be castrated.[247] In any case, it is preferable

---

[244] See *Minĥat Ĥinuĥ* Commandment 291, that aside from the prohibition of sterilization, there is a prohibition of causing injury. Therefore, although most Torah authorities (following Rambam in this matter) say there is no prohibition of sterilization for Gentiles, they are nevertheless forbidden to do so in practice, by the prohibition of causing injury to one's self or others.

[245] See *Shulĥan Aruĥ Even HaEzer* 5:12, which states that a Jewish woman is permitted to drink a contraceptive liquid (and in our days, to take a contraceptive medication in other forms, such as birth-control pills), because she is not obligated in the Torah's commandment to "be fruitful and multiply," which is incumbent only on Jewish men. Accordingly, both male and female Gentiles are similarly not expressly commanded to do this.

[246] See *Igrot Moshe, Even HaEzer* vol. 3, ch. 15.

[247] This can be done for the purpose of safeguarding the man's potential victims from being sexually harassed by him.

to accomplish this with drugs, and as a short-term solution, the offender can be sedated with drugs.

If a woman will suffer greatly from pregnancy or in childbirth, and certainly if pregnancy will endanger her life, she is permitted to have herself sterilized. It is preferable for her to accomplish this by taking a drug, instead of resorting to a surgical procedure.[248]

3. If a man or woman has already undergone some type of sterilization operation, or if someone is naturally infertile, it is nevertheless still forbidden for the person to undergo any additional sterilization operations, unless there is a medical necessity.[249]

4. Transgender operations (sexual reassignment surgery, or SRS) – either performed to change parts of a man's body to a female form, or parts of a woman's body to a male form – are forbidden, at least on the grounds that this is a destruction of the body. (See also Part VI, topic 2:7, for the implications in regard to forbidden relations.)

Moreover, it seems that a transgender operation is also forbidden on the grounds that it nullifies and contradicts the purpose of creation,[250] just as it is prohibited because of this reason for a Gentile to cross-graft different species of fruit trees, or to cross-mate different species of animals. This is explained in Part IV, topic 8:15 and fn. 277 there.[251]

5. It is permitted for a woman to do an act that prevents pregnancy – for example, to insert a sponge or other contraceptive device into her

---

Moreover, for purposes of healing from illness, it is permitted to make incisions, operations, or other medical procedures upon a person, because of medical necessity. Castration of a chronic sex offender can be considered as medically necessary for him. See *Responsa Minĥat Yitzĥak,* vol. 5, sec. 12.

[248] See *Igrot Moshe Even HaEzer* vol. 3, ch. 12.

[249] This is obvious, because the sterilization operation would constitute a destruction of the body.

[250] *For that reason, it is also forbidden for an adult or a child to take or to be given gender-altering hormone drugs, that bring out physical characteristics of the opposite gender in a person.

[251] See *Sho'el U'Maishiv*, vol. 4, part 3, ch. 108, regarding the opinion that sterilization is forbidden for Gentiles even though they are not commanded to "be fruitful and multiply." This source presents a similar logic.

vagina in order to prevent conception from taking place. It is also permitted for her to perform contraceptive measures after relations to prevent conception from the outset, such as using a liquid douche.[252] But if conception has already taken place, it is forbidden to take any action that will cause her fetus, or her implanted fertilized egg, to abort, because an act of intentional abortion is included in the Noahide prohibition of murder. (See topics 1:10-14 above for more details.)

6. The Rabbinic authorities debate as to whether a Gentile man is allowed to spill his seed "in vain," referring to deliberate actions other than permitted intercourse. Some authorities hold that it is forbidden to do so on the grounds that this is likened to killing a fetus.[253] See Part VI, Chapter 5, for details of this rule.

However, when there is legitimate overriding medical need, for instance, for purposes of necessary medical testing, it is permissible for a man to emit semen by means other than permitted intercourse, since this is not considered to be a prohibited destruction of his seed, or wasting it in vain.[254]

7. No sin is greater than murder. Even those sins of the utmost spiritual severity, namely outright idol worship or cursing God's Name, do not entail destruction of civilization, and they are classified as "transgressions between man and God." However, murder is classified as a "transgression between man and his fellow man," and does constitute a destruction of civilization. Whoever bears the sin of murder without proper repentance is considered an absolutely wicked person (and he has no portion in the World to Come), and not even the sum total of all the Divine service and good deeds that he accomplishes in his life can outweigh the gravity of this sin, as it says,[255] *"A man that is laden with*

---

[252] See Part VI, topic 5:5.

[253] *Furthermore, it is an act that degrades the man's health for no constructive purpose (i.e., it is committed "in vain"). See Part VI, topic 5:1. In contrast, permitted marital intercourse between a husband and wife, even if there is no possibility of conception for whatever reason, is considered to be a constructive purpose for the man's emission of his semen.

[254] See responsa *She'ilat Ya'avetz* vol. 1, ch. 43; *Aĥiezer* vol. 3, 24:4; and *Igrot Moshe Even HaEzer* vol. 1, ch. 70-71.

[255] Proverbs 28:17.

the blood of any person shall hasten his steps unto the pit; none will support him."[256] And without full repentance and atonement his prayers are not accepted either, as it says,[257] "*And when ye spread forth your hands, I will hide My eyes from you; yea, when ye make many prayers, I will not hear; your hands are full of blood.*"

8. But if a murderer accomplishes a complete repentance for all of his actions, his prayers are accepted by God, and there is hope for him that he will be forgiven by God on the Day of Judgment.[258] And it is entirely fitting that he should go to the graveside of the person he killed, and ask the person's soul to forgive him.[259]

One who truly repents for this sin should make a complete repentance, including increasing his acts of loving kindness and his charitable giving, and providing sustenance to those who are poor and living in pitiful conditions. Perhaps in the merit of this sincere penitence, God will grant him life. It is also good for him to exile himself from his place of residence and his station in life, for exile atones for the sin of murder, as was explained above in Chapter 4.

---

[256] Rambam, *Laws of Murderers* ch. 4 and *Laws of Repentance* 3:6 – "[Unrepentant] spillers of blood have no portion in the World to Come."

[257] Isaiah 1:15.

[258] See Rambam, *Laws of Prayer* 15:3; *Shulĥan Aruĥ Oraĥ Ĥayim* 126:35.

See Rema *Oraĥ Ĥayim* 53:5, that a Jew who murders intentionally cannot lead the prayer services in a synagogue, even if he repents, since he carries a bad name [and the same would apply to a Gentile in regard to leading a communal prayer service]. *Mishnah Berurah* 53:22 rules leniently in this regard; therefore, it would seem that if he repents and later prays as an individual, his prayers are accepted.

(Note *Midrash Rabbah* on Deut. ch. 35, that "repentance [alone] atones for all sins **other than murder**, as it says 'Whoever sheds the blood of man, by man his blood shall be shed.' " Still, Rambam, *Laws of Repentance* ch. 1, writes that murder is one of the sins that repentance, the Day of Atonement [for a Jewish sinner], and suffering atone for during the person's life.)

[259] Tractate *Makkot* 5b, where it relates the story of Rabbi Yehuda ben Tabbai, and the explanation by Ritva on that section. Rambam, *Laws of Repentance* ch. 2, writes that if the person who one offended passes away, one should go to the deceased person's grave and ask forgiveness.

9. The sin of bloodshed is so severe that if someone kills just one person, it is as if he has destroyed the entire world. Thus does the Torah say about Cain, in reference to his murder of Abel (Gen. 4:10): *"The **bloods** of your brother cries out to Me."* It does not say *"the blood of your brother,"* but rather *"the **bloods** of your brother"* – meaning the victim's blood and the blood of the offspring he would have had until the end of all generations.

Therefore, God created the first man, Adam, as a lone individual, to teach that if anyone murders even one person,[260] it is as if he has destroyed the entire world, for behold, from one person (Adam) the entire world population was brought forth – including Ĥava (Eve), who was brought forth from Adam. And conversely, if someone saves one person's life, it is as if he has saved the entire world.

Another reason why God created Adam as a lone individual was to teach the value of peaceful relationships – that a person should not say to another, "My father is greater than your father," or other types of inflammatory statements. Also, God did so to refute the polytheists who would claim that there are many deities in the spiritual realms (saying that each of these deities created a primordial person).

Mankind produces many coins from a die and they are all similar, but the Holy One blessed be He, the King of all kings, creates every person in the image of Adam and Ĥava, and yet no two people have the same features, to teach us that every human being is significant in his own right. Therefore, each person should rightfully be permitted to say, "The world was created for my sake"[261] – that is, for the sake of the good deeds and the service to God and mankind that He sent me to accomplish in the physical world.

---

[260] This version is used by Rambam in his commentary on Mishna *Sanhedrin* 4:5 (see R. Kapach ed.), as explained in *Laws of the Sanhedrin* 12:3. This is the version in the Jerusalem Talmud, and *Avot D'Rabbi Natan* 31:2.

[261] See Mishna, Tractate *Sanhedrin* 37a and Rashi there; Rambam, *Laws of the Sanhedrin, ibid.*: "*Each* person is obligated to say, 'The world was created for my sake,' " (including Gentiles in this fundamental principle).

PART VI

THE PROHIBITION OF FORBIDDEN RELATIONS

Including Precepts Relating to Marriage, Divorce, Marital Relations, and Being Alone with a Forbidden Partner

This section explains details of the following seven prohibitions that are included in this commandment to Gentiles and its offshoots:

1. Not to commit sexual relations that are between a man and the wife of another man.

2. Not to commit sexual relations that are between a man and his mother.

3. Not to commit sexual relations that are between a man and his maternal sister.

4. Not to commit sexual relations that are between a man and a woman who had been married to his father.

5. Not to commit homosexual relations. An offshoot of this prohibition is not to engage in lesbian sexual activities.

6. Not to commit bestiality (sexual relations of a person with an animal or a bird).

7. For a man and woman not to have close physical contact that could arouse physical desire, if they are forbidden by this commandment to have sexual relations.

This section also includes details of the prohibition against spilling semen "in vain", which is an offshoot of the prohibition of murder.

INTRODUCTION

by Arthur A. Goldberg,[1] *J.D., B.C.P.C., C.R.S.*

Past Secretary, National Assoc. for Research & Therapy of Homosexuality

We live in a strange time, a time when moral relativism appears to be ascending and moral absolutes descending. The culture in which we live has created a world with an unprecedented confusion of values, accelerated by social changes occurring at a pace that would have been unimaginable even a generation ago. This new vision of morality (which, in reality, mirrors much of ancient paganism) is often rationalized as a virtually all-permissive, "anything goes" social system founded on a concept of universal "tolerance." Unfortunately, this concept of tolerance is, in actuality, simply a facade used to mask an agenda of sexual licentiousness.

Starting in the 1960's, this brash new vision – masked as either civil rights, diversity, or tolerance – has inundated western society with a barrage of propaganda and half-truths that are carefully designed to convince us (contrary to the weight of clinical evidence) that homosexuality, transgenderism, incest, bestiality, pedophilia, and many other sexual "freedoms" are simply alternative lifestyles that must be accepted as genetically predetermined and therefore entitled to the same degree and kind of protection as racial and religious diversity. However, such false messages run directly contrary to God's eternal truths and, indeed, our own common sense. By tolerating a permissive sexual agenda, we ignore at our peril the warning of the prophet Isaiah who said (5:20), "*Woe to those who speak of evil as good and of good as evil; who make darkness into light and light into darkness; they make bitter into sweet and sweet into bitter!*"

These admonitory themes are crucial in the area of sexual morality and the roles of sex, marriage, and the family within our lives. As explained in the Written Torah and Talmud, a main accomplishment of the sexual prohibitions is rejection of unbridled licentiousness that leads to the disintegration of society. History confirms what we learn from the Torah. The British anthropologist J. D. Unwin's comprehen-

---

[1] Author, *Light in the Closet: Torah, Homosexuality, and the Power to Change*, Red Heifer Press, Los Angeles, 2nd printing 2009.

sive and classic study of 5,000 years of history chronicles the historical decline of 86 primitive and civilized societies during that period. He found that "the regulations of the relationship between the sexes" are the very foundation of civilized society.[2] Unwin discovered (contrary to his personal philosophy and inclination as a social liberal) a distinct correlation between increasing sexual freedom and social decline.

This part of *The Divine Code* involves a number of precepts for Gentiles, including prohibitions of some specific sexual relationships, and precepts relating to marriage and sexual relations within marriage, categories of appropriate or inappropriate marriage partners, and divorce. As indicated above, these precepts of the Noahide Code are fundamental to an ordered society. It is also important to note that the One God commands fundamental sexual laws for all mankind, in all societies, Jew and non-Jew alike. Non-Jews who observe their laws of the Seven Noahide Commandments, as part of the Torah of Moses, have accepted the Written and Oral Torah as their moral frame of reference. The Oral Torah explains that these righteous people from all the nations have a share in the future World to Come.[3]

It is essential to understand the Torah sources for these laws in the context of their traditional meanings. *P'shat* is the plain meaning of the text, the foundation point of Torah study. Rashi explains that even the level of plain meaning must be based on both text and context, and does not always correspond to what a lay reader takes to be the literal meaning. Let us examine some concrete examples within the context of sexual morality.

(1) Lev. 18:22 is an oft-quoted prohibition involving homosexuality: "You [males] shall not lie with a man as one lies with a woman; it is a *to'eviah* (abomination)."[4] This verse unequivocally prohibits homosexual activities as an abomination to God. However, as explained by the Talmud,[5] the word *to'eviah* can also be viewed as an acronym for three other Hebrew words: "*to'eh, attah, bah*," which means "you have

---

[2] J. D. Unwin, *Sex and Culture*, Oxford Press, 1934.

[3] Rambam, *Laws of Kings* 8:11; *Mishnat Rabbi Eliezer*, sec. VI.

[4] As explained in the following chapter, the source verse that prohibits homosexual activity by Gentiles is Genesis 2:24, which obligates a man not to engage in any sexual activity other than with his permitted wife.

[5] Tractate *Nedarim* 51a.

been led astray." Read that way, the term *to'eivah* transmits an urgent spiritual imperative while simultaneously providing instruction and support for the redemptive process of growth. After all, if someone is led astray, is making a mistake, or is even deliberately transgressing, the Torah teaches that God provides a process to transform oneself and the behavior that needs correction. It is called *teshuvah* (repentance). What is *teshuvah*? It is an internal, transformational process in which behavior change becomes the desired outcome. It involves a rebirthing of the soul, a returning to the undefiled spiritual state in which the person was created, and a process by which a person undertakes a solemn commitment to live in accordance with God's will once it becomes known to him.

Understanding this imperative, Rabbi Shmuel Kamenetsky wrote a letter of endorsement in March 2000 to my organization, JONAH (Jews Offering New Alternatives for Healing – www.jonahweb.org), in which he stated, "Anything that the Torah forbids, the human being is able to control. Many times, additional professional assistance is needed to control these deviations, such as psychologists, psychiatrists, and Rabbinic authorities." In other words, those who have engaged in the acts prohibited by Lev. 18:22 can find help through the spiritual practice of *teshuva*h, combined with emotional, spiritual, and intellectual re-adaptation. Rambam explains[6] that *teshuvah* involves understanding and regretting a past failing, changing present patterns of thoughts, feelings and behaviors that came about because of that past, and resolving to do things differently in the future. The secular clinical methodology for overcoming homosexual inclinations and behavior (referred to as "gender affirming processes") mirrors the process of *teshuvah*. Jewish tradition teaches that a person retains the ability to transform him or herself and modify his or her thoughts, feelings, or behavior patterns. There is no blemish of sin that cannot be washed away, no spiritual wound that cannot be healed. Indeed, Torah teaches those who are emotionally wounded, ill, or distraught to heal through *teshuvah*, medical attention, and counseling. Thus, by understanding the deeper implications of Lev. 18:22 and the connection between *to'eviah* and *teshuvah*, we learn how God set forth a path of healing for those who have violated the prohibition of homosexuality.

---

[6] Rambam, *Laws of Repentance* 2:2.

(2) Lev. 22:24 concerns transgender activities. The *P'shat* of this sentence tells us not to offer to God that which has its testicles crushed, torn or cut, and further commands "neither shall you do these in your land." But there is more to understand. The Talmud in Tractate *Shabbat* 110b clarifies the meaning of "in your land" as referring not to the land of Israel (as one might assume) but rather to one's own body, making the point that no one may choose to be castrated (unless disease makes it necessary for preserving the person's life). It is clear that sexual reassignment surgery or a regime of hormone pills to change physical characteristics of one's sex are prohibited.

(3) Lev. 18:21 literally says, "You shall not give any of your children to pass through [the fire] for *Moleĥ* ..." According to the Oral Tradition, this commandment prohibits an insidious form of child sacrifice. Some suggest that the *Moleĥ* prohibition was inserted into the chapter on sexual immorality because this cult targeted innocent and defenseless children. Thus *Moleĥ* can also be seen as a symbol for the sexual or psychological abuse of children. Indeed a salient feature of both pedophilia and the cult of *Moleĥ* is the willingness to sacrifice the well being of a child for the sake of gratifying one's own desires. "Education" programs on sexuality found in our public school systems often explain and normalize alternative sexual practices, a process that denigrates not only the individual but also society as a whole. Children are supposed to be a source of blessing to the entire community. But if their innocence, their outlook, their hopes and their selfhood are sacrificed by the society in which they live, for the sake of greater sexual "freedom," then that society, in effect, sacrifices those children to a type of *Moleĥ*. Moreover, by defiling a child, the abuser attacks God's image that resides within that child (the child's soul), and violates the sacred responsibility with which we have been entrusted to honor and guard that image.

(4) In Lev. 18:24-30, the Torah expressly implicates the sexual immorality of the Canaanites as one of the main reasons God took the Holy Land away from them and transferred it to the Israelites: "Do not become contaminated through any of these [acts]; for through all of these the nations that I expel before you became contaminated ... do not commit any of these abominations (*to'eviot* in Hebrew) ..." When the Torah reminds us here that the Canaanite occupants of the land are being expelled because of their abhorrent sexual practices *that were*

accepted as normative by their society, we need to look further to determine what acts are included. The Torah refers to the same widespread manifestations of sexual excess and moral corruption that brought down entire peoples and cultures throughout history (some of which are documented in the Unwin studies spoken about previously). Hence the paramount importance of sexual moral standards and self-control. As the author, Rabbi Weiner, teaches in the following chapters, the prohibited acts and their offshoots include (but are not limited to): incest, bestiality, adultery, male homosexuality, female homosexuality (lesbianism), spilling male seed, fornication, and transgenderism (gender confusion).

It is important to note that the Commandments themselves are not open to interpretations that are divorced from the traditional understanding of the text. Unfortunately, certain parties have attempted to develop a new theology, one in which the *halaĥah* (Torah Law) is "liberated" from its moorings in Talmud and set adrift upon the rough seas of human whims and crafty rationalizations.

Reformist camps in many religious denominations have twisted the concept of traditional interpretations of the Written Torah into a purported license to liberalize, bowdlerize, and even delegitimize the Commandments as they see fit, particularly in justifying homosexuality, but also in supporting other sexual confusions. In other words, they seize upon the Talmud of the Sages – that was compiled by devout Rabbis who were skilled in deep understanding of the authentic Mosaic Torah tradition – as a pretext for reinterpreting the Commandments in an unauthorized way. They claim this "allows" them to innovate compromises with the "dictates" of our times.

The reformist approach is antithetical to every authentic Scriptural and Talmudic source. It involves self-deception and playing fast and loose with the Torah's text, tradition, history, and logic. This attempt to fashion a pro-gay and sexual-liberationist theology is exactly what the Torah expressly prohibits (Deut. 17:11): *According to the teaching that they [the Sages] will teach you and according to the judgment that they will say to you, shall you do; you shall not deviate from the word that they will tell you, right or left.*

The Torah does, however, explicitly recognize that the sex drive is one of the most powerful forces influencing human behavior, and it certainly recognizes how difficult it is for almost anyone to be totally free of illicit thoughts, fantasies, lusts and arousals (and how much more so in today's commercially hyped culture of sexual indulgence and exploitation). When unchecked, these drives adversely affect both the individual and the society in which s/he lives. The Torah acknowledges that all the sexual acts it prohibits are within the potential range of human sexual expression. It further recognizes that if left uncontrolled and unchanneled, as Unwin documented, the effect of practicing these prohibited activities is to bring civilized society to the point of disintegration and collapse, thus undermining the very purpose of creation. God therefore ordained and defined a controlled and beneficial outlet for such a powerful and potentially destructive force, and that outlet is heterosexual marriage. However, even here, within the sanctity of the marriage relationship, God prescribed specific sexual boundaries, as explained in the following chapters.[7]

In summary, it is evident that nowhere are the traditional limitations on Torah interpretation more crucial to society than in the area of sexual morality. It is for that reason that this section is so refreshing. It provides authentic Torah learning on true sexual morality as conceived in God's eyes, and the text is to be commended for its clarity and forthrightness. If these laws and obligations are followed, humankind will hopefully not *self*-destruct. God provided a rainbow as evidence of His covenant that He will not again destroy the world. The seven colors of the rainbow correspond to the Seven Noahide Laws – the foundations of a Godly and ordered society. But because God endowed mankind with free choice, there is the ever-present question whether a society will heed them – particularly the admonitions of sexual boundaries and proscriptions. These are set forth in this volume as a codex of laws involving sexuality. If Gentiles live their lives consistent with this Biblical framework of morality, then the rainbow can also represent a multilevel system of spiritual wholeness that enables them to live righteous lives and have a share in the World to Come. This then becomes the opportunity for a covenant between humans, and a basis upon which we can create a world of wholeness and holiness.

---

[7] The Noahide Code constitutes God's *baseline* for a just and moral society. A society that honors this Torah-based morality cannot support legislated or officially condoned acceptance of more permissive sexual boundaries. However, restrictions beyond these minimums may be instituted. See, for example, Chapter 4 regarding polygamy, and the minimum age for marriage.

CHAPTER 1

Categories of Sexual Partners and Acts that are Forbidden

1. Six sexual acts are forbidden to Gentiles as capital sins,[1] and an adult who participates willingly in any of these is liable:

(a) intercourse between a male and his father's present or former wife who is not his mother;
(b) intercourse between a male and his mother;
(c) intercourse between a male and a female who is another man's wife (i.e., adultery with a married woman);[2]
(d) intercourse between a male and another male;[3]
(e) bestial intercourse[4] in which a male person is the active partner and any other species of creature (male or female) is the passive partner, or in which any person (male or female) is the passive partner and a mammal is the active partner;
(f) intercourse between a male and his sister from his mother (i.e., his full sister or his maternal half-sister).

The five prohibitions (a) – (e) above can be learned from a single verse,[5] "Therefore a man shall leave his father and his mother and cling to his wife, and they shall become one flesh." Respectively:

(a) "a man shall leave his father" refers to his father's wife, according to the Oral Tradition;
(b) "and his mother" refers to the simple meaning;
(c) "and cling to *his* wife," but not the wife of another man;

---

[1] *These acts are capital sins by Divine decree. Intercourse in this context means penetration of one partner's vagina or anus by the head of a male partner's organ. However, any other type of sexual contact between these listed partners is also forbidden. A ruling government may forbid intercourse between other close relatives, or other types of sexual acts, if it is deemed beneficial for society. See topic 9.

[2] This is explained in detail in Chapter 3. The acts that make one liable for a capital sin are explained in topic 1:14.

[3] See Chapter 2.

[4] See topics 2:8-10. All manners of bestiality with any types of creatures are forbidden. Topic 2:9 explains that liability to capital punishment is not incurred if a male non-mammal is the active partner.

[5] Genesis 2:24.

(d) "to his *wife*" (*b'ishto* in Hebrew, which is feminine), but not to another male;
(e) "and *they* shall become *one flesh*," specifying human partners (for a man and woman combine as one flesh in a conceived child);[6] this excludes relations with domestic animals, wild animals, birds, etc., with which humans cannot conceive and become "one flesh."
(f) It is also written,[7] "... she is my sister, the daughter of my father, but not the daughter of my mother, and so she became my wife;" this statement by Abraham teaches that the Noahide Code forbids relations with a sister or half-sister from the same mother, and permits marriage with a half-sister from the same father.[8,9]

Although all the above forbidden relations that are referred to in the cited verse, "Therefore a man shall leave his father ...," are mentioned there in reference to "a man," the same prohibitions apply to women as well, as the verse concludes, "and *they* shall become one flesh," in which women are included.[10]

Therefore, a Gentile woman is forbidden to have relations with: her stepson (even after she is widowed or divorced from his father); her

---

[6] Rashi on Genesis 2:24; Tractate *Sanhedrin* 58a.

[7] Genesis 20:12.

[8] Rambam, *Laws of Kings* 9:5 and *Laws of Forbidden Sexual Relations* 14:10.

[9] Rashi on Genesis 20:12. It appears clear that the original source of this prohibition is not from this verse, since it only *informs* us through Abraham's statement that relations with a sister from the same mother are forbidden, but not relations with a half-sister who is only from the same father. *Margaliot Hayam* (Tractate *Sanhedrin* 58b, note 3) says that this detail was not originally given to Adam with all its specifications, which is the reason why Cain was allowed to marry a full sister. (There were twin sisters who were born with him and with his brother Abel, in order that the world could be populated through their children; see Rashi on Genesis 4:1.)

But the Jerusalem Talmud, *Yevamot* ch. 11, p. 62, says that the original prohibition of relations with a maternal sister is from the cited verse, "Therefore a man shall leave his father and mother and cling to his wife, and they shall become one flesh." The Talmud there discusses a question of whether the prohibition includes only a sister from the same mother (i.e., either a full sister or a maternal half-sister), or also a paternal half-sister. See the first footnote to topic 14 below.

[10] Tractate *Sanhedrin* 57b.

son; any man other than her husband if she is married; an animal; or her full brother or her half-brother from her mother. The same precepts apply to these forbidden relations for a woman as for a man.

2. A Gentile man is liable for relations with his mother. This applies even if she is not married to his father, or never was married to his father – for example, if he was conceived from his mother being seduced or raped by his father.[11]

3. A Gentile man is liable for relations with a woman if she has ever been his father's wife, even if she is not his mother. This prohibition continues under all circumstances, including after his father's death,[12] or after she was divorced from his father[13] (even if his father later died, or if she remarried and the relations would also be forbidden as adultery). The woman remains forbidden to him for her entire life.[14]

The designation of a woman as the "father's wife" applies only after she actually became married to the father (as marriage is defined in Chapter 3 below). In this context, the marriage bond of "husband and wife" between Gentiles is established when the father and the woman have normal sexual relations with the intention to consummate a marriage relationship.[15]

However, a Gentile woman does not become designated as the "father's wife" if they did not intentionally consummate a marriage bond through normal relations. This applies, for example, if they only

---

[11] Rambam, *Laws of Kings* 9:6.

[12] *Ibid.*

[13] Rabbi Yonatan Shteif, *Mitzvot HaShem*, p. 392.

[14] Based on the explanation in topic 1:14 below, a Gentile man is also liable for a capital sin if he has anal intercourse ("abnormal relations") with a woman who has been his father's wife (unlike the case of committing the sin of adultery with the Gentile wife of any other man by abnormal relations, for which a Gentile man is not liable to capital punishment; *all the other forbidden relations in topic 1 apply for either normal or abnormal intercourse*). This prohibition remains in effect, even after one's father's ex-wife remarried.

[15] Ramban on Tractate *Yevamot* 98a; *Sefer HaĤinuĥ*, Commandment 191.

had "abnormal relations,"[16] if they had normal relations only for promiscuity (but never for marriage), or if the woman was forced (by rape or seduction).[17] In all these cases, the woman does not become the "father's wife," and she is permitted to marry the man's son.

Any female domestic partner of a man's father has the same status (regarding forbidden relations) as a wife with a formal marriage contract,[18] so she would be liable for relations with her partner's son.

4. A Gentile man is liable for relations with his sister or half-sister from his mother in all cases (even if they do not have the same father), regardless of whether he or she was born from his mother through married, adulterous or promiscuous relations.[19]

5. A Gentile man is forbidden to have relations with his mother, or his sister or half-sister from his mother, regardless of whether either he or they are free persons, or if any of them have been enslaved. In all these cases, a man and his mother, his full sisters, and his maternal half-sisters retain their status as forbidden partners for sexual relations.[20]

Likewise, any of a man's sons are forbidden to have relations with

---

[16] *This is an expression for the act of heterosexual anal intercourse. For Gentiles, this act does not consummate a marriage bond, even if the partners have that intention.

[17] Rambam, *Laws of Forbidden Sexual Relations* 2:4 and 2:11.

[18] From *Parashat Derahim*, p. 7 and 20, a Gentile man is liable for adultery through relations with another man's "concubine," as he would be through relations with another man's fully married wife; see topic 4:10 below. (In Torah Law, a "concubine," or *pilegesh* in Hebrew, is a woman who establishes her home with a man and engages in marital relations with him, but without a formal marriage contract or a secular marriage license.)

[19] Rambam, *Laws of Forbidden Sexual Relations* 2:2-4.

[20] Tractate *Sanhedrin* 58b and Rambam, *Laws of Forbidden Sexual Relations* 14:17 and 14:19, imply that only for the Biblical category of "Canaanite slaves" in the Torah Law for Jews (see Exodus 20:20-21 and Rashi there), there is no status of family relationships or marriage. But any other enslaved Gentile is still bound by the Noahide Code, and has the status of relatives and marriage like a free person; see topic 3:11 below. (The *Midrash* that Shimon married Dinah after her rescue is discussed in *Sheva Mitzvot HaShem*, Volume II.)

any woman whom he ever married. This applies even[21] if the son, his father, or the woman were enslaved. (For example, if the father was married to a slavewoman,[22] as will be explained below in Chapter 3, she is forbidden to have relations with any of her husband's sons for the rest of her life. This applies even after the father dies, or after he separates from the slavewoman whom he had married, as will be explained below in Chapter 4.)

6. There are other sexual relations that are not in the category of capital sins for Gentiles, but they are nevertheless forbidden:[23]
- a full sister or maternal half-sister of a man's mother is forbidden to him (but a paternal half-sister of his mother is permitted to him);[24]
- for a full sister or maternal half-sister of a man's father, some Rabbinical opinions hold that she is forbidden to him[25] (but the main opinion is that she is permitted to him).[26]

A paternal half-sister of a man's father is permitted to him.[27]

7. The Torah Law itself did not forbid a Gentile man from marrying his daughter,[28] but this has been rejected from Biblical times as a disgusting practice.[29]

If a Gentile man divorces his wife or she dies, he may then marry her daughter from another man. In fact, a Gentile man (who is permitted within Torah Law to have multiple wives) may be married to a woman

---

[21] As can be inferred from the preceding footnote.

[22] *This is a term for an enslaved woman or girl (*shifĥa* in Hebrew).

[23] Some authorities say these are forbidden as abominations to God, though Rambam (*Laws of Forbidden Sexual Relations* 14:10) rules that they are permitted for Gentiles. (See footnote 72 below.)

[24] Ramban on Tractate *Yevamot* 98; *Shulĥaṇ Aruĥ Yoreh De'ah* 269:3.

[25] *Shaĥ Yoreh De'ah* 269:4, based on *Tosafot* and Rosh, who follow the stringent opinion of Rabbi Eliezer in Tractate *Sanhedrin* 58a.

[26] *Shulĥan Aruĥ Yoreh De'ah* ch. 269, based on Rambam, Ramban and *Sefer Mitzvot Gadol*, who follow the lenient opinion of Rabbi Akiva in Tractate *Sanhedrin* 58a.

[27] Tractate *Sanhedrin* 58b.

[28] Tractate *Sanhedrin* 58b; *Shulĥan Aruĥ Yoreh De'ah* 269:3.

[29] *Ramban* on Genesis 19:32; Rashi on Genesis 20:1.

and her daughter (his stepdaughter) at the same time,[30] but it is an abomination.[31] Within Torah Law, a Gentile man may be married to a woman and her granddaughter (from her daughter or from her son).

8. A Gentile man is permitted to marry his ex-mother-in-law[32] after his wife dies or is divorced from him. (If he marries a woman and her mother at the same time, it is not forbidden by Torah Law, but it is an abomination, as stated in topic 7 above). Within Torah Law, a Gentile man is not forbidden to marry his maternal or paternal grandmother.

A Gentile man is permitted to marry his uncle's ex-wife, his brother's ex-wife, or his son's ex-wife, if she was either divorced or widowed.[33]

Torah Law permits a Gentile man to marry his niece,[34] and to marry two sisters.[35]

9. The relations considered in topics 6-8 above are not forbidden for Gentiles within Torah Law, and they are therefore not liable to punishment for any of them within the Noahide Code. If Gentile societies see a need to impose upon themselves extra restrictions and enforcedly prohibit some or all of those relations, they are permitted to do so,[36] as explained in Part I, topic 3:10.

10. For every one of the forbidden relations that are capital sins, both

---

[30] Ramban, Rashba and *Nemukai Yosef* on Tractate *Yevamot* 98.

[31] *Sifra* on Leviticus 18:3; R. Yonatan Shteif, *Mitzvos HaShem* p. 398. See footnote 72 below.

[32] *Nemukai Yosef* on Tractate *Yevamot* 98.

[33] Ramban and *Nemukai Yosef* on Tractate *Yevamot* 98; *Shulĥan Aruĥ Yoreh De'ah* ch. 269.

[34] For this is even permitted from the outset for a Jew; see Rambam, *Laws of Forbidden Sexual Relations* 2:14, and *Shulĥan Aruĥ Even HaEzer* 2:6. From Tractate *Sanhedrin* 58b, this also applies to Gentiles.

[35] See Ramban and *Nemukai Yosef* on Tractate *Yevamot* 98, who prove this from the fact that Jacob married two sisters (Genesis ch. 29).

[36] See Tractate *Avodah Zarah* 36b and *Tosafot Sanhedrin* 56a. See also Rashi on Gen. 34:7 in regard to the rape of Dinah, and Ramban on Gen. 38:24 in regard to how Judah judged that Tamar should be executed (before he was told the true facts of the case). See *Likkutei Siĥot*, vol. 5, pages 147 and 190.

the man and the woman are equally liable.[37] This applies only to a partner who is of mature age, and who acts voluntarily. But one who is not of mature age or who is forced is not liable to punishment.[38]

A woman who is raped by a forbidden partner is not liable to punishment. In contrast, how could a man be considered forced to act as the active partner in sexual intercourse, because a male's erection only happens willfully (i.e., if the man desires the relations)? This can apply if forcers convince the man that they will kill him unless he has the forbidden relations (e.g., with a forbidden relative or married woman). The man is then being forced to do this; he is not required to give up his life to avoid it,[39] and it is permitted for him to submit to having relations with the forbidden relative or married woman. However, this only applies if the woman consents to have the relations, even if she is forced to consent on pain of death.[40] But even if the man is being threatened with death, he is *not* permitted to physically force the intercourse upon a woman against her will, even if she is not forbidden to him by Torah Law. Even if she is single and not a relative, the man has no permission to do so (since it would constitute forceful rape), even if he is being forced to do so with a threat of death if he does not (as explained in Part V, Chapter 2).[41]

The same applies if a man is forced to commit homosexual relations.

11. If intercourse with a forbidden partner was being physically forced upon a woman, but in the midst of the act (after he had entered her) she began to desire the relations, this does not make her liable for

---

[37] Tractate *Sanhedrin* 57b and Meiri there.

[38] Rambam, *Laws of Forbidden Sexual Relations* 1:9,13,14,17,18.

[39] Rambam, *Laws of Kings* 10:2.

[40] See *Minĥat Ĥinuĥ* Commandment 296 (section 4), that even though a Gentile man may have relations with a forbidden woman to avoid giving up his life, the forbidden woman does not have permission to voluntarily submit in order to save him. She is only allowed to submit if she herself is being threatened with death if she does not.

[41] Rabbi Zalman Nehemiah Goldberg doubts this ruling (meaning that if a Gentile man is being forced under threat of death to rape a woman, he might possibly be permitted to do so in order to save his life). This is discussed in Part V, topic 2:5.

punishment. For once the forced relations begin, it may not be possible for her to hold back from desiring it.[42]

This also applies to a woman who starts having intercourse by mistake (for example, if she initially thinks the man is her husband), and in the middle of the adulterous relations she realizes that he is another man. Then she is not liable, even if she allows the relations to continue (because she is the passive partner, and not the active partner). However, if a man was forced to have forbidden intercourse because he was already erect, or if he mistakenly thought she was his wife and permitted to him (and during the relations it became known to him that she was forbidden), then he should support himself motionless on his fingers and toes (so he derives no pleasure) until the erection is lost and then withdraw. If he does not do so, then his willful continuation of the act is not considered forced, and he is liable.[43]

12. It has previously been explained in Part I, topic 4:4, that Gentiles do not become obligated in their commandments, or liable for their transgressions, until they are knowledgeable, mature, and responsible for their actions. This age is a subject of Rabbinical debate. Some authorities say that this is achieved at 13 years for a boy, and 12 years for girl, provided that the person has developed at least two pubic hairs. Others say that it depends on the person's individual level of mental maturity, and even if the boy or girl has not yet reached this age (13 or 12 years, respectively) but is already intellectually mature, then he or she is obligated to observe the Noahide Commandments.

A practical example is seen in regard to marriage. A girl will be liable for the capital sin of adultery with a man other than her husband, but only if she has reached the age when she can become truly married according to Torah Law. Conversely, there is no status of true marriage for those who are minors according to Torah Law, since they do not have the maturity of mind to accept upon themselves a marriage bond. This is explained in topics 3:1-6 below.

It is fitting not to allow boys at the age of 13 or girls at the age of 12 (or less) to enter into marriage, as most people at those respective ages do not have the maturity to accept upon themselves a bond of

---

[42] Rambam, *Laws of Forbidden Sexual Relations* 1:9.

[43] Rambam, *Laws of Forbidden Sexual Relations* 4:11, and *Minĥat Ĥinuĥ* Commandment 35, state that this is not considered a mistaken transgression.

marriage, and it would be closer to promiscuity (even if a marriage was contracted).[44] Rather, a higher minimum age should be set by communities at which to allow and recognize marriages. This should be the age at which most people in that community can be considered as having maturity and responsibility for their actions. Nowadays this is usually around the age of 17 for boys and girls (sometimes slightly older or younger, depending on the country and the community).

13. It has been explained that a minor child is exempt from liability for violations of the Noahide Commandments. Therefore, if two Gentiles had forbidden relations and one was of mature age and the other was a minor child, the one of mature age is liable, and the child is not.[45]

Heterosexual relations with an underage child are only considered within Torah Law to be true intercourse with a boy if he is at least nine years old, and with a girl if she is at least three years old. If a child is younger than this age, the act is considered to be in a different category of sin than sexual intercourse.[46] Therefore, liability for a capital sin within the types of forbidden relations does not take effect for

---

[44] See footnote 129 below, which explains why the minimum age for full marriage (within the Torah Law for Gentiles) can be higher than the minimum age at which one becomes liable for the Noahide Commandments in general, since if a Gentile's marriage is not recognized by the society, then according to Torah Law it is not considered to be a full marriage. (I.e., if a society does not accept that a 14 year-old girl is old enough to marry, then if she becomes a man's domestic partner with or without a marriage contract and she then has relations with another man while she is still 14, they will not be liable as adulterers, since she cannot yet be fully married.) This follows the opinion of Rambam, who holds that within the Noahide Code, the marriageable age is also dependent on the decision of the society as a whole, together with the decision of the mature partners who wish to become husband and wife. This takes precedence over the wishes of a boy or girl who has reached maturity at a younger age and desires to become fully married. (These and related issues are covered in Chapters 3 and 4 below.)

[45] Rambam, *Laws of Forbidden Sexual Relations* 1:13-14.

[46] **Such an act is definitely forbidden, because it is a licentious fornication*; see topic 3:7 below. If physical or mental harm to the child is included, that is also obviously forbidden (see Part V). A society should enact laws to punish those who inflict sexual molestation on children, and to restrain them from having access to children if they are not rehabilitated.

heterosexual relations with children below those ages (three years for a girl, and nine years for a boy), and even if the other partner is above the age of majority, he or she is not liable for a capital sin for forbidden relations.[47]

14. All of the forbidden relations are prohibited for either normal or abnormal intercourse. Both of the forbidden partners are liable for their engaging in either manner of relations,[48] with the exception of the sin of adulterous relations with a married woman.

In the case of adulterous relations with a married woman, although abnormal intercourse is also prohibited, a capital sin is only incurred

---

[47] *Ibid.* As explained in *Sheva Mitzvot HaShem*, Volume I, Part I, footnote 92, the disagreement as to whether a child reaches an age of liability based on personal maturity, or if it depends on reaching a certain age, is only regarding matters that depend on intellect and knowledge. However, regarding physical capacities, such as whether the relations are in the category of true sexual intercourse, there is no difference between Jews and Gentiles; a boy reaches this point at age nine, and a girl at age three. This can be inferred from Tractate *Avodah Zarah* 36b and Meiri there; from Rambam in *Laws of Impurities Imparted by Sitting and Reclining*, ch. 2; and from Rambam in *Laws of Kings* 9:5.

This is unlike the opinion in *Minĥat Ĥinuĥ* (Commandments 35 and 190), which says that for Gentiles, forbidden sexual relations are like other forbidden things, that are not limited to a minimum time or quantity, and therefore liability for forbidden relations would not be limited by a minimum age; see the last footnote to topic 2:1 below.

[48] Rambam, *Laws of Forbidden Sexual Relations* 1:10; *Kesef Mishneh Hilĥot Melaĥim* 9:7.

Kesef Mishneh explains that the specific exemption is only regarding adultery with another man's wife. The prohibition for any other forbidden relations is from the verse "Therefore a man shall leave his father and his mother ...," which precludes *any* type of sexual relations with the forbidden family members. But the prohibition of adultery is learned from the continuation of the verse, "...and he shall *cling* to *his* wife, and they shall become one flesh," which specifies capital liability for intercourse with another man's wife only when it is in the manner of "becoming one flesh" (referring to the manner of conceiving a child, which is only by normal intercourse, and the Torah refers to this act as "clinging"), as explained in topic 3:1 below.

for normal intercourse.[49]

15. "Forbidden relations" (*giluy arayot* in Hebrew, which literally translates as "revealing the nakedness") between a man and a woman refers only to sexual intercourse by inserting the male organ into a female's abdominal orifice (her vagina or anus). Any other type of physical contact is not called the act of having sexual intercourse (i.e. "relations"). Nevertheless, all acts of sexual contact with a forbidden partner are abhorrent, and are forbidden.[50]

Forbidden *intercourse* occurs as soon as the male organ enters by a certain amount: the insertion of just the entire head (the thick part at the end) of the erect male organ brings liability for a capital sin, even if the male does not insert his entire organ, and even if he has not completed the intercourse or expelled semen into the woman.[51] But less insertion than this is called "kissing" of the organs, and is not

---

Regarding a man's maternal sister, this is unclear (because of the doubt as to which words in Genesis are explicitly presenting this as a Divine commandment). It may be that the prohibition of relations with a maternal sister is included within the words "... and he shall *cling* to *his wife*," to exclude, as well, a woman who is not fit to be his wife – namely, his maternal sister – and if this is the case, then abnormal relations with her would also not make them liable for a capital sin (since it is not "clinging"), even though it would still be forbidden. Or, it may be included within the words, "Therefore a man shall leave his father and his mother..." (since a man's mother and his maternal sister are in the same category for incest), and a man and his maternal sister would be liable for relations in either manner. It is stated clearly in *Kesef Mishneh* that the prohibition of relations with a maternal sister does not stem from the fact of her being unfit to be a wife for her maternal brother, but rather due to their being very close relatives within Torah Law, and therefore the prohibition must be learned from the words, "he shall leave his father and his mother..." See last fn. to topic 3:10 below.

[49] Rambam, *Laws of Kings* 9:7.

[50] Rambam, *Pirush HaMishnayot* on Tractate *Sanhedrin* ch. 7.

[51] Jerusalem Talmud, Tractate *Kiddushin* 1:1, as written specifically for Gentiles; this is the implication of Rambam, *Laws of Forbidden Sexual Relations* 1:10, that by definition, just the "kissing" (i.e., touching) of the organs by forbidden partners does not constitute the severity of a capital sin.

called actual intercourse in Torah Law[52] (but rather forbidden contact).

16. If a man has forbidden relations with a sleeping woman, or if a woman has forbidden relations with a man who has an erection during his sleep, the one who is awake is liable for a capital sin, and the one who is sleeping is exempt.[53]

Regarding one who is intoxicated, see Part I, topic 4:5, that one who has not reached the degree of intoxication of Lot[54] (who was unaware of his daughter's relations with him during any part of the act) is still liable for his or her actions.

17. If forbidden intercourse takes place when the man's organ is not erect – i.e. his organ is completely limp, such as might be the case when the man is very ill, or if he is impotent (either permanently or only temporarily) – then even if it is inserted into the woman's orifice by hand, the forbidden partners do not become liable for a capital sin through this forbidden act as long as there is no erection.[55]

A man who has relations with the corpse of a forbidden partner – whether a female, or an animal, or another male – does not become liable for the capital sin of forbidden relations.[56] (Nevertheless, it is forbidden to commit this act with any corpse. This certainly violates the sin of spilling semen as discussed in Chapter 5 below, and it is in the category of the abominations that are discussed in topic 1:15 above.)

There is no reason to differentiate between Jews and Gentiles in this matter; see also *Minĥat Ĥinuĥ* Commandment 35, section 12. However, Meiri, on *Sanhedrin* 57, writes that Gentiles are not liable for forbidden relations if there is only insertion of the head of the male organ (and not total insertion of the organ, for the word "clinging" in the verse would indicate a complete insertion according to that opinion; this would require Meiri to say that there is a disagreement between the Babylonian Talmud and the Jerusalem Talmud on this detail).

[52] *Rambam Pirush HaMishnayot*, *Yevamot* ch. 6 and *Sanhedrin* ch. 7.

[53] Rambam, *Laws of Forbidden Sexual Relations* 1:18.

[54] See Genesis 19:33-35.

[55] *Ibid.*, 1:11.

[56] *Ibid.*, 1:12; Rashi on Tractate *Sanhedrin* 78a.

18. Artificial insemination is the medical insertion of a man's sperm into a woman's womb. It is a subject of discussion within Torah Law as to whether this is permitted with the sperm of a man who would be forbidden to have actual relations with the woman, either due to their blood relationship, or on account of adultery if she is married to another man.[57] It is clear that there is no liability to capital punishment for the male sperm donor or the woman in this procedure,[58] because "forbidden relations" only applies to an act of two partners joining in forbidden intercourse.[59]

---

[57] The later responsa (*Igrot Moshe Even HaEzer*, vol. 1, ch. 10 and 71; *Minĥat Yitzĥak*, vol. 4, ch. 5; *Minĥat Shlomo*, vol. 3, ch. 78) deal with this for Jewish men and women, in regard to what might produce the birth of a *mamzer* (a Jewish child born from relations between specific categories of forbidden partners). This can also be referenced to Rashi's comment on the word "perversion" in Leviticus 20:12, that it refers to "… mixing of the seed of the father with the seed of the son" within the son's wife. However, all of this is regarding the Torah Law for Jews.

In contrast, a Gentile is only prohibited by the verse, "Therefore he shall leave his father and his mother, and cling to his wife…" But artificial insemination is not considered "clinging," since "clinging" in this verse refers to the act of normal sexual intercourse.

However, in the responsa of *Shevet HaLevi*, vol. 3, ch. 175, he writes that the injunction is that a child must come from a father and mother who are permitted to each other, and not from one man and another man's wife. He derives this from the verse, "Therefore a man shall leave his father and his mother and cling to his wife..." If so, then this applies to Gentiles as well (and according to this opinion, a married woman would be forbidden to receive artificial insemination with sperm from another man, although there would be no liability to capital punishment).

[58] *However, a man who donates his semen to a sperm bank by expelling it, but not in the process of intercourse, violates the prohibition of spilling semen; see Chapter 5. The later Torah authorities only permitted a man to spill his semen on a case-by-case basis for the purpose of needed medical testing. If a married couple is not able to conceive through normal intercourse, but artificial insemination is possible, the sample can be collected after they engage in normal intercourse (for example, with the husband wearing a condom, which is permitted for Gentiles; see Chapter 5).

[59] *Igrot Moshe, ibid.*

CHAPTER 2

The Prohibitions of Homosexual and Bestial Relations

1. A male is forbidden to engage in anal intercourse with another male,[60] whether an adult or a minor,[61] of any age.[62]

Both male partners in this transgression are liable for a capital sin if they are consenting adults (i.e., each is liable if he was not forced).

A minor boy who participates in this act with an adult male is not liable.[63] If it is the adult male who enters into the minor boy, the adult is liable to capital punishment regardless of the age of the boy (and regardless of whether the boy is a Gentile or a Jew).[64] However, if it is the minor who inserts his organ into the adult male, the adult is liable to capital punishment only if the minor's age is nine years or older. (If

---

[60] *All types of same-sex erotic contact are forbidden, as will be explained.

Anyone struggling with the emotional, physiological and/or psychological dimensions of SSA (same-sex attraction) is encouraged to read *Light in the Closet: Torah, Homosexuality and the Power to Change.* This book addresses 23 categories of "sexual brokenness," which are behaviors, desires or fantasies that are inconsistent with the Torah's designation of heterosexual marriage as the only context for intercourse that is blessed by God. It insists that no one should be denied the right to receive information on, and access to, the known effective means of gender-reaffirming counseling and treatment for sexual disorientation. It includes discussions of relevant Torah Law for Jews and Gentiles, and indicts the permissive (or even promotive) attitudes, found in many countries, about indulgence in homosexual relations.

Orthodox Rabbis agree that homosexual acts bring harm upon a person and that professional counseling should be available to help individuals overcome SSA; see *Siĥot in English*, vol. 30, p. 120-130. The National Association for Research and Therapy of Homosexuality (narth.com) works for the right of anyone with unwanted SSA to receive effective therapeutic treatment, and for the right of professionals to offer that care. Abundant information, including resources to locate participating local therapists, is available on this site.

[61] Rambam, *Laws of Kings* 9:5-6.

[62] Radvaz and *Kiryat Sefer*, *Hilĥot Melaĥim* ch. 9. Radvaz writes that this is learned from the verse Genesis 2:24, "and cling to his *wife*, and they shall become one flesh," which excludes intercourse with any other male.

[63] Rambam, *Laws of Forbidden Sexual Relations* 1:14.

[64] *Minĥat Ĥinuĥ* Commandment 209.

the male who inserts his organ is younger than nine years old, this does not fall within the Torah's definition of "sexual intercourse" with a male,[65] as explained above in topic 1:13, and neither partner would be liable to capital punishment for this sin.)[66]

2. A man should not seclude himself alone with another man who is suspected of desiring to commit homosexual acts, in an area that is not readily open to public access or view (either in a city or in a field), so that he should not come to a transgression.[67] Likewise, one should not let a male child or adolescent stay alone with such a man as his private

---

[65] *Needless to say, the legal system should still specify significant penalties for sexual molestation of minors, even if capital punishment does not apply according to Torah Law, as a deterrent to such sinful and morally corrupt behavior. See the comment to topic 1:13 above.

[66] *Minĥat Ĥinuĥ* (Commandment 209) differs, and rules that for Gentiles, no exemptions are placed on an adult's liability for acts of forbidden intercourse.

Rabbi Zalman Nehemiah Goldberg notes that the author is following the reasoning in topic 1:13 above, but it appears to him that in regard to Gentiles, there is a difference of Rabbinical opinion as to whether the adult is liable for capital punishment in this case of an adult male who is sodomized by a boy who is less than 13 years old, and therefore a Noahide court of law would not apply capital punishment in such a case, because of the doubt.

The author responds that Rabbi Goldberg's opinion is like that of *Minĥat Ĥinuĥ*. This opinion – which holds that if an adult (male or female) is entered into by a minor boy (less than 13 years old) for forbidden relations, the adult will be liable if the boy is nine years old or more – is dependent on the argument (mentioned in topic 1:12) among Rabbinical authorities as to whether the status of legal maturity for a male Gentile is necessarily reached at age 13. According to the opinion that the boy's legal majority depends not on his age, but on his intellectual maturity, the liability for forbidden intercourse in this situation should also not be limited to only apply if the boy is nine years old or more. Thus it could be possible that the adult might not be liable for this intercourse even if the boy was 12 years old, but still not intellectually mature.

See the author's explanation in footnote 47 above, that physical growth is not part of this debate, and therefore the minimum age for Torah-law status of sexual relations of a young male is equal to that for Jews (9 years old).

[67] Rabbi Zalman Nehemiah Goldberg says there appears to be no prohibition upon a Gentile of being alone together, unaccompanied, with a person whom he is forbidden to have relations with.

student, apprentice or worker, or send a male youth to a destination under his escort, because he is suspected of desiring to commit homosexual acts.[68]

3. Two men may not sleep in the same bed, and surely not two bachelors.[69]

4. It is forbidden for females to practice lesbianism, and this is considered an abomination, as it says,[70] "Do not perform the practice of the land of Egypt in which you dwelled; and do not perform the practice of the land of Canaan ..." The Sages explained the practices of the land of Egypt:[71] "What would they do? A man would marry a man, *a woman would marry a woman*, a man would marry a mother and her daughter, and a woman would marry two husbands." Thus we see that lesbianism is clearly a repulsive and abhorrent practice.[72]

However, we find (in *Avot DeRabbi Natan* ch. 1, *Mishna* 5) that Adam took on extra precautions, as we see that he told Ĥava (Eve) not to touch the Tree of Knowledge. (He only erred in not telling her that his precautionary enactment was not a Divine commandment). (See also *Avot DeRabbi Natan* ch. 2, Mishna 5, that Job took on an extra precaution not to look at unmarried women.) This needs further analysis.

[68] Rambam, *Laws of Forbidden Sexual Relations* 22:5.

[69] *Ĥelkat Meĥokek* and *Beit Shmuel Even HaEzer* ch. 24.

[70] Leviticus 18:3.

[71] *Sifra* on Lev. *ibid.*; Rambam, *Laws of Forbidden Sexual Relations* 21:8.

[72] *Sifra* and Rambam, *Pirush HaMishnayot Sanhedrin* ch. 7. But in that portion of Leviticus on relations that are forbidden for Jews, it mentions other relations that are permitted to Gentiles, and includes them all in calling them "abominations," and even says that the Canaanites were destroyed because they practiced them. If so, how could it be said that those other relations are permitted for Gentiles (including a Gentile man having relations with his father's full sister, or with a woman who had been his uncle's wife, his daughter-in-law, or his sister-in-law)?

There is a debate in Tractate *Sanhedrin* 56b as to whether we can infer that these are additional prohibitions for Gentiles, from the fact that the Canaanites were punished for them, and certainly they must have been warned about them. The Torah law follows the opinions that this alone is not a justification to say that Gentiles are forbidden in the acts mentioned there.

5. An androgyne (a person born with male and female genital organs) is considered a male in the context of homosexual relations, and therefore any man who commits anal intercourse with an androgyne is liable for a capital sin,[73] and the androgyne is likewise liable (regardless of which is the active or passive partner). If a man had relations with an androgyne into the vaginal orifice, neither is liable for a capital sin. An

---

Therefore, we also have no proof that it should be forbidden for them to have marital relations with those relatives.

It is possible to say that there are different levels in the abominations that the Egyptians committed. For example, the Torah teaches that if a Jewish man marries two sisters, he causes two women who normally love each other to come to hate each other, since they will be vying with each other for the closer relationship with the husband. This negative transition would logically be worse if it was perpetrated upon a mother and her daughter, and such an action would thus be an abomination for Gentiles, and it would also be this aspect of the action that the Canaanites were punished for. The other relations mentioned are of lesser abhorrence, due to this logic, and therefore would only be forbidden to Jews (since they must conduct themselves in a more holy manner than Gentiles), but they would be permitted to Gentiles.

Ibn Ezra (on Leviticus 18:26 and Deuteronomy 31:16) says that these actions are especially forbidden as abominations in the Land of Israel, which has a higher degree of holiness, and this is why the Canaanites who lived there and practiced them were judged more harshly and punished for them. However, this cannot be the only reason to forbid them, since the verse says (Leviticus 18:3), "Do not perform the practice of the land of *Egypt* …," and equates those with the abominations practiced by the Canaanites, as the *Sifra* cited above relates that these were originally the actions of the Egyptians.

An additional explanation is that God punished the Canaanites for making these abominations into "abominable legal statutes" (Leviticus 18:30), meaning that they were set up as statute laws, causing two sisters to marry one man, even contrary to their natural sibling affection, and this is an abhorrent standard. This is also implied from the words of the *Sifra* there: "… in the statutes that they set for themselves and their ancestors; and what did they do? A man would marry … a mother and her daughter." This is unlike a case in which a man and two sisters (or another pair of women who would be forbidden together for a Jewish husband under scriptural law, but allowed for a Gentile) would agree to live together in the manner of a polygamous marriage, when it is not forbidden by the Noahide Code. As an isolated case, this *in itself* would not be called an "abomination" for Gentiles.

[73] Rambam, *Laws of Forbidden Sexual Relations* 1:15; *Sefer HaĤinuĥ* Commandment 209. ("Androgyne" is the Talmudic term for hermaphrodite.)

androgyne may marry a woman.[74]

6. [A person whose gender is not yet know, because the genitals are covered over with a mass of flesh, is called a *tumtum* in Hebrew.] A man who commits anal intercourse upon a *tumtum* is not liable, if it is not yet know whether the *tumtum* is a female or male.[75] (If this *tumtum* was the man's sibling from his mother, he is liable in any case,[76] because the intercourse is either homosexual if the *tumtum* is male, or it is with his maternal sister if the *tumtum* is female.)

7. As explained in Part V, topic 9:4, sexual reassignment surgery is forbidden because it is damage to the body that is not medically required, and it is also for a licentious purpose. Sexual reassignment surgery (SRS) does not change the person's status in Torah Law as a male or female. If a man who underwent SRS is the passive partner in anal intercourse with another man, both are liable for the capital sin. If the other man inserts his organ into the transsexual's new "female" orifice, neither is committing the act of the capital sin,[77] but it still constitutes forbidden intimate contact.

See *Minĥat Ĥinuĥ* Commandment 209, who writes that the verse (Leviticus 18:22), "You shall not lie with a man as one lies with a woman; it is an abomination," is only stating the commandment for Jews, not the commandment for Gentiles. However, the author argues that this is forbidden, since intercourse between a male and an androgyne is not considered "a man shall ... cling to his *wife*" (Gen. 2:24; the Hebrew word for *wife* refers only to a woman). Just as male homosexual intercourse is forbidden from this verse as explained in topic 1:1, likewise it is forbidden for a male to engage in active or passive anal intercourse with an androgyne.

[74] Rambam, *ibid.*

[75] *Ibid.*

[76] Also, there is no provision in Torah Law that a Gentile can only be liable for judgment in a court of law if he had first been given a clear warning as to the prohibition, to give him the opportunity to stop committing the sin in the presence of eye witnesses (in which case a precise warning could not be given, not knowing what to warn the transgressor, because it is not known whether it is his sister or male brother). A Gentile is liable for judgment in a court of law even without a warning.

[77] As is the rule for the corresponding intercourse with an androgyne; see topic 5 above.

Likewise, a female who undergoes SRS remains a female.[78] If a male sodomizes her, or if she sodomizes a male with her new "male organ," or if she sodomizes another female who underwent SRS, neither partner has committed the capital sin of male homosexual anal intercourse. Obviously if she enters her new "male organ" into another female, that is not an intercourse that would bring liability for a capital sin (but rather it is forbidden as lesbianism).

An androgyne whose male genitals were removed, to leave him resembling a female, still retains his status as an androgyne male.

8. The prohibition of bestiality committed by a male or female person does not depend on the age of the animal.[79] For a male person, it is a capital sin if he enters his organ into the orifice of a male or female creature of any species, or if he causes a male mammal to have relations with him (into his anus).[80] Likewise, a woman who causes a male mammal to have relations with her is liable for a capital sin,[81] whether through vaginal or anal intercourse.[82]

---

[78] *Thus a female who transgressed and underwent SRS is only permitted to have relations with a person who was born male (even if that person also transgressed and underwent SRS). Even in surgically reassigned relationships such as these, the partners who are permissibly intimate should be living as a married heterosexual couple (see Chapter 4).

[79] Rambam, *Laws of Kings* 9:6.

[80] Meiri on Tractate *Sanhedrin* 54, regarding a Gentile.

*It is forbidden for humans to copulate with any other species. But if a person brings a male *non*-mammal creature to insert its male organ into herself or himself, there is no liability to capital punishment, for the creature's organ does not function in the manner of the "intercourse" that is commanded about in the Torah.

[81] Rambam, *Laws of Forbidden Sexual Relations* 1:17. Tractate *Sanhedrin* 57b teaches that both men and women are equally prohibited in forbidden relations from the words (Genesis 2:24) "and **they** shall become one flesh." Since this is the source that teaches the prohibition of bestiality (topic 1:1), it is obvious that men and women are equally prohibited in bestial relations, as it says in *Minĥat Ĥinuĥ* Commandment 211.

[82] See *Kesef Mishneh Laws of Kings* 9:7.

In all these cases, the man or woman is liable for capital punishment, but it is not required to kill the animal.[83] If a court feels that it is necessary to kill the animal so as to remove a stumbling block from the public, or as a penalty for the transgressor, they have the right to do so.

9. Whether it was a domestic or wild mammal, bird or *sheretz* animal (as defined in Part IV, topic 1:7), female or male, that a man entered his organ into for bestial relations, the man is liable for a capital sin.[84] A man (or woman) who brings a mammal to commit anal intercourse upon himself (or vaginal or anal intercourse upon herself) is liable for a capital sin.[85] If a male bird is brought to insert its male organ into a male or female person, this does not fall within the Torah's definition of bestial intercourse, and as such would not make a man or woman liable for a capital sin,[86] although it is nonetheless forbidden.

10. For bestiality committed by a man or a woman, and for male homosexuality, one becomes liable when just the full head of the male organ has entered (including the corona), even without penetrating further or completing the intercourse, whether it is the male organ of a man or of an animal, and whether the entrance is into the orifice of a person or an animal.[87]

---

[83] The precept to kill the animal only applies in the case of a Jew who commits bestiality; Rambam, *Laws of Kings* 9:6.

[84] *Maggid Mishneh Hilĥot Issurei Bi'ah* ch. 1, based on Tractate *Bava Kama* 54b. A man commits a capital sin if he is the active partner in relations with any type of animal, based on the verse "and they shall become one flesh." "Becoming one flesh" from bestial intercourse between a person and a mammal (or a non-mammal) does not happen, and therefore it is a capital sin. But if a bird or other non-mammal inserted into a human, it is not considered actual sexual intercourse at all, so liability for a capital sin does not apply.

[85] Rambam, *Laws of Forbidden Sexual Relations* 1:16-17.

[86] Tractate *Zevaĥim* 85b.

[87] Rambam, *Laws of Forbidden Sexual Relations* ch. 1:16; Jerusalem Talmud Tractate *Kiddushin* ch. 1.

CHAPTER 3

The Prohibition of Relations with Other Men's Wives

1. Adultery with the wife of another man is forbidden for Gentiles (even if the wife has these relations with her own consent and/or with the consent of her husband).[88]

If the wife (the adulteress) consents to committing adultery, both she and the man (the adulterer) who has forbidden relations with her are liable for a capital sin, if they have relations in the normal manner. The conditions for adultery apply after the woman has consummated her marriage with her husband through having normal relations with him.

But if another man has abnormal relations with her after she consummated her marriage, or either type of relations with her while she was only engaged (or after she had completed a wedding ceremony but she did not yet consummate the marriage by having marital relations), then neither she nor the other man are liable for a capital sin, as God said to Abimelech,[89] "Behold you are [on the brink] to die because of the woman you have taken, for she has been *possessed by [her] husband*" (*b'ulat baal* in Hebrew).[90] How did she become fully married to her husband (and thereby forbidden to another man)? It was through normal marital relations, as understood from the Hebrew phrase.

---

[88] This is meant to distinguish the transgression of adultery from the transgression of kidnapping, and in particular to clarify what commandments are violated if a man commits rape. If a man steals a married woman and forcefully commits relations with her, he is violating two separate capital sins of theft and adultery (which will be explained in Part VII, Chapter 10), but the woman is exempt, as explained in Chapter 1 above regarding rape. The case "with the consent of her husband" stresses that even according to the statement in *Minĥat Ĥinuĥ* Commandment 35 (see footnote 99 below), based on Rashi, adultery with rape is also considered stealing from the husband. Even if the husband consents, the capital sin of adultery still applies, for which the man will be liable. Therefore, if a Gentile married woman who resides with her husband for marriage purposes allows any other men to cohabit with her (for example, if she engages in prostitution), whether or not the husband gives his consent, both the woman and her other partner(s) are liable for adultery.

[89] Genesis 20:3.

[90] Rambam, *Laws of Kings* 9:7.

A Gentile man who transgresses by having relations in the abnormal way with another man's Gentile wife is not liable for a capital sin. The source for this rule is from the verse,[91] "...and *cling* to *his* wife" – a man's *clinging* must be only to *his* wife, and not to the wife of another man. This command not to have adulterous relations with the wife of another man refers to the act of "clinging" (*davak* in Hebrew), which specifies that liability for capital punishment in adultery applies only for normal relations.[92]

Although there is no capital liability involved, it is abhorrent[93] for a man to have relations with another man's betrothed woman, or with a married woman in the abnormal way, and such actions incur punishment by the Hand of Heaven.[94] A Noahide court must impose

---

[91] Genesis 2:24.

[92] Tractate *Sanhedrin* 58b.

[93] *Tosafot Sanhedrin* 57b, and *Bava Batra* 16b regarding a *me'orasah* – a woman who is betrothed (engaged) to a man without yet having had normal relations with him for the sake of consummating the marriage. *Tosafot Rid*, on *Bava Batra* there, writes that though there is no liability for a capital sin if another man has relations with her, there is a prohibition, as the Talmud says there, "he transgressed five sins," including this act. How much more so does this apply to one who cohabits with another man's wife in the abnormal way.

[94] One of the sins of the Generation of the Flood was that men would habitually grab (i.e. kidnap) women from under their wedding canopies and rape them, as stated in Rashi's explanation on Genesis 6:2, and in *Bereishit Rabbah* 26:5. It is also explained, in *Bereishit Rabbah* there, that this was legalized, or at least there was no legal or social judgment or punishment for it, and all the dignitaries and prominent men were involved in this sin. Still, it is clear that any sin is made up of several parts, each one separately being forbidden. From this it is clear that even if a man cohabits by consent with a woman who is only betrothed to another man (so there is no rape or complete stealing involved), even though this is not as severe as the sin of the Generation of the Flood, it is still abhorrent and prohibited.

An apparent proof is from Tractate *Sotah* 10a, where it explains that Judah asked Tamar, "Did your father accept an acquisition on your behalf?" – meaning, did her father marry her off as a minor? Judah asked this, even though there is no capital sin for a minor Gentile girl in such a case, as there would be with a fully married adult woman who would be liable for adultery (see topics 4 and 5 below). Thus, we see that a Gentile *me'orasah* (betrothed woman) is forbidden to other men, although there is no liability of capital sin.

punishments for such actions,[95] even though there is no specific commandment for Gentiles stated in the Torah in regard to these sins.

2. There are two terms used for marriage regarding Gentiles: (a) a "woman who has had relations with a husband" (*b'ulat baal*) is a "fully married woman," with whom adultery is a capital sin; and (b) a "betrothed woman" (*me'orasah*), with whom it is forbidden for another man to have relations,[96] but it is not a capital sin. The betrothed woman has not established a marriage bond and is not considered married within the Torah Law for Gentiles; the couple only agreed to become married in the future, and perhaps made some formal commitment. Still, her betrothal makes her prohibited to have relations with other men, since such an act would be akin to stealing.[97]

Even if a woman cohabited with her husband-to-be before they participated in a wedding ceremony (e.g., before they entered their wedding canopy), if those relations were not for the purpose of consummating marriage, but were done only in a provisional promiscuous way, the woman is not called a *b'ulat baal* (one who has been wedded through marital relations), and liability for adultery has

---

[95] Clearly, this obligation rests on Noahide courts within the commandment for legal statutes (*dinim* in Hebrew).

(It is implied by *Bereishit Rabbah loc. cit.*, and Ramban's explanation on Genesis 6:2, that when dignitaries and other prominent people sin with the public's knowledge, it automatically brings about a general attitude of lawlessness. If courts do not enforce such matters for prominent people, it shows the general population that those types of sins are allowed. From this it is inferred that court officials do not only have a responsibility to bring sinners to judgment. They must also act with restraint themselves, in order to uphold standards of righteousness that will keep most people from sinning.)

[96] *Tosafot Rid Bava Batra* 16b, and this is implied by Tractate *Sotah* 10a and Rashi there, as mentioned in footnote 94 above. According to those opinions that a Gentile "acquires" his wife (see footnote 99 below, and the end of topic 5 below), adultery with a betrothed woman would be a theft, since the woman was acquired by her husband. Even if this is not the actual Torah Law for Gentiles, it will apply if a society decides that Gentile wives are acquired by their husbands, in which case adultery with a betrothed woman would be considered stealing from the husband, as is written in *Likkutei Sihot* (cited in the next footnote).

[97] See *Likkutei Sihot*, vol. 30, p. 31, and footnote 14 there.

not yet taken effect upon her.[98]

3. Cohabitation by Gentile partners can bring the consummation of a marriage bond only if it is done in the normal way. If the relations were done only in the abnormal way, the woman is not considered married, and if she later has normal relations with another man, the transgression of adultery would not apply, and there would be no liability of the partners for a capital sin.[99]

---

[98] This is clear from Rambam, *Laws of Marriage*; see footnote 101 below.

[99] *Parashat Deraĥim* p. 19; *Ritva Kiddushin* 9b; *P'nei Yehoshua Kiddushin* 13b; *Ĥizkuni* Genesis 38:7,26.

Minĥat Ĥinuĥ Commandment 35 (section 16) writes an opinion that a Gentile man can "acquire" a woman in marriage through cohabitation, even in an abnormal way, and that abnormal intercourse will also consummate her status as a fully married woman (as is written by Riva on *Parshat Vayeshev*). Indeed, the general opinion of *Minĥat Ĥinuĥ* is in accordance with the opinion of the Jerusalem Talmud, Tractate *Kiddushin* at the beginning of ch. 1, that a Gentile man "acquires" a wife (through their act of intercourse) (and according to the Jerusalem Talmud – but not accepted as the practical Torah Law – he has no way to divorce her). This is also the opinion of Rashi on *Sanhedrin* 57b, regarding the sin of (a) an invading enemy Gentile soldier who kidnaps and cohabits with a local married woman, and (b) a Gentile master who specifies his slavewoman for his slaveman, and then he (the master) cohabits with her. Rashi says that the transgression in each case is that the man is *stealing* a woman who was already "acquired" by another man. (The author argues that even according to the Jerusalem Talmud and Rashi – who have the opinion that acquisition of the wife happens through marriage by normal relations – it is logical that they would agree that abnormal cohabitation does not establish a marriage bond, about which Genesis 2:24 expressly says, "and *cling* to his wife.")

However, it is clear from Rambam's words that his opinion runs counter to this, as he says in *Laws of Marriage* 1:1: "Before the Torah was given, when a man would meet a woman ... and he and she desired to marry, he would bring her to his home, conduct relations in private and thus make her his wife. Once the Torah was given, [only] the Jews were commanded that when a man desires to marry a woman, he must acquire her as a wife [through a formal contractual agreement] in the presence of witnesses."

[By Torah Law, a Jew can acquire a Jewish wife by either marital relations, or a traditional written contract, or by giving her something of value. The Sages prohibited Jewish marriage by intercourse (Tractate *Kiddushin* 12a).]

The act of normal intercourse happens when at least the full head of the male organ is inserted into the woman's vagina.[100] For consummation of a marriage bond, this must be done with both partners intending to become bound in marriage, with their free consent.[101] This excludes relations that are merely promiscuous.

(This acquisition specified in the Torah Law for Jews does not mean that the husband owns his wife, but rather that with her consent, he acquires all of her personal financial assets and the income she may earn during their marriage, with the exception of any of her assets that she specifically excludes from that acquisition by a pre-nuptial agreement.) This implies that in the Torah Law for Gentiles, (a) there is no automatic acquisition of the wife or her personal financial assets when the marriage is consummated by normal relations, (b) an acquisition agreement is not necessary for the marriage, and (c) an acquisition is never part of the essential marriage bond.

This is also clear from Rambam, *Laws of Kings* 9:8, which says (counter to the Jerusalem Talmud, *loc. cit.*) that a married Gentile can divorce, and does not inherently require a divorce proceeding or a divorce document in order to dissolve his or her marriage bond. Rather, it will be dissolved if at least one partner dissents from the marriage bond, *and* the woman leaves or is sent away from the husband's domain (or he leaves from her domain), and she goes on her own independently. (More details of Gentile divorce are presented in Chapter 4.) [This demonstrates that according to Rambam, there is no acquisition by the husband of the wife or her personal financial assets in a Gentile marriage, because if there were an acquisition, the woman would not have the right to leave the marriage without the husband's consent.]

It is clear to the author that the Torah Law for Gentiles follows Rambam's opinion: Gentiles do not have "acquisition" of wives through marriage (i.e., marriage *of itself* does not transfer any special economic rights from the wife to the husband). Rather, consummation of the marriage by normal cohabitation with this intention only accomplishes the marriage bond itself, as it says, "and *cling* to *his wife*." Just as this act is required for making one liable for adultery, it is required for attaining the Torah-law status of marriage, and no economic rights are transferred unless it was enacted as a decree of civil law.

[100] Jerusalem Talmud Tractate *Kiddushin* 1:1. This appears simple, since in Genesis 20:3, the use of *"b'ulat baal"* to specify Gentile marriage refers to the sexual act of marital relations. In Torah Law, the initial stage of the act (the insertion of the head of the male organ) is sufficient to be considered "intercourse," in regard to giving the woman a status of marriage.

[101] This is the meaning of Rambam, *Laws of Marriage* 1:1 as explained in *Maggid Mishneh* and *Kiryat Sefer* there, and Responsa of Rivash ch. 398.

Marital Status of Minors

4. It has previously been explained in topic 1:12 that there is no status of marriage for minors, who have no mature appreciation for marriage, and if they cohabit it is not done for the purpose of full marriage. Therefore, the term *b'ulat baal* for a woman only applies when both partners have the status of adults, at which point their cohabitation can be for the purpose of marriage.[102]

If a Gentile man cohabits with a Gentile minor girl who is living as the spouse of an adult man, or with an adult Gentile woman who is living as the spouse of a minor boy, both partners are exempt from liability for a capital sin of adultery, since the minor girl and the adult woman in these cases are not considered to be fully married. Rather, they are only forbidden to another man to the extent that a betrothed woman would be forbidden.[103]

This is also clear from the law of one who cohabits with a woman who was seduced by his father, who is not considered his father's wife since their cohabitation was not done with marriage in mind (as explained in topic 1:3).

[102] See *Minĥat Ĥinuĥ* Commandment 35 (sections 13 and 19), that a Gentile needs to cohabit with the intention of acquiring the woman for marriage, and if he does not have that intention, another man who cohabits with that woman afterwards is not liable for adultery. Although *Minĥat Ĥinuĥ* holds that this intention is needed for the acquisition (see his opinion there, explained in footnote 99) – and it has been explained that the final ruling is that there is no need for this acquisition – the intention for marriage is still needed to reach this status, and a minor does not have a capacity for legally mature decisions.

Therefore, when *Minĥat Ĥinuĥ* says there that an adult Gentile woman can cause herself to be acquired by a minor (as is the opinion of *Ĥemdat Yisrael Hilĥot Melaĥim* 9:10), and that through her own knowledgeable intention alone she can bring herself to be acquired by another person (even a minor), that is only according to his opinion that acquisition is a factor that applies in the establishing of the Gentile marriage bond. However, as explained above by the author, (a) this intention is needed specifically for creating the status of marriage, and not as a mere acquisition, and (b) for marriage, the responsible intention of both partners is needed. However, if she specifies herself for the minor, it is possible that she has the status of a *me'orasah* with betrothal to the minor.

[103] Tractate *Sanhedrin* 52b states, "a married woman – to exclude the wife of a minor." This applies to Gentiles as well.

5. If a father marries off his minor daughter,[104] she has the status of betrothal (a *me'orasah*) until she reaches legal majority for marriage. Regardless of whether the minor girl had relations with her "husband," it is forbidden for another man to cohabit with her, because she is still betrothed. But one who does so is not liable for adultery, which he would be if he had relations with a man's fully married adult wife.[105]

Likewise, within the Torah Law for Gentile marriage, a minor girl (though she has no complete intention for marriage[106]) may be permitted to marry if she agrees. (In the Noahide Code, this is not considered licentiousness for Gentiles.) She continues in the status of a betrothed

---

This could not be only a scriptural decree for Jews (as *Minĥat Ĥinuĥ* Commandment 35, section 19, implies), since one must follow the logical reasoning that there can only be a status of marriage if the relations are with a woman who is capable of becoming fully married, and this cohabitation must be with the full intention for marriage (which minors do not have). If those conditions are not fulfilled, no liability for adultery can apply.

[104] But due to the rule that for Gentiles there must be cohabitation with full intention to commence marriage, she remains in the status of a *me'orasah* (betrothed) as long as she or her husband is a minor.

[105] Since for Gentiles, marriage depends on the conditions of cohabitation, and the cohabitation of a minor does not include full intention for marriage, a minor girl cannot achieve fully married status.

[106] See *Gur Aryeh* Genesis 27:57 regarding the marriage of Rebecca (Rivkah), that by the Noahide Code, a father has no jurisdiction over his daughter to marry her off as a **full** wife while she is a minor; see *Minĥat Ĥinuĥ* Commandment 35, section 13, and Commandment 190, section 5.

Even though Rashi writes on Genesis 25:20 that Rebecca married Isaac when she was three (based on a calculation of the time from the binding of Isaac until his marriage), it is possible that he is following the opinions that the age of legal majority is reached when mental maturity is achieved (which Rebecca would thus have had at the age of three); see *Likkutei Siĥot*, vol. 10, p. 71. However, in footnote 48 there, it is written that this is Rashi's opinion in his simple explanation of Torah, but as a ruling in Torah Law he holds that she was married of her own accord with the status of a minor. (Rebecca's father died before she left home, as explained by Rashi on Genesis 24:55.)

A minor girl's father has the jurisdiction to marry of his minor daughter, as implied from Tractate *Sotah* 10a, that Judah asked Tamar, "did your father accept an acquisition on your behalf?"(meaning, did her father marry her off as a minor?). It is just that since a minor girl has no mature consent, if she married she would only be forbidden to other men as a betrothed girl.

girl[107] until she reaches the age of legal maturity for marriage.

6. It appears that a minor girl such as this who was married and cohabited with her husband, but did not do so after she reached maturity, cannot truly be called a *b'ulat baal* or a fully married woman. These two partners will not become fully married (with the girl becoming a *b'ulat baal*) until she has normal relations with him again after she reaches maturity, as part of her marriage with him.[108]

7. It is not fitting for an adult woman to marry a minor boy, since this is considered licentiousness. However, if an adult woman dedicates herself to a minor as her husband, she takes on a status of a *betrothed* woman. She is forbidden to have relations with another man as long as she is living in this condition of marriage with her husband who is a minor.[109] If she commits the forbidden relations with another man, they are not liable for a capital sin of adultery. However, they would be liable if she is fully married to an adult (e.g., if she has marital relations with her young husband after he reaches the age of majority).

However, *Tosafot* (on *Yevamot* 61b, and *Da'at Zekenim* on Genesis 27:57) hold that Rebecca was 14 years old when she became married to Isaac, so she had the status of an adult at that time, and not a minor.

[107] See Tractate *Sotah* 10a and Rashi there, that Tamar married Judah's son Er while she was a minor (without being married off by her father, who had died). Thus we see that even though a minor girl has no full intention for marriage, she is allowed to live as a married wife. It is also seen from Rashi (as cited in the previous footnote) that Rebecca married with her own mature intention, even if she was a minor in age. See topic 3:2 and footnote 94.

[108] This appears to be the case, and their relations before the girl reaches maturity only bring her into a status of betrothal; see topic 3:2 above.

[109] See Rambam, *Laws of Forbidden Sexual Relations* 21:25, and *Tur Shulĥan Aruĥ Even Ha'Ezer* 1:3; marrying off a minor son is considered to be instigating licentiousness (unless there is a dire need, e.g., to save a life).

However, *Beit Shmuel* there (note 4) brings dissenting opinions that this is not considered to be in the category of licentiousness, and it is allowed from the outset. Even that which the *Minĥat Ĥinuĥ* discusses (see footnote 102), regarding an adult woman who marries herself to a minor, is only in regard to her legal status, but he nevertheless considers this to be licentiousness. Nevertheless, if she does so she is still considered a *me'orasah* (betrothed), and she is forbidden to a have relations with another man.

Precepts Related to Adultery by a Gentile with a Jewess

8. There is a difference in the Noahide Code between adultery committed by a Gentile man with a married Jewess (including even a Jewess who is a minor, whose father married her to an adult Jew), in contrast to adultery committed with a married Gentile woman.

Since a Jewess is acquired in marriage or betrothal to a Jew, she can have a status of marriage before cohabitation. Therefore a Jewess who is betrothed to a Jew is also called a "married woman," and a Gentile would be liable for adultery if he cohabited with her, just as a Jewish man would be. (In this unique instance, the Gentile adulterer would be subject to the same means of execution as a Jewish man would be, which the Torah specifies as strangulation. If she was also a Jewish betrothed virgin minor up to the age of 12½ years, the specified means of execution would be *s'kilah*,[110] which is inaccurately translated as "stoning.") The source for this is found in a commandment addressed to the Jews, in the verse[111] "*Any man* shall not approach his close [female] relative to uncover the nakedness...;" the term "any man" comes to indicate that there is an additional precept regarding a Gentile who commits a sexual transgression with a Jewess. The Oral Torah explains that the Jewess in this case is a wife who is only betrothed, with whom a Gentile man would be liable for adultery, and he is to be judged and sentenced according to the laws of adultery by Jews.[112]

But if a Gentile man cohabits with a Jewess after she had relations with her Jewish husband, he is liable to the same punishment as if he had cohabited with the Gentile wife of another Gentile man.[113]

Even if this Jewess only cohabited with her Jewish husband in an abnormal way, Torah Law specifies that she still becomes the Jew's full wife and is a *b'ulat baal*, and a Gentile man would be equally

---

[110] *This means of execution does not correspond to the common conception of stoning. The four methods of execution commanded in the Torah, and the details of what type of *Beit Din* court (Jewish or Noahide) has jurisdiction to carry out these different punishments, will be explained in the section on the Noahide Commandment for Courts of Law.

[111] Leviticus 18:6.

[112] Tractate *Sanhedrin* 57b.

[113] Rambam, *Laws of Kings* 9:7; this is execution by decapitation.

liable for relations with her (just as for adulterous relations with a fully married Gentile woman).[114]

9. A Jewess who lives as a domestic partner with a Jewish man without ever having been acquired by him through a traditionally witnessed, contractual marriage agreement (as defined by Jewish Law) does not have the status of a married woman in Jewish Law, and a Gentile who cohabits with such a woman is not liable for the capital sin of adultery.[115] (Such actions are, of course, strictly forbidden.)

10. There is another difference between the laws regarding adultery with a Jewess who is married to a Jew, versus with a married Gentile

---

[114] By Torah Law, a Jewess becomes married to a Jew through acquisition by means of cohabitation, even in an abnormal way, as explained by Rambam, *Laws of Marriage*, ch. 3, and thereby she is called *b'ulat baal*. In contrast, the Noahide Code specifies that for Gentile marriage, abnormal relations do not bring a Gentile woman into the status of *b'ulat baal*, as explained in topic 3:3 above. [The Sages forbade Jewish marriage by marital relations, so Jews must become married through a traditional witnessed contractual agreement.]

[115] See Responsa of *Tzemaĥ Tzedek Even HaEzer* ch. 138, that discusses at length if a *pilegesh* ("concubine") of a Jew needs a *get* (a traditional document of Jewish divorce) if the relationship is terminated. It appears clear that according to the opinion that for a Jewish *pilegesh* this is not required, surely she is not a fully married woman according to the Torah Law for Jews, and therefore a Gentile who transgresses and cohabits with her would not be liable for the capital sin of adultery. This is also clear from *Responsa of Ramban* ch. 284, cited in *Beit Shmuel* 26:2, that a Jewish man is not liable for adultery if he has relations with another Jew's *pilegesh*. This is also implied from *Rema Even HaEzer* ch. 10. This is also the opinion in *Igrot Moshe Even HaEzer* vol. 1, ch. 73-75, that a Jewess who lives specifically and permanently with a man, but without a traditionally witnessed Jewish marriage, is not considered married and does not need a *get*.

Even though a Gentile *pilegesh* is considered married to the Gentile man, since this is not the case for a Jewish *pilegesh*, a Gentile man therefore would also not be liable for a capital sin if he had relations with a Jewish *pilegesh*, as she is not married to her Jewish partner within Torah Law. The general rationale is that in order to have liability for the capital sin of adultery, which is only with a fully married woman, a Gentile woman has to be fully married in the context of the Noahide Code for Gentiles, and a Jewish woman has to be fully married in the context of Torah's precepts for Jews.

woman. A Gentile is only liable for a capital sin of adultery with another man's Gentile wife if he (the adulterer) has normal relations with her (see topic 3:1). On the other hand, if the married woman is a Jewess, he is liable even if he cohabits with her in an abnormal way, as is the Torah's law for Jews.

Therefore, a Gentile who cohabits with a betrothed Jewish woman (or one who has only entered her wedding canopy), even in the abnormal way, is liable for adultery, and the penalty from a *Beit Din* court would be strangulation, as it would be for a Jewish adulterer. If she was also a virgin minor up to the age of 12½, the specified penalty would be *s'kilah* (see footnote to topic 8 above).

If, however, a Gentile cohabits with a Jewess in either the normal or the abnormal way, after she had relations with her Jewish husband, he is judged (and liable to punishment) according to the Noahide prohibition of adultery.[116]

---

[116] From Rambam, *Laws of Kings* 9:7, a Gentile is liable for cohabiting with a Jewess who is the wife of a Jew, even for cohabitation in the abnormal way, as Radvaz there and *Or HaĤayim* Genesis 20:4 explain according to Rambam. The reason is because the adulterers in this care are judged by the Torah's law for Jews regarding this transgression, which specifies that they are fully liable for adultery by either normal or abnormal relations.

Minĥat Ĥinuĥ Commandment 35, sections 14 and 15, explains that the implication from Rambam is that the Gentile is liable, yet logically it seems not so, since such cohabitation does not fall under the parameters of " 'and cling to his wife' – and not another man's wife," whether the Gentile cohabits with a Jewess or Gentile woman.

Seemingly, this would be correct logic, for regarding a Jewish betrothed woman, she has already received the status of marriage in the Torah's law for Jews, and she is already called the wife of another man. By comparison, a sin through cohabitation depends on the prohibitions in regard to the manner of the cohabitation, and in this regard a Gentile is not liable for adultery by abnormal relations, since even for a Jewess this is not considered "clinging."

The explanation, based on the *Kesef Mishneh* (see footnote 48), is that a Gentile is liable for cohabitation in the abnormal way with all forbidden *relatives*, and **only for the prohibition of adultery with a Gentile married woman does the Torah add the extra specification of "clinging."** The reason for this lighter prohibition is that the Gentile married partners can easily divorce when they wish to do so, and just as they were married through cohabitation in the normal way alone, so too, a violation of this marriage is only done the same way (by normal relations). This is in contrast to relations

Marriage of an Enslaved Woman[117]

11. If a Gentile master designates his slavewoman for his male slave and the slave cohabits with her,[118] and subsequently the master or another man cohabits with the slavewoman, the master or the other

---

with other forbidden partners (who are permanent relatives, such as a man's mother or his full sister), with whom *any type* of cohabiting is forbidden. As explained in footnote 48, this is the difference in the verse (Genesis 2:24) that teaches the forbidden relations for Gentiles that make one liable for a capital sin: a Gentile man must "separate" from his specified permanent relatives (*ya'azov* in Hebrew, which means *total* separation – from *either type* of cohabitation), and any wife with whom he "clings" (*davak* in Hebrew, which means normal relations) must be only his own wife.

In contrast, a Jewess, in order to be called married, must be acquired as a wife by a Jewish man, and her marriage can only be terminated with a special divorce document (called a *get* in Hebrew). So she and her Jewish husband cannot terminate their marriage as easily as a Gentile couple can, which can be just by terminating their commitment and their clinging one to another. Thus, if a Gentile commits adultery with a married Jewess, he is liable for a capital sin regardless of whether it is by normal or abnormal relations.

Another possible explanation is that this forbidden cohabitation with a married Jewess is included in the additional teaching learned from the verse (Leviticus 18:6) that uses the term *"any man,"* as explained in topic 3:8. Since in the Torah's law for Jews, one is also liable for adultery with a married Jewess by abnormal relations, a Gentile will be liable for this as well if he commits this act with a married Jewess.

117 *Modern-day slavery is a severe and widespread problem. Especially grave is the sin of kidnapping young girls, God forbid, and selling them for sex slavery. Part VII, Chapter 9, deals with the precepts against kidnapping any person. The precepts regarding a minor girl or an adult woman who is forced against her consent to live with a man are covered in topic 4:6 below.

118 Ran *Sanhedrin* 57, Radvaz and *Kiryat Sefer Hilĥot Melaĥim* 9:8.

It is clear that this is the opinion of Rambam, *Laws of Kings* 9:7-8, that without cohabitation, no woman is ever considered a *b'ulat baal*. The details (that she needs to be living together with him, and that she needs to be known in the community as the slave's wife), are explained by Ran, who writes that if there is cohabitation only, without living together with the public's knowledge, a slavewoman's relationships are usually presumed to be promiscuous only. Thus, in order to establish for herself and for the community that she is designated for this man only, all these conditions need to be met.

man is liable for adultery, but not until the slavewoman becomes known in the community as the slave's wife.[119] This applies even though the master can separate her from the slave whenever he wants, and it will be considered a valid divorce, as will be explained in Chapter 4 on the laws of divorce. As long the master has not separated them, he or another Gentile man would be liable for adultery with her, as they would for any other married woman.[120]

If however, the master singled her out for his slave, but the slave has not yet had relations with her, or he has had relations with her but the matter has not been made public, another man will not be liable for adultery if he has relations with her. Likewise, if her master had specified her for a free man,[121] after which she has the status of a concubine, then even though the master can separate her from the man whenever he wants, the master would be liable for adultery with her as long as she is known publicly as the free man's wife or concubine.

If the master did not specify a husband for his slavewoman, yet it is known publicly that she lives permanently with a certain slave or free man, and the master does not protest and allows her to do so, another Gentile man will be liable for committing adultery with her.[122]

---

[119] Rambam, *Laws of Kings* 9:8. The simple meaning of "designates a slave-woman... When [the master] separates her from his slave," implies that if her master so designates her, even if this is initiated against her will, then once her marital relationship is known publicly, another man who cohabits with her is liable for adultery. Since the slave and the slavewoman are living publicly as man and wife, it is assumed legally that she has accepted this.

[120] A slavewoman who is married in this way is forbidden to have relations with another man, even if she, or the master, or his male slave that he designated her for, or even all of them consent. This is contrary to the opinion in *Minĥat Ĥinuĥ* Commandment 35, section 22, that it can be allowed by consent, according to which the only problem is the one cited by Rashi, who says that it is like stealing (since a theft does not occur if the slave consents). Rather, the practical ruling is that this is forbidden due to her status of marriage, which consent for having other partners does not change, as explained in the beginning of this chapter.

[121] *Minĥat Ĥinuĥ* Commandment 35, section 21.

[122] (*A fortiori* from that which a slavewoman is prohibited, even if the master forcibly married her to the slave.) However, if he allows his slavewoman to live publicly in this relationship, then she has the status of a married woman.

In any situation that a man will be liable for adultery if he cohabits with a slavewoman, she will also be liable, unless it is a case of rape.

12. It appears that a *minor* slavewoman who is specified by her master to be a partner for his adult male slave is not considered to be the wife of the slave, since as a minor she does not attain any status of marriage by her own accord, and the master has no legal right of ownership over her to the extent that he can cause her to have a status of marriage.[123] Therefore, another man who has relations with her is not liable for the sin of adultery.

13. It appears that a Gentile woman who specifies herself for a Gentile slave has the law of a concubine, and is forbidden as a married woman, and another man who cohabits with her is liable for adultery.[124]

---

[123] Rabbi Zalman Nehemiah Goldberg questions this: a master can specify his *adult* slavewoman as a *wife* for his male slave against her will (see footnote 119), so why then can the master not do the same for his *minor* slavewoman, since he does have the power to specify the minor slavewoman as a *concubine* for his male slave?

In response, the author cites Ran on Tractate *Sanhedrin* 57a, that a Gentile cannot legally acquire the body of his slavewoman, to have authority to force a marriage. Still, if a master forcibly specifies his adult slavewoman for his male slave, she is then considered married, only because it is assumed that she then accepts this marriage on herself publicly, with conscious knowledge. (This stringency makes other men liable for committing adultery with her.)

In contrast, a minor girl can be forced to marry, but she will still not consequently have the mature intention for marriage, and therefore, her relations are considered mere licentiousness. At most, she is possibly considered to have the legal status of betrothal, and another man who cohabits with her would not be liable for adultery. See above, topic 3:5.

[124] See topic 4:10 below.

In *Sheva Mitzvot HaShem*, Volume II, the author writes here about the Torah's laws regarding a Canaanite maidservant. The Canaanite slaves discussed in the Torah had a unique status. They underwent a *partial* religious conversion to Judaism, so that they were neither Gentiles nor full-fledged Jews, and this especially affected their status in regard to permissible marital relations. A Jewish master of a Canaanite maidservant could designate her for his Jewish servant (see Exodus 21:4 and Rashi there).

Partners with Whom there can be no Status of Marriage

14. Just as a Gentile woman who is married to a Gentile man is forbidden to have relations with another Gentile man, she is also forbidden to have relations with a Jew, as it says,[125] "and cling to his wife"[126] (which implies that just as a man's "clinging" should be only with his wife, so to, a woman's "clinging" should be only to her husband, as explained in topic 1:1 above). However, neither of them[127] (the married Gentile woman and the Jew) would be liable for a capital sin of adultery with each other in the judgment of a Noahide court.[128]

These Torah Laws applied only in a time when the 50-year Jubilee cycles could be observed (Leviticus 25:8-13), which is when all of the twelve Tribes of Israel were settled in their respective assigned areas in the Land of Israel. This condition ended 100 years before the destruction of the first Holy Temple.

Since these laws are not applicable today, the editor has omitted them from the text, and a short note of explanation is inserted here on this topic:

In practical terms, a designated Canaanite maidservant would be forbidden to other men as if she were a married woman, since the Torah does call her a "wife" in Exodus 21:4: "If his master gives him a wife..." But a Canaanite maidservant does not have the capability in Torah Law to become *fully* married (Rambam, *Laws of Forbidden Sexual Relations* 14:19). Therefore, other men, either Jews or Gentiles, would have no liability to capital punishment for cohabiting with her, since this would not constitute actual adultery, even though she was designated by her master to be his servant's wife.

[125] Genesis 2:24.

[126] *Tosafot Avodah Zarah* 36b and other *Rishonim* Rabbinical authorities, as cited in footnote 128 below.

[127] Tractate *Sanhedrin* 52b states about the Jewish man in this case: "to the exclusion [from liability to a death penalty] for a wife of 'others' [i.e., non-Jews]." See Rambam, *Laws of Forbidden Sexual Relations* 12:10.

[128] Rambam, *Laws of Forbidden Sexual Relations*, *ibid.*, states, "whether a single or married [Gentile] woman … because through her the Jew came to sin." This implies that she is not liable for this as a prohibition of adultery within the Noahide Code. The reason is that the married woman is not transgressing the prohibition against a man "clinging" to another man's wife, since she is not able to become the Jew's wife according to Torah Law, as stated by Rambam, *Laws of Forbidden Sexual Relations* 14:19. This is also written by *Birkei Yosef* on *Even HaEzer* in ch. 16, as well as *Sha'ar HaMeleĥ*

15. There is no status of marriage in a relationship with a forbidden relative, such as a man who lives as a domestic partner with his mother, or with his full sister or his maternal half-sister, in the manner of a married couple. The same applies if a man lives as a domestic partner with a woman who was his father's wife, after she is widowed or divorced from his father. If another man cohabits with one of these women during their relationship with the forbidden partner, the other man is not liable for adultery.[129]

---

on Rambam, *Laws of Forbidden Sexual Relations* 12:2, and others. This is also the opinion of some other *Rishonim* authorities (Ramban, Rashba, and seemingly Rashi on Tractate *Sota* 26b). The implication is that if the Jew is not liable for the prohibition of adultery, the Gentile woman is not either.

However, Ran (on *Sanhedrin* 52b) writes she is liable for adultery in the judgment of a Noahide court. This also appears to be the opinion of *Tosafot* (*Sanhedrin ibid.*, and Tractates *Kiddusin* 21b, and *Avodah Za*rah 36b), Ra'avad (cited by Rashba on *Kiddushin* 13b), *Sefer Mitzvot Gadol* (Negative Commandment 103) and *Tosafot HaRosh* (on Tractates *Sanhedrin* and *Kiddushin*, *ibid.*), who say that a Jew transgresses his positive commandment to "cling to *his* wife" and not the wife of another man, and they would say that the Gentile woman would likewise be liable also, because she is transgressing her command (which carries liability to capital punishment), see *Minĥat Ĥinuĥ* Commandment 35, section 12.

[129] *Parashat Deraĥim* (*Drush* 1, p. 19) discusses whether there can be a status of marriage with a forbidden relation, and he comes to the conclusion that an acquisition of a wife cannot exist in the context of a prohibition.

As well, even according to Rambam's opinion that Gentiles do not have the status of acquisition in marriage, but rather just the condition of being married, it must be clarified whether marriage can exist with a forbidden partner.

Seemingly, the verse Gen. 2:24 that forbids certain relations for Gentiles – "Therefore a man shall leave his father and his mother and cling to his wife" – implies that a woman who can fall under the category of clinging cannot fall under the category of required leaving, and vice versa. If so, if a woman is living in a marriage relationship with a forbidden relation, she is not called "his wife", and another man would not be liable for adultery for cohabiting with her (as is written in *Ĥasdei David* on *Tosefta* of Tractate *Avodah Zara*).

Although *Minĥat Ĥinuĥ* (Commandments 35 and 191) holds that the precept that marriage cannot exist with a forbidden relation only applies for Jews – which therefore implies that for Gentiles, there can be an acquisition of a forbidden relation in marriage – still, one could reason that marriage for Gentiles must also conform to society's definition of a valid marriage (in any

16. It is explained in topic 4:14 below that from God's explicit command in the Torah, there is no status of actual marriage between Jews and Gentiles.[130] Therefore, a Gentile man who became "married" to a Jewess, or a Gentile woman who "married" a Jew, is not considered married according to the Torah Law for Gentiles or Jews. Another man who cohabits with a Jewish or Gentile wife that is involved in such an intermarriage is not liable for the sin of adultery, as he would be liable with a *b'ulat baal*[131] (and neither is the woman liable for adultery).

---

aspects that are stricter than Torah Law requires for them), and "their personal consent is nullified by the opinion of society." This would apply if a man lives in a domestic relationship with his daughter, which is not forbidden for Gentiles by Torah Law, but we see from Torah that it was rejected in practice (see topic 1:7 above). Does the woman in such a relationship have a status of marriage, in which case another man who cohabits with her is liable for adultery, or does she not have a status of marriage, and he is exempt?

It appears that the ruling should be that for partners who are not accepted by society for marriage – even if they are permitted by Torah Law – their cohabiting is not considered marriage, but rather licentiousness, and it cannot be called "clinging to a wife."

Rabbi Zalman Nehemiah Goldberg holds that it is not correct to rule that "their personal consent is nullified by the opinion of society." For in his opinion, it would logically imply that if a marriage is not legally documented, another man would not be liable for committing adultery with the woman.

The author supports his own view by noting that a slavewoman who was designated for a slave cannot receive a status of marriage with him until it is publicly known, and hence accepted, for until then, their relations are considered mere licentiousness in the eyes of society (see topic 3:11 above).

[130] See *Shevut Ya'akov* vol. 1, ch. 20, which does not find any aspect of marriage status between a Jew and Gentile, and only refers to the monetary aspect of such a "marriage" in the context of the country's secular laws.

*The true identity of a child as a Jew or a Gentile by birth is *matrilineal*; it follows the identity of the *mother* who conceived the embryo and carried it through pregnancy until the child's birth. This is stated explicitly by God in the Torah (see Rashi on Deuteronomy 7:4). On the other hand, the membership of a born-Jewish person in one of the Twelve Tribes of Israel is *patrilineal*, based on the tribe of the born-Jewish father. Therefore, a child who is born to a Jewish woman and a Gentile father is fully Jewish, but without membership in any of the Twelve Tribes; see Rashi on Lev. 24:10.

[131] *Minĥat Ĥinuĥ* Commandment 35, section 21.

CHAPTER 4

Precepts Related to Marriage, Fornication and Divorce

1. Even though Gentiles are not commanded to "be fruitful and multiply,"[132] it is nevertheless God's will that every man who is able should marry a woman and have children from her, as He said to

---

[132] It is explained in Tractate *Sanhedrin* 59b that Adam was commanded to be fruitful and multiply, but at the giving of the Torah at Mount Sinai, this command was removed from Gentiles, and it remained only for the Jews. [Likewise, this applies to any pre-Sinai commandment that was recorded by Moses in the Book of Genesis or the Book of Exodus up to the account of the covenant and the revelation at Mount Sinai, but which was not repeated to Moses on Mount Sinai. (But the Seven Noahide Commandments, and the extended Noahide Code, were commanded to Moses on Mount Sinai as the Torah Laws for Gentiles; see the author's Introduction to this volume.) Henceforth, beginning from the giving of the Torah's Laws to Moses on Mount Sinai, the original commandments from before Mount Sinai are only binding on Jews, and not on Gentiles.] This is also the opinion of *Tosafot* on Tractate *Yevamot* 62a.

Nevertheless, this only means that Gentiles have no explicit commandment about this. But as a logical necessity for the establishment of society, they are obligated to do so. As explained in Part I (*Fundamentals of the Faith*), Chapter 3, topics 8-10, there are logical obligations for Gentiles, and since marriage is a way of accomplishing the settling the world and is God's will, it is obvious that they are obligated in general to involve themselves with this task. This would fit with the opinions that Gentiles are obligated by the verse Isaiah 45:18 to "make the world settled" (*yishuv ha'olom* in Hebrew; see footnote 138), and it is possible that this is due to the logical obligation contained in it.

The practical difference is that if Gentiles were expressly commanded to procreate, then they would be obligated to do so even if it would cause them discomfort or trouble. But since the obligation stems only from a logical reason, they are only obligated to do so if there is no logical reason not to do so. An individual Gentile is thus exempt if he would experience any serious discomfort as a result of fulfilling it. This is written in the responsa of *Ĥatam Sofer Even HaEzer* ch. 20, that since only Jewish men are obligated in the commandment to "be fruitful and multiply," therefore a Jewish woman is not obligated to endure pain in order to fulfill this (but she may do so by her choice). The same logic applies to Gentiles. See also topic 5:1.

Adam and Ĥava (Eve):[133] "Be fruitful and multiply." Likewise, God told Noaĥ after the Flood:[134] "And you, be fruitful and multiply; teem on the earth and multiply on it."[135]

2. A man should marry a woman, and she should be an established wife for him, as it says,[136] "Therefore a man shall leave his father and his mother and cling to his wife, and they shall become one flesh." This is the means of establishing a society, which is accomplished through a man bonding with his wife and having children with her, as it says,[137] "The Lord, Creator of the Heavens; He is the God, the One Who fashioned the earth ... He did not create it for emptiness; He fashioned it to be inhabited ..." Thus it is God's will that people should settle the world.[138]

---

[133] Genesis 1:28.

[134] Genesis 9:7.

[135] *Aruĥ HaShulĥan* on *Even HaEzer* ch. 1, section 5. See Tractate *Yevamot* 63b and Rashi on Genesis 9:7 (said to Noaĥ), that anyone who abstains from procreating is compared to a murderer, since the verse Genesis 9:6 regarding the prohibition of murder is juxtaposed with verse 9:7 regarding procreation. This implies that there is Divine punishment for a Gentile who deliberately does not fulfill this obligation to procreate, unless the person has a valid reason. As explained in Part I, topics 3:8-9, even though Gentiles are not commanded to give charity (according to Rambam), Sodom was destroyed because they nullified all acts of kindness and charity from their midst. This means that a society can receive punishment if there is widespread behavior that opposes morality, even if it does not go against any express Divine command; and it appears that the same applies to the issue of procreation.

[136] Genesis 2:24.

[137] Isaiah 45:18. The Sages used the phrase "make the world settled" to refer to this verse. We cite the phrase several times, always referring to this verse.

[138] See Tractate *Gittin* 41 and *Tosafot* there. A male or female Canaanite slave who becomes half-free enters a unique status and is forbidden to marry any person. Thus when a Jewish master owns a half-free Canaanite slave, he is forced to set the slave free entirely so that the person will be able to fulfill his or her existing obligation to "make the world settled," as Rashi explains there (as does *Tosafot Bava Batra* 13a). It appears from these opinions that the same applies to all Gentiles in that they are obligated by the cited verse "... He did not did not create it [the world] for emptiness; He fashioned it to be inhabited ..." See *Likkutei Siĥot* vol. 5, p. 159, footnote 63.

This injunction includes two separate details: (a) marrying a wife and living with her in an established manner, and (b) having children with her. Therefore, even if a Gentile man is unable to have children and fulfill the injunction to "make the world settled" in this way,[139] he should still marry and live in an established manner with a Gentile wife, since that is also a manner of the settling of the world, as it says:[140] "The Lord God said: 'It is not good that man be alone; I will make him a helper corresponding to him.' "

3. A woman, as well, should endeavor to marry a man and establish a

---

But the opinion of Rambam (*Laws of Slaves* 7:7) is that we *force* the master to fully free a half-freed Canaanite slave due to his or her freed half, which otherwise can't observe the *obligation* to "be fruitful and multiply," because no marriage is allowed in that condition (i.e., no one can legally cohabit with the half-freed Canaanite slave). This is also clear from *Maggid Mishneh Hilĥot Issurei Bi'ah* 12:16, in his explanation of Rambam's opinion. In other words, they hold that there is no universal *commandment* to "make the world settled," and where this clause is mentioned, they understand it as referring to the Jewish commandment that Jewish men *must* "be fruitful and multiply."

The question of the degree of obligation centers on whether or not there is an extra commandment to "make the world settled," beyond the Torah's Jewish commandment to "be fruitful and multiply." According to *Tosafot* there is a separate commandment to "make the world settled." According to Rambam, by contrast, this statement by the prophet does not constitute a Divine commandment to "make the world settled," but it is rather addressed to the Jews as a strengthening of the Jewish commandment to "be fruitful and multiply," and not as a separate commandment.

It is possible that they only debate regarding the obligation of a Jewish woman and a Canaanite slave, who are obligated in the prohibitive Jewish commandments of the Torah; but all opinions agree that Gentiles at least have a logical obligation to "make the world settled," but it does not have the force of an explicit Divine commandment.

139 See *Nodah BiYehudah Even HaEzer* ch. 6, that (a) based on Ramban, a man who is unable to father children is not obligated in this aspect of "making the world settled," and (b) this man should still become married, as the verse says (Genesis 2:18) "It is not good that man be alone," but this does not fall within the category of the obligation to "make the world settled."

Thus it is not a complete obligation that one has to trouble himself for. But as a logical obligation, even in this case a person is morally obligated.

140 Genesis 2:18.

family, as this is God's will, and a fulfillment of the injunction to "make the world settled."[141] Nevertheless, even though it is fitting to be married and have children, Gentile women or men for whom marriage or having children would be very burdensome are not obligated to cause themselves distress in order to fulfill this obligation.[142]

4. It has been previously explained in Chapter 3 that a woman is only considered fully married if she had normal relations with an adult man whom she is permitted to marry, with her consent and with their intention for marriage. If, however, she only goes through a formal wedding ceremony, she is not yet considered fully married.

It is appropriate for Gentiles to establish wedding ceremonies, so that their marriages will be obvious and known to all (the ceremony, e.g. a wedding canopy,[143] is a betrothal of the bride, and afterwards she becomes fully married by marital relations with her husband in private).

Still, if a Gentile man and woman both consent to live together as domestic partners[144] (although they have not had a wedding ceremony or certified their marriage), and they behave publicly as husband and

---

[141] See *Beit Shmuel Even HaEzer* 1:2, which discusses if women are obligated to "make the world settled," and deliberates based on two answers in *Tosafot* (of which one follows the same line of logic as Rambam, as explained earlier in footnote 138). *Magen Avraham Oraĥ Ĥayim* 153:9 states that a woman has this obligation, and the later authorities agree.

The only practical question is regarding a Jewish woman. But for Gentile men and women, all opinions agree that there is a logical obligation – for all who are able – to "make the world settled" in this manner, as long as it does not cause pain or distress for the person (but disregarding this obligation on account of a wrong viewpoint or illegitimate reasons is morally a sin).

[142] See Tractate *Yevamot* 65b in regard to the wife of Rabbi Ĥiyah who had great pain from a childbirth, and then drank a substance that made her sterile (after verifying that this was permitted for women). See footnote 132.

[143] *Rashi, on Genesis 6:2, cites this as a custom before the Flood.

[144] Rambam, *Laws of Marriage* ch. 1.

*This applies in societies where such conduct is accepted by the public as normal. But in societies where the public does not accept this as a normal state of marriage (but rather as a type of licentiousness), the couple's private decision does not make the woman completely married, so if another man cohabits with her, he and she will not be liable to capital punishment as adulterers. See footnote to topic 3:15 above, and topics 3:9, 4:8, 4:10, 4:14.

wife for an extended period of time, the woman is judged as fully married, since it is assumed that a woman and man living together in this way have had relations with the intention of marriage.[145]

Therefore, while the woman is known to be living together with her male partner, she is forbidden to any other man.[146] If she does have relations with another man, both he and she are liable for adultery, since she has already become a *"b'ulat baal"* (see topic 3:1 above).

5. For Gentiles, the consummation of a marriage bond, in and of itself, does not obligate the husband to provide for his wife or children, or to have relations with her on a regular basis or as a commitment.[147] Such matters depend on the country's laws and customs, and/or any legally or morally binding stipulations made between the wife and husband.[148]

---

[145] *This assumption is presumed to be true unless it is proven otherwise, as a matter of Torah law. Therefore, all the conditions mentioned above (i.e., when a woman is considered a *b'ulat baal*, and through what specific act, etc.) are not necessary to be investigated if a couple is openly living together and behaving publicly in the manner of a husband and wife. In that case, they are presumed in Torah law to be fully married unless proven otherwise, as explained here. Furthermore, a Noahide court may enforce that presumption in terms of liability for relations of the woman with another man.

[146] *This applies even if she and her domestic partner have not had normal relations for the sake marriage, and even if he is not physically capable of engaging in marital relations (e.g., due to illness or advanced age), and certainly if they had a wedding ceremony or they registered as married.

[147] *Nevertheless, a husband is obligated to honor his wife and be involved with her well-being, and a wife is obligated to honor her husband. The Sages said (*Bava Metzia* 59a), "A man's house is blessed solely due to his wife." When there is peace, love and trust between a couple, blessing and success shine in the house. As part of the due respect between a pious couple, they should consult between themselves in conducting the affairs of the home, including the raising and education of their children, with true partnership. The Sages said (*Pirkei Avot* 4:1), "Who is honorable? One who honors the creations" (i.e., he even honors people whose only apparent praise is that they are creations of God). Surely, then, spouses must honor each other, both in private and in public. (See *Seven Gates of Righteous Knowledge*, p. 122.)

[148] *Rabbi J. Immanuel Schochet has provided a basic text for a "Noahide marriage contract," with the stipulation that it should be verified (and adjusted if necessary) to be a valid contract by the standards of the secular legal system under which the couple will be registered as married:

Exemplary Noahide Marriage Contract

By the Grace of God

On the _______ day of the week, the ___ day of the month of __________ in the year 20'__ in the civil calendar, corresponding to the ___ day of the Hebrew month of ___________ in the year 57__ since Creation according to the calendar of the People of Israel, here in the community of ___(city)_____ , (state/province) , (nation) , the bridegroom _____(name)_____ said to the bride ____(name)_____ : "Be my wife according to the laws of the Torah of Moses as they relate to *B'nai Noaĥ*, the Children of Noah. I pledge to respect, honor and maintain you conscientiously and in honorable fashion as becoming of ethical and honorable people, and assume all the responsibilities incumbent upon a loving and faithful husband, living with you as husband and wife according to universal custom and providing you with all necessities of life."

Miss _____(name)______ agreed to become his wife, and pledges to honor and respect her husband and to assume all the responsibilities incumbent upon a loving and faithful wife, living with him as wife and husband according to universal custom and maintaining a harmonious household.

Mr. _____(name)______ , our bridegroom, made this declaration: "I accept upon myself all moral, emotional and financial obligations of this marriage contract. I also accept upon myself to provide all necessities of life for any children God may bless us with, until at least their age of secular majority or marriage. I declare and affirm that all my present and future properties and possessions shall be liable to these undertakings during my lifetime, and after my lifetime, from this day and forever, as may be deemed by a Bet Din of Orthodox Rabbis all consistent with the Torah laws for *B'nai Noaĥ*."

The obligations of this marriage contract were accepted by our bridegroom, Mr.___(name)____, and by Miss ____(name)____, according to all the strictest usages of all marriage contracts according to the prevailing civil laws and social norms. A binding acceptance of this contract by Mr.____(name)____, the bridegroom, and Miss ____(name)_____, his bride, regarding everything written and stated above, is made by both, by affixing their signatures to this document before the affirming witnesses:

_______(groom's signature)_______ _______(bride's signature)_______

Affirmed and signed on the above date before:

________________________________ (Witness)

________________________________ (Witness)

6. A woman who is forced against her consent to live with a man is not considered married,[149] and if another man cohabits with her, both are exempt from liability. (It appears that even if a woman married by her consent, and then wants to separate from the man, but he is forcing her to stay with him and not letting her leave, then she is not considered fully married. Thus if another man cohabits with her in this situation, neither of them are liable for the sin of adultery.)

7. A Gentile man is permitted in Torah Law to marry off his minor daughter[150] to any allowed partner who is fitting in his eyes (as explained in Chapter 3). It is thus fitting for a girl's father or head of the household to be involved with marrying off all the daughters (even as adults) to fitting matches. Nevertheless, it is only fitting to marry off a minor or adult daughter with her knowledge and consent.[151]

It is the custom of certain nations, families or clans that the father or another relative decides whom a woman should marry, and they then force her to marry that man, with the woman having no choice to protest against the marriage. This is contemptible and improper. Nevertheless, once this is done and the woman is referred to by all as this man's wife, she is considered fully married, and another man who cohabits with her is liable if she is at least twelve years old.[152]

---

[149] See Ramban, *Milĥamot Sanhedrin* ch. 8, *Nemukai Yosef Sanhedrin* ch. 8, and Ran *Pesaĥim* beginning of ch. 2, that forced marriage is not considered binding. (Part VII, Chapter 9, deals with the precepts against kidnapping.)

[150] *In modern communities the minimum age for marriage should be regulated, as written in topic 1:12. In societies where it is the custom to marry off young daughters, since usually this is done under responsibility of the parents, the precepts written here apply, even though a bride who is a minor is only considered to be betrothed. See topic 3:5 above.

[151] Tractate *Kiddushin* 41a; Rambam, *Laws of Marriage* 3:19; and Rashi on Genesis 24:57 on the words "let us ask for her [Rebecca's] consent": "From here we see that one cannot marry off a woman without her consent."

[152] This appears correct from the law (topic 3:11) of a master who designates his slavewoman as a wife for his slaveman, and after these two slaves have begun living together with marital relations as a husband and wife, the master is liable for adultery if he cohabits with her. Even if the slavewoman was forced into this type of marriage by her master, it is nevertheless considered a full marriage once the public recognizes it; i.e., even if it was initially against her will, by default it is assumed that she agrees after it is publicly known.

When it is clear the entire time that she cries and protests against the marriage, it is forbidden for her husband to force her to have relations, and as long as she does not willingly consent to have relations with him, she is not a *b'ulat baal* (completely married). Nevertheless, if and when she is silent and accepts and does not protest her marriage, even though she did not agree to it at first, then this is sufficient for her to be considered by all as his wife, and to be fully married.

8. It is allowed within Torah Law for a Gentile man to marry multiple women (if there is full public knowledge). If the courts decide to forbid polygamy or set boundaries on this, they have the ability to do so.[153]

9. However, a woman may only be married to one man at a time, and if she becomes "married" to two men, she is considered married only to the first one she had relations with for the purpose of marriage, and she and the second man are liable for the capital sin of adultery. It is related in Torah sources that God considers the marriage ceremony itself of a woman wedding an additional man to be repulsive.[154]

10. If a woman specifies herself for one man's cohabitation, but she is not considered fully married regarding the secular government's laws and assigned rights (i.e., they are only "living together"), then she is still considered a concubine in the perspective of Torah Law. This

---

Rabbi Zalman Nehemiah Goldberg points out that this brings up a new rule, that marriage can be considered binding through the acknowledgement of society; if a man marries off his daughter, it is possible that the only reason she is considered married is because the father has full jurisdiction over his daughter, as we find (Rambam, *Laws of Slaves* ch. 9) that a father has the power to sell his daughter into slavery, so he can also marry her off – this matter requires further deliberation.

The author responds that this can only explain the case of a father selling his minor daughter. But the matter being dealt with here includes the marrying off of an adult daughter, for whom it appears that the father has no jurisdiction to sell her into slavery.

[153] See note 129, that it appears that if a Gentile man violated his society's accepted code of conduct (that forbids polygamy) by taking a second wife, the second marriage is not considered binding and is only licentiousness, and another man who cohabits with the second wife is not liable for adultery.

[154] *Sifra* Leviticus 18:3.

practice is permitted for Gentiles, and the woman is considered fully married if their shared-home relationship is publicly known.[155] If another Gentile man cohabits with her, both are liable for adultery.[156]

11. If one cohabits with an unmarried woman without intention of marriage, whether or not the matter is known publicly, it does not render her married to him or give her a status of a *me'orasah*, and it is mere licentiousness. Although such relations are not clearly forbidden for Gentiles, it is a repulsive act, even if done in a temporary fashion.[157]

---

[155] *A necessary length of time has not been identified. But the deciding factor is that a couple who are "living together" are considered married when they are known publicly to be living together on a permanent basis in the manner of a husband and wife, and they are not embarrassed about this or trying to hide the fact.

[156] The Torah Law authorities debated whether a Jewish man (other than a Jewish king) is permitted to have a Jewish concubine. See Rambam and Ra'avad, *Laws of Marriage* ch. 1, and *Shulĥan Aruĥ Even HaEzer* ch. 26. According to Rambam there and in *Laws of Kings* ch. 4, it is forbidden since she is not being fully married. But for Gentiles it is definitely permitted.

We find many areas in Scripture that refer to concubines; see Genesis 22:24, and Rashi on Genesis 22:20. Rashi on Genesis 25:6 says that a concubine is a wife who receives no marriage document. See Ramban there, that a concubine has no marital rights. The custom in Biblical times was to provide a "full wife" with a living stipend and other contractual obligations upon the husband, but a woman who agreed to be married without such rights was called a "concubine" (*pilegesh* in Hebrew). Likewise a slavewoman who is taken for marriage is considered as a concubine.

The liability of a man who cohabits with another man's concubine is debatable; see Responsa of Rivash 398 who deliberates about this. But the *Parashat Deraĥim* ch. 1 (p. 7 and 20), explains that a Gentile concubine is a full wife in terms of adultery, and there is no difference in the Noahide commandments between a contractual "full wife" and a concubine; only for a Jew is there is a difference, since a Jewish concubine is not acquired in marriage, nor is she married with a ceremony under a wedding canopy. This is the opinion of Rambam, who holds that when a master specifies his slavewoman as a wife for his slaveman, that slaveman alone may have relations with her, and any other man would thereafter be liable for doing so (until the master publicly severs this relationship between his two slaves). Surely the same applies for a concubine who designates herself to a man, and she is considered a fully married woman within the Noahide Code.

Rashi on *Sanhedrin* 57a argues with the opinion followed by Rambam in regard to this designated slavewoman, and holds that the transgression committed by another Gentile man who has relations with her is that he is stealing her, but not committing adultery, since a slavewoman has no official status of marriage. Still, it seems that Rashi would accept Rambam's opinion regarding a concubine, since she has a share in freely agreeing to the relationship (and therefore it is her free consent that gives her the status of a married woman). This is in contrast to a slavewoman, who has no consent in the matter because she is under the complete jurisdiction of her master.

[157] Rambam, *Laws of Marriage* 1:1, writes that before the Torah was given at Sinai, "a man would meet a woman on the street... give her money and co-habit with her... once the Torah was given, prostitution was forbidden." This implies that for Gentiles, however, it is not forbidden, and there is no express prohibition in Torah for Gentiles not to practice it. However, Ramban on the verse Gen. 2:24, "and cling to his *wife*," implies that this verse excludes clinging in an animalistic way of meeting a woman in the street and engaging in licentious relations with her (whether or not she asks for any payment).

From Ramban, it seems that although there is no express prohibition of prostitution for Gentiles, it is prohibited as an immoral act that conflicts with the command in this verse. Rabbi Zalman Nehemiah Goldberg comments:

(a) Based on the words of Rambam cited above, it does not appear correct to conclude that prostitution is abhorrent and is forbidden for Gentiles; we also see that Judah acted in this way with Tamar, and it seems illogical that he would perform an action that was actually forbidden. (Rambam's *Guide for the Perplexed*, vol. 3, ch. 49, explains that the episode of Judah and Tamar was permitted.) The only prohibition stated in this regard is in the Torah, addressed to the Jews. As well, it is explained by Rambam (*Shorashim* of *Sefer HaMitzvot*) that a reason for the verse (Leviticus 19:29), "Do not profane your daughter to prostitute her, so as not to defile the land and fill it with licentiousness," is that a Jew should not come to unknowingly marry a woman who was conceived by his father with a prostitute. But a Gentile, on the other hand, may marry his paternal half-sister, and therefore this reason cannot be even included within one of the other Noahide prohibitions.

(b) However, the verse that is cited in the next topic (I Kings 14:24), "And also prostitution was in the land, and they did all the abominations of the nations etc.," implies that this practice is considered abhorrent for Gentiles. It is possible that it is only permitted for them (and this applies to the situation of Judah) in a temporary fashion, but not for a woman to practice prostitution on a regular basis. But from Judah's statement (Genesis 38:23), "lest it become a disgrace for us (if it becomes known)," it is implied that the society at that time would have considered his action as somewhat abhorrent.

From God's words,[158] "Therefore a man shall leave his father and his mother and cling to his *wife*, and they shall become one flesh," it is the natural and appropriate way for a man to marry a woman and establish a family. One who deviates from this path is mistaken, and acts against God's will in His creation of mankind and their character.

Furthermore, those who engage in promiscuous relations commit animalistic actions (and this is even worse than the animals, since an animal has no comprehension to understand any other way, unlike a human, to whom God has given a superior intellect), as this is the way of animals – that a male typically cohabits with any female that appears ready before it. This is why all living creatures were created at the outset as females and males, since this is fitting for their nature. In contrast, Adam the first man was created alone, and only after he searched and discovered that he needed a mate did God give him the first woman as his partner. This shows us that the correct way for a man is to look for a specific wife, and to build a life-partnership with her, instead of acting as an animal with casual sexual relationships.

God also differentiated the humans from animals in the way that they should cohabit. Animals have no mutual understanding of their mates at all. This is why God created animals so that their natural way of mating is that the male enters the female from behind, and does not see

---

In response, the author cites Tractate *Avodah Zarah* 36b: "Shem's court prohibited prostitution." However, Rashi on Gen. 38:24, and the *Midrash* there, say that Tamar was sentenced to die only because she was a daughter of Shem (Malĥizedek, a "priest of God;" see Rashi on Gen. 14:18), implying that others would not have been executed for this. The Talmud *loc. cit.* says that Shem's decree was only for one who cohabited with an idolater (which is what Judah assumed when he judged her), but it did not apply to cohabitation with another observer of the Noahide Commandments. (See Tractate *Sotah* 10a, that before having the relations, Tamar told Judah, "I am a convert," and Rashi explains there that then, this meant, "I have abandoned idol worship.")

According to another opinion (debated in the Jerusalem Talmud, Tractate *Kiddushin* 1:1), once one Gentile man cohabits with a Gentile prostitute, she becomes "married" to him, and all Gentile men who later cohabit with her commit adultery and are liable. In that opinion (which also holds that Gentiles cannot divorce), one would have to say that because Judah held that he was permitted to have relations with a prostitute, this debate in the Jerusalem Talmud must only apply to the Torah Law after Mount Sinai.

[158] Rashi on Genesis 2:24, and Ramban *loc. cit.* in the previous note.

her face at all, which is reflective of the fact that an animal has no understanding or love in this act. In contrast, when a man and woman are involved in relations, it should be when they have mutual love and understanding between themselves, which is a personal bonding relationship aside from the purpose of procreating.

Proper human cohabitation is termed "knowledge" in the Torah, as it says,[159] "And Adam ***knew*** Ĥava his wife." Therefore, the anatomically natural means of cohabitation for a man and woman is face to face, through which they will share their mutual recognition and love. But a person who cohabits in harlotry acts in an animalistic fashion, in that the couple has no mutual recognition or love.

Thus the prophet related (Isaiah 45:10), "the world was not created to be empty, but rather to be settled," and licentiousness is not a way of establishing populated and settled societies in the world. Instead, it is chaotic and harmful to society.

12. This is all said concerning a woman who from time to time acts licentiously. But one who acts this way frequently with any man is essentially a prostitute, and it is forbidden for Gentiles to allow such a woman in their midst.[160] This behavior causes the world to be full of prostitution and moral abominations, as it says,[161] "Do not degrade your daughter as a harlot, so as not to defile the land, and [do not] fill it

---

[159] Genesis 4:1. In many places in Scripture, the verb "to know" *("yodah")* is used for the union of intercourse. In comparison, see Rashi on Genesis 18:19, that God's expression regarding His affection for Abraham, *"yeda'ativ"* – meaning love and honor, is from the same root word. In contrast, the cohabitation of animals is called "mating" (*"sar'bi'ah,"* in Leviticus 19:19).

[160] See I Kings 14:24, "And also prostitution was in the land, and they did all the abominations of the nations etc." *Targum Yonatan* translates this as "a wayward woman," implying that this is an abhorrent thing for Gentiles.

It appears that based on the concept explained in this chapter, the verse commanding Gentiles to "make the world settled" forbids them to do any action that logically causes a destruction of society, so prostitution must therefore be banned. For the verse calls it "an abomination," and it is known that many evil actions are done in conjunction with the prostitution industry, including kidnapping, theft, murder, injury, bribery, drug addiction and child abuse. Prostitution itself leads to rampant adultery and the decay of society.

[161] Leviticus 19:29.

with licentiousness."[162] The courts are obligated to prevent the people of their land from doing so, and to close down all brothels and fine and punish all men and women who practice or promote prostitution.[163]

13. Even a woman who cohabits with a certain number of men who she especially chooses, and not with just any passerby, is practicing licentiousness, and she is neither married nor a concubine. This practice is forbidden to Gentiles. This was one of the abhorrent practices of the Egyptians (mentioned above in topic 9, and in topic 2:4), that "a woman would marry two men." (However, if she goes from one to the next, without establishing a home with any one of them, this is not considered adultery, since she does not cohabit with any single one for the purpose of marriage, and they are therefore not liable for adultery.)

14. It is permitted for Gentiles of any nation or race to marry each other as they wish, aside from the forbidden relations cited in Chap. 1.

However, it is forbidden for a Gentile man to marry a Jewess, or for a Gentile woman to marry a Jew, or for a Gentile to live with a Jewish person in a way of marriage, as God commanded the Jews:[164] "You shall not marry into them: do not give your daughter to their son, and you shall not take their daughter for your son."[165] Not only is this

---

[162] See Rambam, *Laws of a Mature Virgin* 2:17, and *Shulĥan Aruĥ Even HaEzer* ch. 177, that this verse is said in reference to any type of prostitution. Even though Ramban in his arguments on Rambam's *Book of the Commandments*, Foundation 5, argues with Rambam and holds that the only prohibition is for a forbidden relation or marriage, but not for two single people, it is clear that he agrees that such an action is abhorrent, and he is only arguing with Rambam as to whether one is liable to be punished for this. The verse brought in the main text here is not an illustration of liability, but rather a proof of the abhorrence of the practice.

[163] See *Shulĥan Aruĥ Even HaEzer* ch. 177, and Rashi on Num. 22:5, that the nations had accepted extra precautions regarding forbidden relations, but the Gentile prophet Balaam gave them (the Midianites and Moabites) advice to commit licentiousness (as an attack on the Jews). This implies that it breaks down the norms of society, which Gentiles are commanded to protect.

[164] Deuteronomy 7:3.

[165] From this verse, we know that it is forbidden for a Jew to marry a non-Jew, as the Rambam rules in *Laws of Forbidden Sexual Relations* 12:2, and the *Shulchan Aruch* rules in *Even HaEzer* ch. 16.

forbidden for a Jewish person, but it is therefore also forbidden for a Gentile, as it is impossible to form a marriage without the participation of both partners, and the Gentile would thereby be a partner to this sin.[166] The verse says "and cling to his wife," which specifies a woman who is fitting for him to cling to. But a marriage arrangement between a Jew and a Gentile, between whom there is no status of true marriage, is not considered a real marriage, but rather licentiousness for both

---

[166] Even though Gentiles are not expressly forbidden to do this, since it is clear that such a thing is forbidden by the Torah, it shows that it is against God's will and is forbidden.

In addition to this main reason, Gentiles as well are included in the prohibition, "Do not put a stumbling block before the blind," as explained in Part I, Chapter 4. This is the reason why a Gentile woman is liable for cohabiting with a Jew, as explained by Rambam in *Laws of Forbidden Sexual Relations*, Chapter 12; this is also written in *Mitzvot Hashem*, p. 427.

Rabbi Zalman Nehemiah Goldberg comments that as opposed to the case of a Jewish man who cohabits with a Gentile woman, where the Torah law is that zealots may kill him while he is committing the act in public, they are not allowed to do so for a Gentile man who cohabits with a Jewess, as explained in *Milĥamot* Tractate *Sanhedrin* 74.

Nodah BiYehudah (vol. 2, *Even HaEzer* ch. 150) learns this from Rambam, who exempts a Gentile who cohabited with a Jewess. The reason for this differentiation is that if the woman is Jewish, the child is also Jewish, while the ruling is more stringent for a Gentile woman whose child would not be Jewish. See *Ĥemdat Shlomo Yevamot* 47, where it discusses this issue.

The author responds that the authorities (*Tosafot*, Rosh, Ramban, Rashba and Ritva on *Yevamot* 47, and *Maggid Mishneh Hilĥot Isurei Bi'ah* 13:8) rule that it is forbidden for a Gentile man to marry a Jewess, and this is the ruling in *Tur Shulchan Aruch Yoreh De'ah* 268:11, although the reason is not given there. The main reason, though, is as given above – a marriage must have two partners. If the marriage is prohibited, it is a prohibition for both partners.

This can also be seen from the Torah's law that a Jewish divorcee or harlot who marries a Jewish priest (*kohen*) transgresses the prohibition given to him that he must not marry her, as explained in Tractate *Yevamot* 84b and *Tosafot Ĥagigah* 14b. This basic explanation is consistent with the ruling by Ran in the beginning of ch. 2 of Tractate *Kiddushin*, that a Jewish woman is not obligated to exert herself to perform the commandment to "be fruitful and multiply," which is incumbent only the Jewish man, but once she is properly married, she becomes a partner in fulfilling it.

partners.[167] If they transgressed this prohibition, there is no status of marriage between them, and another man who cohabits with the woman is not liable for adultery.

(This is not comparable to the case mentioned above in topic 10, in which a Gentile woman who lives permanently with a Gentile man as a concubine is considered fully married, and is liable to capital punishment for adultery. This is because her permanent relationship is not considered licentious, since she is fitting to be fully married to him, and they are publicly known to be living together in the manner of a husband and wife.)

15. Even licentious relations of a Gentile man with a Jewess, or a Jewish man with a Gentile woman, are forbidden. This prohibition is more severe than that of a Gentile man and woman who have relations that are merely licentious.[168]

There is no prohibition for a Gentile man to have relations with a Gentile woman during her menstrual period.[169] A Jewess, however, is forbidden to have any relations during her menstrual period,[170] and therefore a Gentile man has an additional prohibition against having relations with her during her period (beyond the general continuous prohibition of a Gentile having relations with a Jewess, since he is also

---

[167] Rambam, *Laws of Forbidden Sexual Relations* 12:2.

[168] See Rambam, *Laws of Forbidden Sexual Relations* ch. 12, that a Gentile woman is liable in a Jewish court for cohabiting with a Jew. Even though it is understood that a Gentile man is not liable for having relations with an unmarried Jewess, the prohibition of their licentiousness appears to be the same.

See Rashi on Numbers 22:5 in regard to Balaam, who specifically tried to lead the Jews to sin through wanton relations with Midianite and Moabite women. Although Rambam says that Gentiles were not prohibited from being licentious, it appears that this sin in the cited story of Bilaam was worse, because it was intended for the purpose of leading the Jewish men astray. From this we learn that causing a Jew to sin through licentiousness is a more severe transgression than the licentious behavior itself.

[169] This is clear from Rashi on Tractate *Avodah Zarah* 36b, and Tractate *Sanhedrin* 82a.

[170] See *Yaarot Devash* vol. 1, p. 21a, and vol. 2, p. 142, that a man who cohabits with a Jewess during her menstrual period, whether he is a Jew or a Gentile, is guilty of sin. It appears that this is akin to that which has been explained, that the man is a partner with her in her sin.

presenting an added stumbling block for her, by participating in her additional sin of having relations during her period).

16. The court of Shem, the son of Noaĥ, issued a decree that it was forbidden for a woman to have licentious relations with an idolater, since this would cause her to be drawn after him to idolatry.[171] Included in their decree was that a woman should be liable to capital punishment for this. This is why Judah sentenced Tamar to death, because he assumed that she had cohabited licentiously with an idolater.[172] Although it is not clear if Shem's court decreed a punishment for a man who had licentious relations with a woman idolater, it is clear that they forbade a man to marry an idolatress and bring her into his home, with permission for her to practice her idolatry there.[173]

The decision of Shem's court to include a death penalty in this decree was only temporary. Once the Torah was given at Mount Sinai and the Seven Noahide Commandments were set within it forever (as explained in the author's Introduction to this work), we do not find that there is any precept that includes liability to capital punishment for that act. Rather, a Noahide court in any country may (as explained in topic 1:9 above, if it has been granted the authority) make its own additional decrees and determine the (non-capital) penalties if those are violated.

Nevertheless, the decree of Shem's court that one should not marry an idolater still stands,[174] whether it would be the wife or the husband as the idolater. It appears that even if two people are already married,

---

[171] Tractate *Avodah Zarah* 36b.

[172] Genesis 38:22, and as explained in Tractate *Avodah Zarah*, *loc. cit.*

[173] Although from the Talmud there, one may understand that the decree was not applied to a man who cohabits with an idolatress, it appears that this is because the discussion in the Talmud only talks about those relations in the context of licentiousness, and that is explicitly written in the Torah, in the account of the judging of Tamar. But logically, it would forbid a man to marry an idolatress, just as a woman is forbidden to marry an idolater. This is clear in *Or HaĤayim* Genesis 38:26.

[174] This is clear from Tractate *Avodah Zarah, loc. cit.*, that determines, from the decree of Shem's court, the nature of the prohibition after the Torah was given. [This does not contradict what is mentioned in fn. 132, that according to Tractate *Sanhedrin* 59(a,b), any pre-Sinai Divine commandment that was recorded by Moses in the part of the Torah preceding the revelation at Mount

but one begins to serve idolatry and is not willing to give up these ways, the other partner is obligated to divorce and separate.

17. In any Gentile marriage, if the two partners wish to separate, they may divorce at any time that either so desires. When the man sends the woman away from his house with the intention that she should not return to him, or when she leaves of her own accord with the intention not to return, they become separated, and she is considered divorced and single, and is not married anymore in the judgment of Torah Law. Within the Noahide Code, there is no need for Gentiles to have a divorce document.[175] Nevertheless, it is preferable if there is a formal civil procedure for divorce in the society (such as a legal document or court record). See topic 19 below.

Sinai, but was not repeated to Moses after that time, was removed from Gentiles, and it remained only for the Jews. Since the decree of Shem's court was not a precept from God, it was not removed from the Gentiles.]

*This can be viewed as based on the Noahide Commandment of *Dinim* (Judgments), to have courts that establish rules for society. As explained in topic 1:9 above, a Gentile society may institute decrees to help banish idolatry and/or harmful sexual activities. Since the decree of Shem's court (Tractate *Avodah Zarah* 36b) was recorded in the Torah in reference to the story of Tamar in Genesis 38:24, it was given eternal eminence.

From the *Midrash*, Shem started teaching Divine precepts shortly after the Flood, and he explained that the Flood occurred because those precepts were transgressed. (Shem was 98 years old when the Flood came; see Rashi on Genesis 10:21. From *Tanna DeVei Eliyahu* 20:10 and 24:10, Shem prophesied for 400 years to **all** nations of the world, but they did not listen to him. See also *Yalkut Shimoni*, beginning of *Parshas Balak*, that this occurred after the Flood.) Alternatively, the decree could have been a response by Shem (who was the king Malĥizedek of Salem/Jerusalem; see Rashi on Gen. 14:18) to the idolatry that was being spread in the world by the king Nimrod in Babylon. At this time in history, around the time of the Tower of Babel, most of the world's population knew of Shem and his court. (This is obvious from *Tanna DeVei Eliyahu*, *loc. cit.*, that states that Shem prophesied "to all nations.") Shem was recognized after the Flood as God's prophet (see Rashi on Gen. 25:22), and a foremost spiritual leader of the world (although he was eventually surpassed by Abraham as a spiritual leader).

[175] Rambam, *Laws of Kings* 9:8.

To dissolve the state of marriage, this divorce must be a resolute decision for permanent separation.[176] But if they only have intention to leave each other for a period of time and then return to each other (perhaps having in mind that they may have relations with others in the interim), this is an abhorrent practice, and this leads to behavior that is under the category of a woman becoming married to two men (discussed above in topics 2:4 and 4:9).

In the reference to a decision for "permanent separation," the meaning is that at the time they separate, they have made this resolute decision. However, if they change their mind afterwards and decide to return to each other in marriage, they are permitted to do so, even if the woman remarried in the interim, and her second husband divorced her or died.[177]

18. A slavewoman whose master specifies her as a partner for his slave is considered married, as explained above in Chapter 3. When is she considered divorced and single again? When her master separates her from the slave (even by force), and "uncovers her hair in public."[178] In the earlier times of the Sages who codified these Torah laws, a married woman (even a slavewoman) would not uncover her hair in public, so uncovering her hair in public would be a sign that she was single.[179]

---

[176] See Rabbeinu Ĥananel, brought by Rabbeinu Beĥaye on Genesis 20:2, that a woman who was forced by fear into divorce is not considered fully divorced; however, it appears that she also is not fully married, and one who cohabits with her after her forced divorce is not liable to capital punishment for adultery.

[177] See *Tosafot* on Tractate *Sanhedrin* 56b, and Ran on *Sanhedrin* 57b, that there is no prohibition for a Gentile to remarry his divorcee, even after she was remarried to another man whom she subsequently divorced.

[178] Rambam, *Laws of Kings* ch. 9. It appears that the necessity for this special action was due to the fact that the slavewoman and slave lived on the master's property the entire time, and there was no way for them to divorce in the regular manner of free people; see Ran on Tractate *Sanhedrin* 58b.

*This does not mean that she merely revealed her hair briefly or discreetly in public. Rather, her master forced her to walk about in full public view with her hair uncovered, or she could decide to act in this manner on her own.

[179] Rashi on Tractate *Sanhedrin* 58b.

As well, if this slavewoman uncovered her hair in public of her own accord, and her master was not forcing her to stay with the slave that he had specified her for, she was considered divorced.[180]

In other times and places, a slavewoman who separates from a designated slave must do a public action, or act in some obvious way according to the customs of that place, to publicly inform others of her separation from the slave. After that she is considered divorced. For example, the master might be careful to prevent his single female and male slaves from being alone together. If he selects a slavewoman and a slaveman to be together as a married couple, they will be considered divorced when he separates them from each other and prevents them from being alone together.

19. Since it was established that at any time, a Gentile woman or man can separate from their partner and they are considered divorced, why is a married woman who cohabits with a stranger liable for adultery? Perhaps she could be considered single when she shows that she wishes to have relations with a second man and not the first? This is because her actions show that she does not fully want to leave her first husband, since she has not moved out from his home and abandoned their partnership. Rather, she has acted licentiously while remaining in a relationship with her husband, and therefore this is adultery for which both the woman and the other man are liable.

However, if she leaves her husband's home permanently and goes to live with another man, she is not considered married to the first. Rather, she is a divorcee and is permitted to the second man.

Since it may be easy for her to make that move, and it is possible that she might leave her husband for a short time for another man and then return, and it is impossible to know if she made a firm decision to leave her husband, it is proper to set up a formal procedure for a divorce through the courts. This way, a woman will not give the appearance of being married to two men, to whom she goes back and forth whenever she desires.

---

[180] This is the implication of the previously cited Rashi. It appears that Rambam would agree as well, and that he writes, "when the master chooses for the slavewoman to separate," to demonstrate the master's authority in this issue (see footnote 119 above). This does not negate a step she does on her own to divorce from her slave-husband.

20. A married Gentile woman who committed adultery, even intentionally, is not forbidden to her husband, and if they both wish to continue with their married life together, they may do so.[181]

21. A married woman whose husband dies becomes single.[182] If her husband dies, but before she finds out about his death, she cohabits with another man, she is exempt from liability to punishment for adultery. That is because her marriage became nullified in any case through her husband's death, even though she had no knowledge of this.

Editor's note: If a Gentile woman contracts a marriage with a man who is too old to perform intercourse, or injured in a way that makes intercourse impossible, the woman will only have the status of betrothal. Nevertheless, the courts can still impose the status of legal marriage, making it more strictly forbidden for the woman to have relations with another man. But if it is obvious to everyone that there cannot be a consummation of the marriage, then they are not fully married, and the woman would not be liable to capital punishment for adultery within the limits of Torah Law.

---

[181] Ran *Sanhedrin* 57b.

[182] This is apparent; and this is also the opinion of the *Ramban Yevamot* 97b, and *Minĥat Ĥinuĥ* Commandment 35, part 2, and R. Ovadiah Bartenurah and Riva's explanations on Genesis 12:12.

CHAPTER 5

Precepts Related to Spilling Semen, and Contraception

1. Men are forbidden to spill their semen "wastefully" (as this term is explained below).[183]

This sin is grave and is punished by God, as we find that this was one of the sins of the Generation of the Flood, and one of the reasons that caused the Flood,[184] as it says,[185] "As all flesh has corrupted its way *upon the earth*" (meaning that the men habitually ejaculated their semen upon the ground).

We also find that Judah's sons Er and Onan were punished by God for doing so, as it says[186] "And it was that when he [Onan] came to the wife of his [deceased] brother [Er], that he spilled his seed to the earth, so as not to give children to his brother... and his actions were evil in the eyes of God, and He killed him as well."

Anyone who spills semen "wastefully" is compared to a murderer, as it says,[187] "your hands are full of blood."[188]

The Torah-law authorities debated the reason for this pre-Sinai

---

[183] *The use of the term "spilling" in this context is meant to reflect the following definition. It is forbidden by Torah Law for a man to deliberately emit semen when it is not being emitted within his woman partner, in midst of their allowed manner of cohabitation, which is vaginal or anal intercourse (this applies unless there is an instance of an overriding medical necessity for him to do so, as explained below).

If a man (or boy) brings on an ejaculation in some other way, he is said to be spilling his semen wastefully. This applies to a man who does this to himself by his own action, and to one who allows someone else to do this to him.

A man is not held liable for a sin if he unconsciously emits semen during his sleep. However, if he deliberately intends and acts in such a way that this will happen after he falls asleep, it is considered to be close to a deliberate transgression.

[184] Tractate *Niddah* 13a and Rashi there; Tractate *Sanhedrin* 108b.

[185] Genesis 6:12.

[186] Genesis 38:9.

[187] Isaiah 1:15.

[188] Rambam, *Laws of Forbidden Sexual Relations* 21:18.

prohibition for Gentiles.[189] Some said that it is an offshoot of the

---

[189] The opinion of *Tosafot* in Tractate *Sanhedrin* 59b is that a Gentile, who is not commanded to "be fruitful and multiply," is also not forbidden to spill his semen. This is also the opinion of Rabbeinu Tam in *Tosafot Niddah* 13a, *Kesubot* 39a, and *Yevamot* 12b. This opinion of *Tosafot* seems questionable, based on Tractate *Niddah* 13a, that this was one of the sins that caused the Flood, and on *Yevamot* 34b, that Er and Onan were punished by God for this act. A possible explanation is that they lived before God gave the Torah, and before the Torah was given, Gentile men were still subject to the commandment to "be fruitful and multiply" (see Rashi on Gen. 1:28). Therefore, they were punished for spilling semen, which violated that command.

However, *Ramban Niddah* 13 says that the prohibition of spilling semen is independent of the command to "be fruitful and multiply" (to which Rashba, Ran, and Ritva obviously agree there, since they cite his words). The later Rabbis debated about the reason according to Ramban for this prohibition. It seems that it is deemed to be akin to murder, as the Talmud says (Tractate *Niddah* there), "those who slaughter children." This is also stated by *Mateh Aharon* (brought in *S'dei Ĥemed Ma'areĥet Zayin*, ch. 20). *Mishneh LiMeleĥ* (*Laws of Kings* 10:7) explains that according to Ramban, everyone – including even all those who are not commanded to "be fruitful and multiply" – is forbidden to cause spilling of semen, as it says, "*all* flesh had corrupted its way upon the earth" (Genesis 6:12).

The later Rabbinical authorities ask (*Encyclopedia Talmudica* vol. 11, "Spilling Semen") where the source for this prohibition is in Torah, as it is not expressly written anywhere in the Hebrew Bible. Therefore, *Torat Ĥesed* (*Even HaEzer* ch. 43) explains that according to *Tosafot*, spilling semen is a transgression of the command to "be fruitful and multiply" (and therefore for Gentiles, spilling semen was only a transgression of the pre-Sinai command), whereas Ramban holds that it is a post-Sinai Rabbinical injunction. Based on this, the prohibition for Gentiles would be more lenient, if it existed at all.

However, it appears that the prohibition of spilling semen *is* written in Torah, but not as an explicit prohibition. This is explained in the responsa *P'nei Yehoshua* vol. 2, *Even HaEzer* ch. 44 – that it is forbidden since the Torah writes that the actions of Er and Onan were "wicked in God's eyes" (Gen. 38:7,10). The meaning of his words is that anything the Torah expressly says is "wicked in God's eyes" is forbidden for everyone, although it is not written expressly as a prohibition. It is possible that this does not contradict the opinion of *Tosafot*, who are referring to the practical reason for the prohibition, which would explain that this is not an explicit commandment (to Gentiles, and therefore there is no specific punishment for this act in a court of law), but it is still taken into account that the Torah calls it wicked.

prohibition of murder, since the semen could have been used to give birth to children, and one who spilled it is considered murderous (accordingly, it is still forbidden after Mount Sinai). Others say that it was forbidden before Mount Sinai, because one who did so was neglecting the directive to "be fruitful and multiply" that was commanded to Adam and Noaĥ. Since they were commanded about this, they were also given the prohibition against spilling semen. It was only after the giving of the Torah at Mount Sinai that the directive to "be fruitful and multiply" was no longer a Divine commandment for Gentiles, so from that time on, they were no longer liable to capital punishment for spilling semen.

According to all opinions, it is clear that this remains a corrupt act and is counter to acting in the proper way to establish a corrected and settled society, as it says, "The world was not created to be empty, but rather to be settled." Since this action is "empty" and corrupt,[190] it is logical that it is forbidden. It is also expressly written in the Torah of Moses that it is an action that is evil in God's eyes, and it is therefore forbidden in the Noahide Code.

Another point regarding this transgression is that it is a destructive act that causes long-term physical and mental (emotional) damage to the person. One who falls into a regular habit of this behavior causes actual damage to himself, and it is forbidden within the Noahide Code to commit self-damage, as explained in Part V, Chapter 6.[191]

The Sages taught that a man's semen is the strength of his body, his body's life-force, and light of his eyes, and if a man habitually

---

(It is possible that such a prohibition, though not written expressly in any Torah verse, is even more severe than one that is expressly written, since the Torah clearly says that God killed Onan for this. Even though *Tosafot* says that this was only due to the fact that it was expressly forbidden before the giving of the Torah, it still shows the severe negativity of the action, which logically should indicate that it is forbidden. Ramban, on the other hand, would even say that the prohibition and liability to Divine punishment remained the same afterwards, even though it is not written expressly.)

[190] *Levush Even HaEzer* ch. 23, *Aruĥ LaNer Niddah* 13.

[191] We see that the later Torah authorities permitted one to do this on a case-by-case basis for the purpose of needed medical testing, and as written in Part V, Chapter 6, one may cause or allow damage to his body if there is a truly accepted need to do this, in which case the emission of the semen is not considered to have been done "in vain."

ejaculates overly much, his body and his physical power are weakened, and his life span is shortened. This even includes a man who makes it his habit to engage overindulgently in *permitted* sexual relations, beyond his expected conjugal duties to his wife – his old age advances upon him prematurely, his strength is weakened, his eyesight diminishes, his mouth and his armpits emit foul odors, and his hair falls out, to name a few of the resulting physical problems and malfunctions that the Sages warned of. With this loss of strength, various pains and medical susceptibilities will come upon him. The wise doctors of earlier generations said that one man in a thousand dies from unrelated illnesses, and the rest die from physical problems that develop from their excessive sexual relations [and masturbation].[192]

2. The only circumstance mentioned in the Torah in which one received punishment for this was if he was already married, and he deliberately spilled his semen so as to prevent his wife from becoming pregnant, as Er and Onan did. However, one who has the ability to marry and have relations with his wife, thereby removing himself from the natural urges to spill his semen, but does not do so and rather spills his semen deliberately, is wicked and has done an evil action similar to that of Er and Onan.

3. This prohibition only applies to one who spills semen deliberately

---

Similarly, it appears to the author that if one has an intense urge to cohabit with a prostitute, it is better that he spill his semen and not cohabit with her (even if she is unmarried), since both actions violate the command for Gentiles to "make the world settled," and cohabiting with a prostitute causes a greater destruction of the society at large than his own (self-damaging) act of masturbation. (Also, there are those that say that one who cohabits with a prostitute, by default, also transgresses the prohibition of wasteful emission of semen – see *Otzar Ha'Poskim* vol. 9, p. 90b – since it is not done for the purpose of marital relations [as well as the fact that prostitutes use methods of contraception to avoid pregnancy, and those men who use their services are drawn away from the positive obligation to father and raise children]. So the act of relations with a prostitute is the same as if the man spilled his semen on his own, and better that he transgress only one prohibition rather than two.)

[192] Rambam, *Laws of Personality* (*Hilĥot De'ot*) 4:19.

by his own action or by allowing this to happen, as one who arouses himself through contact with a woman and thereby expels semen but not in the process of intercourse;[193] even one who cohabits inside a woman and then expels semen outside transgresses this sin.[194]

However, a Gentile man who has intercourse with his wife is not considered as having wasted semen, even if it will definitely not lead to conception, since this is necessary for the establishment of love between husband and wife, and the preservation and peace of their marriage.[195] Therefore, it is permitted for a Gentile to cohabit with his wife even if she is unable to give birth (such as a post-menopausal or infertile woman), since this is the way of marital cohabitation.

This permitted cohabitation may take place either through the normal way (i.e. vaginal intercourse), or the "abnormal way" (i.e. anal intercourse), since both are called "the way of cohabitation;" see below in topic 7. But ejaculation by any other way, such as oral intercourse, constitutes the prohibition of "spilling semen."

4. It was explained in Part V, Chapter 9, that it is forbidden for a man or woman to undergo elective surgical sterilization, since this is damaging the body, and there are permitted means of temporarily or permanently suppressing fertility through oral medicines that do not damage the body physically. They are permitted for Gentile men and women, since it is not the rendering of infertility that is prohibited for Gentiles, but only the infliction of physical damage.

---

193 Rashi on Tractate *Niddah* 13b says that this is wasting semen in vain.

*Therefore it is forbidden for a man to gaze at pornography and allow himself to be aroused by this, because it is very likely that this will lead to the spilling of his semen.

194 Rambam, *Laws of Forbidden Sexual Relations* ch. 21.

195 Responsa of R. Asher, brought in *Beit Yosef Even HaEzer* ch. 23; Rema, Bach, and *Beis Shmuel* in *Even HaEzer ibid.* Marital relations are necessary for the establishment of love between husband and wife, and the preservation of their marriage. See topic 4:2, that marriage is a union that establishes a normal society, even when couples cannot conceive children. Keeping the immediate family ties (the bond and love between a husband and wife) is indeed a **positive** aspect of the marital intercourse that gives the act itself purposefulness. So even if there is no chance of conception, the act is not done "wastefully."

Nevertheless, a man or woman should not use these methods unless there is a great need involved; but one who does so for no dire reason abandons the nature and normal way of the world, since God created the reproductive organs for the purpose of conceiving and giving birth to children.

5. A woman who does not wish to become pregnant may do certain actions (before relations or afterwards) to prevent the *conception* (the fertilization of the egg).[196] As explained before in Chapter 4 above, Gentiles are not obligated to have children if they do not wish to do so, since they are not commanded to "be fruitful and multiply."

However, once a woman has become pregnant, it is forbidden for her to have an abortion, unless the pregnancy is endangering her life. A woman who willingly submits to an elective abortion (and the one who performs an elective abortion) for any other reason is a murderer of the unborn fetus, as explained in more detail in Part V, topics 1:10-14.

---

[196] The Torah-law authorities argue whether a Jewish woman may use a contraceptive method before or after relations, and the opinions have been gathered in *Encyclopedia Talmudica*, Vol. 11, "Spilling Semen," and *Otzar HaPoskim* Vol. 9 (*Even HaEzer* ch. 23, part 5).

It appears that the entire discussion in the Talmud, Tractates *Kesubot* 39 and *Yevamot* 12, regarding a Jewish woman using contraceptives is only regarding the couple's neglect of the Jewish command to "be fruitful and multiply," but this is not equated with the prohibition of emitting semen in vain, as then it would be totally forbidden, even if there would otherwise be physical discomfort for her (see Rosh brought in *Shulĥan Aruĥ Even HaEzer* ch. 23, that it is forbidden for a husband to expel semen outside after cohabiting, even if the wife has an obstruction that would cause her pain otherwise). The reason that certain contraceptive methods are permitted for Jews is that they allow the act of unobstructed marital cohabitation to still take place, even though it is not possible (due to the contraceptive used) for the wife to become impregnated by the semen that her husband emitted into her (see *Torat Ĥesed Even HaEzer* ch. 44, part 21-23, and other opinions brought in *Otzar HaPoskim ibid.* ch. 17, part 15), and therefore many Torah authorities permit this if it is needed for the sake of a Jewish wife's health.

The reason that this is not considered wasting semen is explained in *Yam Shel Shlomo Yevamot* ch. 1, section 8, that in cohabitation there are two parts: to "be fruitful and multiply," and to cohabit as marital relations. Where the latter is being fulfilled, it cannot be said that the action is spilling semen wastefully, although "to be fruitful and multiply" may be neglected.

6. It is permitted for a Gentile man to wear a condom that blocks the flow of semen, and this is not considered spilling semen as long as he is emitting it during vaginal or anal intercourse with his wife.[197] However, this use of a condom is only permitted on a temporary basis.

If there is a dire need,[198] such as if his wife is not well and does not want to conceive because it would endanger her life or damage her

---

[197] Rabbi Zalman Nehemiah Goldberg advises further analysis. The author responds that the later authorities (brought in *Encyclopedia Talmudica* vol. 11, on "Spilling Semen," and *Tzitz Eliezer* vol. 9, ch. 51) discuss whether a condom is equal to an intra-uterine device (IUD), or if a condom is worse since it interposes between the flesh of the husband and wife, so their act would not be considered actual intercourse. In a situation where this is direly needed, it is permitted since, like an IUD, one does not intend to wastefully emit semen – see responsa of Aĥiezer vol. 3, ch. 24; responsa of Maharshag vol. 2, ch. 243; and responsa of *Pri HaSadeh*, vol. 3, ch. 53.

See *Igrot Moshe* (*Even HaEzer* vol. 1, end of ch. 63) regarding Jews; it is clear from his words that the matter would be more lenient for Gentiles; as we find that Rema (*Even HaEzer* ch. 25) permits abnormal relations.

(In this regard, using a condom is equal to an IUD or abnormal relations, since the man's organ is entering into the woman in the manner of normal cohabitation, but it is done so as to prevent conception. The only forbidden action is full intercourse initially and then emitting semen outside the body [coitus interruptus], whereas with a condom, the man is ejecting semen within the body of the woman. She therefore receives the full pleasure in the entire process of the cohabitation, and because this purpose is achieved, therefore this is not considered to be emitting the semen wastefully.)

It may be added that the later Torah authorities (see *Otzar HaPoskim* vol. 9. p. 17) all agree that one is liable in a court of Torah Law for cohabiting with a forbidden partner even with a condom, from which we see that Torah considers it to be full cohabitation, and therefore it should be permitted for Gentiles to use a condom in cohabitation with their wives.

[198] See *Igrot Moshe Even HaEzer* vol. 4, ch. 70, who permits a woman to use an IUD as a contraceptive because of personal needs (even not for health reasons), since it is necessary for marital relations that maintain peace between the couple. The prohibition he discusses regarding condoms is for Jews, who are forbidden to make complete separation between the husband's semen and the wife's flesh. For a Gentile, this would be completely permitted (see footnote 197). Nevertheless, it appears that it is more proper for Gentiles to use an IUD or other contraceptive than a condom if possible, and only if the wife cannot or does not wish to, her husband may wear a condom.

health, it is permitted. Otherwise it is forbidden for one to do so exclusively, in order to constantly have relations while preventing pregnancy as a matter of mere pleasure and convenience (as is the case with one who constantly has abnormal relations; see the next topic).

The leniency for use of a condom only applies when a man does so with his wife, since he is having normal marital relations, and this is an act of establishing and maintaining the marriage bond. By contrast, one who acts licentiously with a woman outside of marriage, preventing conception by use of condom, has transgressed the prohibition against spilling semen.

7. It is not forbidden for a Gentile to have "abnormal" (anal) heterosexual relations.[199] Although it is impossible for his wife to conceive in this way, it is not considered to be wasting semen, since he is cohabiting with her.[200] (Still, this is a repugnant act, and it is called "an animalistic action," since God created human anatomy differently than animals, whose natural way is that the male cohabits with the female from behind, and does not see her face at all. This general repugnance applies to abnormal intercourse in any position. However, there is no prohibition that forbids this.)

This leniency for abnormal relations only applies if the man does so in a temporary fashion, for the purpose of his own pleasure. But if he does so constantly in order to prevent pregnancy, it is forbidden, and he is considered to be intentionally spilling his semen.[201]

---

[199] Tractate *Sanhedrin* 58b according to the opinion of Rava. We do not follow the opinion of Rabbi Ĥanina there, that it is forbidden since it is not a way of "clinging," from which it would also obviously be forbidden to do so with another man's wife, or even a single woman. Even if the opinion follows Rava, it is still possible that this is only permitted with one's own wife, since it is done in a way of love within marriage, but with any other woman it is merely considered emitting semen wastefully and is forbidden.

[200] *Tosafot Yevamot* 34b, *Rema Even HaEzer* ch. 25.

[201] See *Tosafot Sanhedrin* 58b and *Yevamot* 34b. The reason, explained there, is that Er and Onan were punished because they specifically intended for Tamar not to *ever* get pregnant. But one who does so occasionally for his own pleasure or by his wife's wishes (and not specifically over the long term for the purpose of preventing pregnancy) does not transgress this prohibition. This is clear from *Tosafot Rid Yevamot* 12, and this is how later authorities (e.g., *Igrot Moshe Even HaEzer* vol. 1, ch. 63 part 3) explain *Tosafot*.

CHAPTER 6

Guarding Against Forbidden Relations, and Following Ways of Modesty

1. A man is forbidden to have close physical contact with a "forbidden relation" (i.e. any woman whom Torah Law forbids him to cohabit with), even if the contact is in ways other than cohabiting, such as hugging or kissing, or touching her body in a way of desire, as it may lead him to cohabit with her. Of course they may not sleep together, even if they are sleeping in their clothes, as all these actions lead one to sin.

He must likewise distance himself from all actions that arouse his inclination to desire sinful cohabitation: he may not beckon to a forbidden relation with his hand, or wink at her, joke with her, or become lightheaded with her, and he may not gaze at her beauty,[202] because all these actions can lead one to sin.[203]

---

[202] See *Avot D'Rabbi Natan* 2:5.

[203] See *Bereishit Rabbah* 70:12 on the verse "Jacob kissed Rachel and wept," that explains that he wept because he was suspected of lewdness for kissing Rachel (an unmarried girl of marriageable age), since the generations after the Flood took extra precautions to avoid the sin of forbidden relations. How much more so, a man should not kiss another man's wife. (It is also said in *Bereishit Rabbah* 80:6, in regard to the abduction and rape of Dinah, that the generations after the Flood took extra precautions to avoid forbidden relations. But it is possible to say from there that they only took extra precautions regarding forbidden actions such as the rape of virgins. However, what is clear from both sources is that those generations guarded themselves not only from adulterous relations, but also further restrictions (guarding against forced or consenting relations with single women and girls.)

See *Minĥat Ĥinuĥ* Commandment 188, that discusses whether there is an express prohibition for Gentiles not to have physical contact (even less intimate than sexual relations, such as kissing or hugging) with a forbidden relation. *S'dei Ĥemed* vol. 3, ch. 38, in the name of Ĥida, refers to the responsa of *Ĥavot Ya'ir* ch. 108, that implies that there is no prohibition in this matter.

(This requires further analysis, since there it refers to a single Jewess, and not a married woman or the others who are forbidden for sexual relations within the Noahide commandment. However, from Ĥida's statement that Gentiles are forbidden equally as Jews in regard to the prohibition of a married woman, it is implied that Gentile men are also forbidden to have less intimate types of physical contact with another man's wife. It is possible that

Just as it is forbidden for a man to do these things, it is also forbidden for a woman to do such actions that will arouse a man to desire to sin with her.

2. A mother may hug and kiss her son, and likewise a father may hug and kiss his daughter, as this is not done in a way of sinful desire but rather of a parent's love to a child.[204] The same applies to a grandfather with a granddaughter, a grandmother with a grandson, or a brother with a sister who is a minor (i.e. if she is younger than 12 years old).[205]

However, for a man's mature sister or other female relatives, though the way of the world is to kiss and hug them, and this is not intended for sinful desire but rather respect or friendship, and there is no prohibition involved, this custom nevertheless does lead to forbidden contact. It is therefore proper, as much as possible, to avoid this.[206]

3. A father may sleep in the same bed as his daughter when she is a minor, even with full body contact, and likewise a mother may do so with her son, until the children reach the stage that the daughter is embarrassed to stand naked before her father, and the mother before her son. Even at a later age in childhood, it is permitted for them to sleep in the same bed as long as they are clothed (as is the law for

---

Ĥida only refers to the prohibition upon Gentile men in regard to relations with a married Jewess [see topic 3:8 above], and the only forbidden physical contact for Gentiles is that which is learned from the Jewish commandments, i.e. adultery, but not from their own forbidden relations in the Noahide Code.)

It seems more likely that Gentiles are not commanded in this area at all. *Mitzvot Hashem*, p. 479, states that by logical reasoning, Gentiles are forbidden to have physical contact that could lead them to forbidden relations; thus, the prohibition stems from a logical obligation.

[204] Rambam, *Laws of Forbidden Sexual Relations* 21:7, and *Shulĥan Aruĥ Even HaEzer* ch. 21. Even though it concludes there that such contact is only permitted until the child matures or gets married, *Beit Shmuel Even HaEzer* 21:14 explains that this limitation is only regarding the prohibition of sleeping together, and it does not refer to a prohibition of kissing or hugging an adult of the opposite gender (who is not one's spouse); this type of contact is permitted between parents and their adult children.

[205] *Ĥelkat Meĥokaik* and *Beit Shmuel Even HaEzer* ch. 21.

[206] *Shulĥan Aruĥ Even HaEzer* ch. 21.

hugging and kissing),[207] until they grow up and begin to reach puberty (a girl at the age of 12, and a boy at the age of 13). It is likewise permitted for a brother and sister to sleep in the same bed until they both reach close to the age of puberty.[208]

4. Every woman is obligated to act in a modest way, and not to cause others to err through her dressing and acting in a way that brings them to sinful thoughts, and thereby closer to sinful actions, as the Torah says,[209] "You shall not put a stumbling block before the blind." For in a similar manner, an immodest woman causes others to sin through her way of dressing and acting, and since she is the one responsible for leading others to sinful desires or to actual sinful behavior, God will punish her accordingly.[210]

Any woman above 12 years old, whether single or married, should wear modest clothes that cover her whole torso until her collarbone, her legs until her knees, and her arms until the elbow.

The significance of modesty for men and women is not only that it prevents many sins, but also that it is the correct expression of respect for God's creation of mankind in His image. Thus, covering one's body shows fear of God and respect for mankind. Conversely, it is despicable for a person to walk naked in public, and one who does so shows an attitude of disbelief that there is a God to respect, or that God watches every action of a person, or that all of mankind is created in the image of God. Rather, a person who does this obviously views human beings like animals that can walk shamelessly among their fellow creatures with no clothes.[211]

---

[207] *Shulĥan Aruĥ Even HaEzer ibid.*, and *Beit Shmuel* 21:14.

[208] This appears to be the meaning of *Beit Shmuel* there in the name of *Taz*.

[209] Lev. 19:14. Rabbi Zalman Nehemiah Goldberg notes that he previously explained that there is no such prohibition for Gentiles (see Part I, topic 4:6).

[210] See *Pirkei D'Rabbi Eliezer* ch. 22 and *Targum Yonatan* Genesis 6:2: "The women of the Generation of the Flood used to walk around revealed below their waist." (By this it is logical that they were also punished by the Flood, and not just the men who kidnapped, raped and wasted semen, since by their actions the women were partners in the sins that were perpetrated, because their walking around naked aroused the desires of the men.)

[211] See Tractate *Yevamot* 63b, *Tana De'vei Eliyahu Rabbah* ch. 31, *Tana De'vei Eliyahu Zuta* ch. 10, and *Shulĥan Aruĥ Oraĥ Ĥayim* ch. 2.

5. A man should not intently gaze at the form of a woman in a lustful way, even if she is single, as Job said in his righteousness (Job 31:1), "I have made a covenant with my eyes not to look upon a virgin."

It is, however, permitted for a man who is seeking a wife to look at a single woman's face, to see if she is fitting in his eyes to be his wife. It is not only permitted, but encouraged, that a man should be well acquainted (non-physically) with the woman he wants to marry, to be sure that she finds favor in his eyes.[212]

6. It is forbidden for one to desire or lust after another man's wife.[213] Rather, a man should control his inclination and his mind so as not to think about any attraction to her, and thereby not come to sin.

7. It is forbidden to be involved in any matter that is intended to cause sin and lust, or that is likely to lead to this. It is therefore forbidden to participate in mixed dancing or lightheaded gatherings of mingled men and women, and it is forbidden to go swimming where there are mixed men and women,[214] since all these activities bring people close to, or actually to, sins and licentiousness.

It is likewise forbidden to watch lewd movies, or to read publications or view Internet sites that include lewd pictures or stories, since all these arouse a man's lustful thoughts.[215] A wise man should be careful in this matter, and he should especially watch over the upbringing of his children, and guard them from involvement with these things.

It is the obligation of a society's legal system to ban pornography and punish those who publicize these abominations, since these are things that cause the public to sin.[216]

8. Even though one's wife is permitted to him in any way of non-injurious physical contact, nevertheless, a wise man should calculate his actions and act with respect and love towards his wife, and not in a

---

[212] Based on Rambam, *Laws of Forbidden Sexual Relations* ch. 21.

[213] *Sefer HaĤinuĥ* Commandment 416. See below in Part VII, topic 1:18.

[214] See *Rema Even HaEzer* ch. 21, and *Beit Shmuel Even HaEzer* 21:10.

[215] *Therefore, a Gentile woman should not sing in the presence of men with enticing words and in immodest ways that will be a stumbling block for them. A married Gentile woman should be additionally strict in this matter.

[216] *Shulĥan Aruĥ Oraĥ Ĥayim* 307:16.

way that is only lustful, in order that he not remove himself from proper societal conduct. He should also not have relations with her while thinking of another woman, and they should not have relations when either he or she is intoxicated from alcohol or drugs, or angry, or feeling hateful toward the other.

It is forbidden for a man to force his wife to have relations, since she is not his property to be forced to act on his every whim, even to the point that he can force her to have relations. Rather, mutual marriage can only exist when she consents to the relations they are having. As explained above, she can divorce from him at any time she wishes, so forcing her to have relations is similar to doing so with a stranger.

Likewise, a man should not have relations with his wife in public, but rather only in privacy. It is appropriate that the legal system should punish those who do not act accordingly.[217]

Even the ways of physical affection between men and women, such as kissing and hugging, or lying together, should be done privately,[218] in order not to arouse lustful thoughts of those who would see them in public. In general, a person should act in a way that reflects respectably upon himself, and not in an animalistic fashion.

9. It is proper that a married woman cover her hair when outside her house or in the presence of men other than her husband.[219]

10. A man should not be appointed to guard a women's institution, even if he is trusted and upright, as there is no true guardian for prohibited licentiousness. (If a male guard is necessary, the institution should contract for a licensed guard with a professional security company, so he will be restrained by his strict legal accountability.)

---

[217] Based on Rambam, *Laws of Forbidden Sexual Relations* ch. 21.

[218] See *Rema Even HaEzer* ch. 21.

[219] Tractate *Sanhedrin* 58a states that this was the custom of Gentile women in Talmudic and earlier times, as a clear sign to distinguish married women from single women. Even though it is not customary for Gentile women to do so nowadays in many societies, a modest and pious married woman should nevertheless cover her hair. (This is required for Jewish women once they have become married as defined within Torah Law.)

It is forbidden for a married man to appoint a male guardian over his home while he is away, in order not to lead his wife to commit sin with the guardian.[220]

11. A man naturally lusts for and desires forbidden relations. Therefore, it is fitting that he subjugate his inclination in this matter and behave with extra piety (i.e., one should take upon himself extra precautions, even if they are not explicitly commanded, in order to distance himself from sin), and to cultivate pure thoughts and state of mind (i.e., to turn his thoughts to proper and pure matters, since he naturally thinks of lustful things), and to refine one's behavior and character, in order to be saved from his natural desires.

A person should always distance himself from abhorrent things and from suspicion, and things that awaken thoughts of lust. A man should not walk behind a woman along the street, which will cause him to contemplate her form and her manner of walking. He should go out of his way to avoid walking by a brothel or the place of a prostitute.

He should be wary of being alone with a woman who is forbidden to him, as this brings on sin. He should also distance himself from lightheadedness and lewdness, since these are the main causes of sinning with forbidden relations. He should not remain a bachelor for many years, because marriage brings a man to abide by a higher moral standard[221] (since he can train himself to think of relations only with his wife, and not with any other women).

The most effective way to accomplish this, as the Sages say, is for a man to turn his mind to intellectual or financial[222] pursuits, and expand his mind intellectually, since lustful thoughts only overcome a person whose heart and mind are empty of wisdom.[223]

---

[220] Rambam, *Laws of Forbidden Sexual Relations* ch. 22.

[221] *If a man is considering delaying marriage while he pursues an advanced education and/or advancement in a career, it is worthy for him to seek wise advice about this. It might be better for him overall to find a wife sooner, and then advance through his education and career as a married man.

[222] See Tractate *Kesubot* 59b: "Idleness leads to lewdness and corruption." There is no natural difference in this regard between men and women.

[223] Based on Rambam, end of *Laws of Forbidden Sexual Relations, ibid.*

CHAPTER 7

Prohibitions Related to Being Alone with a Forbidden Partner; The Stringency of the Sin of Forbidden Relations

1. It is forbidden for a man to seclude himself with another man's wife, or with a woman who has at any time been a wife of his father. (These restrictions apply if she is not his close relative, i.e., his mother, sister or daughter.) This is a safeguard against the sin of forbidden relations.[224]

2. It is permitted for a man to be secluded with his mother, daughter,[225] granddaughter,[226] or grandmother, and even to live in the same home with one of them, exclusively and permanently.

It is also permitted for one to be secluded with his sister[227] or his aunt,[228] but only in a "temporary" fashion. (This means that it is

---

[224] The prohibition of seclusion for Gentiles is not stated explicitly, but such seclusion is logically wrong, as it is the greatest cause of forbidden relations, as written by Rambam, end of *Laws of Forbidden Sexual Relations.*

See Tractate *Yevamot* 47b: "Naomi said to Ruth: seclusion is forbidden for us [Jews]," and Rashi explains this as the prohibition of seclusion with the wife of another man. [Naomi was teaching Ruth the stringencies of Judaism, before Ruth converted.] This implies that when Ruth was a Gentile (before her conversion), it was not forbidden for her. It is possible that for a Jew, this is a Torah-law prohibition, and is only a logical prohibition for Gentiles. Or perhaps she was referring to the commandment regarding a *sotah* (a Jewish wife who was suspected of having adulterous relations with a man whom her husband had formally warned her not to be secluded with, as described in Numbers 5:11-31). This Jewish commandment does not apply to Gentiles.

*Topic 17 below explains that this prohibition was not expressly commanded by God to Gentiles. Rather, it is an added logical precaution that helps people to guard themselves from the temptation to engage in adultery or other forbidden relations. See the following topics in this chapter for explanations of where, when, and how this precaution applies.

[225] *Shulĥan Aruĥ Even HaEzer* ch. 22.

[226] *Baĥ Even HaEzer*, beginning of ch. 22.

[227] See *Beit Shmuel* and *Ĥelkat Meĥokaik Even HaEzer*, beginning of ch. 22.

[228] See Responsa of *Igrot Moshe Even HaEzer* vol. 4, ch. 64; *Tzitz Eliezer* vol. 6, 40:20; *Encyclopedia Talmudica* vol. 23, p. 667.

permitted to even sleep over for one night, or even a few nights, as a guest in a home that belongs the other person, but not in a permanent fashion.[229] It appears that they need to sleep in separate rooms, in which case this is permitted even if the house is locked, and even if their bedrooms are not locked. However, they should not sleep in the same room, since that would be immodest.) A Gentile man is permitted even to be secluded with these relatives after they have become married, because a decent person has no lust for these close relatives.[230] However, it is forbidden for one to be secluded with his daughter-in-law or mother-in-law, even in a temporary fashion.[231]

3. Any restriction involving seclusion with a sister is only after she and the brother have grown up and left the home of their parents. But as long as they are being raised together in their parents' home, there is no prohibition of seclusion.[232]

4. If parents have adopted a child, it appears that there is no prohibition for the father to be secluded with an adopted daughter or a mother with an adopted son, or an adopted child with his or her adoptive sibling of

---

[229] See *Igrot Moshe ibid.*; Responsa of *Shevet HaLevi*, vol. 5, ch. 201.

[230] See *Encyclopedia Talmudica* vol. 23, p. 669.

[231] *Igrot Moshe Even HaEzer* vol. 4, ch. 63; *Tzitz Eliezer* vol. 6, 40:20. They say their words regarding a Jew, and the same is surely true for a Gentile.

[232] See *Igrot Moshe Even HaEzer* vol. 4, 65:11, regarding Jews. The Torah Law is surely more lenient for Gentiles, as described here.

*The righteous practices in topics 2 and 3 were established not only for the safeguarding of individuals from actual sin, since upright people are distant from actually committing sinful relations with their relatives, or adultery. These restrictions also greatly benefit individuals and the society at large, by instilling attitudes of modesty, humility, respect for proper intimacy, fear of sin, and fear of God. In this light, it was common for the righteous Sages to tell their students (Tractate *Kiddushin* 82b), "Watch me because of my daughter," and "Watch me because of my daughter-in-law," to teach their students not to be embarrassed about strictness in these matters, and to distance themselves from a situation of forbidden seclusion. If a righteous Sage, who despised the very thought of sin and considered such actions to be completely repulsive, would be so careful, how much more so should his students, who were not so completely righteous – and how much more so should we.

the opposite gender. This applies if the family follows the common practice to conceal from the adopted child that he or she was adopted, and they treat the adopted child as a natural child in the family.[233]

This only applies until the adopted child has matured. But after a person has found out that he or she was adopted, and has left the house, seclusion with members of the adoptive family is restricted according to the same rules as for any other unrelated persons.

Likewise, a man who marries a woman who already has a daughter, and a woman who marries a man who already has a son, are permitted to be secluded with the stepchild as long as the couple lives together peacefully, since stepparents will treat stepchildren as their own children, out of love and respect for their spouse. Furthermore, stepparents will fear that any wrong action with a stepchild will become known and cause estrangement from the spouse.[234]

(This only applies to decent, upright people. But it is forbidden to be secluded with immodest and suspected people in any situation, with the usual exception of a person with his or her natural parent, child, sibling or grandchild of the opposite gender.)

5. The main restriction against seclusion applies to a married woman and another man, since Gentiles are liable for the severe prohibition of adultery.

It is righteous to extend this to seclusion between a single woman and a married or single man, lest they become aroused to commit licentious actions with each other. Since people's hearts are naturally drawn to this, it is therefore the practice of pious people to be especially cautious.

6. The prohibition and restrictions against seclusion apply to the woman just as they apply to the man, just like the precepts in the previous chapter regarding forbidden contact and immodesty between

---

[233] See *Igrot Moshe Even HaEzer* vol. 4, 64:2-3, and *Tzitz Eliezer* vol. 6, 40:21, in regard to Jews, and the same is surely true for Gentiles.

[234] Even though regarding Gentiles, we don't say that a man's wife surely guards him (see later, topic 10), there is nevertheless a difference: a woman would be less likely to remain quiet after discovering that her husband had cohabited with her daughter, and she would not allow him to do so, more so than if he had cohabited with any other woman. See fn. to topic 7:13 below.

forbidden partners.

7. In the daytime, the prohibition of seclusion only applies in a closed place, or in an area where it is unlikely that anyone else will pass by. But in a place where the door is open or there is a large window that is uncovered, and it is likely that a person will pass by and see all that is happening in the room with clear visibility,[235] there is no prohibition for forbidden partners to be alone together in that place.[236]

This applies in the daytime, or at night in a lit-up room that is adjacent to an area like a main street where people pass by constantly.[237] But where these conditions are not met, and it is not possible for people to see what transpires inside, or there are no passersby who will be able to see into the room, the restriction against seclusion applies.[238]

If the door is closed but not locked, and there are regularly people coming in and out during the hours that the man and woman are together inside, there is no prohibition of seclusion, since they will be afraid of being discovered.[239] If this is not the case, the closed door is considered as if it is locked, and the prohibition of seclusion applies.

8. There are Rabbinical authorities who say that a window or door open to a public area only helps for a married woman and another man who are unfamiliar with each other. But if they know each other and are comfortable with each other (such as relatives, a man and woman who were raised together, or a man and his remarried divorcee, or close friends), or if either one is immodest, they are forbidden to be alone together in that situation.[240] There are also authorities who are more lenient about that situation,[241] and one may rely on the lenient opinion in a time of temporary necessity.

---

[235] *Shulĥan Aruĥ Even HaEzer* ch. 22.

[236] *Ezer Mikodesh Even HaEzer ibid.*; *Misgeret HaShulĥan* 152:10.

[237] *Birkei Yosef Even HaEzer* 22:10.

[238] Responsa of *Radvaz* vol. 1, ch. 121; *Be'er Haitev Even HaEzer* 22:9 in the name of the *Knesset HaGedolah.*

[239] Responsa of *Radvaz ibid.*; responsa of *Mabit* vol. 1, part 287; *Binyan Tzion* vol. 1, ch. 138; *Ezer Mikodesh Shulĥan Aruĥ Even HaEzer* 22:9.

[240] *Ĥelkat Meĥokaik Even HaEzer* 22:13.

[241] *Taz Even HaEzer* 22:8; *Birkei Yosef* brought in *Pisĥei Teshuva Even HaEzer* 22:9.

9. If a married woman and another man are the only people in a house with two bedrooms, the man should not sleep in one room if the married woman is sleeping in the other room, even if each locks their own room separately, and each one would be unable to gain access to the other's room without consent. Why is this? Since the outside door is locked (or if it is unlikely that anyone else would happen to walk in), they should not be secluded in this way, because they may become drawn into sinning with each other.[242]

10. The restriction against seclusion applies when a Gentile man is alone with one or two women, even if his wife is one of them, since his wife might not prevent him from sinning with another woman.[243] A man may be secluded with three women.[244]

A woman should not be alone with two men unless one of them is her husband, because he will prevent her from sinning.[245] It is also permitted for her to be secluded with three men.[246]

---

[242] See *Igrot Moshe Even HaEzer* vol. 4, 65:19.

[243] Since a Gentile's wife is not assumed to guard him, as is written in Rambam, *Laws of Forbidden Sexual Relations,* ch. 22, and *Shulĥan Aruĥ Even HaEzer* ch. 22. (Neither are his mother, daughter, or sister assumed to guard him. See *Otzar HaPoskim* p. 51; *Igrot Moshe Even HaEzer* vol. 2, ch. 15, and vol. 4, 65:8; and *Tzitz Eliezer* vol. 6, 40:14.)

[244] This is clear from *Shulĥan Aruĥ Even HaEzer* 22:6: "many men with many women," which the Torah authorities say refers to a minimum of three. How much more so is one man permitted to be secluded with three women, since they would be embarrassed from each other. This is also clear from Rema there, section 5, based on Rashi.

[245] This is because a man is jealous of his wife and guards her. (For Gentiles, the Torah Law is that a wife is assumed to be afraid of sinning while together with her husband, but not if he is just elsewhere in the town. Although *Ezer Mikodesh Even HaEzer* 22:3 permits a Jew to be secluded with a Gentile woman while her husband is in the same town, it is possible that this is because the Jew, at least, will be embarrassed and afraid of her husband. A similar distinction is also made by *Igrot Moshe Even HaEzer* vol. 4, end of 65:8.)

[246] From the translation of the *Mishneh Torah* that is brought in *Shulĥan Aruĥ Even HaEzer* 22:5, it is implied that a Jewish woman may not even be secluded with many men, and there is no number given there.

It is also forbidden for two women to be secluded with two men,[247] unless one of the pairs are married, or a mother and son, a father and daughter, or a brother and sister,[248] or if one of them is elderly, or a minor [who is old enough to differentiate an act of relations].

All these laws only apply to upright, decent people, in a populated area during the day. But in the night or in a unpopulated area, a woman may not be secluded even with three men,[249] or a man with three women, or two women with two men, even if one of the pairs is specifically a married couple, as one person may leave (or fall sleep, if it is night), and the other pair will be left in a situation of seclusion.[250]

But a man with four women,[251] or a woman with four men, or three women and three men, may be secluded even at night or in an unpopulated area. This is only the case if they are not sleeping together in the same room, in which case one should be stringent, even if each one is in his or her own bed.[252]

It nevertheless appears that one may rule leniently for a Gentile woman, since the prohibition for Gentiles is based on logic, and one may rely on Rema's opinion there, that it is permitted for a woman to be secluded with two upright men. However, this leniency of Rema should only be used in a time of great need; see topic 7:17 below.

That which is written in *Shulĥan Aruĥ Yorah De'ah* ch. 153, that it is forbidden for a Jewess to be secluded with many Gentile men, even if their wives are with them, is possibly referring to a case in which they are immoral, as explained in *Taz* and *Shaĥ* there, or it may be a stringency, as explained in the opinion of *Sha'ar Yosef* (*Ĥida Horiyot*, responsa ch. 1).

247 See *Shulĥan Aruĥ Even HaEzer* 22:5, and the opinion of *Baĥ*, Rashal, *Ĥelkat Meĥokaik* and *Beit Shmuel* there, that the *Shulĥan Aruĥ* forbids it.

248 Based on *Tzitz Eliezer* vol. 6, 40:14. It appears that the reason is that specifically a brother and sister are embarrassed to sin before each other. In any case where the man and woman are not so capable, nor naturally tending, to sin with each other, there is no prohibition of seclusion.

249 *Rema Even HaEzer* 22:5.

250 *Pisĥei Teshuvah Even HaEzer* 22:2.

251 See *Rema* there, that at night it is permitted for a woman to be secluded with three upright men, which implies that also at night or outside the town one more is needed. Therefore, also for a Gentile, about whom it has been written that he should not be secluded with less than three women, the rule would be that at night he needs one more to be present.

252 See *Misgeret HaShulĥan* 152:8, and *Tzitz Eliezer* vol. 6, 40:13.

11. The restriction against seclusion applies even if there has been a large gathering of men and women, after which a few are left together alone in that place. If the rules in this chapter for permitted seclusion are not met, they are forbidden to remain in this situation, and they must leave the secluded area.

12. It is permitted for a Gentile man to be secluded by day with two women who dislike each other. This is because each woman is afraid to sin before the other, as she is afraid that the other would not cover up (and would reveal) a licentious act that she witnessed taking place.

Likewise, it is permitted for a Gentile man to be secluded with two wives of another man, or with a woman and her daughter-in-law, or with a woman and her stepdaughter, for the same reason.

It is likewise permitted for a Gentile man to be secluded with a woman and a minor child (a girl or a boy) who already knows the meaning of cohabitation (and who would relate to others what transpired), and who would not be drawn into a licentious act (the age for this is around the age of five and older).[253] This is because the adult woman would not sin before a child of that age, since the child would speak to others of what was witnessed.[254]

It appears that if there is an elderly man or woman present who is lucid (see topic 18 below, that there is no prohibition of seclusion with elderly people), there is no prohibition for a younger man and woman to be secluded there, since they will be embarrassed to cohabit in front of the elderly person, and they will be afraid that the elderly person would reveal their actions.[255]

13. It is permitted for a Gentile man to be secluded with a woman and her daughter or granddaughter, whether a child (in the age range explained in topic 12 above) or mature, since they are embarrassed to act inappropriately before each other. Likewise, it is permitted to be secluded with one's wife and her sister.[256]

---

[253] See in *Encyclopedia Talmudica* vol. 23, p. 716.

[254] *Shulĥan Aruĥ Even HaEzer* 22:10.

[255] This reasoning is written in a responsa of the Radvaz, vol. 3, ch. 481.

[256] See *Igrot Moshe Even HaEzer* vol. 4, ch. 64. The reason for the prohibition of seclusion with two women or two sisters is because they will cover up for each other. But with one's wife and her sister, though we rule that a Gen-

14. There is a prohibition of seclusion even in an open area, such as in a part of a field or park that is out of public view. Likewise, traveling in a car outside the city limits, or in secluded places in a city, or in a deserted public area of a city at night, is forbidden by these rules.[257] One may be lenient when traveling along roads where there are cars driving by constantly, even if one is doing highway driving at night.[258]

This leniency only applies to short drives, less than a day long, for which they will have to return to their homes to sleep. But to travel together for a few days, or for pleasure traveling, one should be more stringent in all the laws of seclusion, as explained before in topic 10 regarding seclusion in an unpopulated place or at night.

15. All the aforementioned limits (topics 10-14) apply only to upright people. They must still take precautions to guard themselves from forbidden relations, and therefore they must prevent themselves from becoming secluded together within these limits. But if there are immodest and immoral men, a woman may not even be secluded with ten of them,[259] nor may even many women, as the men may seduce them.[260] It is likewise forbidden for a man to be secluded with immodest women, even if there are three or more of them, as they are not embarrassed in front of each other at all. But it appears that there is no prohibition of seclusion if many upright men are with many immodest women. However, it is forbidden for an upright man or

---

tile's wife will not be able to guard him from cohabiting with another woman, it is obvious that he has some embarrassment before her, and the sister is embarrassed to have relations with him before his wife, and vice versa. These sisters do not have equal status; one is permitted to him, and one is forbidden (for licentious relations), so they are embarrassed before each other.

257 See *Beit Shmuel Even HaEzer* 22:15 in the name of *Baĥ* and Rashal, that the prohibition of seclusion is more severe while traveling. The reason is simply that they are together for a longer time, and therefore extra precaution is necessary. Nowadays, when travel is usually shorter, there is room to be more lenient, as written by the *Ezer Mikodesh Even HaEzer* 22:5.

258 *Igrot Moshe Even HaEzer* vol. 4, 65:3, and *Tzitz Eliezer* vol. 6, 40:15.

259 *Rema Even HaEzer* 22:5.

260 The implication of *Ritva Kiddushin* 80 in the name of Ramban, *Ĥelkat Meĥokaik Even HaEzer* 22:9, and *Beit Shmuel* 22:11.

woman to be secluded with many immodest men and women,[261] as he or she may become seduced to act like them. If, however, there is an opening to a public area, or the crowd is so large that people would not act licentiously since it is in public, one is permitted to be there.[262]

16. If there is a group of men, and some of them are immodest, one must follow the majority[263] in regard to whether it is forbidden for a woman to be secluded with them, and only if less than half are immodest is it permitted.

17. The prohibition of seclusion was not expressly given to Gentiles, but it is rather a precaution to guard one from forbidden relations. Therefore, if there is a great need for a Gentile to be in a certain place, but there is a Gentile of the opposite gender there and they will be secluded, but they are each busy (e.g., with their occupation), and neither the man or woman are suspected of being licentious, it appears that they may be thus secluded in a temporary fashion (although it is preferable that they have a window or door open to a public area, or if this is not possible, that there is a stranger or an older child with them).

If two men need to be in an area where one or two women are also found, they can be lenient in being secluded if they are busy with their occupation, and they are not suspected of immodesty.[264] Still, they should not be secluded for an extended period of time, as they will become fond of each other (and will be comfortable with each other).

A man whose business requires dealing with women (e.g. a perfumer or makeup artist or hairdresser, or one who sells articles like jewelry or clothes to women), may not be secluded with one or two women even temporarily, for he is comfortable with them, and they are comfortable with him.[265] This applies in a closed area, but if a door is open to

---

[261] See *Misgeret HaShulĥan* 152:6, and Responsa of *Shevet HaLevi* volume 5, ch. 202.

[262] *Ĥelkat Meĥokaik Even HaEzer* 22:9, and *Pisĥei Teshuvah Even HaEzer* 22:5 in the name of *Birkei Yosef.*

[263] See *Pisĥei Teshuvah Even HaEzer* 22:4, in the name of the Responsa of *Shav Yaakov* part 19.

[264] In such a case, it is possible to follow the leniency of *Rema Even HaEzer* 22:5. This is also the opinion of Radvaz in his Responsa vol. 3, ch. 481.

[265] See *Tur Shulĥan Aruĥ Even HaEzer* 22:7, and *Ĥelkat Meĥokaik* 22:11.

public view, there is no prohibition of seclusion (see topic 8 above).[266]

18. There is no prohibition of seclusion for Gentiles with elderly people who have already lost all lust for licentiousness. Therefore, an elderly man may be secluded with a younger woman, or an elderly woman with a younger man, since they would not normally be drawn into licentious acts.[267]

It appears that it is not forbidden for a Gentile to be secluded with a minor (a man with a girl below the age of 12,[268] or a woman with a boy below the age of 13),[269] since children at that age do not have a lust for forbidden relations as do adults, and most adults do not desire to cohabit with minors. (The main reason for the safeguarding prohibition of seclusion is the possibility of licentious desires.) *This only applies if the adult is not suspected of having any desire to abuse children or force relations upon them.* For this reason, it is forbidden to leave one's children with a known or suspected pedophile.

---

[266] *Birkei Yosef*, brought by the *Piŝhei Teshuvah Even HaEzer* 22:9.

[267] For Jews this is forbidden, since the prohibition of seclusion for them is explicit in the Torah, whereas Gentiles may be lenient about this, since their prohibition is only a logical one. See Responsa of Radvaz vol. 3, ch. 481, who uses this logic as part of a permission he gives for a specific situation.

[268] *Ezer Mikodesh Even HaEzer* 22:3. Likewise, it is explained by Rashi, on Tractate *Kiddushin* 81b, that the normal male inclination only begins to lust for a girl if she is old enough that her breasts are formed and she has grown pubic hair; see *Rosh Kiddushin* (there, part 25), that this is close to age 12.

[269] See Rambam, *Laws of Forbidden Sexual Relations* ch. 22, and *Shulĥan Aruĥ Even HaEzer* ch. 22, that a Jewish man or woman is even forbidden to be secluded with a girl or boy, respectfully, who is just old enough for intercourse relations. However, it appears that this does not apply to Gentiles. The main Torah prohibition for a Jewish man or woman is seclusion of a man with another man's wife. It was the Sages who eventually introduced the prohibition of seclusion of a man with a single woman, and in this they did not differentiate regarding her age. By contrast, as explained above, the prohibition for Gentiles in this regard is based on logic, and therefore only that which logically could lead to sinful cohabitation is forbidden to them. Therefore, this would not prohibit seclusion of a *normal* man with a young girl, or a *normal* woman with a young boy.

19. A doctor involved in his practice is permitted to be secluded with a woman patient, even if he is checking and thereby touching her body. Since he is involved in his work and is afraid to sin with the woman, as this would bring a bad reputation, and he would lose his occupation and good name, this is allowed. Still, it is proper for a nurse, guardian or helper to be in the room, or close by, during the examination,[270] and the door to the examination room should be left unlocked.

20. A sick man who has no one to take care of him except a woman is not suspected of sinning with her, if he is so sick that he has no desire for her, in which case he is not forbidden to be secluded with her. It is, however, forbidden for the woman helper to live with him for an extended period of days and nights.

On the other hand, it is forbidden for a sick woman to be secluded with a male helper, since he might have relations with her, unless he is a doctor and will be afraid to damage his reputation, as mentioned.[271]

21. The rules mentioned above regarding the prohibition of seclusion are for Gentiles; the details of this prohibition for Jews are stricter.

It is forbidden for a Jewess, whether adult or minor (even if she does not understand the meaning of intercourse relations), single or married, to be secluded together with any adult male who is not her close Jewish relative.[272]

One or two Jewish women may not be secluded together with any number of Gentile men (unless an upright Jewish man is present who is watching over each Jewish woman). This applies even if there are any Gentile women who are also present. It appears that it is even forbidden for many Jewish women to be secluded with many Gentile men (if there is suspicion that this may lead to rape;[273] if there is only

---

[270] *Igrot Moshe Even HaEzer* vol. 4, ch. 65; *Otzar HaPoskim* vol. 9, p. 72; *Tzitz Eliezer* vol. 6, 40:12.

[271] See *Encyclopedia Talmudica* vol. 23, p. 655; *Shulĥan Aruĥ Yoreh De'ah* 195:15-16; Shaĥ *Yoreh De'ah* 195:19.

[272] *Shulĥan Aruĥ Even HaEzer* ch. 22.

[273] See *Shulĥan Aruĥ Yoreh De'ah* ch. 153, that it is forbidden for a Jewess to be secluded with many Gentile men, even if their wives are with them. It is logical that the same would apply to many Jewish women or girls being secluded with many Gentile men.

suspicion that it may lead to seduction, three or more Jewish women may be secluded with many Gentile men). Three Jewish women may be secluded together with one Gentile man.

A Jewish man may not be secluded with a Gentile woman, whether she is single or married, or with two Gentile women. Although it has been explained previously that it is befitting that a Gentile man not be secluded with a single woman, this is forbidden to Jews by Torah Law.

Although Gentiles are not bound by the same stringencies as Jews in regard to the rules of forbidden seclusion, nevertheless, since a Jew is forbidden to transgress them, if a Gentile causes a Jew to come to sin, the Gentile may be punished for this.[274] It is therefore proper that Gentiles should know what is forbidden to Jews, if it is something that may involve a Gentile as well. With this knowledge, a Gentile can merit to separate a Jewish person from a transgression (even if the Jew is not knowledgeable or careful about such things).

However, the later authorities write (see *Pishei Teshuvah* and *Ezer Mikodesh Shulhan Aruh Even HaEzer* 23:3) that in places where there is severe punishment for rape, one may be more lenient and let a group of Jewish girls go among Gentiles, since we are not afraid that the group will be seduced. But there is concern that one or two women might be raped or seduced, God forbid.

A Jewess may not be secluded with a Gentile man even if her husband is in the same town. The leniency brought by the Torah-law authorities, that she is afraid of her husband and will not allow herself to be seduced, only applies to possible seduction by a Jew, as *Sha'ar Yosef* writes in his Responsa, ch. 3.

[274] See the wording of Rambam, *Laws of Forbidden Sexual Relations* 22:3, and *Shulhan Aruh Even HaEzer* 22:2 – "What can be deduced is that if a [Jewish] man secludes himself with a woman with whom he is forbidden to do so, whether she is a Jewess or a Gentile, both are liable to receive stripes for rebellious conduct" – which simply implies that this is forbidden by Jewish Law, as *Tzafnat Pane'ah* writes on *Laws of Forbidden Sexual Relations* there. However, *Bah Even HaEzer* 22 states that a Gentile woman is *not* liable to a punishment of stripes from a court of law if she commits an act of prohibited seclusion.

The Stringency of the Sin of Forbidden Relations

22. As explained in Part I, topics 1:5-10, any Gentile who recognizes the existence of the One God, and accepts upon himself the yoke of God's Kingship and the responsibility to keep the Seven Noahide Commandments from the Torah of Moses, will merit to be resurrected to receive a portion in the future World to Come. This person has elevated himself to become a Pious Gentile (a *Ĥassid*).

A Gentile is judged by God according to the majority [of the weightiness in God's eyes] of his actions and ways. The weighing of a person's deeds, to decide what is the majority for the person's judgment, is done by God alone (see Part I, topic 9:6).

If a Gentile's good deeds outweigh his unrepented sins, then his soul will be saved from *Gehinom*, and he will merit a reward for his soul in the Heavenly realm directly after his passing.

If his good deeds and unrepented sins are exactly balanced, then his soul will still be saved from *Gehinom*, but not because he is found righteous in judgment. Rather, God will tilt a balanced judgment toward kindness.[275]

However, that only applies to one who does not have the sin of forbidden relations in his judgment of being half sinful. If unrepented forbidden relations are part of a Gentile's judgment of being half sinful, his soul is assigned to *Gehinom* for twelve months of purification, and afterwards it will have a correction (to receive reward in the Heavenly realm for the good deeds that the person did).[276]

This is a stringency regarding Divine judgment of the sin of forbidden relations for a Gentile, more than the judgment for deliberate violations of the commandments prohibiting theft or eating meat that was severed from a living animal. But the prohibitions of idol worship, blaspheming God's Explicit Name, and murder are the most severe of all, in that one who did not repent from deliberately committing any of

---

[275] *Even if a person's unrepented sins outweigh his good deeds, God will always grant the person a reward for his good deeds, either during his lifetime or after his passing.

[276] Tractate *Rosh Hashana* 17a, according to *Tosafot* there.

these three sins has no reward at all for his soul in the Heavenly realm.[277] See Part I, topic 1:10, and also Part V, topics 9:7-8.

The liability to Divine punishment refers to one who did not repent from his sin. One who did the correct repentance is forgiven by God.

---

[277] *From the above teaching of the Talmudic Sages – that if a Gentile engaged in forbidden relations and did not repent for committing those transgressions, his soul will go through a temporary period of cleansing in *Gehinom* for those transgressions after he passes away (if his soul is not judged worthy of going directly to receive its spiritual reward) – it is obvious that they are speaking about someone who was acting with sinful intent when he committed those relations, because it was available in his society to learn that it was forbidden (either as spiritual commandments or as enforced laws in his society).

From Part I (Fundamentals of the Faith), the last footnote to topic 1:12:

> Rambam writes in *Laws of Kings* 10:1 that a Gentile is liable for transgressing a Noahide commandment due to negligence, since he should have learned it. But it seems that Rambam is only referring to a situation in which the general community knows the law this person transgressed, yet he excluded himself and didn't learn it. If most of the members of the community don't know this law, one of these individuals is not liable unless he was previously warned, since it was impossible for him to learn it in his situation. Since the laws of God are true and just, such a person is not liable under these unavoidable circumstances.
>
> [However,] it is clear that this only applies to the Noahide commandments that need to be taught (since they are not dictated by logic), such as details of the prohibitions against worshipping idols and eating flesh that was taken from a living animal. But for the logical prohibitions such as stealing and murder, it is obvious that a community is obligated to learn and know them, and individuals have no excuse for ignorance of the main points of these precepts.

PART VII

THE PROHIBITION OF THEFT

This section explains details of the following two obligations and ten prohibitions that are included in this commandment to Gentiles and its offshoots:

1. Not to steal money or property that belongs to others.

2. Not to kidnap a person.

3. According to Ramban: not rape a woman (in addition to the prohibition against inflicting harm on another person, which is an offshoot of the prohibition of murder).

4. Not to defraud another person, which occurs when money or property of another person enters one's possession permissibly, and he then refuses to return it.

5. Not to withhold the wages due to a worker.

6. Not to commit extortion.

7. Not to cheat in buying or selling in regard to the worth of the merchandise.

8. Not to cheat in buying or selling by using false weights or measures.

9. Not to covet the property of another person, nor for a man to covet another man's wife.

10. Not to damage another's property.

11. To return a lost or stolen object to its rightful owner. This obligation includes freeing a kidnapped person.

12. To ask forgiveness of a person whom one stole from, wounded, or harmed in any other way.

INTRODUCTION

by Rabbi Moshe Weiner

Jerusalem, Israel

The prohibition of theft is unique in that it affects almost every aspect of a person's life, since humans are social beings who must deal with each other continuously, in buying, selling, exchanging, etc. People are always dealing with others, either in person or remotely. The focus of this commandment is to accept and honor another person, his needs, and his possessions, as the Sages taught (Tractate *Avot* 2:12): "Rabbi Yosay said, 'Let the money of your fellow be as dear to you as your own.' " Theft in its different forms causes corruption that deteriorates and endangers the society, until the brink of destruction.

This lesson was learned by humanity in ancient times, from the Generation of the Flood. From what occurred to them, we see how harsh is the punishment for theft. The decree of their annihilation was only *sealed* because they committed rampant theft, even though they were very sinful with respect to all of their divine commandments,[1] as it says (Gen. 6:13), "The end of all flesh has come before Me *because the world is full of robbery*, and behold, I will destroy the world."

For all the Noahide Laws, the basic command is from God Himself to mankind. These are basic necessities that mankind cannot evade at any time or in any way, and they were given to human beings to maintain their proper existence. Therefore, you must realize that the truth of these commands is that they are for your good and the good of the whole world. The other unique point is that in order to justly accept others as equal to yourself, you must honor them and their property. This requires sensitivity, insight and positive feelings toward others. This comes from recognition that you, exactly like your fellow human beings, are created by the same One God, for a general duty and purpose. Therefore no individual is so more important than another, to say that his needs come totally before the needs of another person. Hence, keeping this command keeps you continuously aware of the Almighty, Who is continuously creating and watching everyone and everything with His Divine Providence, for the specific purposes that

---

[1] Tractate *Sanhedrin* 108a, cited by Rashi on Genesis 6:13.

He expects from mankind in general and each person in particular.

Another focus of this command (which is only another aspect of the first point) is your need to be just and truthful. You must contemplate that being just and truthful is not only for the upkeep of society, but also for your own sake and benefit. Being truthful is being correct with yourself, and this makes you fit to recognize your own true virtues, capacities, needs, and duties. No one knows each individual person and his needs better than the Creator Himself.[2] The only way you can maximize your abilities is by doing your duty in being the person God created for the special purposes He has planned for you, by cleaving to His commandments and the patterns He set out for the lifestyle He assigned for mankind – as opposed to the lifestyle He assigned for the animals. But you need a vessel in which to receive this pattern of life, to accept it and manage to live accordingly. This vessel is truth.

This explains the special importance of the prohibition of theft. You are obligated to be extremely careful not to steal, since there are many details. A person's nature is to covet others' possessions, and his evil inclination tricks him with false excuses for why this is permissible. These details help you to focus on God, His Truth, and your own truth.

Within the Seven Noahide Commandments, each one has a negative aspect ("Do not commit…"). At the same time, each one has a *positive* aspect and teaching that molds you into a better person. You should exert extra effort to learn and understand the general prohibition of theft and its details, so you can merit to be careful and not to transgress it even by mistake. Likewise, it is an obligation to contemplate your actions, in order not to fall mistakenly into theft, since this is likely to occur when you are not taking careful notice of your actions.

Learning the details of the prohibition of theft will correct your thoughts, your actions, and you as a person. This in turn allows you, and eventually all humanity, to appreciate the truth and justice of God's being the King over the entire world. The fulfillment of the Noahide Laws, and especially the laws of theft, help to perfect the world under the Kingship of the Almighty (the opposite of the world's destruction that was caused by the Generation of the Flood). With this we can merit the fulfillment of God's promise (Isaiah 11:9), "They will not harm or destroy on all My holy mountain, for the earth will be filled with the knowledge of God as water covering the sea bed."

---

[2] See Rambam, *Fundamentals of the Torah* 2:8-10; *Likkutei Amarim* p. 60a,b.

CHAPTER 1

The Prohibition of Theft

1. An adult Gentile is warned about the prohibition of theft, and can be subject to capital punishment in a court of law for this transgression.[1] This applies to one who forcefully robs or secretly steals money or any movable property, or kidnaps a person, or withholds the wages of his employee or other similar acts, and even to an employed

---

[1] Rambam, *Laws of Kings* 9:9.

See *Shulĥan Aruĥ HaRav, Laws of Robbery* topic 23: "Gentiles are prohibited to commit theft and extortion, just like Jews, since this is one of the Seven [Noahide] Commandments, and they are liable for capital punishment for robbing by force or stealing from another person." *Extortion* is the act of using overbearing power or authority, or usury, to compel another person to *sell* something of value. Note that a prohibition of extortion is mentioned there, but not in regard to capital punishment. This implies that no punishment is specified within the Noahide Code. The reason for this, it seems, is that within the Noahide prohibition, only outright theft brings liability to capital punishment. But for an act of theft that involves no real monetary loss (or a monetary loss so small that no one would be concerned about it; see topic 4 below), a Gentile is not liable to capital punishment.

Therefore, it seems that a Gentile who steals land should not be liable for capital punishment, since land itself is not considered (within Torah Law) to be actually transferred to the ownership of the thief (since it can't be physically moved from the owner's possession). For stolen movable objects, although they must be returned intact to the rightful owner, Torah Law specifies (see Chapter 2) that even if a Gentile returns the object he stole, he is still liable in a court for the capital sin of theft. By contrast, stolen land is not acquired by the thief. Rather, it stays in the legal jurisdiction of the rightful owner, even if he is unlawfully denied access to his land. Therefore, since there is no real loss of ownership, the one who seized control of the land has no liability for capital punishment (but he is subject to the civil laws of the country). (However, if a person consumes produce from the land he stole, the produce becomes movable once he picks it, and he is liable for capital punishment just as he would be for stealing other movable objects.)

The author notes that it is hard to accept an alternate view that a Gentile is liable to capital punishment for theft of land, for the Talmud asks in Tractate *Avodah Zarah* 71b: "If the thief did not acquire the object by moving it, how should he be liable to capital punishment?" It is logical that if a Gentile thief does not acquire the item he stole, he is not liable for capital punishment.

harvester who eats from his employer's produce without permission.[2] For all such acts, a Gentile is liable for a capital sin,[3] and one who commits any of these types of transgressions is considered as a robber.[4]

2. What is considered *robbery* (*gezelah* in Hebrew), which is committed by a *robber*? This is when someone takes the money or a belonging of another person by open force – for example, if one forcibly took moveable objects away from the owner who was holding them, or if he committed any of the following types of acts in view of the owner and against the owner's will: he entered the owner's property and took away items, or he seized an animal and used it, or he ate some of the fruit that was growing there, or anything similar to these cases. One

---

Rabbi Zalman Nehemiah Goldberg disagrees with the author's opinion that a Gentile is not liable to capital punishment for stealing land. This discussion is presented in *Sheva Mitzvot HaShem*, Vol. II, *Laws of Theft*, footnote 1.

[2] See Chapter 12 below regarding the details of the laws of a worker.

[3] *There is a fundamental difference between a person's liability to punishment in a court, and his power to cleanse his soul from liability in the eyes of God. The sin of a Gentile thief in the judgment of God can be removed by proper repentance, but only if the stolen object is returned, or if its value is paid back when returning it intact is not possible. (See topic 2:1.)

[4] Rambam, *Laws of Kings* 9:9, states: "A Gentile is liable for theft ... Whether one forcefully robs or steals money, or kidnaps a person, or withholds the wages of an employee and the like ... for all of these he is liable, and he is considered as a robber ..." *Kesef Mishneh* explains that for a Jew, all these transgressions are prohibited by *separate* commandments, whereas for a Gentile they are all within the general prohibition of theft. Therefore, in regard to what types of theft are prohibited, everything that is prohibited for a Jew as monetary theft is also prohibited for a Gentile.

This appears to have a correspondence to the opinion of Ramban on Gen. 34:13, that Gentiles are responsible for all types of monetary matters as part of the Noahide commandment for Courts of Law (*Dinim* in Hebrew). Ramban views this as a positive (i.e., obligatory) commandment. Thus according to Ramban, a separate negative (i.e., prohibitory) Noahide commandment (which carries liability to capital punishment) only applies for stealing money or movable objects by an action of theft. A difference between this approach of Ramban and that explained in *Kesef Mishneh* is in regard to the prohibition of cheating (which is discussed below in Chapter 5).

who commits any such forceful actions is considered to be a *robber*.[5]

What is considered *thievery* (or *theft*, which is *geneivah* in Hebrew), which is committed by a *thief*? This is when someone takes another person's money or belongings secretly, without the owner's awareness – e.g., one who stretches out his hand and takes money from another's pocket without the owner being aware, and any similar action.[6]

In the Noahide Laws there is no difference between theft and robbery by a Gentile. Therefore, in every place in this work or other works of Torah Law where either of these terms is used, these two types of actions are considered to carry equivalent liability for Gentiles.

3. A Gentile who forcibly takes another person's money commits robbery and is guilty of a capital sin. (The same principles apply for robbery of movable items.)

This includes one who takes his victim's money by physical threat or blackmail, saying that if it will not be given to him, he will then kill the victim or inflict harm in another manner (physically, or by embarrassment, etc.). Even though the victim then *gives* the robber or blackmailer the money by his own consent, because of the threatened harm, it is outright robbery.[7]

There is another type of forcible acquisition of items, called *extortion* (*ĥamas* in Hebrew). This occurs when one forces his victim to *sell* him an object,[8] even at its correct value. This is similar to

---

[5] Rambam, *Laws of Robbery* 1:3. If someone used another person's animal, but without intention to steal the body of the animal, and instead he intended to use it only for a short time, he is considered as one who borrows without permission, which is tantamount to robbery. Nevertheless, for a Gentile, such an action would not be a capital sin, since he does not make the owner actually lose the item, but rather only causes an indirect loss to the owner.

[6] Rambam, *Laws of Theft* 1:3.

[7] Rashi on Tractate *Bava Kama* 67a translates *"anas"* as an "extorter." However, the term "force" used here in our text is meant in reference to armed robbers and the like, who take from the victim by threats of harm. But as for one who extorts money or belongings, it has been explained earlier (in footnote 1) that he is not liable to capital punishment. Thus we cite Meiri on *Bava Kama* 67a, where he translates *"anas"* as referring to armed robbers.

[8] *The sin of extortion also applies if one is forced to exchange his money or take a loan on interest (see Chapter 6), or if one person pressures another to sell an item to a third party (who may or may not know the sale is forced).

robbery, and it is forbidden for Gentiles to commit such acts because of the Noahide prohibition of theft.[9] (See Chapter 6 for full details.)

4. There is no set minimum amount for the prohibition of theft. Even if a Gentile stole the smallest amount of money *that a person would be concerned about*, he is guilty of the capital sin of theft.[10] This applies

---

[9] See Rambam, *Laws of Selling* ch. 10. There are two types of extortion:

(1) Person A pressures person B to sell him an item, until B consents and does so. B's consent (although given under duress) makes the item acquired by the buyer (A, who is the extorter). Such an act is forbidden under the prohibition of coveting.

(2) The extorter forcibly grabs the item, but then leaves due payment.

The second act is clearly theft, and the thief must return the item, since the owner never consented to the sale (even though the owner took the money that was left behind, because he was left without any choice in the matter). The first type of extorter, on the other hand, is not obligated to return the item, and the sale is valid. As stated in fn. 1 above, all types of extortion are forbidden to Gentiles under the general category of theft. However, in regard to the first type of extortion, since the sale is valid (i.e., the owner consented to the sale in the end), there also is no liability to capital punishment for this extortion. In contrast, even though in the second case the thief who grabbed the item then left money to make a "purchase," this still does not save him from the liability to capital punishment for committing theft.

It appears that a source for the prohibition of extortion by Gentiles can be learned from the Book of Jonah. After the Gentile people of Nineveh were warned, they returned all their extorted belongings. Tractate *Taanit* 16a explains that if there was a stolen board that was built into a house, they broke up the house to remove and return the board. Meiri, on *Taanit* there, explains that the reason why they could not simply pay the previous owner for the board is that this would still be tantamount to extortion of the second type, since the previous owner whom they took it from never consented to having his item taken in the first place, even if he would be reimbursed for it later. Although it may be explained that the people of Nineveh went beyond the letter of the law in their repentance, it can nevertheless be seen clearly that to forcibly take an item and leave money for it is certainly forbidden.

[10] Rambam, *Laws of Kings* 9:9. The reason given for this in Tractate *Sanhedrin* 57a is that the victim of the theft would not forgive the theft. But if it is such a small item that no one would mind (such as a sliver of wood), it is not considered as having any monetary value, and one who takes such an item without permission would be exempt from capital punishment. This is also written in *Hamra V'hayei* on Tractate *Sanhedrin* 59a.

even if he stole less than the value of a *perutah* (a Hebrew term for the smallest coin in circulation – e.g., a penny in the United States).[11]

If the value of the item taken is so small that *no one would be concerned about it* – for example, if one pulled a sliver of wood from another's crate or fence to use for picking his teeth – such a thing is permissible, and there is no prohibition of theft involved. Nevertheless, it is a righteous characteristic to hold oneself back from this as well.[12]

This is only said about pulling off one or two slivers of wood, which the owner would not be concerned with at all. But if many people would come, and each would pull off one sliver, and through that the whole wooden piece would be destroyed, it is obvious that this would matter very much to the owner, and it is forbidden as theft.[13] Similarly, regarding a vessel that is made of many small pieces, such that each piece alone is not considered to have any monetary value, it is still forbidden to take even one piece from the vessel. For if many people were to come and take just one piece, the whole vessel would be entirely destroyed, and this certainly would matter to the owner.

Likewise, this applies regarding stores that provide plastic or paper bags at the check-out line for their customers' purchases: if in the eyes of the society, one such bag is not considered to have any monetary value, then the owner would surely not be concerned if just one bag

---

[11] In Torah Law, even less than a *perutah* is considered significant in regard to theft by a Gentile, but for a Jew, a *perutah* is the smallest amount that is considered to be significant. One point of this rationale is that the Gentile thief considers that the small amount he deliberately stole is significant.

[12] *Shulĥan Aruĥ HaRav, Laws of Robbery* topic 1.

[13] See *Beit Yosef* and *Sefer Meirat Einayim Ĥoshen Mishpat* 359:4, that the reason for the righteous practice of not taking a stalk of straw from a bundle is that the owner would lose his whole bundle if many people do this. Their wording implies that there is no actual prohibition for an individual to do this, within Torah Law. But it appears that this only constitutes a "righteous practice" if it is one single person who is refraining from taking the stalk, because the owner would not mind this minimal loss. But if there are actually many people involved and each one is taking out one stalk, surely the owner would mind this, and it is either theft or an extortion perpetrated by a multitude of people, which is clearly forbidden. From *Midrash Rabbah* (Gen. ch. 31), the sin of extortion of the Generation of the Flood was that a merchant would bring out beans, and each person would come and take one bean (worth less than a *perutah*) without paying, until the box was empty.

were taken without permission. Nevertheless, it is forbidden to take even one shopping bag without the permission of the owner,[14] for if many people would come along and each one would take one bag without making any purchase, the owner would suffer monetary loss, and this certainly matters to him.[15]

5. If a first Gentile steals something that is worth even less than a *perutah*, and a second Gentile comes and steals it from him, both of them are thieves and liable to capital punishment because of theft.[16]

If the stolen item is still in its original condition, the first thief therefore has not fully acquired it (i.e., if it has not been physically changed while in the first thief's possession, Torah Law requires that he must return the stolen object itself intact to its owner, instead of making a monetary reimbursement, as will be explained in Chapter 2). Still, *even in this case*, the second thief is guilty of theft.[17]

However, if someone took a stolen item from a thief (even by robbery or theft) to save it and return it to the rightful owner, he is not liable. [He should try to do so openly to avoid the appearance of hidden theft, and he would need to prove his intent to be exempted by a court – for example, with witnesses who were told what he would do, and why.] It is surely not considered theft if the owner took his own object back from the thief.[18] These points are explained in Chapter 4.

---

[14] *It is not sufficient to ask permission from an employee who is not authorized to decide on behalf of the owner. If one does not get proper permission to take a bag, he can avoid theft by making a small purchase.

[15] This is not comparable to the case of pulling off slivers of wood, since it is unlikely that more than one person would come and take slivers, and therefore the owner does not mind. But it is a usual occurrence for almost all of the customers to take a bag from the store for their purchases, causing an expense to the merchant, and surely the merchant would mind when people who are not buying merchandise from the store take the store's bags.

[16] Rambam, *Laws of Kings* 9:9. Although Rambam uses the case of an item worth less than a *perutah*, the example is given to show the full extent of the law, which surely would apply to theft of an item worth more than a *perutah*.

[17] The author postulates that Radvaz rules this way because although the first thief does not rightfully own the object, the fact that he plans to benefit from it, and the second thief steals this benefit from him, is enough to make the second thief liable (i.e., he causes financial loss to the first thief).

[18] For a Gentile, there is no prohibition to take one's items back from a thief.

6. It is forbidden for a person to steal from another, even if the other person had previously wronged him monetarily (see topic 4:12). It is also forbidden to steal in the following cases, and each one is a thief:

(a) in order to aggravate a person, or to play a joke on him, but with no intention to keep the stolen money or item (i.e., the only intention is to temporarily pain or trick the owner, and then afterwards to return the item);[19] for this, the thief is not liable to capital punishment;

(b) robbing or stealing any item (or money) with the intention to pay back money,[20] even if one intends to pay more than the stolen item is

---

[19] See Tractate *Bava Metzia* 61b: "It is forbidden to steal with intention [only] to anger, or with intention to return or reimburse," and the Sages determine this from a verse in the Torah. In *Shulĥan Aruĥ HaRav*, *Laws of Robbery* topics 2 and 3, it says simply that this is a Torah prohibition, but he brings an opinion that it is only a Rabbinical prohibition for Jews. It seems very clear there that the first opinion (that it is prohibited for Jews by the Torah) is the more accepted one, and this is the opinion of Rambam in *Sefer HaMitzvot* Negative Commandment 244 and of *Sefer HaĤinuĥ* Commandment 224. Therefore, it is clear that Gentiles are forbidden to do so as well.

Rabbi Zalman Nehemiah Goldberg notes that there is a difference between (i) one who steals with intention to *return* the object, and (ii) one who steals with intention to *reimburse* for the object, since the thief in case (ii) is causing the owner to lose the actual item (even though he will not lose any monetary value), whereas the thief in case (i) intends to cause no loss at all, and is only forbidden to do this on a practical basis because the action is one of theft. In case (ii) the thief commits actual theft (for which a Gentile may be liable to capital punishment, unless it is merchandise ready to be sold).

The opinion of *Minĥat Ĥinuĥ* Commandment 224, that there is no commanded prohibition upon Gentiles for the act of theft in and of itself (e.g., if it is done to aggravate and anger a person, in contrast to the forbidden theft, which is done for the purpose of causing monetary loss), seems problematic, since all prohibitions upon a Jew in regard to theft also apply to Gentiles (as explained in footnote 4), and the act of theft itself is clearly forbidden to a Jew. (It seems that *Minĥat Ĥinuĥ* is following Ramban's opinion mentioned in the last footnote to topic 1:1 above.)

In general, it seems that although there is no conclusive proof that a Gentile is liable to capital punishment for an act of theft in which there is no actual loss caused (as in the example here – because the thief did not intend to take ownership of the stolen object), it is still forbidden.

[20] Rabbi Zalman Nehemiah Goldberg notes that *Yad Ramah* (on *Bava Batra* 16a) permits this for a Gentile. Regarding merchandise, see topic 9 below.

worth, or to replace the older stolen item with a new and better item (and the intention is for the good of the one from whom he is stealing);[21]

(c) stealing an item without permission in order to use it with the intention of returning it, and even with the intention to pay for the time it was used; this is considered to be one who borrows without the owner's permission, and such a person is a thief, but he is not liable to capital punishment (see Chapter 7).

There is no difference in situations (a) – (c) whether the person stole secretly or robbed openly. In either manner these are all forbidden.[22]

7. It is also forbidden to steal from relatives or to take something of theirs without their knowledge, to use it *without permission*. This applies even if one knows with certainty that if his relative learned that he did this, the relative would be happy that he benefited in this way.[23] As long as permission has not been given, this is forbidden as theft.[24]

A person should not say, "I will steal and apportion the money to poor people,"[25] for this is considered doing "a *mitzvah* (meaning, a meritorious and good deed) that comes about through a sin." This is disgusting and hateful in the eyes of God, and is not considered a good deed at all. (See below in topic 2:27).

8. In addition, one may not steal from a person who is not careful in guarding his money or other belongings. This applies even if the intention of the thief is only to teach the careless person a lesson (that he should pay more attention and be careful in guarding his belongings), and not to take something to keep for himself, but rather he intends to return it at a later time.[26]

---

[21] Rambam, *Laws of Theft* 1:2; *Shulĥan Aruĥ Ĥoshen Mishpat* ch. 348.

[22] There is no difference for Gentiles in these cases between robbery and theft, as explained (regarding Jews) by *Shulĥan Aruĥ Ĥoshen Mishpat* 359:2.

[23] *Shulĥan Aruĥ HaRav, Laws of Found Objects* topic 4.

[24] *Leĥem HaPanim* on *Kitzur Shulĥan Aruĥ* ch. 182. (See also topic 8.)

[25] *Leĥem HaPanim ibid.* in the name of *Sefer Ĥasidim.*

[26] From *She'iltot* ch. 4, it is forbidden to steal even from one who is not careful about guarding his possessions, in order to teach him to be careful, even if the intention is to return the item. He compares this rule to one who steals with intention to reimburse the owner, which is forbidden (topic 1:6).

But if a person is not mentally or physically able to guard his wealth, it is permissible for his family members to take his possessions in order to watch them for him (even if they must be taken in a manner of theft), or to appoint a guardian who will take care of his possessions, in order that they will not go to waste (for example, in the case of a person who lost his mental abilities and is wasting his wealth). It is thus permissible for a debilitated person's spouse or mature child to take the person's possessions (without permission and in a manner of theft) in order to guard them, if the debilitated person is not watching these things properly, and they are in danger of being lost or stolen.[27]

9. Regarding objects designated for sale (e.g., merchandise in a store), for which the manner of payment is known and recognized by the merchant and customers, it is permitted to take this merchandise and pay for it *in the accepted manner*, even though the merchant who sells it is not present and is unaware at the time. This is not considered theft (of the type discussed above in topic 6), if this is the desire and agreement of the owner. (For example, in some stores, a buyer takes merchandise and places payment money in a box prepared by the owner, even when the owner and his workers are not in the store; or the owner may appoint his employees to collect payments from the customers.)

---

[27] *Sefer Ĥasidim* ch. 585. It is logical that there is no prohibition of theft involved, since (e.g.) the child's intention is only to safeguard the money and possessions of his debilitated parent. Presumably the same can be said for any other person who comes with proper intentions to guard a debilitated person's possessions. This is not comparable to one who steals with intent to pay back, when the owner is in full control of his mind and is guarding his possessions. A mentally or physically debilitated person, by contrast, cannot safeguard his possessions, and therefore it is not considered theft if one tries to save those possessions and guard them. (Likewise, a custodian of a minor's funds may spend them for the minor's good as allowed by civil law.)

Rabbi Zalman Nehemiah Goldberg notes that this is obviously correct in the case where the owner is fully demented. (Regarding someone who is sane, but is just a spendthrift, it is unclear whether one may take and hold his possessions for the purpose of returning them later.) A similar ruling is found regarding a person standing at the open grave of a deceased relative, and out of extreme grief he is throwing vessels into the grave, and the vessels will become ruined or lost. It is a meritorious deed to save the vessels. If one does save them, it is obligatory for him to guard them, and he is responsible for them and for returning them when the owner's mind becomes settled.

Therefore, it is permitted to take such merchandise and pay for it with money through a second person[28] (who is trusted and reliable in the eyes of the owner), and this is not considered theft, because he has not acted secretly, and the second person is aware of the transaction. Likewise, it is not considered robbery, because the owner willingly allows it. This is referring to a transaction conducted specifically in a public manner.

From this it can be seen that even if a person who is squandering his money is sane, it is meritorious for another person to save the money by legal means in order to return it later. If the money is returned to the person while he is incapable of guarding it, such as a person addicted to gambling or drugs, the one returning the money is liable for any such wasteful loss.

(If possible, one should seek legal permission and authority for this financial guardianship, through the civil court system. It remains doubtful that one could be allowed to steal at the outset in order to save an addict's money, or if it would only be allowed when the addict begins to make his wasteful purchase. Furthermore the obligation of returning lost objects is not a commandment for Gentiles, so this intention can't override the prohibition of theft. More clarification of these issues is needed, and situations must be considered on a case-by-case basis.)

[28] In regard to transferring a purchase payment to a merchant through his employee, we may say that the hand of the employee is like the hand of his employer, and therefore the employer (the merchant) acquires the money as soon as the employee receives it. See *Shulĥan Aruĥ Ĥoshen Mishpat* 270:3.

But the transfer of a purchase payment to a Gentile merchant through someone who is not his employee seems to be dependent on whether a Gentile can appoint a legally binding emissary. In any event, it appears that clearly, a Gentile merchant can receive a payment through his trusted friend who is not his employee, and (disregarding the subject of appointing emissaries) it is because the merchant obviously will consent that this trusted friend will receive a payment for him. Even if one would say that by Torah Law, the merchant has not yet acquired the money (and therefore, for example, a merchant can still retract a sale as long as the money has not entered his own hand), nevertheless, there is no issue of theft involved, since the merchant consents and trusts this process.

In addition to the logical explanation above, many Rabbinical opinions say that when one pays in cash through a third party whom the merchant trusts, it is considered a complete and finished transaction (and not a transaction on credit that requires the appointment of an emissary), even if the buyer paid for and took the merchandise without the merchant knowing. This is explained by Rabbi Akiva Eiger on *Shulĥan Aruĥ Ĥoshen Mishpat* ch. 359.

However, it is forbidden to do such things secretly in a manner that resembles theft,[29] since it may accustom a person to making transactions regularly in a secretive manner, and lead him to committing real theft.

In contrast, if a person took merchandise with the intention of paying for it, but then without permission he did not pay for it immediately, this is theft and is forbidden.[30] Similarly, if a person takes an item and pays money without the merchant's awareness (inconsistently with the merchant's original intention for how the item will be sold), such an act would be forbidden as a manner of theft (similar to a person who steals with intention to pay back later, as explained in topic 6), since he is acting secretively. Furthermore, it may accustom him to paying at a later date without permission, which is actual theft.

It appears that it is forbidden to take merchandise and leave a prepared check as payment without permission, because the owner does not wish to receive checks in the same way he anticipates to be paid with cash.[31] It is obvious that the buyer is not allowed to leave his own merchandise or belongings without permission as payment for the merchandise he is buying, because a seller wants money as payment, not other items. However, if it is known that the owner agrees to a certain means of payment, by receiving a check or specific items in

---

[29] See *Shulĥan Aruĥ Ĥoshen Mishpat* 359:2 and Shaĥ there, and *Shulĥan Aruĥ HaRav, Laws of Robbery* topic 2. These sources explain that there is permission to take merchandise through paying a middleman without the merchant knowing, but only if the transaction is made honestly and openly.

[30] It is clear that the rule above (the first paragraph of this topic) specifically applies only when this is satisfactory to the merchant. But it can be assumed that a merchant would not want someone to take merchandise from his store in order to pay later without his permission, for until he receives money he would not consent, and he is not interested in running after the person for the money he is owed, as explained in *Sefer Meirat Einayim* 359:8.

[31] See Rema *Ĥoshen Mishpat* 205:1, regarding the case of one who put another under duress until he sold an item. Such a sale is only valid when the payment is in cash, and certainly not in an I.O.U. ("I Owe You") note, since not everyone relies on an I.O.U. in the same way.

*In regard to leaving one's credit card information for payment, this would depend on the individual business. Some businesses consistently (or at some times) consider a credit card payment as equivalent to cash, or even better than cash. The deciding factor is the policy of the merchant.

exchange for his sold merchandise, then it is permissible.[32]

10. The above law refers to a situation in which the buyer's item that is exchanged is equal in value to the merchandise that he took (in the opinion of the merchant). For not all merchants are equal in their opinion of the value of exchanged merchandise, and most want only money in exchange for a sale.

However, the buyer may intend to additionally benefit the merchant, by exchanging (through a middleman who is trusted by the merchant) an item that is greater in value than merchandise he is taking. This applies if it will bring profit to the merchant, and if it seems clear that the merchant will be happy to gain this item that is higher in value (and if this is being done specifically in a place that uses such bartering and exchanges in the markets, and buyers pay with items they wish to give to the sellers).[33] With these conditions, and if time is of the essence and the matter is pressing, or for a great need (such as a sick person who needs the merchandise for health reasons), but the owner is not present to agree to the sale and the exchange, then it is permissible for a buyer to benefit the merchant by making the exchange and leaving it in the care of a middleman whom the merchant trusts with such matters. In this scenario, there is no theft or extortion involved.[34]

---

[32] It appears that if the merchant trusts the check of a friend or knows that the buyer is a trustworthy person, then even when he does not usually accept checks from unknown people who come into the store, it is permissible for that trusted buyer to take the merchandise without the merchant's knowledge and leave a check, since for this person, the merchant considers his checks to be as good as cash, and the merchant is presumably happy with the sale.

[33] This is logical, for regarding a matter that is a burden to a person and is not habitual, although he will profit through it, it cannot be assumed that he will consent to it. Likewise, it is clear that this also depends on the type of profit being made. For example, a merchant of clothes is not interested in selling fruits and vegetables in the market, even though he will be able to make double the profit of the clothes he sells in his store. However, it can be assumed that he consents to expend a small amount of effort in order to sell a diamond worth a thousand times his merchandise.

[34] This is only permissible when there is almost no doubt that the merchant would consent to the sale, at which point we say that he is surely benefiting from this, and it is a valid sale. If not, it is forbidden. (Therefore, permission is given for this only when it is done openly and not in a secretive manner.)

However, if a person does not need the merchandise urgently and there is no pressing need, he should not take it by exchange without the knowledge of the merchant, who might not want an exchange even if it is worth more than his own merchandise.[35] It is superfluous to mention that if the merchant is present, then the buyer is permitted to carry out such an exchange only with the owner's awareness and permission.

It appears that in this case (when the buyer exchanged an item of higher value than the merchandise that he took), even though it is permitted to do so (since we assume that it is for the benefit of the merchant, and therefore he would agree to it), nevertheless, if the merchant later protests when the exchange becomes known to him, saying that he did not want this exchange, then the buyer must return the merchandise that he took if he still has it intact within his possession.[36] If he no longer has it intact, then he must pay for it with

---

Permission is given in *Shulĥan Aruĥ HaRav*, *Laws of Found Objects* topic 5, for a household member to give food to a poor person if it is standard practice for the master of the house to allow this. It is sufficient for the master of the house to have a general knowledge and consent that this is the policy, even if he doesn't know about and consent to a specific occurrence.

In summary, a person only has permission to take a belonging without the owner's knowledge if the owner had revealed previously that in any situation, or in this particular situation, he would consent to this item being taken (such as some food from his home, or a fruit from his orchard). It is also important to consider whether the owner applies this consent to anyone, or only to some specific people.

35 *Taz Ĥoshen Mishpat* ch. 359 follows the opinion that one cannot appropriate a credit or other benefit for another person (in such a case) without his knowledge, so unless one knows that the merchant is accepting of an exchange for his merchandise, there is a possibility of extortion involved.

However, if one leaves a proper payment of ready money in place of an item for sale, the merchant is surely happy about the sale, and this seems to be completely permissible from the outset, since it is surely beneficial to the owner (this difference is the reason for the separation of topics 9 and 10).

36 This is implied from the *Ketzot HaĤoshen Mishpat* 359:1. See *Encyclopedia Talmudica* vol. 12, p. 137-8 (with references to the authorities who write this), that even though it is the rule that one can benefit another person without his knowledge, this is only based on a general assumption that the person appreciates this. But if a person protests the benefit (in this case, the exchange), it is clear that it is not considered that the acquisition was made, even if extra value was given in his favor.

money (and the item he wished to exchange is returned to him intact). But if the buyer paid for it with cash and the transaction was conducted through another person whom the merchant trusts, the owner may not cancel the sale, for it is accepted regarding monetary transactions that if a buyer paid money and received his merchandise, it is impossible for either the buyer or the seller to cancel the transaction (without the consent of the other party).

11. There is no difference between robbery or theft that is committed against an individual, a community, or partners who share possessions. Even if a person stole something whose value was less than a *perutah* from a communal fund or from communal possessions, he is still considered a thief, and he is liable to capital punishment for the theft.

Anyone who benefits from communal funds (or from a service provided by an individual or a group of people, for which a fee is legally charged), without paying the money that is due (according to the law), has committed a "withholding of due payment" (examples are: one who withholds his employee's wages, or one who refuses to repay a dept, or one who rides in a public bus or a private taxi and then does not pay); this is the same as a thief, as explained in Chapter 12.

12. When a person enters another's property to steal, the point in time at which he is considered a robber or thief is at the moment when he raises the object he is stealing, or when he draws the object to himself by some other means and removes it from the property of the object's owner (whether the thief brings it to his own adjacent property, or into the public domain, or into another person's private property).[37] Therefore, if one only drags an object within the owner's property from one place to another, but does not remove it from the owner's property, and does not raise it or set it inside his own vessel, he is still

---

It appears that regarding barter of merchandise, we make the exception that if one party shows discontent with the barter, the exchange is voided. But regarding payment in cash, which everyone is content to receive as payment, if the merchant leaves an object in his store for sale with the clear intention that he wishes to sell it at a specific price, any ready money payment is considered as having his consent, so the merchant cannot invalidate the sale.

[37] *Shulĥan Aruĥ Ĥoshen Mishpat* ch. 348, 351. See *Biur HaGra* 348:4, that when a thief drags an item to outside the owner's property, the act of theft is considered to have been committed (even if he did not raise up the item).

not guilty of theft, and he is not liable to capital punishment.

13. The above law refers to a situation in which the thief stole an item from its owner's property, or if he stole an item that its owner had placed on the property of a third person. (Even if someone placed his belonging in the property of another person without that property owner's permission, it is nevertheless forbidden for the owner of the property to steal that object;[38] see Chapter 4 below.)

However, one who robs or steals from another in the street (or in any public place that is not owned as private property) is considered a thief from the moment that he takes the object from the victim, or from the victim's container, and carries it away from the victim or places it in his pocket or inside his own container.[39]

14. If two accomplices robbed or stole, either by taking a belonging or by kidnapping, they are both guilty (similar to what is explained about accomplices to murder, in Part V, Chapter 1). See Chapter 3 below.

15. The laws of theft apply equally to men and women.[40]

16. The prohibition of theft applies equally to one who steals from an adult or from a minor.[41]

---

[38] It is unclear if this type of theft makes a Gentile thief liable to capital punishment, since the property owner is just taking an object that was placed in his property without his permission. This can be comparable to one who raises a lost object with intention to steal it, for which a Gentile is exempt from capital punishment (see *Sheva Mitzvot HaShem*, Vol. II, Part 7, ch. 15, fn. 504) since it did not come to his hand through sin. Likewise in this case, it is permissible for a Gentile to raise the object to remove it from his property.

See also topic 15:17 below, regarding the law of one who carelessly leaves his object unattended. In both cases, it is forbidden to steal these objects.

[39] See *Encyclopedia Talmudica* vol. 5, p. 459, and responsa Maharit *Ĥoshen Mishpat* ch. 88, that one is not considered a thief in Torah Law until he makes an acquisition of the stolen object.

[40] This is clearly the law regarding a Gentile, as seen in Tractate *Sanhedrin* 57, and it is likewise written by Rambam, *Laws of Theft* 1:7, that for Jews, a woman is equally as liable for theft as a man.

[41] See *Sheva Mitzvot HaShem*, Vol. II, *Laws of Theft*, footnote 46, as to whether stealing from a minor carries liability to capital punishment.

A minor who stole is exempt from capital punishment. If a minor steals and the money or object is intact, the court is responsible to have it removed from the possession of the minor who stole it, and it is to be returned to the owner. If the stolen money or object is no longer intact, the minor is exempt from paying restitution (and his parents are also not obligated to pay for the financial loss). Even after the minor becomes an adult, he is not obligated to pay for the theft if the stolen money has been spent or if the stolen object has been lost or ruined.

Although there is no capital punishment for a minor, it is proper for a court to punish minors who steal, in accordance with their mental and physical maturity and the severity of the theft, in order that they not become accustomed to stealing or harming people in other ways.

17. Regarding a Gentile slave who committed theft, if the stolen object or money is still in existence, then it must be returned to the owner immediately. But if it was lost, then the master of the slave is exempt from payment. This is because the master is not responsible for the harm perpetrated by his slave, since the slave has his own mind and the master cannot always guard him from stealing (or the slave might steal or do other damage with the intention of causing damage or loss to his master). Once the slave is freed, he is obligated to pay restitution for his theft, and for any other harm he committed.[42]

18. It is forbidden for a Gentile to *covet* the money of other people.[43] The definition of one who covets is one who not only desires another person's belonging or his house, etc., but he also pressures the other person to sell the item to him, until the point that the owner does sell it to him (or the owner may be pressured to give it as a gift, until he finally does). Even if he gives him a large amount of money for the

---

[42] Rambam, *Laws of Theft* 1:10.

[In a country where slavery is legal,] a slave does not own any of his own money. Therefore, if he committed theft, he cannot pay restitution if the money or object he stole is no longer available to be returned (so an alternative punishment should be applied, as written by Rambam *ibid.*).

Courts that do not apply capital punishment for theft should still apply some type of strict punishment. All courts should also force a convicted thief to pay restitution, as explained in Chapter 2.

[43] *Minĥat Ĥinuĥ* Commandment 38.

item, he is still considered to be one who covets.[44] However, if an object is designated for sale, and the person pressures the seller to reduce his price in the way of all buyers and sellers who haggle back and forth over a price, there is no prohibition involved.

Even if one has transgressed the prohibition of coveting, the sale is not cancelled.[45] The one who coveted retains the object, and it is his according to the law, for the final result was that the seller was appeased, and it was not taken from him by force.

Similarly, one who pressures his friend to give him a certain gift has the status of one who covets his friend's money, and this is prohibited.[46]

19. It is also forbidden for a Gentile to desire another person's belongings. This refers to anyone who desires his friend's house, field, vessels, or any other item (which could possibly be purchased), and he mentally plans or desires in his heart to gain that physical item.[47]

The reason for these prohibitions is that they are included in the prohibition of theft, for the result of coveting and desiring is theft.[48] (Desiring another man's wife is also forbidden, since it can lead to the sin of adultery, which is also related to theft; see Chapter 10 below.)

See *Shulĥan Aruĥ HaRav*, *Laws of Robbery* topic 23: "A Gentile is prohibited to rob and extort as is a Jew." (Extortion is forbidden based on the prohibition of coveting.) *Seder Eliyahu Rabbah*, ch. 24, says that Shem, son of Noaĥ, told people, "You shall not kill, you shall not commit adultery, you shall not kidnap, you shall not bear false witness, and *you shall not covet*."

44 Rambam, *Laws of Robbery* 1:9; *Shulĥan Aruĥ Ĥoshen Mishpat* ch. 359.

45 *Maggid Mishneh, Laws of Robbery* ch. 1.

46 Rabbeinu Yonah, *Sha'arei Teshuvah* 3:43.

47 Based on Rambam, *Laws of Robbery* 1:10.

48 This reason for the prohibition of coveting is given by Rambam *ibid.* 1:11.

Therefore, it is also forbidden for a Gentile to lust after another man's wife. For even though he obviously will not be able to "acquire" her as this applies to property, it is possible that he could offer enough money to convince the couple to divorce, and he would then be able to marry her (this is the transgression of coveting, which is prohibited within the Noahide commandment regarding theft). The main point is that whenever there is a possibility of theft, there is also a prohibition to covet, and there does exist a prohibition of theft in regard to adultery, as will be explained in Chapter 10 below.

CHAPTER 2

Laws of Returning Stolen Objects, and Restitution for Theft

1. A Gentile who steals money or an object from another person is obligated to return it, even if the stolen money is less than the worth of a *perutah*.[49] If he does not return it himself, the court should forcibly

---

[49] We find different opinions among the *Rishonim* Sages [*circa* 1000-1500 C.E.] that seem to indicate a disagreement about this point. Analysis of their positions, however, shows that there is agreement that in practice, a thief should return what he stole. The disagreement is about whether this is only a moral obligation (to God and to the victim of the theft), or if there is an additional Torah-law obligation that should be enforced by a court of law. Tractates *Eruvin* 62a and *Avodah Zarah* 71b state: "A Gentile who steals less than a *perutah* cannot return it." Obviously the phrase "cannot return it" alludes to a deeper concept, because in practice, a thief can certainly choose to go and return what he stole, if he wants to, and the victim of the theft will be pleased about this. From a Torah-law perspective, however, there are two interpretations. (1) According to the explanations of *Tosafot*, Meiri, and Ritva on *Eruvin* and *Avodah Zarah* there, of Ra'avad on *Avodah Zarah* there, and of Rashba and Ran on *Eruvin* there, this statement means that returning what was stolen does not acquit the thief from liability to capital punishment for his transgression, but he must nevertheless return what he stole (and he should be compelled to do so by the court, if he does not do so voluntarily). (2) Rashi, on the other hand, holds that this means that since a Gentile is liable to capital punishment for theft, the court does not have a right to force him to return the object (which would make him additionally liable to receive a second punishment of lesser severity – namely, returning the stolen item).

Rashi holds that if a thief is *actually being judged* by a court for capital punishment, the court cannot force him to also return the object or pay back its value. Nevertheless, Rashi would clearly agree that if the item is still intact, the victim of the theft can take the initiative on his own to take back the item, because it still belongs to him.

It is also clear (and Rashi would agree) that if the thief wishes to fulfill his obligation before God in order to complete his repentance (regardless of whether or not he is sentenced to any punishment from a court), he must ask for and receive forgiveness from the victim, and also return the stolen item (or reimburse its value if it is no longer intact). This is found in the responsa *Yad Eliyahu* ch. 40.

take away the object or money he stole and return it to the owner.[50] If the stolen object is not intact, the court should force the thief to pay for the value of the object he stole.

Even though he returns the stolen object, the thief is not exempt from punishment in the court. Likewise, even if the thief is liable for capital

---

Although Gentiles do not have a specific positive commandment to return stolen property, they are nevertheless obligated in the "positive action" side of the prohibition of theft. This means that a Gentile thief is obligated to take action (returning the stolen object if possible, and if not, then reimbursing its value) to stop his transgression of theft from continuing. This is comparable to the commandment for Gentiles to establish a righteous court system, which would also include a prohibition against inaction of the court system. This is surely the case regarding theft, as explained in Chapter 3 below that theft is a continual sin so long as the thief holds onto the stolen property (see *Zeĥer Yitzĥak* ch. 12-13, and *Likkutei Siĥot* vol. 17, p. 209-210).

This has practical applications, such as the case when a person inherits a stolen item or steals unintentionally, and then later finds that he has the stolen item in his possession. He is not liable for capital punishment if he does not take the positive action of returning the stolen item, although he is obligated to do so.

Another difference in the above matter, as explained in Chapter 6, is that an extorter (who convinces a merchant through duress to agree to sell an item to him) acquires the extorted object, and the court cannot forcibly remove it from him, since the sale is valid. But in regard to making amends, the extorter must return the extorted item. Otherwise, he is considered a thief in regard to his obligation before God, unless the victim of the extortion readily forgives and fully agrees to the sale that was made through extortion.

Proof for this can be brought from Tractate *Taanit* 16a, which says that the people of Nineveh, in order to *fully* repent, destroyed parts of their houses in order to return stolen beams to their rightful owners. Meiri on *Taanit ibid.* writes that they did not exempt themselves by merely reimbursing the owners with money, since that would still be considered extortion.

[50] We don't say that the court does not deal with matters worth less than a *perutah*. According to the explanation in the preceding note, a Gentile thief is obligated to return even less than a *perutah*, since it is considered to have significance to the thief and to the owner (who might not forgive this). The meaning of the Talmud's words *loc. cit.*, "It cannot be returned," is that the thief should be tried in court with liability to capital punishment, and he cannot be exempted from punishment by returning the stolen object (even though this is needed to bring forgiveness from God).

punishment in court, this does not exempt him from returning the stolen object, or paying restitution (as above). If he is not willing to do so, the court should forcibly remove the stolen item or the due amount of restitution money from him and give it to the victim of his theft.[51]

If a Gentile steals from a Jew the value of less than a *perutah* (either money or an object of some worth), even though he is liable to capital punishment for this (as explained above in footnote 11), he is not obligated to return it.[52] If he stole the value of a *perutah* or more from a Jew, he must return it.[53]

2. As explained in Part V, Chapter 3, a thief who approaches secretively to steal is considered a murderous pursuer, and he accepts the risk that others may try to kill him (as Torah Law permits) if he is discovered breaking in to steal. Even in this case, a Gentile thief must return what he stole. This is not limited to the actual objects he stole, but he must even reimburse the owner for any objects he broke or lost, whether at the time of his undercover theft, or after his getaway.[54]

For a summary of topics 3-17, refer to the flowchart after topic 17.

3. One who stole or robbed must return the stolen object intact. If the object was lost, he must pay the victim the value of the object. This is based on the verse,[55] "And he shall return the stolen object he stole," as

---

[51] *Tosafot* and the other authorities mentioned above say that liability to capital punishment does not exempt the thief from payment, since for Gentile transgressors, a more severe punishment does not negate a smaller one.

[52] Tractate *Sanhedrin* 57a.

[53] *Tosafot* and Rashba *ibid.* (in footnote 49).

[54] For Gentiles, (as explained above in topic 2:1) liability to a more severe punishment does not nullify liability to another, less severe punishment.

Rabbi Zalman Nehemiah Goldberg adds that a Gentile thief is obligated to pay even for an item that broke by accident, only because of his negligence.

[55] Leviticus 5:23. It is clear from the discussion in Tractate *Avodah Zarah* 71b that there is no specific positive commandment from the Torah that a Gentile thief must return the object he stole.

Nevertheless, the verse Lev. *ibid.* is part of the Torah's prohibition of theft. This means that *as long as the object remains stolen, the Gentile thief is obligated to return it, since otherwise he is continuing his action of theft* (as the Sages explained:[56] "If [the stolen object] is as it was when he stole it, he shall return it intact [and he may not exempt himself from this obligation by paying its value]; but if it is not [in that condition, for example, if it was lost, broken, or sold to another person and the victim already *despaired* **(i.e., gave up hope)** of recovering it], it is only money that he is required to pay [to the victim]."[57]

The obligation to return the stolen object (rather than paying for its value) applies only if the victim of the theft demanded that the original object be returned, or if he was silent about the issue. If the victim is satisfied with being paid money in exchange for the object, it is permissible for the thief to pay, and the item itself will be considered as purchased property rather than stolen property[58] (but the thief is still liable to capital punishment for his transgression).

4. Likewise, if a stolen object has been altered, although it is still intact in the thief's possession, once it has changed from its original condition, the thief acquires it. This applies to a *permanent* change, in which the item will not return to its original condition. Even if the

---

explained above in footnote 49). For a Jew, returning a stolen object is a positive Torah commandment, separate from his prohibition of theft. Just as *Sefer HaĤinuĥ* Commandment 416 explains that a Gentile is forbidden to covet, which is part of his general prohibition of theft, also any Torah prohibition upon a Jew that relates to theft is included in the Noahide commandment that prohibits theft, as explained above in footnote 4. Therefore, the obligation to return stolen property is also included in the Noahide Code's prohibition of theft.

[56] Tractate *Bava Kama* 66a; Rambam, *Laws of Robbery* 2:1-2.

[57] Although the source for this difference is from the verse Lev. *ibid.*, "… he shall return the robbed item that he robbed, or the proceeds of his extortion…," which is part of a positive Jewish commandment, nevertheless, it is possible to say that the difference between whether the original object is intact or not is also a logical one, and therefore it also applies to Gentiles.

*Torah Law teaches that if a victim of theft or loss "despairs" of regaining the object, in most cases his ownership of it is cancelled; see topic 18. This *legal* term means that the owner of the missing object no longer has any expectation that it will be returned. He therefore relinquishes his mental attachment as its owner, and he accepts that it now belongs to whoever has found or taken it.

[58] *Aruĥ HaShulĥan Ĥoshen Mishpat* 360:1.

victim of the theft has not despaired of recovering the object, the thief is not required to return the object if it was permanently altered, but he is obligated to pay for its worth at the time of the theft (or its worth at the time it was altered, as explained below in topic 16).[59]

If there is a *provisional* change in the object, which can be changed back to the original condition, then if the victim despairs *before* the thief made this change, the thief acquires the object with the combination of the victim's despair and the provisional change (but he must still reimburse the victim for the loss).[60] If the victim did not despair before this change was made, the thief does not acquire the object, and it must be returned intact to the victim (even if the victim did despair *after* the object received the provisional change).

When is it considered that a person despaired of regaining a stolen object? If the person says about this, "I'm upset over my loss," or makes any similar statement or any action that implies his despair, this proves that he has despaired of recovering the stolen object or money.

If the person *does not* make such a statement or action, an assumption can be made that depends on how the object was stolen:

(a) If the object was stolen by open force, and the robber can be identified, this is referred to in Torah Law as a "typical robbery." In this case, we do not assume that the victim despairs, since he hopes to recover his loss from the robber through the court system.[61]

(b) If the object was stolen secretly, and the victim does not know who the thief is, this is referred to in Torah Law as a "typical theft." There is an opinion that in this case, the victim probably despaired of recovering his loss.[62] Since the thief has not been identified, we assume that the victim has already despaired of recovering the object.

There is also a differing opinion[63] that a Noahide court does not rule that a Gentile victim has despaired of regaining a stolen item, even

---

[59] Rambam, *Laws of Robbery* 2:1; *Shulĥan Aruĥ Ĥoshen Mishpat* ch. 353, 360. The responsa *Sha'alee Tzion Kama* vol. 2, ch. 16, proves from *Ĥok Ya'akov* (*Laws of Passover* ch. 448) that this precept also applies to Gentiles.

[60] This ruling is the opinion of *Tosafot*, Rosh and *Tur*, mentioned in *Shulĥan Aruĥ Ĥoshen Mishpat* 353:2 and 360:2.

[61] *Shulĥan Aruĥ Ĥoshen Mishpat* ch. 361.

[62] Rema *Ĥoshen Mishpat* ch. 368.

[63] Shaĥ *Ĥoshen Mishpat* 368:1.

regarding a "typical theft," until there is a witness who clearly overheard the victim saying that he regrets that he suffered a loss, or some other proof of that he has given up hope of regaining the item.

5. If one stole wood and made a vessel from it, or wool and dyed it, or a stone and carved it, these are considered permanent changes, and through these a thief acquires the stolen objects. By contrast, if the thief stole wooden planks and nailed them together to make a box, this is not considered a permanent change, since the planks can be returned to their original state by disassembling the box. Likewise, if one stole yarn and made a garment from it, this is not considered a permanent change, since the yarn can be returned to its original state.[64]

If one stole large beams and cut them into boards, or wood and cut it into large beams, this is considered a permanent change (since the name of the stolen item has changed), and the thief acquires them.[65]

If one stole a bar of metal and made vessels from it, he has not acquired them, since it is possible to melt the vessels and return the metal to its bar state. If, however, he stole a vessel and melted it, this is considered a permanent change, for even if it would be made back into a vessel in the form it had before, it is considered an entirely new item.[66] The same applies to any material with this property (such as glass or plastic).

This is the general rule: the stolen item is not considered as having undergone a permanent change unless (a) it cannot be changed back to its former state, as the item was before it was stolen, and (b) due to this change, the item receives a new name. If it *can* be changed back (even if it has a new name due to the change), the thief does not acquire it.[67]

The above applies only if the victim has not already despaired. If he has despaired, and then later the thief makes a provisional change that brings with it a change of name (for example, making a vessel out of

---

[64] See *Kesef Mishneh* and *Leĥem Mishneh* on Rambam, *Laws of Robbery* 2:12, who question Rambam's opinion there that if one makes threads into a garment, this is considered a permanent change.

[65] Rambam, *Laws of Robbery* 2:14; *Shulĥan Aruĥ Ĥoshen Mishpat* ch. 360.

[66] Rambam *ibid.* 2:11-12, and *Shulĥan Aruĥ ibid.*

[67] *Tur*, *Shulĥan Aruĥ ibid.*, and Rema on *Shulĥan Aruĥ ibid.*

stolen metal), then the thief acquires the changed object, and only needs to return the value of the original stolen object to the victim.[68]

6. If a stolen item was changed but its name did not change at all, the thief does not acquire it, even if the item does not return to its previous state. For example, if a thief stole large beams and then cut them down to small beams, since they still have the name of "beams" and this did not change, the thief does not acquire them. Without a complete change of name,[69] a permanent change has not occurred, and the item is considered as still intact. In this case therefore, even if the victim despaired, the thief must return the item.

7. Even though we have explained that through a permanent change, the item becomes acquired by the thief, and he need only pay back the value of the item and not the item itself, this only applies *post facto*, once he has already changed it. However, it is forbidden for the thief to change the item he stole in order to acquire it (or even for some other reason), since in doing so he adds to his theft. With this action, the thief is fully removing the item from the jurisdiction of the previous owner, which is an additional theft. Even those types of changes by which the item does not become acquired by the thief (for which examples were given above) are forbidden for the thief to make. This applies just as it is forbidden for the thief to use the item he stole (as explained below in Chapter 3). Rather, it is an obligation for the thief to return the stolen item, intact, to its owner.[70]

8. If a thief stole a young animal and it grew to become an adult animal, this is considered a permanent change occurring at the hand of

---

[68] Based on the opinions of *Tosafot* and Rosh, that through a provisional change along with despair of the victim, the thief acquires the item (as explained in *Shulĥan Aruĥ ibid.*).

[69] Rabbi Akiva Eiger on *Shulĥan Aruĥ Ĥoshen Mishpat* ch. 353, based on *Tosafot* Tractate *Sukkah* 30b.

[70] *Shulĥan Aruĥ HaRav*, *Laws of Robbery* topic 10, explains that it is forbidden for another person to buy a stolen item from the thief, since in doing so the buyer completely removes the original owner's jurisdiction over the item. How much more so it is forbidden for the thief himself to make a permanent change in the item, since this is complete theft, as explained in *Netivot HaMishpat* 34:5. See footnote 49 above.

the thief, and he thereby acquires it even if the victim has not despaired, (and even though the thief himself did not cause the change, and it occurred on its own; nevertheless, since it is universally recognized that its name has changed, this is considered a permanent change).[71] In such cases, the thief is only obligated to return the value of the stolen animal at the time of the theft.[72]

Conversely, if one stole a weak animal and fattened it, or a healthy animal and weakened it, Torah Law does not consider this a change at all, and it must be returned intact. If the animal became fattened through the thief feeding it, the animal's added value belongs to the thief,[73] as will be explained in topic 10.

If the animal he stole weakened because he did not feed it or watch it sufficiently, and needless to say if he injured it (even if it can be returned to its original state of health), the thief must pay the victim for the loss in value he caused (in addition to returning the animal).[74]

It is unclear whether a Gentile thief is liable to a *separate* sentence of capital punishment for making this permanent change. The practical difference occurs if, for example, (a) there were no witnesses to the theft itself, but there were witnesses who knew it was a stolen object, and they saw a person (the thief) making a change in it in order to acquire it, or (b) the original act of theft was committed in error. The same applies if one buys a stolen item from the thief before the victim despairs, and, knowing that it was stolen, this buyer makes a permanent change in the item to remove it from the original owner's jurisdiction. Based on the explanation in footnote 1, the buyer, or the thief in situations (a) or (b) mentioned here, would not be liable to capital punishment just for making the change in the stolen item, since that does not cause any additional monetary loss to the victim, beyond the value that was stolen at the time of theft.

71 Shaĥ *Ĥoshen Mishpat* ch. 353.

72 Rambam, *Laws of Theft* 1:13 and *Laws of Robbery* 2:14; *Shulĥan Aruĥ Ĥoshen Mishpat* ch. 353.

73 Rambam, *Laws of Theft* 1:11; *Shulĥan Aruĥ Ĥoshen Mishpat* ch. 354.

74 See *Taz Ĥoshen Mishpat* ch. 363 and Shaĥ *Ĥoshen Mishpat* 363:7, from which it appears that if the animal was permanently weakened due to the thief's negligence, he is liable for the depreciation like one who damages, or like a watchman who did not guard the item sufficiently. Obviously, if the animal was permanently weakened by a direct action of the thief (e.g., if he forced it to do overly strenuous labor), then he must pay for the depreciation. This is explained in *Sefer Meirat Einayim Ĥoshen Mishpat* 363:8.

9. If a stolen item is in the hands of the thief and it has not been changed, it must be returned to the victim, whether it is before or after the victim despairs. The difference is that if the victim despaired of recovering the stolen item, any naturally occurring increase in its value after the owner despaired should be repaid to the thief.[75]

For example, if the stolen item was in the hands of the thief and the victim did not despair, and it increased in value on its own, such as if the thief stole an animal when it was pregnant and it then gave birth, or when it had a full coat of wool and he then sheared it, he must return the stolen animal, and the wool or offspring as well.[76]

If the victim despaired of recovering this stolen animal, and it then gave birth or its wool was shorn, the thief acquires the offspring or wool due to the victim's despair.[77] The thief must return only the actual stolen animal. If this is not possible (for example, if the animal afterwards died or was lost), he repays the value it had at the time of

---

[75] *Topic 9 is speaking about a change that comes about by itself, which is a natural change that occurs to the object, but it does not completely change it bodily into a different type of object. These laws are primarily speaking in regard to a living object (e.g., an animal) that experiences a peripheral type of change (e.g., growth of additional wool, or of a fetus) that automatically increases its value. A question arises as to whether this incremental increase in value should be considered a significant change, such that the thief would acquire the body of the animal. The opinion followed here (from Rambam and *Shulĥan Aruĥ*) does not consider this to be a significant change, so it only considers that (a) the thief acquires the increase in value (e.g. the additional wool or offspring), (b) the thief acquires this increase only after the victim despairs. A different Rabbinical opinion (from Ra'avad, Rosh and Rema) considers these changes to be like the permanent changes a thief would make to a stolen object. So even if the owner never despaired, in their opinion, the thief acquires the changed animal [plus the increased value], and he only needs to repay the monetary value of the animal at time of theft.

[76] Here, the repayment for stealing the animal is to return the actual animal itself, and likewise, if the offspring or shorn wool are also intact, they must be returned to the victim, instead of paying their monetary value. See *Sefer Meirat Einayim Ĥoshen Mishpat* 354:1. (If the animal and its offspring and/or shorn wool are lost from the possession of the thief, he must pay for their full value.)

[77] Rambam, *Laws of Theft* 1:11, and *Laws of Robbery* 2:2,6; *Shulĥan Aruĥ Ĥoshen Mishpat* ch. 354 and 362.

the theft (for example, the value of this cow that will soon give birth, or of a sheep that will soon be shorn).[78]

The same law applies if the thief returns a stolen animal that increased in value after it was stolen, while it was in the thief's jurisdiction (for example, a stolen cow that became pregnant or a stolen sheep that grew more wool,[79] or in any similar case). *If the owner had previously despaired of regaining the object* (between the time of the theft and his demand for its return), then the increase in value (for example, from an offspring or added wool) belongs to the thief (even if the victim demanded return of a stolen animal while it was still pregnant or unshorn).

If this object contains the increased value within itself (for example, if the cow is still pregnant or the sheep is still unshorn), then by the enactment of the Sages (in order to encourage repentance and restitution), the thief acquires the increase in value. If the victim takes back this object that increased in value (for example, the pregnant cow or unshorn sheep), then according to this rule, he should pay the increased value to the thief. If the increased value has been separated from the object while in the thief's jurisdiction, that belongs to the thief (for example, the thief keeps his born calf from the stolen cow that became pregnant, or his increased wool that was shorn from the stolen sheep that grew more wool), and he need only return the stolen animal itself, as it was at the time of the theft.[80] (If the owner never despaired, in all cases everything is returned to the owner, with its increased value, as explained in the second paragraph of this topic.)

The explanation of this ruling, according to this view of Rambam and *Shulĥan Aruĥ loc. cit.,* is that according to Torah Law, a thief does not acquire any of these benefits, since they accrue naturally from the stolen item, and they must all be returned to the owner. But to encourage thieves to make amends, the Sages enacted that a thief acquires any benefit that accrues from the stolen item after the victim despairs of recovering the loss (so the thief will more readily agree to return at least the item itself that he stole). (See topics 24 and 31 below for further consideration of this principle by Noahide courts).

[78] Shaĥ *Ĥoshen Mishpat* 354:3 and *Taz ibid.*

[79] *Tur*, *Sefer Meirat Einayim* and Shaĥ *Ĥoshen Mishpat* ch. 354, in their explanations of Rambam's opinion.

[80] Rambam, *Laws of Robbery* 2:6; *Shulĥan Aruĥ Ĥoshen Mishpat* 362:7-8.

There are those that differ about this, and hold that if the appreciation in value comes through *any change* (even a natural change) in the object while it is in the thief's jurisdiction (for example, offspring that was born or wool that was sheared, or the stolen animal became pregnant or grew more wool), then even if the victim has not despaired of regaining the loss, it is considered that a permanent change in the stolen object occurred, and the thief acquires the changed object and all of the increased value (for example, the animal along with its offspring or its shorn wool), and he is only required to reimburse the owner for the value of the object at the time of the theft.[81]

If the thief was brought to a Noahide court while the stolen animal was still in its original condition (e.g., still pregnant, or still not shorn), then even if the owner had despaired in the interim, since this is not a permanent change in the object, the thief has not acquired it, and he must return it intact.[82] However, if the victim despaired and there was an increase in value in the object itself, the thief returns the object and receives payment from the victim for the increased value.[83] If the victim did not despair, he need not pay anything at all to the thief for any increased value in the stolen object itself.

10. This only applies to appreciation in value that comes of its own to the stolen item. But if it appreciated due to the efforts of the thief (i.e., it appreciated in value through the thief expending money on it – for example, if he fattened the animal), the appreciation in value belongs to the thief even if the owner did not despair. When the thief returns the stolen property, he may claim the increased value from the owner.[84]

If the stolen item changes permanently while in the hands of the thief (e.g., a stolen young animal that matures into an adult, as in topic 8),

---

[81] Ra'avad, Rosh, and Rema *Ĥoshen Mishpat* ch. 354.

[82] In such a case, there is no change in the jurisdiction of the thief over the item he stole – for example, there is nothing new that develops from a stolen sheep if it was already pregnant at the time of the theft and had not yet given birth. Therefore, it must be returned as is. This appears clear from Rema *Ĥoshen Mishpat* ch. 354.

[83] *Sefer Meirat Einayim Ĥoshen Mishpat* 354:2, 362:16; Shaĥ *Ĥoshen Mishpat* 354:4.

[84] Rambam, *Laws of Theft* 1:11; *Shulĥan Aruĥ Ĥoshen Mishpat* ch. 354.

he acquires it, and its increase in value, even before the owner despairs, and he need only reimburse the owner for the value of the stolen item at the time of the theft.[85]

11. A stolen item that did not have a bodily change, but its current market value increased, must be returned intact to the owner, even if the owner despaired, and the thief has no claim to any of it.[86] This is not comparable to an increase in intrinsic value that comes from a change in the stolen item itself, such as offspring or wool (as explained above in topic 9), by which the thief has an acquisition (of the item itself according to the second opinion there, or only the increase in its intrinsic value according to the first opinion). In contrast, an increase in market value itself does not constitute any change at all in the object.

Likewise, if its market value depreciated but is still intact, even if the owner has not despaired, the thief can return the intact item and say, "Your [stolen] item is before you" (i.e., the loss of market value belongs to the owner).[87]

12. If one stole an animal and eventually it grew old, or it weakened in such a way that it cannot regain its original strength (for example, if it developed a disease for which there is no cure, or in the similar case of one who stole fruits that afterwards rotted or wine that afterwards

---

Likewise, if the thief stole a ewe and expended effort to bring a ram to get her pregnant, this is considered appreciation in value that comes from the thief's actions, for which he may claim reimbursement from the owner. If this ewe gave birth while in the jurisdiction of the thief, whether the owner despaired or not, the offspring belongs to the thief.

This is clearly the case, even according to Rambam's opinion (mentioned in topic 9 above), since this is not an increased value that came on its own, but rather through the efforts of the thief, who takes the increased value that is due to his efforts. Therefore, if this sheep gives birth, the offspring (that the thief caused to be conceived) belong to the thief, even if the owner does not despair.

[85] Rambam, *Laws of Theft* 1:12, and *Laws of Robbery* 2:14; *Shulĥan Aruĥ ibid.*

[86] Rambam, *Laws of Robbery* 2:16; *Shulĥan Aruĥ Ĥoshen Mishpat* ch. 362.

[87] Rambam, *Laws of Robbery* 3:4.

soured), it is considered as if the thief stole a vessel and broke it, for which he must pay its value at the time of the theft. Likewise, if the object was lost or burned or the like, he must reimburse the owner for its value at the time of the theft.

However, if the thief stole an animal, and after this it weakened but its strength could be restored, or he stole fruits and a fraction of them (less than half) spoiled, he can return what he stole and say "Your [stolen] item is before you."[88] This only applies if the deterioration happened on its own, and it was not the result of any negligence by the thief. However, if the thief is responsible for the deterioration, he must pay the item's worth at the time of the theft (as explained in topic 8), and he cannot say, "Your item is before you."

13. If one stole a coin and afterward the government invalidated it, there is an opinion[89] that he must pay the owner the value, in valid currency, that the coin had at the time of the theft. However, if the coin is still valid in another country, even if it is invalid in the country the owner lives in, the thief may return it and tell him, "Your [stolen] item is before you."

Another opinion says that even if the coin has been invalidated everywhere in the world, the thief may still return the coin intact and tell the owner, "Your [stolen] item is before you."[90] This only applies if he comes to return the very coin he stole. But if he wants to replace it with another coin, he is not able to claim "your [stolen] item is before you," and he must instead reimburse the owner with a comparable value in valid currency.[91] It appears that this argument applies

---

[88] Rambam, *Laws of Robbery* 3:4; *Shulĥan Aruĥ Ĥoshen Mishpat* ch. 363.

[89] Rambam *ibid.* and *Shulĥan Aruĥ Ĥoshen Mishpat ibid.*

[90] Rema *Ĥoshen Mishpat* 363:1, and Shaĥ *Ĥoshen Mishpat* 363:5.

Rabbi Zalman Nehemiah Goldberg points out that this applies only in the case when the coin has real worth for the value of its metal, even though it is used for currency in a specific denomination.

However, it seems clear that if one damages a silver goblet or piece of jewelry, it is considered a complete, directly-caused loss, since he destroys their form. This is unlike a coin, which *in reality* has only the worth of the metal it is stamped on (this difference is also mentioned in Shaĥ *Ĥoshen Mishpat* 386:7).

[91] Shaĥ *Ĥoshen Mishpat* 363:4.

specifically to *coins* that have value based on the worth of the metal that they are stamped on (such as those used in olden times).

Nowadays, when a coin is worth more than the value of the metal in it (due to the laws of the government, and likewise for paper currency), if the government would invalidate the currency (and it would also be worthless in other countries around the world),[92] the thief would need to pay from new currency equal to the value of the invalidated currency at the time of the theft. This is because an indirect cause for money loss is considered as if it is directly caused.[93]

Likewise, if one steals an amount of money, and the value of the money goes down (in its market value – i.e. due to inflation), the thief cannot return other coins or bills (of the same type) in the amount that he stole, but must instead pay the market value of the money at the time of the theft.

---

[92] If, however, this paper currency bill would have value in other countries, it has the same law as a coin that was invalidated by the government, and as explained before, all opinions hold that the thief can say, "Your [stolen] item is before you."

[93] This is comparable to the law of one who burns another person's I.O.U., as is explained in *Shulĥan Aruĥ Ĥoshen Mishpat* 386:2. *Aĥiezer* vol. 3, ch. 37, writes that this only applies if he did so intentionally. If he did so accidentally, he is exempt from an obligation to reimburse.

Even according to Rema *Ĥoshen Mishpat* ch. 386, who rules that one is exempt for causing indirect financial damage, this is because it is only in regard to the law of one who damages – such as one who rubs out the face of a coin that someone else owns (thus removing its denomination value) or who *pushes* another person's coin into the sea (such that it is permanently lost, and he does not take possession of it at any point). By contrast, if one steals a coin, acquires it and then pushes it into the sea (or if one steals an I.O.U. and then burns it), once this person is liable for theft, he also becomes obligated to return the value that the stolen item had at the time of the theft, and he cannot be considered exempt from this payment just because the damage was indirect, as explained in Shaĥ *Ĥoshen Mishpat* 386:13,20 and Maharshal *Bava Kama* 9:17. It is different in the case of a coin that the government invalidated after the theft, since the thief did not cause the invalidation through his actions, and he can return that item intact. Therefore, in any case that an object was stolen, and through this it was damaged – even if the damage was caused later and indirectly – the rule is that "if the start of the damage is with negligence, and the damage at the end is due to unpreventable circumstances, the perpetrator is liable." See Meiri *Gittin* 40.

14. If one steals a check or IOU and it becomes outdated, or it becomes invalid after the theft for other reasons – and surely if the thief destroys the document – the thief must reimburse the owner for its worth at the time of the theft, and he cannot say, "Your item is before you."[94]

15. If a thief stole merchandise that is ready for sale, which has a high value during the market season but not during the rest of the year, and he came to return it during the rest of the year, then according to the first opinion (in topic 13) he is not able to say, "Your item is before you." Instead, he must also pay back the depreciation in value he caused by preventing the owner from selling it during the market season. According to the second opinion (as mentioned there), he may still return it and say, "Your item is before you."[95]

16. If one stole an item and it became completely ruined (for example, an animal and it died, or a vessel and it was destroyed, or wine and it soured), or the stolen item was lost (or sold or given away after the owner despaired of regaining it), and now (at the time of the thief's

---

[94] Based on the previous footnote.

Rabbi Zalman Nehemiah Goldberg notes that the author's opinion, that one who steals is also considered as causing financial damage, fits with the opinion of *Netivot HaMishpat* (*Ĥoshen Mishpat*, ch. 25), who argues with *Ketzot HaĤoshen*. *Ketzot HaĤoshen* there, 25:1, says that one who steals unintentionally (such as one who thought the item he was taking was his own) is exempt, and only in regard to damage do the Sages say that a person is always capable of damaging, and thus is liable for not guarding himself even from unintentionally damaging. *Netivot* argues there that if one stole by mistake, this may be included in the element of damage as well.

The author responds: See *Ĥidushei Rav Ĥayim HaLevi* on Rambam, end of *Laws of Robbery*, that any thief must also pay for damages. See *Maĥaneh Efraim*, *Laws of Robbery* ch. 7, who says that as long as the person is unaware that he is stealing, he is not liable for theft, and this is also written in *Mekor Ĥayim Laws of Pesach* 454:2. (It is possible that according to all opinions, one who steals purposefully is liable for damages, and the above argument between *Netivot* and *Ketzot HaĤoshen* is in regarding to stealing unintentionally.) Regarding one who steals a check unintentionally, see in the previous footnote that according to *Aĥiezer*, a Gentile who causes unintentional financial loss is exempt.

[95] *Pitĥei Teshuva Ĥoshen Mishpat* ch. 363.

court case) the market value of that type of commodity has *decreased*, the thief must pay the victim of the theft for the stolen item in the amount of its value at the time of the theft.

Likewise, if the market value of that type of commodity has *increased*, then if the damage or loss of the stolen item happened on its own,[96] the thief only needs to pay for the market value that the item had at the time of the theft.

However, either before or after the victim despaired of regaining the stolen item, if the thief ruined it (for example, he slaughtered the animal, or broke the vessel, or drank the wine) or lost it due to his negligence (or sold or gave it away after the owner despaired), the judgment is that the victim was financially damaged. Therefore, the thief must pay the value of the item at the time he destroyed it, or at the time he caused it to leave his possession.[97]

17. If one stole an item, and it then became broken or its value decreased (on its own, or by the actions or negligence of the thief), this loss of value is not evaluated. (I.e., the thief cannot fulfill his obligation by giving back the broken item and reimbursing the owner for the decrease in value caused by the breakage or depreciation.) Instead, we evaluate the value of the vessel at the time of the theft (or

---

[96] "On its own" is the wording of *Rambam* and *Shulĥan Aruĥ*; see *Sefer Meirat Einayim* 354:7 and 362:20, that this is to exclude any damage that occurred due to negligent safeguarding, for which the thief would need to reimburse the owner for the value of the item at the time **it was lost**, just like any damager. This is also the opinion of *Taz Ĥoshen Mishpat* end of ch. 362. (However, *Ketzot* and *Netivot* ch. 354 argue against the opinion of *Sefer Meirat Einayim*, and say that as long as the thief did not directly damage the stolen item, he need only reimburse its value at the time of the theft. See *Pitĥei Teshuva Ĥoshen Mishpat* ch. 354).

[97] Rambam, *Laws of Theft* 1:14 and *Laws of Robbery* ch. 3; *Shulĥan Aruĥ Ĥoshen Mishpat* 354:3 and ch. 362.

Rabbi Zalman Nehemiah Goldberg notes that the issue of whether one who steals (and the item appreciated in value, and later the thief damaged it or the like), must pay for the item's worth at the time of the theft or its loss is an argument between *Ketzot HaĤoshen* and *Netivot HaMishpat Ĥoshen Mishpat* ch. 34; the author's opinion [inside] fits the opinion of *Netivot HaMishpat*, whereas *Ketzot HaĤoshen* there disagrees and holds that the thief may reimburse in the amount of the worth at the time of the theft.

at the time of the breakage or depreciation, if the thief caused the loss after the item appreciated in value while in his possession, as explained earlier). The thief needs to pay this full higher value to the victim of the theft, and the broken or depreciated item belongs to the thief.

If the owner wishes instead to keep the broken vessel for himself, and receive payment from the thief for the depreciation in value, the owner may choose this option.[98]

However, if a thief stole an animal and slaughtered it, he must pay for the entire animal, and its carcass belongs to him. Even if the owner wants to keep the slaughtered animal, he cannot force the thief to give him the carcass and pay the difference in value of a whole, live animal. Since slaughtering the animal is a permanent change from a live animal, the thief acquires it.

---

[98] Rambam, *Laws of Theft* ch.1 and *Laws of Robbery* ch. 2; *Shulĥan Aruĥ Ĥoshen Mishpat* ch. 354, 362. *Magid Mishneh* explains that this is speaking about a case in which the object's name is not changed by the breakage (rather, it only depreciated in value). But if its name was changed, this would constitute a substantial change, and regardless of what the owner preferred, the thief would acquire the stolen object and would only be obligated to reimburse the item's worth at time he broke it.

This enactment (that the thief must fully reimburse, and cannot give back the broken item and pay only the difference in its worth) is for the benefit of the victim of the theft. Therefore, if he desires, he can force the thief to return the broken stolen item, just as any other stolen item that is still intact.

Magid Mishneh asks why the law is that one who breaks a vessel, although he is changing it, does not acquire it with this change; he answers that this case is referring to a vessel *that can still be used in its original manner*, and therefore has not undergone a permanent change. See *Taz Ĥoshen Mishpat* ch. 354. Their intention appears to be that a provisional change is the middle ground between a complete change, for which the thief acquires the stolen item based on Torah Law, and no change, for which the item should be returned to the owner. In this middle ground, it was possible for the Torah Sages to make varying enactments as they saw fit. Likewise, in this case of a broken vessel, the enactment is for the better of the victim of the theft, such that if he desires, he can force the thief to return the item, just as any other stolen item that is still intact.

Flowchart for Restitution from Theft, Topics 2:3-17

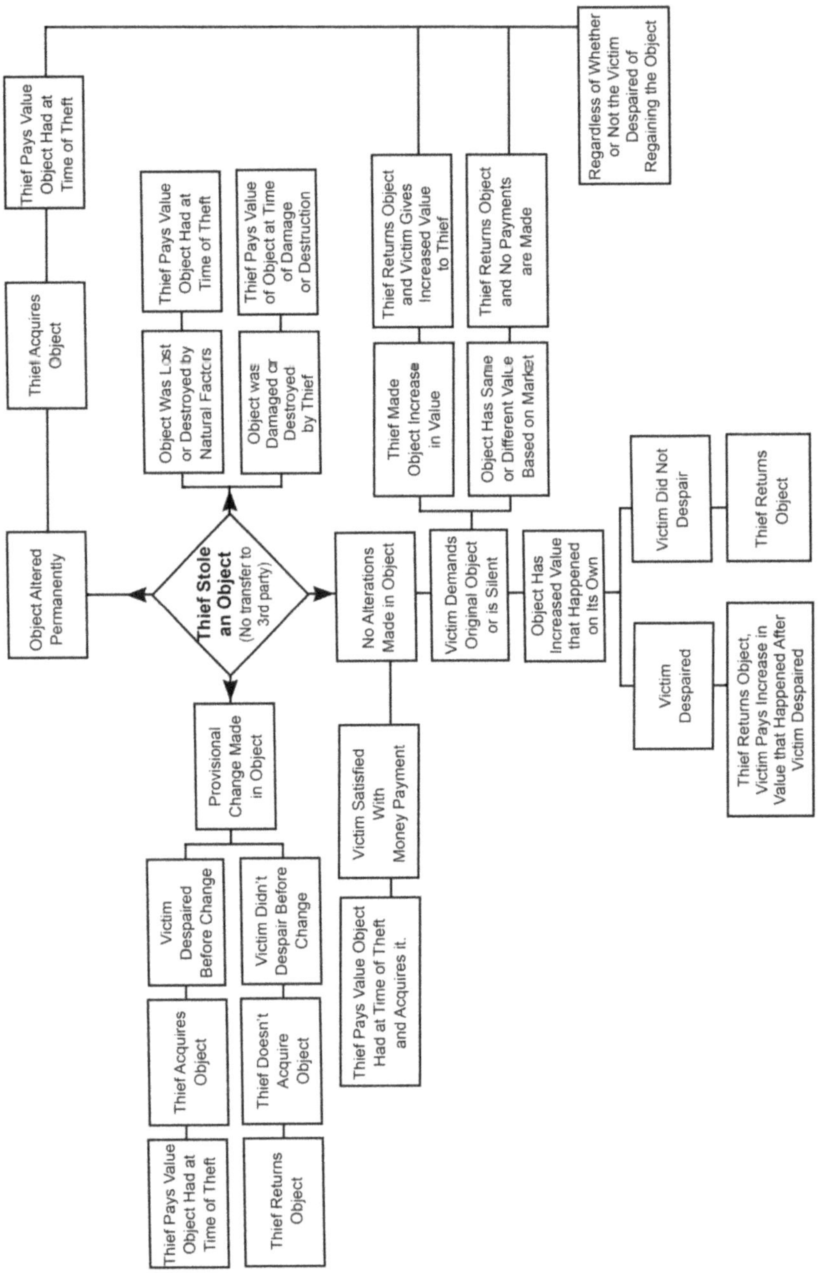

18. If a thief steals an item and sells it to another person, the obligation of the thief (or one who buys it from the thief) to return the original item depends on whether or not the owner despairs, and at what point he despairs:

(a) If the owner despaired of recovering the item before the sale, the buyer acquires it with the owner's despair and this change of jurisdiction.[99] The thief then only needs to reimburse the owner for the value of the stolen item.[100]

(b) If the owner did not despair and the item is still intact, the buyer

---

[99] Rambam, *Laws of Robbery* ch. 2 and *Laws of Theft* ch. 5; *Shulĥan Aruĥ Ĥoshen Mishpat* ch. 353, 356.

[100] The rulings in this topic follow *Tur* and *Rema Ĥoshen Mishpat* ch. 353 and 356, that the owner's despair combined with the change in jurisdiction make the item fully acquired by the one who buys it from the thief, and he is entirely not obligated to compensate the victim. Therefore, it is clear that the victim can demand reimbursement for the entire value of the item, and if it appreciates in value between the time of the theft and the sale, the thief must pay for the value at the time of the sale (as explained above in topic 16). Their opinion is that a transfer in jurisdiction over the item (for example, if it was sold by the thief after the owner despairs) does bring acquisition of the item, since it is coming into the buyer's jurisdiction legally, being that it is no longer owned by the victim at all (because of his despair).

However, Rambam, *Laws of Robbery* 5:3, holds that if the owner despairs of recovering an item that was robbed from him, and the second person is thereby able to buy the item from the thief (even if he knows that the item he is buying is stolen), this only means that he is able to keep the item, but he is still obligated to pay its value to the original owner. This is also the ruling in *Shulĥan Aruĥ Ĥoshen Mishpat* ch. 353 and 356. This is because his view is that the buyer is merely committing a second act of theft in completely removing the item from the owner's jurisdiction, even if he is doing so unwittingly.

It appears that this whole argument exists only where the owner is not able to force the thief to pay for theft, at which point it is disputable whether he can demand it from the buyer, or where the item appreciated in value after the theft, where there is more money involved that can be demanded from the buyer; otherwise there is no reason that he should not get it from the thief, and the buyer should not have to pay.

does not acquire the object. It must be returned intact to the owner,[101] and the buyer can demand the value of the item from the thief who sold it to him illegally.[102]

(c) If the owner did not despair of regaining the item at the time of the sale and did so only afterwards, there is an argument between the Torah-law authorities as to whether the buyer acquires it with this despair and the change of jurisdiction. There are some opinions[103] that the buyer acquires the item and it need not be returned intact, and the thief only needs to reimburse the owner for its value. According to other opinions,[104] the buyer does not acquire the item even if the owner despaired after the sale, so it must be returned intact.

A change of jurisdiction completes acquisition, even if the buyer

---

The reasoning seems that the obligation to return the item always remains on the original thief who originated the theft, and even where the buyer bought the item intentionally, knowing it was stolen, he was not the one who actually stole it. His only obligation comes from the positive command (in Jewish Law) to return a stolen item, or because practically the item belongs to the owner, so he can demand it back; or alternatively, because his continued use and possession of the item is theft. However, the main obligation to return the item is to correct what he did originally, and this only applies to the thief himself. (See Rambam, *Laws of Theft* ch. 5 and *Laws of Robbery* ch. 5, that the buyer is only transgressing for assisting the thief [but not as an act of theft itself]).

101 It therefore appears that one who buys a stolen item from a thief is not considered a delinquent debtor, and although the owner can demand it back, this is only because the stolen item does not belong to the buyer, and not because he is transgressing any prohibition of theft or delinquency.

102 This is the law based on the Written Torah. However, the Sages enacted that the owner should not be able to remove the object from the buyer unless he [the thief who reimburses the buyer] pays for its worth. Also, there is another enactment from the time of the Early Sages that one must always return the stolen object to the owner, even after he despairs and the item changes jurisdiction, as these details are explained in *Shulĥan Aruĥ Ĥoshen Mishpat* ch. 361. These laws have not been included here, since [as will be explained in topic 31] every country and court has the ability to construct its own legal enactments for the better functioning of the community.

103 Rambam, *Laws of Robbery* ch. 2, and *Laws of Theft* ch. 5; *Shulĥan Aruĥ Ĥoshen Mishpat* ch. 353, 356.

104 Rosh, *Tur* and Rema *Ĥoshen Mishpat* ch. 353, 356.

knows the item he bought was stolen, and knows that through his buying the item, it will be completely removed from the owner's jurisdiction. Although the buyer is forbidden to make this purchase (since he would be an accomplice to theft, as explained in Chapter 3), nevertheless, this change of jurisdiction accomplishes the acquisition, and the item need not be returned intact to the owner.[105]

This is all said in reference to the basic law. But if the buyer wishes to make complete amends, because it is a righteous character trait not to benefit from stolen property (such as if he knew that the item was stolen, and he therefore has sinned in buying it; or even if he did not know at all that it was stolen, and he bought the object innocently, but afterwards he found out that it was stolen), he should return the item intact to the owner, and not benefit from the stolen item.[106]

19. A change of jurisdiction happens only by a sale or gift that is given by the consent of both parties in the transaction. Therefore, if the thief forced the buyer to buy the stolen item (or to take it as repayment for a loan), this is not considered a change of jurisdiction, and even if the owner despaired of recovering the item, it must be returned to him.[107]

Therefore, if a second thief stole the item from the first thief, and the item is still intact, it still must be returned to the owner, even if he has previously despaired of recovering it. This is because there is no change of jurisdiction without the consent of the one who gives up the item (in this case, the first thief, since it was stolen from him).[108]

20. If the buyer of a stolen object has not acquired it with the change of jurisdiction, since the owner did not despair, then if he destroys the object or loses it through his negligence, or if he sells it to a second buyer, then the owner can make a demand in court to be paid for the stolen item, either from the thief or the first buyer.[109] (In this situation,

---

[105] *Sefer Meirat Einayim Ĥoshen Mishpat* 361:5.

[106] *Darkei Moshe* and *Sefer Meirat Einayim Ĥoshen Mishpat* 363:8.

[107] Rema *Ĥoshen Mishpat* 361:5.

[108] This is clear from Rambam, *Laws of Robbery* 1:17.

[109] Rabbi Zalman Nehemiah Goldberg notes that this law is derived from Tractate *Bava Kama* 111b: if one stole and the owner did not yet despair, and another person consumed the stolen item, the owner can demand payment either from the thief or from the second person.

the first buyer has removed the owner's jurisdiction from the item. For example, the owner despaired after the first buyer acquired the item but before he sold it to the second buyer, so the second buyer fully acquires the item with the owner's despair and the change of jurisdiction.) Even though the first buyer is not a thief, and even if he had no idea that the item was stolen,[110] nevertheless, since the item is not his, he is responsible for the loss that he caused.

In this situation, what amount does the first buyer of the stolen item owe to the victim of the theft? He must pay for the part of the value that is over and above that which the thief is obligated to pay. (The thief must reimburse the owner in place of returning the stolen object, since it is no longer in the thief's jurisdiction). For example, a thief stole an item worth $100, and it appreciated in value and is now worth $120 before he sells it to a buyer. The buyer then destroys it or causes its value to decrease. Then the thief must pay the owner $100, and the buyer must pay him $20. If it is impossible for the owner to demand payment from the thief, he can demand the whole sum from the buyer. This only applies if the buyer intended to acquire the stolen item.

However, if a second person only intentionally damaged the stolen item (for example, he ate stolen food that the thief gave him to eat), or if a second thief stole it from the first thief, he has not acquired it legally (whether or not he knew that the item had been stolen; and even if he intends to acquire the item for himself, but he does not wish to receive it legally, and therefore he is merely a damager). Therefore, if the item has a permanent change while in the jurisdiction of the second person by which he acquires it, or if he loses it (even if not by his negligence), or if he eats it or ruins it in some other way, then since the victim of the theft did not despair of recovering the object at the time it was changed or lost,[111] it still belongs to the victim. In this case, this second person who damages the item (after he receives, buys, or steals it from the thief) is considered as if he himself also stole it from the owner. Therefore, the owner can demand full payment for the theft

---

Rashba, Mordeĥai and Meiri on Tractate *Bava Kama* 111b explain that as long as the owner has not despaired, even an unsuspecting buyer from the thief is liable for any damages that occur to the item.

[110] *Maĥaneh Efraim Laws of Robbery* ch. 7.

[111] *Netivot HaMishpat Ĥoshen Mishpat* 361:3.

either from the first thief or the second person,[112] or half from each. Likewise, if the stolen item depreciated or appreciated in value between the first theft and the transfer to the second person, the owner can demand payment from both of them. For example, if the stolen item *depreciated* in value, and the owner received payment from the second person for the amount that it lessened in value after he received it from the first thief, then the owner can demand the rest of its value (at the time of the theft) from the first thief. If it *appreciated* in value, and the first thief paid the owner only the amount it was worth at the time of the theft, the owner can then demand from the second person to pay him the amount that it appreciated in value once it came into his hands.[113]

If, however, the owner despaired of recovering the object before the second person caused the loss, the owner can only demand payment from the first thief (for the amount that it was worth at the time of the theft, or of his despair).[114]

21. This all applies regarding a second person who bought or stole a stolen item from the first thief. But if someone finds a stolen item that a thief lost, or if he temporarily has a stolen item that a thief gave him to hold for safekeeping, and he knows that the item was stolen, he is forbidden to return the item to the thief (since he would be helping the thief to continue in his sin). Instead, he should return it to the rightful owner. Nevertheless, if he returned it to the thief, the owner cannot demand from him the value of the stolen object[115] (since a person who safeguards a stolen object for the thief does not intend to receive it for

---

[112] Rabbi Zalman Nehemiah Goldberg notes that it appears that if the object was changed, it depends on the argument explained above in footnote 97.

[113] Since both of them are thieves who must pay the reimbursement to the owner, as explained in *Tur* and *Shulĥan Aruĥ Ĥoshen Mishpat* ch. 361, therefore the laws that apply to a change in the value by the first thief, as explained before (in topic 16) apply as well to both.

[114] *Shulĥan Aruĥ Ĥoshen Mishpat* ch. 361.

[115] *Shulĥan Aruĥ, ibid.* 348:7. Even though Rema writes there that the owner can demand payment from the one who returned the stolen object to the thief, since he caused the owner a loss, this is only because for a Jew, there is an obligation to return the item to the owner, just like any lost object. For a Gentile, there is no Torah Law to return a lost object.

himself,[116] and there is no Torah law that a Gentile must return a lost object to its owner). [For the laws of a watchman in general, see Chapter 7. If a watchman was asked to guard a stolen object and he failed to do so as required, and he is obligated to pay for the loss he caused, it is obvious that the owner of the object may demand this payment from him (as long as the owner has not despaired, as explained topic 20 above).]

22. If one stole and gave the object to another person as a gift, then if the owner despaired before the thief gave the gift, this is considered a change of jurisdiction. Then the thief need only return the value of the stolen object to the owner, and the gift remains in the possession of the one who received it. If the owner did not despair, and the object is still intact, it must be returned to the owner.[117]

However, if one stole an item and his children inherited it, this is not considered a change of jurisdiction, and even if the owner despaired, the inheritors are obligated to return it, if is still intact. If it changed and is still in their jurisdiction, they must pay its value to the victim of the theft, even if he despaired. If the object was lost, they are exempt from making reimbursement.

If the inheritors destroyed the stolen item (e.g., food that was eaten, or firewood that was burned), whether during the life of the father [the thief] or after his death, then if they destroyed it before the owner despaired, they are obligated to reimburse the owner, and if they destroyed it afterwards, they are exempt.[118]

23. If one stole an item and then it was lost, broken or stolen from him, this is the thief's responsibility, and he needs to pay for the full value of the stolen item, even if the damage was unpreventable. This only applies once he removed the object from the owner's property, or raised it or placed it in his vessel (see topics 1:12,13). But if it is still in the owner's property, and the thief has not raised it above three hand-

---

[116] See *Shulĥan Aruĥ Ĥoshen Mishpat* 348:6, *Sefer Meirat Einayim* 348:14 and *Biur HaGra* there, topic 21.

[117] Rambam, *Laws of Robbery* ch. 2; *Shulĥan Aruĥ Ĥoshen Mishpat* ch. 362.

[118] *Shulĥan Aruĥ Ĥoshen Mishpat* 361:7. See there and Rambam, *Laws of Theft* ch. 5, regarding the obligation of the orphans to pay the debts of their father; it appears that a Gentile is exempt in this regard.

breadths from the ground,[119] then it is still in the owner's jurisdiction, and the thief is not obligated to pay for any unpreventable damages that occur, unless they were caused through his action of theft.[120]

24. If one stole an object and built it into a building, by Torah Law, the thief should return the stolen item intact (for example, a wooden construction beam), and he is held responsible to even take apart the building if that is the only way to remove the item. However, the Sages instituted that he is not obligated to destroy the building, and may instead pay for the item's value.[121] This enactment is for the benefit of those who wish to repent, so it should not be too hard for them to make amends, since returning the item would be too expensive if it would be necessary to take apart the building to remove it. This applies to any stolen item that is still intact but was built into a larger structure (such as a building, a vehicle, a vessel, etc.).[122]

It is also unclear if a Gentile is bound by the law that if the father left property for the children, that property is under lien to any debts he had prior to his death.

[119] See *Shulĥan Aruĥ Ĥoshen Mishpat* 198:2.

[120] For example, if one stole a sheep from the owner's pen and was pulling it away, and then it died while still in the owner's property, the thief is exempt, since the death was an unforeseen circumstance that was not caused by his actions of theft. If he raised it or removed it from the property of the owner, the thief must pay for the cost of the sheep. If the sheep pen was in a forest, once the thief prods the sheep to move and hides it in the trees and brush, it is considered stolen and the thief is obligated to pay for any unpreventable damage that occurs to it, up to the full value of the sheep. See Rambam, *Laws of Theft* ch. 2; *Shulĥan Aruĥ Ĥoshen Mishpat* 348:4.

[121] *A Jew who follows the Rabbinical enactment of monetary reimbursement in this case also fulfills the Torah's Jewish commandment of returning the stolen object. For Gentiles, it is questionable if their obligation in this case is fulfilled through monetary reimbursement, even if an empowered Noahide court would permit this leniency. See the ends of footnotes 9 and 49, on what Tractate *Taanit* 16a teaches regarding the repentance of the Gentiles of Nineveh: "[The Sage] Shmuel says that even if they needed to destroy their houses to remove a stolen beam [they did so]." Therefore, it still needs to be clarified whether a Gentile *must* return the stolen object itself in this case, instead of paying a reimbursement.

[122] *Gittin* p. 55; Rambam, *Laws of Robbery* ch. 1; *Shulĥan Aruĥ ibid.* ch. 360.

25. A Gentile who steals and is required to return the item itself or its value, is not obligated to expend effort to return it to the hands of the owner. He may instead let the owner know that he has the stolen item, in order that the owner may come to pick it up from him.[123]

If he stole from a person in the city and wanted to return it to him in the wilderness, the choice is in the hands of the owner. If the owner wants, he can receive the item there, and if not, he may tell the thief, "I only wish to accept it in the habited area, since it may be unsafe to accept it in the wilderness [lest it be stolen or lost there]." At this point, the stolen item is still in the jurisdiction of the thief and under his responsibility, until he returns it in the habited area. If the thief is reimbursing the owner for the value of the stolen item, the same applies to this money.[124]

26. If someone steals from a person and wishes to return the money to the victim in a hidden way (for example, to include the amount of the stolen money in another deal that he is making with him, such as if the thief subsequently bought merchandise from the victim for $100, and he adds the amount he stole into the stack of payment money), he can fulfill his obligation in this way. If the thief returns the money into the victim's wallet that contains other money already, he has also fulfilled

---

It appears that since we don't find this enactment made for Gentiles, the Sages did not make it for them. This is also written by Ĥatam Sofer *Gittin* 55, and responsa *Hitorerut Teshuva Ĥoshen Mishpat* ch. 28. This matter is in the hands of the Noahide court to decide, and they can make a general law that one must return the item itself, or that reimbursement is sufficient.

[123] This is implied in Rema *Ĥoshen Mishpat* ch. 367 and Shaĥ 367:3. [Since the logic and reasoning behind this law is questionable (as discussed in the Hebrew text of *Sheva Mitzvot HaShem*, Part VII, footnote 128), we have left the words of Rema as they are in the *Shulĥan Aruĥ*, even though it seems correct that the thief would be obligated to expend effort to correct his wrong and bring the theft (or payment) back to the owner. (Rabbi Yaakov Eliezrov notes: it should be mentioned that *Sefer Meirat Einayim* 367:2 holds that the reason for this is to make it easier for the thief to make amends, for otherwise it would be fitting to obligate him to bring the item to the owner. Therefore, this depends on whether we say that this enactment of the Sages applies to Gentiles or not.) Still, it is reasonable that a Noahide court can make the same legal enactment to make it easier for the thief to make amends.]

[124] Rambam, *Laws of Robbery* ch. 1; *Shulĥan Aruĥ Ĥoshen Mishpat* ch. 366.

his obligation, since a person checks his wallet frequently, and the victim will see the returned money along with the other money. If the victim can count the money, even if he does not recognize the difference, the law is that this exempts the thief. If the thief returned the money into an empty wallet (that is not being checked), he is not yet exempted, and he is still responsible for stealing the money, until he notifies the victim that he returned it. (The same rules apply if the thief returns the money through a third party.)[125]

This only applies if the victim knew about the theft. If he did not know about it at all, and the thief returned the item to the place he stole it from (even money to an empty wallet), he fulfills his obligation.

(The above applies to a theft of a non-living item. But if one stole an animal and returned it to its owner's pen, he must inform the owner. Even if the owner then counts it without knowing the difference, it doesn't exempt the thief. This is because the animal that was stolen became used to a new path of travel and a new location, and it might go off again on that path, toward that place. Since the owner now needs to pay more attention to this animal, to watch that it will not leave, the thief must inform the owner.)[126]

27. One who stole from many people and does not know (or remember) who they are, so he is not able to return what was stolen from them, should give the value of the stolen items to pay for things that are needed by the community (such as digging wells that will supply water for the community), in order that those from whom he stole will be included in deriving benefit from them. But if this thief recognizes someone as one of his victims, he is obligated to return what he stole from this person, and he cannot suffice with this known victim having benefit from the community assistance that he paid for.[127]

He should not take any recognition or appreciation (or tax deduction) for his public assistance, since this honor does not belong to him; he is only returning a theft from the public.[128]

One who steals from one of two people and is unsure of which one,

---

[125] Rambam, *ibid.*; *Shulĥan Aruĥ Ĥoshen Mishpat* ch. 355.

[126] Rambam, *Laws of Theft* ch. 4; *Shulĥan Aruĥ, ibid.*

[127] *Shulĥan Aruĥ Ĥoshen Mishpat* ch. 366; *Shulĥan Aruĥ HaRav, Laws of Robbery* topic 8.

[128] *Igrot Moshe Ĥoshen Mishpat* vol. 2, ch. 88.

should return the full amount to both if he wishes to fulfill his obligation to God.[129]

28. If the victim of a theft dies before the item is returned, the thief must return it to the inheritors of the victim, if it is in the same form as when it was stolen. If not, its value must be reimbursed to them.[130]

29. If one stole an item and had benefit from its use (such as one who stole an animal and used it for plowing or carrying packages), then even though he stole and benefited from this use, the item can be returned and there is no obligation to repay the value of the benefit as well, if the stolen item did not depreciate in value as a result. Even though there is a loss to the owner during the time that he would have used the item, this does not come as a direct damage from the thief; rather, it is only an outcome that was caused.[131]

This only applies if he stole once or twice incidentally. But one who is accustomed to steal other's property and return it later should be penalized to return an amount equal to what it would have cost him to rent the stolen item, or as is otherwise seen fit by the court.[132]

30. If one stole an item that is suitable for rent (for example, a rental car) with intention not to return it, and it is still in its same condition, it can be returned, and the thief does not need to pay the rental fee for its use. If he damaged it, he needs to pay the owner for the cost of repairing it, and for the resulting depreciation of the item. If the person intended to take it as a loan to be returned later, he has committed theft, and he must also pay for the cost to rent the item. The owner is also allowed to require repayment for any decrease in the item's value that was caused by this use.[132] If the thief rented the item out to another person, he must also return the rental money to the owner.

---

[129] *Shulĥan Aruĥ, ibid.* ch. 365; *Shulĥan Aruĥ HaRav, ibid.* topic 34.

[130] Rambam, *Laws of Robbery* ch. 8; *Shulĥan Aruĥ, ibid.* ch. 367.

[131] This is not comparable to the case in topic 2:13 above, when a Gentile is liable to pay for an indirect cause of loss (such as one who burnt an IOU note, or stole a bill and caused its value to decrease), since there the damage is caused by his actions. By contrast, if the perpetrator is only preventing the owner from receiving profit, he is exempt from any loss that is indirectly caused through his actions.

[132] Rambam, *Laws of Robbery* ch. 3; *Shulĥan Aruĥ, ibid.* ch. 363.

31. All the details of returning a stolen object that are explained in this chapter are either obligated by the Torah or are laws that were set up by the Jewish Sages. (Most of the laws in this chapter are the Jewish Torah laws in regard to theft. Another law enacted by the Sages is that the buyer of a stolen item should be compensated for the purchase price he paid. [This compensation is paid by the owner of the stolen object, at the time it is returned to him.] This is called "*takanat hashuk*" in Hebrew, which is a legal enactment that protects the regular procedure for sales in the market – for if a buyer would not be compensated when he has to return a stolen item to the rightful owner, he would be reluctant to buy merchandise in the market.)

It is permissible for the government or court of every nation to set up laws for the return of stolen items as they see fit, as long as this is beneficial for society, and then these laws are obligatory for the citizens. These include such laws as paying interest on stolen money, or payment for the use of stolen items, or any other penalties that seem fit.[133] It is forbidden for them to permit theft, or to permit a thief to benefit sinfully by acquiring or not returning the items he steals, or to remove all liability from a thief for restitution to his victim. In these matters, they are only allowed to determine the procedures for returning what was stolen, and for compensating the victim, and the manner of disciplining a thief.

32. One who stole is obligated to ask for forgiveness from the victim whom he stole from. The thief has no forgiveness from God until he returns the object and/or any required reimbursement (according to the laws discussed in this chapter), and asks for forgiveness from the victim for the trouble he caused. (He should continue to ask for forgiveness until the victim is appeased, even if this involves other reasonable actions that are needed to appease him).[134]

---

[133] Rema *Ĥoshen Mishpat* 355:7.

[134] Rambam, *Laws of Repentance* 2:9. Rabbi Zalman Nehemiah Goldberg notes that it is unclear why one who damages (but does not injure) does not need to ask for forgiveness, but one who steals does. See *Leĥem Mishneh* on Rambam, *Laws of Injury* 5:9, that a thief benefits from the theft and causes anguish to the victim, but a damager is not getting a benefit from the victim's anguish. Also (see *Likkutei Siĥot* vol. 32, p. 115), one who steals removes the item from the owner's jurisdiction, which is a personal harm, but a damager does not take jurisdiction over the monetary loss he caused to the victim.

CHAPTER 3

The Prohibitions of Aiding or Having Benefit from Theft or Buying Stolen Property, and the Laws of Unintentional Theft

1. It is forbidden to assist a thief or robber in his crime in any way, and likewise one who sees a theft or robbery and is silent is a sinner.[135]

2. If two people steal or rob with a partnership action (e.g., both together drew a sheep out of the owner's property), they are both liable for the capital sin of theft. Each must pay half the value of the stolen item. If each one separately held the object in his possession, the owner can demand the full payment from either one he wants.[136]

If one of the two people was accomplishing the act of theft, and the second was *only* assisting him, the one assisting is exempt from receiving capital punishment or paying any damages.[137] However, this only applies if the stolen item has not entered the property of the assistant. If it does enter the assistant's property, he has an obligation to return the object to the owner, and if he does not do so, he must pay restitution, as explained above in topic 2:20.

Likewise, if a thief is sent to steal and bring the stolen item to the one who sent him, the owner can demand restitution from either the thief or the one who sent him.[137]

3. One who hires or sends another to commit thievery or robbery is not liable in court as a thief (see Part I, topic 4:6 and the footnote there, and Part V, topic 1:5), even though he is liable to punishment by God as one who causes another to sin. (And the courts are empowered to

---

[135] Rema *Ĥoshen Mishpat* ch. 356. See Ibn Ezra Lev. 19:11 – "Why is the prohibition against stealing given in the plural? To say that one who sees a theft and remains silent is considered a thief." This means that theft refers to any concealment from a rightful owner. Though it is possible to say that this applies only to one who witnesses an undercover thief, and will be able to discourage his intentions by scaring him, but not to one who witnesses an armed robbery, it is nevertheless logical that one is obligated to do all in one's power to prevent a robbery due to the command of having a righteous justice system, as explained in Part I, Chapter 4.

[136] See responsa Ĥatam Sofer *Ĥoshen Mishpat* ch. 131.

[137] *Shulĥan Aruĥ Ĥoshen Mishpat* ch. 348.

deal with and punish such actions through civil laws and penalties, as explained in Part V, topic 1:8.) If the thief brings the stolen item to the one who sent him to steal (the sender), this is not considered a change of jurisdiction by which the sender can acquire the item.

4. If one tricks another into stealing an object for him (e.g., by saying that the object really belongs to him, and the one being sent is unaware of the theft he is committing), the sender is obligated to return the object and is responsible for anything that happens to it.[138]

5. It is forbidden for anyone to benefit from a stolen item,[139] since the actual use of the item is included in the prohibition of theft. This applies even if the owner despaired of recovering the object,[140] as long as the object is intact and in the hands of the thief. As long as the thief is obligated to return the stolen object, his continued possession and use of the object is considered an ongoing transgression of theft.[141]

---

[138] See *Darkei Moshe Ĥoshen Mishpat* ch. 348, and *Shaĥ* there, topic 6.

[139] Rambam, *Laws of Robbery* ch. 5; *Shulĥan Aruĥ Ĥoshen Mishpat* ch. 369.

[140] See *Netivot HaMishpat* 361:2, that this only applies if the despair came after the loss. However, one who despaired before the actual loss, such as if one saw robbers coming and gave up, this is considered a full loss, and any other person has permission to benefit from the [ownerless] object. The proof is from the law (*Ĥoshen Mishpat* ch. 368) that if one saves an object from the hands of the robbers, it belongs to him (the "saver"), because of the owner's despair (even though it has not changed jurisdiction, and the despair itself does not make the object acquired by the saver). The logical difference between the two cases is that if the object is still in the owner's hands, he can consent for it to belong to the saver. But once the robbers have taken the object, they have an obligation to return it to the owner, so it cannot leave his jurisdiction even with his despair (unless it is sold or permanently changed).

[141] It appears that the prohibition against using a stolen object is part of the prohibition of theft, *a fortiori* from the case of one who borrows without permission, which is also considered theft (a transgression extending over the entire period the thief retains the object), and is not just a penalty instituted by the Sages. It also appears that there are two prohibitions regarding the use of the stolen object: (1) the use of the object against the owner's will, which is itself a type of theft, and (2) a prohibition decreed by the Rabbis against any use of a stolen object, even if there is no objection from the owner. The second prohibition can be seen from *Shulĥan Aruĥ HaRav, Laws of Robbery*:

Likewise, anyone who borrows without the owner's permission is considered a thief (as will be explained in Chapter 7). This applies not only to the one who intends to return the item after using it, but even if other people use it after he has taken it, they also commit the transgression of theft, since they are also borrowing without the owner's permission.[142]

6. If an object stolen had a complete change while in the hands of the thief, by which he acquires the object (and is only obligated to repay the original owner for its value, as explained in Chapter 2), it is then permitted for anyone, including the thief, to use the object.[143]

7. It has been previously explained in Chapter 2 that even though a thief acquires the stolen object if it has a complete change while in his possession, it is forbidden to intentionally make this change, since this furthers the scope of the theft by completely removing the object from any connection to the jurisdiction of the owner. Similarly, one who buys a stolen object is further removing the jurisdiction from the owner (through the owner's despairing of recovering the object, and the change of jurisdiction from the thief, as explained there). The buyer therefore sins through buying the object and aiding the thief.[144]

In the first sale of a stolen object, the one who actually fully transgresses the prohibition of theft is the one who sells the object, since his action furthers the theft.[145] The buyer, even if he is aware that

---

(1) from topic 10 there, that one may not even ride on a stolen animal, although this use would not bother the owner, and (2) from topic 11 there, that it is forbidden to walk through a stolen house or field (which is probably a use that the owner is not particular about, and even if he is, it is possible that for unmovable property, borrowing without the owner's permission is not considered theft) – hence, the prohibition is only a decree by Sages.

[142] Rabbi Zalman Nehemiah Goldberg comments:

Regarding one who borrowed an object without the owner's consent, it is considered that the object is still in the owner's possession, since there is no intent to steal it indefinitely. Therefore, if anyone else damages it, the owner can demand payment equally from the person who borrowed it and the person who damaged it. See topic 2:20 above.

[143] *Shulĥan Aruĥ HaRav, Laws of Robbery* topic 23 and *Oraĥ Ĥayim* 11:12.

[144] Rambam, *Laws of Robbery* ch. 5; *Shulĥan Aruĥ Ĥoshen Mishpat* ch. 369.

[145] See footnote 70, that there is no capital sin for this furtherance of the theft.

the object is stolen and that his action is completing the transfer of the object out of the jurisdiction of the owner, is only considered an assistant to the thief, and not as a thief himself (and he is therefore exempt from the harsh punishment for theft).[146]

8. Regarding an object that was not fully acquired by the thief, the object is considered stolen in the hands of the last holder. (E.g., if the owner has not yet despaired of recovering the object and no permanent change has occurred to it – regarding which it was explained in Chapter 2 that there is no change of jurisdiction, and the object still belongs to the owner, even if the buyer had no idea that the object was stolen and he was only informed after the fact; or if a second person robbed the object from the first thief, in which case the object does not change jurisdiction, as explained in topic 2:19). It must be returned to the original owner, and it is forbidden to make use of or have benefit from the object, in the same way that this is prohibited for the thief. It is also forbidden for another person to buy the stolen object from this last holder.[147]

It appears that if the buyer knew that the object was stolen and he made a complete change in the object in order to remove it fully from the owner's jurisdiction, he is transgressing the prohibition of theft.[148]

If the victim of the theft despaired of recovering the object, there is no prohibition for the buyer to use it (even if he sinned in buying it, because he knew at the time of the purchase that it was stolen).[149]

---

[146] Rambam and *Shulĥan Aruĥ, ibid.* The reason he himself is not considered a thief is because without the thief selling him the item, he alone would be unable to make a jurisdictional change in the article. For even if he instead stole it from the thief, it would not change jurisdiction, and the requirement to return it to the original owner would still stand, as explained in topic 2:19.

[147] *Shulĥan Aruĥ HaRav Laws of Robbery* topic 11. This is also apparent from *Shulĥan Aruĥ HaRav Oraĥ Ĥayim* 649:6.

[148] Rabbi Zalman Nehemiah Goldberg notes: This seems to concur with the opinion that making a permanent change in the item is considered theft.

[149] See *Shulĥan Aruĥ HaRav Laws of Robbery* topic 11, that although one transgresses through buying stolen property, it is henceforth permissible to use it (if the victim despaired of recovering it), since the object no longer has any connection to the original owner. It is only while it still is in the hands of the thief that it is forbidden for anyone to use it – including the thief – since he is obligated to return the object itself, as explained in topic 5 above.

9. It is forbidden to buy a stolen object from the thief (unless it has undergone a complete change by which the thief acquires the object, as explained in topic 6), and this is a great sin, since it strengthens the hands of those that sin, and causes them to continue on to other thefts. For if there are no buyers, there is usually no reason to steal. Regarding this matter, it is written (Proverbs 29:24), "One who divides with a thief hates his [own] soul" (since in the end he will also be caught and punished for assisting the thief).[150] If however, his intention is for the owner's benefit, in order to return the object, it is permitted to buy the stolen object from the thief.[151]

10. It is forbidden to buy or benefit[152] from any item that can be assumed to be stolen. If it is assumed that most items of a certain type in the market are stolen, it is forbidden to purchase any of them.

In any case that one is suspicious of a sale, such as when the seller tells the buyer to hide the product being sold, it is forbidden to participate in the sale.[153]

11. It is forbidden to buy an item from a known thief, unless one knows specifically that the thief has such an item that rightfully belongs to him. Even if the thief has a majority of identical items that are stolen and a minority of these items that legally belong to him, one may be lenient and assume that the item being sold is legally owned by

---

150 Rambam, *ibid.* and *Laws of Theft* ch. 5; *Shulĥan Aruĥ ibid.* chs. 356, 369.

151 *Shulĥan Aruĥ HaRav Laws of Robbery* topic 9.

152 *Ibid.*, topic 20.

153 Rambam *Laws of Theft* ch. 6; *Shulĥan Aruĥ ibid.* ch. 358. In a place where most shepherds steal, one may not buy from them any wool, milk or goats, since these can be assumed to be stolen. Certain items that one can assume have been given to the shepherd (or he may take) with the owner's permission, such as the milk or cheese he carries outside the city limits, are permissible to buy from the shepherd. However, if the shepherd has these items and is working close to an inhabited area, it is assumed that he has stolen them, since the owner would not give him permission to take them.

A shepherd who sells four or five sheep or cattle out of a small corral is not assumed to have stolen them, since the owner would be aware of the loss. Rather, he is assumed to be making the sale legally. One also may not buy fruit from a field's watchman in a place where the watchmen are suspected of stealing, as he may be selling the fruits from the field he has been watching.

the thief – unless it is clearly known that this item itself is stolen.[154]

12. It is forbidden to benefit from the money of people who are known to be thieves and can be assumed to have stolen all their possessions and merchandise, since they have no legal business or profession.[155]

13. It is forbidden to benefit from stolen money. Therefore, one may not do business with or accept a present from thieves, since the money one receives from them is stolen. Even a small amount of benefit is forbidden (such as exchanging currency without paying the thief), since the money can be assumed to be stolen. If the money is not definitely stolen, some opinions permit such a type of benefit. If one owes money to a thief and pays with a larger sum, it is permitted to accept change of a smaller sum in return, since this is considered saving money from the thief.[156] It is also forbidden to pay a thief for an exchange of his money, since this is considered as aiding theft.[157]

The above rules apply if the buyer is not afraid that the thieves will injure him. But if he feels threatened by them, he may buy their merchandise or exchange currency with them (at the minimum needed).[158]

14. One may not buy items from children (or slaves) unless it can be assumed that the items belong to them or that they are selling them with the consent of the owner.[159]

15. If a craftsman or a tailor (who received an item to fix, or materials to make an item) has leftover scraps from the materials, one should deal with these scraps in the manner prescribed by the law of the

---

[154] *Shulĥan Aruĥ HaRav Laws of Robbery* topic 10.

[155] *Ibid.*, topic 12.

[156] See *Shulĥan Aruĥ ibid.* 369:4 and *Shulĥan Aruĥ HaRav ibid.* topic 12.

[157] It appears that there is no argument at all that this is considered assisting the thief. Only regarding exchanging currency are there differences of opinion, as this may or may not be considered minimal benefit for the thief.

[158] This is apparent from the general permission to save one's own life even at the expense of another's money. Even though it is explained in Chapter 4 that this only applies in a life-threatening situation, it appears that in regard to the *lesser* prohibitions of benefiting from theft and aiding theft, it is permissible even for the sake of preventing extreme anguish and threat of distress.

[159] Rambam *Laws of Theft* ch. 6, and *Shulĥan Aruĥ ibid.* ch. 358

country. If the accepted practice is to return them to the owner, one is obligated to do so, and keeping them is stealing. In places where the custom is not to be particular about them, they belong to the craftsman or tailor who fashioned the item.[159]

Likewise, one may not buy factory products from the factory workers, unless the factory owner clearly allows them to sell the products they are working with. Otherwise, it can be assumed that the owner is particular regarding his merchandise, and the workers are stealing it and selling it on the side, in which case it would be forbidden to buy it from them.

16. One may not *purchase* items from a businessman whose profession is to take in those types of items that belong to his customers, do improvements or repairs or some other service on those items, and return them to their owners, since such a sale can be presumed to be a theft. (This includes a sale item that contains material taken without permission from a customer's item.)

What is one permitted to purchase from him? If it can only be assumed that he is making a *provisional* change in part or all of an item that was entrusted to him for service and return, and then selling it, it is permissible to buy it from him. This is because it is only presumed, and not known with certainty, that part or all of the sale item was stolen. See topics 2:4,5. (For example, the person is hired to take his customers' woolen blankets and comb off "wool flocking" that he should return with the blankets, so it can be used for stuffing pillows. He also sells this type of pillows. Although this is only a provisional change in the wool flocking, one may buy the pillows because the wool flocking is only presumed to be stolen.)

But if part or all of the sale item is *definitely* known to be stolen, it is forbidden to buy it, since the change in the item was only provisional, and not permanent. If a *permanent* change was made it (see topic 2:4), it is permissible to buy it from this businessman, even if it is certainly stolen (since he has taken the item out of the owner's jurisdiction).[160]

17. What is the ruling if robbers stole items from a person, and later

---

[160] *Shulĥan Aruĥ* and Rema *Ĥoshen Mishpat* end of ch. 358; *Shulĥan Aruĥ HaRav, ibid.* topic 23. If threads are woven into a garment there is a difference of opinion on whether or not this is a permanent change in the threads.

returned to replace them with other items[161] – and the items in their possession are presumed, but not definitely known, to be stolen?

On the *assumption* that the items are stolen, then *if* it can be assumed that the owners would have despaired of recovering their items, it is permissible for this person to accept these items in exchange for what was stolen from him. This is not considered benefiting from theft, because (1) the robbers gave the items to him in exchange for what they stole from him, so this exchange is like a sale, and (2) it is *not certain* that the actual items being exchanged were stolen.[162]

However, if it is *known* to him that the replacement items are certainly stolen, it is forbidden for him to accept them, since it is a direct benefit from theft.

If one bought a stolen item, and it is known that the owner has not despaired of recovering it, the buyer must return it to the owner.[163] But if it is assumed that the owner has despaired, it belongs to the buyer *post facto*.[164] Nevertheless, it is praiseworthy for the buyer to be stringent and return the object to the owner if possible.

18. If one gives a vessel to a craftsman to fix, and the worker returns a different but similar item, it is permissible for the owner of the original item to take this new item from the craftsman (since it can be assumed

---

[161] The Mishnah *Bava Kama* 114 uses the example of a robber who returned an item of the same kind as the one he stole, such as one who stole an article of clothing and returned a different article of clothing. It is not clear what would be the case if a robber stole, for example, a donkey, and returned money in its stead to appease the owner. It seems that the permission given to take an item from the robber that is comparable to the one he stole is because it is like saving money from him. Therefore, there should seemingly be no difference in regard to what item is returned, even if it is a dissimilar item.

[162] This means that since the victim of the theft is receiving a similar item in exchange for his stolen one, it is considered a sale and change of jurisdiction; and since the original owner of the returned item probably has despaired, the receiver acquires it legally. Although there is another prohibition involved, namely benefiting from a person for whom most of his possessions have been acquired through theft, nevertheless, since the victim does not know specifically that this item was stolen, he may receive reimbursement for the value of his stolen item from the thief, so he will not completely lose out.

[163] See Rambam, *Laws of Robbery* 5:10; *Shulĥan Aruĥ, ibid.* ch. 369.

[164] *Imrei Ya'acov* topic 102 on *Shulĥan Aruĥ HaRav, ibid.* topic 14.

that the craftsman has permission to sell the item from the previous owner). But if the craftsman's wife or child returned the different item to him, it is forbidden to take it, since they may have switched it without the other owner's permission. Likewise, if the craftsman tells the receiver, "Take your object," and he knows that it is not his, it is forbidden for him to receive it.[165]

19. One who mistakenly takes items belonging to someone else (e.g., one who switches coats mistakenly at a wedding hall) may not use the other's belongings after he discovers the error. Even if the second person is using the first person's item (even intentionally), the first person has no permission to steal from a thief, and he cannot take the law into his own hands (in such circumstances), as explained in Chapter 4. If the second person asks for his item to be returned, without returning the first person's item, the first person must do so despite the fact that his item was lost.[166] (This applies if his item was accidentally taken, as in the case of the switched coats at the wedding hall. However, if he sees that the other person clearly stole his property, he can take or keep the other's coat in place of his own.)[167]

This all applies only if there was a mistaken mix-up. If one sees clearly that the other switched his clothes for the first one's better pair,

---

[165] Rambam, *Laws of Robbery* ch. 6; *Shulĥan Aruĥ Ĥoshen Mishpat* ch. 136.

[166] *Shulĥan Aruĥ, ibid.*; *Shulĥan Aruĥ HaRav, Laws of Robbery* topic 30.

[167] Rabbi Zalman Nehemiah Goldberg comments:

It appears that the statements of the *Shulĥan Aruĥ Ĥoshen Mishpat* (in the preceding footnote) that the person whose coat was switched must return the coat left with him to its owner, despite the fact that he has lost his own, only applies if the other person took his coat by mistake and not with intention to steal. If there was intent to steal, even though one may not take the law into one's own hands, he may *hold the other's coat as a deposit* until his own is returned. He may likewise go to court and demand his coat from the other person, and they can sell the thief's coat (in the other's possession) to compensate for the theft. This applies even in the case that his own coat still is intact in the hands of the thief, since he can just as well say that the coat in his possession was his own. Even if one switched possessions with another by mistake, it appears that each one can sell the one he holds for its value, since the other person who took his item needs to pay for its use (unlike a thief who takes the item intentionally), and in using the other's coat he is paying off the other's debt to him.

it is permitted for the victim to use the thief's clothes in exchange.[168]

20. Likewise, if one who leaves his clothes with a launderer, who then mistakenly switches his clothes with those of another customer, it is forbidden to use the other person's clothes. One must return them even if his own clothes were lost.[169] If much time has passed and the other person has not gone back to retrieve his clothes, it is permitted for the one who lost his own clothes to use the other's clothes, since the other person is presumed to have despaired of recovering his clothes, and the launderer has reimbursed him.

21. Even one who did not steal on purpose, but rather received another's item mistakenly, is nevertheless required to return it, and it is forbidden to use it. (If the item is lost or broken after he uses it, he is obligated to compensate the owner according to the law of a borrower, unless the owner has despaired previously.)[170]

22. However, if one knows that an object or money does not belong to him and is not ownerless, but rather it belongs to another, but he errs and thinks that he may use it without permission, he is considered a thief. (And he is liable for this, since this is not considered an innocent mistake, since he should have been knowledgeable of the laws of theft, as explained in Part I, Chapter 4).

---

[168] Ben Ish Ĥai *Parshat Teitzei* Law 10.

[169] *Shulĥan Aruĥ, ibid.*; *Shulĥan Aruĥ HaRav Laws of Robbery* topic 30.

[170] *Shulĥan Aruĥ, ibid.* 361:7. If one inherits stolen items and consumes some of them before the owner despairs of recovering them, he is obligated to repay for the consumed items. On the other hand, he does not have to repay for what he consumed after the owner despaired. It can be deduced that if one took another's property by mistake, he must pay for any use that happened before the owner despaired. It appears that this comparison can be drawn, since the inheritor of the stolen items has not committed a theft intentionally.

See *Maĥaneh Efraim Laws of Robbery* ch. 7, that if there is no intention to steal, there is also no obligation for compensation. Nevertheless, such a person would be called "one who uses another's possessions without permission," regardless of how it is approached. If he finds out only after he uses it that it is not his, and still decides to use it, he does so without permission. And if he thought the whole time that it was his own, he is nevertheless obligated to repay, for he is like one who damages another's property.

CHAPTER 4

Laws of Saving Oneself or One's Property at the Expense of Another's Money; Taking the Law into One's Own Hands

1. One who finds himself in mortal danger may save himself by taking another's money, and this is not transgressing the prohibition of theft, since the prohibition of theft is pushed aside for saving a human life. Nevertheless, he should not take another's money or belongings unless he plans to return the full value when he is able to do so.[171] (This means that saving a life overrides the prohibition of theft, but it does not take away the obligation to compensate the owner, and it does not allow the person to steal more than is needed to save his life. However, if he knows that there is no possibility that he will be able to pay back, he is still allowed to save himself through another's money, since the whole reason for the obligation to pay back is the prohibition to steal. Once this prohibition is overridden by the obligation to save a life, the only reason for the obligation to pay back is his ability to do so.)[172]

If however, one is not in mortal danger, but instead has pain or a disease and wants to take another's money in order to save himself from pain, it is forbidden to do so, even with intent to compensate. Likewise, to save oneself from an oppressor who wishes to cause pain that is not life threatening, it is not permitted to use another person's money. Surely, it is forbidden to save one's own money through taking another person's money.[173]

2. It appears that it is even permitted to take another person's money to save one's own limb.[174]

---

[171] *Shulĥan Aruĥ Ĥoshen Mishpat* ch. 359. See Part IV, Chapter 6, that a Gentile is not obligated to give up his life for the Seven Noahide Laws (except for murder), even in a case of severe illness; the same applies to theft.

[172] Apparently based on the ruling of *Shulĥan Aruĥ ibid.* Although one should not take without intention to pay back, it is clear that if it would be impossible to pay back, the person would still be allowed to steal to save his life.

[173] *Shulĥan Aruĥ HaRav ibid.* topic 2. (A Gentile should be liable for capital sin if he steals money to save himself from pain; it may be that he is exempt from punishment, since it is pain, or other duress, that is forcing him to steal.)

[174] See *Shulĥan Aruĥ HaRav Laws of Monetary Damage* topic 10: "[It is permissible] if there is a danger to life or limb." See Part V, topic 2:5.

3. It is also permissible for a third-party (e.g., an onlooker) to save someone's life or limb by using another person's property, and this is not considered stealing.[175]

4. It is also permitted for a person to borrow without permission – an act normally deemed as theft – in order to save his life. If it is an item that is normally rented, one must pay back the amount usually required for its rented use. (See above, topic 2:30.) Therefore, if one stole a rental car in order to save a person's life, he must pay the amount of the rental fee for the length of time he takes it. If it is not a rental car, he is not obligated to pay any rental fee for this use (but he must pay for or replace the amount of gasoline he used).

5. If one is a victim of theft, he may forcibly take the law into his hands and take back his belongings that were stolen, and he is not considered a thief for doing so[176] (subject to the restriction in the next

---

[175] See *Korban Netanel* (*Bava Kama* topic 6:12) based on Rosh there, that otherwise, people would be hesitant to save other people; it is logical that the same applies to Gentiles. *Igrot Moshe Ĥoshen Mishpat* vol. 2, ch. 36, states that this only applies to one who damages other people's money, but if one borrows to save another person, he is obligated to repay.

It is unclear if the same law applies if the person whose money he is taking or damaging is present. Do we say that the person coming to steal in order to save himself is considered a "pursuer" in the mind of the victim of the theft, who will fight to the death for his money, and then it comes down to the thief saving his life through that of another, which is obviously forbidden?

Rabbi Zalman Nehemiah Goldberg notes:

This does not follow the laws of a pursuer. For a Jew, it would not apply since the second person is obligated to give up his money to save the "thief," who is therefore rightfully taking money. It would seem, then, that the same applies to a Gentile. Although a Gentile is not obligated to give money to save another person, stealing is nevertheless permitted to save a life. Thus, if the victim of the theft thwarts the one who comes to steal to save a life, he would be doing so illegally.

[176] *Shulĥan Aruĥ, ibid.* ch. 4. *Ha'amek Sh'ailah* 2:3 states that only a Jew is "allowed to take the law into his own hands" in this manner, but this does not seem to be correct, since there is no logical reason for differentiation between a Jew and a Gentile in this matter. It appears that a Gentile may also steal back what is his (see Minĥat Ĥinuĥ Commandment 224), and even forcibly, provided that he does not strike the thief if he is Jewish (Part V, topic 6:3).

topic). Rather, he is merely saving his own property.

Therefore, if the thief does not allow the owner to reclaim his stolen item, the owner can strike the thief until he allows the owner to take it back, if the owner has no other recourse. The owner is not required to take the thief to court in order to demand the return of his stolen item, since a person may use any means available (other than serious injury or murder) to him to recover a stolen item that is still intact. Even if this would require no extra effort on his part, he does not need to bring the matter to court, and he is permitted to settle it on his own. However, the owner should *not* go secretly to steal the object back from the thief, unless he has no other recourse, since he will then be acting like a thief. In any case when a person is allowed to recover his own belongings, he is permitted to send another person to recover the object for him.[177]

6. This only applies if the owner can prove his ownership of the item in court. If he cannot prove this, he may not seize his item from the thief, and he may definitely not strike the thief. (In this case, the owner would be liable to punishment by the court if he strikes the thief.) Even after the fact, if the owner seized his unproven belonging, his action will be futile if the thief takes the case to court, because the court will confiscate it from the owner who seized it, and return it to the thief. The owner can only take back and retain his unproven stolen item if he does this secretly, so he could deny that the matter ever happened.[178]

7. It is not permissible for a victim of theft to steal another item of similar value from the thief (even if the original stolen item is not intact or recoverable anymore, in which case the thief would be liable to pay back the value in money or with a similar item, as explained in Chapter 2). This is because it is forbidden to steal a thief's personal items. Instead, a victim should demand compensation in court if he is

---

[177] Rema *Ĥoshen Mishpat* ch. 4. At the outset it is forbidden for Jews to exact judgment through a Gentile individual or court, because of their obligation to seek judgment through an Orthodox Jewish court, if possible. Thus a Gentile may recover his belonging (exact judgment for himself) through others.

[178] *Shulĥan Aruĥ HaRav Laws of Robbery* topic 29. Rabbi Zalman Nehemiah Goldberg comments that it appears it would be permitted for the victim to steal back his own object secretly (even if he cannot prove his ownership).

not able or willing to take back his stolen item on his own.[179]

It is nevertheless permitted for the victim to seize money from the thief, equal to (but not more than) the value of the stolen item, since the thief is obligated to give him restitution in this amount,[180] and in all such cases, the victim may take the law into his own hands.

This does not only apply to a victim of theft, who may steal back his item from the thief. Even one who rents out an item and is not paid the rental fee, or if he was hired for a job and he was not paid, or if he gives a loan and the borrower does not wish to repay[181] (according to the agreed stipulations), then as a victim of nonpayment, he may seize any money owed to him, in the same way as a victim of theft. In all these cases, a person may take the law into his own hands.

8. Although, as explained, in general one is not allowed to take the law into one's own hands, this applies only if the restitution is taken in a way of stealing, such as seizing an item in restitution for an unpaid loan or for a different stolen item. However, it is permitted to seize an item as collateral until the matter is settled in court, and this is not considered theft. This applies whether it is taken as collateral for payment on a purchase, or for a late payment for a service provided, or for the return of a stolen item, or for repayment of a loan.[182]

9. It appears that even if the thief sold the stolen item, if the victim never despaired of recovering it – in which case the law is that it must be returned intact – the original owner can take the law into his own hands and forcibly take his item from the buyer (even though the sale was done without the buyer being aware that the item was stolen).[183]

---

[179] *Shulĥan Aruĥ HaRav Laws of Robbery* topic 27. (It appears that this is not a Torah prohibition, as will be explained in topic 10; once the thief has stolen, all of his possessions are on lien for his debt to the victim of his theft.)

[180] Taking the monetary value of one's stolen item is like taking back the stolen item itself. See *Sho'el U'Maishiv*, ed. 3, vol. 1, ch. 371.

[181] Rema *Ĥoshen Mishpat* ch. 4, in the name of Rivash.

[182] *Shulĥan Aruĥ, ibid.* 97:14. (Although it is forbidden for a Jew to seize collateral for a loan, since there is a Torah prohibition for him to enter the house of the debtor to demand collateral, this is not prohibited for Gentiles.)

[183] This is implied from Rema *Ĥoshen Mishpat* ch. 4, in the name of Rivash: "Or he found it [a deposited item] in the hand of another," and there is no logical difference between seizing a deposit or one's stolen item.

10. If a worker steals fruits from the field he is working in, the owner may deduct the value of the fruits from the worker's salary.

However, if a sharecropper steals from the fruits that he must share with the landowner, it is forbidden for the landowner to deduct from the sharecropper's portion of the fruits, just as it is forbidden to steal from a thief. (The sharecropper took the fruits not as his contracted portion, but as a theft, and as explained above in topic 7, one may not steal something else in compensation for something of his that was stolen.)[184] Nevertheless, this is not considered completely as a theft, and if the owner went and took a comparative amount of fruits from the sharecropper in restitution, he is not judged in court as a thief, and that which he has seized may not be taken from him.[185]

The same law applies to any partnership in which one of the parties stole from the shared merchandise or money.

11. The above is said regarding seizing the belongings or money of a person who stole or who owes a payment. A Gentile may, however, hold on to an item that was entrusted to his care by a person who stole from him or who is overdue on paying on a debt, in order to collect the person's overdue payment (even though there is no surety that it may be legally correct for him to keep the entrusted item[186]), and he does not need to return it until his judgment is handed down in court.[187]

12. Anyone who mistakenly seizes another's item, thinking that it either was his or rightfully should belong to him as a legal judgment, is not judged as a thief, even if the court determines that the item was not rightfully his. Likewise, if one was harmed or injured in a way that would usually bring him a monetary award in court from the damager, then although the victim is forbidden to seize this money, until the court makes a judgment, the victim is not judged as a thief if he seizes the money.[188] But after court determines that the defendant has no monetary obligation to the plaintiff, then the plaintiff is considered a

[184] Tractate *Berahot* 5b; *Shulhan Aruh HaRav Laws of Robbery* topic 27.

[185] Responsa of Rosh, principle 64, part 1 (see above, topic 1:5).

[186] See *Sefer Meirat Einayim Hoshen Mishpat* 4:3, and *Urim V'Tumim* 4:2.

[187] Rema *Hoshen Mishpat* ch. 4.

[188] If the pain inflicted can obligate the perpetrator for restitution, and the victim then seized this money from him, the victim isn't considered as a thief.

thief if he still goes ahead and seizes the money. If the plaintiff has seized money already and the court determines that he is obligated to return it, any hesitation on his part transgresses the prohibition against withholding pay (as mentioned above in topic 1:1).

13. If some type of damage is happening to a person's property (for example, a river is flooding his land), he is *not* allowed to divert it from his property if doing so will cause this damage to occur to another person's property, since it is forbidden save one's own property by causing financial damage to someone else. Before the damage actually occurs, though, it is permissible to prevent it from befalling his property, even if this action will cause damage to another, e.g. if a river is flooding its banks and will soon be overflowing into his field, if it has not yet reached his field, he may build a blockade even if by so doing he causes it to flood a neighbor's field; once it already has begun to damage his field, however, he may not do so, as this is removing damage from oneself onto another.[189]

14. If one is incurring sudden damage, one may not use another's belongings (even if he was borrowing them) without the owner's consent in order to save his own belongings, even if he intends to repay any damage that would occur to the other's belongings. For example, if someone's barrel of honey broke and he has in his house a barrel of wine borrowed from a friend, he may not pour out his friend's wine in order to save the contents of his own barrel. This applies even if his honey is more valuable than his friend's wine, and he intends to reimburse his friend for the cost of the wine. Likewise, one whose bee colony swarmed into his neighbor's property and landed on a branch of his tree, may not cut off this branch in order to return his bees, even if he intends to repay the value of the branch, as one is not permitted to

---

(See *Shulĥan Aruĥ HaRav, ibid.* topic 1.) It is obvious that the victim has no permission to do so at the outset, as no person may take the law into his own hands unless it is clear that he is taking something that already belongs to him. Since restitution for damage can only be assessed by a court, any seizure of restitution before the court renders judgment is prohibited. Nevertheless, since the perpetrator has a monetary obligation to the victim, the victim is not liable for theft if he seizes it.

[189] *Shulĥan Aruĥ HaRav Laws of Monetary Damage* topic 2.

save his own money at the expense of another's without the other person's consent, and doing so is considered theft.[190]

15. If a belonging of another person is causing damage to one's property, and he is not able to save his own property without causing damage to the other's belonging, he is permitted to save his own property, and he need not be held back by the other's damage. Later, the other person may take him to court to recover the damages incurred. Nevertheless, he is obligated to cause as little damage as possible to the other's property while saving his own; and although by the strict letter of the law he is not required to go to this effort, it is nonetheless righteous behavior to cause as little damage to the other's property as possible.[191]

Therefore, if someone else's ox attacks one's own ox with intention to kill it, then if it is possible for him to pull the attacking ox off without harming it, he should do so. If it is impossible to stop the attacking ox in any way other than to strike it or even kill it, it is permissible for him to so, in order to stop it from killing his own ox.[192]

Likewise, if another's birds or beasts are entering his shop or yard and are damaging his property, he should first warn the owner, and if the owner still does not restrain them, it is permissible for him to forcibly remove them, even if this causes them injury. If he must put out too much effort to remove them without causing them injury, then legally he may even strike or kill them in order to protect his belongings.[193] (He may not, however, take them for himself, since the owner has not declared them ownerless.)

---

[190] Rosh (*Bava Kama* 114) and Rambam *(Laws of Robbery* 6:14) disagree as to whether a person can destroy another's cheap items to save his own expensive ones with intention to reimburse the owner for the damage. This hinges on whether this was one of the stipulations made by Joshua when he divided the Land of Israel among the Jews. Otherwise this is considered theft, since it was never permitted for Gentiles. It is arguable whether they can make that enactment on their own. Without that, it is forbidden for Gentiles.

[191] Based *Shulĥan Aruĥ HaRav Laws of Monetary Damage* topic 5.

[192] See *Shulĥan Aruĥ ibid.* ch. 383 and *Shulĥan Aruĥ HaRav ibid.*

[193] *Shulĥan Aruĥ, ibid.* ch. 397, forbids a Jew to kill such animals. because a Jew is obligated to return a lost object to another Jew. A Gentile is not obligated to return a lost object, so he may kill the trespassing animals that are causing a nuisance for him, after ample warning to their owner.

Similarly, if branches of a neighbor's tree have grown over one's own yard, he may cut them off, since he is not obligated to endure damage from another person.[194] (He should give the cut branches to the neighbor if he didn't provide ample warning. If he did warn his neighbor and the alternatives offered were too much effort, he may proceed to cut them off. When he cuts the neighbor's branches that are over his own property, he makes them legally ownerless, and he can acquire them for himself).

16. It was explained above (topic 1) that it is permissible to save one's own life at the cost of another's money or property, although one should do so with the intent to pay it back when possible (or with the conditional intent that he will pay it back if the court determines that he is obligated to do so). Therefore, if someone is forcing or coercing a person to show him the money or property of another (third) person, or even forcing him to steal another's money, then if the force is life-threatening, this action is permitted. But if it is not life-threatening, the coercion does not make it permitted to steal the other's money, or even to show where the money is hidden so the thief may steal it or force it out of the possession of the owner.

However, if money or an item is deposited with someone to safeguard, and a robber comes to force it from him, he may hand it over to the robber. In this case, he need not suffer harm or unreasonable distress in order to save the depositor's money, since it can be presumed that this is the condition upon which he agreed to safeguard the deposit.

17. Suppose one is asked by another to rent out an area to store produce, and he did not agree, and the owner of the produce then tricked him into storing it by giving a promise that he did not fulfill.

---

[194] If one's neighbor lit a fire outside, he can take the law into his own hands to prevent the fire from coming onto his own property. The Torah Law says that the fire occurred in the neighbor's field by no fault or desire of his own, so the would-be victim may save his own property even at the expense of the neighbor's property, since it is as if the neighbor's property itself is causing the damage. The case would be comparable to a neighbor's ox fighting with his own ox, without the neighbor's knowledge. Then he may remove the neighbor's ox, and even if he causes injury to it by doing this, he is exempt from paying for the damage. See *Shulĥan Aruĥ Ĥoshen Mishpat* ch. 383.

When the produce-owner has acted deceitfully, the owner of the storage space can act likewise; he may hire workers to throw the produce out into an ownerless area, and then pay them from it.

It is then an act of righteousness to inform the produce-owner about the action he has taken, so that the produce-owner can go and gather up the remaining produce that was tossed into the ownerless area.[195]

18. If the owner of the produce did not act deceitfully, but rather moved his produce into the other's storage without the knowledge of the storage owner, then if the storage was intended for rent (for similar items), the storage-owner has no right to throw the produce into the street or another ownerless area until he notifies the produce-owner. If the area was not intended for storage, it is permitted to first throw it out and then notify the produce-owner afterwards. But if he hires workers to do this, it is not permitted to pay them from the produce.[196]

19. If a person filled up another's yard with his barrels of wine or oil or the like, without the consent of the yard's owner, the yard-owner may enter and exit his yard, and need not take care to not damage the barrels. But he is not permitted to damage them intentionally. Rather, he may remove them into the street[196] (for although the owner of the barrels transgressed a prohibition by putting them in his property, this does not allow the yard-owner to steal or damage in return).

20. There is no obligation to return an envelope sent with a return stamp if the recipient has no intention of replying. Rather he may throw it away, or use it for his own needs. Likewise, if one receives a catalog in the mail, there is no obligation to accept it, return it, or safeguard it. Since those who send such articles in the mail have essentially declared these items to be ownerless, and the sender never requests payment for them, the recipient may take them for free if he so wishes. He is not considered as having benefit from stolen property, and he is not responsible at all for the item being sent, so he does not have to safeguard or return the item.

---

[195] The warehouse owner must let the produce owner know that he will throw it out if it is not removed, due to the obligation of returning a lost object. Since this does not apply to Gentiles, the author wrote that it is a righteous trait, and not an obligation, to inform the owner of the produce about this.

[196] *Shulĥan Aruĥ HaRav Laws of Borrowing* topic 9.

CHAPTER 5

Theft Incurred by False Measurements, and the Prohibition of Cheating or Misinforming Another Person

1. A seller who knowingly or negligently weighs merchandise for a buyer with scales that are faulty, according to the fixed measures of the government (whether in dry or liquid measures), or according to that which is agreed upon between the two parties, or in a measurement of land, is a thief.[197] Even if the difference is less than the value of a *perutah*, the perpetrator is still a thief.[198] He is obligated to return the amount or value of the purchase that was stolen from the buyer.[199]

Even if it was done mistakenly by the seller, he must return the amount overpaid (as explained later, in topic 12 below).

2. The seller needs to correct his scales and weights in order that they are exact and working properly, for otherwise the seller would be a thief. Likewise, one needs to make sure that one's instruments for

---

[197] Rambam, *Laws of Theft* 7:1,9; *Shulĥan Aruĥ HaRav, Laws of Measures and Weights* topics 1,2. See *Minĥat Ĥinuĥ* Commandment 258, which states that it is clear that Gentiles are included in this prohibition as well as Jews, and are liable for transgressing it.

*If one sells *pre-packaged* merchandise by weight or volume, he should show the *net* weight or volume, which excludes the tare weight or empty volume of the packaging. It is understood that the cost of the packaging is included in the profit he makes on his sales.

[198] Rambam, *Laws of Theft* 8:7; *Shulĥan Aruĥ Ĥoshen Mishpat* 231:6; *Sefer HaĤinuĥ* Commandment 258, *Shulĥan Aruĥ HaRav ibid.*

*This applies to cases of an avoidable difference in the measured value, due to the person's deceit or negligence. However, no measurement can be truly exact, because every measuring instrument has an inherent limit of the smallest fraction of a measurement unit that can be resolved on its measurement scale. When a buyer agrees that a certain measuring instrument will be used, he implicitly agrees that he accepts the inherent limit of its accuracy. The fractional deviation of an honest measurement from the true value will vary *randomly* over multiple measurements – sometimes larger and sometimes smaller – and each party in the sale implicitly agrees to accept either the small loss or benefit that will randomly come from the measurement device that they have agreed to use.

[199] Rambam, *Laws of Theft* 7:8; *Shulĥan Aruĥ HaRav ibid.*, topic 2.

measuring land are exact.[200]

Therefore, it is forbidden for a seller to knowingly or negligently cause an instrument for measuring weight (as a basis for a sale price) not to measure correctly (e.g., storing a weight in salt), in order to steal from the buyer. Likewise, one who measures liquid in a vessel should not pour quickly, since that will cause it to appear fuller from the froth, which is stealing from the buyer. The same applies for other types of instruments or vessels used for measuring commodities for sale.[201]

A seller must wipe down his weights and scales so nothing is stuck to them, which would cause the measured weight to be too high. Before weighing an item for sale, or between a few measurements, the seller must verify that his scale measures zero when nothing is on it. (One who is scrupulous will correct for the weight of the bag or box.)

3. The sin of stealing from another person through false measurements is more severe than other types of theft, since one who does so is like a judge who judges perversely, as it says,[202] "You shall not do wrong in justice, in measurement, in weight, or in volume." The Sages[203] derived from this verse that one who steals by using false measurements is like a judge who gives a perverse judgment. Therefore, a Gentile who commits this sin transgresses both the prohibition of theft and the Noahide commandment to have a correct justice system.

Not only is the seller who uses the false weights a thief. Even one who has no personal monetary gain from the incorrect measurement, and who gives a benefit for another party, is considered a transgressor[204] (such as a thief who steals just for the sake of theft), and one who corrupts justice.

It is clear from Rambam and *Shulĥan Aruĥ* that he must return even a small amount overcharged in this way, although in regard to the Torah's laws of theft, less than a *perutah* is not considered money. This is because in buying and selling, the Torah is extremely exacting about measuring equipment, and one must return even a small amount obtained by this means of transgression.

200 Rambam, *Laws of Theft* 8:1. *Rokeaĥ* ch. 366 writes that Gentiles are obligated to keep correct measurements.

201 Rambam *Laws of Theft* 8:7.

202 Leviticus 19:35.

203 *Torat Kohanim* on Leviticus 19:35.

204 Rabbi Zalman Nehemiah Goldberg comments:

4. Every government is obligated to establish laws for all residents in their country in regard to keeping their weights and measuring instruments exact for sales, whether regarding merchandise or land, and these laws must also require that all the residents of the country should be exacting and careful about the weights and measures set up and agreed upon by the nation's citizens. One who changes from these standards of measurement to the detriment of the buyer or the seller is considered a thief.

The government also needs to set up a system of police and inspectors to enforce these laws, in order that there be no opening for those who sell merchandise to steal by using faulty measures. These inspectors should frequently check the measuring instruments and the measuring methods, and punish and fine those who violate the laws.[205]

5. Even if a merchant does not use a faulty measuring instrument that he owns, it is fitting that he not keep one on his property. Rather, he should destroy it, or change it in a way that it will not be able to be used for measuring merchandise that is sold. If not, he may come to mistakenly use it, or another may find it and use it, leading to a transgression of the prohibition of theft.[206]

Likewise, a person should not hold on to a contract of obligation that has been paid, unless he writes clearly on the document that it was paid. If not, it may lead him to inadvertently or deceitfully demand the debt from the debtor a second time.[207]

See the wording of Rambam, *Laws of Theft* 8:3, and Tractate *Bava Metzia* 61b and Rashi's explanation there: "One should not use the same rope for measuring land in the summer that he used in the winter. During the winter it is wet, so the rope will stretch, and during the summer, it will be dry and tight." It appears that the one who is measuring is committing a sin, even if he himself will not be getting any unfair benefit from the false measurement.

[205] Rambam, *Laws of Theft* 8:20.

[206] See *Minĥat Ĥinuĥ* Commandment 602, which says there is no prohibition for a Gentile to possess weights or other measuring instruments that are false.

Nevertheless, it is logical that one should distance himself from this, as it can lead one to transgress.

[207] See *Shulĥan Aruĥ HaRav, Laws of Testimony* topic 53, based on Tractate *Ketubot* 19a, that quotes the verse, "Do not allow transgression to dwell in your tent."

6. It is forbidden for a seller to "cheat" a buyer (*defined as a legal term in topic 10 below*), whether in pricing (beyond a maximum percent of the worth of an item, such as telling a buyer that the item is worth $2 when it is only worth $1), or in the amount being sold (e.g., if a seller *tells* a buyer that he is selling him a kilogram of merchandise, and in actuality he sells him less), or regarding the measurement of land (e.g., if a seller says that the land being sold is a hectare in area, and it is actually less). One who "cheats" another in these ways is a thief, and this is prohibited as part of the Noahide prohibition of theft.[208]

This applies as well to other types of business, such as a renter or contractor (when a contractor receives payment based on the work he does), or exchanging currency or the like. In any case in which there is unjust financial gain for either party, and either party misleads the other, this falls under the prohibition of cheating.[209] It is likewise prohibited for the seller of a house or other property to claim a false value that is not in accordance with the real market value. (When multiple potential buyers are actively bidding against each other, if those who are still in the bidding desire to bid above the market value

---

[208] Cheating is part of the prohibition of theft; see *Tur Ĥoshen Mishpat* ch. 227, and commentaries there. It is therefore forbidden to Gentiles. *Minĥat Ĥinuĥ*, Commandment 337, states that Gentiles are liable for a capital sin by cheating in transactions of monetary value, since it is part of the Noahide prohibition of theft (according to Rambam), or it violates the Noahide obligation to set up a system of justice (according to Ramban). (This is subject to the understanding of the measurement principles explained in the editor's notes to topic 5:1.)

There are three parts to cheating, which have varying relevance to Gentiles. (1) The seller knows that his item is overpriced, and yet he deceives the buyer – this is forbidden to Gentiles. (2) Both the seller and buyer are negligently mistaken about the value of the item – here too, this is considered theft and is forbidden to Gentiles. (3) The buyer *mistakenly* overvalues the item and *offers* a too-high price to the seller, who knows better but is then quiet and accepts (or vice versa, if the seller *mistakenly* undervalues the item and *sets* a too-low price, and the buyer knowingly accepts) – here, in the Torah Law for Jews there is an obligation between one Jew and another Jew of returning a lost object, but this does not apply within Torah Law for transactions between Gentiles, or between a Jew and a Gentile.

[209] Rambam, *Laws of Selling* 13:17; *Shulĥan Aruĥ Ĥoshen Mishpat* 227:35, and *Shulĥan Aruĥ HaRav, Laws of Cheating* topic 9.

in order to obtain the property, or any item at auction, this is permitted.)[210]

7. It is forbidden for the merchant to cheat the buyer, and in doing so he would be deemed a thief; it is likewise forbidden for the buyer to mislead the seller to give him a wrong price estimate on the product he is buying.[211] Likewise, partners who divide their property may not cheat each other in taking more than that which is due to them.[212]

8. Since cheating in business transactions is theft, one who does cheat another must return the object received unfairly, or compensate the difference in price, or invalidate the sale. The court system in every country is obligated to judge with laws against cheating[213] and establish laws for return of unjust gain. This includes laws that define if and when cheating invalidates a sale, and what percentage of a sale price above or below the true worth of an item is the level of cheating (*by its legal definition*) that invalidates a sale, and the minimum amount of cheating that necessitates returning the extra money that was gained by cheating.

9. *The Noahide prohibition of "cheating" only applies to deception in doing business*. But if the buyer knows the correct worth of an object

---

[210] Although there is an argument among the Sages as to whether the prohibition of cheating exists in regards to real estate property, *Minĥat Ĥinuĥ* Commandment 337 says that for Gentiles, since this prohibition is part of the prohibition of theft, they are surely liable for cheating in the sale of land. (See footnote 1 above, which explains that this is not subject to capital punishment. Nevertheless, it is possible that only if one cheats in the measurement itself is he not liable to capital punishment. But if the cheating is in the valuation of the property, it is possible that a Gentile would be liable just as in any other money transaction.)

*But if someone bids up the price when he has no intention of buying, this is the general type of deception that is forbidden for Gentiles, since it is dishonest and a form of lying. See topics 24 and 27 below.

[211] Rambam, *Laws of Selling* 12:1; *Shulĥan Aruĥ Ĥoshen Mishpat* ch. 227; *Shulĥan Aruĥ HaRav, Laws of Cheating* topic 1.

[212] Rambam, *Laws of Selling* 13:12; *Shulĥan Aruĥ Ĥoshen Mishpat* ch. 227.

[213] Ramban on Genesis 34:13.

for sale, yet he is in a pressing situation and needs it urgently, and the merchant takes advantage of this situation to sell him the merchandise at an inflated price, this is not considered deception, and is not forbidden for Gentiles. Likewise, if the seller knows the value of his item but he desires to sell it for less (e.g., if otherwise he will have no buyers), the buyer may take advantage of this situation to get a lower price. This is not considered deception, and it is permitted for a Gentile.[214]

10. There was uncertainty among the Sages as to whether "cheating" *in buying and selling* is completely like theft, in which case it is therefore forbidden in even the smallest amount, or whether it is only forbidden – and thus considered as theft and deception – when it is at or above a certain minimum percent for an item that has a <u>*set value*</u> (see topic 14 below). Because of this doubt, the Sages established a definite boundary for cheating that is forbidden and must be repaid.

The Sages established that the cheating that the Torah forbids in buying and selling is set at a sixth or more of a total *set value* of the sold object,[215] such as selling an object whose set value is $6 for $7,

---

[214] See *Ketzot HaĤoshen* 227:1, which states that one who exploits another's dire straits to sell him an item for more than (one-sixth) its value has committed the transgression of cheating.

It appears that he says so only regarding Jews, and not for Gentiles. The difference is that a Jew's prohibition of cheating includes two types: (1) the prohibition to cheat another by extorting money through deception, and (2) the prohibition to cheat another by establishing a wrong price, even if the other party agrees to it, but is doing so because he is in dire straits and is forced into buying. The first Jewish prohibition is logically a type of theft, since the other person is being deceived, so it is forbidden for Gentiles as well. On the other hand, the second Jewish prohibition does not include any deceit, and therefore it is not forbidden to Gentiles.

[215] **Any* difference in price from the *set value* that is called a "sixth" in the common terminology of the local people is definitely cheating, since people are generally not willing to forego the loss when they are overcharged by more than their understanding of a "sixth." But most people are willing to tolerate an overcharge that is less than a "sixth" *in their eyes*.

A *set value* (or set price) is usually one that is set by the government or local authorities. Regarding items that *do not* have a set value, *which applies in most cases for free economies*, see topic 14 below.

since it is the way of the world to tolerate up to one-sixth extra as the cost of dealing with merchandise, and not as theft.[216]

This only applies regarding an overcharge beyond the set value of the merchandise. But any mistake in the measure, weight, quality, or amount of an object is considered theft, and the perpetrator must return the money received from such theft even for the smallest amount, since people are fastidious in this matter.

Likewise, the way of the world is to be fastidious regarding the amount of money received for a sale, and the buyer would be bothered by even the smallest discrepancy from the amount he required to pay, such as 99¢ instead of $1.00, and this is considered theft.[217]

11. Likewise, in a place where certain staples are sold at a set price in every market (such as bread and milk), if one sold it for even the smallest amount over the set market price, this is considered theft, since these items are not being sold in the manner of regular merchandise, and the people will be fastidious about even the smallest change of price for these staples, and are not tolerant of any extra charge.[218]

Exchange of different countries' currencies is commonly done with an additional charge for the exchange. If the principal bank of the country sets the comparative values of currencies, this is considered as having a set price in the market, and anyone who deviates from this rate, even to the smallest degree, transgresses the prohibition of theft, and is a thief. However, regarding the *fee* one takes for the exchange, which may require more effort for some currencies than for others, this depends on the discussion in topic 10. In a place where there are numerous moneychangers, and their currency exchange fees are considered like buying and selling, then the overcharge above market value that is forbidden is 1/6. But if there is only a set fee, then charging anything over that set fee is considered as theft by deception, with no minimum permissible limit.

---

216 Rosh *Bava Metzia* ch. 4; *Shulĥan Aruĥ Ĥoshen Mishpat* ch. 227. *Minĥat Ĥinuĥ* Commandment 337 writes that these two possibilities exist for Gentiles as well.

217 *Shulĥan Aruĥ Ĥoshen Mishpat* ch. 232.

218 *Aruĥ HaShulĥan Ĥoshen Mishpat* 227:2,7; *Maĥaneh Efraim Laws of Cheating* topic 7.

12. The prohibition of cheating is dependent on the deception of the second party. Therefore, the perpetrator should not say to himself, "maybe elsewhere (in a place where prices are generally higher) this item is really worth the amount I am charging, and therefore I am justified in charging more," since an item's worth is only decided according to the time and place of the sale. One who overcharges (by 1/6 or more) by setting his price based on irrelevant calculations is cheating, and he deceives the buyers.[219] Whether the seller overpriced the item and cheated the buyer (even if by mistake), or the buyer underpriced the item and cheated the seller (even if by mistake), the party that made the unjust gain must compensate the other for the unjust loss.[220]

However, if the first party *who received the loss* did so *due to his own error*, and the second party gained due to this error, the second party is not considered as having cheated the first party. For example, if the seller knew that an item was only worth one dollar, and the buyer *offered* him two dollars thinking that this was the correct amount for such an item, the seller need not point out the buyer's mistake, and it is permissible for him to accept the price set by the buyer. A Gentile is not required to point out that the other party made a mistake *in setting* the item's sale price, and he is not required to pay compensation for this after the sale.[221] (This is the letter of the law, which means that he has not committed theft. But obviously this involves some dishonesty. To avoid this, the government may establish rules for vendors, such as clearly writing or affixing the correct current price on each item. See topic 8 above.)

13. However, an error in the amount of the money handed over in a sale (for example, if the price is $100 and the buyer by mistake handed

---

[219] *Shulĥan Aruĥ HaRav, Laws of Cheating* topic 1.

[220] Even if one cheats another by mistake, he must return the money, as explained in *Shulĥan Aruĥ HaRav, Laws of Cheating* topic 2, based on Rambam, *Laws of Selling* ch. 12.

[221] See Rambam, *Laws of Robbery* 11:4; *Rema Ĥoshen Mishpat* 348:2; *Shulĥan Aruĥ HaRav, Laws of Robbery* topic 4, *Laws of Cheating* topic 11, and *Laws of Weights and Measures* topic 2. Since Gentiles are not obligated to return a lost object, and here the mistaken party is giving money out of his own free will, the receiver has no obligation to return it.

over more than $100, or if the seller by mistake gave extra change), this is not considered a permitted error (allowing the one who benefits to keep the extra amount without the other's knowledge). Rather, it is a mistaken theft. *Therefore, the extra amount received by mistake must be given back.*

Similarly, a mistake in adding the prices of the items being sold is considered mistaken theft,[222] and even the smallest mistake must be returned. This applies, for example, if the buyer included two objects of different price in a single sale, and the seller by mistake sold them together for twice the individual price of the more expensive item; or if the seller counted incorrectly and charged more for a number of same-priced items than the correct multiple of the item's individual worth (such as counting 9 apples as 10 by mistake, at $1 each, for a total charge of $10).

Even if the one who received the loss from the miscalculation was the one who made the error, and he inadvertently benefited the other party, there is an obligation to return the mistaken amount when it is discovered. This case is not considered like one who makes a mistake in *setting the value* of the merchandise that benefits the other party, which (as explained in the previous topic) is permitted to be kept by the other party who benefited. (In that case, the one losing out consented on his own to the agreed price for the item, and his mistake in setting the item's value is not like a mistake in calculating the total

---

Rabbi Zalman Nehemiah Goldberg comments that this matter is not so clear, since it says in Tractate *Bava Metzia* 26 that one who sees another person drop a coin, and takes it before the person despairs of recovering it, transgresses the prohibition of theft. In the present discussion, it may therefore be forbidden for a Gentile to take this money from the mistaken giver, even though he has no obligation to return a lost object.

The author responds that this case is actually more lenient than that of another person's dropped coin, since in that case the second person is causing the completion of the loss, whereas in our case, the buyer is completely at fault for offering more money than the item's true value. This may be better compared to one who takes the dropped coin after the owner despairs. Also, the case in Tractate *Bava Metzia* possibly may not be referring to a Gentile, and as will be explained in Chapter 15, a Gentile has no obligation to return a lost object.

[222] *Shulĥan Aruĥ HaRav, Laws of Robbery* topic 4, and *Laws of Cheating* topic 11.

amount of money to be transferred.) In this case, however, since one party did not agree that the amount of funds being transferred was calculated correctly, then even if he himself took the loss, nevertheless his mind was not in agreement with the act, and therefore the one who benefited from the mistake is considered as having committed a mistaken theft.

14. *For items that have* no set value*, and the buyers in the area can choose to do business with many different merchants (including telephone, mail order, and Internet sales), each charging more or less than the average price, there is no cheating involved in selling or buying at these different prices.* However, if an item has a set value (like currency), one who wishes to sell it for more than its worth may do so, on the condition that he tells the buyer its true worth, and that he only agrees (for whatever reason) to sell it for more. If the buyer still agrees to the sale, there is no prohibition involved.[223]

Likewise, if the buyer is not prepared to pay the price that the seller is asking (even if this is the set market value of the merchandise), and he only agrees to buy at a lower price, this is not considered to be theft or cheating (as would be the case if he deceived the seller about the item's value).[224]

---

[223] Rambam, *Laws of Selling* 13:4; *Shulĥan Aruĥ Ĥoshen Mishpat* 227:21; *Shulĥan Aruĥ HaRav, Laws of Cheating* topics 3, 4.

[224] Rabbi Zalman Nehemiah Goldberg comments:

See *Ketzot HaĤoshen* 227:5, that even if the buyer knows that an item he is buying is overpriced beyond 1/6 of its set value, it is still considered cheating, and this is only permitted *if the seller knows that the buyer knows* that the item being sold is priced more than 1/6 above its set value, because then the buyer is agreeing to the overcharged price *and* agreeing that he will not have a grievance against the seller for having cheated against him.

The author responds:

It appears that this does not apply to Gentiles, as explained in footnote 208. Therefore, in this case, since the buyer actually knows and agrees to the overcharged price, there is no transgression of cheating, regardless of whether or not the seller intends to cheat him. The law explained in *Shulĥan Aruĥ Ĥoshen Mishpat* ch. 227 does not apply to Gentiles – that in transactions between Jews, if the buyer being cheated knows that the price is inflated, and as he buys the item, he is planning to demand restitution for the cheating, he can rightfully demand it from the seller in a Jewish court.

Some specialty items are only sold occasionally in the marketplace, as special transactions, and their true present set value is not known to the general public (although there *is* a true present set value that can be determined by those who are experts about this type of item). Then even if it is usual for this specialty item to be sold in that place, if the merchant is overcharging a buyer by more than 1/6 of the set value, he must let him know of the deviation from the true present value. If he does not, he is considered to be stealing from the buyer by cheating.

The same applies for a stranger who is not familiar with the ways of the local merchants, but he wishes to do business with them. If an item has a true present set value, the merchant must either inform the buyer about this, or about how the market operates. If the merchant fails to do so, and he deceitfully overcharges this buyer by more than 1/6 of the item's set value, this is considered cheating.

15. The laws of deception and cheating also apply to very expensive items, such as diamonds and precious gems, and it cannot be said that surely they have no true set value, or that since those involved in their trade are experts who recognize their worth, it is sure that the buyer is willingly paying the price set for the merchandise. Rather, since there is a set value known to experts, anyone who deceives another in buying or selling by more than 1/6 of the value of such items transgresses the prohibition of cheating.[225]

For expensive items that have no regular market value and are sold to masters of a certain trade, or collector's items such as artwork, there is no cheating involved in setting a price. However, *if one of the parties* does not recognize the true quality of the item being sold, and thinks that it is a cheaper valued item, this is considered deception and is forbidden.[226]

Likewise, for a one-time sale with an announcement or mutual understanding that the item has no set value or price (such as an auction sale), there is no issue of deception.[227]

---

[225] See *Shulĥan Aruĥ Ĥoshen Mishpat* 227:15 regarding a Torah scroll and precious gems.

[226] See *Aruĥ HaShulĥan* 227:7.

[227] See responsa of Rosh, Principle 13, brought in *Maĥaneh Efraim Laws of Robbery* topic 24.

16. One who sells merchandise that is defective and does not inform the buyer is considered as having stolen from him.[228] Conversely, it is forbidden to buy with forged checks or counterfeit money. It is also forbidden to exchange these false items for real money, because this is stealing from the other party. Afterwards, he may unknowingly do business with the false money or checks, and others will be cheated.[229]

Likewise, one who pays with a check, while knowing that he will not have enough money in his bank account to cover the amount, has committed theft and deception.

17. Any deception by misrepresentation in business is forbidden, such as externally enhancing the appearance of an animal or vessel so it looks nicer than it actually is (for example to color used vessels so they appear new, or to feed an animal liquefied bran so that it will appear fatter), since in doing so he deceives the buyer to believe that the item is new or improved in value.

It is, however, permitted to color new vessels so that they appear nicer, and included in this permission is the practice of giving a discount on another item if one buys the first one. This is even permitted if in doing so he raises the price, since the buyer accepts the higher price of the new item because of this nicer appearance or the extra item included.[230]

18. It is forbidden for a meat vender to soak raw meat in water in order that it should appear fresher or fatter.

Needless to say, it is forbidden for a meat vender to soak the meat in water before freezing it, so the customer will be paying extra for the weight of the ice in the meat. This is pure deception, unless this is the known practice of all butchers in the area.[231]

19. It is forbidden to mix old merchandise with new merchandise, such as fresh produce with old produce, so that the buyer will think that he

---

[228] *Rambam, Laws of Selling* 18:1; *Shulĥan Aruĥ Ĥoshen Mishpat* ch. 228, *Shulĥan Aruĥ HaRav, Laws of Cheating* topic 11.

[229] *Shulĥan Aruĥ HaRav, Laws of Cheating* topic 10.

[230] Rambam, *Laws of Selling* 18:2; *Shulĥan Aruĥ ibid.*; *Shulĥan Aruĥ HaRav, Laws of Cheating* topic 18.

[231] *Shulĥan Aruĥ HaRav, Laws of Cheating* topic 19.

is receiving only fresh produce.

However, if the merchant receives stock produce from a number of providers and then mixes it all together, and this practice is known to all, he does not need to notify his customers. But if he mixes in a significant amount of the lower-grade produce and sells the lot as if it were higher-grade produce, that is considered theft and deception.[232]

20. It is forbidden to sell land or merchandise to another person if it has a lien against it, unless the seller provides this information to the buyer. It is also the responsibility of the buyer to investigate this. Nevertheless, it is clear that under normal circumstances, a buyer would not want to give money for something that would later have to be disputed in court with others, and therefore the seller must provide this information.[233]

21. Some food merchants set out a tray of sample food for their customers, or potential customers, who come by or into their shops. If someone goes to the shop and eats from those samples when he already knows he is not going to buy anything there, he is considered a deceiver and thief, since the business owner does not consent to this.[234]

22. If the buyer and the seller agree on a certain deal, although it is permissible by law for either to back out before the legal sale is made, such an action is not done in good faith, and one who does so is a liar and sinful.[235]

Regarding one who begins the sale, such as one who gives over part of the merchandise and then decides to invalidate the sale (and causes grief or a loss to the other party), the Sages said, "The One who

---

[232] *Shulĥan Aruĥ HaRav, Laws of Cheating* topic 20, 21.

[233] *Ibid.*, topic 17.

[234] Ben Ish Ĥai, *Parshat Teitzei* law 9. See Tractate *Shabbat* p. 129, and *Shulĥan Aruĥ HaRav Oraĥ Ĥayim* 156:20, that if someone is starving and he only has a few coins, which are not enough to make a food purchase, he may eat one of the samples and offer the merchant a coin in return, and he can repeat this at other merchants until he feels his life returning – but this is only allowed because it is a life-threatening matter.

[235] See Rashi on *Bava Metzia* 49a, that one who does not deal honestly transgresses a Scriptural injunction.

exacted punishment from the Generation of the Flood will exact punishment from one who does not stand by his word."[236] (However, if the other party also agrees to terminate the sale, there is no ill will involved, and certainly no punishment is due).

This only applies if there is no defect in the merchandise. If, however, the buyer found a defect (or that the seller tricked him significantly), it is permissible for him to back out of the sale, and he is not considered untrustworthy.[237]

If the value of the merchandise being sold increased, or either party sees that there will be a loss because of the sale, there are Torah authorities who say that there is no need to incur a loss, and it is permissible to back out of the sale. Others are of the opinion that this is still called untrustworthy.[238]

If unforeseeable and unpreventable circumstances occurred, such as the merchandise became extremely hard to procure, or the buyer could not obtain the money for the sale or he lost the money, it is permissible to cancel the sale and this is not considered untrustworthy, even if doing so will cause the other party a loss.[239]

23. If one makes a promise to another person in monetary matters, or promises to give another person a gift, it is forbidden to back out, since

---

[236] See Rambam, *Laws of Selling* 7:1. Although he writes there, "He has done an action unworthy of a Jew," his intention is that the court curses the person who acts in that manner. However, it is clear that one who backs out from a business deal even before the money changes hands (even if he is not cursed by the court) has not dealt honestly, and this is sinful. This all applies to Gentiles as well; see *Kol Bo'ai Ha'Olam*, p. 95.

[237] See Shaĥ *Ĥoshen Mishpat* 204:2, whether one can back out of a sales transaction if the item is overpriced by a sixth of its actual value. (The Torah Sages ruled that if an item is more overpriced than this, it is considered a valid justification for canceling a sales transaction). If a blemish or defect is found in the item that actually lowers its value or desirability, it is clear that the buyer is permitted to back out from the sale, since it is an erroneous transaction.

The amount of cheating that would necessitate an invalidation of a sale seems to depend on the law set by the Gentiles for themselves in any particular country (see topic 8).

[238] See *Shulĥan Aruĥ Ĥoshen Mishpat* 204:2,12.

[239] See *Shulĥan Aruĥ Ĥoshen Mishpat* 204:2.

this is breaking a trust.[240] (It appears that if the other party harmed him after the promise was made, it is permissible to go back on his word.)

This only applies if the promised action is something that is feasible to be done by the one who made the promise. But if he exaggerates to the point that the other party does not believe him, there is no obligation for him to complete what he promised.

We learn the prohibition of using unjust measurements from these verses:[241] "You shall not do wrong in justice, in measurement, in weight, or in volume. You shall have correct scales, correct weights, a correct *ephah* [a unit of dry measure], and a correct *hin* [a unit of liquid measure] – I am the Lord your God." The Sages expounded from this:[242] "a correct *hin*" can be read as "a correct *hein*" [a correct "yes"], meaning that your "yes" should truly be a "yes," and your "no" should truly be a "no." This means that a person should keep his word and be trustworthy.[243]

24. Just as it is forbidden to deceive someone in business in accordance with the laws of theft, it is also forbidden to deceive another person even when no financial loss is involved (for example, selling meat of an animal that died of disease, but presenting it as if the animal had been slaughtered for food).

Likewise, when someone presents himself as if he is doing a favor for another person, but he truly is not, this is a forbidden deception.[244]

25. It is forbidden to cheat on a test (or buy the correct answers) in order to receive a reward or good grades in school, since this is deception and fraud. Even if this does not affect one's grade, the deception alone is forbidden.[245]

26. A valid copyright is a true right, and it is forbidden to steal it, or to copy the item that is copyrighted without the copyright-owner's

---

[240] See *Shulĥan Aruĥ Ĥoshen Mishpat* 204:8.

[241] Leviticus 19:35-36.

[242] Tractate *Bava Metzia* 49a.

[243] Rashi on Tractate *Bava Metzia ibid.*

[244] *Shulĥan Aruĥ HaRav, Laws of Cheating* topic 12. Responsa of *Hitorerut Teshuva Ĥoshen Mishpat* ch. 18 says this prohibition also applies to Gentiles.

[245] *Igrot Moshe Ĥoshen Mishpat* vol. 2, ch. 30.

permission, subject to the legal limitations on copyrights that the courts of the land have established.

27. Part of the prohibition of deceiving is also the prohibition of lying, and although this is not part of the prohibitions that were commanded to Gentiles, it is logical that one should be forbidden to do so (unless it is necessary for saving a person's property or well-being, or to avoid embarrassment or insult to another person). This can be seen from what Jacob told Laban,[246] "Why have you deceived me?"[247]

---

[246] Genesis 29:25. See *Likkutei Siĥot* vol. 5, p. 141-148.

[247] *When Jacob asserted this complaint to Laban, Laban took pains to make an excuse and justify himself, thus showing that he agreed that his deception of Jacob was considered a sin. Likewise, when Jacob complained against Laban (Genesis 31:41) that the terms of his wages in sheep were changed 100 times (as explained in Midrash *Bereishit Rabbah* 74:3), Laban tried to justify this by saying that he was the owner of all of Jacob's flocks, and everything else that Jacob possessed.

CHAPTER 6

The Prohibitions of Extortion and Forcing a Purchase

1. It is forbidden to forcefully take the possessions or money of another person, because of the prohibition of robbery. Any type of extortion of money is considered robbery, and is forbidden to Gentiles as part of the Noahide prohibition of theft.[248]

How is the transgression of *extortion* defined? This happens when someone forces another person to accept an object for exchange, even in exchange for money, and even if more than its value is given,[249] whether it is real estate[250] or a moveable object.[251] How much more so does this apply if one forcefully takes something, but he lays out the full money payment before the victim. This is considered extortion and robbery, and it is forbidden just the same as outright theft.

It is also extortion if one compels another person to buy a certain item from him, and he takes the person's money by force as payment. Even if he leaves the item (whose value is not less than the amount of money that he has taken) in front of the victim, this is considered extortion and robbery.[252] (And he transgresses just like someone who actually took money by robbery and left a security in exchange for his debt, for this is considered to be robbery, and not a loan).

Any type of compulsion to buy or sell against the will of the other party is considered forcing, regardless of whether it is done by physical strength or by any form of threat – for example, one who says that if

---

[248] *Shulĥan Aruĥ HaRav, Laws of Robbery* topic 23: Gentiles are forbidden to practice extortion, as are Jews. This is also written in *Rokeaĥ* ch. 366. A proof for this can be brought from Jonah 3:8 – "and from the extortion in their hands," as explained in footnote 9.

[249] *Yam Shel Shlomo Bava Kama* 6:26.

[250] See *Shiltai Giborim Sukkah*, beginning of ch. 3 in the name of Riaz.

[251] Rambam, *Laws of Selling* ch. 10, *Shulĥan Aruĥ Ĥoshen Mishpat* ch. 205.

[252] See Rema *Ĥoshen Mishpat* ch. 205, that this is considered completely theft, and a Gentile who does this would be liable for a capital sin. There is an argument among the Torah-law authorities if there is a prohibition of theft involved when the victim of the extortion agrees to the sale being forced on him, or if this only involves the prohibition of extortion itself. But if the victim doesn't agree, all opinions hold that this is considered complete theft.

the other will not sell to him, he will inform on him or he will turn him over to the mafia or the government, or he will steal the item.[253]

2. But if the one who compels another to sell threatens him (by saying that if he does not, he will cause him to suffer, or kill him, or harm him another way), and because of this threat, the person *willingly agrees* to sell to him, this is not defined as extortion, but rather as a *forced sale*.

What is the difference in definition and Torah Law between extortion and a forced sale? Extortion (a form of robbery) is committed when the robber takes an object by force and leaves money, and the victim *never intended or agreed to sell – so there is no sale*. But in a forced sale, the one who gives in accepts the payment and agrees to the sale, *post facto*, because he avoided harm and received full payment.[254]

Whether or not the victim of a forced sale explicitly said "I agree," since he took the money into his hand with acceptance, this is considered *post facto* to be his agreement to the sale. Therefore, the transaction cannot be cancelled, because he *consented* to the sale.

This only applies if the seller did not issue a protest before he made the sale, by telling two witnesses: "Know that the reason I am selling this item (or property) is that I am being compelled against my will." But if the seller *did* make such a statement before witnesses (that such and such a person is forcing him to sell him the item, and he sells it to him only because he is forced, but in truth he does not desire to sell), and if witnesses are aware of the force, this nullifies the transaction. Then the item or property should be returned to the victim, and the money paid should be returned to the one who committed extortion.[255]

3. When is a forced sale a complete sale? This is only when the seller receives the full price. Likewise, a forced gift is not considered a gift. If the forcer takes the item but does not give the full price, this is not extortion, but robbery[256] (and is punishable just as other types of theft).

---

[253] See Rambam, *Laws of Selling* 10:4.

[254] See Tractate *Bava Kama* 62a; *Netivot HaMishpat* ch. 205; *Maĥaneh Efraim Laws of Robbery* ch. 26.

[255] Rambam, *Laws of Selling* 10:1,2; *Shulĥan Aruĥ Ĥoshen Mishpat* ch. 205.

[256] *Shulĥan Aruĥ Ĥoshen Mishpat* 205:4.

4. If one forcibly takes an item against the will of the owner and gives payment in full, or if he forcibly takes a person's money and leaves an item of equal value in exchange, then this *extortion* is complete robbery, since the other party did not agree to sell his item or to part with his money. Indeed, there is no sale when the second party is forced against his will, even if the forcer gives more in exchange than the worth of what he took. The stolen item or money must be returned, and then the payment from the forcer must be returned.[257] For Gentiles, this mode of robbery is a capital sin. Even if the forcer made a cash payment, this makes no difference, because it is robbery if the owner did not agree to sell. The payment or exchange that was left by the forcer, but not accepted by the victim, is considered as a gift or deposit (until what was stolen is returned).

It seems that at a later time, if the victim makes known to others that he now *accepts* the exchange as a desired sale with payment in full (even though when the robber took the item or money, it was against the victim's will), then *post facto* the robber retains jurisdiction over what he stole, and the ownership transfers to him. From then on, the victim has lost his right to demand in court that the robber must return what he stole (even if the victim eventually changes back to his original opinion).

5. Gentiles are not liable to capital punishment by a court for compelling a forced sale (although theft in general is a capital sin for Gentiles). The reason for this (as explained in footnote 1) is that even though the owner has distress over the incident, he accepts the sale and he does not lose any net monetary value.

Although the courts do not give capital punishment for forcing a sale, the forcer will nevertheless be punished harshly by God for this sin. Furthermore, if the courts do not establish laws and punishments that will deter this, people will be less stringent in general, and they will think that if they also commit extortion or rob a small amount, they will avoid the authority of the court. This tendency to leniency obviously applies to robbing something that is less than a *perutah* in value. It also applies to stealing small amounts of money that people

---

[257] Ra'avad *Laws of Robbery* ch. 1, and *Shulĥan Aruĥ Even HaEzer* ch. 28.

will normally not take the trouble to claim in court, and for which they will not normally call on law enforcement to report the robbery.[258]

6. It was explained that a forced sale is considered a complete sale because the seller agreed (as a result of the force). Therefore, it is impossible for the seller to retract, or to demand in court that the forcer return the object he paid for (i.e., the court will not make a judgment against the forcer). However, in order to accomplish complete repentance for this in God's eyes, so that the forcer will be forgiven for his sin, this requires that he return the sold item that is in his possession,[259] to the one from whom he took it by force and compulsion. Alternatively, he should appease the person who he forced to sell, and receive forgiveness from that person for whatever was taken.

---

[258] See *Bereishit Rabbah* ch. 31, that the Generation of the Flood committed rampant acts of extortion of less than a *perutah*, so no individual could be identified for judgment in court, yet many people were financially ruined. Because they destroyed the society this way, their sentence of destruction by God was sealed. This applies not only to this specific type of theft mentioned here – but rather all other types of stealing by which one circumvents the civil laws, or for which the law is not exacting enough, or in regard to judges who do not punish those who steal less than the value of a *perutah*.

[259] This was the repentance accomplished by the people of Nineveh, as written in Jonah ch. 3; see the first footnote to topic 2:1 above. See also topic 2:24.

CHAPTER 7

Laws of Borrowing, Renting, Responsibility for an Entrusted Item, and Holding Collateral for a Loan

1. One who borrows or rents an item or an animal from another individual is permitted to use it in accordance with the verbal or written agreement they made. Their agreement determines the conditions they established for the lending or renting. As a general rule, a person is obligated to guard what he borrows or rents, but his degree of responsibility for damage or loss depends on the type of agreement.[260]

What is the responsibility of a *borrower*? A borrower is responsible for any damage, theft or loss that occurs to the borrowed item (unless it is damage to the item that happens as a direct result of its being used in a normal manner to do the task for which it was borrowed). This applies even if it happens through forces beyond his control; i.e., even though he was guarding it properly, he was not at all able to save the borrowed item, because it was lost due to some great outside force. For example, even if the item was stolen by armed thieves or lost through

---

Definitions of terms: a *bailment* is a contractual delivery of goods in trust from a *bailor* to a *bailee* for a specific purpose. An example is a farmer (the bailor) who entrusts (as a bailment) an amount of his produce to another person (the bailee) who will keep it in a storehouse. Another example is a person (the bailor) who entrusts a letter to a mail carrier (the bailee), who will deliver it. The bailee is either a *paid watchman* or a *nonpaid watchman*.

[260] Ramban states (on Genesis 34:13), "[God] commanded them [the Children of Noah] concerning laws of theft, overcharging, withholding wages, the laws of bailees,* [etc.]... comparable to the civil laws about which Israel was commanded..." He did not mean that the laws of watchmen are the same for Gentiles as for Jews. Rather, both are commanded about this. There are Torah commandments for Jews regarding responsibilities of watchmen, while Gentiles are required to establish similar laws as part of their general commandment to have a system of laws and courts. Most of the Jewish laws of watchmen are simple and logical, and they are mentioned here in regard to the basic requirements of restitution payments by negligent watchmen.

Rabbi Zalman Nehemiah Goldberg notes that one can add a proof for this from *Shita Mekubetzet Bava Metzia* p. 94, where he writes that if one make his own stipulations for payment with a watchman, the stipulations are binding even if they conflict with the basic Torah law.

an unexpected natural disaster, or a borrowed animal was killed by large wild beasts, or anything similar to these cases, the borrower is responsible to pay the owner for the loss.[261]

But if an animal died as a result of doing the work for which it was borrowed, or if an item broke while it was being used to do the task for which it was borrowed, the borrower is exempt from liability according to Torah law – if the borrower did not deviate from the normal use of that animal or that item, or alternatively, from other conditions of use that had been agreed upon between the lender and the borrower.[262] For example, if a donkey was borrowed to carry its normal-size load over its usual distance and terrain, the borrower is exempt from liability if it died while working under these conditions.

2. What is the law of a *renter*? A renter is liable for lesser incidents that are beyond his control – for example, if the item is stolen or lost even though he guarded it properly in the normal manner that was expected. But he is exempt regarding drastic incidents that are totally beyond his control, from which he could not have guarded the object at all – for example, if a rented animal was killed or stolen by armed robbers, or a vessel was broken in a natural disaster that he could not save it from, such as a major earthquake (even though he had been watching over the item properly).[263]

On the other hand, if he did not watch the item properly, he is liable

---

[261] This is identical to the Torah law for Jews, as it is explained by Rambam in *Laws of Rentals* 1:2. Rashi on Tractate *Avodah Zarah* 15a writes that a Gentile borrower is liable for unavoidable damage. It seems that he intends that this is identical to the laws for Jews. Based on this a Gentile borrower would be liable in a similar way as a Jew, as this is a logical law: since the borrower has complete benefit from his use of the borrowed item without paying any fee, he is also financially liable for any damage to the item – unless it gets damaged while being used in its normal manner, since that is considered to be a loss that would even be beyond the control of the lender (the owner) when he himself is using it in his own domain. Likewise, it is logical that a watchman (a guard) who is paid should have some liability, since he benefits from the payment he receives. But he does not have liability for losses beyond his control, because he does not have permission to benefit fully from the item. For further explanation of this case, see topic 8 below.

[262] Rambam, *Laws of Borrowing* 1:1; *Shulĥan Aruĥ Ĥoshen Mishpat* ch. 340.

[263] Rambam, *Laws of Rentals* 1:2; *Shulĥan Aruĥ Ĥoshen Mishpat* ch. 303.

for any damage or loss that happens to the item as a result of his negligence. (But if the item was damaged due to circumstances that were forced upon him that had nothing to do with his improper watching, i.e., the damage would have occurred even if he would have watched properly, then in such a case he is exempt from liability.)[264]

3. Allowed borrowing can only take place with the awareness and permission of the owner, but one who borrows without the permission of the owner is a thief. If the borrower took the object from the jurisdiction of the owner without the owner's permission, even if he did not intend to steal it but only to use it and afterwards return it, this is forbidden and considered as theft. If person A permissibly borrowed an item, and then person A loaned it to person B without the permission of the owner, this is forbidden, and both person A and person B are considered to be a thief.[265] See topic 6 below.

Even if a person did not remove an object from the possession of the owner, but he used it without permission on the owner's property, this is prohibited because it is considered borrowing without the owner's consent.[266] This applies even if the usage did not cause any damage or wear to the item at all[267] (but it is not a capital sin, since the item did

---

[264] *Shulĥan Aruĥ ibid.* 291:6,9; *Sefer Meirat Einayim Ĥoshen Mishpat* 291:10

[265] Rambam, *Laws of Robbery* 3:15. It seems that one who borrows without the consent of its owner is a robber according to Torah law, and therefore a Gentile who does this would be liable for a capital sin if he removes the item from the owner's jurisdiction without the owner's permission.

See *Shulĥan Aruĥ ibid.* 292:1, "he is *like* a robber," referring to a watchman who guards an object for its owner, and *uses* it without the owner's permission but doesn't cause financial loss to the owner. But if a person borrows an item from the owner's property without permission, he is an actual robber, even if he intends to keep it in his possession only for a short while. The difference between these cases is the extent to which the unauthorized user is liable to pay for damages that happen to the item while it is in his possession. A borrower who takes the item from the owner's property without permission is also liable for unpreventable and unforeseeable damages. Possibly, even if the watchman uses the object in a way that the owner would protest, but he is not removing it from the authorized location, he is not liable for a capital sin.

[266] *Shulĥan Aruĥ HaRav Laws of Borrowing (Hilĥot She'ilah)* topic 5; *Shulĥan Aruĥ HaRav Hilĥot Hefker (Laws of Finding Lost Objects)* topic 2.

[267] See *Shulĥan Aruĥ ibid.* 292:1, and *Shulĥan Aruĥ HaRav ibid.* topic 28.

not leave the possession of the owner).

When does this apply? This applies to an item for which it is accepted that a person would be strict about its use by others. It even applies for an item that most people would not be strict about others using (because the possibility of it getting ruined is very unlikely), and only a minority of people would be strict about it because of a farfetched concern. For such an item, it is prohibited for a person to borrow it unless the owner consents, even though the person is certain that it will not be ruined. As long as it is without the permission of the owner, it is prohibited as a type of theft.

On the other hand, if a person knows that the owner of the object is not strict at all regarding its being used (in a normal way), it is permissible for him to use this object in this manner without the owner's consent (if he does not remove it from the owner's jurisdiction), and he is not a thief. (For example, if a person has permission to enter someone's home, he may sit on the couches or chairs without asking for the owner's consent.) This is certainly the case for an item that cannot be damaged at all, and no person would be concerned about how others use it. For example, it is permitted to sit on a stone fence that is built around a person's field, for no one is concerned about such a thing.[268]

4. Even if it is known that a person is the owner's good friend, and that the owner would be happy to hear that this friend benefited from his possessions, nevertheless, as long as the owner has not given permission, it is considered to be borrowing without the owner's consent. But if the owner made known his opinion that it is fine with

---

[268] *Ibid.*, in *Hilĥot She'ilah* topic 5 and *Hilĥot Hefker* topics 5 and 28.

Rabbi Zalman Nehemiah Goldberg notes: this only applies if the owner knows that people are using his item and he does not mind. Otherwise, it is like the law of a lost object while the owner has not discovered his loss; if the owner has not yet despaired of recovering the item, others may not use it, as written in *Shulĥan Aruĥ HaRav Hilĥot She'ilah* topic 4.

The author responds: it seems that the owner's consent would be necessary in order to avoid it being considered theft if there is some type of physically identifiable deficiency that the use would cause to the object. But if there is no deficiency caused to the object – in other words, there is no theft of the item itself – then all that is needed is the general knowledge that such use would not bother the owner. See *Imrai Yaakov* on *Shulĥan Aruĥ HaRav ibid.*

him if a certain person would benefit from his possessions and make use of them, then it is permitted for that person to borrow the items even though the owner is not aware of it at the time, and he is not considered a thief.[269]

5. If one takes an item without the owners' knowledge and his intention is not to borrow it but to pay rent for it, this is still considered borrowing without the owner's knowledge, and it is forbidden.[270]

If an item is meant to be rented, and the owner usually rents it to anyone at a set price, it is permitted to take the item from the owner's house without his knowledge and pay him the rental fee for the item. But if the members of the owner's house stop a person from taking the item for rent, and how much more so if the owner makes it known that he does not want to rent it out at that time, it is forbidden to take out the item at that time.[271]

6. One who borrows or rents an animal or other moveable object is not permitted to lend it or rent it to another person without the owner's permission, because it is possible that the owner does not wish for his item to be in the hands of that other person, and it is forbidden to transgress the will of the owner, regardless of what his reason is (for example, the owner may believe that the other person is not reliable). But if it is normal for the owner to always trust a certain person in important matters (such as borrowing this item), it is permissible for the first borrower to lend the borrowed item to that trusted person,

---

[269] See *Shulĥan Aruĥ HaRav Hilĥot Hefker* topics 4 and 5. The leniency provided in topic 5 there is not because the one using the object is a friend, but rather because such use would not bother the owner if it was done by anybody. Nevertheless, it appears that it can also apply if the owner makes it clear that he does not mind if a certain friend uses one of his objects. The same law can be seen also from the law (mentioned in topic 6 below) that one watchman can give over his responsibility to another watchman if the owner is used to relying on the other as well.

[270] See Rema *Shulĥan Aruĥ Ĥoshen Mishpat* 308:7, and *Maĥaneh Efraim Laws of Robbery* ch. 15 and 16, that if the stolen item was meant to be rented, he is not considered a robber, but rather he is using it without the consent of the owner (which applies if he afterwards pays the rent; otherwise, he is considered a delinquent debtor).

[271] See Rema *ibid.* 308:7, and *Shulĥan Aruĥ HaRav Hilĥot She'ilah* topic 7.

provided that the second person guards the object according to all the obligations that were incumbent upon the first borrower who became responsible for it.[272]

7. One who hires transportation (a vehicle or an animal, and the owner provides his hired driver – such as a taxicab service) may substitute another passenger or another load during the journey, without informing the owner beforehand. For example, in the middle of the journey, the passenger left and brought the driver a substitute passenger, or let off part of his load and brought on a new load in its place. The driver has a justified grievance against the first passenger, who changed their understood agreement by bringing in a substitute passenger or a substitute load which the driver did not originally have in mind to transport.

But if the owner's agent is not present (for example, one who rents a car from a car rental company, and the company does not provide a driver), the original renter is not permitted to rent it to another person without the knowledge of the owners.[273]

---

[272] Rambam, *Laws of Rentals* 1:4; *Shulĥan Aruĥ ibid.* 291:2 and chs. 307,342.

[273] Rambam *Laws of Rentals* 5:4-5; *Shulĥan Aruĥ ibid.* ch. 311.

*The following is an explanation and expansion of topic 7.

It is common that a transport-service business owned by an individual or a corporation will own a vehicle or an animal, and hire a driver to pick up and deliver local packages or local passengers with luggage, up to a limit on size and weight, as contracted between the customer and the owner. If the customer (a passenger) decides to end his ride before reaching the agreed destination, the driver may take on a different passenger who pays to travel with luggage or packages along the remaining part of the planned route (in conformity with the owner's limits on size and weight), even without the knowledge of the owner – if the owner has not made any rule against this.

For example, if the passenger cut short his trip in the midst of the planned route, the driver may take on another passenger who wishes to go toward the destination that was originally planned. Similarly, the original passenger may drop off a part of his items along the way, and he may replace that with other items. However, the owner of the delivery service may have a grievance against the driver or the new passenger, if this is a passenger whom the owner did not want to do business with, or an item which the owner did not want to transport. Even more so, the owner may have a grievance and a financial claim against the driver if he takes on extra passengers, or extra packages for delivery, along with the contracted passengers or packages.

8. A watchman who is entrusted with an item, with the sole responsibility of watching over it (so he is called a *guard*, as opposed to a *borrower* or a *renter*) is forbidden to use the item, for it was deposited with him only to be guarded. If he guards it for free, his responsibility is to watch it as any guard would normally watch it, and if he guards it appropriately, then he is not liable for anything that would occur to the item that is beyond his control. But if he was negligent in guarding it, then he is required to pay for any loss that occurs (for example, if it was stolen or lost), even if it was beyond his control.[274]

If the watchman is paid for guarding the item, the law regarding this case is the same as that of a renter who is liable for lesser incidents that are beyond his control, but not liable for incidents involving a greater lack of control (when he is guarding the item appropriately). But if he did not guard it properly, he is liable in every case, except for a situation of extreme lack of control, for which the damaging event would have occurred in any case, and is not connected at all with his negligence in guarding (as explained above in topic 2).[275]

All the laws mentioned here regarding the obligations of a paid or nonpaid watchman, a renter and a borrower, are directly from the

---

Any of these considerations may be overridden by any rules and contract terms that have been set in place between the owner and the hired driver.

If neither the owner nor the owner's agent (e.g., a hired driver) is accompanying with the rented transportation (e.g., a car rented from a car-rental company), the renter is not permitted to rent it or loan it to be driven by another person without the consent of the owner. If the renter transgresses and does this, he is responsible for what happens to the rented vehicle while it is being driven by the unauthorized person. Likewise, the renter is always responsible (on his own account, or through any liability insurance that he purchases) for any passengers who are not covered in the rental agreement.

[274] See *Ketzot HaĤoshen Ĥoshen Mishpat* 72:43 and *Minĥat Ĥinuĥ* Commandment 57:6, that a Gentile is exempt from liability if he was negligent in his duty as a watchman. But there are many dissenting opinions, e.g.: *Netivot HaMishpat* 72:53, *Sha'agat Aryeh* ch. 88, *Aĥiezer* 3:37, *Naĥal Yitzĥok* ch. 91.

[275] These laws of renters and paid and nonpaid watchmen are found in Rambam *Laws of Rentals* ch. 1, and *Shulĥan Aruĥ Ĥoshen Mishpat* ch. 291 and 307. See *Ĥizkuni* and *Or HaĤayim* on Genesis 31:39, that Jacob was a paid watchman of the flocks of Lavan, and he would have been obligated to pay for sheep lost due to theft or predators.

Torah.[276] However the borrower, renter or watchman is permitted to stipulate at the outset that he be exempt from liability for damage or loss to the item, or the owner may stipulate that the liability and responsibilities will be greater than that which is obligated within the Torah Law. With any such overriding agreement, the obligations for guarding and responsibility to pay for loss are determined according the agreed-upon conditions.[277]

Similarly a king or other form of national government is permitted to legislate civil laws in these matters, in which case the financial responsibility and the watchman obligations of a guard, a lessee or a borrower will be determined by the civil law.[278] It is also permissible for a government to legislate that the lessee may not be exempted from responsibility by his own testimony alone (for example, if he claims that the guarded item was destroyed by forces beyond his control, which were not seen by any witnesses), but that he must also specifically make an oath to God that he is exempt. Alternatively, the government may decide that the requirement for such an oath will be left to the discretion of the presiding judge in each individual case.

9. One who receives a deposited item without collecting a fee is considered to be a nonpaid watchman only if he accepts financial responsibility for the item. But if he only gives permission to the other owner to leave the item within his possession (e.g., in his house or his yard), this is not a watchman agreement. Rather, the one who receives

---

276 *In *Laws of Rentals* 1:3, Rambam covers one aspect of Torah Law in this area which is unique to Jews, and does not apply to Gentiles. These are the laws regarding a Jew who rents or borrows the use of an animal or an item at the same time that he hires its Jewish owner, and they are based solely on the Oral Torah. For Gentiles, the laws of renting and borrowing are not affected if the owner is also hired or participates in the work at the same time.

277 Rambam *Laws of Rentals* 2:9; *Shulĥan Aruĥ Ĥoshen Mishpat* ch. 296.

278 *Shulĥan Aruĥ HaRav Oraĥ Ĥayim* 440:9. A country's civil law overrides in these areas, since the obligation of a watchman is logical. Even regarding the Torah law for Jews in this area, there are situations that (and accepted ways to) circumvent the basic ways in which a paid watchman is considered liable. See Rambam *Laws of Rentals* 3:2, that the Sages enacted a law in regard to a specific situation in this area. This is called a *"takana"* in Hebrew, which is a legal enactment that protects the regular procedures for doing business, so people will not be reluctant to enter into these agreements.

the item is merely giving permission to its owner to leave the item in this place, and he is not liable for any damage that may happen to it.[279]

10. From what point in time does the responsibility of the watchman end? If the length of time for guarding the item has not been stipulated, then he must guard it until he returns it to the owner. If a time limit has been set, then if this time arrives and the owner has not come to claim his item, there are three possibilities, as follows.

If the item is on the watchman's property, then:

(a) if the watchman was a borrower, then when the time limit arrives, he is from then on considered as a paid watchman, and

(b) if he was a paid watchman from the outset, then when the time limit arrives, he is from then on considered as an nonpaid watchman.

If the watchman was guarding the item on its owner's property, then:

(c) when the time limit arrives, his responsibility ends.

Regarding a nonpaid watchman who accepts responsibility for guarding an item for a certain amount of time, when that time has ended, his responsibility and his liability end, even though the item still remains in his possession.[280]

11. All skilled craftsmen who receive an item which they are to repair are considered to be paid watchmen. They are required to guard the item, and they are responsible if it is stolen or lost, just like a paid watchman. When does the craftsman's responsibility as a paid watchman end? If the craftsman said to the owner, "Take your item, and bring the payment," or "I finished your work," or something similar to this, then from that moment on he is considered a nonpaid watchman. But if he said "Bring the payment and take your item" (so he made known that he would not return the item until he received his payment), he is still considered to be a paid watchman. And if he said explicitly, "Take your item, and I am no longer watching it," then he is exempt from any responsibilities – even those of a nonpaid watchman.

12. Anyone who guards an item (whether or not he is paid to do so) is forbidden to use the item without permission from the owner. Even

---

[279] *Shulĥan Aruĥ Ĥoshen Mishpat* 291:2.

[280] *Shulĥan Aruĥ Ĥoshen Mishpat* ch. 343, and *Pisĥei Teshuva* there, note 1.

though he does not intend to steal the object or lose it, and he only wishes to use it temporarily (and even if he intends to pay the owner if the item would be ruined, broken, or stolen due to his use of it), this is considered "misappropriating the entrusted article", and it is forbidden as theft, since he did not receive permission from the owner.[281]

One who misappropriates an entrusted item in order to use it has the status of one who borrows without the owner's awareness. He has the status of a thief, and from that point on, he is liable with responsibility for the entrusted article as if he were a thief (and not as if he were a watchman). If the item he used is lost or stolen, or it is an animal and it died, then even though he watched it properly and the loss did not occur as a result of his misappropriating the entrusted item,[282] it is irrelevant whether or not it became ruined or lost as a result of his using it. He must pay for it, even if the loss occurred due to extreme circumstances over which he had no control.

The following case is an example. A person agreed to watch a flock of animals, and took some animals from the flock for his own needs. Even though he returned the animals to the flock, this is considered an act of theft. Even if the owner is completely unaware of the temporary loss, and there was no aggravation or loss to the owner because the animals were returned to their place in good condition, this watchman is a thief because he misappropriated the entrusted item.[283] Furthermore, he is responsible for any avoidable loss or damage that may subsequently occur to that item before it is returned to the owner.

13. If the watchman misappropriates the item but only uses it for a benefit that does not cause any loss or damage to the item (and it remains in his possession], and he then returns it undamaged to its place, then even though this misappropriation is prohibited, he is not

---

[281] Rambam *Laws of Robbery* 3:11; *Shulĥan Aruĥ Ĥoshen Mishpat* ch. 292.

[282] See Rambam *Laws of Theft* ch. 4 and *Laws of Robbery* 3:11. Since one who uses an item entrusted to his safekeeping is considered a thief, Gentiles would also be liable for this. However, it is unclear if he is liable to capital punishment, since there is no loss of money through his use of the object.

[283] Rabbi Zalman Nehemiah Goldberg notes the reasoning for this: while the watchman has removed the item secretly from the owner's jurisdiction, the owner is not relying on him to guard it, and it remains in the watchman's possession until he notifies the owner. If a person, unbeknownst to the owner, steals and then returns an item, he is exempt from any further responsibility.

liable for any subsequent loss or damage to that item due to events that are beyond his control. This is because he did not nullify the guardianship which he had accepted upon himself originally.[284]

14. If a person accepted an article to watch over and he later claimed that the item was stolen or lost, then if it is found that he lied and the item was in his possession, he is a thief.[285] How much more so does this apply if he denies that he received the entrusted article that he stole; even if the entrusted item was worth less than a *perutah*), this is still considered complete theft.[286]

Denial of an entrusted article is called theft, because the article is still intact, and denying the owner's possession of the item is considered stealing from him. Therefore, if he denies the existence of an entrusted item which is no longer intact – for example, it was stolen or lost and now he is denying that it still exists – he is then obligated to pay for it, for by denying the entrusted article that he received, he is considered a delinquent debtor. This is not the case regarding one who denies receiving money for a loan. Rather, he is considered a delinquent debtor as explained in Chapter 12, because there is no obligation to return the actual money that was originally received.

15. A person who borrows or rents an item is not exempt from his responsibility if he claims that it was stolen or lost, and he must pay for it. Nevertheless, it is forbidden for him to lie and claim such a thing in order to ensure that the object will remain in his possession. How

---

[284] See Rema *Ĥoshen Mishpat* 292:1, and Shaĥ there.

[285] Rambam *Laws of Robbery* ch. 4.

[286] *Shulĥan Aruĥ ibid.* ch. 294. Here the law is different than for one who withholds payment of wages that are due for a worker, by claiming that he already paid the worker. If the watchman through his testimony is removing the object from the owner's jurisdiction into his own jurisdiction, that is complete theft which is liable to capital punishment. In contrast, if the item entrusted to the watchman was stolen and he later denies that he was entrusted with the item for safekeeping, he is not actually stealing, since the item is already long gone. Rather, he is only denying his responsibility, and according to the opinion of the *Or HaĤayim*, he is exempt from punishment for this denial if the liability is less than the value of a *perutah* (the Hebrew term for the smallest coin in circulation; e.g., a penny in the United States).

much more so does this apply to a person who withholds someone else's item in his possession, and does not wish to return it even though he is willing to pay for it, because this is theft and robbery.

16. A person may lend money on the condition that he takes an item from the borrower as collateral for the loan. If the collateral item is a work tool, and it is customary in that community to rent out that type of tool, the lender who is holding the collateral may rent it out without the owner's awareness and take the rental fee for himself *as a payment toward the amount of the loan*. This is permitted, since the rental fee is more than the depreciation or damage that is caused to the tool by the work that is done with it, and generally the owner will allow it to be rented out in order to reduce the amount he owes for the loan. Nevertheless, from the outset, the lender should not use the collateral item himself, but instead rent it to a third party, since he might be suspected of using it himself and applying less than the fair amount of credit.

But if the collateral is not a type of item that is customarily rented out in that community, the lender who is holding it is not permitted to rent it out to others, and he is not allowed to make use of it for himself, unless the owner knows about this and gives permission. This applies even if the time has come for the borrower (who owns the collateral) to pay back the loan. If the borrower does not pay back the loan when it is due, and the lender wants to collect his money at that point, he should go and sell the collateral item according to the instructions of the court. He may not pawn it to another person, for the collateral is like an entrusted article in the hands of the lender. Just as it is forbidden to misappropriate an entrusted item or to take it as one's own, this is also the law regarding collateral for a loan.[287]

17. A lender may take an item as collateral for a loan, so the lender will be able to collect his debt from the value of the collateral (without making a claim for the loan in court), if the lender explicitly stipulates at the time he gives the loan that if the borrower becomes delinquent in payment, the lender will take permanent ownership of the collateral in place of the loan. If the borrower does not pay his debt by the set time, the lender may keep the collateral according to the condition he set.[288]

---

[287] *Shulĥan Aruĥ HaRav Hilĥot She'ilah* topic 21.

[288] *Ibid.*, topic 24.

CHAPTER 8

Stealing or Encroaching Upon Real Estate Property

1. A person who secretly moves the boundary marker of his property[289] into the property of his neighbor, so as to diminish his neighbor's property and enlarge his own, has committed theft (*gezel* in Hebrew) – even if the area taken is only the width of a finger.[290] Likewise, one who takes over the property of others by force has definitely committed theft.[291] Any produce that the land-thief gathers or eats from this property is also theft, and he is obligated to return the property and the uneaten produce, along with the value of any produce he ate.[292] The same applies for anything else that he takes from the land or uses for his benefit (resulting in a financial loss for the owner).

One who forces another person to sell his property has committed robbery. The Torah Law regarding forced sale of movable goods has been explained in Chapter 6 above.

2. It is forbidden to steal property, even if this is done in order to enhance it and afterwards return it. This is just like the prohibition of temporarily stealing moveable items with that intention (see topic 1:6).

---

[289] *In this chapter, "property" refers to real estate property (land or buildings).

[290] Rambam *Laws of Theft* 7:11, *Shulĥan Aruĥ Ĥoshen Mishpat* ch. 376.

[291] *Although theft of land is not subject to capital punishment within Torah Law (see the following footnote), it is nevertheless strictly forbidden, and the courts are obligated to have and enforce laws against theft of real estate. If a person is forced to sell his property, regardless of whether the forcer buys the property or forces it to be sold to a third person, the forcer is equally guilty within Torah Law.

[292] Rema *Ĥoshen Mishpat* ch. 371. See footnote 1 above, which explains that a Gentile is not liable to punishment within Torah Law for stealing land. This is because he is unable to actually take possession of someone else's land, since he cannot move it into his own rightful domain. On the other hand, if one takes produce from land that is not his, without the consent of the true owner, it is clearly like any other theft, since the produce is like any movable object.

3. Property and buildings have a different status than moveable objects. Moveable objects may be fundamentally changed after the thief acquires them, or at least there is a change in possession, from the victim of the theft to the thief who took the item (as explained in Chapter 2 above). In contrast, stolen property and buildings (and anything attached to the ground in a permanent fashion) will forever remain in the possession of the rightful owner, even if he has despaired of it ever being returned. Even if the thief who stole the property has sold it to a second person, and that person has sold it to a third person, etc., the property or building still belongs to the original owner, and must be returned to him.[293] (But if the land-thief added anything moveable onto the property, he is permitted to later remove it and take it with him because that item is his possession.)

Therefore, one who steals property and then builds a structure on it, or plants crops or trees, does not acquire the property, regardless of any changes he makes, and the property itself must be returned to its owner.[294] Furthermore, even if the thief says "I will uproot these trees that I planted," or "I will destroy the building that I built," he has no permission to do so, because this would lower the value of the property itself.[295] Rather, when the property is returned to its owner, the owner must pay the thief for any expenses that he put out to make changes that raised its value, but not for the value of the upgrade itself. (For example, if the property value increased by $1000 as a result of an

---

[293] *Shulĥan Aruĥ Ĥoshen Mishpat* ch. 371.

Rabbi Zalman Nehemiah Goldberg notes:

The *Netivot HaMishpat* (*Ĥoshen Mishpat* ch. 371), based on Tractate *Bava Metzia* 6, says that for a case in which the judge(s) cannot find a legal justification to return a stolen property (for example, if there is a legal dispute, and the existing laws cannot define who the property belongs to), and this property is not in the owner's jurisdiction, then the owner's despair of regaining the land relinquishes his claim on it. [According to the *Netivot*, when the owner despairs of regaining his property in this legal situation, the ownership still does not transfer to the thief; rather, the property becomes ownerless.]

[294] See Rema *Ĥoshen Mishpat* 360:1, that for Jews as well, there is no leniency for the thief to be allowed to reimburse the victim for the value of the property, and keep the property for himself. Rather, the thief must return the stolen land to the rightful owner.

[295] *Shulĥan Aruĥ Ĥoshen Mishpat* ch. 375.

improvement provided by the thief, but the improvement itself cost only $200, then the owner owes the thief the $200 that he paid out. Also included is the value of the thief's time when he works to make an improvement. For example, if the thief worked 10 hours to make the improvement, doing labor worth a wage of $20 per hour, then the owner owes the thief $200 for the time he invested.) If the expense was more than the improvement is worth, the owner owes only the value of the improvement itself.[296]

If the owner from whom the land was stolen tells the thief to remove the upgrade that was added (for example, if the owner tells him, "Uproot the tree you planted, and go!"), the decision of the owner is heeded, and he is not obligated to pay anything to the thief.[297]

4. Since stolen property itself will never be acquired by the thief, it is forbidden for any person to harvest produce from stolen property. This is forbidden for the thief himself, as well as for all other people, because the harvester is stealing the produce from the owner. Even if the owner has already despaired of having the stolen property returned, the property is not acquired by the thief as a result of the owner's despair. (Furthermore, the produce does not belong to the harvester, and he is obligated to return it to the owner, even if the owner has despaired of regaining his property, as explained in Chapter 2.)[298]

5. If the property was ruined in a natural way (for example, if the property was flooded and all the plants were destroyed), the thief may return the land to the owner, saying "What is yours is before you," and he does not have to pay for the loss in value. But if the thief deliberately caused a loss in value of the property – for example, if he cut down trees or dug holes and thereby caused losses – he must pay the owner for all of the damages he did to the property.[299]

6. Similarly regarding one who stole possession of a house, if he did not benefit from it at all, he must return the house and does not need to

---

[296] *Shulĥan Aruĥ Ĥoshen Mishpat* ch. 372.

[297] *Shulĥan Aruĥ Ĥoshen Mishpat* ch. 375.

[298] Tractate *Sukkah* 30b, *Shulĥan Aruĥ Oraĥ Ĥayim* ch. 649, *Ĥoshen Mishpat* 369:2.

[299] *Shulĥan Aruĥ Ĥoshen Mishpat* ch. 371.

pay for the loss caused to the owner from the fact that he was not able to use his house.[300]

But if the thief did benefit from the house – for example, if he lived in it – he must return it as it is and give the owner a rental payment for all the time he lived in it.[301] If the thief rented the house to another person, he must pay the amount of that rent to the owner.[302] And if the thief damaged the house (or its fixed or moveable contents) in any way, he must pay the owner those damages. When the house is returned to its owner, the owner must pay the thief for any expenses that he put to make changes that raised its value, but not for the value of the upgrade itself. The Torah Law for upgrades or damages to a stolen house is the same in all respects as it is for land property, which was explained above.[303]

7. It is forbidden to use the property of others or public property without permission, even for a limited time, and such use is forbidden (but not punishable) as theft.[304] Therefore, it is forbidden to walk in another person's field or in his courtyard without his permission, if this trespassing matters to the owner. One who does so has the status of one who borrows without the owner's awareness, and he is therefore a thief. If it is known that this trespass would not matter to the owner, it is permitted. Similarly, it is forbidden to park one's car on someone else's property (even if it is a parking lot) without the owner's permission [and the unauthorized user is liable for any physical damages that he causes].

It is also forbidden to benefit from a stolen house or property, even to pass through them as a shortcut or to take shelter there from rain or

---

[300] *Tur* and Rema *Ĥoshen Mishpat* 363:6; the reason for the exemption is that it is only an indirect cause of damage, which did not come about from the actions of the thief, but rather because of the inability of the owner to use his house. For this type of loss due to an indirect reason, payment cannot be imposed upon the thief by a court, within Torah Law. See footnote 131.

[301] *Shulĥan Aruĥ Ĥoshen Mishpat* 363:6 and 369:2.

[302] *Shulĥan Aruĥ Ĥoshen Mishpat* 363:5,10.

[303] *Shulĥan Aruĥ Ĥoshen Mishpat* 375:6.

[304] See *Shulĥan Aruĥ Oraĥ Ĥayim* ch. 637, that it is forbidden to build a personal sukkah booth in a public domain, as it involves stealing property.

for similar reasons, because it is forbidden to benefit from stolen items, as explained above in Chapter 3.[305]

8. The Sages forbade a person to block or ruin a thoroughfare that is used by many people, and it is unnecessary (in this scenario) to determine if the person is claiming that he has a right to obstruct the thoroughfare because the land is ownerless. For even if the public has been using a thoroughfare in a private field or yard, and the owner was aware of this and allowed it (by not making any protest), the public has thereby gained the right to continue using it, due to the fact that they have already been using it regularly with the owner's consent.

It is forbidden for someone to take away the public's right to use an existing thoroughfare. Even if a person ruins it with some other intention (for example, if it passed through his field, and he plowed over it), and he provides a replacement thoroughfare for the public, he is still obligated to return the first one to them. This applies even if the second one is better and flatter than the first, because he is not able to exchange anything with the public without everyone's consent – for perhaps there will be someone who prefers the first thoroughfare, because it is closer to him than the new one. If the owner of the land nevertheless goes ahead and does make a replacement thoroughfare, and the public makes use of it, it is forbidden for him to afterwards destroy it. This is because the public has already gained the right to use it as well, since they have already done so with his awareness and permission.[306]

On the other hand, if the public trespassed and made a thoroughfare through private land in opposition to the owner, and he protested [even

---

[305] It is explained in *Shulĥan Aruĥ Ĥoshen Mishpat* 369:2, and *Shulĥan Aruĥ HaRav, Laws of Robbery* topic 11, that it is forbidden to benefit from a stolen house or field. Likewise, it is clear that it is forbidden to trespass, if this is against the will of the owner of the property, and this is considered theft. This is also clear from Rashbam on Tractate *Bava Batra* 57b.

This topic (8:7) clarifies that even if a particular person generally does not mind for others to have the small benefit of walking in his property, the situation changes if someone steals his property. It then becomes forbidden for anyone other than the owner to walk there, because it is forbidden to derive benefit from a stolen item, even if the owner wouldn't mind.

[306] *Shulĥan Aruĥ Ĥoshen Mishpat* ch. 377; *Shulĥan Aruĥ HaRav*, *Laws of Robbery*, topic 33.

by merely posting a "no trespassing" sign], that thoroughfare will not be under the jurisdiction of the public, and the owner may block it off in any manner he wishes.[307]

However, there are some Torah authorities who are of the opinion[308] that nowadays, it is permitted for a land owner to ruin a thoroughfare that the public has made on his property, and he does not need to first make a protest that the public is trespassing, because according to government law, he can always stop trespassers from passing through his property. Therefore, the owner's silence about the unauthorized thoroughfare on his property is meaningless and is not considered a *de facto* permission.

This is similar to one who makes barriers (for example, walls or fences) in his yard and leaves an area outside of the barrier, along the side of a public path or street, where he permits the public to walk (for example, a sidewalk). Since he widened the width of the area that is designated for public travel, he may not afterwards block off that path he provided, because it is forbidden to ruin a thoroughfare which has been permitted to and used by the public.

Both of the opinions cited above accept that if the public caused damage to the property (for example, if they broke down trees or fences on their way), then if the owner becomes aware of this but doesn't make any protest, he is foregoing his rights over this path in favor of its use by public as a thoroughfare. Since the owner decided not to issue any form of protest in this situation, that is considered *de facto* permission, and the public may continue to use the path.

It is possible to initially ensure that the public will not be able to gain thoroughfare rights in a private area. This can be done by erecting a permanent fence around the property border, or by hanging signs that warn others not to trespass, or by any other means that are accepted by the community or the legal system as a way to ensure a property owner's right to prohibit trespassing. In this way, the public will not

---

[307] *Sefer Meirat Einayim Ĥoshen Mishpat, ibid.*

[308] See *Imrei Yaakov* on *Shulĥan Aruĥ HaRav*, *Laws of Robbery ibid.* in the name of many Torah authorities, that nowadays, in places where property boundaries are all written down in the country's court records, the owner of the property would feel no need to protest the public's use of his property, and therefore his silence is in no way considered as consent. See Rema *Ĥoshen Mishpat* 417:2.

gain usage rights to any thoroughfare through the property, even if they trespass and the owner remains silent, because the public has been duly warned.[309]

9. One who goes without permission and lives in another person's building or open land, or who takes over and uses the property without permission, is a thief, as has been explained, and this land-thief is obligated to stop living there. Nevertheless, if (for example) it is a house that is vacant and not usually rented out, or a field that is unused and unplowed, the land-thief does not have to pay any rent for the benefit he received from living there, for the benefit gained by the thief did not cause any loss to the owner.

On the other hand, if this real estate property is generally rented out, and the thief has therefore caused a loss of money to the owner by occupying the house or the field, he must reimburse the owner according to the Torah Law regarding anyone who causes damage.

However, if the owner tells this land-thief, "Leave my property," yet he continues to live in the house or the field without permission, he is required to pay rent, even though the owner is not losing any money as a result of his living there.[310]

10. One who rents or borrows a house is free to sublet it to others, provided that there will not be a larger number of occupants than those who were included in the original agreement with the owner.[311] (The guidelines of one who borrows a house or land are not like those for one who rents or borrows movable items. For movable items, the renter or borrower is not permitted to rent or lend them out to others without obtaining the owner's permission, for the reason stated above in topic 7:6.) Nevertheless, in today's society there are more expenses involved in maintaining a home, and it is common for disputes to arise between the owner and the renter regarding who is financially responsible for these expenses or any damages. Thus, it is fully expected that the owner would not wish the renter or borrower to sublet to others without obtaining his consent. Therefore, the

---

309 See *Shulĥan Aruĥ Ĥoshen Mishpat* ch. 417.

310 Rambam, *Laws of Robbery* 3:9; *Shulĥan Aruĥ Ĥoshen Mishpat* 363:6.

311 Rambam, *Laws of Rentals* 5:5; *Shulĥan Aruĥ Ĥoshen Mishpat* ch. 316; *Shulĥan Aruĥ HaRav, Laws of Borrowing*, topic 2.

guidelines for renting or borrowing a house are nowadays the same as for movable objects, in this regard; i.e., it is forbidden to sublet or lend them to others without assurance of the owner's permission.[312]

11. Invasion of privacy is considered to be a non-monetary damage, and within Torah Law, a person has a right to prevent others from invading his privacy. Needless to say, it is forbidden to look at another person or his property in a way that could damage him with the "evil eye."[313] Similarly, one may not stand next to a person's grain field and gaze into it when the grain has grown and is standing upright, because it could be damaged by an "evil eye." Even in regard to watching another person's activities or work in situations when he need not be afraid of any damage from an "evil eye," it is forbidden to invade the privacy of his home, since he may not want anyone to know of his personal activities and what is going on there.

Therefore, if two neighbors use separate designated areas in the same courtyard, they are required to build a separation between their individual areas so that one should not see the activities of the other within the courtyard or within the other's own home. If they have not built the separation yet, each is forbidden to peer into the other's personal domain and his activities there.

Needless to say, it is forbidden for a stranger who does not have legal rights to a private courtyard to intrude there and look at the

---

312 See *Maggid Mishneh, Laws of Borrowing ibid.*, where it explains the difference between movable objects and land in this regard – that there is not usually any damage to the land itself, and therefore the owner would usually not be upset. However, nowadays people are very concerned over any property damage, so this would not apply – especially since there may be issues of contention between the renter and the owner, and the owner may not want any further interference or complication from any third parties. See *Imrei Yaakov, Laws of Borrowing ibid.*, which deals with this at length.

313 *The "evil eye" is a name given to harmful negative energy which is created as a result of a person looking at another person or his belongings or property with envy or ill-feeling. The Talmud explains that the "evil eye" can only affect a person if he is worried about such a thing, whereas it does not affect a person who ignores this issue. The most powerful protection against evil forces is the force of goodness, which is especially actualized with sincere prayer, generous charity, and conduct that is guided by Torah-based morality. (*Adapted from Chabad.org.*)

owners' activities or into their houses without their knowledge and consent. Regarding this type of intrusion, even if the house owner sees and does not protest, the intruder has no permission to do so, since it is possible that owner is keeping silent due to embarrassment.[314]

12. Therefore, it is forbidden for a person to make a new opening in the outside wall of his house and build a window there, if it would be opposite an existing window of his neighbor, or to build a new door opposite his neighbor's door, because his neighbor will be embarrassed about this new access to look into his home, and as a result, the neighbor will feel pressured to decrease his activities in that area of his home. Creating this opportunity for invasion of a neighbor's privacy is a type of personal damage. If one's neighbor does give permission to make a new window looking out onto his private property (e.g., an elevated window that looks down into a fenced-in yard or patio), he can say that this permission was only for his neighbor to get more light, but not for him to stand and look at all his activities in his personal property, and he can force him in court to make a barrier to obstruct that view. The same applies with all types of personal damage by intrusion of privacy.

This only applies if there is no public domain separating between the neighbors, and only if the one who is making a new window is gaining access to see into the other's window or yard space that was originally private. However, regarding windows that are already open to the public domain and are placed low enough so that those walking in the street can see into them the whole day, a neighbor is permitted to make a new window or door opposite that existing window. If the person

---

See Rashi on Numbers 24:2, that Balaam sought to instill an "evil eye" upon the Israelites who were encamped in the wilderness. But then he saw that the entrances of their tents were not aligned opposite each other, so each family could not peer into its neighbor's tent. Because of their obvious respect for each other's privacy, Balaam was motivated to bless them instead, as recorded in verse 24:5 and Rashi there.

[314] *Shulĥan Aruĥ Ĥoshen Mishpat* ch. 378, and *Shulĥan Aruĥ HaRav, Laws of Monetary Damage* topic 11. It appears that the laws of liability for privacy invasion are incumbent on Gentiles as well, since any use and benefit at the expense of another against his will, or even without his permission, is considered theft and monetary damage.

protests that it will be an invasion of privacy, the one who is making the new window can tell him that no matter what, that space is already open to the view of public passersby, so his privacy will not be lessened any more than the existing situation. If, however, a person has a window in a second or higher story floor, into which the public passersby cannot look, he can prevent the neighbor adjacent to him from visually intruding on his privacy – for example, by forcing the neighbor to make a visual barrier if he makes a new window that would allow a view into his home.[315]

It appears that it is also forbidden to look at another's mail or documents without permission, since this is an intrusion of privacy.

13. Just as there is a prohibition against moving a property border to steal land, likewise one is forbidden to copy material that is copyrighted, without permission from the copyright owner. This applies, for example, to assuming unauthorized rights on a book which another person wrote or printed, or reprinting another person's book without the owner's express consent.[316]

Copying computer programs or digital recordings that are protected by copyright is forbidden as theft, if the copyright owner has not given his permission.[317]

14. One cannot take over the job of another worker (even by providing an agreement that is more favorable to the employer), since this amounts to stealing the livelihood of the first worker.[318] Likewise, if one person is negotiating to rent a house, another person may not approach the owner with a better offer, since by doing so he is stealing

---

[315] *Shulĥan Aruĥ Ĥoshen Mishpat* 154:3; *Shulĥan Aruĥ HaRav, Laws of Monetary Damage* topic 12.

[316] See Rema *Ĥoshen Mishpat* 292:20; *Sho'el U'Meishiv* vol. 1, ch. 44; *Beit Yitzĥok Yoreah De'ah* vol. 2, ch. 78; *Hitorerut Teshuva Ĥoshen Mishpat* ch. 24.

[317] *Igrot Moshe Oraĥ Ĥayim* vol. 4 ch. 40. It appears that just as it is forbidden to copy them, it is also forbidden to have benefit from the copies, just as any benefit from theft is forbidden.

[318] *Shulĥan Aruĥ Ĥoshen Mishpat* 237:2; *Shulĥan Aruĥ HaRav, Laws of Ownerless Objects and Invasion of Property*, topic 12. See *Tosafot Kiddushin* 59a which says, "It is as if he is stealing that which belongs to the other."

the rental home of the other person. However, if it is during the season when new rental contracts are being made (for example, when many students come to rent at the start of a new college semester), and the rental prices are fluctuating, it is permissible for people seeking rentals to present counteroffers to the landlords.[319]

In all cases, if one person steals the existing livelihood, sustenance or living arrangements of another person, this is included in the prohibition of theft.

15. If a worker was trying to make an arrangement to work for an employer, and a second worker comes and knowingly makes this arrangement before and in place of the first worker, then the second worker has transgressed the prohibition against encroachment on another person's rights to property and livelihood. He is called a wicked person,[320] since with a small amount of effort, he could have made the same arrangement with another employer, and instead he is taking away another person's livelihood without justification.

Likewise, if one is negotiating to rent or buy land, a house, or movable objects, and a second person comes and precedes him to buy or rent it, this action is immoral, and the second person is called a wicked person. This only applies if the second person could find a similar item or property, even if it will require a little more effort, and he is deliberately grabbing the opportunity from the first person. But if there are no available opportunities comparable to those being offered to the first person, or if the deal is very advantageous, he is not called evil for trying to procure that opportunity for himself, even though his action is detrimental to the other person who was trying to obtain it.

Also, this only applies if the other parties had already completed a verbal agreement, but had not made a legally binding contract or signed an agreement to formalize the deal. If there was no agreement yet between those parties, another person is morally allowed to put forth a competing offer in order that the renter or seller will accept his terms, and he will receive the business agreement or the purchase.[321]

---

[319] See Rema *Ĥoshen Mishpat* 237:1; *Shulĥan Aruĥ HaRav*, *ibid.* topic 11.

[320] Tractate *Kiddushin* 59a, according to *Tosafot* there.

[321] *Shulĥan Aruĥ Ĥoshen Mishpat* ch. 237; *Shulĥan Aruĥ HaRav, Laws of Ownerless Objects and Invasion of Property,* topics 10-11.

16. It is permissible for an employer to suggest to the workers of another employer that they should change their place of work and come to work for him.[322]

17. It is permissible to open a new store next to another person's store, even though it will cause the other person to have this new local competition in his business. Even if the new store lowers the prices and gives out gifts to the customers in order to draw in more business, this is not considered encroachment on property rights, because the owner of the new store can say to the other store owner that he is free to do the same thing as well.[323]

Although the above mentioned practices in topics 15-17 are permitted, a pious person will nevertheless distance himself from these practices or anything similar, and he will not encroach upon the business of another person at all.[324] The Sages have commented[325] that the verse[326] "[he] who has done his fellowman no evil" refers to one who does not encroach upon another's business. Thus, doing such a thing in any way is called "evil."

Similarly, if one sees another person trying to gain through a certain good investment deal, even though as explained above (topic 15) it is permissible for him to preempt that deal to gain it for himself, this is nevertheless not a pious action or character trait. There are those among the Sages who say that he is called "wicked" for doing this.[327]

---

[322] *Avnei Neizer Ĥoshen Mishpat* ch. 17.

[323] Rema *Ĥoshen Mishpat* 156:5; *Shulĥan Aruĥ HaRav, Laws of Ownerless Objects and Invasion of Property,* topic 13.

[324] Rambam, *Laws of Ethics,* end of ch. 5; *Shulĥan Aruĥ HaRav, Laws of Ownerless Objects and Invasion of Property,* topic 13.

[325] Tractate *Makot* 24a.

[326] Psalms 15:3.

[327] Rashi and Ramban on Tractate *Kiddushin* 59a.

CHAPTER 9

The Prohibition of Kidnapping; Stealing Enslaved Persons

1. A Gentile who kidnaps a person – whether the kidnapper was male or female, and whether the victim was male or female, an adult or even one day old[328] – has committed a capital sin that is part of the Noahide prohibition of theft.[329] This applies whether the kidnapper took the victim through theft (in secrecy), robbery (with force), or coercion.[330]

2. To what do these three terms refer to? Kidnapping in a way of theft happens, for example, when the kidnapper lures a child into his own property and locks him up there, and this applies even if the child has no comprehension of the thief's actions.

Kidnapping in a way of robbery happens when the kidnapper takes a person away forcibly, even if he does not force the victim to serve him at all.[331] In any such case the kidnapper is liable, regardless of the reason for the kidnapping.

Coercion involves forcibly enslaving the victim or forcibly selling him as a slave, telling him that he will be injured if he does not comply.

3. A kidnapper is liable for theft due to his act of kidnapping the victim, regardless of whether he subsequently enslaved the victim, or sold the victim to others, or imposed nothing further upon the victim.

Therefore, if a third party acts only as an agent between the seller and the buyer of a kidnapped victim, or if he himself sold the victim

---

[328] It appears clear that if a kidnapper steals a newborn baby from the hospital, or even if the kidnapped baby was born in a field (i.e., not in the property of the baby's mother or father), he is still liable. This applies especially because within Torah Law, a minor child is always in the father's jurisdiction (barring any civil-law ruling to the contrary). See topic 9 below.

[329] See Rambam, *Laws of Theft* 9:6,9.

[330] Meiri on Tractate *Sanhedrin*, p. 56. This is also the opinion of *Kesef Mishneh* on *Laws of Kings* 9:9, that kidnapping in a way of thievery (i.e. secretly) or robbery (i.e. by open force) is the same.

[331] See *Minĥat Ĥinuĥ* Commandment 36, that although a Jewish kidnapper is not liable to capital punishment unless he forcibly sells the victim, these details do not apply to a Gentile, who is liable to capital punishment for the theft itself, just like stealing another person's movable objects.

who only afterwards was enslaved by the buyers, the seller is not liable for a capital sin.[332]

Although a person who sells kidnapped people into slavery is exempt from capital punishment if he is not a kidnapper, it is a great sin and deserves harsh punishment. The ruling government may (on an as-needed basis) execute such a person, if they determine there is a need to do so. At least, it is the obligation of the court system to punish these types of sinners, for sake of establishing a moral society (and in fulfillment of the commandment to make a system of justice).

4. One who kidnaps a younger brother, or a legal guardian who kidnaps an orphan in his care, or a homeowner who kidnaps one of the family members who eat at his table, or a teacher who kidnaps a student who is studying under him in the teacher's home, is considered a kidnapper and is liable. This applies only if the victim was originally in the kidnapper's domain, and the kidnapper takes the victim by thievery or robbery to another property.[333]

5. The kidnapper is not liable until he brings the victim into his jurisdiction and/or forceful control in a manner of **theft**. If he only ties up the victim in the victim's own domain, he is exempt from capital punishment, because the victim has not been stolen.[334] If he places the

---

[332] The prohibition of selling a kidnapped Jew is commanded only to Jews (Rambam *Laws of Theft* 9:2), whereas selling a kidnapped victim is not a commanded prohibition for Gentiles. Therefore a Gentile who commits only this act is not liable to capital punishment, but clearly it is forbidden, and it is expected that a court of law would give some punishment to a Gentile for any involvement in kidnapping, even if capital punishment does not apply.

[333] A condition of the prohibition for a Jew to kidnap and sell another Jew is stated in Exodus 21:16 – "and if he [the victim] is found in his hand" [i.e., in the kidnapper's domain, where he was taken by kidnapping]. This excludes a victim who was continuously under the kidnapper's jurisdiction, as explained by Rambam, *Laws of Theft* 9:5, but this does not apply to Gentiles.

[334] See Rambam, *Laws of Theft* 9:3. Rashi on Tractate *Sanhedrin* 85b explains that one is not liable for kidnapping a Jew until he removes the victim from the place where the victim was, and brings the victim into his jurisdiction and control. It is logical that the same applies to Gentiles, since a Gentile is not liable for stealing an animal or movable object until he removes it into his own property. See Rambam, *Laws of Theft* 2:16.

victim on his shoulder (or carries the victim in his arms), or places the victim in his (the thief's) vessel or vehicle, or on his animal (such as a horse), in order to move him to the thief's own property, that is the point in time at which he is considered a kidnapper and is liable.[335]

If the victim was persuaded to enter the kidnapper's property by the victim's free will, and there the kidnapper locked him up so that he could not go anywhere freely, this is an act of kidnapping.[336]

6. It is forbidden for another person to buy the victim from the kidnapper, since this is like receiving stolen property. If another person does buy the victim from the kidnapper, the buyer is obligated to free the victim.[337] This applies even if the victim had been forced into slavery for many years and had children during this time of captivity. Furthermore, one who enslaves the kidnapped victim's children transgresses and is obligated to free them.[338]

A kidnapper is obligated to release his victim, just as a thief is obligated to return what he stole (Chapter 2 above). The kidnapper is also obligated to ask forgiveness from his victim for any anguish that the victim suffered through the kidnapping, as is the case for anyone

---

[335] See Ramban on Exodus 21:16 in regard to Jews; see also *Tosafot Sanhedrin* 85b which is unsure as to the ruling here (in regard to Jews). Nevertheless, regarding Gentiles, we follow the logic that kidnapping is like theft of movable objects, and a kidnapper will become liable in a similar way as a thief, upon bringing the victim into his jurisdiction and control.

[336] Since the victim was deceived, then even though he entered the kidnapper's property willfully, when the kidnapper locks up the victim it is surely against the victim's will, and that is considered kidnapping. Even if a kidnapper locks up his victim in a place that is ownerless or belongs to a third party, that place is considered a domain of the kidnapper since he restrained his victim to stay there, and he is liable. See *Ketzot HaĤoshen* 348:2 and *Netivot HaMishpat* 341:9 that the same applies to one who steals an animal.

[337] *Tur Yoreah De'ah* 267:14, Ra'avad and Rashbah on Tractate *Gittin* 37b. It is unclear if a Gentile is liable for enslaving a victim who was kidnapped by someone else, or if the only liability is for the act of kidnapping itself.

[338] A victim of theft relinquishes ownership of the stolen item if he despairs of regaining it, but this does not apply to a *kidnapped* person who was enslaved or to the children he had during that time. We do not say that they resigned themselves to being slaves, since a kidnapping victim can never truly despair of regaining his freedom (see Tractate *Bava Kama* 68b).

who inflicts physical injury or financial damage on another person.

The kidnapper is obligated to repay the victim for the value of his work that was lost while he was unable to do his job,[339] and for any physical injuries that the kidnapper caused.

If a subsequent enslaver (a third party) inflicted physical injury on the victim that included emotional pain and embarrassment, the enslaver must pay the victim for those damages (see below in Chapter 11). But the kidnapper or a subsequent enslaver are not obligated to pay damages for the victim's emotional distress, embarrassment or fear due to being enslaved or held captive, since those are *indirect* results of the kidnapper's actions.

7. Anyone who forcibly uses a person (regardless of the person's age or gender, if it is without valid permission and against the person's will) commits a sin (which is a type of theft resembling kidnapping,[340] but it is not liable for punishment from a Noahide court). This applies even if the use had a value of less than a *perutah* (such as leaning on the person; see topic 1:4 above for the definition of a *perutah* coin). This applies even if the user does not forcibly move the person into his

---

[339] See Tractate *Sanhedrin* 91a, which recounts that it was successfully argued before Alexander the Great that Egypt should reimburse the Jewish people for the wages that were owed to the 600,000 male Israelites who had been forced into slavery, whom God redeemed in the Exodus from Egypt.

[340] *Leḥem Mishneh Laws of Servants* 1:8. This is comparable to the law of one who grabs another person's slave and uses him for his own work, which is forbidden as an act of theft (Rambam, *Laws of Robbery* 1:3, 3:7). Likewise, one who forcibly uses a free person for work commits the transgression of theft. However, regarding whether there is any liability to capital punishment for this, or under what conditions, it appears that it depends on the argument discussed in the next chapter, in topic 10:1.

According to Rambam's opinion (explained in topic 10:1), it seems that the laws regarding stealing a human are comparable to those regarding theft of a movable object, for which there is no liability to capital punishment unless the person takes the object with the intention to acquire it (or even borrows it but removes it from the owner's jurisdiction without permission). However, if he borrows the object without permission while it remains within the owner's jurisdiction, and he does not intend to steal it, he is exempt from capital punishment, although he transgresses (if the owner would mind that he borrowed it). See topic 7:3 and the footnotes there.

(the user's) own property. Even forcibly using a person in the public domain, or in the used person's own property, is forbidden.

Parents, however, are exempt from this rule in regard to their own children, since a parent may force his or her own children to do work, as explained below in topic 9. It seems that a guardian appointed for orphans may similarly force them to do work as a way of educating them. See Part V, topic 6:7.

8. The liability of a Gentile who rapes a woman is explained in topic 10:1. However, one who forcibly takes a victim into his property for the purpose of rape, even if he immediately frees the person and does not commit rape, is liable to capital punishment for kidnapping.[341]

9. From Biblical times until a few years ago, there have been nations where the government's laws allowed servitude, and this is addressed within the Noahide Code.[342] In nations with such laws, it is permissible for an adult Gentile to *voluntarily* sell himself as a servant.[343]

Likewise, *if it is permitted by the government's laws*, a Gentile father

---

[341] This is the opinion of Rambam, *Laws of Kings* 9:9 and 9:14, regarding the story of Dinah, that Shechem was liable for the death penalty for kidnapping her into his property (Genesis 34:2). See topic 10:1 below.

[342] *The Torah set forth revolutionary legal and moral standards for humane treatment of slaves and servants, 3330 years ago, while at the same time dealing with the practical fact that people would continue to regard the work of their servants, and the very bodies of their slaves, as economic commodities that were subject to the laws of buying, selling and theft. With that in mind, the remaining topics in this chapter deal with this subject only as it relates to the prohibition of theft by Gentiles, in Torah Law.

There is nowhere in the world today where full slavery (ownership of people as property) is legal. However, forced possession or servitude of non-incarcerated people, whether illegally or with the acceptance of the society, is still present in all countries. Thus it remains as a moral issue of international concern, including in regard to economic exploitation of children.

[343] *For example, see Genesis 47:19, in which the Egyptians approached Joseph during the years of famine, and requested for him to acquire them as servants to the Pharaoh, along with their land, in exchange for bread to eat and seed for crops. In Ramban's explanation of this verse, he writes that the people requested to be acquired as servants, and Joseph was permitted to accept their request. But instead, he acted leniently and acquired them only as serfs who would work as sharecroppers.

can sell his Gentile child into servitude if the child is a minor, in which case there would be no liability for this action itself, either for the father or the person who is buying his child from him as a servant.[344]

In nations where the laws of the land forbid servitude, it is obviously forbidden for a father to sell his child as a servant, or for a person to buy a child as a servant.[345]

10. In the rest of this work, we use the terms ***bondservant*** and ***full***

(It is explained in *Ha'amek Davar* that he did this for the benefit of the government. If he would have acquired the people as servants, the government would be responsible to feed them all, even if they were slack in their work. As sharecroppers, they would primarily be working for themselves and their families. Thus they would have a greater personal incentive to work, and this would increase their productivity.)

See also Genesis 50:18 which relates the actions of Joseph's brothers after the passing of their father Jacob: "His brothers also went and fell before him and said, 'We are ready to be your servants!' " Joseph was permitted to accept their request, but instead he acted kindly and refused.

[344] Rambam, *Laws of Slaves* 9:2; *Shulĥan Aruĥ Yoreh De'ah* 267:17. See *Igrot Moshe Yoreh De'ah* vol. 1, topic 162, that it seems clear in Torah Law that a Gentile mother can sell her minor children as servants *(where the law of the land permits)*, especially if their father put them under her jurisdiction. It also seems clear that Gentile parents can only sell their Gentile children as servants *(where the law permits)* if they are still minors (boys younger than 13 and girls younger than 12), as written in *Tzafnat Paneaĥ Tinyana* p. 64, since they are still under their father's full jurisdiction. This can also be understood from Tractate *Yevamot* 48a and Ritva's explanation there.

This is seen from Leviticus 25:45, with the caveat that the Oral Torah teaches that when a Gentile purchases another Gentile as a servant or a slave, there is no actual ownership of the person, but rather only the rights to the fruits of the person's labor. This rule is stated by Rambam in *Laws of Slaves* 9:5. According to this rule, if a Gentile parent sold his or her Gentile sons or daughters into servitude when they were minors, it is logical to say that they become free as a matter of Torah Law when they reach the age of 13 or 12, respectively. (It is also clear from this rule that if a Gentile voluntarily sells himself or herself as a servant to another Gentile, and this servant then has a child, the child is born as a free person.)

[345] Governments may rightfully decide to outlaw servitude. Nevertheless, even if it is prohibited by the civil law, a death penalty may not be imposed upon a Gentile father for selling his own Gentile child as a servant, since the Torah does not classify that as kidnapping or as theft in general.

slave for two different situations. We define *bondservant* as a person who works in servitude for a master in accordance with the law of the land, but he is not owned as the master's property. We define *full slave* as a person whose body is the property of his master, according to the laws of a "rightfully empowered" king, such as those in Biblical times.

This refers to a king whose subjects willingly accept that his sovereignty gives him the legal right to kill people who rebel against him.[346] Thus, he holds accepted full jurisdiction over his subjects' bodies. In Torah Law, this includes the power to hold sway over a subject's or captive's body as a monetary object, *in certain conditions*.

Such a king has a range of power to make decrees and set punishments (as explained in Chapter 14 below, and in *Sheva Mitzvot HaShem* Part VIII *(Dinim)*, Chapter 15). For example, if this king decrees that anyone who breaks a certain law or does not pay his due taxes will be sold into full slavery as the punishment, the purchaser acquires this slave's body as a legally binding sale,[347] and the Noahide prohibition of kidnapping does not apply to this situation.

11. If an empowered king makes a law that captives taken in war may be sold as full slaves, it is binding in practice.[348] A prisoner captured in war and forced into slavery by the law of this king has a status of a full slave, and one who buys this slave acquires his body as full monetary property. But if a person sells himself as a bondservant, his body is **not** acquired as property by the master. For the differences between these cases see *Sheva Mitzvot HaShem*, Volume II, Part VII, topics 9:11-15.

12. If any valid government institutes a jail sentence for violating certain laws, even up to life imprisonment, this is not considered kidnapping, but rather it is permitted as the law of the land.[349]

---

[346] See Joshua 1:18, that Joshua was accepted by his people as such a king.

[347] Rambam *ibid.* 9:4. The principle of "the law of the land is the law" is explained in topic 10:4, and in *Sheva Mitzvot HaShem*, Part VIII, ch. 15.

[348] Rambam *ibid.* 9:4, regarding the binding nature of such decrees.

[349] See Rambam *Laws of Courts* 24:9.

*A justified jail sentence with humane conditions is not tyrannical, but the Torah tradition discourages punishment by imprisonment. Imprisonment deprives the transgressor of his God-given, life-long task to use his abilities in ways that contribute to society.

CHAPTER 10

The Prohibition of Rape, and Laws of Taking Captives

1. One who rapes an unmarried woman – whether she is free or a slavewoman,[350] whether vaginally or anally – transgresses a prohibition by causing her pain and embarrassment.[351] The act of rape also includes a prohibition theft, because it steals her state of mind and her honor, and the rapist is using her against her will.

There are opinions that a Gentile is liable for capital punishment from a Noahide court[352] for raping a free woman, as part of the prohibition of theft, even if he does not force the victim into his own

---

[350] See topics 4 and 5 below.

[351] Rape is prohibited as a matter of bodily injury, and it inflicts damages due to pain and embarrassment, as explained in Chapter 11 below. This is also clear from the many places in the Hebrew Bible where the rape of a woman is referred to as "causing anguish."

[352] On Genesis 34:13, in the story of the rape of Dinah (who was a virgin), Ramban says that a Gentile is liable to capital punishment from a Noahide court for committing rape, because it is a type of theft. Ramban also holds that a Gentile who permanently injures another person is liable for the death penalty. It would seem that a Gentile who rapes a virgin female is liable to capital punishment for both reasons: for the permanent bodily damage of breaking her hymen, and for the act of rape. If a Gentile rapes a non-virgin female, if there is no permanent damage in the victim's body, there is still the liability of theft due to act of rape itself, in Ramban's opinion.

According to *Minĥas Ĥinuĥ* Commandment 35, topic 22 (and many others) this is also the opinion of Rambam, *Laws of Kings* 9:14, that Shechem was liable to capital punishment for the act of raping Dinah.

However, this is not necessarily the meaning of the words of Rambam, as it is possible to say that Shechem was liable for the death penalty for kidnapping Dinah into his own property, and not for the rape. It may be the opinion of Rambam that a Gentile has no liability for capital punishment for the act of raping a woman without kidnapping her. This is also the opinion of Meiri on *Sanhedrin* p. 56.

This also appears to be the opinion of Rashi on Tractate *Sanhedrin* 57a, that one who has relations with a captive married woman is liable for theft from her husband. He does not mention theft of her dignity and body in regard to herself, or that relations with an unmarried woman should carry the capital punishment for the act of rape itself.

domain. However, if he does kidnap the woman and forces her into his domain, he is liable according to all opinions for committing theft, even if he does not rape her, as explained above in Chapter 9. The laws of one who kidnaps and rapes a slavewoman are explained in topic 5.

2. A girl below the age of 12 years[353] does not have the maturity to accept marriage (as explained in Part VI, Chapter 1). Therefore one who seduces a minor girl for relations is considered as having raped her,[354] because a minor cannot take care to guard herself, and this is therefore forbidden within the prohibition of theft.

According to the opinion (see topic 1 above) that Gentiles are liable to capital punishment for rape, they are likewise liable for seducing a virgin minor as part of the prohibition of theft.[355] But if a non-virgin minor is seduced, although it is forbidden, the seducer is not liable for capital punishment (even according to this opinion).[356]

Rashi on Genesis 34:7 quotes Midrash *Bereishit Rabbah* 80:6, that after the Flood, the leaders of the nations made a decree against engaging in sexual immorality (to guard against people falling into the sexual transgressions that contributed to causing the Flood). The Midrash says that included in that decree was not to rape virgins, so this logically implies that before this decree, it was not forbidden from the outset as a clear transgression of God's commandment against theft. (On the other hand, rape of a married woman was forbidden from the outset as an act of adultery.)

[353] See Part I, topic 4:4, and Part VI, topic 1:12, as to whether the transition to majority for Gentiles is dependent on age (upon turning 13 for boys and 12 for girls), or on the individual's psychological maturity.

[354] In Torah Law, the seduction of a minor is considered to have the same legal status as rape, as explained in *Yevamos* 33b and 61b, since a minor is not considered to have the level of independent mature knowledge.

[355] Ramban on Gen. 34:13 says that a Gentile is liable for theft if he commits rape or seduction. It appears that he refers only to seduction of a minor, which would be theft of her consent, which she is not mature enough to give.

[356] Though seduction of a minor is akin to rape, it is different in that the victim must be compensated for her pain in the case of rape, but not in case of seduction. (See the last topic in this chapter and the footnote there for an explanation of the different types of compensation that the offender may be obligated to pay.) In the Torah Law for Jews, one who seduces a minor who is not a virgin is exempt from the additional standard penalty for seduction of a virgin minor (Rambam, *Laws of a Virgin Maiden* 2:10).

3. If a married Gentile woman has abnormal relations with another man, neither of them are liable to capital punishment for committing adultery. Nevertheless, there is a prohibition involved, as explained in Part VI, Chapter 3. There is also a prohibition of theft involved (even if it was done with her consent), because they are doing it without the consent of her husband, and therefore the other man is considered to be stealing her from her husband.[357] However, this type of theft is not liable to capital punishment. Therefore, if she has abnormal relations with another man, they are also exempt from capital punishment for theft. But if a married woman is raped abnormally, this is the same as the rape of an unmarried woman, as explained in topic 1 above.

Rape of a betrothed woman involves no capital transgression of forbidden relations (as explained in Part VI, Chapter 3), and there is no capital sin of theft from the *future* husband.[358] Nevertheless, this is a violent and despicable act, and completely forbidden.

4. One who seizes booty in a war acquires it, as will be explained in Chapter 14, and it is not considered theft.[359] However, this only applies to property seized from conquered enemy territory or a vanquished army, or (if an empowered king – defined in topic 9:10 above – has decreed that it is permitted) to ownership and enslavement of the conquered people who are captured in the war. However, a Gentile man cannot acquire his slavewoman's body to the extent of forcing

---

In regard to Gentiles, one who seduces a virgin minor is liable monetarily (in addition to any criminal penalty which the society's laws may impose) if, in that society, extra money would be paid to her father for her hand in marriage if she were a virgin bride, which is more desirable. For a minor who had already lost her virginity, since there would be no change in the amount that would be paid to her father, there is not considered to be any significant degree of theft that would make the seducer liable for capital punishment.

[357] *Minĥas Ĥinuĥ* Commandment 35, topic 22. He proves this from Rashi on Tractate *Sanhedrin* 57a, that regarding both a captive married woman, and a slavewoman whose master specified her for a specific slave, if the woman's captor or slavemaster has relations with her, he is liable for theft of the marriage from her husband. Likewise, abnormal relations with a married woman is forbidden because it is considered as stealing from her husband.

[358] *Tosafot*, on *Bava Basra* 16b and *Sanhedrin* 57b; see also Part VI (The Prohibition of Forbidden Relations), first footnote to topic 3:1.

[359] Rambam *Laws of Slaves* 9:4; *Shulĥan Aruĥ Yoreh De'ah* 167:18.

upon her a marriage without her consent,[360] and to do so is forbidden as theft (kidnapping).[361]

The laws of a ruling government are binding in regard to economic matters, but not in regard to forcing the absolution of a valid marriage (i.e., to decree an override of the Noahide prohibition of adultery, nor may they override any other of the Seven Noahide Commandments, which includes the prohibition of rape). Therefore, if a Gentile king makes a decree that his subjects may take married women captured in war from another nation as wives, this law is not binding (and the king transgresses the Noahide commandment to have a righteous legal system). Even during a war, and even if the ruling government has given permission, a Gentile transgresses the capital sin of adultery if he forces a captured married Gentile woman to marry him – if neither the woman nor her husband have despaired of continuing their marriage together, so their marriage bond has not been terminated. As long as the captured woman still remains in her bond of marriage, another man who takes her for a wife has also committed theft against her existing husband, and he is obligated to return the woman to her husband.

5. If one raped a woman who prostitutes herself for pay, it appears that the rapist is not liable for theft (other than in the view of the opinion mentioned above in topic 1). He is also not considered a delinquent debtor, since she never agreed to have relations with him, and there was never any payment agreed upon. Rather, his offense is limited to damaging her body and causing pain (and any expenses she incurs due to medical treatment and loss of work time), so he is liable to pay for those damages he caused (see topic 8), but this is not considered theft.

If one is delinquent in paying for any services of a prostitute that they agreed upon for a certain pay, he is considered a delinquent

---

[360] As Tractate *Sanhedrin* 59a says in regards to a captive woman, "They are not considered acquirable [to the extent of forcing them into marriage];" see the explanation of Ran on *Sanhedrin* 57a.

[361] *Sanhedrin* 59a, and Rashi there, explain that a Gentile has no ability to remove the married status of a married woman who is taken captive.

debtor and is liable for theft (as will be explained in Chapter 13).[362]

6. As we have explained, there is disagreement among the Torah sages as to whether a Gentile is liable to capital punishment for rape, within the scope of the Seven Noahide Laws. This means that there may be an obligation on a Noahide court to impose the death penalty for committing rape, but since there is no definitive ruling within Torah Law on this matter, a Noahide court is not required to do so. Nevertheless, it is still an obligation for the courts to give harsh punishment to rapists, for the sake of upholding safety and morality in the society. Therefore, the legal system is allowed to set the death penalty for rape, if it is determined that there is a need to do so for this reason.[363]

7. Within Torah Law, one who rapes is obligated to pay his victim compensation for the five traditional categories of damages – permanent injury, pain, expenses for medical treatment, loss of work time, and embarrassment – as is anyone who injures another person (as explained in Chapter 11 below). Likewise, one who seduces a virgin minor is liable to pay compensation for the damages caused.

One who rapes an adult or a minor, or one who seduces a minor, must ask her forgiveness for pain and embarrassment caused to her, like anyone who injures another, as explained below in Chapter 11. (He is not obligated to ask forgiveness from her family, although he causes them mental anguish and embarrassment, since one is only obligated for direct damage he caused to his victim, and not any indirect damage that resulted from his actions.)

---

[362] *It seems that if the acceptance of payment for prostitution is made illegal within a society's civil laws, a court is not obligated to enforce payment to a prostitute from someone who agreed to pay for the services and afterwards did not, nor to force one who raped a prostitute to pay compensation on account of causing a loss of work time due to bodily injury.

There may not even be a moral obligation to make such payments, because prostitution (whether criminalized or legalized by the ruling government) is a sinful behavior that destroys the morality, order and well-being of society (see Part VI, topics 4:11-12, and the footnotes there).

[363] See *Likkutei Sihot*, vol. 5, p. 190, that measures taken by the nations to prevent sins and immorality **may include** even the death penalty, and this is an application of the Noahide commandment to establish a system of justice.

CHAPTER 11

Bodily Injury and Damaging Another's Property

1. It is forbidden to injure another person's body or cause pain or embarrassment. There are two reasons for this: (a) injury is included as part of the Noahide prohibition of murder, as explained in Part V, Chapter 6, and (b) injury is considered a form of theft – if one person injures another, it is treated in the same manner in Torah Law as if the victim's property was damaged,[364] and this is forbidden under the Noahide prohibition of theft.[365] Within the prohibition of murder, it is forbidden to embarrass or cause distress to another person even if there is no actual monetary loss being caused, but there is no obligation within that prohibition to pay compensation for the embarrassment or distress that was caused. If a person is injured in a way that causes monetary loss, the one who caused the injury is obligated to pay compensation to the injured person.

---

[364] Tractate *Sanhedrin* 2b states, "What is the difference between one who damages a person's body, and one who damages a person's money?" meaning, there is no difference, since both types of damages have the same laws of compensation. This is also written by Ran on *Sanhedrin* 58b.

[365] This is the implication of *Tur Shulĥan Aruĥ* ch. 378, that one who damages property commits the sin of theft.

See Ran on *Sanhedrin* 58b, that it appears that there is no liability to capital punishment for a Gentile who hits another Gentile, if there is no loss of life. This runs contrary to the opinion of Ramban (Gen. 34:14), that bodily injury is included within the Noahide prohibition of theft. A clear distinction can be made between hitting that causes a loss of money through bodily injury, for which a Gentile would be liable to capital punishment for theft according to Ramban, compared to hitting that only causes pain or emotional anguish.

Nevertheless, the idea that bodily damage should be considered theft is not mentioned by Rambam or any other Torah-law authority other than Ramban. There is a clear difference: when one damages a person's body, unlike stealing an object, the perpetrator does not take away and hold any item belonging to the person he injured. Rather, he only indirectly caused a monetary loss to the victim. See *Likkutei Siĥot* vol. 34, p. 53, and *Leĥem Mishneh Laws of Injury* 5:9 regarding the difference between a thief, who needs to receive forgiveness from the victim, versus one who injures, who is only required to reimburse the victim for his loss. See also Part V, last footnote of topic 6:2.

2. One who injures another must give five separate compensations for the five traditional categories of damages in Torah Law: permanent injury, pain, expenses for medical treatment, loss of work time, and embarrassment.[366] Various types of injuries will require the offender to pay all or some of these types of compensations, in varying relative amounts, depending on how many areas of damage are involved.

For example, if one person cut another person's eye or blinded him, he must compensate him for all five categories. If he caused an injury to another person's hand that will eventually heal, he need not pay for damage due to permanent injury, as there will be no lasting physical effect. If there is also no need for medical attention, he need only

---

[366] Rambam, *Laws of Injury and Damages* ch. 1.

In *Sheva Mitzvot HaShem*, Vol. II, Part V, topic 6:1 (footnote 196 there), Rabbi Zalman Nehemiah Goldberg commented:

It is logical that all types of physical injury can be likened to stealing, as we see from the *Tur*, beginning of *Laws of Injury* (*Ĥoshen Mishpat* ch. 378), and Rabbeinu Yonah on Tractate *Avot* (*Ethics of the Fathers*) 1:1. It is questionable if embarrassment can be considered like stealing, although the Torah obligates a Jew who embarrasses another to make restitution, even though there is no monetary damage. It is likewise unclear whether causing another to lose money by injuring him to the point that he is unable to do his job is also part of the prohibition against stealing. It is also unclear if Gentiles are liable to pay all the five traditional categories of damages, since Rambam's opinion is that those penalties may only be levied by a *Beit Din* court of Jewish Torah scholars who have received **classical** ordination (*semiĥa* in Hebrew) [which was the direct line of ordination beginning with that which Moses passed on to Joshua; this did not continue past the 4th or 5th century C.E., due to the persecution of the leading Torah scholars by the ruling governments]. Since that level of ordination ceased long ago, there is no court which can levy these penalties on a Gentile.

The author responds:

See *Minĥat Ĥinuĥ* Commandment 49, topic 26, which is unsure whether these penalties apply to Gentiles (since there is no explicit mention that they are obligated in them, and they already have the greater liability within Torah Law to capital punishment for matters of theft). In topic 38, *loc. cit.*, he leans toward saying that a Gentile has no obligation to pay for causing embarrassment. *Or HaĤayim* on Genesis 34:27 says that after Shechem raped Dinah, her brothers took the penalty of her embarrassment from him, and seems to say that this penalty applies to all Gentiles, and it is not cancelled because of their greater liability to capital punishment for matters of theft.

compensate for damages in the categories of pain, loss of work time, and embarrassment. If there is no loss of work time, this category is also not included. If the injury did not occur in front of others, and the wound is on a non-visible area of the body,[367] the offender would only compensate for the pain, since compensation for embarrassment only applies if others are aware of it.

If one person struck another in public but did not cause any serious pain, such as slapping someone on his cheek, he need only pay for the category of embarrassment. The same applies in all other cases: the types of compensation required are based on the types of damages incurred from the injury.[368]

3. A person is considered predisposed to damaging at all times. Therefore, whether the perpetrator damaged with intention or not, was awake or asleep, or intoxicated, he must fully pay for the bodily or property damage he caused, if it could have been prevented by taking appropriate care.[369] If, however, a person causes damage due to circumstances beyond his control, he is not obligated to pay compensation.[370] For example, if a person ascended to a roof or

---

As for the reasoning of *Minĥat Ĥinuĥ* that there is no explicit mention of these five penalties applying to Gentiles, it is possible that they are obligated to keep them on a logical basis; just as it is forbidden for a Gentile to strike another person, it is also logical that he should pay compensation for the physical injury, no less than he is obligated to pay for property damage. It appears that this is included in Ramban's ruling that the Noahide commandment for a justice system includes judging personal-injury cases and penalizing offenders.

The objection raised by Rabbi Goldberg – that Rambam views these fines as court-imposed penalties, and they can only be judged by a Jewish *Beit Din* court of three judges with classical *semiĥa* – seems not to be an issue. That limitation applies only for Jewish offenders. There is no requirement for Gentile judges to receive ordination, and they need only one judge to decide a case. Therefore, it is clear that they may judge civil cases, including the five categories of damages, in the way they see fit.

367 Rambam *Laws of Injury and Damages* 2:2, and Ra'avad there; *Shulĥan Aruĥ Ĥoshen Mishpat* 421:7.

368 Rambam, *ibid.* ch. 2; *Shulĥan Aruĥ ibid.* ch. 420.

369 Rambam, *ibid.* 1:11; *Shulĥan Aruĥ ibid.* ch. 378.

370 *Shulĥan Aruĥ ibid.* 378:1.

climbed a ladder, and he could not have known that it would break under him (for he reasonably assumed it was strong), but it broke and he caused damage when he fell, he is exempt because the damage was unforeseeable.[371] Likewise, if someone places his object next to a person who is sleeping, or lies down next to him, and the sleeping person turns over and damages the object or injures the person lying next to him, the sleeping person is not obligated to pay compensation, because he had no knowledge of the situation in which he was likely to cause damage. Therefore, he was not able to be wary and take care.

Conversely, if someone ascends to a roof and falls down due to a foreseeable wind, or lies down to sleep next to vessels or another person and turns over in his sleep and causes damage, he is obligated to pay full compensation for the damage he caused. However, he need not compensate for embarrassment. The reason for his obligation in the other four categories is that he was negligent, for he should have been careful (for example, not to go to sleep near anything that he might damage while sleeping). Since he did not take this care, he is liable for the damage, which he is predisposed to causing. However, he is exempt from paying for embarrassment, because the special payment for embarrassment is only incumbent on someone who *intended* to damage (even if there is no intention to cause embarrassment).[372]

4. If one caused a person to become an invalid temporarily, so the person was confined to his sickroom and suffered a loss of work time, that is the only category of damage that must be compensated.[373] Likewise, if a Gentile locked someone up (even in the person's own room, which the person was already in at the time), he is obligated to compensate the person for any work time that was lost.[374]

5. If one strikes a woman and causes her to miscarry, he is obligated to

---

[371] See Rambam, *ibid.* 1:12; *Shulĥan Aruĥ ibid.* 378:2-3, 421:11.

[372] Rambam, *ibid.* 1:10; *Shulĥan Aruĥ ibid.* 421:1.

[373] Rambam, *ibid.* 2:11; *Shulĥan Aruĥ ibid.* 420:17.

[374] *Shulĥan Aruĥ ibid.* 420:11 says that for such a case (mentioned in the parentheses in the main text), in a *beit din* court, a Jew would be exempt for indirectly causing damage, and only liable in the judgment of God. By contrast, a Gentile is liable to reimburse a victim for indirect damage, as written by *Aĥiezer*, brought in footnote 93 above.

compensate the woman for her injury and pain, and also to pay the value of the fetus to her husband (or to her, if she is single).[375] Even if the woman died as a result of the injury, and the perpetrator is liable to capital punishment for causing her death, he still must compensate the value of the fetus to her husband. (If her husband died after the miscarriage, this compensation should be paid to his heirs.)

6. There is no obligation to pay compensation to a person for pain or embarrassment if there was no bodily offense. For example: for a slap in the face or a strike that did not leave any lasting injury, or if one spit on another's body, the offender must pay compensation for pain and/or embarrassment. But one that embarrassed another with words, such as cursing or belittling, or spit on the ground before him, is exempt from paying any type compensation, since he did not touch or affect the other person's body. Nevertheless, one who deliberately causes distress or embarrassment to another person by using words or actions (without making any physical contact) has committed a transgression, even though he has no obligation to pay compensation (because no contact was made with the body of the offended person).[376]

7. One who scares someone and causes physical or mental illness without making contact with the victim's body, or one who screams into another's ear and deafens him, must pay compensation for the damage he caused under all the categories of damages.[377] Although no

---

[375] Rambam, *ibid.* 4:1; *Shulĥan Aruĥ ibid.* ch. 423.

The *Minĥat Ĥinuĥ* Commandment 49, topics 34 and 41, is uncertain if a Gentile is liable to pay compensation for causing the fetus to die (when the miscarriage was an outcome of hitting the woman). It seems that this should be an obvious liability if she was hit intentionally; even though a Gentile is liable to capital punishment for killing a fetus intentionally, there is no law for Gentiles that having a greater liability exempts one from paying compensation for a simultaneous lesser liability.

[376] Rambam, *ibid.* 2:7 and 3:5,7; *Shulĥan Aruĥ ibid.* 420:38.

[377] See Rambam, *ibid.* 2:7; *Shulĥan Aruĥ ibid.* 421:25,32; *Sefer Meirat Einayim Ĥoshen Mishpat* 421:26. Although the Torah Law for a Jew is that one who scares another person, or one who screams into another's ear and deafens him, without making contact with the victim's body, is exempt from liability in court and only liable in God's judgment, this exemption is because a Jew is not liable for indirect damage, whereas a Gentile is liable.

physical contact was made, the scream or scare had a physical effect. This can be compared to one who shoots a person with an arrow; even though there is no bodily contact with the victim, the arrow is considered as if it were being held in the shooter's hands.

The situation is different if one distressed another person with words, which then caused him to be adversely affected psychologically, or if he scared someone and it caused the person to turn around suddenly and get injured from stumbling. Within Torah Law, the perpetrator is not obligated to pay compensation, because his actions did not directly cause damage. Rather, the harm occurred only as an indirect result of the actions. (However, a court has permission to make him pay a fine, if it sees fit to do so.)

8. It is forbidden to damage another person's property, even with intention to compensate the owner, just as it is forbidden to steal with intention to return the stolen object (see topic 1:6 above).[378] In contrast, it is permissible to damage another's property if this action is clearly to the owner's benefit;[379] since it is permitted to cause pain to a person's body if it is beneficial to the person (as explained in Part V, topic 6:5), it is surely permissible to do similarly with his property.

9. It is forbidden to damage another's money in any way, whether the damage is caused through action or speech, even if the damage is caused indirectly.[380] For example, it is forbidden for a passerby to tell someone who is about to buy merchandise that the product is not worth the price, even if this is true, since he causes monetary damage with his speech to the one who is selling the merchandise.[381] However, if the buyer asked his advice as to whether the price was fair or not, he may tell him the truth.

10. It has already been explained (in Chapter 1 above) that one who

---

[378] Rambam, *Laws of Monetary Damage* 5:1; *Tur* and *Sefer Meirat Einayim* on *Ĥoshen Mishpat* ch. 378; *Shulĥan Aruĥ HaRav, Laws of Monetary Damage*, topic 1.

[379] See *Likkutei Siĥot* vol. 34, pp. 52,53.

[380] Tractate *Bava Batra* 22b; Rambam, *Laws of Monetary Damage* ch. 5; *Tur Ĥoshen Mishpat* ch. 378.

[381] See *Shulĥan Aruĥ HaRav, ibid.*

coerces another to give him money is considered to have committed full robbery. It is forbidden to assist such a coercer, such as showing him where the victim's money is kept (unless it is a matter of life and death, such as if a coercer tells someone that unless he reveals the location of another person's money, he will kill that person, as explained in topic 4:16). It is forbidden to hand over another's money to a coercer under the prohibition of theft, and handing another's body over to a coercer is forbidden under the prohibition of injury.[382]

It has been explained in topic 4:13 that it is forbidden to remove a damage that is occurring to oneself by putting it on another person.

11. It is forbidden to place an obstacle in public property, for this is prone to cause damage to other people or their property. If one digs a pit in a public thoroughfare and does not properly cover it, and a man or animal falls into it and is injured, or a load on the animal was damaged, the one who dug the pit must compensate the person who was physically or financially damaged. Likewise, one who unlawfully leaves an object in public property or an obstacle which can cause damage is obligated to pay for any damage or injury caused.[383]

---

[382] See Rambam, *Laws of Injury* ch. 8.

[383] See Rambam, *Laws of Monetary Damage* ch. 12. It appears that the inference in the Talmud (based on the verse in Exodus 21:33), " 'And an ox or donkey falls there': an ox and not a person, a donkey and not vessels," cannot be applied to Gentiles.

Rabbi Zalman Nehemiah Goldberg comments:

There is no source given for why a Gentile should be liable for the damages of his pit. There is no reason to give him liability due to the actions of his body, since this was through an indirect cause. The liability of a Jew is based on a special law of the damage caused by a pit, but for a Gentile, just as there is no liability for the damage caused by one's ox, there should also be no liability for the damage caused by one's pit. However, in *Birkat Shmuel* (*Bava Kama* ch. 2), he writes that one whose pit causes damages to vessels is obligated in God's judgment, as with any case of indirectly caused damage. Therefore, if we would say that any matter for which a Gentile is liable in God's judgment, he can also be liable in court, there is room to make him liable to pay damages.

The author responds:

See Tractate *Bava Kama* 38a and *Tosafot* there ("He stood"), which imply that the damages caused by a pit or fire apply equally to Jews and Gentiles.

12. If one places his vessel in the public domain, and it is broken by people who are walking by, and consequently a person or animal was injured by the broken pieces, then (whether it was the injured person who broke the vessel or someone else) the owner of the vessel is liable to pay for the damages. Even if he declared the broken pieces ownerless, he is not exempt from any damage they cause, since his placing the vessel in that location was a negligent act.

If the owner was holding the vessel, and by unpreventable circumstances it broke while he was walking in the public domain, and another person was injured by the broken pieces, the owner of the vessel is exempt from paying for any damages. Nevertheless, the owner is obligated to gather up the pieces and remove the danger from the public domain. If he does not do so, although he is exempt in a Noahide court, he is liable to punishment from God for causing damage through postponing removal of the pieces as required.

This exemption in a Noahide court only applies if he declared the broken pieces to be ownerless after they broke by unpreventable circumstances. If he did not do so, and instead intended to collect the pieces as his property, then the owner is liable for any damage caused by their being in the public domain, as in the case of one who digs a pit in the public domain (see topic 11 above). The same applies to all similar cases, such as one whose animal stumbled and fell in the public domain, and he did not stand it up, and then another person's animal stumbled over the fallen animal. Then the fallen animal's owner is obligated to pay for all damages caused to the second animal or its load, because he did not declare his animal to be ownerless.[384]

Although the details of these laws as they are written in the Torah apply to Jews, there is no exclusion given in regard to Gentiles, and there is a logical need for the courts to judge such cases of direct and indirect damage.

There is only a specific exemption given for Gentiles in regard to one's animal causing damage, as this is a very indirect cause of damage – merely that the animal's owner did not guard it correctly, and the animal did damage on its own. But if the damage is caused solely through the action of the owner, and the nature of the action makes the damage likely to happen, the owner should logically be liable if he did not take reasonable precaution to avoid it. It is also clear from Ramban (on Genesis 34:13) that Gentiles are liable to pay for damages caused by their pit or fire (at least).

384 Rambam, *Laws of Monetary Damage* 13:8; *Shulĥan Aruĥ Ĥoshen Mishpat* ch. 412.

Likewise, if one's automobile was involved in an accident, and since he did not remove it from the road it caused damage, then if he is responsible for the accident, he is also responsible for any subsequent damage caused by the presence of the wreck. If he is not the responsible party, he is considered a victim of unpreventable circumstances, and is exempt. Therefore, if he intends to send his damaged car to a mechanic or the like, it is still considered his car, and he is liable for any subsequent damages it causes due to being left on the road – if he has the ability to remove the car from the scene of the accident, and he is lazy and does not do so (even though the accident was not his fault). If he is unable to remove the car, he is considered not at fault for unpreventable damage that is subsequently caused. If he declares the car to be ownerless, he is exempt from any further damage.

13. One who was walking on the road, and his body or an object he was carrying caused damage to another person's body or property, is obligated to pay compensation for the damage caused.

For example, if one was walking with a bundle and stumbled and fell, and he was able to stand up and clear the way but he procrastinated, and therefore a second person stumbled over him (or the fallen bundle), then he is liable for the damage caused to the second person. But if he did not have an opportunity to stand up in time and clear the way, he is considered a victim of unpreventable circumstances and is exempt from paying for the damage. The second person, however, is exempt from any liability for damage caused to the first person, who had no permission to create an obstacle in public domain. The first person is exempt from any liability if he warns the second person, and the second person is then liable for any damage he causes, unless he was not able to avoid it.[385]

14. If one lit a fire in his property and did not properly guard it, and the fire spread to another's property and burnt a field or haystack which

---

Rabbi Zalman Nehemiah Goldberg comments that it is not so clear that this law also applies to Gentiles. It is possible that they would be exempt from all such liabilities, just as a Gentile is exempt if his ox damages another's ox.

[385] See Rambam, *ibid.*; *Shulĥan Aruĥ Ĥoshen Mishpat* ch. 413.

had hidden items inside it,[386] then he is liable to pay for any damages caused by his fire. Obviously, one who sets fire to another person's field or haystack is considered to be causing direct damage, and he is liable to pay in full for any damages caused.[387]

If one was properly guarding a fire in his own property, and the fire got out of control because of an unforeseeable event and spread to another's property and caused damage, then it is considered to be a result of unpreventable circumstances, and he is exempt from financial liability. This would be the case if the fire jumped over a river, a pond, or a wall or the like – events that could not have been expected to happen according to reasonable expectations.[388]

15. If one gave a hot coal to a deaf-mute, a mentally deranged person or a minor, who are not responsible for their actions, and the recipient caused damage from a fire that he started with the coal, then a Noahide court does not require the one who gave over the coal to pay for the damage. Nevertheless, in God's judgment he is liable to pay compensation. This only applies if the hot coal on its own would not have started a fire, but the irresponsible person fanned it on his own and brought out a flame which caused the damage. Since the nature of a hot coal left alone is to cool down, the judgment by the Noahide court is that both the original person and the recipient are exempt.

If one gave a live flame to one of these types of people, who then caused damage with it, the original person is liable for any damage

---

[386] It appears that a Gentile should not be exempt for his fire's damage to another's hidden items. The exemption in the Torah law for Jews (regarding hidden objects that are damaged by another Jew's fire) is a decree based on a scriptural verse, and it is not a matter decided on a purely logical basis. Logically, it would be expected that a person should be liable for any damage that he causes to another person's item, whether or not the item was openly exposed at the time.

Rabbi Zalman Nehemiah Goldberg notes to see his previous comment to topic 12 (regarding the liability of a Gentile for damages caused by his pit).

[387] See Ramban on Genesis 34:13, that a Gentile who lights fire to another's haystack is liable for capital punishment for the prohibition of theft. As noted earlier, it is clear that the perpetrator would need to pay for the damage as well. However, it seems from Rambam that one would not be liable to the death penalty for causing damage to property; see footnote 365.

[388] Rambam, *ibid.* ch. 14; *Shulĥan Aruĥ Ĥoshen Mishpat* ch. 418.

caused, since it was his action that caused the damage.[388]

16. Not only is one who starts a fire liable; one is also liable for all damages caused if he blows a fire and causes it to leave its place and burn another's property, or if he bends down the standing grain in another's property towards a fire in an adjoining property and causes the whole field to burn down.[389]

In any case which begins with negligence, even though the damage in the end is caused by unavoidable circumstances, the perpetrator is liable for any damage caused. Therefore, even if one lit a small fire to destroy a small part of another's property, or he lit a small fire and did not guard it properly, and later an unnatural wind caused the fire to damage a much larger area, the perpetrator is liable for all the damages that result from this.

17. Damage that occurs in the same manner as damage from a fire has the same laws. For example, if one puts a stone, a knife or a load on a roof and a normal wind blows it off, and it then causes damage in public domain or another's private property (either when it fell, or later on), the law is that the person is liable for any damage caused.

If a person placed down an object on a fenced-in roof, and an abnormal wind came up and blew it off and it caused damage, the person is free from liability because the occurrence was unpreventable.[390] (See topic 12 above, that if the person knows that the object has fallen into a place where it is a hazard, and he doesn't declare it to be ownerless, then he is liable due negligence if it afterwards causes a damage.)

Likewise, one who pours water or another liquid into another's property (or into public property, in places where he has no right to do so), and this causes damage at the time it is poured, the laws of liability are similar to those relating to fire.[391] If the liquid came to rest and later on, those who were walking in the area got damaged by it, this damage is similar to the category of damage caused by a pit.[392] Either way, the perpetrator is liable for all damages.

---

[389] Rambam *Laws of Monetary Damage* ch. 14.

[390] Rambam *ibid.* ch. 14; *Shulĥan Aruĥ Ĥoshen Mishpat* ch. 411.

[391] See *Shulĥan Aruĥ ibid.* ch. 416, and ch. 417 topic 1.

[392] *Shulĥan Aruĥ HaRav, Laws of Monetary Damage* topic 14.

In places where it is customary to pour water into the public domain (as when the residents of a city have given up their rights to protest about this because they have no other option), although it is permissible to do so, one is still liable to pay for any damage that is caused by his water when it is being poured out, but not for damage it causes later, after it comes to rest).[393]

18. It is forbidden to cause damage to another's property even if this only happens through routine use of one's own property. For example, if one's wall is adjacent to another's, it is forbidden to place something very hot or wet next to his own wall if it may cause damage to the other person's adjacent wall. Likewise, it is forbidden for him to pour water steadily next to his own wall, if it may cause damaging dampness or mold on the other person's wall.[394]

19. It is forbidden for one to do actions in his own house or yard that cause damage or a serious nuisance to others, such as causing a large amount of smoke, stench or noise.[395] It is likewise forbidden for one to build a structure in one's own yard that juts out into the public domain. Therefore, if one's tree has a branch that sticks out into the street or sidewalk area and obstructs those who pass by, he must prune it (even if it is a fruit tree) so it will not cause obstruction or damage.[396]

---

[393] See *Shulĥan Aruĥ Ĥoshen Mishpat* 417:1, and chs. 412, 416.

[394] *Shulĥan Aruĥ HaRav, Laws of Monetary Damage*, topic 14.

[395] *Shulĥan Aruĥ ibid.* 155:34; Rema there, topic 15; *Shulĥan Aruĥ HaRav ibid.* topic 17.

[396] See Rambam *ibid.* 13:24-26; *Shulĥan Aruĥ ibid.* ch. 417.

The branches extending into public property belong to the tree owner, and others do not have permission to take them. Although another person may cut them off, that is based on the law that a person who is being damaged may take the law into his own hands. In essence, however, the responsibility to cut them is placed on the tree's owner, not to cause damage. For all a person's belongings that are surely going to directly cause damage, and he can prevent them from doing so, he is fully obligated to guard them from damaging.

Indeed, where the damaging or dangerous entity extends into the public domain, the court should warn the owner to remove it, since courts are the guardians of the public citizens. But if it enters into another person's private property, that person has his own right to complain to the one who is responsible, or to bring him to court.

20. It is forbidden to make a dovecote in one's own property of it is in an area of fields and gardens, because the doves will cause damage to others' produce. Although the doves are not completely the property of the one who builds the dovecote (as they come on their own from elsewhere), he is nevertheless causing the damage. It is therefore an obligation to distance the dovecote from others' areas of growing produce, by at least 50 cubits. The Torah law states that one need not be concerned that doves might cause damage farther than 50 cubits (approx. 25 meters) from their dovecote.[397]

21. If a privately-owned animal went out and damaged on its own, whether it damaged property (such as eating from a person's produce, or trampling a person's produce or vessels in its path, or injuring or killing another animal or a person), the owner is exempt from all liability.[398] Although it is forbidden to cause damage even through one's animals,[399] and therefore there is an obligation to guard them appropriately, a court is not obligated by Torah law to make the owner

---

Although the Mishnah, in Tractate *Bava Batra* 2:13, says that the victim of the damage must cut the tree himself (and the same applies to *Bava Batra* p. 60), this because the entrance of the tree's branch into a neighbor's property is not always considered to be a damage (and possibly it is beneficial, for the shade it provides). Therefore, until the neighbor complains, the owner of the branches has no obligation to cut off the intruding branch. If he does complain, the owner is obligated to cut back the branch.

397 *Shulĥan Aruĥ Ĥoshen Mishpat* 155:24; *Shulĥan Aruĥ HaRav, Laws of Monetary Damage*, topic 16.

398 Rambam, *Laws of Monetary Damage* 8:5 and 10:1, states that if a Gentile's ox kills another Gentile, the ox is not killed. (However, Ramban, on Genesis 9:5, holds that the ox should be killed, based on that verse: "...of every beast I [God] will demand it...")

399 This can be inferred from Rambam, *Laws of Monetary Damage* 5:1: "It is forbidden to cause damage" (meaning also through one's animals), and also from *ibid.* 8:5 regarding the ox of a Gentile, which implies there that the courts are obligated to make laws that one's animal must be guarded from causing damage, even though the Noahide Commandments do not make one liable to pay for damages that are caused by his animals of their own accord. (It seems that the prohibition Rambam refers to is that of theft, which includes causing damage, as explained in the beginning of this chapter, and this would also be applicable to Gentiles.)

pay for damages caused by his animal of its own accord. Nevertheless, it is fitting that the courts set regulations and fines for this, so that owners of animals will be more careful to guard them.[400]

However, one who sends his animal out to damage – such as one who sends his sheep to pasture in another's field – is considered to be causing direct damage and is judged as a damager (and he is also considered to be a thief).[401] He is therefore liable to pay for any damage that his animal causes.[402]

22. It is forbidden to raise a dog (or other animal) which is vicious and prone to cause damage or injury to others, unless it is guarded and contained properly.[403] One who sends his dog out to attack other people or their animals is liable for all injury or damage caused.[404]

23. A damage which is invisible is still considered damage, and it is forbidden for one to perpetrate such a damage.[405]

For example, a Jew is not allowed to eat various foods, all which have varying levels of ritual stringency. In particular, it is prohibited for a Jew to drink wine if it was touched or moved by a Gentile, either

---

400 This appears correct based on Rambam, *Laws of Monetary Damage* 8:5, which states, "this is a penalty that is imposed on Gentiles." Therefore, the Gentile courts as well can and should give this penalty.

401 Rashi on Genesis 13:7 (based on Midrash *Bereishit Rabbah* and *Targum Yonatan* there) explains that "The shepherds of Lot were evil, and would pasture their flocks in others' fields, and Abraham's shepherds rebuked them for their theft."

402 *Shulĥan Aruĥ Ĥoshen Mishpat* 394:3 – "One who stands up his animal by another person's grain pile is considered as if he is directly causing damage."

403 Rambam *ibid.* ch. 5; *Shulĥan Aruĥ ibid.* ch. 409.

404 It appears that a Gentile is liable for causing damage in this way, as explained in topic 21 above. Even if one sends his animal to harm Person A, and the animal of its own accord harms Person B instead, he is obligated to pay for the damage – for both personal injury and damage to property.

405 See Tractate *Avodah Zarah* 59b; Rambam, *Laws of Forbidden Foods* 13:28; and *Shulĥan Aruĥ Yoreh De'ah* ch. 132: if a Gentile poured a Jew's *kosher* wine which had not been boiled, the Jew may demand from him the value of this wine that was thereby rendered forbidden for Jews. See *Ĥatam Sofer* on *Avodah Zarah* there and *Aĥiezer* 3:37, that as this is an indirect damage for which a Gentile would be liable if he did it intentionally. Also see

before it was sealed, or after it was unsealed, if it had not been boiled (*mevushal* in Hebrew) beforehand. Therefore, it is forbidden for a Gentile to cause a Jew a financial loss by picking up or carrying the Jew's unboiled *kosher* wine if it is unsealed, since damage will be caused to the Jew in that his wine will thereby be rendered forbidden for him to drink. This applies even though there is no physical damage done, and the Jew's loss is only based on a decree of Scriptural or Rabbinical Torah Law. Therefore, Gentiles are forbidden to cause damage of this nature as well.

It is likewise forbidden for a Jew to eat meat that is not *kosher* according to Torah Law. It is therefore forbidden for a Gentile to switch his piece of non-*kosher* meat with a Jew's similar-looking piece of *kosher* meat, even though the damage to the Jew within Torah Law is not physically recognizable.

24. If one caused damage to another, even though the perpetrator gave full compensation in all five categories of damage, he still does not receive atonement from God until he appeases the one who was damaged, and he asks for forgiveness and receives it.[406] The same applies to one who embarrasses or pains another, even when there is no obligation to pay compensation. See topic 6 above.[407]

However, if one damages another's possessions, once he gives compensation for all damages, his liability is discharged, and within Torah Law he is not obligated to ask for forgiveness.[408]

---

the Appendix in this work, topic 17 and the footnote there.

[406] Rambam, *Laws of Injury* 5:9, *Shulĥan Aruĥ Ĥoshen Mishpat* ch. 422.

[407] Rambam, *Laws of Repentance* 2:9.

[408] Rambam *Laws of Injury* 5:9.

CHAPTER 12

The Laws of a Delinquent Debtor and One Who Withholds Payment Owed to a Hired Person

1. A *debtor* is a person who has a legal financial obligation to pay money or goods to someone else (who could be an individual or a corporation). A *delinquent debtor* is someone who does not pay his financial obligation when the contracted time for payment arrives. (For example: someone who does not repay a loan that is due, or does not pay money in exchange for an object that was given to him for safekeeping but he lost it, or does not pay a hired worker who demands payment for work that he did.)

If a delinquent debtor has the ability to pay what he owes but he does not, he transgresses the prohibition of theft.[409] This especially applies to someone who succeeds in not paying a debt because he is stronger than the creditor.[410] It also applies to someone who does not have enough money to pay the debt, but he has possessions he could sell in order to do so. (However, if someone keeps an object that was deposited with him to watch over, or denies ever receiving the object, he has committed an act of outright theft.)

If the debtor lacks the resources to pay his commitment, there is no transgression. This also applies if he has the funds available but he requests additional time to pay, and he receives the permission to delay his payment.

If the debtor constantly pushes off the lender to come back later, and has no intention of actually paying him, he is considered a delinquent debtor, even if he does not say expressly that he will not pay.[411] Needless to say, if one denies a debt that he owes – whether he denies

---

[409] This is based on Rambam, *Laws of Kings* 9:9, that a person who withholds a worker's pay is committing theft. He is considered a delinquent debtor. This is clear from *Kesef Mishneh* there, and Rashi on *Sanhedrin* 57a, and *Sefer HaĤinuĥ* Commandment 228. Ramban writes on Genesis 34:13 that this is a capital sin for Gentiles, as is written in *Minĥat Ĥinuĥ* there.

[410] Rambam, *Laws of Robbery* 1:4, *Tur* and *Shulĥan Aruĥ Ĥoshen Mishpat* ch. 359.

[411] *Sefer HaĤinuĥ* Commandment 228 and *Shulĥan Aruĥ HaRav Hilĥot Gezelah* topic 4.

the existence of the debt or his contract for work that was done for him, or falsely says that he has already paid and has no further obligation – he is considered a delinquent debtor.[412]

2. If a person is in a partnership and he refuses to return the partner's money when he is obligated to do so,[413] he is considered a delinquent debtor. Likewise, anyone who hires a person or rents an animal, vessels or a house, etc., and withholds due payment, is a delinquent debtor.[414]

3. Someone who accepts a service which requires payment (such as travel by bus), and does not pay, is a thief if the payment was required before the service. If the payment is required after the service, he is a delinquent debtor.[415]

If a person bought something on credit (so the sale price remains as a loan to the buyer), and he did not pay the debt at the agreed time, he is a delinquent debtor as long as the full amount remains unpaid. If he cheats the seller on the amount, giving only less than they agreed, he has committed theft, because the seller did not intend at all to give a reduction on the price.[416]

4. A delinquent debtor or one who does not pay a worker is not liable for capital punishment from a court (for theft) unless the person owed demands the money[417] and then the debtor refuses to pay or denies the claim. Nevertheless, even if the person owed does not demand payment, the debtor transgresses the prohibition against being a

---

[412] *Sefer HaĤinuĥ ibid.* and *Sefer HaMitzvot* Negative Commandment 247.

[413] See Rambam *Laws of Robbery* 7:2.

[414] Rambam *Laws of Kings* 9:9 and *Kesef Mishneh* there.

[415] Rabbi Zalman Nehemiah Goldberg notes that if the person decided not to pay at the time he stepped into the bus, it seems that he transgressed the prohibition of robbery at that point, because he would not have been allowed on the bus to begin with if the driver would have known about his plan.

[416] *Shulĥan Aruĥ HaRav Hilĥot Gezelah* topic 4.

[417] This is implied from the wording of Rambam *Laws of Robbery* 1:4 – "when payment was demanded, he forcefully refused to pay." For a Jew as well, the offense takes effect when payment is demanded but he refuses, as explained in *Shulĥan Aruĥ Ĥoshen Mishpat* 339:10.

delinquent debtor as long as he is in violation of his obligation to pay.[418]

However, if the debtor only pushes off the lender to lengthen the time of the loan, and he does not intend to deny or to hold on to the owed money, there is no liability (for capital punishment) for delinquency.[419] Nevertheless, such a thing is forbidden as theft, as the debtor is stealing the lender's livelihood, and many times this turns into a perpetually delinquent debt, due to unpreventable circumstances that happen to the debtor or the person owed giving up on his payment. Regarding this, it is stated,[420] "Do not tell your fellow, 'Go and return, and tomorrow I will give,' though you have it with you."[421]

One who withholds a payment that he is obligated in, or a loan after the due date, transgresses the prohibition against theft from the owner of the money[422] (but he is not liable for capital punishment).

5. One who employs a worker or rents a house or the like is obligated to pay by the stipulated time, and if he pushes off the payment and does not pay, he transgresses the prohibition of being a delinquent debtor, even if the payment was not demanded.[423] If no payment date was set between them, the time for payment is based on the customary payment schedule in that country.

If a worker demands his payment (or even if he did not expressly demand it, and only came to the employer[424] and it is clear that he intends that the employer should pay him), and the employer has the money available but he delays paying to gain time with his money or

---

418 See *Piŝhei Teshuva Ĥoshen Mishpat* 339:7 regarding the Jewish prohibition against withholding payment. It is clear that the same applies to a delinquent debtor.

419 *Kesef Mishneh, Laws of Rental,* beginning of ch. 11, and *Sefer Meirat Einayim Ĥoshen Mishpat* 339:1 in reference to Jews. The same law applies to Gentiles.

420 Proverbs 3:28.

421 Tractate *Bava Metzia* 111a; Rambam, *Laws of Rentals* ch, 11; *Shulĥan Aruĥ Ĥoshen Mishpat* ch. 339; *Shulĥan Aruĥ HaRav Hilĥot She'ilah v'Seĥirut* topic 14.

422 *Bayit Chadash Ĥoshen Mishpat* end of ch. 38.

423 See *Minĥat Ĥinuĥ* Commandment 220..

424 See *Ahavat Ĥesed* ch. 9 and *Netiv HaĤesed* topic 29.

to cause anguish to the worker (or if a renter does the same to a landlord to whom he owes a rent payment), he transgresses the injunction, "Do not tell your fellow, 'Go and return, and tomorrow I will give,' though you have it with you."

If a debtor has the money to pay but he needs to delay because he is too busy at that moment, he may push off giving the payment until a more convenient time. This does not fall under the prohibition "Do not tell your fellow, 'Go and return' ...," because he is not pushing off payment to gain time with his money, but rather because he is temporarily too busy.[425]

6. These rules also apply for one is holding on to an object that was left with him for safekeeping, or who borrows a vessel for a set time. If the owner asks for it to be returned, and the one holding the object continues to do so for undue reasons, he transgresses the prohibition of theft since he causes a loss to the owner of the item and causes him anguish needlessly.[426]

7. A person who leaves his vessel with a craftsman to be fixed is not obligated to pay for the work done until the craftsman informs him that he is finished and returns the vessel. As long as the vessel remains in the craftsman's hands (since it is comparable to an object left for safeguarding), the owner does not transgress the prohibition "Do not tell your fellow, 'Go and return' ...," by withholding the payment, even if the craftsman demands to be paid.[427]

Likewise, if one gave the worker or craftsman a deposit for his work, he does not transgress the prohibition of being a delinquent debtor if he does not pay on time. The same applies to one who leaves collateral for a loan that he must repay (and the collateral is worth the full

---

[425] *Shulĥan Aruĥ Ĥoshen Mishpat* 339:7 and *Shulĥan Aruĥ Harav Hilĥot She'ilah v'Seĥirut* topic 14.

[426] See *Shulĥan Aruĥ Ĥoshen Mishpat* ch. 294 and *Ketzot HaĤoshen* there, and Responsa of Maharit on *Ĥoshen Mishpat* topic 88, who say that one who withholds returning an item for safekeeping is not a thief. Surely they intend that although this person is not liable to the same punishment as a thief, it is surely forbidden, as explained in *Bayit Chadash ibid.*

[427] *Shulĥan Aruĥ Ĥoshen Mishpat* 339:6 and *Shulĥan Aruĥ HaRav Hilĥot She'ilah v'Seĥirut* topic 13.

amount of the loan): if he leaves the collateral in the hands of the lender, then even if he intends not to repay, he is not liable as a delinquent debtor.[428]

However, if one asks a craftsman to make a vessel for him and he does not pay for it, but instead leaves it in the hands of the craftsman, he is liable as a delinquent debtor. The fact that the craftsman holds the vessel holds no bearing, because the person who requested the vessel is withholding the payment from the craftsman.

8. Any case of delinquent payment – such as one who bought merchandise on credit and did not pay, or took a loan and did not repay it, or did not pay a debt incurred for contracting workers – is forbidden to be committed even if the amount being withheld from payment is less than the value of a *perutah* (the coin of smallest value that is in current circulation in that country).[429]

Another opinion is that a Gentile is not liable to capital punishment for delinquent repayment of a debt or loan that is less than a *perutah*, and that it is not comparable to theft which is forbidden for even less than a *perutah* since the victim's money comes into the thief's possession illegally.[430]

9. It appears that a Noahide court can judge all kinds of delinquent payment, even if the dispute is over less than a *perutah*, and force the delinquent debtor to repay his debt.

How would such a case be judged? The one who has the claim against the other would demand it in the court, and the judge would rule on whether the defendant is liable or exempt. If he is found liable, the judge would tell him that he must pay the specified amount. The judge would set a time limit for the payment to be made, or he would decide that the violator must pay immediately. If after the judgment, the violator clearly refused to follow the sentence of the court, he would be liable to capital punishment for theft.

---

[428] *Sefer Meirat Einayim Ĥoshen Mishpat* 339:10; *Shulĥan Aruĥ HaRav ibid.*

[429] This is the implication of Rambam and *Kesef Mishneh, Laws of Kings* 9:9, that any delinquent debtor commits theft, and a Gentile is even liable for this when it involves an amount less than the value of a *perutah*.

[430] *Or HaĤayim* on Genesis 6:11.

10. A delinquent debtor or one who withholds payment for a rental is not forgiven by God until he repays his debt and appeases the other person for the anguish he caused him.[431]

11. In view of the above Torah laws regarding delinquent debtors, questions arise as to whether it is permissible for a person (or possibly for a corporation) to declare "bankruptcy" on his own initiative. By this we mean that he obtains a legal ruling (based on the civil laws of his government) that he cannot repay his full debts to all of his creditors, and the court then absolves him (within the civil law) from paying his debts in full.

If he does not have enough money to pay his debts, and the government's laws permit him to declare bankruptcy, it appears that it would be permissible to do so. And since the law of the government cancels part of his debts, he is thus henceforth exempt from paying in accordance with the court's decision. The rationale for this is that since the government has the power to render a person's money ownerless,[432] his financial obligation to his lenders or creditors has been eliminated to the extent that the court decided. Even if he later becomes wealthy, his previous lenders or creditors have already despaired of collecting his monetary debt because of the legal power of the court.

However, if he has more monetary resources available than the lesser amount that he claims, and that the court therefore orders him to pay, and he uses this bankruptcy law (in a fraudulent manner) to defraud any of his lenders or creditors, then this is cheating. and he is liable for transgressing the Noahide prohibition of theft. In this case, even if he was legally successful in obtaining a declaration of bankruptcy from the court, and consequently his lenders or creditors have despaired of receiving the full amount of the money he owed them (since they are no longer able to demand it from him in court), nevertheless, from God's perspective he is stealing, and he remains obligated to repay his debts in full.

---

[431] *Sefer HaĤinuĥ* Commandment 228.

[432] The authority of the court to declare a person's money ownerless stems from the scope of the Torah law that "the law of the land is the law" *(dina de'malĥuta dina)*, as explained in *Sheva Mitzvos HaShem* Part VIII *(Dinim)*, topic 15:13.

CHAPTER 13

The Laws of a Worker in Regard to the Employer

1. Anyone who is hired for a job needs to keep day and evening hours (the number of work hours per day, and when the work day starts and ends) according to the customary practice of workers who do that type of job in that area. This is because an employer hires workers based on his assumption that they will follow this customary practice. Likewise, a teacher needs to work in the customary way of other teachers in the area, starting and finishing at the normally scheduled times.[433]

2. A worker is obligated not to leave his work unfinished nor waste his work time. He should be meticulous in using the time appropriated. This means that if his employer obligates him to work for a certain amount of time, he cannot waste this time and, in doing so, neglect the work that the employer needs to have done.[434] Nevertheless, he may take time for breaks and to eat, according to the custom of that area.

If an employer hired a worker to do a specific task but did not give him the work to do, or told him to do a task but it was already finished, the above rule does not apply. Nevertheless, the worker is obligated to inform the employer that he is waiting for the work, or that the work was finished, respectively.

3. One may not use his work animal for his own work at night and then rent it out during the day, because this weakens the animal and it therefore cheats the person who is paying to use it. Likewise, a worker may not starve or otherwise afflict himself because his strength will weaken, and he will not be able to work with his full strength. Likewise, a teacher needs to be careful in this matter, and he may not stay awake too much at night because that will cause him to be sluggish in his teaching during the day. For the same reason, he may not overeat, because that will also cause him to be tired and sluggish.

It is forbidden for a teacher to be involved with any other work while he is teaching. Likewise, one who is hired to work in a store (to be a

---

[433] See *Shulĥan Aruĥ Ĥoshen Mishpat* ch. 331; *Shulĥan Aruĥ HaRav Hilĥot She'ilah* topic 10.

[434] *Shulĥan Aruĥ ibid.* ch. 337; *Shulĥan Aruĥ HaRav ibid.* topic 20.

salesperson or to do other types of work) may not be involved in any unrelated work even when no customers are there, because that will distract him from watching what is happening in the store.[435]

4. If someone makes only a verbal agreement to hire a worker to do a job, or to hire a contractor to do some work, either of the parties can unilaterally retract the agreement, and the other one can have no claim (since they did not make a legally binding agreement).

In this case, even if the worker went to the work site and waited one or two hours for the employer to give him the job to do, the employer can still retract. The employer will have no obligation at all if the worker can then find other work and will therefore not have a loss. But if the worker cannot find other work that day, or only some work that will pay less, or if the available work will not provide him with payment that day (if that is what the employer promised, or if that is the custom in that area), the employer must reimburse him for this loss.[436]

5. One of the parties to a work agreement can unilaterally retract only if they did not make a binding agreement. If they did make a binding agreement (for example, if the employer gave the worker an advance payment of part of his salary, or a retainer fee, or they signed a contract), neither of them have legal permission to unilaterally retract from the commitment. If either one does this, he must pay financial compensation.[437] (Needless to say, if the worker then retracted, in any case he must at least return any money that he was given in advance as a down-payment or a retainer fee.)

As well, if any worker or contractor starts the work set out for him, he is considered as having made a formalized legally binding agreement, and this makes both sides responsible for completing the agreed-upon work and payment.[438]

6. An agricultural worker is forbidden to eat from the produce he is working with, whether it is still attached to the ground or it is

---

[435] *Ibid.*

[436] *Shulĥan Aruĥ Ĥoshen Mishpat* ch. 333.

[437] See *Tur* and Rema *Ĥoshen Mishpat* 333:1.

[438] *Maggid Mishneh Hilĥot Seĥirut* ch. 9 as brought in the *Beit Yosef*; Rivash and Shaĥ *Ĥoshen Mishpat* 333:14.

detached, without the knowledge and permission of the owner, and needless to say he may not collect from the produce and place it in his own vessels (i.e., to take it for himself). If a worker takes produce from a field or orchard without the knowledge of the owner (even if it is a small amount which he knows that the owner would not mind),[439] this is considered theft.[440]

Likewise, a worker is not permitted to use the hirer's work tools without his permission. For example, a worker at a factory may not use the factory phone without the owner's permission.

7. A Gentile is not obligated to allow his hired worker, or his working animal, to eat from his produce that is being worked on in his field. Nevertheless, it is an attribute of kindness for him to allow this during the time of the labor if it involves cutting, threshing, harvesting or similar types of work with edible produce, which is the way that a Jew is commanded: "You shall not muzzle an ox while it threshes."[441]

8. If any craftsman received a solid piece of material from a customer who commissioned him to make a vessel from it, and he has some leftover material when he finishes the work, he must return to the customer any pieces which a person would normally be fastidious about. If he does not do so, he has committed theft. But if it is not the way of the people in that area to be fastidious about this, he may keep the leftover pieces for himself.

For example, a tailor who has a little leftover material from what was provided to him to make some clothing, or a carpenter who has small nails or screws left over from what was provided to him to make a piece of furniture, may keep those materials if it is not the way of people to be fastidious about them.[442]

---

439 See Tractate *Sanhedrin* 26b, Rambam *Laws of Testimony* 10:5, and footnote 34 above.

440 See Shaĥ *Ĥoshen Mishpat* 333:1, and *Shulĥan Aruĥ HaRav Hilĥot She'ilah* topic 29, from which it is apparent that if a Gentile field-worker eats from the produce of the field, but the Gentile field-owner is particular about him not eating and has no obligation to feed him, he would be committing theft, whether it is during or after the time he is working.

441 Deuteronomy 25:4.

442 *Shulĥan Aruĥ HaRav Hilĥot Gezelah* topic 22.

CHAPTER 14

Government Authority; Laws of Land Conquered in War

1. Who is considered a valid king? A person who is appointed or accepted[443] by a majority of the citizens of the country to rule over them. If a valid king establishes a valid law for all the citizens of the country, they are legally bound to follow it.[444] But if someone rules over a nation or a part of a nation despotically, he and all his officials are considered like a band of robbers, whose laws are not binding (and any taxes that he takes are theft on his part).[445]

Even though wars of aggressive conquest over other nations are forbidden as theft for Gentile governments[446] (as opposed to wars of self-defense, which are permitted), the land which a valid king conquered in any type of war is fully considered to be his acquisition. Therefore everyone in the vanquished land must follow the laws of the king who conquered them, the same as if they had willingly accepted his kingship, even though they fell under his rule through conquest, and the king's taxes that he applies to them are not considered theft.[447]

---

443 *For example, it may be a tradition in a country that once a king is established as the ruler, one of his children will inherit that position after him, and the people will automatically accept him as their new king. If it is the custom of a country that they will accept a woman to rule over them as their queen, she assumes all the traditional powers and status of a "king."

444 *It must be remembered that God, Who is the King of the universe, constantly watches and judges the actions of every person. Even if a government and the majority or the entirety of a society will decide to make laws that permit acts which are always forbidden by Torah Law, such as types of murder or forbidden relations, there is no substance to those laws in God's eyes, and there is no permission to engage in those "legal" activities. See topic 10:4 above.

445 Rambam, *Laws of Robbery* 5:11-18; *Shulĥan Aruĥ Ĥoshen Mishpat* ch. 369.

446 See *Sheva Mitzvot HaShem*, Part VIII, ch. 16, and *Ĥatam Sofer Ĥoshen Mishpat* Responsa 54.

447 See Rambam: *Laws of Robbery* ch. 5 and *Laws of Slaves* ch. 9; *Shulĥan Aruĥ HaRav: Hilĥot Hefker* topic 3 and *Hilĥot Gezelah* topic 15; and *Oraĥ Ĥayim* 649:10.

2. Any governing body chosen or appointed by the people of a country has the same authority as a king. Therefore, any country (or province, state, or city within a country) that is run by a government is under the rule of the "king."[448] Any place in this chapter where the word "king" is written, it refers to the local, regional and national governing bodies, and "the laws made by the king" are binding laws.

3. The laws of the king are only binding regarding a matter that is equally incumbent upon the whole population, such as a tax which falls on everyone equally (or in which the percentage taken is based on defined ranges of income levels or property ownership). If, however, the king rules that only a specific person or ethnic group is required to pay a certain tax, this law is not legally binding, and is only extortion and robbery.

Likewise, a government law is binding if it concerns a matter that has benefit for the king or is good for the country as a whole, but not if it was made for the sake of a specific matter between two people.[449]

Therefore, if the king decreed that someone who violates a certain rule will have his property seized, and he enforces this, another person may buy such property from the king since it was taken lawfully. However, if the king forcefully took property and his action was not based on laws that are binding on all the citizens, it is robbery. Therefore, it is forbidden to buy that property from the king, and one who does so does not lawfully own it, since property cannot be acquired through theft, as explained above in Chapter 8.[450]

4. If a king gets angry at one of the citizens of his country (for defying

---

[448] This is clear, as the reason that the laws of the king are legally binding is because his authority was accepted by the people of the country, as explained in the wording of the aforementioned Rambam, *Laws of Robbery*. This is also obvious from Rashbam *Bava Batra* 54b and Ritva *Bava Batra* 55a in the name of Ramban, who say that a new decree of the king is not legally binding until the majority of the country's people accept it. This would be the case with any governing group for whom the people of the country accept their rules.

[449] *Shulĥan Aruĥ* and Rema *Ĥoshen Mishpat* ch. 369, *Shulĥan Aruĥ HaRav Hilĥot Gezelah* topic 19.

[450] Rambam *Laws of Robbery* ch. 5; *Shulĥan Aruĥ Ĥoshen Mishpat* ch. 369.

him or the like,[451] meaning that his anger is justified based on the laws and conduct of kings), so he took the person's field, house, or other possessions, this is not considered theft. Others are permitted to have benefit from this property and to buy it, and the original owner can have no claim against them for this acquisition. It is the right of a king to take the possessions of a citizen who disobeys or defies him (if the nation's law allows this), and this is lawfully binding and not theft.[452]

5. One who evades taxes levied by the king is a thief, as he is stealing from the money of the government.

A question may be raised, based on what was explained in topic 5:12 above, that cheating is only forbidden when one buys something from another and does not pay for it, but that which is only the error of the seller does not involve any prohibition of cheating. Seemingly, also in tax evasion, a person is not giving exactly complete information about his property and business, and therefore, could a person claim that the government is taking a mistaken amount, so it is not forbidden to cheat by not paying the full tax?

The answer is that all the land of the country is considered as if it belongs to the king and is subservient to him, so a tax evader is considered as having stolen an existent item that belongs to the king, and he is actually a thief, not just a cheater.[453]

6. If one is required to pay a tax, he may not conceal his required tax money from tax collectors who are employed by the government, if they are working lawfully and not stealing.

If a tax collector is illegally taking more money than the tax that is due and keeping that for himself, without permission from the king (i.e. he takes more than the amount that is allotted to him by the king), this is utter theft. It is therefore permissible to hide the portion of the money that is being demanded unlawfully.

---

[451] See *Piŝhei Teshuva Ĥoshen Mishpat* there, topic 1.

[452] Rambam and *Shulĥan Aruĥ Ĥoshen Mishpat*, *ibid.*

[453] See Rambam *Laws of Robbery* 5:11 ("He steals the portion of the king"), *Shulĥan Aruĥ Ĥoshen Mishpat* 369:6, and *Shulĥan Aruĥ HaRav Hilĥot Gezelah* topic 15, that for a Gentile this is considered complete theft, not just pushing off a loan. For a Gentile, pushing off payment of a loan is considered delinquency, and is forbidden.

Any possessions that tax collectors seize unlawfully are considered to be stolen, and it is forbidden for others to benefit from them.[454] The same applies to property that is seized unlawfully by a policeman.

7. If tax collectors seized someone's animal or possessions and offered him a substitute, it is permitted for him to accept the substituted item from them. For if they are doing so lawfully, it is clearly permitted, and even if this was done unlawfully, and they are thieves, nevertheless, the original owner of the substituted item has already despaired of recovering his object, which was surely also stolen by the unlawful tax collector. The person thus receives ownership of the substituted item through the original owner's despair and the change of jurisdiction (see topic 3:17 above). However, one who wishes to be scrupulous and go beyond the letter of the law should act piously and return any item for which he knows its rightful owner, in order not to benefit from stolen possessions.[455]

8. A king may demolish private houses or take parts of private fields to build a needed wall or a road, and this is not considered theft, because it is the law of the government that this is done for the benefit of the country.

Likewise, if the king establishes a law that any citizen who does a certain crime will be sold as a slave, this law is legally binding.[456]

9. Any country conquered in war is the acquisition of the conquering king, and the king may do whatever he wishes with this land – to sell it to whomever he sees fit, or give it as a gift, and even to enslave the inhabitants, and this is not considered theft, since the conquest by the king is as a full acquisition.[457] Therefore (as explained above in topic 1), any decree made by the king for a land he conquered is legally binding, and the inhabitants of that land are obligated to accept the decree, because they are essentially subservient to him.

---

[454] See Rambam and *Shulĥan Aruĥ*, *ibid.*; *Shulĥan Aruĥ HaRav Hilĥot Gezelah* topics 15,16.

[455] Rambam and *Shulĥan Aruĥ*, *ibid.* See *Shulĥan Aruĥ HaRav Hilĥot Gezelah* topic 14.

[456] Rambam and *Shulĥan Aruĥ*, *ibid.*

[457] Based on the references in footnote 447 above.

10. Any area in a country that is not private property, such as streets and highways, city squares, rivers, forests, deserts, lakes, and the like, is the property of the nation's king (or government), and he may do whatever he desires with it.[458] Therefore, any privilege over such property that the king assigns to a specific person (or corporation), such as renting a forest to someone for cutting lumber, or a desert for excavating ore, or a river or lake to catch fish, and all similar privileges – whether the king rents them out, sells them completely or gives them as a gift – is considered to be under the full ownership and/or jurisdiction of this individual, and anyone who benefits from such places without the consent of the king's assigned owner or renter is stealing.[459]

However, a non-private area which a king acquired through conquest but left ownerless, and as of yet did not exercise his privilege to own it (such as a forest, a river, wilderness land, or other area that is open for communal use), is considered completely ownerless, and anyone is permitted to benefit from it. This is not considered stealing from the king, as long as the king has not done any action or showed his desire to make the conquered area forbidden to be used by others, and he has not sold, gifted or rented it to anyone.

By contrast, any private property in an area which a king conquered remains in the jurisdiction of the private owners, so long as the king has not exercised his right to seize it for himself. No one other than the conquering king has permission to remove property from the ownership of the private individuals in the conquered area.[460]

---

[458] *For the great majority of the nations that have coastlines, the width of the coastal waters over which they have claimed sovereignty is 12 nautical miles (22.2 km) or less, and their claims for limited control and economic rights typically extend farther.

For more information, see https://en.wikipedia.org/wiki/Territorial_waters. The law of a nation *(dina de'malĥuta)* is binding on its own citizens regarding control of its coastal waters, but not on citizens of another nation, unless the two nations have mutually accepted a law (a treaty) about this, e.g. an international standard definition. But if there is no treaty, one nation (and its citizens) are not obligated (at their own risk) by the coastal-water claims of the other nation.

[459] *Shulĥan Aruĥ HaRav Hilĥot Hefker* topic 3.

[460] *If a king declares that the people in an area he conquered are his slaves (see topic 9), he acquires ownership of their private property.

CHAPTER 15

Laws of Ownerless Items and Finding Lost Objects

1. A person may declare any item or money he possesses to be ownerless, which he does by removing it from his property and saying "this item is ownerless." At that point his jurisdiction leaves from the item, and any person who wishes to claim it may do so. He need not necessarily mention this with his mouth; as long as his actions show that he does not desire the item anymore, it becomes ownerless.[461] Likewise, any item that can be assumed to be ownerless, such as an item lying in an open-access public garbage heap, is considered ownerless, and anyone can claim it.[462]

Likewise, a person can declare his land or house ownerless,[463] through abandoning them and leaving them deserted and open for all. Then anyone who wishes to lay claim to the house or land may do so.

How can a person lay claim to an ownerless item? If he wishes to acquire a movable object, once he raises it from the ground or drags it into his property, he acquires it.

With Torah law, one can only acquire abandoned landed property through an act of manifesting ownership (*chazakah* in Hebrew). This is accomplished by doing any positive beneficial action that is recognized as demonstrating one's jurisdiction over the property, such as fencing in a plot of land, or making a useful opening in an existing fence (e.g., for a gate), or affixing a lock to the door of a house.[464] However, if there is a law made by the government that one can only have jurisdiction over landed property with a document or a registered filing for the asset under his name, this law is binding, and until this has been accomplished there can be no complete legal jurisdiction.[465]

One who sees an item that can be acquired, or a lost object, and only

---

[461] Shaĥ *Ĥoshen Mishpat* ch. 261.

[462] See Rema *Ĥoshen Mishpat* 260:11.

[463] *Shulĥan Aruĥ Ĥoshen Mishpat* ch. 273.

[464] Rambam, *Laws of Sales* 1:8-16.

[465] See Rambam, *Laws of Acquisition and Gifts* 1:15.
Rabbi Zalman Nehemiah Goldberg comments that Rambam is speaking there about a case in which a Jew buys landed property from a Gentile. By Torah law, acquisition of landed property by a Gentile is accomplished by payment.

calls out "I wish to acquire it!" or a similar statement, does not gain jurisdiction over the item.[466] The only ways to establish ownership are those described above; see topic 16:6 below.

2. Public deserts, forests, rivers, lakes, oceans, and any things in them are deemed ownerless. Since they are not under the jurisdiction of any specific person, no one is able to have any claim over anything in these places. Only the king or government of the country can claim jurisdiction over these places, as explained in the previous chapter (topic 14:10) Therefore, it is permitted for anyone to harvest fruits from a public forest or to trap animals, fowl or fish in these places (subject to the government's regulations), since from the outset they do not belong to anyone.[467] If, however, the king sold such an area to a specific person (or a corporation), or gave it as a present or rented it out, it belongs to that person, and anyone else who then takes something of value from there is considered to be committing theft.[468]

If the king (or the government) forbids or limits trapping, fishing, or logging, etc., in an ownerless area, it is a binding law. That activity is then also correspondingly forbidden or limited by Torah law, because violating it would be theft from the king.[469]

3. If an object or money is found deserted in a public place (e.g., on a street), and there is no indication of whom the owner is, one can assume that the owner has declared it ownerless or has despaired of recovering it. Therefore, it is considered to be an ownerless object.

Likewise, it is possible that the government will see a need to require a document of acquisition to complete the transfer of ownership [whereas in Torah law, the acquisition of land by a Jew is accomplished when he does an act of manifesting ownership (*ĥazaka*)]. Rambam does not actually deal with the case of landed property that became ownerless, and it does not seem logical that a king would decree that one cannot acquire an ownerless landed property unless he has a document.

466 Rambam, *Laws of Robbery and Lost Property* 17:1; *Shulĥan Aruĥ Ĥoshen Mishpat* 273:11 and ch. 268.

467 Rambam, *Laws of Acquisition and Gifts* 1:1,2; *Shulĥan Aruĥ ibid.* ch. 273.

468 *Shulĥan Aruĥ HaRav*, *Laws of Ownerless Property and Invasion of Property* topics 2, 3.

469 This is explained in *Biur Halaĥa* (on *Mishna Berura Oraĥ Ĥayim*) 637:2.

This applies whether the object was abandoned willfully, or by coercion (for example, if robbers stole it and then threw it into another place, so the owner despaired). It is then permitted for any person who finds it to acquire it, which is accomplished by lifting it up or drawing it into his own property.

In regard to a **stolen** object, in general it can be assumed that the victim despairs of recovering it (even if he has a good identifying sign for it), for it is assumed that he does not know the identity of the person who stole it, and therefore he is not able to chase the person down and get his object back (see topic 2:4 above).[470] However, if a robber stole from someone and the victim knows who it was, so he is able to report him to the police, and if it is a place where it is usual for police and judges to recover stolen objects from robbers, then it is assumed that the owner has not despaired. But if the robbers are not known, or it is known that it will be impossible to regain the stolen object from the robber, it is assumed that the victim despaired of recovering it.[471]

4. A Gentile is not obligated to return a lost object that has not come into his hand.[472] Therefore, if he sees a lost object, even if he knows whom it belongs to, he is not required to return it to its rightful owner, or to inform the owner that it is in that specific place, even though this will cause a loss to the owner. Likewise, a Gentile is permitted to "cover his eyes" from a lost object (i.e., ignore the fact that it is lost) until he later hears that the owner despaired of finding it, and he can then pick it up and claim it for himself.

---

[470] See topic 2:4 above regarding the debate among the Sages about whether we assume that the average victim of theft despairs of recovering a stolen object. This has a practical application (as explained there) for whether one who buys the stolen object needs to return the object itself to the victim, or just its value. But it can be deduced that one who *finds* a stolen object need not return it, because he can rely on the opinion that the victim despaired. (The owner of a found stolen object cannot enforce his claim of ownership in a Torah-based court, since the debate about this in Torah law is unresolved).

[471] See *Shulĥan Aruĥ Ĥoshen Mishpat* ch. 368, and 369:5, regarding the law concerning extorters who took away a property.

[472] Rambam *Laws of Robbery* ch. 11; *Shulĥan Aruĥ Ĥoshen Mishpat* ch. 266; *Shulĥan Aruĥ HaRav Hilĥot Metzia* topic 38; responsa *Chavot Yair* ch. 79.

Moreover, if a Gentile found a lost object in a public or ownerless area and did not know whom the owner is, and he picked it up to acquire it for himself, then even if he found out later whom the owner was (after the owner despaired of recovering the object), he is not obligated to return it. This is because the prohibition of secretive theft by a Gentile only applies to stealing something from the land or a possession that the victim owns or rents – for example, his car or his vessels, or his clothing (i.e., a pickpocket). If the lost object is located on public or ownerless property, then anyone who finds it and permissibly raises it in order to acquire it (thinking that it is ownerless) is not stealing from another's property, and since he is not intending to acquire something that belongs to someone else, his act is not immoral.

5. Different considerations apply if the owner of the lost object did not yet despair of recovering it, and the finder takes it:

(a) Whenever the finder knows whom the owner is, if at some point he conceals the object from the owner with the intention to acquire it after he knows or can rightfully assume that the owner has despaired, he is acting immorally by intending to hide another person's property. Therefore, it seems that he is morally obligated in God's eyes to return the object (or to inform the owner that he has it and that it can be retrieved), even after he later finds out that the owner has despaired. If he does not fulfill this obligation, he is deemed sinful (see topic 8:17 above),[473] even though he has not committed theft.

---

[473] This appears clear from a law in Tractate *Kiddushin* 59: if a poor person is scrounging for a piece of food that he sees and is close to his reach, and a second person observes this and grabs it before the first person can reach it, the Talmud calls the second one an evil person. *A fortiori*, the same applies if someone is trying to recover his lost object, and another person hides it so he will acquire it after the owner despairs of finding it. See Rosh on *Kiddushin* (end of 3:2), that if a poor person is in the top of an olive tree cutting off ownerless olives for himself, whoever takes the olives that fall down is considered to be stealing (because it is a deviation from social norms; see topic 16:6 below), since the poor person is relying on being able to get them. This is also the ruling of *Shulĥan Aruĥ Ĥoshen Mishpat* ch. 370. Therefore, for the cases mentioned in the main text, one should return a found object to its owner if he knows who that is, in order to fulfill his obligation in God's eyes (even though that is not strictly required).

Furthermore, if the finder of a lost object keeps it for himself, he may not **use it** until he knows or can validly assume that the owner despaired. If it is an animal, he must care for it properly during this interim time. In order to pay for its food, if it is a work animal, he may hire it out, and if it is a poultry bird that lays eggs, he may sell its eggs. If he pays from his own resources, he may demand reimbursement from the owner when the owner makes his claim. If it is produce that begins to spoil, it may be sold. The money from sold produce, or the excess money from the hire of the animal or the sale of the eggs, may be used by the finder as a loan from the owner, until the owner makes his claim or he has despaired.[474]

(b) If the finder does not know whom the owner is at the time he takes the object, and then at a later time he learns whom the owner is and that the owner had already despaired, the finder is not obligated in God's eyes to return it.

6. If a lost item is found on someone else's private property, and the finder knows that it doesn't belong to the person who owns that property, the finder has no right to take and claim it, since the owner of the private property should acquire it when the person who lost it despairs of regaining it. But if the finder had taken it, once the person who lost it despaired, (and the property owner never acquired it) – after the fact it seems that neither the former owner nor the property owner can claim the object from the finder.[475]

7. When does one acquire a lost object that he found?

If any lost object is found in a public area with many Gentile passersby, whether the object has an identifying mark or not, it can be assumed that the owner has despaired of recovering it. This applies if the Gentiles (who are the majority in that area) are known to keep the lost objects they find, so therefore it is likely that the owner has assumed that a passerby has found and kept the object, and that it won't be returned (as explained below in topics 11 and 12). Because it is assumed that the owner despaired, the object is considered to be ownerless, as explained above, and it is permitted for anyone to take it

[474] Rambam, *Laws of Robbery and Lost Property* 11:14, 13:15-17,19.

[475] See topic 16:3, and Rambam *Laws of Robbery and Lost Property* 17:8-9.

and keep it as their acquired object.

Even if the finder knows the owner at the time he raises the object that he found in this type of public area, it is clear that it is permitted for him to take it in order to acquire it for himself due to the owner's assumed despair, and this is not considered to be theft. (But as explained in topic 5, if the finder knows that this owner did **not yet** despair, and he nevertheless hides the object until the owner despairs, he is sinful. Even so, after the owner eventually despairs – at which point the finder acquires the object – a Torah-based court cannot force the finder to return it.)

If someone who lost an object **despaired of recovering it**, which makes the object ownerless, he is forbidden to forcibly take it back from someone who finds it, because he would be stealing it from the finder who legally acquired it.

However, if the owner of the lost object **has not despaired** (as explained below in topics 11 and 12), and he demands the object back from the finder – after proving his ownership with his knowledge of identifying marks, or with witnesses who saw him drop the object – by Torah law the finder must return it (since he only acquires the object when the owner has despaired of recovering it, thereby rendering it ownerless). In this case, after the owner has proven his ownership and that he did not despair, if the finder then continues to hold the object and does not return it, the finder is considered to be a robber. (If the owner takes this case to a court and proves his continuing ownership, then if the court is unable to recover the object for the owner, he is permitted to take it forcefully from this robber. This is a situation in which a person may take the law into his own hands; see Chapter 4.)

8. If a finder raised a lost object with intention to return it to the owner (whether or not he knew who the owner is), when does he acquire it?

If he subsequently found out that the owner had already despaired of recovering it at the time it was found, then by default he has already acquired the object that had been in an ownerless state, because the owner's despair is the decisive factor. (After that happens, the one who lost it cannot lawfully demand that it be returned, because the finder was not serving as a guardian or an acquirer of the object on his behalf).[476]

---

[476] Responsa *Beit Shlomo*, vol. I, *Oraĥ Ĥayim* ch. 57.

Even if at the time the finder raises the object, he knows whom the owner is and picks it up for the purpose of returning it, but then later he changes his mind and decides to keep the object concealed from the owner (in order to acquire it later after the owner despairs), this is not considered forbidden theft, and the owner cannot legally demand it from the finder after he despaired. (Regarding the finder's moral obligation in this case to return the object, see topic 5 above.)

9. Everything above regarding returning a lost object is explaining either the basic required Torah law or the clear moral obligation for Gentiles. However, whenever the finder knows whom the owner is, it is pious to go beyond the letter of the law and return the lost object, or inform the owner, in any case. By doing this, a person will be promoting the ways of peace and an ethical society. It not only avoids situations that can cause hostility between people, but it also goes beyond this and increases friendship and love.

If one needs to spend money in order to inform the owner, he may charge the owner compensation for his expenditures,[477] up to the value of the object.

However, if the owner of the lost object is a wicked evildoer, it is not considered an act of righteousness to return his lost objects to him, for in doing so, the finder would be strengthening those who do evil.[478]

10. In a place where the government requires people to return a lost object even if the owner has despaired of recovering it, this is a binding law.[479] In this case, one who does not return a lost object is considered to be holding stolen property in his hand,[480] and even after the owner has despaired, the finder is considered to be withholding a

[477] It is clear that a Gentile is not obligated to put out effort for free to return a lost object, because he is not required to return it. Even a Jew who *is* required to return a lost object is only obligated to expend effort, but not money, as explained by Rambam, *Laws of Robbery and Lost Property* 13:15, and *Shulĥan Aruĥ HaRav Hilĥot Metziah* topic 33.

[478] See Rambam, *Laws of Robbery and Lost Property* 11:3.

[479] Rema *Ĥoshen Mishpat* 259:7.

[480] It is unclear if a Gentile is liable to capital punishment for this type of theft. Torah law says that this type of government law is binding, as explained in *Shulĥan Aruĥ HaRav Hilĥot Hefker* topic 3.

required payment.

11. There is a case in which it is assumed that a person has despaired of recovering an object that he lost. This applies if there is no identifying sign associated with the lost object, and therefore the owner has no way of proving that it is his. Even though it is possible that the owner will be identified at some point, nevertheless, a finder is permitted to take and acquire the object because of this assumption that it is ownerless (due to the owner's assumed despair). The finder is then not required to return it to the owner, even if he knows who the owner is. Even if the owner comes and claims that it belongs to him, he does not have authority to forcibly take the object from the finder.

There is also a case in which it is assumed that a person has **not** despaired of recovering a lost object, or a number of objects that he lost at one time. That is to say, it is assumed that he still maintains ownership of the thing he lost. This applies if:

(a) the object was lost in a field or a place where there are few people, so the owner still hopes to find it there when he will search for it, **and**

(b) it has a unique identifying sign: for example, by a mark or something else on it that is unique, or by its unique weight or dimensions, or its unique location, or – if it is a collection of items – the amount or types of the items, or how they are placed (such as a purse full of currency that can be identified by its physical construction and design, or the details of the money or other items in it).[481]

In this case, if the owner comes and demands the object from the finder, and he gives an identifying sign, it must be returned to him.

The result of a government law that the object must be returned is that it is still considered to be the property of the one who lost it, even if he despaired of recovering it. Based on this, a finder who disobeys the government's law to return the object is like one who hides an item for safekeeping and denies having it (as explained above in topic 7:14), and this is committing theft. Nevertheless, it appears that within Torah law he is exempt from punishment if the owner has despaired; although he is obligated to return the object if that is the government's law, it is not considered complete theft if he does not, since it did not come into his hand through stealing.

[481] Rambam, *Laws of Robbery and Lost Property* 13:5.

12. However, if an object was lost in a place like a busy city street, then even if the owner knows a clear identifying sign, it is assumed that he immediately despairs when he realizes that it is lost, because surely one of the many passersby will find it and take it for himself.

But if the busy place where the object was lost is in an area where the people are accustomed to returning lost objects to their owners, (such as in the streets of Jewish cities where most people do this, or if there is a civil law that people must return lost objects, or if most of the people are righteous Gentiles who take upon themselves to do this[482]), then if there are identifying signs for the object, it is assumed that the owner has not despaired, because he hopes that he will get it back.[483]

13. That which is explained above – that a lost object is considered to be ownerless if there is no identifying sign, or it was lost in a busy public area where most people take and don't return lost objects – is only an assumption. But if, in fact, the owner nevertheless does not despair, and he is searching for the object, then the object has not become ownerless *(hefker)*. In that case, a person who finds the object is not able to acquire it – even if it has no sign and it fell in a busy public place;[484] however, if the owner comes and demands it from the finder, the burden of proof is on the owner to show that he did not despair of recovering it.

The above applies only if the owner has some way to prove that the object is his, even though he does not have an identifying sign, and therefore he did not despair. But it does not apply if there is no way to

---

[482] And also if most of the people are Jews; see *Imrei Ya'akov, Laws of Findings* topic 38.

[483] Rambam, *Laws of Robbery and Lost Property* 11:7, and *Shulĥan Aruĥ Ĥoshen Mishpat* 259, regarding a city that has a majority of Jewish inhabitants. It appears that the same applies in a city where the Gentile inhabitants are accustomed to returning lost objects (either because of the law of the land, or out of righteousness, since they are not commanded to do so), and therefore the owner still hopes to recover the lost object by identifying it.

[484] This is clear from the Torah-law authorities who write that (in a usual case), it can be assumed that it was lost (see Rambam, *Laws of Robbery and Lost Property* 14:2), for this is given as a generality, but not as the only possibility, so there can be an exception. We do not say that a person's thoughts are considered nullified to the attitude of the general population, since this is only said in cases when the object is unrecoverable by anyone.

prove that the object is his, for it could just as well have been lost by someone else. For example, if one drops a common coin or a bill of paper currency, as soon as it leaves his sight and he does not know its location (such as if it fell in an unknown place on a street, or into sand dunes), then even if he cries out that he is not despairing of recovering it, and he is exerting effort to find it, he is nevertheless considered to have despaired.[485] For even if he finds the same type of money, he cannot prove it was the money he lost, so his efforts are like one who searches randomly in a street or a field, hoping he will chance upon some money (and his shouting that he doesn't despair is in vain). Therefore, if one sees another person drop money and subsequently leave it out of sight, he may pick up the money and keep it even if he knows the owner, since he is acquiring an object that is ownerless because the owner despaired.[486]

14. A person can only despair of recovering his lost object if he knows it was lost. But as long as he does not know that it left his control, there is no aspect of despair (even in circumstances in which he would immediately despair if knew of the loss; for example, if his money fell in a busy public area and it had no identifying signs).[487]

For example, if one's object is being washed away in a river or the sea, even if he is screaming that it is his and he is trying to recover it, his efforts are considered null to the general consensus that it is unrecoverable, as explained in *Shulĥan Aruĥ HaRav Hilĥot Metziah* topic 19. There are many situations (e.g., when one knows the exact spot where he lost an item, or he hopes that his friends will recover it, or he has witnesses that he lost it) when one surely does not despair of recovering it.

[485] Tractate *Bava Metzia* 25b; *Shulĥan Aruĥ HaRav Hilĥot Metziah* topic 8.

[486] Tractate *Bava Metzia* 26b; Rambam, *Laws of Robbery and Lost Property* 14:9, *Shulĥan Aruĥ Ĥoshen Mishpat* 262:14.

*Many nations print paper currency which has a unique serial number on each bill. If the owner knows the serial number of the bill he lost (which people very rarely notice), that can serve as an identifying sign, but only if there is a witness who saw that the money fell from that person. The same applies for any type of sign on a piece of money that is negotiable currency. Even if the owner wrote or engraved his name on the money, it is not accepted by itself as proof of ownership, for the owner might have spent it and transferred it to someone else. See Rambam, *ibid.* 14:10.

[487] Rambam, *Laws of Robbery and Lost Property* 14:5.

Therefore, if someone saw a person unknowingly drop an object, and then he saw another person pick it up for himself, so he went and told the owner about all of this (which the owner did not yet know, so there was not yet any aspect of despair), the owner can then go and legally claim the object from the person who took it (which he can do in this case even if there are no identifying signs, for he has the testimony of the witness, including that when the finder took the object, the owner was still unaware that it was lost). On the other hand, if the person who dropped the object had already realized and despaired about it for whatever reason, the finder has therefore already acquired it.

Likewise, if someone is unaware that he dropped an object, and he sees it in the hand of a person who found it, it still belongs to him, for he never despaired of finding it (since he didn't know that he lost it).

However, it can generally be assumed that a person knows that he lost an object, because most people are constantly watching their belongings and are aware when something is missing. Especially if one lost money from a wallet or purse, which a person usually checks frequently and will know when some is missing (and if it is a situation in which he is likely to despair of finding it), it can be assumed that he did already despair.

15. The following rule applies to fruits such as figs, that become ruined by falling on the ground. If such a fruit tree in an orchard is leaning over a public path, and one finds fallen fruits in the path under that tree, it is permitted to take them, even though the owner does not know that they fell. This is because the owner knows that it is normal for these fruit to fall, so he will naturally despair of them when they fall on the public path, and then they are ownerless. However, it is forbidden for a passerby to harvest them from the part of the tree that overhangs the public path, even if he knows they will fall soon due to their ripeness, for that is theft. (In the orchard's private area, taking fruit without permission is always theft.)

If they are fruits that do not become ruined when they fall down, such as oranges and apples, then in a similar situation, if the owner is accustomed to leave the fallen fruit ownerless, since he does not put out effort to gather them (because passersby either take them from the path or ruin them by walking on them, or animals or insects eat them), they are considered ownerless and one may take them. But if the owner is not accustomed to leave them ownerless, and comes to collect them – and surely if he clearly indicates that he does not want others to take them – it is forbidden to take them, for that is theft.[488]

16. Even though a Gentile is not required to return a lost object (as explained earlier), if one finds a contractual document and wishes to return it, he must know whom to return it to. If one finds a document of sale or gift (i.e., a document that testifies about a previous transaction), and it is validated with witnesses' signatures or it is notarized, and it is clear that it was given to the buyer of an item or the receiver of a gift, then the listed recipient is the person whom it should be returned to.

If one finds a promissory note (for a debt), and the lender confirms that it had been given over to the borrower (because the debt has been paid or canceled), the borrower is the one whom it should be returned to. However, if the borrower says that the lender dropped it, and surely if he does not admit anything about its status, the finder should not return it to either one, because it has lost its validity by not being properly guarded.[489]

If one finds a check, then if the writer confirms that it was in the hand of the payee, the payee is the one whom it should be returned to. If the writer does not confirm this, the writer is the one whom it should be returned to (or to the listed payer, if the writer is serving as an agent for the payer).

17. If someone intentionally abandons his property (e.g., he left his animal untied in a barn with the door open and without a guard, and his animal ran away, or he tossed his wallet into the street and he left), it can be considered ownerless. (However, there are some opinions that it is not ownerless and is forbidden to be taken, and that doing so is still considered theft).[490] If someone then takes it (even if he knows whose it was), the owner does not have a right to take it back.

---

[488] *Shulĥan Aruĥ Ĥoshen Mishpat* ch. 260, and *Shulĥan Aruĥ HaRav Hilĥot Metziah* topic 6.

[489] *Shulĥan Aruĥ*, *ibid.* ch. 65; *Shulĥan Aruĥ HaRav Hilĥot Eidut* topic 49.

[490] See Rambam, *ibid.* 11:11; though a Jew is not obligated to return an intentionally abandoned item, it is forbidden for him to take it, as this is theft. He rules that the owner's intentional loss does not make the item ownerless until he declared it to be ownerless, as written in *Shulĥan Aruĥ, ibid.* 261:4.

However, it is forbidden to take a person's animal from his open barn, or to pick up his wallet from his courtyard even though it was left unguarded. Although the owner would be causing his own loss, nevertheless, as long as a person's object is still on his property, it is not considered ownerless, and it is forbidden for anyone else to take it from there (for that is theft). (See topic 1:8 as to whether it is permissible to take a person's object with intention to guard it for him).

18. An object is only considered lost if it is found in a way that looks as if it was accidentally dropped or it accidentally fell out of the owner's control – for example, fruits that are strewn in a public area without any order, or an object that looks like it was dropped or forgotten. The same applies if it is clear that an object was forgotten for an extended period of time, such as something that has grown dusty or was sunk into dirt. In all these cases, the object is considered to be lost, and it is assumed that the owner has despaired of recovering it.

However, an object that was set down in a guarded place is not considered lost and is forbidden to be taken.[491] How so? If one finds a farm animal pasturing normally in a field, it is not considered lost. But if it was found wandering on a path where it is not usual for such animals to go, or at nighttime when shepherds usually bring these animals into a pen, it is assumed that the owner lost this animal.

Any object that looks like it was placed in its spot intentionally is forbidden for anyone to touch or take, for it is assumed to have been placed there by the owner for a short period of time and is not

---

However, the opinion of the *Tur*, Rema and Shaĥ *Ĥoshen Mishpat* 261:4, and *Shulĥan Aruĥ HaRav Hilĥot Metziah* topic 16, is that it is considered ownerless and is allowed to be taken.

Rabbi Zalman Nehemiah Goldberg comments that Rambam is referring there to a case in which the owner knows where the object is, but he is not guarding it sufficiently. But if he completely forgets about it, or other people moved the object to another place without his knowledge, it is assumed that the owner despairs – at which point it becomes ownerless – even if it has an identifying mark, since anyone who finds it has no obligation to return it.

[491] It is clear that if an object was found arranged in a way that looks like it was placed there intentionally, it is not considered to be lost, and one who takes it is considered to be a thief (regardless of whether the finder is a Jew or a Gentile), as explained in *Netivot Hamishpat Ĥoshen Mishpat* 260:4.

ownerless or lost at that point. For example, if one finds a vessel with its contents and lid in place, or a folded garment, next to the road or next to a fence, it is assumed that it was deliberately placed there and is not lost. An overturned vessel with its contents spilled out, or a disarrayed garment on the side of the road, are assumed to be lost.

If someone found an object that did not appear to be lost and took it into his house, then if this happened only a short time ago, he should return it immediately to its place where he found it. But if he keeps it with him for a period of time in which it is possible that the owner came to look for it, and having not found it, despaired of recovering it, then if it has an identifying mark, the finder must announce what he found and return it to the owner based on the identifying signs, so that the owner can recover what is rightfully his.[492] If there is no sign for the owner to identify the object by, and it was placed in a location and in a way that it looked as if it was hidden there and was not lost, then since the finder took it unlawfully, he should not use it. Instead, he should guard it until it is clear to the extent of his capabilities and understanding whom the object belongs to, in order to return it.

If there is no sign by which the owner could identify the object, and a long period of time passed, so it is clear that the owner has despaired, it appears that it is permitted for the finder to keep it for himself.[493]

---

[492] Rambam, *Laws of Robbery and Lost Property* 15:1; *Shulĥan Aruĥ Ĥoshen Mishpat* ch. 260; *Shulĥan Aruĥ HaRav Hilĥot Metziah* topic 12.

[493] In a similar situation for a Jew, the Torah-law authorities argue. Rambam, *Laws of Robbery and Lost Property* 15:1 (and *Shulĥan Aruĥ Ĥoshen Mishpat* 260:9-10) hold that it is permissible for the finder to take possession of the item, as he acquires it when it can be assumed that the owner has already despaired. This seems problematic, since the item came into the finder's hand through sin, and it should not be acquired by theft. See *Sefer Meirat Einayim* there, topic 42 and *Netivot Hamishpat* topic 13, who explain the reason for this, that at the time he took it, it was unintentional theft, since he intended to return it, and not to steal it. It is just that he did not know that when there is uncertainty as to whether an object was placed down intentionally or not, one should not take it. Therefore, it is not considered as if the item came to him through sin.

Many opinions argue with Rambam, including the *Tur* and Rema there, and say that a Jewish finder should not take the item for himself, but should instead keep it set aside, because it is forbidden to benefit from stolen property.

(This applies to an object that was only assumed to have been placed intentionally. But if it was certain at the time when the finder picked it up that it had been placed intentionally and was not lost, it appears that it is forbidden for him to benefit from the object forever, since that is the rule for any type of theft, as explained in topic 2:27 above).

19. The law for a lost object only apples to something that became lost from its owner. But if the owner is actively trying to retrieve the object, and can do so although with much effort, it is not considered to be lost, and one who takes it before the owner gives up his effort is a thief; this is not considered acquisition through raising a lost object, but rather grabbing another's money. This applies, for example, to possessions that were swept away by a river (and are therefore not considered completely lost, unlike the cases in the following topic which are unable to be rescued, and are therefore considered ownerless),[494] or if the owner was involved with them and they fell, and he is trying to find and recover them.[495]

20. If an object is lost at sea, or in a flooding river which is flowing rapidly, or it sank in a deep river, or if a wind blows the object very far away, or an animal or bird took the object and cast it in a place that the owner cannot see, one who finds it afterwards is able to acquire it from its now ownerless state. This applies even if the owner knows identifying signs for the object, and everyone knows that this object

---

If it is a Gentile who took the item, he can rely on the opinion of Rambam *post facto*, that the reason that it is stricter for a Jew is that there is a possible Torah prohibition of theft involved, yet there is no prohibition for a Gentile in situations of possible sin, as was explained in Part IV, "The Prohibition of Eating Meat that was Separated from a Living Animal," topic 6:8. But if he knew when he took the item that it was put there intentionally and the owner did not despair of recovering it or declare it ownerless, it is possible that even according to Rambam he is liable to return it to the owner, and he is forbidden to benefit from it just like any stolen item. (Even if his transgression was intentional, as he thought that it is permissible to take it in order to bring it to the owner or to guard it, nevertheless, the action is one of sin.) This is also written in responsa of Radvaz, ch. 2285.

[494] *Tur* and Rema *Ĥoshen Mishpat* 259:7.

[495] This is clear from *Bava Metzia* 26b: one who saw a coin fall from one of two people [who are together] must return it; see *Tosafot* there ("that it fell").

belongs to this specific person. Even if the owner sees it in the finder's hand and is standing and screaming that it belongs to him, since this object is considered to have been lost from him and all other people, he certainly had given up on recovering it (as soon as he realized that is was lost to such a degree). The fact that it was recovered later is only a chance occurrence which does not affect its ownerless state.[496]

If the owner was able to save it and was running to recover it, calling out that he lost the object, the object is not considered ownerless and one who finds it while this is happening is unable to acquire it for himself.[497]

21. If a caravan was travelling in the desert and a band of thieves came to raid their possessions, and they were unable to save them, but then one person came and saved any items, they belong to him, since the owners despaired of recovering them. If they were able to save the objects themselves, and it is just that this person went and saved them first, he must return them to their owners.

If they were able to save their objects but only with much effort, then anyone who saves the objects must return them to their owners, unless he clearly said "I am saving them for myself." For when the group heard him say that, they should have pushed themselves to try to save their possessions on their own, and their inaction shows that they despaired of recovering them. The one who saved the items can therefore acquire them from their ownerless state.

The same rules apply in similar situations, such as when the sea is about to flood a person's property, or a person's object is being swept away by a river or snatched by an animal, and the owner is able to save it (whether with or without much effort), but another person went ahead and saved the object before the owner.[498]

22. If a person's property catches on fire and he is not able to save an item – neither he, nor the firefighters who come to put out his fire – then if another person comes and saves the item, whatever he saves

---

[496] Rambam, *Laws of Robbery and Lost Property* 11:9-10 and 14:4; *Shulĥan Aruĥ Ĥoshen Mishpat* 259:7.

[497] Rema *Ĥoshen Mishpat* 259:7.

[498] Rambam *Laws of Robbery and Lost Property* 12:8-9, and *Shulĥan Aruĥ Ĥoshen Mishpat* ch. 259.

belongs to him. Since the owner was unable to save it from being burned, he despaired of recovering it, so the one who then does save it acquires it for himself (within the Torah law).[499]

The laws mentioned above regarding saving another person's object from destruction by a fire or a river or the like, from which the owner is unable to save it, are only in reference to the Torah laws regarding these circumstances. However, if the government's law states that anyone who saves someone else's object from a destructive calamity, when the owner cannot save it, must return the object to the owner; or that one must return someone's object that he saved from thieves; or that any lost object which the owner despaired of regaining must be returned – that becomes the binding law, as explained earlier.[500]

In contrast, if a person could have saved an item of his from a destructive calamity by making a great effort, but he did not, and someone else comes and saves it for himself (and he calls out that this is his intention), then the owner has effectively despaired and declared it ownerless. Then the government has no overriding law to require that the object must be returned, since a governing power can only mandate the return of objects that have been lost to everyone, but not when the owner has declared his object ownerless through his tacit acceptance that others can make the effort required to save it and acquire it for themselves.

---

[499] Rema *Ĥoshen Mishpat* 264:5.

[500] *Ibid.* 259:7.

CHAPTER 16

Maintaining Peace in Society by Forbidding Acts Similar to Theft

1. There are actions that are not fully considered theft, yet the Rabbinical Sages forbade them because they are a danger to peaceful society. In particular, these are actions that involve a perpetrator and a victim, in which the victim will feel as though he was robbed. This may lead to the victim killing or stealing from the perpetrator in revenge. Although the following wrongful actions are not fully considered to be theft, if a person uses one of these tactics to receive an object, he must return it in order to maintain a peaceful society.[501]

2. It was explained in Chapter 15 that seas, open rivers and open forests are ownerless, and a person may hunt in them or set out traps for fish or animals (subject to the government's restrictions). Therefore, if someone set out a trap that does not have the legal status of being a vessel (for example, a fishnet), and then another person came and took a captured animal or fish from the trap before it was found and retrieved by the trap's owner, this is not fully considered as theft. Why? The trapper has not yet acquired it because (a) it has not yet come into his hand, and (b) this trap is not a complete vessel, so something in it does not automatically becomes his. Nevertheless, it is forbidden for another person to take the trapped creature, so that a breakdown in the peace of the society will be avoided.

If, however, the trap was a complete vessel and an animal or fish entered it and was trapped, the owner of the vessel acquires it. The acquisition takes place by the Torah law that a person's vessel acquires

---

[501] See Rambam *Laws of Acquisition and Gifts* 1:3; *Shulĥan Aruĥ Ĥoshen Mishpat* ch. 273 and 370; *Shulĥan Aruĥ HaRav Hilĥot Hefker* topic 6. And even though in *Shulĥan Aruĥ Ĥoshen Mishpat* ch. 370 it is written that an acquisition that is decreed by the Sages to be forbidden cannot be reclaimed in court, it is nevertheless an obligation on the person to return it, as explained in *Shulĥan Aruĥ HaRav Hilĥot Hefker ibid.*

It is clear that a Gentile who commits this type of immoral acquisition, which was forbidden by the Sages, is exempt from liability to capital punishment for theft, as in all these cases, the item being taken is not really owned by anyone else. Rather, the Sages only placed it in one person's possession at the outset, to promote the ways of peace between people.

for its owner something ownerless that comes into it. Therefore, one who takes a trapped animal from another person's trap that is a complete vessel is fully liable for the transgression of theft.[502]

3. However, it is forbidden to hunt in a field, forest or river that is privately owned, as this would be using the other's property without permission. Nevertheless, if one traps an animal, bird or fish in one of these places, it belongs to the intrusive trapper.

However, if someone traps creatures that are constrained to be in a corralled area, such as a fish hatchery, or a fenced-in valley that contains animals, since the area is closed off and guarded, the area and all that is in it belongs to the owner, and the trapper does not acquire anything.[503] This applies even if effort would be needed to trap the animal or fish, such as in a case where the enclosure was very large.

4. Doves in a dovecote and pigeons living on a roof typically have come freely from elsewhere and are now dwelling on a person's private property. Although they are currently within the owner's property, they can still go and come freely since they are not being constrained. Therefore, they are not completely considered as belonging to the property owner, even though they are inside his dovecote, or living on his roof. Likewise, the bees in a hive that they have made in a beekeeper's field are not constrained. Nevertheless, it is forbidden to take any of these birds or bees from another person's property, and not even when they go out from that property into a third person's property. In order to establish a more moral world, the Rabbinical Sages decreed that these valued creatures (bees for their honey, and birds which are taken for food) are considered to belong to

---

502 *Shulĥan Aruĥ Ĥoshen Mishpat* 273:13 and 370:4; *Shulĥan Aruĥ HaRav Hilĥot Hefker* topic 3.

503 *Shulĥan Aruĥ Ĥoshen Mishpat* 273:13; *Shulĥan Aruĥ HaRav Hilĥot Hefker* topic 4. Even though for a Jew, his real-estate property acquires for him any ownerless thing that comes into it, and one who then takes that object is fully a thief, this does not apply for a Gentile's real-estate property, because it does not acquire ownerless objects. (This is learned from the Torah laws of a representative messenger (a *shaliaĥ*), which do not apply to Gentiles). Nevertheless, taking an ownerless object from the property of a Gentile was forbidden by the Sages, since doing so could result in a breakdown of a peaceful society.

the owner of the property where they make their nests.[504]

5. If one person shakes fruits from an ownerless tree with intention to collect and acquire them, and then a second person comes and picks them up from the ground, the second person acquires them for himself according to Torah Law. (Since the first person did not yet establish his ownership by lifting up the fruit from the ground for himself – or by placing them into his vessel, or letting them fall into his vessel – therefore the second person acquires them by his act of lifting them for himself.) Nevertheless, to preserve the ways of peace, this was decreed as forbidden, and the fruit must be treated as belonging to the person who shook them off from the tree with the intention that he would take them for himself.[505]

6. Any object that was previously ownerless or lost, that a person finds within four cubits (about six feet) of himself, belongs to him (provided that he intends to acquire it), even if he has not yet picked it up. This Rabbinical enactment was made for the sake of peace in the world. Once a person is standing close to an ownerless object that he desires (although he has not yet technically done an action to acquire the object), he has already established in his mind that he has acquired it. If anyone else would then step up and take it, this would begin a quarrel. Therefore, a second person may not take it at that point, and if he does, he must return it to the first person.

This only applies in an open area that is ownerless and which is not crowded with many people, such as a public field or the sides of a public domain. In the middle of a public path where the passersby are walking close to each other, and each one does not have his own personal space of four cubits in which to be able to acquire an object through its close distance to him alone, one only acquires an object through raising it. Even if he spread his garment over it, or it struck him while it was falling from above, he does not acquire it until he raises it.

If the object is on another person's property, even if the property

---

[504] Rambam *Laws of Robbery* 6:14; *Shulĥan Aruĥ Ĥoshen Mishpat* ch. 370; *Shulĥan Aruĥ HaRav Hilĥot Hefker* topic 6.

[505] *Shulĥan Aruĥ Ĥoshen Mishpat* ch. 370; *Shulĥan Aruĥ HaRav Hilĥot Hefker* topic 5.

owner is not present in order to see it, the finder cannot acquire a nearby lost object only by virtue of it being within his four cubits.[506]

There are some Torah authorities who, regardless of the situation, forbid a person to take an object that another is trying to pick up and acquire, and someone who does this is called a sinful person. Anyone who pushes ahead and takes a lost object or a business opportunity that another person is trying to acquire is a sinful person.[507] See topic 8:17.

7. It is forbidden to steal an object found by a young child, as this destroys peaceful society.

If the child received an item as a gift, or as payment for work, and he is at the stage of maturity when he can discern between a coin and a plaything, such an act is full theft. If he has a lower level of maturity, the prohibition is only one of destroying peaceful society.[508]

8. A guest who eats a meal from a homeowner which he knows is more than the homeowner can afford has committed an act akin to theft, since the homeowner does not want to give him that much food, or food which is that expensive, and only does so since he is embarrassed to tell the guest otherwise.[509]

9. It is forbidden to steal another person's advantage, such as one who jumps ahead in a line in which others are waiting, as he is stealing their advantage and time.[510]

---

[506] Rambam *Laws of Robbery and Lost Property* 17:9; *Shulĥan Aruĥ Ĥoshen Mishpat* ch. 268; *Shulĥan Aruĥ HaRav Hilĥot Hefker* topic 7.

[507] *Shulĥan Aruĥ Ĥoshen Mishpat* ch. 237.

[508] *Ibid.* 243:15 and ch. 370; *Shulĥan Aruĥ HaRav Hilĥot Hefker* topic 8 and *Hilĥot Meĥirah* topic 10.

[509] Rambam, *Laws of Repentance* 4:4.

[510] Rabbi Zalman Nehemiah Goldberg notes that the rule "first comes, first served" is said in reference to litigants coming before a court for a judgment (*Shulĥan Aruĥ Ĥoshen Mishpat* ch. 15), but that is only after the judge has started to judge one case, he may not stop and take another case instead. But if he didn't start yet, he may take a different case than the one that is waiting next in line. Still, it is probable that jumping ahead in a line is forbidden since it disturbs the business; for example, if one jumps ahead in a line at a bank, it disrupts the business and causes a loss to the bank.

10. Those who make profits from gambling are not committing theft. Nevertheless, it is not fitting that a person should be involved in such pursuits, but rather with matters which establish a productive world order.[511]

11. It is forbidden for one to raise a type of dog or cat that is dangerous for young children. If such an animal gets loose, it is forbidden for one to return the animal to the owner, and anyone who finds it may kill it, and use its fur, as it is considered ownerless.[512] The same applies for anything which is a danger for the public. Since it is permitted for one to kill it or destroy it, therefore if someone steals it for himself, a Torah-based court cannot force him to return it or pay restitution.

12. It is unclear if it is permissible for a Gentile to steal or rob an idol or another prohibited object that is linked to idol worship, even if his intention is to destroy it or to turn the owner away from idol worship. Either way, it appears that the thief is not liable for capital punishment for theft, and he need not return the prohibited object that he stole.[513] (See Part II, "The Prohibition of Idolatry," topic 7:2.)

13. One is obligated to be extremely careful regarding the prohibition of theft, as there are many details, and the nature of a person is to covet

---

511 See *Shulĥan Aruĥ Ĥoshen Mishpat* ch. 370.

512 Rambam *Laws of Robbery and Lost Property* 15:17, *Shulĥan Aruĥ Ĥoshen Mishpat* ch. 266.

513 It seems from the story of Rachel (Genesis 31:19) – "And Rachel stole the idols that belonged to her father" – as Rashi comments there based on *Midrash Rabbah*, that she intended to separate her father from idol worship, and *Gur Aryeh* explains there that therefore, this is not considered theft, so it appears that it is permissible.

It appears that since there is an obligation to destroy idols, and when they are existent they are a stumbling block for those that serve them, so this is comparable to a dangerous thing, as explained above in topic 11. Therefore, one who steals or damages them is exempt. Although the owner of the idols is able to nullify them and use their monetary value, and therefore one who damages them would be stealing from the owner, the same can be said for a dangerous pet, which is worth money but is nevertheless considered ownerless. Surely, one can say this about idols.

the money of others, so his evil inclination tricks him with various excuses for why it is permissible.

Therefore, one should make extra effort to be careful about this prohibition, and he should learn and know its details very well, in order not to transgress it even by mistake. It has already been explained in Part I, "Fundamentals of the Faith," Chapter 4, that one who transgresses a Noahide commandment because he was negligent and did not learn, and therefore thought that it was permitted, is liable to punishment, for he was obligated to learn and know what he is prohibited from doing.

Likewise, a person is obligated to contemplate and judge the actions he is doing, in order that he not fall mistakenly into theft, as this is likely to occur when one is not being careful.

14. We see how harsh the punishment for theft can be from the Generation of the Flood. The Sages teach[514] that although the people of the generation were very sinful, God's decree of their annihilation was sealed only due to their sins of robbery, as it says,[515] "God said to Noaĥ, 'The end of all flesh has come before Me, for the earth is filled with robbery; and behold, I am about to destroy them from the earth.' "

There are cases in which a person will receive severe retribution from God for committing theft, similar to a kidnapper (see Chapter 9 above) or a murderer (see Part V).[516] When might this judgment be made? This can happen if his theft left the victim with no money, which caused the victim to die of hunger, or similar cases in which the robber causes the victim to die from other circumstances, because of his financial loss. Since these situations can't be fully evaluated by mortals, it is understood that God will consider any theft according to His true understanding of the situation – which may be as severe as a case of murder or manslaughter – and He will judge accordingly.[517]

---

[514] Tractate *Sanhedrin* 108a, cited by Rashi on Genesis 6:13.

[515] Genesis 6:13.

[516] See Tractate *Bava Kama* 119a, and *Sifri Devarim* 32:43 – all *extortion* that the Babylonians committed against the Jews is considered as if they spilled innocent blood (i.e., a capital sin). See also Rambam, *Laws of Robbery and Lost Property* 1:13; *Shulĥan Aruĥ Ĥoshen Mishpat* 359:3.

[517] See Rashi's explanation of Deuteronomy 1:9.

Part VIII

Establishment of Laws and Courts

Details of the following nineteen obligations and seven prohibitions, that are included in this commandment and its offshoots, are explained in this section and in *Sheva Mitzvot HaShem*, Vol. 3 *(Dinim)*:

1. For a Gentile society to establish laws and ordinances.

2. For a Gentile society to establish courts in which judges will adjudicate regarding issues and transgressions that involve the Seven Commandments

3. For judges to adjudicate in court cases regarding all other matters that pertain to maintaining a stable society.

4. To compel and strive to guide Gentiles to accept and fulfill the details of their Seven Commandments and behave in a good and upright way. This includes the obligation to educate others in good and proper ways of life.

5. Not to cause someone to err or deviate from proper ways of living, nor cause someone to have an obstacle in his life, nor lead someone to transgress one of the Torah's laws that he is obligated to observe.

6. To involve oneself in charity and acts of kindness for the poor and needy.

7. To work on self-improvement, and to educate and guide oneself in proper character traits, attitudes and ideals. This includes fulfillment of all logical obligations, such as the obligation for Gentiles to honor their parents.

8. To ensure that the people are being correctly and fairly judged within the courts, which includes appointing only judges and police officers who are qualified and fitting for their positions.

9. For empowered Noahide courts to judge matters of the Seven Commandments according to the relevant Torah laws; other cases that involve laws which are agreed upon by the society should be judged according to the understanding of the judges, within the proper guidelines.

10. To distinguish between deliberate, inadvertent, or coerced transgressors, and to apply the correct standards for judging those different types of cases.

11. To judge righteously and without perversion of justice.

12. Not to accept a bribe that touches upon the judgment of a court case.

13. To ensure that the judges and witnesses are men in capital cases that involve transgression of any of the Seven Commandments.

14. That a qualified person is to judge or be a witness in a case involving transgression of one of the Seven Commandments, even he is a close relative of a person who is involved in the case.

15. For a judge not to remove himself from judging due to worry or fear about reprisals that might be made against him.

16. To judge cases that involve transgression of one of the Seven Commandments through valid witnesses.

17. In the opinion of Maimonides: for a valid witness to come forward to a court to give testimony that he knows about a case that involves transgression of one of the Seven Commandments.

18. Not to give false testimony to a court of law.

19. To investigate and determine whether the testimony given to a court of law is true or not.

20. Not to receive invalid testimony in a court of law, in courts cases that involve transgression of one of Seven Commandments.

21. Not to hire a false witness to give false testimony to a court of law.

22. To correctly establish the laws of inheritance for Gentiles.

23. If an adult Gentile transgressed one of the specific Seven Commandments and was convicted for this by a Noahide Court (i.e., a court that judged him in accordance with the Torah laws for Gentiles, and was authorized to do so by the majority of the society), the court is obligated to sentence him to death and carry out the execution (if that is the punishment that is required in the law), rather than accepting a ransom to spare his life. By extension, a court system is to carry out the punishment prescribed by the law of the land for one who has been properly convicted of committing a crime.

24. To establish laws and rules for judging in courts about matters beyond the Seven Commandments that need to be regulated for the society, such as establishing beneficial laws for commerce, according to the understanding of the lawmakers.

25. To appoint police officers to enforce a court's rulings, and by extension, to establish proper laws and rules of government that are agreed upon by the majority of the people, by which "the law of the land is the law".

26. For a Gentile court not to convict or execute someone who prophesies falsely in the name of God, but rather to hand such a false prophet over to be judged by the Supreme Sanhedrin of the Jews, if it is functioning.

INTRODUCTION

The Social Obligation of Justice

by Rabbi Dr. Shimon D. Cowen

Director, Institute for Judaism and Civilization, Melbourne, Australia

The Noahide precept of justice, or *dinim*, is the obligation, incumbent upon societies, to establish the rule of law through courts in every district of the land. It is, however, not simply the establishment of law and order (however that might be) specifically in reference to the Noahide Laws, which have somewhat of a parallel in secular legal philosophy that might be called an order of "natural justice." In actuality, it is the Divine template for human conduct, set out in the Hebrew Bible and its Oral tradition. This is what Rambam intends when he states that the Noahide precept of establishing a system of justice is for the purpose of ruling on the other six universal Noahide Laws. That is to say, justice itself is one of the Noahide Commandments, with its own parameters, and its purpose is to judge in relation to, and to enforce the observance of, the other six Noahide Laws.

In defining the precept of *dinim*, the words of Rambam are "to judge in relation to these six [other] precepts" and this is understood to exclude judgment in certain areas where punishment is given over to the hands of Heaven[1] instead of the courts. Still it would appear that the precept applies to three areas: (a) the actual prescriptions in the Noahide Laws as set out in the Biblical revelation to Moses at Sinai, and elucidated in the Oral tradition which also derives from Sinai; (b) an area of rules and arrangements in the realm of justice, mandated by reason for the purposes of social order, where the rightness of this reason is generally informed by the rationally grasped precepts given to the Jewish people, but for which the same prescription of detail does

---

[1] Such as Rambam details in *Laws of Kings*, 10:6-9. See Rabbi Yehuda Gershoni, *Mishpat HaMeluĥa* on *Laws of Kings* 9:14. Nevertheless, even for those transgressions which are not to be judged by a Noahide court, it is incumbent to publicize and teach those laws and even apply limited punishment to offenders when they are broken, for the transgressions are serious in the eyes of God, and may even entail the spiritual death of the person's soul, as in the case of creating new (man-made) religions and religious commandments, for example.

not necessarily apply to Gentiles as it does for the Jewish people;[2] (c) a domain of adopted stringencies, whereby higher standards of justice (judged by reference to the Jewish ideal of "absolute justice") are taken on and become part of Noahide law.[3]

The normative legal system is thus not a mere reflection of community values or a repository of statutes given by a legislative body, but of the Noahide Code, *within which* community values – including legislated laws and norms – are included so long as these are consistent with the Noahide laws. Judges, lawmakers and the enforcers of law all need to be cognizant of this higher, universal code. Where there is doubt as to the parameters of Noahide law in regard to new matters, the filling of this gap can be done only by a qualified Orthodox Rabbinic authority in the Noahide laws.[4]

The function of *dinim* is also put "negatively": to disallow disorder. Here Rambam writes that the function of courts under Noahide law is to "warn the people" against its infringement. This presupposes a stance of practical responsibility[5] on the part of the State's agencies of justice: both of the constituted sovereign authority and the judiciary.

The precept of *dinim* is important even in societies with high standards of impartiality and freedom from corruption in the administration of justice. This is because personal value judgments and beliefs enter the rulings of judges, resulting in decisions which are at variance with the Noahide Laws. This is seen in rulings permitting homosexual "marriage," elective abortion, and euthanasia. The judge must first and foremost know and be beholden to the Noahide Laws as the ethical conditions for all human-made law and its adjudication.

---

[2] As we find in the general discretion given to the Jewish king and Jewish courts to rectify social order, which are in fact founded on *Noahide* law.

[3] As the Lubavitcher Rebbe learns in the view of Rashi, *Likkutei Siĥot*, Vol. 5, p. 190. See Rabbi J.D. Bleich in *"Mishpat mo'ves b'dinei b'nei Noaĥ"* in the *Sefer HaYovel* for Rabbi Y.B. Soloveitchik, pp. 203-204, where he quotes an opinion that the punishment intended for Tamar (Genesis 38:24) was for her supposed transgression of a prohibition *introduced* by the court of Shem.

[4] See *Likkutei Siĥot* Vol. 29, p. 98, where a Noahide judge is prohibited from "filling a gap," under the general prohibition to a Noahide to *m'ĥadesh da'at* (extrapolate to a new application of Torah Law) (*Laws of Kings* 10:10).

[5] The functions of a Noahide judge are (a) to set forth the relevant rulings and (b) to see to it that they are carried out. See *Likkutei Siĥot*, Vol. 29, p. 98.

CHAPTER 1

The Obligation for a Gentile Society to Set Up a Judicial System

1. Adam was commanded regarding the prohibition of murder and the obligation to establishment justice.[1] God later repeated the prohibition of murder to Noaĥ, and commanded him regarding the punishment of a murderer, as the verses state, "But, your blood of your souls I will demand …; but of man, of man for his brother, I will demand the soul of man. Whoever sheds the blood of man, among man, his blood shall be shed; for in the image of God He made man."[2]

The warning, "But, your blood of your souls I will demand, etc.," refers to the prohibition of murder, while the verse, "Whoever sheds the blood of man, among man, his blood shall be shed...," refers to the commandment to judge and penalize the murderer.[3] The Sages inferred this command from the following explanation of the above verse: "Whoever sheds the blood of man" (referring to the murderer) "among man" (is prosecuted in court by a man who is qualified to testify); "his blood shall be shed" (he is given capital punishment by the court).[4]

Just as Gentiles are commanded to judge the case of the murderer, they are also obligated to likewise bring to justice those who transgress the other Noahide commandments.

The reason for the Noahide commandment of *Dinim* (Hebrew for *Judgments*) – meaning the establishment of a justice system – is clear: to keep order and morality in the world, and not let society degenerate to a state of lawlessness in which people are killing, extorting, stealing and harming each other. In the words of Rabban Shimon ben Gamliel:[5]

---

[1] Tractate *Sanhedrin* 56, Rambam *Laws of Kings* 9:1.

[2] Genesis 9:5-6.

[3] Tractate *Sanhedrin* 57a. There must be a command to all Gentiles to execute a murderer who is found guilty in a just court, for if not, there would be no permission for a court to execute any person. The permission to do so is found in the command, "...his blood shall be shed," and therefore a righteous Gentile society is not only permitted, but also obligated to authorize a just court to execute a murderer. (See topic 11 below for when this can apply.)

[4] Tractate *Sanhedrin* 57b; *Bereishit Rabbah* ch. 34; *Targum Onkelos*, *Targum Yonatan ben Uziel*, Rashi, and Ramban on Genesis 9:5-6.

[5] Tractate *Avot* (*Ethics of the Fathers*) 1:18.

"The world endures by virtue of three things – justice, truth, and peace, as it is stated,[6] 'Administer truth and the judgment of peace in your gates.' " Another reason for this commandment is that in order to keep a spirit of Godliness in the world, one must be concerned with the establishment of a society according to God's will, in which people keep their Divine commandments that concern a person's obligation to God and to one's fellow human beings.

2. What is involved in the obligation of *Dinim*? Gentiles are commanded to set up proper judges and law enforcement officers in every inhabited area and city,[7] who will be empowered to judge in matters of the Seven Noahide Commandments, to urge the people to observe the laws, and punish offenders.[8]

It is an obligation for Gentile judges to decide the correct laws for Gentiles according to their Seven Commandments, such as whether or not a particular action directly violates one of these seven Divine commandments. For example, a qualified judge would decide whether a particular action falls directly under the Noahide prohibition of idolatry, or whether the action is an offshoot of idolatry and is

---

[6] Zeĥariah 8:16.

[7] Tractate *Sanhedrin* 56b and Meiri *ibid.*; Ramban on Genesis 34:13.

[8] Based on Rambam, *Laws of Kings* 9:14. In his words, the seventh Noahide commandment is that "they are obligated to set up judges and magistrates in every major city to render judgment concerning these [other] six commandments and to admonish the people [regarding their observance]." (It appears from his statement that Gentiles are not obligated to appoint judges in every town, which is supported by his later statement in *ibid.* 10:11, "The Jewish Court [one that follows Torah Law] is obligated to appoint judges for these resident [*Ger Toshav*] Non-Jews [who are residing in the Land of Israel among the Jews]" – assumedly, these are lower judges and officers of law to carry out the judgment in smaller cities.) With this opinion, he disagrees with Ramban (on Genesis 34:13), who is of the opinion that these judges are only to judge monetary matters. However, it is clear even according to Ramban, although he does not state it explicitly, that one who transgresses one of the six prohibitory Noahide commandments is liable, and also that no one may give him any punishment for transgressing them unless he is given a fair trial. This can also be seen from the fact that Ramban does not mention the obligation to judge a murderer, although it is clear from the scriptural text that this is required.

therefore forbidden yet not punishable; or whether a woman is considered married and forbidden to another man; or whether a sum of money belongs to a specific person, and therefore another person who takes it would be liable for stealing; and all similar matters.[9]

The ruling explained earlier in Part I, topic 5:4 – that because of their prohibition of making a new religion, a Noahide Court may not on its own decide a question that arises about the *halaĥa* (Torah Law) regarding one of the Seven Commandments, and must rather let a Jewish Court decide the *halaĥa* – applies to establishing a **new** ordinance in regard to one of the Seven Commandments. However, they are permitted to clarify whether a certain situation falls under a category of the pre-defined Seven Commandments, and into which category it falls, as this would not be considered an establishment of a new law.[10]

Within the scope of the Seven Noahide Commandments, the prohibition against establishing a "new commandment" only applies to those aspects of the commandments that were given by God Himself as part of the Torah of Moses from Sinai, since the establishment of Torah Law is not in the jurisdiction of Noahide Courts. The Noahide Courts may, however, establish the rules in regard to other laws that they take upon themselves, or matters that should be logically and morally binding, or monetary and business laws and the like, which the various countries have established for themselves.

In summary, a Noahide Court is not permitted to change the framework of the Torah's laws of *Dinim* for Gentiles. Examples of such forbidden changes would be deciding that there is no obligation to have a court rule on monetary laws, or changing a detail of *halaĥa* in one of the other six Noahide Commandments. They have jurisdiction, though, to make decisions regarding monetary cases according to their understanding, and if they decide to change one of the laws that they have previously decided regarding monetary cases, they may do so as well.

The command for court judges to admonish the people about following the laws includes the obligations to teach the society what is

---

[9] Responsa of *Yad Eliyahu*, ch. 38: "The main obligation of *Dinim* is to make clear rules, such as where there is doubt of whether an action is stealing; and even to clarify these laws before litigants come to court." Also see Responsa *Maĥaneh Ĥayim*, vol. 2, ch. 22.

[10] See *Likkutei Siĥot*, vol. 29, p. 98.

forbidden and permitted, to warn them regarding these matters, and to have a system for preventing the people from transgressing the laws.[11]

This includes the obligation of Noahide Courts to oversee the education system in the country, and to set the curriculum in a way that will teach the populace that which it must know, including: belief in God; the acceptance of the "yoke of Heaven" and the fulfillment of their Divine commandments, including all the details of the Seven Commandments; and all other moral obligations that are logically incumbent on Gentiles.[12]

A Noahide Court is also obligated to judge a Gentile in all situations of possible transgression, to decide whether and how the convicted transgressor is liable to be punished, and to carry out that punishment.

3. The Noahide commandment and obligation of *Dinim* is not only for Gentiles to judge and punish transgressors, but also to take care about the morality of society. This includes making moral laws to guard the populace from sinning,[13] and any other laws necessary for the establishment of a just and peaceful society.[14]

Gentiles are therefore obligated within their commandment of *Dinim* to make righteous and beneficial laws that are effective for all the country, in all matters between people, such as laws in the areas of:

---

[11] Responsa *Maĥaneh Ĥayim ibid.*; *Ĥemdas Yisrael* 9:29.

[12] To quote the Sages in Tractate *Sanhedrin* 56b: "and He commanded them *dinim,* as it is stated (Genesis 18:19, regarding Abraham) 'For I know him, in order to command his children and house after him, that they may keep the path of God.' " The simple meaning of the verse is a reference to educating one's children about God's laws. It is clear from Rambam's words in *Laws of Kings* 9:14, "to admonish the people," that educating the people about God's laws is an obligation upon the courts as well.

[13] See *Roke'aĥ*, ch. 366: "Gentiles are commanded as part of their obligation of *Dinim* to fix the weights and measures." (This includes the obligation on the court to routinely check the stores to see if their weights, measures and scales are correct, as Rambam explains in *Laws of Theft* 8:20 in regard to the obligation of officers of the Jewish courts.) This applies in addition to the obligation of each individual to check his or her own weights and measures to avoid cheating, as explained above in Part VII, ch. 5.

[14] In the wording of Rambam in *Laws of Kings* 10:11, "…so that the world will not become decadent," or as in the wording of Meiri in Tractate *Sanhedrin* 56, "the laws of *Dinim* prevent the sins of theft and extortion."

theft (e.g., requiring a thief to reimburse his victim),[15] cheating, payment of a hired worker, holding back a worker's pay, obligations regarding watchmen, rape or seduction, monetary damages (e.g., by a person damaging someone financially, or by a person allowing his property to damage someone bodily or financially), bodily injury, lending and borrowing, other business transactions, and requirements for the courts to administer justice according to these laws.[16] (In Part VII, the main laws of the Noahide Code are already outlined regarding theft, cheating, holding back a worker's pay, the obligations and pay of watchmen, rapists or seducers, monetary damages, and bodily harm.)

The people who write these laws which Gentiles may establish for themselves, and the judges who rule on the applications of these laws, must establish them according to their knowledge of the true needs of the country's population and the establishment of a moral society. They do not necessarily need to follow the Torah's monetary laws for Jews. Rather, they may rule similarly or differently based on their view of what is necessary for the specific society of their country. The laws must obviously conform to logical and moral standards, and they must not be like the evil and cruel laws of the Biblical city of Sodom, on account of which God utterly destroyed that metropolis.[17]

4. How does the obligation of *Dinim* for Gentiles to judge regarding their Seven Commandments (as explained above in topic 2) differ from their obligation to judge in monetary matters and other laws that their courts have decided on their own (as detailed in topic 3 above)?

A Noahide Court's judgment of the Seven Commandments from God may only follow the guidelines that the Torah of Moses has estab-

---

[15] See Part VII, ch. 2, that a Noahide Court is permitted to pass judgment on the amount required for compensation for theft. They are also permitted to widen or narrow the prohibition of theft to specific circumstances. However, the basic prohibition of theft is ordained by God, so theft cannot be made permissible. The same applies for the prohibition of cheating: although a Noahide Court may determine logically what is considered cheating and at what point a sale is invalid, they cannot nullify the Divinely-ordained prohibition of cheating.

[16] Ramban on Genesis 34:13; *Sefer HaĤinuĥ* Commandment 58; Rashi on Tractate *Gittin* 9b.

[17] *Kol Ba'ei Ha'Olam*, p. 93.

lished,[18] and they may not nullify or change these commandments or the punishments set for them.[19] If a Noahide Court fails to administer this judgment, it has failed to observe the commandment of *Dinim*.[20]

However, the court may judge monetary laws and other matters that fall under their jurisprudence, according to their own understanding. For example, they may decide what penalty to set for a rapist[21] (who raped a woman who is not forbidden to him for marriage within Noahide Law, so he is therefore not liable to capital punishment from a Noahide Court on account of any of the basic Seven Noahide Commandments). The lawmakers may establish the penalty as either capital punishment or any other punishment that appears to them to be correct for their society. Likewise, they can decide to base their judgment on the testimony of one witness, or only at least two witnesses, or by their own examination of the evidence (including testimony from the victim), or by the confession of the defendant. The same applies to all other details of the judgment.

They can also judge a person who causes bodily harm to another according to their own decision, and if they decide to let the accused person go free based on the circumstances of the incident or a specific testimony, they have the permission to do so and are not considered as

---

[18] Based on God's command to Moses, as explained in the author's Introduction to *Sheva Mitzvot HaShem*, footnote 7.

[19] *Mishneh Halaĥot* vol. 7, ch. 255.

[20] This is clear from the opinion of Rambam, *Laws of Kings*, end of ch. 9; he is of the opinion that if the judges do not do so, they are liable. Even Ramban, who argues and says that they cannot be liable for inaction, still agrees that they have not fulfilled the commandment of *Dinim*.

[21] See in Part VII, ch. 10, that one who rapes a woman (who is not forbidden to him for marriage within Noahide Law) is not held liable to capital punishment in a Noahide Court, since it does not fall within the category of one of the absolute Noahide Commandments. Therefore, this matter is within the jurisprudence of the society's lawmakers. This can be compared to the story of Judah and Tamar, in which she was initially sentenced to capital punishment (for assumedly having had relations with an idolater, which was declared by the court of Shem as forbidden and punishable by death); this enacted prohibition was one of the extra standards (beyond the Noahide Commandments) that was imposed by societies after the Flood to hold people back from idolatry and licentious sexual relations. (This explanation is brought in *Tosafot Sanhedrin* 56, and *Likkutei Siĥot* vol. 5, p. 190.)

failing to keep the commandment of *Dinim*.[22]

However, it is the obligation (as part of their commandment of *Dinim*) of these judges (or the society's lawmakers, as implied and understood in this context) to establish laws in the areas that fall under their jurisdiction, and they are forbidden to let such issues go completely ignored – for example, by deciding that one who rapes or injures another will not undergo any judgment or penalty. Any such lack of response to these matters (especially in an area where there is clearly a need for such laws) constitutes a failure to observe the commandment of *Dinim*. The determination of particular laws in these areas, and the penalties for their transgression, falls under the court system's own jurisprudence.

If there are no permissible witnesses or judges within the rules for Noahide Courts (yet there is, nevertheless, still an obligation to adjudicate in matters of the Seven Commandments), the existing court has permission to reach a judgment according to their own understanding. However, if the court excuses itself from judging the case altogether, they have failed to uphold the Noahide Commandment of *Dinim*.[23]

In this work, from this point on, all laws will be divided into two categories: (a) "fixed laws" – those commanded by God, and (b) "resolved laws" – those involving areas other than the other six Noahide Commandments, or situations in which the judges cannot make a judgment within the Torah Laws for Noahide Courts (e.g., due to lack of acceptable witnesses), in which case they should judge according to laws of the land and their own justice system.

5. The Noahide Commandment for *Dinim* is obligatory for everyone in the whole society, both upon the community[24] as well as upon the

---

[22] This is based on the explanation in Part VII, ch. 11, that one who injures another is not liable for transgressing the prohibitions of theft or murder (although Ramban is of the opinion that it would be considered theft), and therefore it is up to the court's decision as to how they will judge such a case.

[23] It appears that even according to Rambam (see topic 9 below), they are not liable for not keeping the commandment of *Dinim* under these circumstances, since there is no truly valid case for them to rule upon, according to the exact standards of justice within the purview of Noahide Law (and therefore this is not considered to be annulling the commandment of *Dinim*).

[24] This obligation falls more heavily on the ones who preside over the country, as they are in more control than the individuals within the country.

individual.[25] Although the obligation to establish a court system is upon the whole community, there is more responsibility placed in the hands of the ruling members of the society, who have the ability to determine that a system of laws will be established, and to fix any perversion in the judicial system.

6. The commandment for *Dinim* includes two general obligations: the positive command to establish justice, and the negative prohibition against perverting justice.[26] The positive command includes many details, among them the appointment of appropriate judges, the establishment of appropriate laws (including civil laws), and the obligation of the courts to judge and admonish the populace, as explained earlier. The negative prohibition includes the perversion of justice in any way, and includes many details,[27] such as:

- the prohibition for a judge to change the correct judgment because of his own wickedness, or because of a bribe or some reason that is not legally relevant, or to accept a bribe at all (see topics 2:4-8);
- the prohibition for a witness to testify falsely;
- the prohibition against changing the correct judgment in any way,

---

Historically, this can be seen from what happened to the Generation of the Flood (Genesis ch. 6-7), the people of Sodom (Genesis 19:1-25), and the city of Sheĥem (Genesis ch. 34, as explained by Rambam, *Laws of Kings* 9:14). Those calamities happened because the laws of *Dinim* were not kept. Although the original sins of these populations may have been in a particular area, such as idolatry, the lack of a valid system of justice made the proliferation of other serious sins even more widespread, and it was therefore decreed by God for their entire societies to be punished more severely. See Responsa *Maĥaneh Ĥayim*, vol. 2, *Oraĥ Ĥayim* ch. 22, p. 62.

[25] This is clear from Rambam, *Laws of Kings* ch. 9, in regard to Sheĥem. This can also be seen from the discussion in Tractate *Sanhedrin* 57b regarding whether women are obligated in the commandment of *Dinim*, which shows that this is an obligation upon the individual.

[26] Tractate *Sanhedrin* 59a.

[27] Rashi on *ibid.* 59a, Meiri on *ibid.* 57, and Ramban on Genesis 34:13. (This is unlike the Torah's commandments for Jews, which are divided into many individual detailed commandments, 613 in number, whereas the Noahide Commandment of *Dinim* is the overall general commandment that includes all these related details, as explained in Part VII, last footnote to topic 1:1.)

or intimidating a plaintiff, a witness or the judges from the process of obtaining a correct judgment.

All such matters constitute perversion of justice and failure to uphold the commandment of *Dinim*.

The individual's obligation of *Dinim* includes coming to court for a judgment, and not taking matters into one's own hands with coercion.[28] See Part VII, topics 4:5-8, regarding when it is permissible for a Gentile to take matters into his own hands in a monetary dispute.

7. There is an opinion that part of a Gentile's obligation of *Dinim* is to respect judges and not curse them.[29] Included in this injunction is the prohibition against cursing a king or ruler of the country, since the ruler is responsible for establishing the law and order in the country. This follows the concept in the verse (Exodus 22:27),[30] "You shall not curse a judge, and you shall not curse a leader among your people."

8. Although a Gentile woman is not obligated in the commandment of *Dinim*, she is nevertheless obligated to uphold the law, such as when she is asked by the court to testify in certain cases (see *Sheva Mitzvot HaShem*, Part VIII, Chapter 9), and she is surely forbidden to obstruct the law or societal morality (see topic 6 above).[31]

9. A Gentile is liable to capital punishment for transgressing the injunction of *Dinim* that is commanded by God to all Gentiles, in

---

[28] See *She'iltot*, ch. 2, regarding the Torah Law for a Jew, and *Ha'amek Sha'aloh* ch. 2, regarding the Torah Law for a Gentile.

[29] See *Shulĥan Aruĥ Ĥoshen Mishpat* 8:4, which says that the community must honor a judge, clearly implying that it is forbidden to disrespect him. See also *Ĥemdat Yisrael* on Rambam, *Laws of Kings* ch. 9, that the prohibition for a Gentile to curse a judge comes from the Noahide prohibition of cursing God. This is also implied from Rashi on Tractate *Sanhedrin* 56b. See also *Mitzvot HaShem* by Rabbi Yonatan Shteif, p. 377.

[30] See *Mitzvot HaShem*, p. 453.

[31] See Meiri on Tractate *Sanhedrin* 56, that all the Noahide Commandments apply equally to men and women. It appears that although Gentile women are not liable for capital punishment for obstructing justice (as written in *Mesheĥ Ĥoĥmah*, that for this reason they were not killed along with the men of Sheĥem), it is still forbidden for them to hinder the process of justice at all.

regard to those aspects of *Dinim* that are set Torah Laws. Therefore, a judge who perverts and changes the law intentionally, due to his own wickedness or a bribe, deserves capital punishment.[32]

Regarding a court or individual judge that neglects the duty to judge a case involving one of the Seven Noahide Commandments,[33] there is an argument among the Torah-law opinions. Rambam[34] is of the opinion that any party involved in the neglect of the duty to judge is liable – be it the individual judge, the court or any witness who fails to testify. Ramban[35] disagrees and holds that one can only be liable to capital punishment for doing a forbidden action (for example, a judge who delivers a perverted judgment), but not for a neglectful inaction.

10. It is forbidden for someone acting as an individual to execute a person who has transgressed one of the Seven Noahide Commandments. Rather, the offender must be judged by a court[36] and receive his penalty from the court. One who goes ahead and kills the transgressor

---

The determination as to whether a woman can be liable for bribing a judge may be dependent on an argument between Rambam and Ramban. Rambam (as explained in *Sheva Mitzvot HaShem*, Part VIII, ch. 10) is of the opinion that one who knows a relevant testimony but willfully does not testify is liable, so one who actively gives a bribe is liable. It is possible that Ramban, who says that one who gives false testimony is liable, may not agree that one who gives a bribe is liable, since the former directly obstructs the judge from making a just decision, whereas the latter is merely assisting the transgression of the judge; therefore, the judge would be the liable party, since he accepted the bribe and carried out the deed of perverting his judgment.

32 Tractate *Sanhedrin* 57a.

33 It is clear that even according to Rambam, a Gentile would only be liable for not judging a transgression of the Seven Noahide Commandments, and he is not liable for not judging monetary matters or the like.

34 Rambam, *Laws of Kings*, ch. 9. See *Sheva Mitzvot HaShem*, Part VIII, topic 10:6 and footnotes there.

35 Ramban on Genesis 34:13. This is also the opinion of Ran (Rabbeinu Nissim), on Tractate *Sanhedrin* 56.

36 *Sefer HaĤinuĥ* Commandment 409, based on the verse, “And the murderer shall not be killed until he stands trial” (Numbers 35:12). Although this command is a specific precept given to Jews, it appears that as part of the laws of *Dinim*, a court must judge an accused murderer, rather than individuals taking the law into their own hands.

before the court has decided on a death penalty is considered as failing to uphold the command of *Dinim* (in addition to his sin of murder – and for that alone he is liable to capital punishment – unless the accused was a murderer who escaped from the court, as explained in Part V, topic 1:25, and *Sheva Mitzvot HaShem*, Part VIII, Chapter 13).

As part of the prohibition of failing to uphold the commandment of *Dinim,* it is also forbidden to appoint any person to a court if the person is not qualified to judge, either to judge a case or to carry out a judgment from the court. (This does not include a monetary dispute, in which the two parties may appoint a mediator to reach a settlement for them; that is a valid act under the commandment of *Dinim*, as explained in Chapter 3 below.)

11. All the precepts mentioned above comprise the main components of the commandment for *Dinim*, as given for all Gentiles by the Torah of Moses. **The Rabbinical authorities of our generation wrote that the Torah Laws concerning an obligation for Noahide Courts to administer capital punishment apply *only* if the majority of the society's population believes in the One True God and specifically observes the Seven Noahide Commandments as Divine commandments that they accept upon themselves.** In that situation, an individual who leaves the behavioral boundaries of the society to transgress one of those commandments is liable to the specified punishment from a Noahide Court.

If, however, the majority of the society's population does not believe in the One True God and observe the Seven Noahide Commandments (for example, if as a whole they regularly permit transgression of at least one of these commandments), the courts of that society are not permitted to sentence a transgressor of one of the Seven Noahide Commandments to receive the death penalty on the basis of the Torah Law.[37]

---

[37] See *Ĥazon Ish Bava Kama* 10:16, that if Gentile witnesses and judges do not fully keep the Seven Noahide Commandments, due to this being the case for society at large, then even though they are considered trustworthy by society and do observe law and order (and uphold the command for *Dinim* as such), they are nevertheless forbidden to charge someone as liable for the death penalty, since these witnesses and judges do not accept the "yoke of Heaven" and their Seven Commandments.

(However, if the courts decide that it is necessary to apply the death penalty for murder in order to bolster the safety of the society, they are permitted, but not required, to execute convicted murderers.)[38]

12. Even if most of the Gentiles in a certain country do not abide by the Seven Noahide Commandments as Divine precepts, but instead they observe the basic obligations of some of the Noahide Commandments based on their own morality and logic – for example, abiding by the prohibitions of theft and murder, and judging transgressors in an upright manner, by establishing their own courts to sentence transgressors for theft, murder, injury and the like, and to decide in monetary cases – this is considered for them as a *partial* fulfillment of their commandment of *Dinim*.

Likewise, if the courts in such societies do not sentence violators of the Seven Noahide Commandments to capital punishment, but rather sentence them to confinement in jail or other punishments,[39] they are nevertheless keeping the principle of the commandment of *Dinim*, in that they are keeping society from reverting to chaos, and the main

---

See *Igrot Moshe Ĥoshen Mishpat* vol. 2, ch. 68, by Rav Moshe Feinstein. **For the author of the present work, it is obvious that Rav Feinstein's opinion is that the non-Noahide Gentile courts in our modern secular societies may not impose a death penalty, even for murder, unless they see that extenuating circumstances are forcing them to do so specifically for murderers, as when the society becomes unchecked in transgressing this basic command.**

[38] *It is clear that the permission to execute convicted murders must be applied based on uniform guidelines that are set by the society's legal system, and not based on case-by-case personal whims or prejudices of individual judges or others who are assigned to declare what punishment will be given.

[39] However, if the majority of a society correctly accepts all of the Noahide Commandments, then it appears that in the opinion of Rambam, if there is an empowered court that fully accepts the Noahide Commandments as given by God and correctly judges cases within the Seven Commandments according to the commandment for *Dinim*, but it decides as an option not to execute a convicted Gentile transgressor who is liable to capital punishment according to the Torah Law – then it has not fulfilled the commandment of *Dinim*. In such a case, the judges themselves are liable in the opinion of Rambam (but not in the opinion of Ramban, as explained in topic 9 above).

purpose of this commandment is to establish a society that protects its citizens from being wronged by one another.[40]

Therefore, an observant Noahide who has the ability and knowledge to judge is permitted and has a duty to become a judge for a non-Noahide Gentile court, in order to establish law and order in the society as much as possible, even if (due to the circumstances in his country) he is unable to administer justice by the guidelines of the Noahide Code. Likewise, an observant Noahide who is able to give testimony on a certain matter, or has reason for a lawsuit against another person, must go to these courts and testify or bring the case before them, because those judges for the country are bringing a degree of righteousness and morality to the society.

(If it is clear that the justice system of the country is corrupt, it is forbidden for a person to participate in such judgments, either as a judge, witness, or litigant.)

There is no obligation for observant Noahides to set up their own Noahide Courts if they are a minority in a country that has a generally just society.

13. Every nation and country is obligated to appoint judges in order to bring justice to them (as explained above in topic 2). In every district there should be a court, and in every city there should be one or a number of judges. There should also be a highest appellate court to deal with issues that apply to the whole nation, and to oversee all the lower courts to make sure that they are judging correctly and keeping their obligation to abide by the command for *Dinim*.[41]

---

[40] As explained by Rashi on Genesis 11:9, God's destruction of the Generation of the Flood, and of the metropolis cities of Sodom, was a harsher punishment than that given to the Generation of the Tower of Babel, who were not destroyed but only dispersed with 70 different languages. God applied these different punishments because the former people sinned against both God and their fellow men, whereas the latter only sinned against God, and not against their fellow men.

[41] This is comparable to the Jewish commandment to set up a Supreme Court, called the Great Sanhedrin, which is to be responsible to oversee the lower courts, as explained by Rambam, *Laws of Courts* 2:8 and ch. 5, and Ramban on Deuteronomy 7:18.

However, no Gentile court of one nation has permission to judge people of another nation.[42] This applies equally to judging all the people of a foreign nation, or one community within a foreign nation, or one detail of their affairs, since the people of one nation do not have jurisdiction to judge the people of another nation.

Therefore, there is no Torah-based obligation for any Gentile nation to extradite a foreigner who has fled from his own country's justice system, although they may do so if they wish. However, it appears that as a logical moral code for all societies, if the country that is holding the fugitive from justice knows that the person deserves to be brought to trial for committing a crime, it is proper to extradite the fugitive, in order to support justice and morality for the whole world.

---

[42] See Responsa of *Maĥaneh Ĥayim* vol. 2, *Oraĥ Ĥayim* ch. 22, in explanation of the words of Rambam that the people of Sheĥem were liable for not exacting justice: there is nonetheless no obligation for one city to judge the lawless society of another city. In this opinion, it was for this reason that Jacob was angry at his sons Shimon and Levi for executing judgment when they were not obligated to do so. This is the simple understanding of the words of Ramban on Genesis 34:13: "However, the matter was not given over to Jacob and his sons that they should execute justice against them [the Canaanites]."

See also Ramban on Genesis 19:8 and Deuteronomy 16:18, and *Sifri* and Malbim on Deuteronomy 16:18.

CHAPTER 2

The Prohibition Against Perverting the Course of Justice or Taking a Bribe

1. Every judge is commanded and warned to judge righteously,[43] as it says, "You shall not commit a perversion of justice; you shall not favor the poor and you shall not honor the great; with righteousness shall you judge your fellow."[44] It also says, "Do not pervert the judgment of your poor person in his grievance."[45] It also says, "You shall not pervert the judgment of a proselyte or orphan."[46] The Bible repeatedly warns a number of times about the perversion of justice,[47] especially concerning the perversion of justice for those who are weak, because the judge has to strengthen his resolve to the utmost to protect their rights before violent and strong people who try to oppress them, and the judges are likely to ignore their distress.

2. It is forbidden for a judge to pervert a judgment, which includes convicting the innocent or vindicating the guilty,[48] whether in monetary cases or in cases of capital offense. Even regarding a defendant who is known to be wicked, it is forbidden to pervert the judgment by condemning him if there is insufficient evidence to prove that he violated the law in the case that has been brought to the court.[49] This is stated regarding monetary cases in the verse, "Do not pervert

---

[43] From *Ĥasdei Dovid Tosefta* end of Tractate *Avodah Zarah* and *Minĥat Ĥinuĥ* Mitzvah 235, this is also obligatory on Gentiles as part of their commandment of *Dinim*.

[44] Leviticus 19:15.

[45] Exodus 23:6.

[46] Deuteronomy 24:17.

[47] See Rambam, *Laws of Courts* 20:12.

[48] Rambam, *ibid.* 20:6.

[49] See *Ĥatam Sofer Likutim* ch. 14, and *Minĥat Ĥinuĥ* Commandments 81 and 233, that this verse also applies to Gentiles. Obviously, the judge must use his discretion when a case has reasonable doubt; it is only prohibited for him to make judgment based on a personal estimation of the righteousness of a litigant. See *Sheva Mitzvot HaShem*, Part VIII, topic 5:9.

the judgment of your poor person in his grievance."[50] (About this, the Sages explained that "poor" means poor in observance of his commandments, meaning that because he is sinful, he has no merits in the eyes of the judge.) And regarding cases of capital offense, it is stated, "do not execute the innocent or the righteous."[51] If "the innocent" is stated, what extra meaning is added by "the righteous"? It refers to a defendant who should be declared "righteous," i.e. not guilty, in his court trial, because even if he is known to have committed crimes in the past, there is not enough legal evidence to convict him in the present case, and certainly the judge must therefore not take this opportunity to have him put to death.[52]

It is obvious that it is forbidden for a judge to pervert justice for the sake of someone whom he wishes to gain favor from or to promote, for whatever reason. Judges are warned against all these things,[53] which are all included in the precept of, "you shall not commit a perversion of justice," that was cited above. Someone who violates one of these prohibitions has transgressed the Noahide commandment of *Dinim*.

3. What is included in the prohibition of "you shall not favor a poor person"? It is forbidden for a judge to have mercy on a poor person in judgment, and he should not say to himself, "This man is poor, and his opponent is rich, and it is appropriate that the rich man should support the poor man [because he needs charity]. Therefore, I will award the monetary judgment to the poor man, and as a result he will be supported in dignity."

The prohibition of "you shall not respect a great man" means that if a case comes before a judge between a rich wise man and a poor simple man, the judge should not favor the rich wise man. For example, the judge should not ask the rich man about his well-being, because with this the judge is showing favoritism, and when the poor man sees this, he will become bewildered and will stumble in his arguments or withhold them, and then the resulting judgment will not be fair. Similarly, the judge should not say to himself, "How can I find this honorable person guilty in judgment, and then as a result he will be

---

[50] Exodus 23:6 and *Meĥilta* there; Rambam, *Sefer HaMitzvot* Neg. Com. 278.

[51] Exodus 23:7.

[52] *Meĥilta* and Ibn Ezra on Exodus *ibid.*

[53] See *Sefer HaĤinuĥ* Commandment 233.

embarrassed? I will declare him to be innocent, and after that I will tell him privately that he is really guilty and responsible to pay the amount." A judge should not do any such things; rather, he should promptly decide and hand down the correct legal judgment, without showing favor to either litigant for any reason.[54]

4. It is forbidden for a Gentile judge to take a bribe, for this directly results in a perverted judgment.[55] Even taking a bribe to give a correct judgment is forbidden,[56] for the Torah declares twice, once in Exodus – "You shall not accept a bribe, for a bribe will blind the clear sighted and corrupt words that are right"[57] – and again in Deuteronomy: "You shall not pervert justice; you shall not show favoritism, and you shall not take a bribe, for bribery blinds the eyes of the wise and perverts just words."[58] Bribery perverts the opinion of the judge, because from the moment he accepts a bribe, his opinion leans (away from the proper and unbiased judgment) because of the bribe that he received,[59] and he does not judge fairly.[60]

It is also forbidden for a judge to take bribes from both litigants, even if he takes an equal sum from both of them.[61]

5. A judge has to be very careful not to take a bribe. If a judge feels that because of some favor that one of the litigants once did for him, his opinion is leaning in that person's favor, he is obligated to invalidate himself from judging in that case, because he might not

---

[54] *Shulĥan Aruĥ Ĥoshen Mishpat* 17:10.

[55] Ramban on Genesis 34:13, in the name of the Jerusalem Talmud.

[56] Rambam *Laws of Courts* ch. 23; *Shulĥan Aruĥ Ĥoshen Mishpat* ch. 9.

[57] Exodus 23:8.

[58] Deuteronomy 16:19.

[59] Rashi on Deut. 16:19 – one may not take a bribe, even to give a just sentence, for once one takes a bribe it is not possible to turn against the giver.

[60] As explained in footnote 27, the Noahide Law of *Dinim* is the overall commandment that includes all the details which for Jews are individual commands, as explained in Part VII, last footnote to topic 1:1. It is also clear from Ramban mentioned earlier that a Gentile judge may not take a bribe even where he has decided to make just sentence.

[61] *Ha'Amek Davar* on Exodus 23:8; *Birkei Yosef*, brought in *Pisĥei Teshuva* on *Shulĥan Aruĥ Ĥoshen Mishpat* 9:3 regarding a Gentile judge.

make a fair judgment.[62]

It is forbidden for a judge to accept a gift from a litigant who gives it in order that he be found innocent in judgment. This prohibition of accepting a gift from a litigant applies even after the judge has completed his deliberation and already decided what his correct legal ruling is, and has already delivered the verdict or stated the law, because this is similar to bribery.[63]

Just as it is forbidden for a judge to take a bribe, so too it is forbidden for a policeman to take a bribe to absolve himself from fulfilling his responsibility.[64]

6. A judge who took a bribe is invalid to judge from that point on, and his judgments are not to be regarded as the law – not in the case in which he took the bribe, and not in any case that he will judge in the future.[65] However, the judgments that he made before he took the bribe are not invalidated.[66]

7. It appears that according to the law, a Gentile judge who took a bribe is not obligated to return the bribe, for it was given to him as a gift.[67] It is clear that the society's legal system has permission to institute that the bribe may be taken away from the judge, and this enactment would be proper. It has already been explained that they are obligated to rescind his decision that he passed, remove him from his position as judge and punish him for taking the bribe (as explained in *Sheva Mitzvot HaShem*, Part VIII, topic 2:9).

8. Just as it is forbidden for a judge to take a bribe, it is obvious that

---

[62] *Shulĥan Aruĥ Ĥoshen Mishpat* 9:1,2.

[63] See Rema *Ĥoshen Mishpat* 34:18.

[64] See *Kli Ĥemda, Shoftim* 97b.

[65] *Shulĥan Aruĥ Ĥoshen Mishpat* 7:9. After a judge has taken a bribe once, he is considered to be a sinful person and is unfit to even testify in court from then on (unless he does complete repentance), and any future cases he judges are invalid. This is clear from *Sefer Meirat Einayim Ĥoshen Mishpat* 9:13.

[66] See *Prisha Ĥoshen Mishpat* ch. 9, *Urim Ĥoshen Mishpat* 9:7, and *Pisĥei Teshuva Ĥoshen Mishpat* 9:10, regarding one who is paid by litigants to judge their cases. Unless there is proof or a very strong reason to believe that he was previously untrustworthy, the past judgments he made are still valid.

[67] See *Shulĥan Aruĥ Ĥoshen Mishpat* ch. 9.

the prohibition also applies to the one who gives it, because he is causing the judge to transgress and pervert justice,[68] and indeed he transgresses the commandment of *Dinim.*

There is no difference between a monetary bribe or any other favor or benefit; it is all considered bribery – for example, when a litigant pays any of the judge's debts,[69] or giving a bribe through others to be given to the judge.[70]

9. The Sages taught that any judge who charges money from litigants in order to judge them, that his judgments are invalid.[71] Even though this was said regarding the judgment of the Jewish people, nevertheless, it is obvious that every society or government of Gentiles is obligated to establish a salary for their permanent judges and officers, that will be arranged from the public funds (of the region or city), so that they should be paid handsomely and not be dependent on getting paid through the goodwill of the ones being judged.[72] This is because a judge who takes money from litigants is acting very similarly to taking a bribe, and this will lead to perversion of justice.

If it is the custom in a certain place that a permanent judge takes an equal sum of money from every litigant that comes before him, then it is permitted, since all the people in that place accept that they will act in this way, and the payment is known and fixed.[73]

10. This above law pertains to a permanent judge (established by the government, or the like), before whom the litigants are forced to be judged. Therefore, the public is obligated to arrange that his salary be

---

[68] *Shulĥan Aruĥ Ĥoshen Mishpat* ch. 9 explains that this is prohibited for a Jew under the Jewish commandment, "You shall not put a stumbling block before the blind." Although that precept is not incumbent upon Gentiles, it has been explained in Part I, ch. 4, that it is forbidden for Gentiles to do this. It is also possible that one who gives a bribe transgresses the prohibition of "You shall commit no injustice in judgment;" see *Or HaĤayim* on Leviticus 19:16, and topic 1:8 and the footnote to topic 1:8 above.

[69] *Panim B'Mishpat* 9:11.

[70] *Ĥatam Sofer Likutim* ch. 14.

[71] Tractate *Beĥorot* 29; *Shulĥan Aruĥ Ĥoshen Mishpat* 9:5.

[72] *Tur Ĥoshen Mishpat* ch. 9.

[73] *Urim Ĥoshen Mishpat* 9:9.

fixed according to their collective opinion, so that he will judge truthfully and fairly. But if a judge is asked by litigants to judge them in a monetary case (as an occasional private manner, and not because it is required by the government's law, so it is considered a type of arbitration), or to arrange a compromise for them, then he is permitted to establish his payment in advance according to the discussion he has together with both of them, because they have willingly accepted his authority over their dispute.[74]

In addition, this payment must be made in advance[75] by both litigants (in front of each other,[76] so that neither of them will suspect the other or the judge); otherwise, it is not a fair judgment. This is because arbitration and compromise are also considered to be types of judgment, and it is forbidden for a judge who arbitrates or arranges a compromise to take bribery or pervert the judgment against one of the sides, for this is theft and a violation of the principles of *Dinim*. And if a litigant tells the arbitrator or the one arranging the compromise, "If you will find me innocent, I will give you such-and-such a sum of money," then that is complete bribery.[77]

11. A judge is permitted to take an additional payment for any other necessary expenses (such as upkeep of his office), but if a judge gives undue raises to his assistants and liberally increases their expenditures or the like (at the expense of the public or a private person), then this person is displaying greed, and it is disgraceful.[78]

12. Included in the precepts of "Do not pervert the judgment" and "You shall not commit a perversion of justice" is the prohibition of causing suffering by prolonging the decision of judgment.[79] This

---

[74] Shaĥ *Ĥoshen Mishpat* 9:7, and *Ĥoĥmat Shlomo* there.

[75] See *Sefer Meirat Einayim Ĥoshen Mishpat* 9:14, that it is sufficient to establish payment before the case begins.

[76] Shaĥ *Ĥoshen Mishpat* 9:6.

[77] See Responsa of *Pani'im Meirot* vol. 2, ch. 159, and *Aruĥ HaShulĥan* 9:6.

[78] *Shulĥan Aruĥ Ĥoshen Mishpat* 9:4.

[79] See Rambam *Laws of Courts* 20:6; *Sefer HaĤinuĥ* Commandment 233. It appears that it is even forbidden to delay a verdict in a capital case, as explained in Rambam *Laws of Courts* ch. 11. See *Sheva Mitzvot HaShem*, Part VIII, topic 13:13.

means holding back from judging a certain case because the court pushes aside upholding the law, especially if it is done by extending the trials of weak people such as orphans and widows. Regarding them it is stated, "You shall not oppress any widow or orphan,"[80] because their souls are downcast,[81] and they do not have the power to demand from the judges to judge their cases promptly (or at all). Regarding judges who prolong in deciding the law for the cases of weak people, the prophet says, "The orphan they do not judge, and the quarrel of the widow does not come to them. 'Therefore,' says the Master, the Lord of Hosts, the Mighty One of Israel, 'Oh, I will console Myself from My adversaries, and I will avenge Myself of My foes.' "[82]

Prolonging the decision of judgment is included in the prohibition of "You shall not commit a perversion of justice" because procrastinating to make a decision in judgment causes the wronged person a loss of time and money as well as great pain, and sometimes, because the judgment is pushed off (repeatedly), the plaintiff loses hope of receiving fair judgment. In this case, both oppression and perversion of justice are committed through the withholding of judgment.

13. Included in the prohibition of extending and pushing off a legal judgment is that which the Sages referred to, "A judgment of a *maneh* [a large sum of money] should be as esteemed in your eyes as the judgment of a small coin."[83] This means that if a case of a small coin comes before a judge and he has begun to hear the case, he should not stop and push it away (thereby delaying the judgment of the case) in favor of hearing another case involving a large sum of money that was waiting next in line. Instead, the legal proceedings and judgment of the case at hand, whether it is a small or large matter, should be judged first.[84] This is also what Moses commanded to the judges of the Jewish

---

80 Exodus 22:21. See *Meĥilta* there, and *Sha'arei Teshuva* of Rabbi Yonah (*Sha'ar Shlishi*, ch. 24).

81 Rambam *Laws of Personality Development* ch. 6; *Sefer HaĤinuĥ* Commandment 65.

82 Isaiah 1:23-4.

83 *Shulĥan Aruĥ Ĥoshen Mishpat* ch. 10.

84 Tractate *Sanhedrin* 8a, *Sefer Meirat Einayim Ĥoshen Mishpat* ch. 10.

people: "You shall not show favoritism in judgment, small and great alike shall you hear."[85]

14. Similarly, a judge is forbidden to delay his judgment of case (meaning, he draws out the judgment for an unnecessary time), by lengthening matters that are clear, in order to cause pain to one of the litigants, or to the one who is guilty. This is included in the rule of "You shall commit no injustice in judgment."[86]

The rule of the matter is this: anyone who pushes off the judgment is unjust; whether it is in carrying out the discussions and judgment, lengthening the judgment, or in carrying out the decision, it is causing suffering by delaying judgment, and it is included in the prohibition of "You shall not commit a perversion of justice."

---

[85] Deuteronomy 1:17. See *Sheva Mitzvot HaShem*, Part VIII, ch. 7.

[86] Leviticus 19:15. See Rambam *Laws of Courts* 20:6; *Shulĥan Aruĥ Ĥoshen Mishpat* 17:11.

CHAPTER 3

Monetary Laws, and Laws of Mediation and Arbitration

1. It has already been explained in Chapter 1 that included in the Gentiles' obligation of the commandment of *Dinim* is the obligation to judge in cases of a claimant and a defendant.[87]

Which are cases of a claimant and a defendant?

This would include every monetary case that arises by the claim for money between a man and his fellow, such as:

- cases of robbery and theft in which the robbed victim claims that the robber should return to him that which was stolen;
- cases of fraud in which the buyer sues the seller for fraud in price or similar things;
- cases of exploitation and an employee's salary in which the exploited claims payment that is due to him;
- cases of guardians in which the one who entrusted his article claims the article entrusted to the guardian;
- cases of lenders and borrowers;
- cases of business transactions such as when one side reneges on the agreement, or when the buyer claims that there is a blemish in that which he purchased, and any claims similar to these,
- similarly, cases of partners who come to divide their possessions.

Any sum of money about which there is an argument between a man and his fellow, and they are not able to come to agreement between themselves about what each of them is due, the court is obligated to judge their case, for the sake of justice and peace.

Also, Gentiles are obligated to judge in cases of bodily harm or harm to life (and the principles of these things have already been explained in the laws of murder and theft), and damages to property or possessions.

It has already been explained in Chapter 1 that these laws are not decided according to Torah as to what is the law for each one of them, but instead it is the responsibility of the Gentile societies and law-makers to discuss these matters and to pass fair laws in each matter

[87] *Sefer HaĤinuĥ* Commandment 58; see *Minĥat Ĥinuĥ* there.

and in each detail of these laws, and to judge in each case as pertains to that situation according to the laws they establish.

2. Included in the commandment of *Dinim* for Gentiles is to make compromises between the litigants,[88] as it says,[89] "that they keep the way of the Lord, doing righteousness and justice," and justice means compromise.

A compromise is a judgment of peace, as it says, "Administer truth and the judgment of peace in your gates."[90] What is a type of judgment that has peace in it (meaning agreement and appeasement between the two sides)? This is a compromise.[91]

3. Therefore, the correct procedure in light of Torah is that initially the judge should suggest and say to the litigants, "Do you desire a judgment or a compromise?"[92] It is also a righteous practice on the part of the judge to attempt to make a compromise between the two litigants and to convince them to do this, and also after he heard their claims and he knows in which direction the judgment will lean, it is still a righteous practice to make a compromise.[93] If they agree to make a compromise, that is preferable to making a judgment, but the

---

[88] Rashi and Meiri on Tractate *Sanhedrin* 56b. See *Mesheĥ Ĥoĥmah* on Genesis 18:19 which God said about Abraham, that compromise ("righteousness" in this verse) precedes judgment, and for Gentiles, even if a judge knows the decision to which the law is inclined, it is righteous to make a compromise between the litigants (and only if they are persistent in demanding a legal ruling should the judge do so).

[89] Genesis 18:19.

[90] Zeĥariah 8:16.

[91] Tractate *Sanhedrin* 6b.

[92] Rambam, *Laws of Courts* ch. 22; *Shulĥan Aruĥ Ĥoshen Mishpat* ch. 12.

[93] *Shulĥan Aruĥ ibid.* 12:2. See *Ethics of the Fathers* 4:7, "Rabbi Yishmael [the son of Rabbi Yosay] said, '[A judge] who refrains from handing down legal judgments [but instead seeks compromise between the litigants] removes himself from enmity, theft, and [the responsibility for] an unnecessary oath; but one who aggrandizes himself by [eagerly] issuing legal decisions is a fool, wicked and arrogant.' "

litigants are not obligated to accept the compromise that the judge will make unless they made a commitment to do so.[94]

Even though it is a righteous practice to make a compromise, if the judge recognizes that there is a real theft or exploitation committed by the defendant, it is a preferred righteous practice to save the exploited person from the hand of the one who exploited him. Therefore, the judge should make an unequivocal judgment, and he should not make a compromise that will cause loss to the exploited and an unfair gain to the exploiter. Only if he has no ability at all to pass judgment and fairness against the wicked person and remove the theft (the stolen goods or payment) from his hands, then he should make a compromise from lack of any better available choice.[95]

4. Just as the judge must create equality between the two litigants and listen to their words equally, so too in a compromise. The compromise that the judge suggests must be equal, and not show preference to one side more than the other,[96] because it says,[97] "Justice, justice you shall pursue." In the doubled language of this verse, one directive for justice refers to justice in judgment, and the other directive for justice refers to justice in compromise.[98]

5. Even after a litigant accepted a compromise in his demands and committed himself to the decision according to the legal procedure, if he finds a proof or testimony that was hidden from him at the time that they made the compromise, and the judgment should be changed in a substantial manner because of that proof, he may go back and change what he accepted because his compromise and his monetary waiver were made in error.[99]

Similarly if the judge erred in the compromise with a very big error that leaned the judgment of the compromise to one side in a manner

---

[94] *Shulĥan Aruĥ ibid.*, 12:7.

[95] See *Pisĥei Teshuva Ĥoshen Mishpat* 12:4.

[96] *Shulĥan Aruĥ Ĥoshen Mishpat* 12:2.

[97] Deuteronomy 16:20.

[98] *Sefer Meirat Einayim Ĥoshen Mishpat* 12:7.

[99] *Shulĥan Aruĥ Ĥoshen Mishpat* 12:14,15 and end of ch. 25; *Sefer Meirat Einayim ibid.* 25:7.

that was not appropriate, the litigant who lost out may appeal and bring it to judgment again.[100]

6. Two litigants are permitted to arrange for themselves one arbitrator or a number of arbitrators who will hear their case and pass judgment.[101] It seems to me that arbitration (by Gentiles) is a sub-category of making a compromise which is part of the commandment of *Dinim*, and just as the judge is obligated to try to make a compromise as explained above, similarly, if the litigants agree to make a compromise between themselves either on their own or through an arbitrator whom they both accept, then this is compared to a compromise arranged by a judge; i.e., it is considered to have fulfilled the commandment of *Dinim*.

That which has been explained in *Sheva Mitzvot HaShem,* Part VIII, Chapter 5, that the regular court should force the two litigants to be judged before it, this applies when one of them or both of them do not want to be judged in any form of law (not in a court, not by a compromise, and not by arbitrators). But if they both agree to a compromise or to arbitration, then that is their prerogative and they are not forced to be judged by the law.[102]

7. Arbitration is similar to a compromise in that they both need binding acceptance, because otherwise each side could renege on it. It is proper that each side should find for himself one arbitrator to be like a judge, and if they want, a third arbitrator as a judge, then they should choose a third arbitrator by mutual agreement, or they should grant permission to the two arbitrators who were already selected to choose for themselves a third arbitrator. The two sides should then write up a document of arbitration in which each side obligates himself to accept this arbitration as binding. And after they do this, neither side is able to disagree with these arbitrators or with their conclusion, or to demand that additional arbitrators be added on to the three[103] (with the

---

[100] See notes of R. Akiva Eiger on *Shulĥan Aruĥ Ĥoshen Mishpat* ch. 12.

[101] See *Kesef Mishneh Hilĥot Sanhedrin* beginning of ch. 7; *Sefer Meirat Einayim ibid.* 13:1.

[102] See *Shulĥan Aruĥ Ĥoshen Mishpat* 3:1.

[103] *Ibid.*, 13:2.

exception of situations in which an error in the judgment is discovered, as mentioned above in topic 5).

8. Even though the process of arbitration is like reaching a compromise, it is similar to judgment (with the agreement of the litigants), in that the arbitrators are discussing between themselves how to judge and decide between the litigants. Therefore, all the prohibitions that apply to the judge in order to prevent perversion of justice also apply to the arbitrator; for example he is not allowed to take a bribe which will distort the judgment, and the arbitrator should not listen to the words of one litigant when not in the presence of his opponent.[104]

Any payment to an arbitrator for his service of arbitration needs to be given by each side equally, because otherwise it would be a case of bribery and distortion in favor of one side.[105]

9. If the arbitrators do not know how to judge or decide in a specific case, and they want to ask for advice from sages or other judges regarding the matter, they are permitted to do so, and the litigants may not prevent them from doing this, since they already obligated themselves with the arbitration.[106]

---

[104] *Pisĥei Teshuva Ĥoshen Mishpat* 13:3.

[105] See *Aruĥ HaShulĥan Ĥoshen Mishpat* 13:4.

[106] See *Shulĥan Aruĥ Ĥoshen Mishpat* 13:6.

CHAPTER 4

Societal Morality and the Obligation of Doing Kindness

1. Though the commandment of *Dinim* is primarily focused on the conduct of the community, with the purpose of creating a just society, each individual is nevertheless part of this community and will necessarily impact society as a whole through his or her actions. Therefore, along with the obligations on the individual to uphold the command of *Dinim* as part of the general scope of the command discussed in topic 1:5 above, there are also additional obligations on the individual's conduct, as a sort of branch of the command of *Dinim*.

Though all these obligations are both logical and ethical and therefore obligatory as discussed in Part I, Chapter 3, they are also considered part of the commandment of *Dinim* since they are the just way to act towards another person, and the purpose of the obligations is identical to that of *Dinim*, which is to make a functional and orderly world.

2. "With righteousness shall you judge your fellow" (Lev. 19:15): This verse teaches us not only about the upholding of justice in the courts, but also the ethical and moral way for an individual to conduct his or herself. The Sages learned from this verse,[107] "Judge each person favorably,"[108] and they also taught regarding the necessity of reaching a compromise in order to preserve peace,[109] and that making peace is part of judging favorably and acting kindly.

3. Part of the obligation of judging favorably is the necessary effort that must be put out to persuade the other person to become more upright. This is the source of the prohibition explained in Part I, Chapter 4, that a Gentile may not lead another to stumble in sin, as it is obligatory to judge another favorably, which includes helping the other person to become more upright.

---

[107] *Torat Kohanim* and Rashi on Lev. 19:15. See Tractate *Sanhedrin* 32.

[108] See Rambam, *Sefer HaMitzvot* Positive Commandment 177; *Sefer Mitzvot HaShem* by R. Yonatan Shteif, p. 490.

[109] See *Ethics of the Fathers,* in: 1:12, "Hillel said: 'Be of the disciples of Aaron, loving peace and pursuing peace..."

It is therefore befitting that any person who can assist others in teaching the foundations of belief in the One God and the obligations of one person to another and to God, must accept this great obligation. As previously explained in Part I, topic 3:1, Moses our teacher was commanded that all people must be compelled to accept the Seven Noahide Laws, and the obligation to persuade people to accept this is not only upon Jews, but also upon Gentiles. Any persons or groups who have influence – be they kings, governments, courts, or any individuals – and who have the ability to persuade and explain to someone about the obligation to observe the Noahide Laws, is required to do so.

4. It is self-explanatory that saving a person's life from a would-be murderer is also an aspect of pursuing justice, and therefore some say[110] that it is obligatory for a Gentile to save another person, based on the above branch of *Dinim* (in **addition** to the obligation explained in Part V, topic 7:3).

5. If two boats are traveling towards each other and at their meeting point there is not enough space for both to pass at the same time without capsizing, one vessel must wait at a wider point until the other passes through. The same applies to two camel drivers that are passing through a narrow precipice in a mountain, where both cannot traverse at the same time or one would fall off; it is incumbent on one of the camel drivers to return backwards and let the other pass. How is it determined which one should go through first? First priority goes to the one carrying a load; if both are equal in this regard, the one who has an easier time turning to the side or back should do so. If both are still equal, then they should compromise between themselves or decide on a compensation for the one turning back (or to make a rotation of turns if this regularly happens).

The same applies to all situations in which a number of people want to do something but cannot do it simultaneously; it is incumbent upon them to act justly in regards to making order and setting priority, even in regards to who goes first when walking up stairs, etc. Regarding

---

[110] See *Ĥemdat Yisrael* (Rambam, *Laws of Kings* 9:9) in the name of *Zeĥuta D'Avraham*, that a Gentile is obligated to save another's life under the command of *Dinim*.

such conduct, the verse says, "Justice, justice you shall pursue,"[111] i.e. one must pursue both a just decision in court, as well as a just compromise if there is no clear priority or weight towards one of the parties.[112]

6. It has previously been explained in Part I, Chapter 3, that the obligations which are logically incumbent, such as honoring one's parents or being kind and charitable, are obligatory upon all Gentiles since they are the ways of upright conduct.

There are Rabbinic opinions which say that Gentiles are obligated to give charity (as an additional active commandment,[113] beyond what is included in the specific Seven Noahide Laws, which only command about refraining from forbidden actions), and this obligation applies both to the community as well as the individual, to help the needy in any way possible.

Even those Rabbinic opinions that disagree and say that charity is not an explicit universal commandment, do agree that it is an obligation as part of the necessity to create a civilized world, by protecting and helping others.[114] It is not permissible, nor is there any justification, for any community to hide from its poor constituents and not make efforts to help them. A community that ignores the poor is comparable to the historic cities of Sodom and Ammorah (Gomorrah), and will eventually be destroyed as they were. Regarding these cities, the prophet Ezekiel said; "Behold, this was the sin of Sodom ... She and her daughters [her suburbs] had pride, fullness of bread and peaceful serenity, but she did not strengthen the hand of the poor and the needy. And they were haughty, and they committed an abomination before Me, so I removed them in accordance with what I saw."[115] The Sages said that the destruction of Sodom and Ammorah was only finally decreed on account of their not upholding the hand of the needy, and

---

[111] Deuteronomy 17:20.

[112] Tractate *Sanhedrin* 32; Rambam, end of *Laws of Murderers*; *Shulĥan Aruĥ Ĥoshen Mishpat* 272:14; *Shulĥan Aruĥ HaRav*, end of *Hilĥot Ovrei Deraĥim*.

[113] *Roke'ach* ch. 366; *Yad Ramah* and *Ĥidushei HaRan* on *Sanhedrin* 57b; and the approbation of *Netziv* for *Ahavat Ĥessed* of the Ĥofetz Ĥayim.

[114] *Likkutei Siĥot* vol. 5, p. 160.

[115] Ezekiel 16:49-50.

because they prevented from their midst all efforts of charity and help to the poor."[116]

7. Charity and kindness are the attribute of Abraham[117], about whom God said,[118] "For I have known (loved[119]) him, because he commands his children and his household after him, that they keep the way of the Lord, doing charity and justice ..." From all of Abraham's qualities, God praised his exceptional kindness.

8. An act of kindness is greater than charity, as it can be done for the rich as well as the poor, and can be done both with money as well as bodily effort (such as visiting the sick, gladdening a bride and groom, and escorting a friend). As well, charity is done only for the living, whereas one can do kindness for the dead as well (such as eulogizing, escorting the bier and burying the dead).[120]

Included in kind actions are visiting the sick, comforting the bereaved, paying for the expenses of the dead and arranging for a eulogy, and burying the dead with honor befitting the deceased and his or her relatives, making wedding arrangements and inviting guests.[121]

9. What is included in making wedding arrangements? It is a great kindness to assist in finding fitting matches for men and women, and the same applies for marrying off one's children, both with assistance in good advice and monetary help.

10. Kindness and charity can be done on many levels. A person should not mistakenly view the act of giving as only a kindness to others, as the act of giving is more beneficial to the giver than the recipient.

---

[116] See Ramban on Genesis 19:5, and Tractate *Sanhedrin* 104b and 109a.

[117] Rambam, *Laws of Gifts to the Poor* ch. 10.

[118] Genesis 18:19.

[119] Rashi on Genesis 18:19.

[120] Tractate *Sukkah* 49b.

[121] Rambam, *Laws of Mourners* ch. 14. See *Roke'aĥ* ch. 366, who implies that Gentiles are obligated to invite guests either because it is a logical obligation or it is part of their obligation of charity. See Rashbam on Genesis 26:8, that the obligation of inviting guests preceded the laws given at Sinai, i.e., that it is part of a commandment to Gentiles.

Anyone who has pity on the poor is pitied by God.[122] Therefore, a person should meditate that he is constantly requesting from God to provide the necessary livelihood, health and all other good things in life, and just as one depends on God to listen to his prayers, so must one answer the requests (and prayers) of the poor. One who has mercy on others is given mercy from Above, but one who closes his ears from hearing the cries of the poor should not wonder why God is not listening to him.

In this vein, the prophet says, "It has been told to you, O man, what is good, and what the Lord does require of you: only to do justly, and to love mercy, and to walk humbly with your God."[123] "To do justly" refers to correct justice in courts; "to love mercy" refers to charity; and "to walk humbly with your God" refers to escorting the deceased and arranging for the expenses of weddings."[124]

"To walk humbly with your God" also teaches that there is nothing finer than modesty, and there is nothing finer in the way of charity than giving to the poor with discretion.

11. There are eight levels of charity, each greater than the next:[125]

1) The greatest level, above which there is no greater, is to support a fellow person by endowing him with a gift or loan, or entering into a partnership with him, or finding employment for him, in order to strengthen his hand until he need no longer be dependent upon others. In this way the poor person need not feel the embarrassment of having to accept alms. Therefore, such charity, by which the poor person is accepting the money in a respectable way, is more praiseworthy than if the poor person is given alms that he is embarrassed to accept.

2) A lesser level of charity than this is to give to the poor without knowing to whom one gives, and without the recipient knowing from who he received. In this circumstance as well, the poor person need not feel embarrassment at being the recipient of charity from any specific person.

---

[122] *Tur* and *Shulĥan Aruĥ Yoreh De'ah* ch. 247.

[123] Miĥah 6:8.

[124] Tractate *Sukkah* 49b.

[125] Rambam, *Laws of Gifts to the Poor* ch. 10, *Shulĥan Aruĥ Yoreh De'ah* ch. 249.

Giving to a charity fund is similar to this mode of charity, and is a great deed, as the giver and receiver do not know who each other are.

3) A lesser level of charity than this is when one knows to whom one gives, but the recipient does not know his benefactor.

4) A lesser level of charity than this is when one does not know to whom one gives, but the poor person does know his benefactor.

5) A lesser level than this is when one gives to the poor person directly into his hand, but gives before being asked.

6) A lesser level than this is when one gives to the poor person after being asked.

7) A lesser level than this is when one gives inadequately, but gives gladly and with a smile, to encourage and pacify the recipient.

8) A lesser level than this is when one gives unwillingly and unhappily, causing the poor person embarrassment.

If one does give, but unhappily and with anger, he loses most of the merit of his giving.[126] One should not allow himself to feel or be openly haughty for the charity he has given, and if one does so, it is fitting that he not only lose his merit for helping the poor, but that he should even be punished (by Heaven for his haughtiness and the embarrassment he has caused to the poor).[127]

It is permissible for another person to publicize a donor's work, so that others will honor the donor and learn from the donor's good actions.[128]

12. A righteous Gentile should strive to give charity for the sake of Heaven alone, and not in order to merit rewards such as a livelihood or health, and surely not for his own honor (as this may cause him to lose his merit). Nevertheless, if one does give charity and then prays to receive some reward for this, the good deed still stands; however, it is not as great as if one gives with a pure heart.[129]

---

[126] Shaĥ *Yoreh De'ah* 249:9.

[127] Rema *Yoreh De'ah* 249:13, Tractate *Bava Batra* 10 in the opinion of Rabbi Yehoshua.

[128] See Rema *Yoreh De'ah* 249:13.

[129] See Tractates *Rosh HaShanah* 4 and *Bava Batra* 10, "one who gives a *selah* coin to a poor person so that his son should live, etc."

13. Helping one who is not needy is not considered charity. Such a person who takes from charitable funds is a thief and a swindler, as he swindles those who think they are giving true charity when this is not the case, and he is stealing the portions of those who are truly needy who now have less available to them.

Likewise, one should not give charity to one who collects unless it is clear that the collector is honest and is collecting for a just cause, as it is possible that the collector is a swindler and is using the community's money in an unnecessary and wrongful way.

This can be seen in the saying of the Sages, "We investigate a request for clothes but not for food," meaning that when a poor person whose identity is unknown says: "I am hungry, provide me with food," we do not investigate whether he is a deceiver (unless he is known to be a deceiver, in which case we do not give him anything). Instead, we provide him with sustenance immediately. However, if he asks for clothes or something less essential, we investigate whether he is a deceiver, and only if it is clear that he is truly in need do we give to him.[130]

14. The greatest charity is redeeming captives, and this holds the highest priority before any other type of charity. One who neglects to help the plight of captives or is lazy in redeeming them (when he is able to do so) is considered as having blood (i.e., murder) on his hands.[131]

15. In all forms of charity, it is proper to prioritize the needy that are closer than those who are farther. One's immediate family members come before the extended family, one's neighbors before the indigent of the rest of the city, and the indigent of one's city before those of the whole country.[132]

---

[130] Rambam, *Laws of Gifts to the Poor* ch. 7; *Shulĥan Aruĥ Yoreh De'ah* 251:10.

[131] Rambam, *Laws of Gifts to the Poor* ch. 8; *Shulĥan Aruĥ Yoreh De'ah* ch. 252. (Note that there are situations in which ransom is not given, so as not to encourage kidnappers, if the ransom is intended as a type of blackmail upon the society to extract money – see *Shulĥan Aruĥ Yoreh De'ah* 252:4.)

[132] *Shulĥan Aruĥ Yoreh De'ah* ch. 251.

16. If a Gentile who observes the Seven Laws desires to give charity through the Jews, it should be accepted from him. This charity money should be given to the Jewish poor, for a righteous Gentile who is in need may likewise receive sustenance from the Jews, and they are commanded to support him if necessary. In contrast, if an idolater desires to give charity through the Jews, it should be accepted from him and given to the Gentile poor.[133]

If a Gentile gives charity through a Gentile charity collector, it is the collector's choice as to which poor people he will distribute the money to, or to which cause he will remit the charity.[134]

17. If a Gentile gave charity to a synagogue, it may be accepted, provided the Gentile says, "I am donating it according to the intent of the Jewish people"[135] (i.e., that the Gentile donor is not going to be involved in deciding how those funds will be disbursed; generally such a gift is accepted, and should be dispersed in the appropriate manner based on the type of Gentile donor as detailed above in topic 16, and in topic 13 regarding gifts of food for the needy.)

Charity to the poor is greater than a donation to a synagogue in that it atones for one's sins, whereas a donation to a synagogue is considered only as a "burnt offering" to God.[136]

18. This does not apply to donations that fund any project for construction, repair or upkeep within the walls of Jerusalem, and surely not to the Temple Mount or the Temple itself, as such funding must only come from Jews,[137] as written in Ezra, "It is not for you [Gentiles] together with us [Jews] to build a Temple for our God;

---

[133] Rambam, *Laws of Kings* ch. 10. Though it says there that the closer the needy person is, the more precedent he has, this does not apply to a collector who is able to distribute as he sees fit, as explained in *Shulĥan Aruĥ Yoreh De'ah* 251:9.

[134] *However, charity money should not be given to, or collected for, any causes that are in violation of any precepts within the Noahide Code.

[135] Rambam, *Laws of Gifts to the Poor* 8:8, *Shulĥan Aruĥ Yoreh De'ah* 259:4.

[136] Shaĥ *Yoreh De'ah* 254:4.

[137] See Tractate *Erĥin* 5; Rambam: *Laws of Endowment Valuations* 1:11, *Laws of Gifts to the Poor* 8:8, and *Laws of Shekalim* 4:8.

rather we, by ourselves, will build [it] ...,"[138] and in Neĥemiah, "... but you [the Gentiles] have no portion nor charity nor remembrance in Jerusalem."[139]

19. The deed of inviting guests is a law enacted by Abraham for his descendants and those who follow in his ways, and is the way of kindness which he exemplified. He would feed the passersby and give them beverages to drink, and would escort them on their way. The reward for escorting is greater than all other ways of attending to a guest.

Indeed, inviting guests is greater than receiving the Divine Presence, as it says, "And he lifted up his eyes and saw, and behold! Three men were standing before him. He saw, and he ran to meet them from the entrance of the tent, and bowed toward the ground. And he said: 'My Lord, if it please you that I find favor in Your eyes, please pass not from before your servant.' "[140] This tells us that Abraham was sitting[141] in prayer before God, yet when he saw the guests, he asked permission from God to interrupt his prayer, and God's revelation to him, in order to take care of his guests and invite them in. Therefore, it can be seen that inviting in guests is greater than receiving the Divine Countenance (in prayer).[142]

Escorting a guest at the conclusion of one's hospitality is greater than inviting a guest into the house, and indeed the Sages say that one who does not escort a guest as he leaves is as if he has spilled his blood.[143] How far must one escort a guest? One should walk the guest through the door and at least 4 cubits beyond the door,[144] and if the guest is a respectable person, the host must escort the guest according to the guest's honor or need.

---

[138] Ezra 4:3.

[139] Neĥemiah 2:20.

[140] Genesis 18:2-3.

[141] *See Rashi on Genesis 18:1.

[142] Tractate *Shabbat* 127a.

[143] Rambam, *Laws of Mourners* ch. 14.

[144] *Sefer Meirat Einayim Ĥoshen Mishpat* 427:11.

THE PIOUS GENTILE AND THE *GER TOSHAV* IN TORAH LAW

1. Rambam writes[1] that a *Ĥasid Umot HaOlom* (lit., a pious person of the nations of the world) is a Pious Gentile[2] who:

(a) has accepted the faith in the One God alone as the only Deity;
(b) has abandoned all forms of idolatry (and anything related to it);
(c) scrupulously observes the Seven Commandments that God commanded to the descendants of Noaĥ, as their details are explained in the Oral Torah from God at Mount Sinai;
(d) observes the Noahide Commandments not because of intellectual conviction, but rather specifically because God commanded this in His Torah and informed us through Moses our teacher that the descendants of Noaĥ were previously commanded about them.

In contrast to this, if a Gentile observes his Seven Commandments based only on his own reasoning and understanding, and not based on these matters of faith, he is not a *Ĥasid Umot HaOlom.*[1]

2. A special condition applies for Gentiles when the Land of Israel is ruled by a fully observant Jewish government, and fully settled in accordance with the 613 Jewish Commandments. This means a time when the Jews of all the Twelve Tribes are settled separately in their assigned areas within the land, so they can observe the fifty-year cycle of *Yovel* (Jubilee), and the *Yovel* cycle is being observed.[3]

In that time, in order for a Gentile to be allowed to live in the Land of Israel, or even to pass through, he will be required to first receive a *formal certification* that he has taken upon himself to be scrupulous in observing the Noahide Commandments, as specified above in topic 1.[4]

A Pious Gentile obtains this certification by making a verbal declaration in the presence of (at least) three Jewish "friends," i.e., a

---

[1] Rambam, *Laws of Kings* 8:11.

[2] *In one form of modern usage, such a person is identified as a "Pious Noahide," or a "Noahide Ĥasid." For a Gentile, acceptance of the conditions listed here constitutes the acceptance of "the yoke of God's Kingship."

[3] *This will require the Messianic ingathering of all the Jewish people from around the world, and the identification of each one's tribal lineage, which will be accomplished by the ruling Messianic king when the spirit of holiness will be resting upon him. See Rambam, *Laws of Kings* 11:1 and 12:3.

[4] Rambam, *Laws of Forbidden Sexual Relations* 14:7-8 and *Laws of the Worship of Stars [and Idols]* 10:6.

convened Jewish court *(Beit Din)* of Torah-observant, God-fearing Torah scholars. The *Beit Din* will then certify his **status in Torah Law** as a *Ger Toshav* (lit., a "Sojourning Foreigner"; pl. *Gerim Toshavim*). This *"Ger Toshav"* confirmation by a *Beit Din* is referred to as "the *acceptance* (*kabalah* in Hebrew) of a *Ger Toshav* by the Jewish people," and it is only permitted during an era when the *Yovel* cycles are being observed.[4] (During such times, this declaration is optional for a Pious Gentile if he lives outside of the Land if Israel, and it is mandatory in order for him to be allowed to live in the Land of Israel.)

A Gentile who does not accept upon himself all of the four principles above, and to observe them faithfully, does not have the designation of *"Ger Toshav,"* and he is not to be accepted as such by a *Beit Din*.[5]

A Gentile who has not received this designation from a *Beit Din* will be forbidden by Torah Law to reside in the Land of Israel when it is ruled according to Torah Law and the Twelve Tribes are settled there.[6]

It is clear that the qualifications of a Gentile to be validated by a *Beit Din* as a *Ger Toshav* includes acceptance of the governing power of the Jewish people over the Land of Israel. (This applies to the Jews' governance of the nation, and not to their Torah observance, so it is clear that if a Gentile does not accept Jewish ownership of the Land of

---

[5] Rambam, *Laws of Kings* 8:10-11. It appears that according to Rambam, this process of Jews bestowing the *Ger Toshav* status upon a Pious Gentile is optional, because it is not included in Rambam's listing of the 613 Jewish Commandments. Ramban (see the 16th commandment in his listing of those not included by Rambam in *Sefer HaMitzvot*) also appears to share this view, that there is a positive Jewish commandment to secure the well-being of a *Ger Toshav*, but he does not count the bestowing of the *Ger Toshav* status upon a Pious Gentile as one of the Jewish commandments. (According to Rambam, the Biblical command to secure the well-being of a *Ger Toshav* is included in the commandment to give charity, as he explains in *Laws of Gifts to the Poor* 7:1.) It is clear that according to all opinions, the commandment upon the Jews is that they are obligated by Torah Law to secure the well-being of a *Ger Toshav*, but they are not commanded to grant that status.

[6] See *Sheva Mitzvos Hashem*, Part VIII, p. 888, topic 4. Ra'avad disagrees with Rambam and maintains that it is only people of the seven Canaanite nations who are forbidden to reside even temporarily in the Land of Israel. Nevertheless, it is obvious that according to Ra'avad, in order for a Gentile to be permitted to reside in the Land of Israel, he must at least be living a moral lifestyle such that he will not lead a Jew toward idolatry or other sins.

Israel, its Jewish government should not allow him to live there).[7]

All of the above applies for all Gentiles, whether male (a *Ben Noaĥ*) or female (a *Bat Noaĥ*).

3. The Jewish people are obligated to secure the well-being of a Pious Gentile who was properly accepted by a *Beit Din* as a *Ger Toshav*. As needed, they must assist him with his settlement into the Land of Israel and his establishment of a livelihood, and even support him with charity if he is not able to support himself.[8] They must save him from any mortal peril that he might encounter, as the verse states,[9] "you shall uphold him [a fellow Jew] – [and even] a *ger* [righteous convert] and a *toshav* [resident Pious Gentile] so that he can live with you."[10]

4. In an area of the Land of Israel that is either governed by Jews or significantly settled by Jews – even before the conditions for observance of *Yovel* are reinstated – any Gentile who has not accepted all of the conditions stated above in topic 1 is forbidden by Torah law from living in those areas, nor may he even pass through temporarily (and the Jews in the position of authority are obligated to enforce this).[11]

5. If a Gentile has not accepted the conditions in topic 1 above, it is not only the Jewish people who are obliged to prevent him (whenever possible) from living among them in the Land of Israel. The obligation also falls upon the Gentile himself, to refrain from living there so long as he is not a Pious Gentile *(Ĥasid Umot HaOlom)* in good standing. Therefore, even if, for whatever reason, the Jewish people are allowing such Gentiles into the Land [or even asking them to come and live there, for whatever reason], it is still forbidden for a Gentile to live there until he has accepted upon himself the yoke of the Seven Laws of Noaĥ (as explained above).[12]

---

[7] See *Sheva Mitzvot Hashem*, Part VIII, p. 886, topic 2.

[8] Rambam, *Laws of Kings* 10:12 and *Laws of the Worship of Stars [and Idols]* 10:2.

[9] Leviticus 24:35.

[10] However, for aid during the Jewish Sabbath that requires actions that are Scripturally forbidden for Jews, the assistance to a *Ger Toshav* must be provided by other Non-Jews. See Rambam, *Laws of the Sabbath* 2:12.

[11] This is clear from Rambam, *Laws of the Worship of Stars [and Idols]* 10:6.

[12] Vilna Gaon, *Aderet Eliyahu* on Deut. 1:5.

A Gentile must not take this matter lightly and think that if the Jewish people in the Land of Israel are not enforcing this restriction, then everyone who lives there is free to practice an idolatrous religion if they choose. Know that God hates idolatry, lewdness, and anything which the Torah refers to as an "abomination", and He considers the Land of Israel holier than any other place in the world. God is more exacting about the behaviors of people there than in any other place.[13]

6. It was explained above in topic 2 that when the Jubilee cycle is not observed, the *Ger Toshav* status is not conferred. However, if a Pious Gentile in good standing voluntarily accepts upon himself the Seven Laws of Noaĥ (as in topic 1), the Jewish government of the Land of Israel may allow him to live there and, if needed, to receive their assistance (see topic 3 above, and topic 7 below).

In this instance, a Pious Gentile does not need to declare his observance of the Noahide Laws in the presence of a Jewish court, since the Jewish people are not conferring the *Ger Toshav* status, regardless. Instead, what is most critical is that the person piously follows the Noahide Laws by his own volition, in which case he is a *Ĥasid Umot HaOlom.*[14] However, unlike Rambam, some Rabbinical authorities[15] maintain that even today, to be considered a *Ĥasid Umot HaOlom*, one must accept upon himself the observance of the Laws of Noaĥ in the presence of a *Beit Din* of three observant Jewish men. (This would apply to any Pious Gentile anywhere in the world, and not only those who wish to live in Israel.) By taking this step, he helps ensure that his obligations to God and his reward are complete.

7. As explained in topic 3, Jews are obligated to secure the well-being of a *Ĥasid Umot HaOlom* who was properly accepted by a *Beit Din* as a *Ger Toshav*. The Torah law of conferring of the *Ger Toshav* status is only in regard to permitting a Gentile to live in the Land of Israel when the *Yovel* is observed, but the obligation upon Jews that is stated in the verse Lev. 24:35 applies to a *Ĥasid Umot HaOlom* at any time.[16]

---

[13] See: Lev. 18:24-28; Rashi on Lev. 18:28; Ramban on Lev. 18:25; Deut. 11:12 and Rashi there; II Kings 17:24-26.

[14] This is Rambam's opinion, as explained in footnote 5 above.

[15] Following the opinion of Ramban on Tractate *Makos*, p. 9.

[16] This is Rambam's opinion, as explained in *Tzafnat Pane'aĥ*, and in *Likkutei*

It is incumbent upon the Jewish people to support a *Ger Toshav* both physically and spiritually. They should encourage him and assist his settlement in the land. They should help him become accustomed to his religious obligations so that his settlement and the observance of his commandments should not seem overly difficult.[17] Obviously, the Jewish people must treat the *Gerim Toshavim* with respect and kindness including visiting their sick, burying their dead, etc.[18]

8. When the acceptance of *Gerim Toshavim* in the Land of Israel applies, the Jewish court must appoint judges for them [those who are living under Jewish jurisdiction], to decide matters for them in accordance with the Noahide Code. The Jewish court can appoint these judges from among the *Gerim Toshavim* themselves, or appoint Jewish judges, as they see fit.[19]

9. It appears that when the Jewish people have legal jurisdiction over the Land of Israel and the Holy Temple is standing, a *Ger Toshav* may not live inside the walled area of Jerusalem that is sanctified by its encompassing walls, but they may pass through or pray there.[20] In all other times, a *Ĥasid Umot HaOlom* may live inside that area.

With that exception, the permission granted to a *Ger Toshav* to live in the Land of Israel applies to anywhere else they may choose to live, even in distinctly Jewish cities.[21] A *Ger Toshav* may even purchase land and a home in the city in which he lives.[22]

It appears that this restriction regarding Jerusalem only applies when the Jewish people have legal jurisdiction over the Land of Israel and

---

Siĥot vol. 26, p. 134. Others (Ra'avad and Ramban, as quoted in *Sheva Mitzvot HaShem* vol. 3, p. 886-7, fn. 6) seemingly disagree, and maintain that *"toshav"* in Lev. 24:35 applies only to a *Ger Toshav* whose declaration was accepted by a *Beit Din.*

[17] *Mesheĥ Ĥoĥmah* on Lev. 25:35.

[18] Rambam, *Law of Kings* 10:12.

[19] *Ibid.* 10:11.

[20] Rambam, *Law of the Chosen House* 7:14.

[21] This is Rambam's opinion (see *Sheva Mitzvot HaShem* vol. 3, p. 892, fn. 25), as opposed to Ra'avad on *Laws of Forbidden Sexual Relations* ch. 14, who maintains that a *Ger Toshav* is permitted to live in the land *outside* a Jewish city, but not inside the city.

[22] *Mishpat Kohen* ch. 63; *Ĥazon Ish Yoreh De'ah* ch. 65.

the Holy Temple is standing. In all other times, a Pious Gentile may live in the Holy City of Jerusalem.[23]

10. A *Ger Toshav* has no obligation to be circumcised,[24] as circumcision is a strictly Jewish commandment. He is, however, permitted to have himself circumcised, as explained in Part I, topics 3:5-7.

If a *Ger Toshav* pledges before a *Beit Din* comprised of three observant Jewish men to have a circumcision, and twelve months pass without him fulfilling his promise (with no valid health reason for not doing so), he is considered to be like an apostate Gentile[25] (a *Min* in Hebrew; see Part I, topic 1:7). The Jewish people then have no obligation to sustain him, and his right to remain in the Land of Israel as a *Ger Toshav* is revoked.

11. When a Gentile husband becomes a *Ger Toshav*, his Gentile wife does not automatically gain that status. If she also wishes to be a *Ger Toshav*, she must make her own declaration before a Jewish court of three observant Jewish men. Similarly, if his Gentile child who has reached the age of majority wishes to be *Ger Toshav*, the child must make his or her own declaration. (The age of majority in Torah law is 13 for boys and 12 for girls. See Part I, topic 4:4, that some Rabbinic authorities maintain that a Gentile youth who has developed a mature intellect at a younger age is bound by the same laws as an adult.)

However, younger children who are still reliant on the intellectual capacity of their parents are included in their parents' *Ger Toshav* declaration. If such children decide later, after they are mature, that they will not follow in their parents' observance of the Noahide Commandments, they are considered to be *Gerim Toshavim* who have cast off the yoke of Heaven (and therefore their right to remain in the Land of Israel is revoked.)

12. So long as a *Ger Toshav* is generally observing the Seven Noahide Commandments, he is presumed to be in good standing. This is so even when his observance has been less than perfect, having transgressed some details repeatedly. Nonetheless, if he is firm in his

---

[23] See responsa of Radbaz, ch. 633.

[24] Rambam, *Laws of Forbidden Sexual Relations* 14:7.

[25] Rambam, *Laws of Kings* 8:10.

belief in the One God and he is observant of that, he maintains his status as a *Ger Toshav*. If he abandons his acceptance of God's rulership in general, or even one of the Noahide Commandments fully, his title and privileges as a *Ger Toshav* are thereby revoked.[26]

13. It was explained in Part I, Chapter 3, that any Gentile is forbidden from observing the Jewish commandments that pertain to the Sabbath, because doing so would be adding a commandment for himself that was not commanded by God. A *Ger Toshav* is included in this prohibition; he may not observe ritual restrictions for the sake of the Sabbath. He is, however, allowed at any time not to be working, if it is not for any religious reason – for example, if it is because he has no other work at hand, or he is on vacation. He is not required to go out of his way to deliberately perform a *melaĥa* (the term in Hebrew for any of the activities that are forbidden for Jews during their Sabbath), so long as he does not consider himself to be observing any restrictions on account of the Sabbath.

These rules apply even for a *Ger Toshav* who is a servant or employee of a Jew in the Land of Israel; during the Sabbath, he continues to publicly do his regular *melaĥa* activities that he does for his own benefit. However, with regard to doing something during the Sabbath on behalf of his Jewish employer, he may not do any *melaĥa* that violates the Jewish Sabbath restrictions. *This prohibition is not upon the Ger Toshav himself, but rather it is upon the Jew who is forbidden to cause his Gentile servant or employee to do any melaĥa during the Sabbath.*[27]

14. According to the basic Torah Law, this prohibition for a Jew applies only to his own Gentile servants and employees. The Sages of the Talmud were stringent in this matter and created additional enactments as a safeguard against transgression. They ruled that a Jew is forbidden to benefit from any *melaĥa* that was done on his behalf by any Gentile during the Sabbath. This applies even if the Jew did not specifically instruct the Gentile to do the *melaĥa*, but the Gentile did it by his own choice because of his desire to benefit the Jew.[28]

---

[26] Ĥazon Ish on *Bava Kama*, topic 10:15.

[27] Rambam, *Laws of the Sabbath* ch. 20; *Shulĥan Aruĥ Oraĥ Ĥayim* ch. 304.

[28] Rambam, *ibid.* ch. 6; *Shulĥan Aruĥ HaRav* ch. 243.

However, if a Gentile did *melaĥa* on the Sabbath for his own benefit, and not specifically to benefit a Jew, a Jew may benefit from it – e.g., if a Gentile erected a ramp so he could ascend or descend, a Jew may also use it after the Gentile does; if a Gentile lit his own candle for his own benefit, a Jew may also benefit from its light. This rule applies for other similar circumstances in which the Gentile's *melaĥa* is for himself, and no additional *melaĥa* is done for another person. (But if the type of *melaĥa* he does on the Sabbath has an aspect of quantity, so he can do more of that *melaĥa* beyond his own need to benefit others (such as drawing water in a public area, in which case he may wish to draw more for others), a Jew is prohibited to benefit from that.[29]

15. There are, however, two exceptions to prohibition for Jews that is stated in the previous topic:

(1) If the *melaĥa* that a Gentile does is primarily for his own benefit, but the act itself is done for a Jew. This applies in the following case:

A Jew hired a Gentile to do a *melaĥa*, the wage has been agreed upon, the Gentile was not instructed that he must complete the job specifically on the Sabbath, the Jew has given him ample time to complete the job without any work needing to be done on the Sabbath, and the *melaĥa* is not done in the home, property, or store of the Jew.

Under these conditions, the Gentile's *melaĥa* that was done for a Jew on the Sabbath is permitted for a Jew to benefit from. This is because the Gentile did it for the sake of his livelihood, and the Jew did not cause him to perform it on the Sabbath, so it follows that the Gentile is choosing of his own volition to do the *melaĥa* on that day, and it is for his own benefit (so that he will be paid).

In contrast, it is forbidden for a Jew to cause a Gentile to do *melaĥa* during the Sabbath under any of the following circumstances (and if this prohibition was violated, a Jew is forbidden to benefit from the *melaĥa* that was done in these cases):[30]

(a) The *melaĥa* is performed by a Gentile in the Jew's home;
(b) The *melaĥa* is performed by a Gentile on the Jew's property;
(c) The Gentile is hired by a Jew only for the day of the Sabbath;

---

[29] Rambam *ibid.*; *Shulĥan Aruĥ* details a few exceptions to these general rules, in *Oraĥ Ĥayim*, chs. 244, 245, and 328.

[30] See *Shulĥan Aruĥ Oraĥ Ĥayim* ch. 244.

(d) The Gentile will be paid by a Jew for each day that he does the *melaĥa* (and one of the days is the Sabbath);

(e) A Jew allotted a certain time in which the *melaĥa* must be performed by the Gentile that he hired, and it is impossible to meet the deadline if it is not done during the Sabbath;

(f) The Gentile's wage has not yet been set, and he does not know if or how much he will be paid.

(2) A Jew is permitted to request or instruct a Gentile do *melaĥa* on the Sabbath for the personal needs of a sick Jew who is in great pain, even if the situation is not life threatening.[31]

16. If a Jew and a Gentile are business partners, there is a prohibition upon the Jew against his Gentile partner doing any *melaĥa* on the Sabbath that is for the sake of the business in which they are partnered. Since they are partners, it follows that the Gentile would be doing *melaĥa* for the benefit of the Jew as well.

The Gentile partner also may not open the shared business during the Sabbath to earn money, even if he does not need to engage in any *melaĥa* on that day (such as a bath house or similar enterprise in which customers pay simply to enter and use the facility, even if it does not require any maintenance to be done on that day). Since the Jew also has a share in the business, the Gentile partner would also be acting as the Jew's agent and causing him to earn profit from the operation of the business during the Sabbath, which is forbidden for the Jew even if it does not involve the performance of any *melaĥa* during the Sabbath.

If the Gentile partner wishes to open the business during the Sabbath and Jewish holy days (*"yom tov"* days), when the Jew is forbidden to earn profit from the business, this is only permitted if there is an absolute agreement between them that any profits generated on those days belong to the Gentile alone, and the Jew has no share in it at all.

If it is difficult to know how much profit is generated on those days, they may create an agreement in which a part of the total profit from the business – corresponding to the best estimate of the profit that was generated on Sabbath and *yom tov* days – will be subtracted and given to the Gentile, and that which remains will be paid out according to the general terms of the partnership.[32]

---

[31] See *ibid.* ch. 328.

[32] See *ibid.* ch. 245.

The laws regarding partnerships between Jews and Gentiles are extensive. The purpose here is merely to provide the central concepts so that Gentiles may be aware of them. In truth, these are obligations of the Jew, not of the Gentile. They are mentioned here for the Gentile reader, so he will know that it is *permitted* for him profit on his own behalf during the Sabbath, it is *prohibited* for him to observe the ritual Jewish commandment to refrain from doing *melaĥa* during the Sabbath, and it is *prohibited* for him to do *melaĥa* on behalf of a Jew during the Sabbath (except in the cases mentioned above in topic 15).

17. Jews have special precepts regarding wine (*yayin* in Hebrew). One manner of serving an idol is by pouring a libation (*neseĥ* in Hebrew) of wine before it. Wine poured in this way is called *yayin neseĥ* and is forbidden for Jews or Gentiles to drink or benefit from it at all (see Part II, topic 9:2). As a safeguard against Jews benefiting from *yayin neseĥ* the Rabbis forbade Jews to have *any* benefit from "high-quality wine" which a non-Pious or non-Muslim[33] Gentile produced or owned, or touched if the container was unsealed. *In this context, "high-quality wine" means any wine or juice of grapes that was not boiled (not 'mevushal' in Hebrew).* As a further safeguard against social mingling of Jews and any Gentiles while intoxicated with wine, the Rabbis forbade Jews to drink any non-*mevushal* wine that was touched by any Gentile while it was in an unsealed container. Rabbinically-forbidden wine is called "their normal wine" (*stam yaynam* in Hebrew).

If a Pious or Muslim[33] Gentile touches unsealed, non-*mevushal* wine, the Jew may not drink it. He may, however benefit financially from such wine (e.g., by selling it or giving it as a gift to a Gentile). Therefore, a Gentile must be careful not to touch unsealed non-*mevushal* wine belonging to a Jew, because that would make it forbidden to the Jew (either totally, or only to drink, as explained here), and doing so is considered damaging another person's property.

18. The Torah laws regarding a *Ger Toshav* who kills inadvertently, and the associated laws of Cities of Refuge[34] in regard to *Gerim Toshavim*, are explained in *Sheva Mitzvot HaShem*, Part V, Chapter 5.

---

[33] Rambam, *Laws of Forbidden Foods* 11:7. See Part II, topic 6:3 and the footnote there. See also Part VII, topic 11:23 and the footnote there.

[34] *See Numbers 35:9-28. These laws apply when *Yovel* cycles are observed.

CPSIA information can be obtained
at www.ICGtesting.com
Printed in the USA
LVHW082219111121
703137LV00013B/608

9 781733 363518